T0325469

THE HISTORICAL PERFORMANCE
OF THE
FEDERAL RESERVE

THE HISTORICAL PERFORMANCE OF THE

FEDERAL RESERVE

THE IMPORTANCE OF RULES

Michael D. Bordo

HOOVER INSTITUTION PRESS
Stanford University | Stanford, California

Hoover Institution Press Publication No. 695
Hoover Institution at Leland Stanford Junior University,
Stanford, California 94305-6003

First printing 2019
26 25 24 23 22 21 20 19   9 8 7 6 5 4 3 2 1

Manufactured in the United States of America

The paper used in this publication meets the minimum requirements of the American National Standard for Information Sciences—Permanence of Paper for Printed Library Materials, ANSI/NISO Z39.48-1992. ∞

Cataloging-in-Publication Data is available from the Library of Congress.
ISBN-13: 978-0-8179-2214-6 (cloth)
ISBN-13: 978-0-8179-2216-0 (EPUB)
ISBN-13: 978-0-8179-2217-7 (Mobipocket)
ISBN-13: 978-0-8179-2218-4 (PDF)

Please see additional information about the original sources of many of the articles included in this volume on pages 597–598, which constitutes an extension of this copyright page.

CONTENTS

Foreword   ix
JOHN B. TAYLOR

Introduction/Overview   xiii

FOREWORD

JOHN B. TAYLOR

THIS BOOK CONSISTS of fifteen fascinating chapters, each one a major contribution in its own right and all written by the distinguished monetary historian Michael Bordo. In many of the chapters, Michael Bordo is joined by notable coauthors, who constitute an amazing list of contributors, including Anna Schwartz, Athanasios Orphanides, John Landon-Lane, Joseph Haubrich, Chris Erceg, Andrew Levin, Ryan Michaels, Michael Dueker, David Wheelock, and Ehsan Choudhri.

As you begin to look through and read these chapters, you quickly realize that the book is much more than a collection of intriguing stand-alone pieces. The chapters are connected and woven together—as Michael Bordo explains in a beautiful introduction—to form a definitive, lessons-packed historical treatment, informed by theory and data, of the Federal Reserve and related markets and institutions.

Like Milton Friedman and Anna Schwartz's *A Monetary History of the United States* and Allan Meltzer's *A History of the Federal Reserve*, Michael Bordo's *The Historical Performance of the Federal Reserve: The Importance of Rules* covers huge expanses of history in a comprehensible way. And, as with these other historical perspectives, it develops and establishes new monetary lessons with great relevance around the world today. Whereas Friedman and Schwartz demonstrated the importance of money, and Meltzer the importance of the institutions, Bordo establishes the importance of predictable monetary strategies and specific policy rules.

As Bordo emphasizes, the "important lesson from the monetary history of the United States and other advanced countries is that the pursuit of stable monetary policy guided by central banks following rule-like behavior produces low and stable inflation, stable real performance, and encourages financial stability." The case for monetary policy rules continues to be one of the most difficult policy issues facing central bank officials and societies more generally today. The evidence that Michael Bordo has uncovered in his research over the years figures importantly in this debate. Connecting the evidence from different historical episodes and periods, as accomplished in this book, further solidifies this evidence and makes it more convincing than ever.

Right from the start, in Chapter 1 on "Rules versus Discretion: A Perennial Theme in Monetary Economics," Bordo concentrates on this key issue. He appropriately and fairly considers alternative views, but he concludes that the case for rules holds up very well against these alternatives. The poor performance during the great inflation of the 1970s as monetary policy deviated from rules is an important, but only one, of many pieces of evidence.

Consider, for example, his finding that both the commodity-based monetary rule implicit in the gold standard period and the fiat-based policy rule during the Great Moderation from 1985 to 2005 were associated with price stability and generally good economic performance. Both periods contrast with the poor performance and poor policy in other historical periods, including the 1970s in many countries.

Indeed, comparing and contrasting economic performance and its associated monetary policy in different historical episodes is a recurrent theme and valuable method used throughout this book. Looking at different real economic performance during different deflationary periods is another example. The book considers (1) the post–Civil War greenback deflation, (2) the post–World War I deflation, and (3) the Volcker disinflation of 1979–1982. Here one can see the beneficial impact of transparency and credibility in policy, which is also different in these periods. This policy difference seems to account for the widely divergent real macroeconomic effects in these three periods when the monetary policy was explicitly deflationary and brought inflation down from high levels.

Often the book usefully digs into important timing differences in central bank decisions and shows that these significantly affect economic performance. For example, the book shows that in both the 1920s and the 1950s the Federal Reserve responded relatively quickly by tightening when the aggregate price level started to rise. In the 1960s the Fed delayed its tightening, waiting until long after inflation began to rise. Thus, the Fed was often too late, and inflation picked up leading to a boom bust cycle.

Bordo goes back further into history to explore the case for monetary rules. He looks at the operations of the Bank of England in the 1820s and 1830s, and contrasts the Currency School, which effectively endorsed a monetary rule tying the money supply to the balance of payments, with the Banking School, which allowed for much more discretion. In reviewing the twentieth century he examines the work of Henry Simons, at the University of Chicago, who made the case for rules that was further pursued by Milton Friedman, who specified the constant money growth rule. The Friedman rule was then improved upon by Bennett McCallum's monetary base-growth rule and by the Taylor rule, which explicitly showed how interest rates should respond to economic developments, and which, in Bordo's assessment, was "widely accepted as the best-practice monetary rule."

The book examines deviations from policy rules and the harm that such deviations may cause, including by showing that episodes in which monetary policy is too easy are often followed by booms and inevitable busts. Consider, for example, the chapter "Does Expansionary Monetary Policy Cause Asset Price Booms? Some Historical and Empirical Evidence," written with John Landon-Lane. It collects data from eighteen countries during the years from 1920 to 2011. Using these data, it estimates the impact of loose monetary policy on housing, stock, and commodity prices. It shows that loose monetary policy—defined as having a policy interest rate too low or money growth rate too high relative to a given rule—has a significant, but temporary, inflationary impact on asset prices. The research with many countries and many time periods shows that asset price inflation follows excessive monetary accommodation.

More generally, the book continually brings history to bear on current policy debates. The chapter "Deep Recessions, Fast Recoveries, and Financial Crises: Evidence from the American Record" written jointly with

Joseph Haubrich, directly relates to debates about the reasons for the recent slow recovery from the 2007–2009 recession. The chapter shows that recoveries from deep recessions in the United States are usually faster than recoveries from shallow recessions. It thereby demonstrates that the slow recovery from the deep recession of 2007–2009 and from the financial crisis was unusually weak compared to recoveries from past recessions with financial crises in the United States.

This finding implies that something else was holding the recovery back, and that something was probably poor economic policy. This view is in direct contrast to the claim made by others that the slow recovery was just what one would expect from a deep recession, with the implication that policy was just fine and that a different policy would do little good. As of the publication of this book, the controversy continues. It could be that current developments affect the debate because economic growth appears to be accelerating to the fastest rate in the recovery, and the improvement has been associated with a change in policy. If this continues, it will give further empirical support to Bordo's hypothesis.

I have had the opportunity to learn much about monetary history and policy from Michael Bordo, especially during the time he has spent at the Hoover Institution over the years, much as I had a similar opportunity to learn from Milton Friedman and Allan Meltzer when they were at the Hoover Institution. I came away with a better appreciation that there is a great deal that one can learn from history, especially when our theoretical models do not always deliver. Michael Bordo makes that crystal clear in this book. He is the person to reach out to on any policy issue relating to monetary history, and there are many such policy issues addressed in this book.

—JOHN B. TAYLOR
February 2019

INTRODUCTION/OVERVIEW

THE FINANCIAL CRISIS OF 2007-2008 and the Great Recession—which officially ended in June 2009, although the subsequent recovery was sluggish—led to massive intervention by the Federal Reserve and other central banks. The crisis was triggered in 2006 by the bursting of a massive housing boom that had been facilitated by permissive government housing policy, financial innovation (subprime mortgages, shadow banking, and securitization), and lax regulatory oversight by the Fed and other agencies. The boom was fueled by the Fed to keep its federal funds rate well below the Taylor rule rate from 2002 to 2005 (Taylor 2009). In the face of financial stress in the fall of 2007, the Fed cut its policy rate by 300 basis points. It also introduced radical extensions to its discount window-lending arsenal, which included, inter alia, the Term Auction Facility (TAF), the Term Security Lending Facility (TSLF), and the Primary Dealer Credit Facility (PDCF) "to unclog the arteries" of the financial system. This shift to credit policy (Goodfriend 2012) involved the provision of credit directly to financial firms that the Fed deemed most in need of liquidity—in contrast to delivering liquidity directly to the market by open-market purchases of Treasury securities and leaving the distribution of liquidity to individual firms to the market. Such targeted lending represented fiscal, not monetary, policy. Credit policy was also a threat to the Fed's independence.

In early 2008 the Fed suspended its funds rate-cutting policy out of concern over a run-up of global commodity prices threatening future inflation. The consequent rise in real interest rates may have generated a steep recession (Hetzel 2012). In March 2008 the Fed arranged a rescue of the insolvent investment bank Bear Stearns on the grounds that it was too interconnected to fail. This led to concern by many over moral hazard. Then, in a dramatic policy reversal in September 2008, the investment bank Lehman Brothers was allowed to fail on the grounds that it did not have sufficient sound collateral to justify a Fed rescue. The resulting global financial panic then led the Fed to quickly cut the funds rate to close to zero and resuscitate the Bretton Woods–era swap network with many central banks. By year's end, faced with the zero lower bound on short-term interest rates, the Fed introduced the unorthodox policy of quantitative easing (QE1) by purchasing both long-term Treasury securities and mortgage-backed securities. This policy succeeded in modestly reducing long-term interest rates and may have aided in arresting the downturn. QE1 was followed by two successive QE strategies whose impact has been less potent. Despite these actions, the recovery remained sluggish at least until 2017; indeed, the current recovery is unique among financial recession recoveries, which are generally more rapid than those of ordinary recessions (Bordo and Haubrich 2017).

Many have argued this record of hyperactive Federal Reserve discretionary monetary policy has prevented the US economy from having a repeat of the 1929–1933 Great Contraction. An alternative view is that had the Fed followed more rule-like policies, including sticking to the Taylor rule, it would have avoided the housing bubble (Taylor 2009). Moreover, even if the housing bubble had continued to inflate and then burst, as it did, more consistent rule-like policies in 2007–2008 could have mitigated the recession and prevented the Lehman Brothers panic in September 2008 (Ball 2018). Finally, providing lender of last resort liquidity to the financial markets in general and not following discretionary credit policy would have preserved Fed credibility and independence and lessoned the policy uncertainty that was an important ingredient in the crisis. An important lesson from the monetary history of the United States and other advanced countries is that the pursuit of stable monetary policy guided by central banks following rule-like behavior produces low and stable inflation, stable real performance, and encourages financial stability.

The modern approach to rules focused on the role of time inconsistency. According to this approach, a rule is a credible commitment mechanism that ties the hands of policy makers and prevents them from following time-inconsistent discretionary policies—policies that take past policy commitments as given and react to the present circumstances by changing policy as given and react to the present circumstances by changing policy (Kydland and Prescott 1977; Barro and Gordon 1983).

The classical gold standard from 1880 to 1914 was based on such a credible monetary rule by defining the dollar as a fixed weight of gold (fixing the price of gold in terms of the dollar) and requiring the monetary authorities to maintain the peg above all else. This rule both precluded discretionary monetary policy and the running of fiscal deficits. It was a contingent rule in the sense that gold convertibility could be temporarily suspended in the event of an emergency, such as a war or a financial crisis not of the monetary authorities' own making (Bordo and Kydland 1995). The gold standard era was associated with long-run price stability and good, real economic performance. The "Great Moderation" period from 1985 to 2005, based on a fiat-based "credibility for low inflation" rule, also exhibited exemplary price stability and real economic performance and had some of the features of the gold standard without the resource and other costs of having a commodity-based currency.

History teaches us that episodes of sustained expansionary monetary policy in excess of the potential growth of the real economy—not policy based on adherence to a credible monetary rule—can create inflation. Sustained slow monetary growth relative to potential growth will lead to deflation and in the face of nominal rigidities will lead to recession.

Expansionary/contractionary discretionary monetary policy based on fine-tuning can exacerbate the business cycle. The record of the Federal Reserve shows that it has often been too late in exiting from expansionary policy as the economy recovers and too slow in recognizing recessions (Bordo and Landon-Lane 2012).

The recent US experience, as well as the historical record for many countries, shows that expansionary discretionary monetary policy can produce asset price booms (in equities, real estate, and commodities) as part of the transmission mechanism of monetary policy. This can lead to future inflation, as was the case in the 1970s. Asset price booms can also end in busts that can lead to financial (banking) crises, as occurred in 2008 and in many other episodes.

Financial crises, as evident in the very recent past, can severely impact the real economy. Banking crises since the 1970s have led to fiscal bailouts, which in turn increased fiscal deficits and national debt. As recently witnessed in Greece, Ireland, Spain, and other countries, debt crises ensue that inevitably result in default (Bordo and Meissner 2016).

Fiscal bailouts can lead to monetization by the monetary authorities and inflation. This can happen via "unpleasant monetarist arithmetic" (Sargent and Wallace 1981) or via the "fiscal theory of the price level" (Leeper 2011).

Finally, price level and inflation variability can lead to and exacerbate financial instability. Unexpected inflation or deflation can damage the balance sheets of firms and financial institutions, leading to restricted lending and insolvency (Schwartz 1995).

In sum, the failure to adhere to rules that produce monetary stability will inevitably produce the dire consequences of real, nominal, and financial instability.

1. The Case for Monetary Rules

There is a long tradition in monetary economics making the case for monetary rules instead of central bank discretion. The classic statement of the case for rules goes back to the Currency Banking School debate of the 1820s and 1830s in England (Viner 1937). The Currency School advocates (McCulloch, Overstone, Longfield, Norman, and Torrens) emphasized the importance for the Bank of England to change its monetary liabilities in accordance with changes in its gold reserves—that is, according to the Currency principle, which advocated a rule tying money supply to the balance of payments. The opposing Banking School (Tooke, Fullarton, and Mill) emphasized the importance of disturbances in the domestic economy and the domestic financial system as the key variables the Bank of England should react to. They advocated that the Bank directors should use their discretion rather than be constrained by a rigid rule (Schwartz 2008). The Currency School argued that following rules was deemed superior to allowing policy to be based on the discretion of even well-meaning and intelligent officials in the face of limited information. The Currency principle was enshrined in the operations of the Issue Department in the

1844 Bank Charter Act, which governed the Bank of England for a century. The Banking principle was embodied in the Banking Department of the Bank of England.

The Federal Reserve, founded in 1913, was based on both the gold standard and the real bills doctrine, which derived from Banking School theory. The basic premise of real bills was that as long as central banks discounted only self-liquidating short-term real bills, then the economy will always have the correct amount of money and credit. Adherence to the real bills doctrine has been viewed as being responsible for monetary and financial stability in the interwar period and even into the late 1970s (Meltzer 2003, 2009).

In the twentieth century the question that followed the Currency Banking School debate was whether monetary policy should be entrusted to well-meaning authorities with limited knowledge or to a rule that could not be designed to deal with unknown shocks. Henry Simons (1936) made the case for rules. Milton Friedman, Simon's student, posited the case in 1960 for his famous k% rule under which the central bank would set the rate of monetary growth equal to the long-run growth rate of real income adjusted for the trend growth rate of velocity. Adhering to Friedman's rule would maintain stable prices.

Friedman argued, based on voluminous empirical and historical evidence documenting how discretionary Fed policies exacerbated US business cycles, that pursuit of his rule would have delivered economic performance superior to that generated by the policies followed by the Fed.

Friedman's (1960) rule, which was based on steady growth of broad money, was improved upon by Bennett McCallum's (1987) base-growth rule with feedback from the real economy and by John Taylor (1993), who developed an interest rate rule based on the policy instruments that central banks were actually using. In his rule, the Fed would set its rate depending on the natural rate of interest and a weighted average of the deviations of inflation from its target and real output from potential output. Taylor (1999) showed how his rule could be converted into a money growth rule that could be used in environments where central banks target monetary aggregates. In the past two decades the Taylor rule has been widely accepted as the best-practice monetary rule.

Pursuit of rules like the Taylor rule or the McCallum rule by maintaining price stability would mitigate real economic instability, avoid asset price booms and financial crises, and prevent financial instability.

2. The Book

This book is a collection of my articles (some written with others) on the importance of monetary stability and the case for monetary rules. The chapters present theoretical, empirical, and historical perspectives to support the case.

2.1. Theoretical Perspectives

The chapters in this section survey the history of the case for monetary rules.

Chapter 1, "Rules versus Discretion: A Perennial Theme in Monetary Economics," examines the classical early nineteenth-century debate in England between the Bullionists and the anti-Bullionists and the Currency Banking School debate that led to the first formulation of the case for monetary rules. I then analyze the case for a monetary rule by the Chicago School (Henry Simons and Milton Friedman). Friedman posited the case for his constant money growth rate rule in 1960. I conclude by revisiting the modern case for instrument rules and the Taylor rule. This approach is based on the seminal work by Kydland and Prescott on time inconsistency.

Chapter 2, "The Importance of Stable Money: Theory and Evidence," was written with the late Anna J. Schwartz. In it we survey postwar developments in monetary theory on the case for stable money and the importance of monetary rules. Our survey begins with Milton Friedman's case for stable money (rules-based monetary policy) and against the pursuit of discretionary countercyclical stabilization policy fine-tuning. We then examine an opposing theory of monetary policy associated with the work of Theil (1967) and Tinbergen (1978), which made the case for discretionary stabilization policy. We then make the case for Friedman's (1968) natural rate hypothesis and the rational expectations hypothesis.

We conclude with the case for a legislated monetary rule and provide empirical evidence in favor of Milton Friedman's constant money growth rate rule.

2.2. Empirical Evidence

Part Two examines the historical and empirical record of economic performance (both inflation and real output) across policy regimes.

Chapter 3, "Monetary Policy Regimes and Economic Performance: The Historical Record" (with Anna J. Schwartz) surveys the historical performance of monetary regimes: the classical gold standard period (1880–1914), the interwar period (1919–1939), the postwar Bretton Woods international monetary system period (1946–1971), and the managed float period (1971–1959). A salient theme in our survey is that the convertibility (into gold) rule that dominated both domestic and international aspects of the monetary regime before World War I has since declined in its relevance. Policy techniques and doctrine developed before World War I proved to be inadequate to deal with the domestic stabilization goals in the interwar period, setting the stage for the Great Depression. In the post–World War II era, the complete abandonment of the convertibility principle and its replacement by the goal of full employment, combined with the legacy of inadequate policy tools and theory from the interwar period, set the stage for the Great Inflation of the 1970s. The lessons from that experience have convinced monetary authorities to reemphasize the goal of low inflation, as it were, thus committing themselves to rule-like behavior.

Chapter 4, "Introduction to 'The Great Inflation: The Rebirth of Modern Central Banking'" (written with Athanasios Orphanides), describes the salient features of the Great Inflation of 1965–1983. It describes how inflation ratcheted up, as loose monetary policy was followed by contraction, but not sufficient to break the back of rising inflationary expectations. Fear of rising unemployment tempered the Federal Reserve's willingness to tighten policy, leading to the phenomenon of stagflation. We also survey the debate over the causes of the Great Inflation. The contending explanations included: expansionary monetary policy (the monetarist explanation); oil price and other commodity price shocks; time inconsistency; political pressure on the Fed; the Phillips curve trade-off; fear of repeating the Great Depression; data mismeasurement; and an expectations trap. Many of the alternative explanations are explained in detail in Bordo and Orphanides (2013).

2.3. Monetary Policy Performance

This section contains six chapters on the performance of the Federal Reserve in its pursuit of discretionary monetary policy.

Chapter 5, "Exits from Recessions: The US Experience, 1920–2007" (with John S. Landon-Lane), examines the record of the Fed's discretionary monetary policy. Specifically, we provide evidence on how the Fed shifted from expansionary to contractionary monetary policy after a recession has ended—the exit strategy. We examine the relationship between the timing of changes in several instruments of monetary policy and the timing of changes in real output and inflation across US business cycles from 1920 to 2007. Based on historical narratives, descriptive evidence, and econometric analysis, we find that in the 1920s and 1950s the Fed would generally tighten when the price level turned up. By contrast, since 1960 the Fed has generally tightened when unemployment peaked, and this tightening often occurred after inflation began to rise. The Fed is often too late to prevent inflation.

Chapter 6, "Deep Recessions, Fast Recoveries, and Financial Crises: Evidence from the American Record" (with Joseph G. Haubrich), focuses on the coincidence of financial crises and economic recoveries. Specifically, we ask whether recessions associated with financial crises have slow or steep recoveries. Our analysis based on all US business cycles since the establishment of the Fed is that recessions associated with financial crises are generally followed by fast recoveries. We find three exceptions to this pattern: the recovery from the Great Contraction in the 1930s; the recovery after the recession in the 1990s; and the recovery since the Great Financial Crisis of 2007–2008. The recent recovery has been strikingly more tepid than the recovery of the 1990s. Factors that can explain the recent experience include policy uncertainty and the moribund nature of residential investment.

Chapter 7, "Credit Crises, Money and Contractions: An Historical View" (with Joseph G. Haubrich), analyzes the relationship between policy-induced monetary changes and credit crises. Using a combination of historical narrative and econometric techniques, we identify major periods of credit distress from 1875 to 2007, examine the extent to which credit distress arises as part of the transmission of monetary policies, and document the subsequent effect on output. Using business cycles defined by the Harding-Pagan algorithm, we identify and compare the timing, duration, amplitude and co-movement of cycles in money, credit, and output. Our regressions show that financial-distress events exacerbate business cycle downturns both in the nineteenth and twentieth centuries and that a confluence of such events makes recessions even worse.

Chapter 8, "Three Great American Disinflations" (with Christopher Erceg, Andrew Levin, and Ryan Michaels), analyzes the role of transparency and credibility in accounting for the widely divergent macroeconomic effects of three episodes of deliberate monetary contraction from high inflation: the post–Civil War greenback deflation; the post–World War I deflation; and the Volcker disinflation of 1979–1982. Using a dynamic general equilibrium model, we show that the salient features of these three historical episodes can be explained by differences in the design and transparency of monetary policy. For a policy regime with relatively high credibility (as in the 1870s), our analysis highlights the benefit of a gradualist approach rather than a sudden change in policy (as in 1920–1921). By contrast, for a central bank with relatively low credibility (such as the Federal Reserve in late 1980s), an aggressive policy stance can play an important signaling role by making the monetary shift more evident to private agents.

Chapter 9, "Aggregate Price Shocks and Financial Instability: A Historical Analysis" (with Michael Dueker and David Wheelock), presents evidence for the hypothesis that aggregate price shocks (often induced by monetary policy) cause or worsen financial instability. Based on two annual indexes of financial conditions for the United States covering 1790–1997, we estimate the effect of aggregate price shocks on each index using a dynamic ordered probit model. We find that price-level shocks contributed to financial instability during 1790–1932, and that inflation shocks contributed to financial instability during 1980–1997. Our research indicates that the size of the aggregate price shocks needed to substantially alter financial conditions depends on the institutional environment, but that a monetary policy focused on price stability would be conducive to financial stability.

Chapter 10, "Does Expansionary Monetary Policy Cause Asset Price Booms? Some Historical and Empirical Evidence" (with John Landon-Lane), uses a panel of eighteen OECD countries from 1920 to 2011 to estimate the impact that loose monetary policy, low inflation, and high levels of bank credit has on housing, stock, and commodity prices. We review historical narratives on asset price booms and use a deterministic procedure to identify asset price booms. We show that loose monetary policy—having an interest rate below the target (Taylor rule) rate or having a growth rate of money above the (Friedman rule) target rate—does positively impact asset prices, and this correspondence is heightened during periods when asset prices grew quickly and then subsequently suffered a significant contraction.

2.4. Monetary History

This section contains several chapters on the history of monetary policy and especially of the actions by the Federal Reserve during the Great Depression. A leading theme is how the record could have been better had monetary rules or rule-like behavior been followed. It concludes with a reflective essay on how the US economy would have fared if it had a central bank in the eighty years before the establishment of the Federal Reserve in 1913.

Chapter 11, "The History of Monetary Policy," surveys the history of central banks since the establishment of the Swedish Riksbank in 1664 and the evolution of monetary policy and its instruments from the gold standard to the present. A key theme that runs through this historical overview is the importance of following a regime dedicated to maintaining price stability.

Chapter 12, "The Banking Panics in the United States in the 1930s: Some Lessons for Today" (with John Landon-Lane), discusses the lessons learned from the US banking panics in the early 1930s for the response by the Federal Reserve to the crisis of 2008. We revisit the debate on illiquidity versus insolvency in the banking crises of the 1930s, providing evidence that the banking crisis largely reflected illiquidity shocks. In the 2007–2008 crisis, the Federal Reserve, under its chair, Ben Bernanke, had learned the lesson well from the banking panics of the 1930s of conducting expansionary monetary policy to meet demands for liquidity. However, unlike in the 1930s, the deeper problem of the recent crisis was not illiquidity but insolvency and especially the fear of insolvencies of counterparties. A number of virtually insolvent US banks deemed to be too big or too interconnected to fail were rescued by fiscal bailouts.

Chapter 13, "Could Stable Money Have Averted the Great Contraction?" (with Ehsan U. Choudhri and Anna J. Schwartz), directly tests whether the implementation of Milton Friedman's constant money growth rate rule during the Great Contraction of 1929–1933 would have largely prevented the disastrous collapse of output that occurred. We simulate a model that estimates separate relations for output and the price level and assumes that output and price dynamics are not especially sensitive to policy changes. The simulations include a strong and weak form of Friedman's constant money growth rule. The results support the hypothesis that the Great Contraction would have been mitigated and shortened had the Federal Reserve followed a constant money growth rule.

Chapter 14, "Was Expansionary Monetary Policy Feasible during the Great Contraction? An Examination of the Gold Standard Constraint" (with Ehsan U. Choudhri and Anna J. Schwartz), reconsiders a well-known view that the gold standard was the leading cause of the worldwide Great Depression of 1929–1933. According to this view, for most countries continued adherence to gold prevented monetary authorities from offsetting banking panics with expansionary monetary policies, thereby blocking their recoveries. We contend that although this may have been the case for small open economies with limited gold reserves, it is not the case for the United States, the largest economy in the world, holding massive gold reserves. The United States was not constrained from using expansionary policy to offset banking panics, deflation, and declining activity. Simulations based on a model of a large open economy indicate that expansionary open-market operations by the Federal Reserve at two critical junctures

(October 1930–February 1931, September 1931–January 1932) would have been successful in averting the banking panics that occurred—without endangering gold convertibility. Indeed, had expansionary open-market purchases been conducted in 1930, the contraction would not have led to the international crisis that followed. As I argue in chapter 15, the pursuit of rule-like policy could have maintained macroeconomic stability.

Chapter 15, "Could the United States Have Had a Better Central Bank? An Historical Counterfactual Speculation," argues that two alternative hypothetical central bank scenarios could have improved the Federal Reserve's track record with respect to financial stability and overall macroeconomic performance in its first century. The first scenario assumes that the charter of the Second Bank of the United States had not been revoked by President Andrew Jackson, and the Second Bank would have survived. Had this scenario been followed, the US central bank would have learned to prevent the banking panics that characterized much of the nineteenth century, and possibly it would have learned, as the Bank of England did, to follow more stable monetary policies.

The second scenario takes as given that the Second Bank did not survive and history evolved as it did, but considers the situation in which the Federal Reserve Act of 1913 was closer to the original plan for a central bank proposed by Paul Warburg in 1910. Had the Warburg Plan been closely followed, the Federal Reserve might have followed more rule-like lender of last resort policies and mitigated the banking panics of the 1930s.

We thank the various presses for permission to reprint the articles in the chapters in this volume.

References

Ball, Laurence M. 2018. *The Fed and Lehman Brothers: Setting the Record Straight on a Financial Disaster*. New York: Cambridge University Press.

Barro, Robert, and David Gordon. 1983. "Rules, Discretion and Reputation in a Model of Monetary Policy." *Journal of Monetary Economics* 12:101–21.

Bordo, Michael, and Joseph Haubrich. 2017. "Deep Recessions, Fast Recoveries, and Financial Crises: Evidence from the American Record." *Economic Inquiry* 55, no. 1 (January): 527–41.

Bordo, Michael, and Finn Kydland. 1995. "The Gold Standard as a Rule: An Essay in Exploration." *Explorations in Economic History* 32 (4): 423–64.

Bordo, Michael, and John Landon-Lane. 2012. "Does Expansionary Monetary Policy Cause Asset Price Booms; Some Historical and Empirical Evidence." *Journal Economia Chilena*, Central Bank of Chile, 16, no. 2 (August): 4–52.

Bordo, Michael, and Christopher Meissner. 2016. "Fiscal and Financial Crises." In *Handbook of Macroeconomics*, Volume 2A, edited by John B. Taylor and Harald Uhlig, 355–412. Amsterdam: North Holland.

Bordo, Michael, and Athanasios Orphanides. 2013. *The Great Inflation*. Chicago: University of Chicago Press.

Friedman, Milton. 1960. *A Program for Monetary Stability*. New York: Fordham University Press.

———. 1968. "The Role of Monetary Policy." *American Economic Review* 58, no. 1 (March): 1–17.

Goodfriend, Marvin. 2012. "The Elusive Promise of Independent Central Banking." Institute for Monetary and Economic Studies, Bank of Japan.

Hetzel, Robert. 2012. *The Great Recession: Market Failure or Policy Failure?* New York: Cambridge University Press.

Kydland, Finn, and Edward Prescott. 1977. "Rules Rather than Discretion: The Inconsistency of Optimal Plans." *Journal of Political Economy* 85 (3): 473–92.

Leeper, Eric. 2011. "Perceptions and Misperceptions of Fiscal Inflation." Paper presented at the 10th Annual BIS Conference: Fiscal Policy and Its Implications for Monetary and Financial Stability.

McCallum, Bennett. 1987. "The Case for Rules in the Conduct of Monetary Policy: A Concrete Example." *Federal Reserve Bank of Richmond Economic Review* 73 (September/October): 10–18.

Meltzer, Allan H. 2003. *A History of the Federal Reserve*. Vol. 1, *1913–1951*. Chicago: University of Chicago Press.

———. 2009. *A History of the Federal Reserve*. Vol. 2, Book 2. Chicago: University of Chicago Press.

Sargent, Thomas, and Neil Wallace. 1981. "Some Unpleasant Monetarist Arithmetic." *Federal Reserve Bank of Minneapolis Quarterly Review* 5 (Fall): 1–11.

Schwartz, Anna J. 1995. "Why Financial Stability Depends on Price Stability." *Economic Affairs* 15 (Autumn): 21–25.

———. 2008. "Banking School, Currency School, Free Banking School." *New Palgrave Dictionary of Economics*. 2nd ed. London: Palgrave Macmillan.

Simons, Henry. 1936. "Rules versus Authorities in Monetary Policy." *Journal of Political Economy* 44 (1): 1–30.

Taylor, John B. 1993. "Discretion versus Policy Rules in Practice." *Carnegie Rochester Conference Series on Public Policy* 39 (1): 195–214.

———. 1999. "A Historical Analysis of Monetary Policy Rules." In *Monetary Policy Rules*, edited by John B. Taylor, 319–48. Chicago: University of Chicago Press for the NBER.

———. 2009. *Getting Off Track*. Stanford, CA: Hoover Institution Press.

Theil, Henri. 1967. *Economics and Information Theory*. Vol 7. Amsterdam: North Holland.

Tinbergen, Jan. 1978. *Economic Policy: Principles and Design*. Amsterdam: North Holland.

Viner, Jacob. 1937. *Studies in the Theory of International Trade*. Chicago: University of Chicago Press.

Warburg, Peter. 1910. "The United Reserve Bank Plan." In *The Federal Reserve*, Vol. 1, edited by Paul Warburg. New York: Macmillan.

PART ONE

THEORETICAL PERSPECTIVES

CHAPTER 1

Rules versus Discretion

A Perennial Theme in Monetary Economics

MICHAEL D. BORDO

Introduction

THE DEBATE OVER RULES versus discretion has been ongoing in monetary economics for over two centuries. The question is, Should a free society allow well-intentioned, even wise, individuals to run monetary policy, or should it be guided by simple and well-understood (automatic) rules? The debate has evolved in its context and theoretical framework over the years, but the main theme is the same.

We survey the issues from the classical debate between the Bullionists and the anti-Bullionists and then the Currency School versus the Banking School in early nineteenth-century England; to the operation of the gold standard convertibility rule in its various manifestations from the mid-nineteenth century until 1971; to the mid-twentieth-century perspective of the Chicago School: Henry Simons and Milton Friedman; to the late twentieth-century perspective that came from the literature on rational expectations and time inconsistency; and to the current discussion on interest rate instrument rules and the Taylor rule.

The Classical Debate; the Bullionists and anti-Bullionists; the Currency School versus the Banking School

During the Napoleonic Wars from 1793 to 1815 there was a significant run-up in inflation and depreciation of the pound on the foreign exchanges following the suspension of specie convertibility in 1797. The Bank of England requested the suspension because it was unable to maintain convertibility according to its charter and also finance government expenditures by the purchase of Exchequer (Treasury) bills at a low interest rate (Bordo and White 1990). The Bank of England's note issue expanded as the intensity of the conflict reached its climax, so that by 1810 prices were rising close to 10 percent per year. During this period there was a debate between some of the leading economic thinkers of the time over the causes of the inflation (Viner 1937). The Bullionists, led by David Ricardo and Henry Thornton, attributed the rise in prices and the decline in sterling to excessive note issue by the Bank of England.[1] The anti-Bullionists, Thomas Tooke and James Fullarton, attributed the inflation to nonmonetary causes, including harvest failures and the ongoing remittances to British allies on the Continent (Bordo and Schwartz 1980). The Bullion Report of 1810, largely drafted by David Ricardo, blamed the Bank for overissuing its notes. As a solution, Ricardo proposed that the Bank follow a simple rule: the Bank should always maintain specie convertibility, that is, it should peg the price of sterling in terms of specie at the official rate of 3 pounds, 17 shillings, and 10½ pence per ounce of gold and allow its note issue to fluctuate automatically with the Bank's gold reserves. In the case of a balance of payments (trade) deficit, the Bank's gold reserves would decline, and the Bank would reduce its note issue. The opposite would occur with a balance of payments (trade) surplus. The rule, in a sense, would stabilize the purchasing power of gold in terms of other goods and services (Laidler 2002).

Specie convertibility at the original parity was restored in 1821, and the Bank returned to its peacetime role. A second debate began in the 1820s between the successors of the Bullionists, the Currency School (McClelland, Lord Overstone, Longfield, Norman, and Torrens), and the successors to the anti-Bullionists, the Banking School (Tooke, Fullarton, J. S. Mill). The Currency School writers focused on the issue of how the

Bank could maintain price stability with a mixed currency system (specie and bank notes). They argued that the Bank should follow the Currency principle, that is, the money supply should behave exactly as it would under a pure specie standard. Thus a gold inflow should lead to a one-to-one increase in the total currency and the opposite for a gold outflow. This principle led to the adoption of Palmer's rule (1827), named after Horsely Palmer, a governor of the Bank of England. Palmer posited that the Bank should keep its security portfolio constant and keep its gold reserves at one-third of its total liabilities. This would allow the Bank's note issue to vary directly with gold flows into and out of the Bank.

The Banking School criticized Palmer's rule and the Currency principle for omitting deposits at the Bank of England and the country banks for not accounting for movements in the velocity of circulation. They also defined money as currency plus deposits, whereas the Currency School defined it as simply currency (coins plus bank notes).

The Banking School argued that the money supply was endogenous and was determined according to the real bills doctrine by the needs of trade. If the Bank discounted only real commercial bills, reflecting the state of the economy, there never would be too much or too little money in circulation. An increase in the note issue by the Bank would always return via the operation of the price-specie flow mechanism and by the Law of Reflux (Schwartz 2008a).

Another critique of the Bank's sole pursuit of the Currency principle was the problem of internal drains, or commercial bank runs in the face of financial distress. The demands for liquidity would reduce the Bank's gold reserves, and via the Currency principle would lead the Bank to tighten monetary policy, thus aggravating the financial crisis. The Banking School believed that discretionary policy was needed to deal with liquidity drains. Serious banking panics in 1825, 1836, and 1839 led to the call for major reform of the Bank of England.

Reform came in the Bank Charter Act of 1844, which divided the Bank into the Issue Department and the Banking Department. The Issue Department would follow the Currency principle. Its balance sheet consisted of a fixed fiduciary note issue of 14 million pounds, and then every additional pound would vary with gold flows into and out of the Bank's reserves. The Banking Department was set up on commercial banking lines. The Bank would accept deposits from commercial banks and other financial intermediaries, and private individuals and would make loans at the discount rate (Bank rate) at rates slightly above the market rate. The Banking Department had reserves of the Fiduciary note issue and some gold.

Although the Bank was following rules-based policy, it was unable to deal with several very serious banking panics in 1847, 1857, and 1866. The problem was that the Banking Department did not have adequate reserves to freely provide liquidity to the financial system in the face of a panic. On several occasions the Bank avoided suspending convertibility by requesting a Treasury letter (a temporary suspension of the Bank's charter), which allowed it to expand the fiduciary note issue as needed. As it turned out, just the news of the issue of the Treasury letter was sufficient to allay the panic in 1847 (Dornbusch and Frenkel 1984) and later in 1866. Another problem with the Bank of England's handling of financial crises was that it attached greater importance to the well-being of its shareholders than to the public in general. In several banking panics (1825, 1847, and 1866), the Bank, concerned over its profitability, acted too late to provide liquidity to the general money market (Schwartz 1986). This led Walter Bagehot, editor of the *Economist*, to state his Responsibility Doctrine urging the Bank, which was privately owned but had a public charter, to put the public's interest first. In his classic book *Lombard Street* (1873), Bagehot also formulated rules for a lender of last resort: in the face of an internal drain (banking panic), lend freely; in the face of an external drain (a currency crisis), lend at a high rate; and in the face of both, lend freely at a high rate.

In the years after 1844 the Bank developed a set of "rules of thumb" to operate as a central bank under the classical gold standard in a world of free capital mobility (Bordo and Schenk 2017). The rules of the game required the Bank to use its discount rate to accommodate gold flows. Thus in the face of a balance of payments deficit and a gold outflow, the Bank was supposed to raise the Bank rate both to encourage a capital inflow and to depress aggregate demand to reduce the demand for imports (raise the balance of trade). In the face of a balance of payment surplus, the Bank

was supposed to lower the Bank rate and encourage capital to leave and
stimulate the economy to increase the demand for imports (reduce the balance of trade) (Bordo 1984).[2]

The gold standard convertibility rule prevailed until the collapse of the
classical gold standard at the outbreak of World War I in 1914. Following
the rule meant that countries would subsume domestic stability concerns
to maintaining the fixed gold parity. The rule followed was a contingency
rule under which the monetary authority would maintain the fixed gold
price except in the event of a major emergency, such as a war when convertibility could be suspended and the central bank could expand its note
issue to raise seigniorage, and the fiscal authorities could run large deficits
to smooth taxes (Bordo and Kydland 1995).[3]

The gold standard rule was successful in the sense that it was associated with stable exchange rates and long-run price stability, and its macro
performance was better than it had been in the interwar period (Bordo
1981). However, many contemporary economists were critical of the gold
standard because it was associated with short-run price level instability and
frequent recessions.

The price level exhibited long swings of low deflation (twenty years) followed by long swings of low inflation (twenty years). These swings in the
price level reflected the operation of the commodity theory of money (Barro
1979), whereby long-run price stability (also known as mean reversion) in
the price level was brought about by changes in gold production and shifts
between monetary and nonmonetary uses of gold in response to changes
in the price level affecting the real price of gold. Thus in periods of deflation, falling prices raised the real price of gold (assuming that monetary
authorities fixed the nominal price). This led to increased gold production
and occasional gold discoveries, in addition to a shift from nonmonetary
to monetary uses of gold, which led to an increase in the world monetary
gold stock and then rising prices. The opposite occurred in periods of
inflation.[4]

Contemporary economists posited that alternative variations of the gold
standard rule could produce price stability (Bordo 1984). W. S. Jevons
(1884) discussed stabilizing a price index. Alfred Marshall (1926) preferred
symmetalism—basing the monetary standard on a mixture of gold and

silver whose value would remain constant with changes in the relative supplies of the two metals. Irving Fisher (1920) developed the compensated dollar, whereby the monetary authorities would change the official price of gold to offset movements in a price index. His proposal was, in essence, a price-level rule. Indeed, in the 1920s his scheme was incorporated in two acts of Congress, which were never passed but which would have required the Federal Reserve to follow a price-level rule (Bordo, Ditmar, and Gavin 2008).[5]

The classical gold standard broke down at the start of World War I. Only the United States maintained the gold dollar peg (although the United States imposed a gold embargo from April 1917 to April 1919). After the war many major belligerents wanted to return to the prewar gold standard at the original parities according to the gold standard contingent rule. Most of these countries came out of World War I with very high rates of inflation and unprecedented levels of outstanding national debt, making resumption a daunting task. The United Kingdom returned to gold at the original parity in 1925, but it did so at the expense of high unemployment (Keynes 1925). France was unable to resume at the original parity because of its high debt and unstable polity (Bordo and Hautcoeur 2007). Germany and other former Central Powers ran hyperinflations. They all restored gold at greatly devalued parities.

The interwar gold standard created at the Genoa Conference in 1922 was a gold exchange standard in which members held both gold and foreign exchange as reserves. The United Kingdom and the United States as center countries backed their currencies with gold. The interwar gold exchange standard lasted only six years. It lacked the credibility of the prewar standard, as most countries were unwilling to let the gold convertibility rule dominate their needs for domestic stability. It also was plagued by maladjustment in the face of disequilibrium parities and nominal rigidities (Meltzer 2003). It collapsed in 1931.

The last vestige of the gold standard rule was the Bretton Woods system established at the international monetary conference in New Hampshire in 1944. Under Bretton Woods, the United States as center country would peg its dollar to gold at $35 per ounce while other countries would peg their currencies in terms of dollars. Unlike the gold standard, the Bretton Woods system was an adjustable peg system whereby members could change their parities in the face of a fundamental disequilibrium brought about, for example, by a supply shock that changed the real exchange rate. Bretton Woods also had capital controls. Like the interwar gold exchange standard, the Bretton Woods system, which had some of the flaws of the Gold Exchange Standard, broke down between 1968 and 1971. A key problem was that the basic rules of the system were not followed. The United States as center country inflated its currency after 1965. Other countries also broke the rules by not allowing the adjustment mechanism to work in the sense that surplus countries like Germany did not allow their money supplies to expand, and deficit countries like the United Kingdom did not allow adjustment through deflation (Bordo 1993).

Rules versus Authorities in the Twentieth Century

The Federal Reserve was founded in 1913 to be the central bank for the United States. The Federal Reserve Act was in part based on concepts from the Currency School versus Banking School debate and the history of the Bank of England (Meltzer 2003, chap. 2). From the Currency School the Fed inherited the convertibility rule of the gold standard. From the Banking School the Fed inherited both the real bills doctrine and the institution of a lender of last resort to allay banking panics.

By the time the Federal Reserve opened its doors for business in November 1914, most of the belligerents in World War I had left the gold standard, and when the United States entered the war in April 1917, an embargo on gold exports was imposed for two years. The Federal Reserve became an engine of inflation financing the government's fiscal deficits. The gold standard became operational after the war, but in the 1920s the Fed prevented the adjustment mechanism from working by sterilizing gold inflows and preventing the money supply from rising. This policy contributed to the global imbalances that eventually led to the breakdown of the interwar gold exchange standard (Friedman and Schwartz 1963; Irwin 2010).

The real bills doctrine guided the Fed's action in the first two decades of its operation, and according to Friedman and Schwartz (1963) and

Meltzer (2003), contributed to some serious policy errors, including the recession of 1920–1921, the Wall Street stock market boom and crash in the 1920s, and the banking panics of the Great Contraction. Indeed, Milton Friedman (1960), following Henry Simons (1936), was highly critical of the independent Federal Reserve for following flawed discretionary policies.

In a seminal article "Rules versus Authorities in Monetary Policy," Henry Simons (1936) made the case for the Federal Reserve to follow rules rather than discretion. Simons posited that in a liberal order (a free society and free market economy), central bank discretion would lead to uncertainty, which would prevent relative prices and markets from operating efficiently, thus contributing to economic instability. He believed that a simple legislated monetary rule would remove the uncertainty of leaving policy decisions to central bank officials. Simons considered a number of possible rules. His first choice was to have a fixed money supply. If prices were flexible, it would lead to deflation as productivity advance would lead to real economic growth. He had reservations with this rule because of measurement issues in determining which monetary aggregate to use; these include: the presence of price rigidities and financial innovation and the development of money substitutes, which would shift velocity. However, he argued that 100 percent Reserve banking could solve the problem of money substitutes (shadow banking). In his scheme commercial banks would become public utilities that just managed the payments system (Friedman 1967; Rockoff 2015). The financial intermediation function of banks would be done by investment banks. Simons also considered tying the money supply to the fiscal deficit and having monetary policy run by the Treasury.[6] Maintaining a balanced budget would also keep the money supply stable.

In the end, he came out preferring a price-level rule, which he argued would avoid the problems associated with a monetary aggregate rule. Prices would be kept stable by the Treasury following a balanced budget and by keeping the money supply constant.

Milton Friedman, in chapter 4 of *A Program for Monetary Stability* (1960), built upon Henry Simons's case for a monetary rule (Friedman 1967).

Friedman, who was a student of Simons at the University of Chicago, further developed Simons's case against discretion. Discretion would lead to uncertainty, which impedes the private sector's decision-making process. He focused his criticism on the Fed's policy of fine-tuning, which was developed in the post–World War II era to offset business fluctuations. Friedman (1953) demonstrated that when the Fed used its policy tools to offset exogenous shocks, it would in most cases aggravate the business cycle. It does this by mistiming its policies because of "the long and variable lags" between changes in monetary policy and its effects on prices and output. Friedman also argued that the correlation between the policy action and the shocks needed to be greater than 0.5 to be stabilizing. Other arguments against discretion included that discretion involves both changes in the guides for monetary policy and changes in its conduct. The guide to monetary policy changed from real bills in the interwar period, to influencing the money market after the Federal Reserve Treasury Accord, to fine-tuning and leaning against the wind in the postwar period. Friedman also argued that discretion did not allow an objective method to judge monetary policy. Finally, he argued that discretion exposes the conduct of monetary policy to political influences.

In a series of articles Milton Friedman and Anna Schwartz documented the long and variable lags of monetary policy and how discretionary Fed policy led to instability in prices and output throughout the Fed's history.[7] The Fed's worst mistake was its key role in precipitating the Great Contraction of 1929 to 1933.

The rule that Friedman favored (and is always associated with) was his constant growth rate of the money supply rule (CGMR), which he first exposited in 1960. However, Friedman had an earlier rule in 1948 that was related to one of Henry Simons's rules. The rule was designed to stabilize the business cycle over time. In Friedman's 1948 rule the Fed would use its open market operations to finance the fiscal deficit over time to ensure a long-run balanced budget and to stabilize the economy. When the level of output fell below the full employment level, automatic stabilizers, such as a decline in tax revenues via the progressive income tax, would lead to a budget deficit that would be financed by an increase in the money supply.

The opposite would happen when the economy faced inflationary pressure. The resultant equilibrating change in income would restore both full employment and budget balance. Nelson (2019) argues that Friedman later changed his mind about this rule as he became more critical of the Keynesian thinking that underlay it.[8]

In chapter 4 of *A Program for Monetary Stability* (1960) Friedman proposed his famous CGMR. He argued that the Fed should set the growth rate of the stock of money equal to the long-run growth rate of real GDP adjusted for the trend change in velocity. The trend growth of real GDP in the century before 1960 was about 3 percent whereas the trend growth in velocity was −1 percent. To achieve price stability (inflation equals zero), money growth would need to be at 4 percent per year. Friedman argued that the Fed should increase money growth at 4 percent, year in and year out. He argued that the rule was simple enough that people would understand it and that adhering to it would eliminate the uncertainty that accompanied discretion.

Friedman was in favor of using M2 as his definition of money (currency plus demand deposits plus time deposits minus large certificates of deposits) on the grounds that it was both a temporary abode of purchasing power (his favored explanation for the use of money as both a medium of exchange and an asset) and that it was the only monetary aggregate where the data existed back to the nineteenth century (Friedman and Schwartz 1970). But he believed that an alternative definition like M1 (currency plus demand deposits) could also work as long as the Fed stuck to the rule indefinitely.

Friedman's CGMR rule, or k% rule, was very controversial. It was criticized for its definition of money, and for its simplicity. Some argued that M2 was inappropriate because the money multiplier was largely determined by the real economy and that a monetary base rule would more appropriately reflect a variable that the Fed actually controlled. Many argued that it did not account for the endogeneity of the money supply (Tobin 1970). Alternative variants of his rule were developed that accounted for feedback from the real economy and short-run changes in velocity (e.g., McCallum 1987). Modigliani (1964) showed that a simulation of the rule over the postwar period did not stabilize the economy. In contrast, historical studies by Warburton (1966) and Bordo, Choudhri, and Schwartz (1995) showed that had the Fed followed the CGMR, then the Great Depression would have been avoided.[9]

Friedman was highly critical of the Fed in the 1950s, 1960s, and 1970s for not paying adequate attention to monetary aggregates in their policy setting. In a number of papers he criticized the Fed for not tightening monetary policy enough to prevent run-ups in inflation and during recessions for waiting too long to follow expansionary policy (Bordo and Landon-Lane 2013). In addition to criticizing the Fed for its destabilizing fine-tuning policy, he also criticized it for using interest rates as both its policy instrument and its target, arguing that had it used the money stock, it could have done better. After Friedman predicted in the 1960s and 1970s that there would be a large inflation, the economics profession and the Fed began to listen to him (Nelson 2019), and the Fed began to pay attention to monetary aggregates in its policy setting. The height of Friedman's influence was reached in 1975, when Congress passed a bill requiring the Federal Reserve to announce its monetary aggregate targets for the future and to report to the Congress every year on how well it performed in hitting its targets. Most of the time, the Fed missed its targets.

The Fed's experience with monetary targeting, which was the closest thing that it came to following Friedman's CGMR, was quite dismal. The Fed's monetary policy strategy was to use a short-run money demand function with lagged adjustment (the Goldfeld [1973] model), and then based on the coefficients of the model and forecasts of real output and inflation, it would set the short-run interest rate in order to hit its money growth target. This strategy, which was used in the 1970s and 1980s by the Fed, the Bank of Canada, and the Bank of England, was abandoned because of the "missing money problem"—that is, velocity kept shifting up in an unpredictable manner, reflecting both financial innovation and changes in financial regulation (Laidler 1985; Anderson, Bordo, and Duca 2017). By the early 1980s the Fed and other central banks abandoned monetary aggregate targeting and shifted to using short-term interest rates as its method to operate monetary policy.

The Modern View of Rules versus Discretion

The rules versus discretion debate has been reinterpreted following the rational expectations revolution in macroeconomics in the 1970s. Seminal work by Lucas (1972) and Sargent and Wallace (1975) posited that in the face of rational expectations under which market agents understood the models that central banks used in their policy making, the central banks as a consequence no longer had an information advantage to conduct discretionary monetary policy. Lucas (1976) demonstrated that with rational expectations large-scale models could not be used to simulate alternative counterfactual discretionary policies without accounting for the rational expectations of the public. Sargent and Wallace (1975) showed that optimal control techniques used in the 1960s and 1970s to design countercyclical monetary policies to offset shocks and smooth the business cycle (Brainard 1967) and to confront Friedman's (1953) critique would be ineffective in a world of rational expectations. In this new macro theoretical context, Kydland and Prescott (1977) argued that discretion, defined as changes in monetary policy based on current information taking the past as given, would not be successful in the pursuit of stabilization policy. This is because market agents with rational expectations would adjust their behavior accordingly. According to them, discretionary policy would be time inconsistent in the sense that if the Fed had announced a policy strategy at time zero, which was supposed to continue indefinitely into the future, and then in the next period, when faced with new information—on the assumption that the public would not change its actions—the Fed changed its policy. When the public caught on and adjusted its behavior, the Fed's policy actions would be stymied. Kydland and Prescott gave the example of the Phillips curve trade-off, arguing that if agents had adaptive expectations (the assumption made by Friedman in his seminal 1968 AEA presidential address in which he argued that in the long run the Phillips curve was vertical), then the Fed could reduce unemployment by following expansionary policy and hence return the economy to the natural rate of unemployment before the public could adjust its expectations of inflation. They argued that with rational expectations, when the Fed followed its discretionary policy, market agents would immediately adjust their expectations so that there would be no effect on unemployment, and the price level would end up at a higher equilibrium level.

Kydland and Prescott argued that the only way the Fed could follow a time-consistent policy would be by committing itself to a rule that would constrain it from changing previously announced policies when circumstances change.

According to Barro and Gordon (1983), even if the Fed did announce that it was following a rule, there would always be a temptation to cheat once circumstances changed, and the advantages of cheating would outweigh the cost. But in that case, the public with rational expectations would catch on, and the policy would be ineffective. They argue that what is required is a binding commitment mechanism where the costs of cheating would be less than the costs of following the rule. In other words, the Fed would need a mechanism that effectively tied its hands (Giavazzi and Pagano 1988). A historical example of such a commitment mechanism was the gold standard rule (Bordo and Kydland 1995).

Modern Instrument Rules: The Taylor Rule

The new approach to rules versus discretion led to important empirical and theoretical work on finding rules that could be the best guides for policy makers. Empirical work by Bryant, Hooper, and Mann (1993), based on a number of large multicountry econometric models incorporating rational expectations, found that instrument rules based on policy interest rates would give the best performance. According to the Taylor rule, the policy interest rate would react to the central banks' two principle policy goals (which in the United States were based on the dual mandate of low inflation and low unemployment[10])—of deviations of inflation from expected inflation and the output gap—performed best in terms of producing the lowest variations. These rules performed better than target rules like Friedman's CGMR. In addition, instrument rules using the policy rate as an instrument outperformed rules using monetary aggregates. Along these lines, Taylor (1993) devised a simple version of an interest rate rule for the United States, as shown in equation (1):

$$i_t = \Pi_t + \Theta(\Pi_t - \bar{\Pi}) + \gamma y_t + R \tag{1}$$

where i_t is the target level of the short-term nominal interest rate (the federal funds rate), Π_t is the four-quarter inflation rate, $\bar{\Pi}$ is the target level of inflation, y_t is the output gap (the per cent deviation of real GDP from its potential level), and R is the equilibrium level of the real interest rate (the natural rate of interest).

Taylor (1993) postulated that the output gap and inflation gaps entered the central bank's reaction function with equal weights of 0.5 and that the equilibrium level of the real interest rate and the inflation target were each equal to 2 percent. This led to equation (2), which is commonly known as the Taylor rule.

$$i_t = 1.0 + 1.5\Pi_t + 0.5y_t \tag{2}$$

A number of other interest rate instrument rules have been used in the past two decades. Some rules (interest rate smoothing rules) have the interest rate reacting to the lagged interest rate (Clarida, Galí, and Gertler 2000). Other rules put a higher weight on real output than did Taylor, while some rules focused on changes rather than levels of the interest rate and the policy objectives (Orphanides 2007).[11]

Taylor initially viewed his rule as a normative rule or as a guide to policy as well as an ex post description of the performance of monetary policy makers. When output is below potential, the rule implies that the Fed should reduce its policy rate sufficiently to reduce the real interest rate. When inflation is above the target rate, the Fed should raise interest rates sufficiently to raise the real interest. Based on the postulated coefficients, the Taylor principle requires that the coefficient on the inflation term be at least 1.5 to reduce inflation.

Taylor (1999b) used his rule to evaluate the performance of monetary policy in the United States across historical policy regimes: the classical gold standard, Bretton Woods, and the current regime of managed floating. Each of the regimes conducted monetary policy differently, but they could be evaluated using the same framework. Taylor found that the coefficients derived from estimating his rule were much lower under the gold standard than in the postwar period and that the coefficients under Bretton Woods were lower than under the managed floating period. He also found that the Taylor principle did not hold during the Great Inflation period of the 1960s and 1970s. He attributed the rise in the coefficients over time to a process of policy learning.

The Taylor rule can also be used to ascertain the extent to which central banks are following rule-like behavior by comparing the actual policy rate to the rate predicted by the Taylor rule. Taylor (2012) and Nikolsko-Rzhevskyy et al. (2014) find that the federal funds rate was closest to the Taylor rule during the Great Moderation era from 1983 to 2003 when Paul Volcker and Alan Greenspan were chairs of the Federal Reserve. Deviations from rule-like behavior were considerable during the Great Inflation period in the 1970s—a regime characterized by Friedman (1982), Meltzer (2012), and Taylor (2012) as discretionary. Beginning in 1965, the Fed gradually fell behind the curve in reducing the rise in both the rate of inflation and inflationary expectations.

There is considerable debate about the causes of the Great Inflation (Bordo and Orphanides 2013, see chapter 1). A key failing was the Fed's unwillingness to keep rates high enough and long enough to break the back of inflationary expectations because of the fear of a political reaction to the necessary recession and rise in unemployment. The appointment of Paul Volcker as Fed chair, with a mandate to end inflation and his introduction of a contractionary monetary policy based on monetary targeting, succeeded by 1983 to reduce inflation to low single-digit levels. Volcker and his successor, Alan Greenspan, elevated the goal of low inflation and maintaining credibility for low inflation to their highest priority.

The rules-based policy ended in 2003 when the Fed kept rates considerably below the Taylor rule to prevent the economy from falling into a Japan-style deflation (Reifschneider and Williams 2000). It is questionable how serious this risk really was.[12] As a consequence, monetary policy was overly expansionary, and some have argued (Taylor 2007, Taylor 2012; Nikolsko-Rzhevskyy et al. 2014; Ahrend, Cournede, and Price 2008; Bordo and Landon-Lane 2013) that this policy was a key contributor to the boom in house prices that burst in 2006, leading to the subprime mortgage crisis of 2007–2008. Taylor (2013), Meltzer (2012), Schwartz (2008b), Bordo (2014), Goodfriend (2011), and others argue that some of the Fed's lender of last resort policies in 2008 involved both credit and fiscal policies, which threatened the Fed's independence. The policy of quantitative easing and forward guidance in effect since 2009 has been viewed as largely discretionary (Taylor 2012). The Fed instituted forward guidance to anchor the public's expectations. Yet it continually changed its announcements with incoming data. In many ways this recalled the fine-tuning policies of the 1950s–1970s. The continued pursuit of discretionary policy has likely contributed to an increase in policy uncertainty since the recent financial crisis. This has contributed to the unusual slow recovery (Bordo and Haubrich 2017) via reduced bank lending (Bordo, Duca, and Koch 2017) and investment (Bloom 2009).

The Taylor rule can be used to evaluate economic performance under rules and discretion regimes using a trade-off (indifference) curve between the variance of inflation and the variance of real output (measured as a percentage deviation from trend), which can be estimated from DSGE models (Taylor 2013). Along each curve the Fed can achieve smaller inflation variability at the expense of greater real variability. The position of the curve depends on the structure of the economy and the size of exogenous shocks. Taylor uses this apparatus to show that the Volcker regime change in 1979 that led to the Great Moderation and the adoption of a rules-based policy was associated with a shift inward of the trade-off curve.[13] Similarly, the movement away from rules-based policy in 2003 and subsequently has led to a shift upward in the curve from its position during the Great Moderation.

Not all economists have accepted the modern case for rules. Benjamin Friedman (2012) argued that in the face of big shocks, like major financial crises, the central bank needs the flexibility to abandon the rule and act as a lender of last resort. However, if one views modern instrument rules as contingent rules like the classical gold standard, then the use of lender of last resort actions during a financial crisis to expand money and liquidity above what would be required in a normal business cycle should not be inconsistent with the case for rule-like policies. On similar lines, Bernanke (2003) made the case for constrained discretion, which meant following rules as a rough guideline but maintaining flexibility to set policy in the face of incoming data. This raises the question of whether it is rules or discretion that is being followed. This introduces uncertainty into decision makers' choice set and defeats the main purpose of following rules made by Simons and Friedman.

Finally, the rules versus discretion distinction has great relevance for international monetary relations. Economic performance (low and stable inflation and high and stable real economic growth) performed best under rules-based regimes: the classical gold standard, Bretton Woods and Great Moderation regimes (Bordo 1993; Benati and Goodhart 2010; Rockoff and White 2015). Moreover, international monetary cooperation worked best under these rules-based regimes (Bordo and Schenk 2017). Deviations from the Taylor rule were lower across countries during the Great Moderation than they were in the period before and also lower than since 2003 (Nikolsko-Rzhevskyy et al. 2014; Ahrend, Cournede, and Price 2008). Meltzer (2012) suggested that if countries were to follow a common inflation target or a Taylor rule, the global economy could be more stable than under discretion. In many ways, countries following common domestic monetary rules under flexible exchange rates would be similar to the fixed exchange rate gold standard period when adherence to the gold standard ensured good economic performance. Under floating rates the real exchange rate would adjust to real shocks, and nominal exchange rate movements reflecting poor monetary policy would be greatly reduced (Meltzer 1987).

Recently the US House of Representatives passed a bill that in some sense echoes the 1975 bill requiring the Federal Reserve to report to Congress on its progress with monetary targeting. This recent bill (HR 3189) would require the Federal Reserve Open Market Committee to decide on a policy rule and to then report periodically to Congress on its performance in following the rule. Like the 1975 act, this new bill would encourage the Fed to follow rules-based policy by clearly stating its policy strategy in advance and then justifying any significant departures from the rule. It would encourage the Fed to reduce its dependence on discretionary policy and move it back toward the good performance that it followed during the Great Moderation.

Conclusion

The nineteenth-century Bullionist and Currency School versus Banking School debates formulated the case for monetary rules instead of discretion. The gold standard convertibility rule, the "rules of the game," and Bagehot's strictures for a lender of last resort were part of the institutional framework associated with good macroeconomic performance by the advanced countries and the establishment of the pre–1914 liberal order.

The middle of the twentieth century witnessed the breakdown of this order and a long period of economic, financial, and political instability and a movement toward discretionary monetary and fiscal policies. Henry Simons (1936) and his successor at the Chicago School, Milton Friedman, revived the case for monetary rules as an essential part of a restored liberal order. Simons proposed a price-level rule while Friedman proposed his constant growth rate of the money supply rule. Friedman was an effective critic of the Federal Reserve's ongoing discretionary regime and by the 1970s was able to influence legislation that influenced the Fed to move toward rules-based policy.

The rational expectations revolution in the 1970s led to a new perspective on rules versus discretion by Kydland and Prescott (1977). Now discretion was not viewed as misguided or mistaken actions by well-meaning officials but as following time-inconsistent policies by not following through on earlier-stated plans. Agents with rational expectations would understand this, negating the effects of the discretionary policy. In this lexicon a rule was a commitment mechanism to prevent policy makers from not following through with their strategy. John Taylor (1993), using models that incorporated rational expectations, developed an interest rate policy rule that reacted to the central banks' key policy goals of price and real output stability in a way to provide optimal performance. The Taylor rule as well as other instrument rules could be used as a normative guide to policy makers but also to evaluate policy strategies ex post. Considerable evidence by Taylor and others convincingly shows that following rules-based policy instead of discretion-based policy leads to better economic performance. This is clearly seen in a comparison of the economic performance of the Great Moderation of 1983–2003 with the Great Inflation period that preceded it and the subsequent period of the housing price boom, financial crisis, and slow recovery that followed it. Policy rules are also important in stabilizing the global economy and in enhancing international monetary policy cooperation.

The historical record makes a strong case for the formal adoption of policy rules today as a guide to monetary policy making. The modern record echoes the experience of the gold standard era of a century ago.

Notes

1. Price indexes had not yet been invented and so by inflation people focused on commodities like the price of wheat and the exchange rate for which there was good data.

2. The Bank of England generally followed the rules of the game, but the central banks of most other countries did not. However, violation of the rules never led them to break the basic gold standard convertibility rule (Bordo and MacDonald 2010).

3. The gold standard contingency rule could also be viewed as a rule or commitment mechanism in the modern sense of Kydland and Prescott (1977).

4. In addition to long swings in the global price level, there was considerable price variability between countries reflecting the operation of the price-specie flow mechanism of the classical gold standard (Bordo 1981).

5. Indeed, Sweden in the 1930s did institute a price-level rule (Berg and Jonung 1999).

6. In 1936 the Fed had de facto lost much of its independence to the Treasury under Secretary Henry Morgenthau. It followed a low interest rate peg to facilitate the Treasury's fiscal expansion under the New Deal and then during World War II. The Fed regained its independence only to conduct monetary policy with the Federal Reserve Treasury Accord in February 1951 (Meltzer 2003).

7. As well as other colleagues, including David Meiselman and Philip Cagan.

8. Friedman, like Simons, considered and then rejected a price-level rule for the same reasons that Simons did, that it would not account for changes in velocity due

to the development of money substitutes, and because of the long and variable lags between changes in the money stock and changes in the price level. He argued that the Fed should target something that it could control, such as the money stock.

9. McCallum (1990) also showed that had the Fed followed his constant growth of the monetary base rule adjusted for feedback from the real economy, then the Great Contraction could have been attenuated.

10. The dual mandate came out of the Employment Act of 1946, which elevated full employment to a leading policy goal of monetary policy. Low inflation (price stability) was already incorporated in the Federal Reserve Act. In the past seventy years, the dual mandate has been interpreted differently by every successive Fed chair. In the 1950s and early 1960s, William McChesney Martin Jr. attached highest priority to low inflation. He believed that maintaining price stability would provide the framework to maintain full employment. Later in the 1970s, Arthur Burns attached greater weight to full employment than high inflation. In the 1980s and 1990s, Paul Volcker and Alan Greenspan attached greater weight to low inflation and, like Martin, believed that maintaining a regime of low inflation would be best for the real economy. Since the recent financial crisis, both Ben Bernanke and Janet Yellen have attached greater weight to full employment and have argued that the dual mandate requires equal attention to both goals.

11. See Taylor (1999b, 5–7) and Taylor and Wieland (2010).

12. Bordo, Landon-Lane, and Redish (2009) make a distinction between "good" productivity-driven (supply side) deflation, as in 1879–1896 in the United States, and "bad" aggregate demand-driven deflation, as in the Great Depression. It is not clear that the low inflation of the early 2000s was a bad deflation.

13. A question that arose was the extent to which the improved economic performance during the Great Moderation reflected good policy or good luck. Stock and Watson (2002) attributed it to good luck whereas Bernanke (2004), King (2012), and Taylor (2013) attribute it to good policy.

References

Ahrend, Rudiger, Boris Cournede, and Robert Price. 2008. "Monetary Policy, Market Excesses, and Financial Turmoil." OECD Economics Department Working Paper No. 597. Paris: Organization for Economic Cooperation and Development.

Anderson, Richard, Michael Bordo, and John Duca. 2017. "Money and Velocity during Financial Crises: From the Great Depression to the Great Recession." *Journal of Economic Dynamics and Control* 81 (August): 32–49.

Bagehot, Walter. 1873. *Lombard Street: A Description.* London: Henry S. King.

Barro, Robert. 1979. "Money and the Price Level Under the Gold Standard." *Economic Journal* 89, no. 353 (March): 13–33.

Barro, Robert, and David Gordon. 1983. "Rules, Discretion and Reputation in a Model of Monetary Policy." *Journal of Monetary Economics* 12 (July): 101–21.

Benati, Luca, and Charles Goodhart. 2010. "Monetary Policy Regimes and Economic Performance: The Historical Record 1979–2008." In *Handbook of Monetary Economics*. Vol. 3, edited by Benjamin Friedman and Michael Woodford, 1159–1236. New York: North Holland Publishers.

Berg, Claes, and Lars Jonung. 1999. "Pioneering Price Level Targeting: The Swedish Experience." *Journal of Monetary Economics* 43, no. 3 (June): 525–51.

Bernanke, Ben S. 2003. "Constrained Discretion and Monetary Policy." Remarks at the Federal Reserve Board of Governors meeting, New York. February 3.

———. 2004. "The Great Moderation." Remarks at the meetings of the Eastern Economics Association, Washington, DC. February 20.

Bloom, Nicholas. 2009. "The Impact of Uncertainty Shocks." *Econometrica* 73 (3): 623–83.

Bordo, Michael. 1981. "The Classical Gold Standard: Some Lessons for Today." *Federal Reserve Bank of St. Louis Review* 63, no. 6 (May): 2–17.

———. 1984. "The Gold Standard: The Traditional Approach." In *A Retrospective on the Classical Gold Standard, 1821–1931*, edited by Michael D. Bordo and Anna J. Schwartz, 23–120. Chicago: University of Chicago Press.

———. 1993. "The Bretton Woods International Monetary System: A Historical Overview." In *A Retrospective on the Bretton Woods System: Lessons for International Monetary Reform*, edited by Michael Bordo and Barry Eichengreen, 3–98. Chicago: University of Chicago Press.

———. 2014. "The Federal Reserve's Role: Actions before, during , and after the 2008 Panic in the Historical Context of the Great Contraction." In *Across the Great Divide: New Perspectives on the Financial Crisis*, edited by Martin N. Bailey and John B. Taylor, 103–26. Stanford CA: Hoover Institution Press.

Bordo, Michael, Ehsan Choudhri, and Anna J. Schwartz. 1995. "Could Stable Money Have Averted the Great Contraction?" *Economic Inquiry* 33, no. 3 (July): 484–505.

Bordo, Michael, Robert Ditmar, and William Gavin. 2008. "Gold, Fiat Money, and Price Stability." *B. E. Journal of Macroeconomics* 7 (1): 1935–1690.

Bordo, Michael, John V. Duca, and Christoffer Cox. 2017. "Money and Velocity during Financial Crises: From the Great Depression to the Great Recession." *Journal of Economic Dynamics and Control* 81 (April).

Bordo, Michael, and William Gavin. 2007. "Gold, Fiat Money and Price Stability." *Berkeley Journal of Macroeconomics: Topics in Macroeconomics* 7 (June): 1–31.

Bordo, Michael, and Joseph Haubrich. 2017. "Deep Recessions, Fast Recoveries and Financial Crises: Evidence from the American Record." *Economic Inquiry* 55, no. 1 (June): 527–45.

Bordo, Michael, and Pierre Cyrille Hautcoeur. 2007. "Why Didn't France Follow the British Stabilization after World War I?" *European Review of Economic History* 11 (1): 3–37.

Bordo, Michael, and Finn Kydland. 1995. "The Gold Standard as a Rule: An Essay in Exploration." *Explorations in Economic History* 32, no. 4 (October): 423–64.

Bordo, Michael, and John Landon-Lane. 2013. "Exits from Recessions: The US Experience, 1920–2007." In *No Way Out: Government Response to the Financial Crisis*, edited by Vincent Reinhart, 117–82. Washington, DC: American Enterprise Institute.

Bordo, Michael, John Landon-Lane, and Angela Redish. 2009. "Good versus Bad Deflation: Lessons from the Gold Standard Era." In *Monetary Policy in Low-Inflation Economies*, edited by David Altig and Ed Nosal, 127–74. New York: Cambridge University Press.

Bordo, Michael, and Ronald MacDonald. 2010. *Credibility and the International Monetary Regime*. New York: Cambridge University Press.

Bordo, Michael, and Athanasios Orphanides. 2013. *The Great Inflation*. Chicago: University of Chicago Press.

Bordo, Michael, and Catherine Schenk. 2017. "Monetary Policy Cooperation and Coordination: An Historical Perspective on the Importance of Rules." In *Rules For International Monetary Stability*, edited by Michael D. Bordo and John B. Taylor, 205–62. Stanford, CA: Hoover Institution Press.

Bordo, Michael, and Anna J. Schwartz. 1980. "Money and Prices in the Nineteenth Century: An Old Debate Rejoined." *Journal of Economic History* 40, no. 1 (March): 61–67.

———. 1999. "Monetary Policy Regimes and Economic Performance: The Historical Record." In *North Holland Handbook of Macroeconomics*, edited by John B. Taylor and Michael Woodford, 149–23. New York: North Holland Publishers.

Bordo, Michael, and Eugene White. 1990. "A Tale of Two Currencies: British and French Finances during the Napoleonic Wars." *Journal of Economic History* 51, no. 2 (June): 303–16.

Brainard, William. 1967. "Uncertainty and the Effectiveness of Policy." *American Economic Review* 57 (May): 41–425.

Bryant, Ralph, Peter Hooper, and Catherine Mann. 1993. *Evaluating Policy Regimes: New Empirical Research in Empirical Macroeconomics*. Washington, DC: Brookings Institution.

Clarida, Richard, Jordi Galí, and Mark Gertler. 2000. "Monetary Policy Rules and Macroeconomic Stability: Evidence and Some Theory." *Quarterly Journal of Economics* 115, no. 1 (February): 147–80.

Dornbusch, Rudiger, and Jacob Frenkel. 1984. "The Gold Standard and the Bank of England in the Crisis of 1847." *Journal of International Economics* 16, no. 1 (February): 233–71.

Fisher, Irving. 1920. *Stabilizing the Dollar.* New York: Macmillan.

Friedman, Benjamin. 2012. "Rules versus Discretion at the Federal Reserve: On to the Second Century." *Journal of Macroeconomics* 34:608–15.

Friedman, Milton. 1953. "The Effects of a Full Employment Policy on Economic Stability: A Formal Analysis." In *Essays in Positive Economics*, by Milton Friedman, 117–32. Chicago: University of Chicago Press.

———. 1960. *A Program for Monetary Stability.* New York: Fordham University Press.

———. 1967. "The Monetary Theory and Policy of Henry Simons." *Journal of Law and Economics* 10 (October): 1–13.

———. 1968. "The Role of Monetary Policy." *American Economic Review* 58, no. 1 (March): 1–17.

———. 1982. "Monetary Policy: Theory and Practice." *Journal of Money, Credit and Banking* 14, no. 1 (February): 98–118

Friedman, Milton, and Anna J. Schwartz. 1963. *A Monetary History of the United States 1867 to 1960.* Princeton, NJ: Princeton University Press.

———. 1970. *Monetary Statistics of the United States.* New York: Columbia University Press.

Giavazzi, Francesco, and Marco Pagano. 1988. "The Advantage of Tying One's Hands: EMS Discipline and Central Bank Credibility." *European Economic Review* 32:303–330.

Goldfeld, Stephen. 1973. "The Demand for Money Revisited." *Brookings Papers on Economic Activity* No. 3.

Goodfriend, Marvin. 2011. "Central Banking in the Credit Turmoil: An Assessment of Federal Reserve Practice." *Journal of Monetary Economics* 58, no. 1 (January): 1–12.

Irwin, Douglas. 2010. "Did France Cause the Great Depression?" NBER Working Paper No. 16350. September.

Jevons, William Stanley. 1884. *Investigations in Currency and Finance.* London: Macmillan.

Keynes, John Maynard. 1925. *The Economic Consequences of Mr. Churchill.* Cambridge: Cambridge University Press.

King, Mervyn. 2012. "Twenty Years of Inflation Targeting." The Stamp Memorial Lecture, London School of Economics. October 9.

Kydland, Finn, and Edward Prescott. 1977. "Rules Rather than Discretion: The Inconsistency of Optimal Plans." *Journal of Political Economy* 85 (June): 473–92.

Laidler, David. 1985. *The Demand for Money.* 4th ed. New York: Harper and Rowe.

———. 2002. "Rules, Discretion and Financial Crises in Classical and Neoclassical Economics." *Economic Issues* 7, part 2 (September): 11–34.

Lucas, Robert E., Jr. 1972. "Expectations and the Neutrality of Money." *Journal of Economic Theory* 4 (2): 103–24.

———. 1976. "Economic Policy Evaluation: A Critique." In *Carnegie Rochester Conference Series on Public Policy*, edited by K. Brunner and A. H. Meltzer. 29:19–46.

Marshall, Alfred. 1926. *Official Papers*. London: Macmillan.

McCallum, Bennett R. 1987. "The Case for Rules in the Conduct of Monetary Policy: A Concrete Example." *Federal Reserve Bank of Richmond Economic Review* (September/October):1–18.

———. 1990. "Could a Monetary Base Rule Have Prevented the Great Depression?" *Journal of Monetary Economics* 26 no. 1 (August): 3–26.

Meltzer, Allan. 1987. "Limits of Short-Run Stabilization Policy: Presidential Address to the Western Economic Association, July 3, 1986." *Economic Inquiry* 25 (January 1987): 1–14.

———. 2003. *A History of the Federal Reserve*. Vol. 1. Chicago: University of Chicago Press.

———. 2012. "Federal Reserve Policy in the Great Recession." *Cato Journal* 32, no. 2 (Spring/Summer): 255–63.

Modigliani, Franco. 1964. "Some Empirical Facts of Monetary Management and Rules versus Discretion." *Journal of Political Economy* 72, no. 3 (April): 211–45.

Nelson, Edward. (2019). *The Economics of Milton Friedman*. Chicago: University of Chicago Press.

Nikolsko-Rzhevskyy, Alex, David Papell, and Ruxandra Prodan. 2014. "Deviations from Rules-Based Policy and Their Effects." In *Frameworks for Central Banking in the Next Century: A Special Issue on the Occasion of the Founding of the Federal Reserve*, edited by Michael D. Bordo, William Dupour, and John B. Taylor. *Journal of Economic Dynamics and Control* 49 (December): 4–17.

Orphanides, Athanasios. 2007. "Taylor Rules." *Federal Reserve Board of Governors Finance and Economics Discussion Papers* (January). Washington, DC: Federal Reserve Board.

Reifschneider, David L., and John C. Williams. 2000. "Three Lessons for Monetary Policy in a Low-Inflation Era." *Journal of Money, Credit and Banking* 32, no. 4, part 2 (November): 936–66.

Rockoff, Hugh. 2015. "Henry Simons on Banking and Monetary Policy." Becker Friedman Institute, Chicago.

Rockoff, Hugh, and Eugene White. 2015. "Monetary Regimes and Policy on a Global Scale: The Ouevre of Michael Bordo." In *Current Federal Reserve Policy under the Lens of History*, edited by Owen Humpage. New York: Cambridge University Press.

Sargent, Thomas, and Neil Wallace. 1975. "Rational Expectations, the Optimal Monetary Instrument, and the Optimal Money Supply Rule." *Journal of Political Economy* 83, no. 2 (April): 241–58.

Schwartz, Anna J. 1986. "Real versus Pseudo Financial Crises." In *Crises in the World Banking System*, edited by Forrest Capie and Geoffrey Wood, 11–41. London: Macmillan.

———. 2008a. "Banking School, Currency School and Free Banking School." In *The New Palgrave Dictionary of Economics*. London: Palgrave Macmillan.

———. 2008b. "Origins of the Financial Market Crisis of 2008." *Cato Journal* 29 (1): 19–23.

Simons, Henry. 1936. "Rules versus Authorities in Monetary Policy." *Journal of Political Economy* 44 (1): 1–30.

Stock, James, and Mark Watson. 2002. "Has the Business Cycle Changed?" In *Monetary Policy and Uncertainty: Adapting to a Changing Economy*, 9–56. Federal Reserve Bank of Kansas City, Jackson Hole Conference.

Taylor, John B. 1993. "Discretion versus Policy Rules in Practice." *Carnegie Rochester Conference Series on Public Policy* 39, (December): 195–214.

———. 1999a. "An Historical Analysis of Monetary Policy Rules." In *Monetary Policy Rules*, 319–48. Chicago: University of Chicago Press.

———. 1999b. "Introduction." In *Monetary Policy Rules*, 1–14. Chicago: University of Chicago Press.

———. 2007. "Housing and Monetary Policy." In Housing, Housing Finance, and Monetary Policy. *Proceedings of the Federal Reserve Bank of Kansas City Symposium*, Jackson Hole, WY. September: 463–76.

———. 2012. "Monetary Policy Works and Discretion Doesn't: A Tale of Two Eras." *Journal of Money, Credit and Banking* 44 (6): 1017–32.

———. 2013. "The Effectiveness of Central Bank Independence versus Policy Rules." *Business Economics* 48 (3): 155–62.

Taylor, John B., and Volker Wieland. 2010. "Surprising Comparative Properties of Monetary Models: Results from a New Database." *European Central Bank Working Paper* No. 1261. November.

Tobin, James. 1970. "Money and Income: Post Hoc Ergo Propter Hoc." *Quarterly Journal of Economics* 84(2): 301–19.

Viner, Jacob. 1937. *Studies in the Theory of International Trade*. New York: Augustus M. Kelly Publishers.

Warburton, Clark. 1966. "Monetary Theory, Full Production and the Great Depression." In *Depression, Inflation and Monetary Policy*, 125–43. Baltimore: Johns Hopkins University Press.

CHAPTER 2

The Importance of Stable Money
Theory and Evidence

MICHAEL D. BORDO AND ANNA J. SCHWARTZ

THE IMPORTANCE OF MONETARY STABILITY derives from the significant independent influence of monetary change on the subsequent course of
economic activity. If money did not matter at all or were of only secondary importance in affecting the flow of spending, income, and prices,
monetary stability would be of little relevance.

Our views reflect theoretical models and the empirical evidence testing
them that establish a close relation between economic stability and monetary
stability, and between inflation and monetary growth in excess of the rate of
real growth. Hence a stable monetary environment is crucial to achieve economic stability encompassing both stable prices and real growth immune to
wide swings. The essential element required to generate a stable monetary
environment is systematic policy, so as to minimize monetary shocks to the
expectations of economic agents. Discretionary policy is unsystematic, hence
fails this test. Increasing the variability of money growth in an attempt to
fine-tune the economy will make the variance of real output greater than it
would otherwise have been. An economy in which countercyclical policy is
followed will end up with unstable money and unstable real output.

Originally published in "The Importance of Stable Money: Theory and Evidence," *Cato Journal* 3,
no. 1 (Spring 1983). Copyright © Cato Institute. All rights reserved.

Postwar developments in monetary theory have shifted the issues that were the original centerpieces of analysis supporting the case for stable money. Correspondingly, the kinds of evidence suggested to test the analysis have changed to reflect the nature of the issues that are highlighted. We examine the developments in chronological order, beginning with Friedman's case for stable money, based on a theoretical argument against the pursuit of countercyclical stabilization policy (section I). Section II then examines the opposing theory of economic policy associated with Theil and Tinbergen and the Phillips curve analysis. That theory holds that countercyclical policy can be employed to stabilize the economy and that stable monetary policy is not decisive for that purpose. Successful countercyclical policy would achieve a standard deviation of money growth that would precisely offset the standard deviation of real economic growth that would otherwise occur, and thereby reduce the variance of real output below that of money. The section concludes with a discussion of the natural rate hypothesis that was the culmination of the Phillips curve analysis. The latest development we cover is the rational expectations hypothesis (section III). In each section we examine the implications of the theory for the stable money view and report the available evidence. In section IV we summarize the case for a legislated rule and present some new evidence for a monetary growth rule. Section V concludes with a brief discussion of the role that a constant monetary growth rule plays in the views of the schools of global monetarism, of Austrian economics, and of the new monetary economics.

I. The Case against Discretionary Monetary Policy

The general case against discretionary monetary policy formulated by Friedman (1953) is that, to function well, stabilization policy must offset random disturbances to economic activity; that is, it should remove the variation in income due to those disturbances. To achieve such a goal, two conditions must be satisfied: one involving timing, and the other involving the magnitude of the policy action. The timing of the policy action should conform to that of the disturbance, and the size of the policy action should be congruent with the size of the disturbance. If both conditions are not satisfied, the policy response will be insufficient and may even be destabilizing.

Friedman (1948, 1953) went on to argue that the lags in the effect of discretionary monetary policy are likely to be long and variable, reflecting both an "inside lag"—the time that elapsed before the monetary authority responded to the disturbance—and an "outside lag"—the time that elapsed before changes in monetary growth affect economic activity. As a result, discretionary policy actions might exacerbate rather than mitigate cyclical disturbances. In addition, Friedman contended that there was no basis for believing that policy makers (and the economics profession) possess the detailed knowledge of the economy's complex interactions and of the lag structure requisite for the pursuit of successful countercyclical policies or for fine-tuning. Furthermore, in his view, even well-meaning monetary authorities were likely to respond to political influences. Politically advantageous, short-run actions by the authorities would ignore the long-run destabilizing consequences. The conclusion Friedman drew from this array of circumstances and from evidence to be considered in what follows was that monetary policy should be based on a legislated rule instructing the Federal Reserve to increase the quantity of money, or high-powered money, on a year-to-year basis at a steady known rate of growth.

Friedman did not allege that such a prescription would yield nirvana. He allowed for the possible accretion of knowledge of the operation of the economy once the rule was adopted that would permit improving it. Adoption of the rule would not eliminate cyclical change, but the rule would remove disturbances arising from erratic fluctuations in the supply of money. The effect would be to reduce the amplitude of the random shocks to real economic growth inherent in the operation of the economy.

Several types of evidence have been used to evaluate the case for a monetary rule, namely: the statistical record of changes in money growth rates and their relation to changes in economic activity; qualitative historical data; and simulations of the hypothetical path of economic activity under an assumed monetary growth rule, compared with the actual path. We first report the statistical and historical evidence.

One body of evidence, of which Clark Warburton was the author, predated Friedman's theoretical case against discretionary monetary policy.

Warburton's writings from the early 1940s, when the Keynesian revolution was in full swing, until the end of his life in 1980, were in the quantity of money tradition and stressed the importance of monetary disequilibrium as the fundamental cause of business fluctuations. At the time that Warburton's views first appeared, attention to the role of money had all but vanished from professional work. His main evidence was based on deviations from trend of quarterly money data for the period 1918–65. He demonstrated that turning points in money preceded those in business, and concluded: "[A]n erratic money supply [was] the chief originating factor in business recessions and not merely an intensifying force in the case of severe depressions" (1966, Intro., p. 9). Warburton also cited, as prime examples of the harmful effects of discretionary policy, the mistakes of the Federal Reserve System that produced the great contraction of 1929–33 and the contraction of 1937–38:

> Since the time of the establishment of the Federal Reserve System, annual deviations in the quantity of money from a reasonable rate of growth have ranged from more than 30 percent excess to nearly 20 percent deficiency. There is no known need for annual variations in the quantity of money, from the estimated reasonable rate of growth, of more than 2 percent, and annual variations in the quantity of money outside this range have been invariably associated with business instability and with inflation or depression. The range of additional variation for seasonal purposes is probably not more than three percent. (1966, chap. 17 [1952], pp. 368–69)

The dismal record of the Federal Reserve led Warburton to strongly favor a legislated monetary rule that would limit the growth rate of money, for a given definition, to 3 percent per annum.[1]

The evidence provided by Friedman and his associates also utilized statistical and qualitative historical data. Unlike Warburton, who expressed the data as deviations from trend, Friedman and Schwartz used first differences of the logarithms of the money series. They then selected turning points in the series from 1867 to 1960, and compared the peaks and troughs in the percentage rate of change of the money stock with peaks and troughs in general business as dated by the National Bureau of Economic Research reference cycle chronology. On average, of the 18 nonwar cycles since 1870, peaks in the rate of change of the stock of money preceded reference peaks by 16 months, and troughs in the rate of change of the stock of money preceded reference troughs by 12 months. On this basis, they argued strongly that: "Appreciable changes in the rate of growth of the stock of money are a necessary and sufficient condition for appreciable changes in the rate of growth of money income"; and, "this is true both for long secular changes and also for changes roughly the length of business cycles" (1963a, p. 53). Using a different methodology over the same period, William Poole (1975) found that the evidence supported the Friedman and Schwartz conclusion.

To the question whether money changes conformed positively to the business cycle with a lead or inversely with a lag, the answer Friedman and Schwartz gave was that the dispersion (measured by the standard deviation) of the leads and lags, as computed under the two interpretations, is uniformly lower when the money series is treated as conforming positively. Serial correlations, furthermore, of expansions with succeeding contractions and of contractions with succeeding expansions display the same patterns for the money change series and a proxy indicator of physical change in general business. Expansions in both series are not systematically correlated with the succeeding contractions, whereas contractions in both series are highly correlated with the succeeding expansions. This evidence supports the positive interpretation of the relation of money *changes* to the business cycle. Otherwise, if inverted conformity were the case and changes in business produced later changes in the opposite direction in money, then the correlations with the succeeding reference cycle phase for money and the physical change in general business measure should be opposite. But the pattern for business *does* reflect, with a lag, the pattern for money.

Statistical evidence provided by Friedman and Schwartz (1963b, p. 594) matched periods with a low standard deviation of year-to-year percentage changes in monetary growth with comparable periods in velocity, real income, and wholesale prices. They also matched periods with a high standard deviation of year-to-year changes in monetary growth with comparable periods in the other magnitudes. In the nine decades, 1869–1960, four periods of comparative stability in money growth were accompanied by relative stability of the rate of growth of output and the rate of change of prices: 1882–92; 1903–13; 1923–29; 1948–60. All other periods were characterized by unusually unstable money growth rates and unusually unstable rates of growth of output and rates of change of prices.

The qualitative historical evidence that Friedman and Schwartz examined also supported the conclusion that erratic money changes, as a result of discretionary actions by the authorities, were accompanied by economic changes in the same direction. Moreover, in a number of episodes when monetary changes had led changes in economic activity, the evidence that the monetary changes were independent of the changes in activity was irrefutable.

We now turn to the simulation studies that compare the hypothetical behavior of the US economy under an assumed constant money growth rate rule with actual economic performance. The evidence is mixed. Friedman (1960) found that a rule would have outperformed discretionary policy in the interwar period, but that the case for the post-World War II period was less clear-cut. For the postwar period, at least until the mid-1960s, most studies (Bronfenbrenner 1961; Modigliani 1964; Argy 1971) concluded that discretionary policy outperformed a 3 or 4 percent monetary growth rule. One inference might be that the Federal Reserve had learned from its "mistakes" in the interwar period. Recently, however, Argy (1979) found that for the period from the late 1960s to the late 1970s, a simulated monetary growth rule for a sample of nine industrial countries would have reduced the variance of real growth considerably below its actual variance.

Finally, Kochin (1979) found that over much of the postwar period US monetary policy was destabilizing. His study, based on an interpretation of the results of several economic models, followed Friedman's (1953) procedure for evaluating stabilization policy.

II. Keynesian Riposte and Return Sally

An analytical development that favored intervention along Keynesian lines was the Theil-Tinbergen theory of economic policy. That approach provided policy makers with an array of instruments—monetary, fiscal, incomes policies—to achieve multiple goals by matching instruments to goals following the principle of comparative advantage. This theory of economic policy combined with the use of optimal control procedures led to a strong case for fine-tuning. It was held that policy makers could devise feedback rules between real economic activity and monetary and fiscal policy that could be applied to offset disturbances to the private sector.

Another development that apparently advanced the case for counter-cyclical policy was the Phillips curve tradeoff. Phillips (1958), Samuelson and Solow (1960), and Lipsey (1960) reported evidence of a stable inverse relationship for the United Kingdom, the United States, and other countries between the rate of change of money wages (alternatively, the rate of change of the price level) and the level of unemployment. The findings led to the view that policy makers could choose, based on a social preference function, between high inflation and low employment, or low inflation and high un-employment, the desired choice to be achieved by discretionary monetary and fiscal policy.

The upshot of these developments was that many economists came to believe that the economy could be stabilized at any desired level of activity. Friedman's objections to fine-tuning seemed to have been circumvented.

Friedman's response came in his 1967 presidential address to the American Economic Association. He argued that the Phillips curve tradeoff was a statistical illusion arising from the failure to account for inflationary expectations. Monetary and fiscal policy could stabilize the economy at some arbitrary level of output or employment, but only temporarily and, even then, only at the expense of accelerating inflation or deflation. Both Friedman (1968) and Phelps (1968) modified the Phillips curve approach by applying the concept of the natural rate employment—that rate consistent with the microeconomic decisions of firms and workers active in the labor force. The natural rate of employment reflects the optimal choice of workers between labor and leisure and the optimal mix of labor and other factors of production for firms in a dynamic economy. According to the "natural rate hypothesis," the natural rate of employment is determined by the intersection of the demand and supply curves for labor, given demographic factors and labor market institutions. Hence deviations of employment from the natural rate are produced only by imperfect information and the costs of acquiring information that affect job search.

One explanation given for such imperfections in information was that employers and workers have different perceptions of changes in real wage rates. It was argued that firms always have perfect information on the prices of their output so that for them actual and expected real wages are always equal. In contrast, workers base their evaluations of prospective real wage rates on their expectations of what the rate of inflation will be over the duration of their contracts. For example, suppose inflation is rising and workers' expectations do not fully reflect the higher inflation rate. Faced with lower real wage rates, firms will be willing to expand employment, which will put upward pressure on nominal wages. The result will appear as a movement along the (short-run) Phillips curve. However, once workers adjust their expectations to the higher inflation rate, they will demand higher money wages. The resultant rise in real wage rates will cause firms to reduce employment to its previous level. The economy will then return to the natural rate of unemployment consistent with labor market forces, *but at a higher rate of inflation.*

The *measured* unemployment rate is thus assumed to depend on the natural unemployment rate and the difference between the actual and expected inflation rates; that is, on the inflation forecast error, with some rate of adjustment of the unemployment rate to the forecast error. As long as the actual and expected inflation rates differ, measured unemployment can differ from the natural rate. However, in the *long run*, actual and expected inflation rates converge, and hence, measured unemployment reverts to the natural rate, though this adjustment process may be sluggish.

The theory of search is an alternative way of explaining unemployment. This theory posits that the natural rate of unemployment is determined by long-run demographic forces, but that deviations from the natural rate are caused by short-run factors affecting the costs and duration of search.

The policy implication that emerged from the natural rate hypothesis was that stabilization policies aimed at reducing unemployment below the natural rate would have only temporary success. Any attempt to achieve permanent results would produce accelerating, and ultimately runaway, inflation. In addition, policies designed to peg the unemployment rate at the natural rate could lead easily to an explosive inflation or deflation if the forces determining the natural rate were to change. Such forces include changes in the labor force skill mix and demographic determinants of the labor force. Thus, the natural rate hypothesis strengthens the case for monetary stability, since monetary instability would produce deviations between the expected and actual inflation rates, causing fluctuations in unemployment and output.

III. The Rational Expectations Hypothesis and the Case for Stable Money

Recent advances in the treatment of expectations supplement the case for monetary stability implied by the natural rate hypothesis. According to the rational expectations hypothesis, economic agents act rationally with respect to the gathering and processing of information, just as they do with respect to any other activity (Muth 1961). This proposition implies that agents will not make persistent forecast errors. If their forecasts turn out to be wrong, agents will learn the reason for their errors and revise their methods of forecasting accordingly. Such an approach seems more reasonable than alternative approaches commonly used to model expectations, such as static expectations that simply extrapolate existing conditions, or adaptive expectations that have the property of yielding continuous forecast errors. Additionally, in contrast to the adaptive expectations approach that uses only past values of the variable about which expectations are to be formed, the rational expectations hypothesis also uses other relevant information.

The rational expectations model assumes that private agents form expectations about the rate of inflation based on their understanding of the economic model that generates the inflation rate, as well as on the policy rule followed by the monetary authorities.

In a model based on rationally formed expectations, Sargent and Wallace (1976) demonstrated that systematic monetary policy would be completely ineffective in influencing real variables. They argued that if the monetary authorities devised a monetary feedback rule, using optimal feedback techniques, according to which the authorities systematically altered the money supply to offset disturbances in real economic activity, then private decision makers would learn the rule and incorporate it into their rational expectations. The thrust of this model—where deviations of output from its full employment (or natural) level can only be produced by an inflation forecast error—is that if expectations are formed rationally, the forecast error cannot be manipulated by systematic (and, therefore, anticipated) monetary or fiscal policy. Indeed, the only way output or unemployment can be altered from its natural rate is by an *unexpected* shock. However, unexpected shocks—monetary or other—have the negative attribute of increasing the level of uncertainty in the economy.

If a negatively sloping Phillips curve were observed, it might result from constant price expectations in a period with *ex post* fluctuations in actual inflation due to unanticipated random shocks that are negatively correlated with *ex post* fluctuations in measured unemployment (Begg 1982, p. 141). Lucas (1973) offered a variant explanation, in a world of rational expectations, for a negatively sloped short-run Phillips curve or, alternatively, a positively sloped short-run supply curve for output, which is determined by lagged output and the discrepancy between actual and expected inflation. Lucas assumed that the economy is characterized by uncertainty, and that competitive firms cannot readily discern whether a change in the price of their output reflects a change in the price level or a change in relative prices. He then demonstrated that other things being equal, the greater the variance of the aggregate price level, owing to greater monetary variability, the more likely it is that firms will mistake a price level change for a change in relative prices. Expansion of output in response to an increase in the level of prices, holding relative prices constant, will ultimately lead to accumulation of inventory, cutbacks in output, layoffs, and more inelastic supply curves and also a more inelastic aggregate supply and Phillips curve. In addition, greater price level variability will be associated with greater resource misallocation because price level variability impairs the ability to perceive the information that prices convey in a market economy.

Brunner, Cukierman, and Meltzer (1980) perceive the problem of extracting the signal from prices somewhat differently from Lucas. For them, the distinction that needs to be made is not the sorting out of aggregate from relative price changes. It is rather the distinction between transitory and permanent price changes. Firms will wait to learn whether a change is permanent before reacting to it and, with great price variability, that process is made more difficult and prolonged than would otherwise be the case.

In any event, price variability reflecting discretionary money variability clearly has negative effects on the economy and reinforces the case for monetary stability. Moreover, the entire enterprise of selecting discretionary policies by simulation of econometric models has been challenged by Lucas (1976). His critique was based on the kinds of equations that are used in econometric models. These are reduced forms of effects on the economy of existing policy arrangements that incorporate the private sector's expectations of policy effects on economic variables. Were the authorities to change the policy rule, the public would adjust its expectations accordingly. Consequently, attempts to forecast the effects of alternative policies without accounting for changes in private agents' expectations are bound to lead to inappropriate policies.

Discretionary policy (defined as policy reacting to the current situation) based on optimal control techniques has been shown by Kydland and Prescott (1977) to be suboptimal and possibly destabilizing in a world of rational expectations. The policy chosen at each point in time may be the best, given the current situation. In the authors' terminology, the policy may be consistent, but it will be suboptimal because the policymaker has failed to take into account the optimizing rules of economic agents. The decisions of agents will change as they come to recognize the change in policy. The example Kydland and Prescott cite is that agents may expect tax rates to be lowered in recessions and increased in booms and make decisions in light of those expectations. Over successive periods, it is not optimal to continue with the initial policy because control theory is not the appropriate tool for dynamic economic planning. Current decisions of economic agents are affected by what they expect future policy to be. A government that attempted to reduce unemployment by increasing the money supply without attention to the rational inflation expectations of private agents would end up with a suboptimal mix of the natural rate of unemployment and positive inflation, despite the fact that it sought to maximize its "social welfare function" by combining the desirability of full employment and zero inflation. The authors conclude (1977, p. 487):

The implication of this analysis is that, until we have . . . [a tested theory of economic fluctuations], active stabilization may very well be dangerous and it is best that it not be attempted. Reliance on policies such as a constant growth in the money supply and constant tax rates constitute a safe course of action. When we do have the prerequisite understanding of the business cycle, the implication of our analysis is that policymakers should follow rules rather than have discretion. The reason that they should not have discretion is not that they are stupid or evil but, rather, that discretion implies selecting the decision which is best, given the current situation. Such behavior either results in consistent but suboptimal planning or in economic instability.

Oversimplication by certain proponents of the rational expectations hypothesis should be noted. A number of factors could lead to nonneutral effects of anticipated monetary growth even in the presence of rational expectations. First, anticipated monetary growth can have effects on the natural rate of unemployment (output) through a real balance effect on the aggregate expenditure function, or by changing the steady state capital-labor ratio and thus affecting the real rate of interest (Buiter 1980).

Second, if the assumption that both government and the private sector have equal access to information is violated when there is a rule for systematic monetary policy, then it is possible for the government to change its policy after the private sector has formed its expectations and thereby affect the inflation forecast error. As a result, output and unemployment can deviate from the natural rate. Such an outcome is also possible in cases where wages are determined by multi-period overlapping contracts (Fischer 1977). In that situation, even if private agents form their expectations rationally, the government can systematically affect output and employment between contract negotiating dates. Third, if the assumption of market clearing is abandoned, yet the assumption of rational expectations is maintained, then it is possible for output to be affected by stabilization policy. Explanations for price stickiness range from the Keynesian disequilibrium approach (Buiter 1980) to price setting behavior in a world of high coordination costs (Cagan 1980).

Fourth, evidence of persistence—that unemployment does not rapidly disappear and bring the economy to full employment—or alternatively, the existence of serial correlation of output and employment over the business cycle, has been advanced as contradicting the rational expectations approach. On the other hand, McCallum (1980) explains persistence within the rational expectations context as reflecting real costs of adjusting the fixed capital stock and other factors of production. For Lucas (1975), persistence occurs because of information lags that prevent "even relevant past variables from becoming perfectly known" (p. 1114), and an accelerationist effect of physical capital. Finally, the rational expectations approach fails to explain how private agents learn from their forecast errors in forming rational expectations (De Canio 1979).

We now turn to the evidence for the rational expectations hypothesis. The evidence most generally cited is that by Barro (1977a, 1977b, 1981) and Barro and Rush (1980). Barro and Rush regressed the unemployment rate over the 1949–77 period on lagged values of a measure of unexpected monetary growth and of expected monetary growth. Expected monetary growth was estimated from a regression of current monetary growth on past monetary growth, the deviation of government spending from its trend, and past unemployment. Such a regression was designed to capture the monetary rule that economic agents perceived. The predicted values of the regression were employed to represent expected monetary growth, and the residuals, to represent unexpected monetary growth.

Barro and Rush found most of the variation in unemployment was explained by unexpected monetary growth, and that expected monetary growth was not statistically significant. They concluded that expected monetary growth is neutral and that only unsystematic elements of monetary policy affect the unemployment rate—a finding that is supportive of the rational expectations hypothesis.

The evidence that Barro has presented—that only unexpected monetary growth explains variations in unemployment—has been challenged. Cagan (1980) argued, following a more traditional approach, that most variations in output and employment can be explained by deviations in money growth from a long-run trend, without invoking rational expectations. Sargent (1976) demonstrated that it is difficult to distinguish Barro's results from those produced by a more traditional approach because of the observational equivalence of natural and unnatural rate theories. For

Sargent, the only way to test a refutable hypothesis is to be able to isolate periods involving a change in clear-cut policy rules. Gordon (1976a, 1976b, 1979) argues that, unless it can be shown that the full effect of a change in nominal income is absorbed by price change, the case for the neutrality hypothesis is not confirmed. In his view, to the extent that some of the effect of expected monetary growth is absorbed by output change, scope remains for stabilization policy. Mishkin (1982) also finds that anticipated movements in monetary growth have effects on output and unemployment that are larger than those of unanticipated movements, but his evidence confirms that expectations are rational.

The rational expectations approach appears to be firmly established, despite unresolved questions including those mentioned above. A clear implication of the literature is that active monetary intervention is likely to lead to large price level changes with little favorable effect on output or employment. Unpredictable policies are likely to increase the degree of uncertainty in the economy and enlarge the fluctuations around the natural rate. The aim of policy should therefore be to establish predictable monetary rules, preferably rules that are easily understood, with full consideration of all the relevant costs and benefits.

IV. The Case for a Legislated Rule

Modigliani's presidential address to the American Economic Association (1977) disputed monetarist views that (a) the economy is sufficiently shock-proof that stabilization policies are not needed; (b) postwar fluctuations resulted from unstable monetary growth; (c) stabilization policies decreased rather than increased stability. He finds that "Up to 1974, these [stabilization] policies have helped to keep the economy reasonably stable by historical standards, even though one can certainly point to some occasional failures" (1977, p. 17). He attributes the serious deterioration in economic stability since 1973 to "the novel nature of the shocks that hit us, namely, supply shocks. Even the best possible aggregate demand management cannot offset such shocks without a lot of unemployment together with a lot of inflation. But, in addition, demand management was far from the best." The failure, he contends, was the result of ineffective use of stabilization policy "including too slavish adherence to the monetarists' constant money growth prescription."

Modigliani's defense of stabilization policies amounts to acknowledging specific failures while asserting overall success, except when exogenous supply shocks occur which "we had little experience or even an adequate conceptual framework to deal with" (1977, p. 17).

Table 2.1 shows the standard deviations of quarter-to-quarter deviations of a two-quarter moving average from a 20-quarter growth rate of M1. The standard deviations are a proxy for unexpected monetary change (shocks) that, according to both older and newer approaches, should be associated with consequent effects on real output and, once fully anticipated, on prices. The table, therefore, also shows the standard deviations of quarter-to-quarter annualized real output growth rates for three postwar subperiods: 1952I to 1960IV; 1961I to 1971II (alternatively, 1973III); 1971III (1973IV) to 1982III.

The variability of the (unexpected) money series declined moderately during the 1960s and until the quarter preceding the Nixon price controls or, alternatively, the quarter preceding the 1973 oil price shock. Over the same subperiods, real output variability also declined, but substantially more than the decline in money variability. In the final subperiods, both money variability and real output variability rose to levels exceeding the ones prevailing in the initial subperiod.[2]

Modigliani's attribution of the serious deterioration of economic stability since 1973 to "too slavish adherence to the monetarists' constant money growth rule" is not apparent in Table 2.1. The inability of stabilization policy to cope with unexpected developments *supports* monetarist views. If policy makers are thought to have an informational advantage over private agents and so able to reduce fluctuations of output around its natural rate, they must be able to make correct inferences about the precise character of current shocks. That does not seem to be the case.

Theory and evidence strongly suggest that a systematic monetary rule is superior to discretion. A fixed rule with no feedback from the current situation to policy instruments, a rule that is simple and preannounced, is the most favorable condition for stabilizing the economy. Any feedback rules that involve government manipulation of the private sector's forecast

TABLE 2.1   Comparative Variability of Monetary Growth and Rates of Change of Real GNP, Postwar Subperiods Quarterly, 1952I–1982III

	Standard Deviation of Quarter-to-Quarter Percentage Changes in:	
Period	Deviations from a 20-Quarter Moving Average of M1 of a 2-Quarter Moving Average (1)	Annualized Real Output Growth (2)
1952I–1960IV	1.93	4.76
1961I–1971II	1.80	3.17
1961I–1973III	1.75	3.20
1971III–1982III	2.11	4.79
1973IV–1982III	2.18	4.89

NOTE: We are indebted to the division of research of the St. Louis Federal Reserve Bank for the data underlying col. 1.

errors is doomed to failure. There is no information available to authorities that is not also available to the private sector.

A fixed, simple, preannounced rule can take a number of forms. For some who are opposed to discretionary policy, the preferred systematic rule is the gold standard rule, for others, an interest rate or price rule. We do not examine the reason such rules have won support from their adherents. The rule we favor is a constant monetary growth rule. It satisfies the requirement for a systematic preannounced policy or regime that economic agents can incorporate in their expectations. It is a rule which can easily be implemented. The case for it, as stated initially by Friedman, is that economists lack adequate knowledge to conduct discretionary policy successfully. A monetary growth rule would obviate monetary policy mistakes. When physicians take the Hippocratic oath, they pledge not to do harm to their patients. Economists should take a similar oath with respect to the instruments that they may be in a position to administer.

The development of the rational expectations approach suggests that public response to stable monetary growth would contribute to the stabilization of the economy. Constant monetary growth will not make the business cycle obsolete. But avoidance of the mistakes of discretionary monetary policy will reduce the amplitude of fluctuations inevitable in a dynamic economy.

V. Divergent Views on a Constant Monetary Growth Rule

Economists who accept the primacy of monetary change in producing changes in economic activity do not all agree that the policy solution is to adopt a rule for constant monetary growth. We may distinguish the views of adherents of global monetarism, Austrian economics, and the new monetary economics.

Global monetarism emphasizes that the world economy is highly integrated with respect both to commodity and capital markets, international price and interest rate arbitrage serving to coordinate national economies. The appropriate unit of analysis, therefore, is not the individual national economy but rather the world. The elements of the doctrine were constructed for a world of fixed exchange rates where the domestic rate of inflation is determined exogenously by the world rate of inflation, and the domestic money stock is determined by the rate of growth of domestic nominal income, set by the world inflation rate. For such an approach, prescribing a rule for domestic monetary growth is pointless. Under a flexible rate regime, however, domestic monetary authorities can control their money supplies *if they choose*. Regardless of the exchange rate regime, global monetarism has not supported a monetary rule for a single nation.

Austrian economics acknowledges the role of monetary policy in producing inflation, and shares the monetarist view that the result of monetary attempts to reduce unemployment below its natural level is accelerating inflation. The chief emphasis, however, is less on these propositions than on the distortions in the production process resulting from monetary expansion. Moreover, in Austrian economics, flexible exchange rates are not the path to domestic monetary control. Hayek, for example, favors fixed exchange rates as a constraint on the government's overexpansion of the domestic money supply. The preferred solution, however, is the abolition of central banks, and the establishment of a commodity money. Hayek recently has advocated the denationalization of money and giving private producers freedom to offer alternative kinds of money. The market would then choose the money that would prove to be stable. Hence no legislated rule would be required.

The new monetary economics enters under the free-market banner. In the system that we are familiar with, money is the product of pervasive government regulation. Had free-market policies prevailed for transactions services, economists of that persuasion argue, a more efficient banking system would have been created, and velocity would have been much different. The new monetary economics therefore opposes a constant monetary growth rule on the ground that macroeconomic performance, under free-market provision of money, could be much better than a rule would have produced. Different schemes have been elaborated by members of this school to replace an inefficiently regulated money stock, but as Hall (1982, p. 1555) writes: "None of them would rely on the concept of a money stock or its stability relative to total income. Whether their macro-economic performance would equal that of a simple money growth rule is still a matter of controversy."

Proposals to change utterly root and branch the existing monetary system strike us as ignoring the enormous attachment of the private sector to arrangements that have become customary. Imposing a system that appeals to visionaries as far more satisfactory than the one markets have adjusted to, given the existing network of regulations, is not the historical way in which alterations in the monetary system have occurred. A complete breakdown in existing arrangements as a result, say, of the catastrophe of hyperinflation would be a prerequisite to adoption de novo of one of the schemes the new monetary economics espouses.

The new monetary economics, by proclaiming that results superior to those of a monetary growth rule are within reach, shares some of the confidence of interventionists. Advocates of a monetary growth rule are skeptical not only about demand management or fine-tuning by interventionists, but also about the prospects that new schemes for settling transactions can be as easily implemented as they can be devised.

Some observers predict that the deregulation process now under way will obscure the quality of moneyness of assets and hence render control by the central bank problematical. We regard this apocalyptic view as unduly alarmist. Not so long ago, it was commonly argued that payment of interest on demand deposits would mean the end of their use as transactions balances. That has not happened, and we do not foresee radical changes on the horizon in the operation of the payments system. The alternatives are not the creation de novo of a set of monetary arrangements or the preservation unchanged of the existing set.

For all the talk of the adoption of monetarism by central banks, their performance gives little indication that they in fact have been influenced by the central message of the doctrine—monetary instability is a potent source of unstable economic performance. Note, for example, the wide swings that have been observed even in a smoothed two-quarter moving average of the US *money* growth rate since 1980—1.9 percent in the second quarter, 5.8 percent in the third quarter, followed by 13.2 percent in the fourth quarter; in the four quarters of 1981, 8.1, 7.1, 4.9, and 3.0 percent; and in the first three quarters of 1982, 8.3, 7.1, and 3.4 percent, with the fourth quarter figure a likely high multiple of the third-quarter figure. Is this monetarism?

A legislated rule has *never* been tried. It is a modest step towards restraining monetary authorities, but both theory and evidence suggest that it could be a giant step toward achieving economic stability.

Notes

1. Warburton (1964, p. 1328). In earlier studies, in the 1940s and 1950s, Warburton advocated a 5 percent annual growth rate in the money stock, inclusive of an adjustment for a projected steady secular decline in velocity of 1.5 percent per year. The shift to a lower proposed growth rate for money incorporated the assumption that the reversal in the trend of velocity in the 1950s—from negative to positive—would continue.

2. Milton Friedman has called our attention to the similarity between the results of a table he constructed for the period 1962I through 1982IV (divided at 1971I and 1973III), and of our table. He calculated a geometric mean of 12-term moving standard deviation of growth rates of M1, M2, and real output. The increase in the variability of M1 from 1962–71 to 1971–82 of 0.26 in his table matches our finding of an increase of 0.31; the increase in the variability of real output he found of 1.61 is almost identical with the increase of 1.62 in our table. For M2, in his table, the increase in variability from the first to the second period is much sharper than for M1—1.21 compared to 0.26.

References

Argy, Victor. "Rules, Discretion in Monetary Management, and Short-term Stability." *Journal of Money, Credit, and Banking* 3 (February 1971): 102–22.

Argy, Victor. "Monetary Stabilization and the Stabilization of Output in Selected Industrial Countries." Banca Nazionale del Lavoro, *Quarterly Review* 129 (June 1979): 155–66.

Barro, Robert J. "Unanticipated Money Growth and Unemployment in the United States." *American Economic Review* 67 (March 1977a): 101–15.

Barro, Robert J. "Long-term Contracting, Sticky Prices, and Monetary Policy." *Journal of Monetary Economics* 3 (July 1977b): 305–16.

Barro, Robert J. "The Equilibrium Approach to Business Cycles." In his *Expectations and Business Cycles*. New York: Academic Press, 1981.

Barro, Robert J., and Rush, Mark. "Unanticipated Money and Economic Activity." In Stanley Fisher, ed., *Rational Expectations and Economic Policy*. Chicago: University of Chicago Press, 1980.

Begg, David K. H. *The Rational Expectations Revolution in Macroeconomics: Theories and Evidence*. Oxford: Philip Allan, 1982.

Bronfenbrenner, Martin. "Statistical Tests of Rival Monetary Rules: Quarterly Data Supplement." *Journal of Political Economy* 69 (December 1961): 621–25.

Brunner, Karl, Cukierman, Alex, and Meltzer, Allan H. "Stagflation, Persistent Unemployment and the Permanence of Economic Shocks." *Journal of Monetary Economics* 6 (October 1980): 467–92.

Buiter, Willem H. "Real Effects of Anticipated and Unanticipated Money: Some Problems of Estimation and Hypothesis Testing." *Working Paper 601*. National Bureau of Economic Research, 1980.

Cagan, Phillip. "Reflections on Rational Expectations." *Journal of Money, Credit, and Banking* 12 (November 1980): 826–32.

De Canio, Stephen J. "Rational Expectations and Learning from Experience." *Quarterly Journal of Economics* 93 (February 1979): 47–57.

Fischer, Stanley. "Long-term Contracts, Rational Expectations and the Optimum Money Supply." *Journal of Political Economy* 85 (February 1977): 191–205.

Friedman, Milton. "A Monetary and Fiscal Framework for Economic Stability." *American Economic Review* 38 (June 1948): 245–64. Reprinted in *Essays in Positive Economics*. Chicago: University of Chicago Press, 1953.

Friedman, Milton. "The Effects of a Full Employment Policy on Economic Stability: A Formal Analysis" (1951). Reprinted in *Essays in Positive Economics*. Chicago: University of Chicago Press, 1953.

Friedman, Milton. *A Program for Monetary Stability*. New York: Fordham University Press, 1960.

Friedman, Milton. "The Role of Monetary Policy." *American Economic Review* 58 (March 1968): 1–17.

Friedman, Milton, and Schwartz, Anna J. "Money and Business Cycles." *Review of Economics and Statistics* 45 (February 1963a, Supplement): 32–64. Reprinted in *The Optimum Quantity of Money.* Chicago: Aldine, 1969.

Friedman, Milton, and Schwartz, Anna J. *A Monetary History of the United States, 1867–1960.* Princeton: Princeton University Press, 1963b.

Gordon, Robert J. "Recent Developments in the Theory of Inflation and Unemployment." *Journal of Monetary Economics* 2 (April 1976a): 185–219.

Gordon, Robert J. "Can Econometric Policy Evaluation Be Salvaged?—A Comment." In Karl Brunner and Allan H. Meltzer, eds., *The Phillips Curve and Labor Markets.* Supplement 1 to the *Journal of Monetary Economics* 1 (1976b): 47–58.

Gordon, Robert J. "New Evidence that Fully Anticipated Monetary Changes Influence Real Output After All." *Working Paper 361.* National Bureau of Economic Research, 1979.

Hall, Robert E. "Three Views of Friedman and Schwartz' *Monetary Trends:* A Neo-Chicagoan View." *Journal of Economic Literature* 20 (December 1982): 1552–56.

Hayek, Friedrich A. *Denationalisation of Money.* London: Institute of Economic Affairs, 1978.

Kochin, Levis. "Judging Monetary Policy." *Proceedings of Second West Coast Academic/ Federal Reserve Economic Research Seminar.* Federal Reserve Bank of San Francisco, 1979.

Kydland, Finn E., and Prescott, Edward C. "Rules Rather than Discretion: The Inconsistency of Optimal Plans." *Journal of Political Economy* 85 (June 1977): 473–91.

Lipsey, Richard G. "The Relation Between Unemployment and the Rate of Change of Money Wage Rates in the United Kingdom, 1862–1957: A Further Analysis." *Economica* 27 (February 1960): 1–31.

Lucas, Robert E. "Some International Evidence on Output-Inflation Tradeoffs." *American Economic Review* 68 (June 1973): 326–34.

Lucas, Robert E. "An Equilibrium Model of the Business Cycle." *Journal of Political Economy* 83 (December 1975): 1113–44.

Lucas, Robert E. "Econometric Policy Evaluation: A Critique." In Karl Brunner and Allan H. Meltzer, eds., *The Phillips Curve and Labor Markets.* Supplement 1 to the *Journal of Monetary Economics* 1 (1976): 19–46.

McCallum, Bennett T. "Rational Expectations and Macroeconomic Stabilization Policy." *Journal of Money, Credit, and Banking* 12 (November 1980): 716–46.

Modigliani, Franco. "Some Empirical Tests of Monetary Management and Rules Versus Discretion." *Journal of Political Economy* 72 (June 1964): 211–45.

Modigliani, Franco. "The Monetarist Controversy or, Should We Forsake Stabilization Policies?" *American Economic Review* 67 (March 1977): 1–19.

Muth, John F. "Rational Expectations and the Theory of Price Movements." *Econometrica* 29 (July 1961): 315–35.

Phelps, Edmund S. "Money-Wage Dynamics and Labor Market Equilibrium." *Journal of Political Economy* 78 (July/August 1968): 678–711.

Phillips, A. W. "The Relation Between Unemployment and the Rate of Change of Money Wage Rates in the United Kingdom, 1861–1957." *Econometrica* 25 (November 1958): 283–99.

Poole, William. "The Relationship of Monetary Decelerations to Business Cycle Peaks: Another Look at the Evidence." *Journal of Finance* 30 (June 1975): 697–712.

Samuelson, Paul A., and Solow, Robert M. "Analytical Aspects of Anti-Inflation Policy." *American Economic Review* 50 (May 1960): 177–94.

Sargent, Thomas. "The Observational Equivalence of Natural and Unnatural Rate Theories of Macroeconomics." *Journal of Political Economy* 84 (August 1976): 631–40.

Sargent, Thomas, and Wallace, Neil. "Rational Expectations and the Theory of Economic Policy." *Journal of Monetary Economics* 2 (April 1976): 169–83.

Warburton, Clark. "Variations in Economic Growth and Banking in the United States from 1835 to 1885." *Journal of Economic History* 18 (June 1958): 283–97.

Warburton, Clark. "Monetary Disturbances and Business Fluctuations in Two Centuries of American History." In Leland Yeager, ed., *In Search of a Monetary Constitution*, pp. 61–93. Cambridge: Harvard University Press, 1962.

Warburton, Clark. "Four Statements." In *The Federal Reserve System After Fifty Years*, vol. 2, pp. 1314–42. Hearings before the Subcommittee on Domestic Finance of the Committee on Banking and Currency, House of Representatives, 88th Cong., 2nd sess. Washington, DC: Government Printing Office, 1964.

Warburton, Clark. *Depressions, Inflation, and Monetary Policy: Selected Papers, 1945–53.* Baltimore: The Johns Hopkins Press, 1966.

PART TWO

EMPIRICAL EVIDENCE

CHAPTER 3

Monetary Policy Regimes and Economic Performance

The Historical Record

MICHAEL D. BORDO AND ANNA J. SCHWARTZ

1. Policy Regimes, 1880–1995

1.1. Definition of a Policy Regime

M ONETARY POLICY REGIMES ENCOMPASS the constraints or limits imposed by custom, institutions, and nature on the ability of the monetary authorities to influence the evolution of macroeconomic aggregates.

We define a monetary regime as a set of monetary arrangements and institutions accompanied by a set of expectations—expectations by the public with respect to policy makers' actions and expectations by policy makers about the public's reaction to their actions. By incorporating expectations, a monetary regime differs from the older concept of a monetary standard, which referred simply to the institutions and arrangements governing the money supply.[1]

Originally published in "Monetary Policy Regimes and Economic Performance: The Historical Record," chap. 2 in *Handbook of Macroeconomics, Volume I*, ed. John Taylor and Michael Woodford (New York: North Holland, 1999). © 1999 Elsevier Science B.V. All rights reserved.

1.2. Types of Regimes

Two types of regimes have prevailed in history: one based on convertibility into a commodity, generally specie, and the other based on fiat. The former prevailed in the USA in various guises until Richard Nixon closed the gold window in August 1971, thereby terminating the gold convertibility feature of the Bretton Woods international monetary system. The latter is the norm worldwide today.

The two types of regimes relate closely to the concept of a nominal anchor to the monetary system. A nominal anchor is a nominal variable that serves as a target for monetary policy. Under specie convertible regimes, the currency price of specie (gold and/or silver coin) is the nominal anchor. Convertibility at that price ensures that price levels will return to some mean value over long periods of time.[2]

Regimes have both a domestic (national) and international aspect. The domestic aspect pertains to the institutional arrangements and policy actions of monetary authorities. The international aspect relates to the monetary arrangements between nations. Two basic types of international monetary arrangements prevail—fixed and flexible exchange rates, along with a number of intermediate variants including adjustable pegs and managed floating.

1.3. Rules vs. Discretion in Monetary Regimes

Alternative monetary regimes can be classified as following rules or discretion. The convertible metallic regimes that prevailed into the twentieth century were based on a rule—adherence to the fixed price of specie. The rule operated in both the domestic and the international aspects of the regime. In the international aspect, maintenance of the fixed price of specie at its par value by its adherents ensured fixed exchange rates. The fixed price of domestic currency in terms of specie provided a nominal anchor to the international monetary system.

Fiat or inconvertible regimes can also be based on rules if the authorities devise and credibly commit to them. At the domestic level, setting the growth rates of monetary aggregates or those targeting the price level are examples of rules. At the international level, fixed exchange rate regimes such as the European Monetary System (EMS) are based on a set of well-understood intervention principles and the leadership of a country dedicated to maintaining the nominal anchor.

This chapter surveys the historical experience of both international and domestic (national) aspects of monetary regimes from the nineteenth century to the present. We first survey the experience of four broad international monetary regimes: the classical gold standard 1880–1914; the interwar period in which a short-lived restoration of the gold standard prevailed; the postwar Bretton Woods international monetary system (1946–1971) indirectly linked to gold; the recent managed float period (1971–1995). We then present in some detail the institutional arrangements and policy actions of the Federal Reserve in the United States as an important example of a domestic policy regime. The survey of the Federal Reserve subdivides the demarcated broad international policy regimes into a number of episodes.

A salient theme in our survey is that the convertibility rule or principle that dominated both domestic and international aspects of the monetary regime before World War I has since declined in its relevance. At the same time, policy makers within major nations placed more emphasis on stabilizing the real economy. Policy techniques and doctrine that developed under the pre-World War I convertible regime proved to be inadequate to deal with domestic stabilization goals in the interwar period, setting the stage for the Great Depression. In the post-World War II era, the complete abandonment of the convertibility principle, and its replacement by the goal of full employment, combined with the legacy of inadequate policy tools and theory from the interwar period, set the stage for the Great Inflation of the 1970s. The lessons from that experience have convinced monetary authorities to reemphasize the goal of low inflation, as it were, committing themselves to rule-like behavior.

2. International Monetary Regimes

2.1. The Gold Standard

The classical gold standard which ended in 1914 served as the basis of the convertibility principle that prevailed until the third quarter of the twentieth century. We discuss five themes that dominate an extensive literature.

The themes are: gold as a monetary standard; gold and the international monetary system; central banks and the "rules of the game"; the commodity theory of money; the gold standard as a rule.

2.1.1. Gold as a monetary standard.   Under a gold standard the monetary authority defines the weight of gold coins, or alternatively fixes the price of gold in terms of national currency. The fixed price is maintained by the authority's willingness freely to buy and sell gold at the mint price. There are no restrictions to the ownership or use of gold.

The gold standard evolved from earlier commodity money systems. Earlier commodity money systems were bimetallic—gold was used for high-valued transactions, silver or copper coins for low-valued ones. The bimetallic ratio (the ratio of the mint price of gold relative to the mint price of silver) was set close to the market ratio to ensure that both metals circulated. Otherwise, Gresham's Law ensured that the overvalued metal would drive the undervalued metal out of circulation.

The world switched from bimetallism to gold monometallism in the 1870s. Debate continues to swirl over the motivation for the shift. Some argue that it was primarily political [Friedman (1990a), Gallarotti (1995), Eichengreen (1996)]—nations wished to emulate the example of England, the world's leading commercial and industrial power. When Germany used the Franco–Prussian War indemnity to finance the creation of a gold standard, other prominent European nations also did so.[3]

Others argue that massive silver discoveries in the 1860s and 1870s as well as technical advances in coinage were the key determinants [Redish (1990)]. Regardless of the cause, recent research suggests that the shift both was unnecessary and undesirable since France, the principal bimetallic nation, had large enough reserves of both metals to continue to maintain the standard [Oppers (1996), Flandreau (1996)]; and because remaining on a bimetallic standard, through the production and substitution effects earlier analyzed by Irving Fisher (1922), would have provided greater price stability than did gold monometallism [Friedman (1990b)].

The simplest variant of the gold standard was a pure gold coin standard. Such a system entails high resource costs and, consequently in most countries, substitutes for gold coin emerged. In the private sector, commercial banks issued notes and deposits convertible into gold coins, which in turn were held as reserves to meet conversion demands.

In the public sector, prototypical central banks (banks of issue) were established to help governments finance their ever expanding fiscal needs [Capie, Goodhart and Schnadt (1994)]. These notes were also convertible, backed by gold reserves. In wartime, convertibility was suspended, but always on the expectation of renewal upon termination of hostilities. Thus the gold standard evolved into a mixed coin and fiduciary system based on the principle of convertibility.

A key problem with the convertible system was the risk of conversion attacks—of internal drains when a distrustful public attempted to convert commercial bank liabilities into gold; and external drains when foreign demands on a central bank's gold reserves threatened its ability to maintain convertibility. In the face of this rising tension between substitution of fiduciary money for gold and the stability of the system, central banks learned to become lenders of last resort and to use the tools of monetary policy to protect their gold reserves [Bagehot (1873), Redish (1993), Rockoff (1986)].

The gold standard, both the pure coin variety and the more common mixed standards, were domestic monetary standards which evolved in most countries through market driven processes. By defining its unit of account as a fixed weight of gold or alternatively by fixing the price of gold, each monetary authority also fixed its exchange rate with other gold standard countries and became part of an international gold standard.

2.1.2. Gold and the international monetary system. The international gold standard evolved from domestic standards by the fixing of the price of gold by member nations. Under the classical gold standard fixed exchange rate system, the world's monetary gold stock was distributed according to the member nations' demands for money and use of substitutes for gold. Disturbances to the balance of payments were automatically equilibrated by the Humean price–specie flow mechanism. Under that mechanism, arbitrage in gold kept nations' price levels in line. Gold would flow from countries with balance of payments deficits (caused, for example, by higher price levels) to those with surpluses (caused by lower price levels), in turn keeping their domestic money supplies and price levels in line.

Some authors stressed the operation of the law of one price and commodity arbitrage in traded goods prices, others the adjustment of the terms of trade, still others the adjustment of traded relative to nontraded goods prices [Bordo (1984)]. Debate continues on the details of the adjustment mechanism; however, there is consensus that it worked smoothly for the core countries of the world although not necessarily for the periphery [Ford (1962), DeCecco (1974), Fishlow (1985)]. It also facilitated a massive transfer of long-term capital from Europe to the new world in the four decades before World War I on a scale relative to income which has yet to be replicated.

Although in theory exchange rates were supposed to be perfectly rigid, in practice the rate of exchange was bounded by upper and lower limits— the gold points—within which the exchange rate floated. The gold points were determined by transactions costs, risk, and other costs of shipping gold. Recent research indicates that although in the classical period exchange rates frequently departed from par, violations of the gold points were rare [Officer (1986, 1996)], as were devaluations [Eichengreen (1985)]. Adjustment to balance of payments disturbances was greatly facilitated by short-term capital flows. Capital would quickly flow between countries to iron out interest rate differences. By the end of the nineteenth century the world capital market was so efficient that capital flows largely replaced gold flows in effecting adjustment.

2.1.3. Central banks and the rules of the game.   Central banks also played an important role in the international gold standard. By varying their discount rates and using other tools of monetary policy they were supposed to follow "the rules of the game" and speed up adjustment to balance of payments disequilibria. In fact many central banks violated the rules [Bloomfield (1959), Dutton (1984), Pippenger (1984), Giovannini (1986), Jeanne (1995), Davutyan and Parke (1995)] by not raising their discount rates or by using "gold devices" which artificially altered the price of gold in the face of a payments deficit [Sayers (1957)]. But the violations were never sufficient to threaten convertibility [Schwartz (1984)]. They were in fact tolerated because market participants viewed them as temporary attempts by central banks to smooth interest rates and economic activity while keeping within the overriding constraint of convertibility [Goodfriend (1988)]. An alternative interpretation is that violations of the rules of the game represented the operation of an effective target zone bordered by the gold points. Because of the credibility of commitment to gold convertibility, monetary authorities could alter their discount rates to affect domestic objectives by exploiting the mean reversion properties of exchange rates within the zone [Svensson (1994), Bordo and MacDonald (1997)].

An alternative to the view that the gold standard was managed by central banks in a symmetrical fashion is that it was managed by the Bank of England [Scammell (1965)]. By manipulating its Bank rate, it could attract whatever gold it needed; furthermore, other central banks adjusted their discount rates to hers. They did so because London was the center for the world's principal gold, commodities, and capital markets, outstanding sterling-denominated assets were huge, and sterling served as an international reserve currency (as a substitute for gold). There is considerable evidence supporting this view [Lindert (1969), Giovannini (1986), Eichengreen (1987)]. There is also evidence which suggests that the two other European core countries, France and Germany, had some control over discount rates within their respective economic spheres [Tullio and Wolters (1996)].

Although the gold standard operated smoothly for close to four decades, there were periodic financial crises. In most cases, when faced with both an internal and an external drain, the Bank of England and other European central banks followed Bagehot's rule of lending freely but at a penalty rate. On several occasions (e.g., 1890 and 1907) even the Bank of England's adherence to convertibility was put to the test and, according to Eichengreen (1992), cooperation with the Banque de France and other central banks was required to save it. Whether this was the case is a moot point. The cooperation that did occur was episodic, ad hoc, and not an integral part of the operation of the gold standard. Of greater importance is that, during periods of financial crisis, private capital flows aided the Bank. Such stabilizing capital movements likely reflected market participants' belief in the credibility of England's commitment to convertibility.

By the eve of World War I, the gold standard had evolved de facto into a gold exchange standard. In addition to substituting fiduciary national monies for gold to economize on scarce gold reserves, many countries also held convertible foreign exchange (mainly deposits in London). Thus the system evolved into a massive pyramid of credit built upon a tiny base of gold. As pointed out by Triffin (1960), the possibility of a confidence crisis, triggering a collapse of the system, increased as the gold reserves of the center diminished. The advent of World War I triggered such a collapse as the belligerents scrambled to convert their outstanding foreign liabilities into gold.

2.1.4. Theory of commodity money. The gold standard contained a self-regulating mechanism that ensured long-run monetary and price level stability, namely, the commodity theory of money. This was most clearly analyzed by Irving Fisher (1922) although well understood by earlier writers. The price level of the world, treated as a closed system, was determined by the interaction of the money market and the commodity or bullion market. The real price (or purchasing power of gold) was determined by the commodity market; and the price level was determined by the demand for and supply of monetary gold. The demand for monetary gold was derived from the demand for money while the monetary gold stock was the residual between the total world gold stock and the nonmonetary demand. Changes in the monetary gold stock reflected gold production and shifts between monetary and nonmonetary uses of gold [Barro (1979)].

Under the self-equilibrating gold standard, once-for-all shocks to the demand for or supply of monetary gold would change the price level. These would be reversed as changes in the price level affected the real price of gold, leading to offsetting changes in gold production and shifts between monetary and nonmonetary uses of gold. This mechanism produced mean reversion in the price level and a tendency towards long-run price stability. In the shorter run, the shocks to the gold market or to real activity created price level volatility. Evidence suggests that the mechanism worked roughly according to the theory [Cagan (1965), Bordo (1981), Rockoff (1984)] but other factors are also important—including government policy towards gold mining and the level of economic activity [Eichengreen and McLean (1994)].

This simple picture is complicated by a number of important considerations. These include technical progress in gold mining; the exhaustion of high-quality ores; and depletion of gold as a durable exhaustible reserve. With depletion, in the absence of offsetting technical change, a gold standard must inevitably result in long-run deflation [Bordo and Ellson (1985)]. Although there is evidence that the gold standard was self-regulating, the lags involved were exceedingly long and variable (between 10 and 25 years, according to Bordo [1981]), so that many observers have been unwilling to rely on the mechanism as a basis for world price stability, and prominent contemporary authorities advocated schemes to improve upon its performance. Others, e.g., Keynes (1930), doubted the operation of the self-regulating mechanism and attributed whatever success the gold standard had before 1914 to purely adventitious acts—timely gold discoveries in Australia and California in the 1850s, invention of the cyanide process in the 1880s, and gold discoveries in South Africa and Alaska in the 1890s.

2.1.5. The gold standard as a rule.   One of the most important features of the gold standard was that it embodied a monetary rule or commitment mechanism that constrained the actions of the monetary authorities. To the classical economists, forcing monetary authorities to follow rules was viewed as preferable to subjecting monetary policy to the discretion of well-meaning officials. Today a rule serves to bind policy actions over time. This view of policy rules, in contrast to the earlier tradition that stressed both impersonality and automaticity, stems from the recent literature on the time inconsistency of optimal government policy.

In terms of the modern perspective of Kydland and Prescott (1977) and Barro and Gordon (1983), the rule served as a commitment mechanism to prevent governments from setting policies sequentially in a time inconsistent manner. According to this approach, adherence to the fixed price of gold was the commitment that prevented governments from creating surprise fiduciary money issues in order to capture seigniorage revenue, or from defaulting on outstanding debt [Bordo and Kydland (1996), Giovannini (1993)]. On this basis, adherence to the gold standard rule before 1914 enabled many countries to avoid the problems of high inflation and stagflation that troubled the late twentieth century.

The gold standard rule in the century before World War I can also be interpreted as a contingent rule, or a rule with escape clauses [Grossman and Van Huyck (1988), DeKock and Grilli (1989), Flood and Isard (1989), Bordo and Kydland (1996)]. The monetary authority maintained the standard—kept the price of the currency in terms of gold fixed—except in the event of a well-understood emergency such as a major war. In wartime it might suspend gold convertibility and issue paper money to finance its expenditures, and it could sell debt issues in terms of the nominal value of its currency, on the understanding that the debt would eventually be paid off in gold or in undepreciated paper. The rule was contingent in the sense that the public understood that the suspension would last only for the duration of the wartime emergency plus some period of adjustment, and that afterwards the government would adopt the deflationary policies necessary to resume payments at the original parity.

Observing such a rule would allow the government to smooth its revenue from different sources of finance: taxation, borrowing, and seigniorage [Lucas and Stokey (1983), Mankiw (1987)]. That is, in wartime when present taxes on labor effort would reduce output when it was needed most, using future taxes or borrowing would be optimal. At the same time positive collection costs might also make it optimal to use the inflation tax as a substitute for conventional taxes [Bordo and Végh (1998)]. A temporary suspension of convertibility would then allow the government to use the optimal mix of the three taxes.[4]

It is crucial that the rule be transparent and simple and that only a limited number of contingencies be included. Transparency and simplicity avoided the problems of moral hazard and incomplete information [Canzoneri (1985), Obstfeld (1991)], i.e., prevented the monetary authority from engaging in discretionary policy under the guise of following the contingent rule. In this respect a second contingency—a temporary suspension in the face of a financial crisis, which in turn was not the result of the monetary authority's own actions—might also have been part of the rule. However, because of the greater difficulty of verifying the source of the contingency than in the case of war, invoking the contingency under conditions of financial crisis, or in the case of a shock to the terms of trade—a third possible contingency—would be more likely to create suspicion that discretion was the order of the day.

The basic gold standard rule is a domestic rule and it was enforced by the reputation of the gold standard itself, i.e., by the historical evolution of gold as money. An alternative commitment mechanism was to guarantee gold convertibility in the constitution as was done in Sweden before 1914 [Jonung (1984)].

The gold standard contingent rule worked successfully for the "core" countries of the classical gold standard: Britain, France, and the USA [Bordo and Schwartz (1996a)]. In all these countries the monetary authorities adhered faithfully to the fixed price of gold except during major wars. During the Napoleonic War and World War I for England, the Civil War for the USA, and the Franco–Prussian War for France, specie payments were suspended and paper money and debt were issued. But in each case, after the wartime emergency had passed, policies leading to resumption at the prewar parity were adopted. Indeed, successful adherence to the pre-World War I rule may have enabled the belligerents to obtain access to debt finance more easily in subsequent wars. In the case of Germany, the fourth "core" country, no occasions arose for application of the contingent aspect of the rule before 1914. Otherwise its record of adherence to gold convertibility was similar to that of the other three countries. Unlike the core countries, a number of peripheral countries had difficulty in following the rule and their experience was characterized by frequent suspensions of convertibility and devaluations.

One author argues that the commitment to gold convertibility by England and the other core countries was made possible by a favorable conjuncture of political economy factors. The groups who were harmed by the contractionary policies, required in the face of a balance of payments deficit to maintain convertibility, did not have political power before 1914. By contrast, in some peripheral countries, powerful political groups, e.g., Argentine ranchers and American silver miners, benefited from inflation and depreciation [Eichengreen (1992)].

The gold standard rule originally evolved as a domestic commitment mechanism but its enduring fame is as an international rule. As an

international standard, the key rule was maintenance of gold convertibility
at the established par. Maintenance of a fixed price of gold by its adherents
in turn ensured fixed exchange rates. The fixed price of domestic currency
in terms of gold provided a nominal anchor to the international monetary
system.

According to the game theoretic literature, for an international monetary arrangement to be effective both between countries and within them,
a time-consistent credible commitment mechanism is required [Canzoneri
and Henderson (1991)]. Adherence to the gold convertibility rule provided
such a mechanism. Indeed, Giovannini (1993) finds the variation of both
exchange rates and short-term interest rates within the limits set by the
gold points in the 1899–1909 period consistent with market agents' expectations of a credible commitment by the core countries to the gold standard rule. In addition to the reputation of the domestic gold standard and
constitutional provisions which ensured domestic commitment, adherence
to the international gold standard rule may have been enforced by other
mechanisms [see Bordo and Kydland (1996)]. These include: the operation
of the rules of the game; the hegemonic power of England; central bank
cooperation; and improved access to international capital markets.

Indeed the key enforcement mechanism of the gold standard rule for
peripheral countries was access to capital obtainable from the core countries. Adherence to the gold standard was a signal of good behavior, like
the "good housekeeping seal of approval"; it explains why countries that
always adhered to gold convertibility paid lower interest rates on loans contracted in London than others with less consistent performance [Bordo
and Rockoff (1996)].

2.1.6. The viability of the gold standard. The classical gold standard
collapsed in 1914. It was reinstated as a gold exchange standard between
1925 and 1931, and as the gold dollar standard from 1959 to 1971. The
gold standard, while highly successful for a time, lost credibility in its
twentieth-century reincarnations and was formally abandoned in 1971.

Among the weaknesses which contributed to its abandonment were the
cost of maintaining a full-bodied gold standard. Friedman (1953) estimated
the cost for the USA in 1950 as 1.5 percent of real GNP. Shocks to the

demand for and supply of gold that produced drift in the price level also weakened support for the gold standard, leading many economists to advocate schemes for reform [Cagan (1984)]. Finally, in a growing world, the gold standard, based on a durable exhaustible resource, posed the prospect of deflation.

The key benefits of the gold standard, in hindsight, were that it provided a relatively stable nominal anchor and a commitment mechanism to ensure that monetary authorities followed time-consistent policies. However, the gold standard rule of maintaining a fixed price of gold meant, for a closed economy, that continuous full employment was not a viable policy objective and, for an open economy, that domestic policy considerations would be subordinated to those of maintaining external balance. In the twentieth century few countries have been willing to accept the gold standard's discipline [Schwartz (1986b)].

2.2. Interwar Vicissitudes of the Gold Standard

The outbreak of World War I in August 1914 led to a massive worldwide financial crisis as investors across the world scrambled to liquidate sterling and other financial assets in exchange for domestic currency and gold. The response to the crisis and the need by the European belligerents for gold to pay for war material led to the breakdown of the gold standard.

After the war the UK and other countries expressed a strong preference to return to gold parity at the original parity following the gold standard contingent rule [see the Cunliffe Report (1918)]. At the Genoa Conference in 1922, the Financial Commission, under British leadership, urged that the world return to the gold standard. However, the system they advocated was a gold exchange standard that encouraged member countries to make their currencies convertible into gold but to use foreign exchange (the currencies of key reserve countries, the UK and the USA) as a substitute for gold. The experts also encouraged members to restrict the use of gold as currency, thus establishing a gold bullion standard, and to cooperate when raising or lowering their discount rates to prevent competition for gold. The motivation to economize on gold was a belief that the world would suffer a severe gold shortage in coming decades.

The gold standard was restored worldwide in the period 1924–1927. It only lasted globally until 1931. The key event in its restoration was the return in April 1925 by the UK to convertibility at the prewar parity of $4.86. It is believed to have overvalued sterling between 5 and 15 percent depending on the price index used [Keynes (1925), Redmond (1984)].[5]

Countries with high inflation, such as France and Italy, returned to gold but at a greatly devalued parity. It took France seven years to stabilize the franc after the war. As described by Eichengreen (1992), the franc depreciated considerably in the early 1920s reflecting a war of attrition between the left and the right over the financing of postwar reconstruction and over new fiscal programs [Alesina and Drazen (1991)]. The weakness of the franc was halted by Poincaré's 1926 stabilization program which restored budget balance, low money growth, and an independent central bank [Sargent (1984), Prati (1991)]. Germany, Austria, and other countries, which had endured hyperinflation, all stabilized their currencies in 1923/1924 and, with the aid of the League of Nations, all returned to gold convertibility at greatly devalued parities.[6]

The gold standard was restored on the basis of the recommendations of Genoa. Central bank statutes typically required a cover ratio for currencies of between 30 and 40 percent, divided between gold and foreign exchange. Central reserve countries were to hold reserves only in the form of gold.

The gold exchange standard suffered from a number of serious flaws compared to the prewar gold standard [Kindleberger (1973), Temin (1989), Eichengreen (1992, 1996)]. The first problem was the adjustment problem. The UK with an overvalued currency ran persistent balance of payments deficits and gold outflows which imparted deflationary pressure, and in the face of sticky prices and wages, low growth, and high unemployment. This also required the Bank of England to adopt tight monetary policies to defend convertibility. At the other extreme, France with an undervalued currency enjoyed payments surpluses and gold inflows. The Banque de France did not allow the gold inflows to expand the money supply and raise the price level. It sterilized the inflows and absorbed monetary gold from the rest of the world.[7] At the same time the USA, the world's largest gold holder, also sterilized gold inflows and prevented the adjustment mechanism from operating [Friedman and Schwartz (1963)].

The second problem was the liquidity problem. Gold supplies were believed to be inadequate to finance the growth of world trade and output. This in turn was a legacy of high World War I inflation which reduced the real price of gold. The League of Nations in the First Interim Report of the Gold Delegation [League of Nations (1930)] tried to forecast the world demand for and supply of gold in the next decade. The Report argued that, unless further attempts to economize on gold succeeded, the world was destined to suffer from massive deflation. That happened in the period 1929–1933, not because of a gold shortage but because of the Great Depression [Bordo and Eichengreen (1998)].

In the face of the perceived gold shortage, following the strictures of Genoa, central banks substituted foreign exchange for gold. This in turn created a confidence problem. As outstanding pounds and dollars increased relative to gold reserves in London and New York, the greater the likelihood that some shock would lead to a speculative attack on sterling or the dollar by foreign holders fearful that they would be unable to convert their balances. Indeed this is what happened to sterling in 1931 [Capie, Mills and Wood (1986)] and to the dollar in 1933 [Wigmore (1987)].

The final problem plaguing the gold exchange standard was a lack of credibility. A change in the political complexion of many European countries (the growth of labor unions and left-wing parties) after World War I made it more difficult to defend convertibility if it meant adopting deflationary monetary policy [Eichengreen (1992, 1996), Simmons (1994)]. Speculative attacks made short-term capital flows destabilizing instead of stabilizing, as they were before World War I. The lack of credibility could have been offset, according to Eichengreen (1992), by increased central bank cooperation but it was not forthcoming. The system collapsed in the face of the shocks of the Great Depression.[8]

2.3. Bretton Woods

Bretton Woods was the world's last convertible regime. It fits within the context of the gold standard because the USA, the most important commercial power, defined its parity in terms of gold and all other members defined their parities in terms of dollars.

The planning that led to Bretton Woods aimed to avoid the chaos of the interwar period [Ikenberry (1993)]. The ills to be avoided were deduced from the historical record: floating exchange rates, condemned as prone to destabilizing speculation in the early 1920s; the subsequent gold exchange standard that enforced the international transmission of deflation in the early 1930s; and devaluations after 1933 that were interpreted as beggar-thy-neighbor actions and declared to be wrong, as was resort to trade restrictions, exchange controls, and bilateralism [Nurkse (1944)]. To avoid these ills, an adjustable peg system was designed that was expected to combine the favorable features of the fixed exchange rate gold standard and flexible exchange rates.

Both John Maynard Keynes representing the UK and Harry Dexter White representing the United States planned an adjustable peg system to be coordinated by an international monetary agency. The Keynes plan gave the International Clearing Union substantially more resources and power than White's United Nations Stabilization Fund, but both institutions were to exert considerable power over the domestic financial policy of the members. The British plan contained more domestic policy autonomy than did the US plan, while the American plan put more emphasis on exchange rate stability.

The Articles of Agreement signed at Bretton Woods, New Hampshire, in July 1944 represented a compromise between the American and British plans. It combined the flexibility and freedom for policy makers of a floating rate system which the British team wanted, with the nominal stability of the gold standard rule emphasized by the USA. The system established was a pegged exchange rate, but members could alter their parities in terms of gold and the dollar in the face of a fundamental disequilibrium. Members were encouraged to rely on domestic stabilization policy to offset temporary disturbances to their payments balances and they were protected from speculative attack by capital controls. The International Monetary Fund (IMF) was to provide temporary liquidity assistance and to oversee the operation of the system [Bordo (1993a)].

Although based on the principle of convertibility, with the USA rather than England as the center country, Bretton Woods differed from the classical gold standard in a number of fundamental ways. First, it was an arrangement mandated by an international agreement between governments, whereas the gold standard evolved informally. Second, domestic policy autonomy was encouraged even at the expense of convertibility, in sharp contrast to the gold standard where convertibility was key. Third, capital movements were suppressed by controls [Marston (1993), Obstfeld and Taylor (1998)].

The Bretton Woods system faced a number of problems in getting started, and it took 12 years before the system achieved full operation. Each of the two key problems in the early years—bilateralism and the dollar shortage—was largely solved by developments outside the Bretton Woods arrangements. The dollar shortage was solved by massive US Marshall Plan aid and the devaluation of sterling and other currencies in 1949. Multilateralism was eventually achieved in Western Europe in 1958 following the establishment in 1950 of the European Payments Union [Eichengreen (1995)].

The period 1959–1967 was the heyday of Bretton Woods. The system had become a gold dollar standard whereby the United States pegged the price of gold and the rest of the world pegged their currencies to the dollar. The dollar emerged as the key reserve currency in this period, reflecting both its use as an intervention currency and a growing demand by the private sector for dollars as international money. This growth in dollar demand reflected stable US monetary policy.

Also the system evolved a different form of international governance than envisioned at Bretton Woods. The IMF's role as manager was eclipsed by that of the USA in competition with the other members of the G-10. According to Dominguez (1993), although the IMF provided many valuable services, it was not successful in serving as a commitment mechanism.

The Bretton Woods system, in its convertible phase from 1959 to 1971, was characterized by exceptional macroeconomic performance in the advanced countries (see Section 4 below). It had the lowest and most stable inflation rate and highest and most stable real growth rates of any modern regime. However, it was short-lived. Moreover, it faced smaller demand and supply shocks than under the gold standard. This suggests that the reason for the brevity of its existence was not the external environment but, as with the gold exchange standard, structural flaws in the regime and the lack of a credible commitment mechanism by the center reserve country.

The three problems of adjustment, liquidity, and confidence dominated academic and policy discussions during this period. The debate surrounding the first focused on how to achieve adjustment in a world with capital controls, fixed exchange rates, and domestic policy autonomy. Various policy measures were proposed to aid adjustment [Obstfeld (1993)].

For the United States, the persistence of balance of payments deficits after 1957 was a source of concern. For some it demonstrated the need for adjustment; for others it served as the means to satisfy the rest of the world's demand for dollars. For monetary authorities the deficit was a problem because of the threat of a convertibility crisis, as outstanding dollar liabilities rose relative to the US monetary gold stock. US policies to restrict capital flows and discourage convertibility did not solve the problem. The main solution advocated for the adjustment problem was increased liquidity. Exchange rate flexibility was strongly opposed.

The liquidity problem evolved from a shortfall of monetary gold beginning in the late 1950s. The gap was increasingly made up by dollars, but, because of the confidence problem, dollars were not a permanent solution. New sources of liquidity were required, answered by the creation of Special Drawing Rights (SDRs). However, by the time SDRs were injected into the system, they exacerbated worldwide inflation [Genberg and Swoboda (1993)].

The key problem of the gold–dollar system was how to maintain confidence. If the growth of the monetary gold stock was not sufficient to finance the growth of world real output and to maintain US gold reserves, the system would become dynamically unstable [Triffin (1960), Kenen (1960)]. Indeed the system was subject to growing speculative attacks, in which market agents anticipated the inconsistency between nations' financial policies and maintenance of pegged exchange rates [Garber and Flood (1984), Garber (1993)]. Although capital flows were blocked in most countries, controls were increasingly evaded by various devices including the use of leads and lags—the practice of accelerating payments in domestic currency and delaying foreign currency receipts in the expectation of a devaluation of the domestic currency [Obstfeld and Taylor (1998)]. Thus successful attacks occurred against sterling in 1947, 1949, and 1967 and the franc in 1968 [Bordo and Schwartz (1996b)].

From 1960 to 1967, the United States adopted a number of policies to prevent conversion of dollars into gold. These included the Gold Pool, swaps, Roosa bonds, and moral suasion. The defense of sterling was a first line of defense for the dollar. When none of the measures worked the dollar itself was attacked via a run on the London gold market in March 1968 leading to the adoption of the two-tier gold market arrangement. This solution temporarily solved the problem by demonetizing gold at the margin and hence creating a de facto dollar standard.

The Bretton Woods system collapsed between 1968 and 1971 in the face of US monetary expansion that exacerbated worldwide inflation. The United States broke the implicit rules of the dollar standard by not maintaining price stability [Darby et al. (1983)]. The rest of the world did not want to absorb dollars and inflate. They were also reluctant to revalue. The Americans were forced by British and French decisions to convert dollars into gold. The impasse was resolved by President Richard Nixon's closing of the gold window, ending convertibility on 15 August 1971.

Another important source of strain on the system was the unworkability of the adjustable peg under increasing capital mobility. Speculation against a fixed parity could not be stopped by either traditional policies or international rescue packages. The breakdown of Bretton Woods marked the end of US financial predominance in the international monetary system. The absence of a new center of international management set the stage for a multipolar system.

Under the Bretton Woods system, as under the classical gold standard, a set of rules was established, based on the convertibility of domestic currency into gold, although under Bretton Woods only the United States was required to maintain it.[9] Also, as under the gold standard, the rule was a contingent one. Under Bretton Woods the contingency, which would allow a change of parity, was a fundamental disequilibrium in the balance of payments, although fundamental disequilibrium was never clearly defined.

Unlike the example of Britain under the gold standard, however, the commitment to maintain gold convertibility by the USA, the center country, lost credibility by the mid-1960s. Also the contingency aspect of the rule proved unworkable. With fundamental disequilibrium being ill-defined, devaluations were avoided as an admission of failed policy. In addition, devaluations invited speculative attack even in the presence of capital controls. Once controls were removed, the system was held together only by G-10 cooperation and once inconsistencies developed between the interests of the USA and other members, even cooperation became unworkable.

In conclusion, under Bretton Woods gold still served as a nominal anchor. This link to gold likely was important in constraining US monetary policy, at least until the mid-1960s, and therefore that of the rest of the world. This may explain the low inflation rates and the low degree of inflation persistence observed in the 1950s and 1960s [Alogoskoufis and Smith (1991), Bordo (1993b)]. However, credibility was considerably weaker than under the gold standard and it was not as effective a nominal anchor [Giovannini (1993)]. Moreover, when domestic interests clashed with convertibility, the anchor chain was stretched and then discarded [Redish (1993)]. This was evident in the US reduction and then removal of gold reserve requirements in 1965 and 1968, the closing of the Gold Pool in 1968 and the gold window itself in 1971. The adoption of the Second Amendment to the IMF Articles of Agreement in 1976 marked the absolute termination of a role for gold in the international monetary system.

With the closing of the gold window and the breakdown of the Bretton Woods system, the last vestiges of the fixed nominal anchor of the convertibility regime disappeared. The subsequent decade under a fiat money regime and floating exchange rates exhibited higher peacetime inflation in advanced countries than in any other regime. An interesting unanswered question is whether the demise of the fixed nominal anchor and the convertibility principle explains the subsequent inflation or whether a change in the objectives of monetary authorities—full employment rather than convertibility and price stability—explains the jettisoning of the nominal anchor.

2.4. The Recent Managed Float and the European Monetary System

As a reaction to the flaws of the Bretton Woods system, the world turned to generalized floating exchange rates in March 1973. Though the early years of the floating exchange rate were often characterized as a dirty float, whereby monetary authorities extensively intervened to affect both the levels of volatility and exchange rates, by the 1990s it evolved into a system where exchange market intervention occurred primarily with the intention of smoothing fluctuations.

Again in the 1980s exchange market intervention was used by the Group of Seven countries as part of a strategy of policy coordination. In recent years, floating exchange rates have been assailed from many quarters for excessive volatility in both nominal and real exchange rates, which in turn increase macroeconomic instability and raise the costs of international transactions.

Despite these problems, the ability of the flexible regime to accommodate the problems of the massive oil price shocks in the 1970s as well as other shocks in subsequent years without significant disruption, as well as the perception that pegged exchange rate arrangements amongst major countries are doomed to failure, render the prospects for significant reform of the present system at the world level remote. Based upon the Bretton Woods experience, major countries are unwilling to compromise their domestic interests for the sake of the dictates of an external monetary authority or to be subject to the constraints of an international exchange rate arrangement which they cannot control [Bordo (1995)].

This is not the case at the regional level where there is a greater harmony of interests than between major countries. Indeed Europe is moving unsteadily towards creating a monetary union with a common currency. On the road to that end, the EMS established in 1979 was modelled after Bretton Woods (although not based on gold), with more flexibility and better financial resources [Bordo (1993b)]. It was successful for a few years in the late 1980s when member countries followed policies similar to those of Germany, the center country [Giavazzi and Giovannini (1989)]. It broke down in 1992–1993 in a manner similar to the collapse of Bretton Woods in 1968–1971. It also collapsed for similar reasons—because pegged exchange rates, capital mobility, and policy autonomy do not mix. It collapsed in the face of a massive speculative attack on countries that adopted policies inconsistent with their pegs to the D-mark and also on countries that seemingly observed the rules, but whose ultimate commitment to the peg was doubted. The doubt arose because of rising unemployment in the latter.

The lesson from this experience is that the only real alternatives for the European countries are monetary union, perfectly fixed exchange rates and the complete loss of monetary independence, or else floating. Halfway measures such as pegged exchange rate systems do not last. Schemes to reimpose capital controls [Eichengreen, Tobin and Wyplosz (1995)] will be outwitted and will only misallocate resources.

The legacy of the gold standard and its variants for EMU is the role of gold as the nominal anchor and of a credible policy rule to maintain it. Cooperation and harmonization of policies under the gold standard was episodic and not by design—in contrast with Bretton Woods, EMS, and EMU. For the EMU to succeed, members must have the same credible commitment to their goal as did the advanced nations to the gold standard rule a century ago. That is, they must sacrifice domestic to international stability.

The advent of generalized floating in 1973 allowed each country more flexibility to conduct independent monetary policies. In the 1970s inflation accelerated as advanced countries attempted to use monetary policy to maintain full employment. However, monetary policy could be used to target the level of unemployment only at the expense of accelerating inflation [Friedman (1968), Phelps (1968)]. In addition, the USA and other countries used expansionary monetary policy to accommodate oil price shocks in 1973 and 1979. The high inflation rates that ensued led to a determined effort by monetary authorities in the USA and UK and other countries to disinflate.

The 1980s witnessed renewed emphasis by central banks on low inflation as their primary (if not sole) objective. Although no formal monetary rule has been established, a number of countries have granted their central banks independence from the fiscal authority and have also instituted mandates for low inflation or price stability. Whether we are witnessing a return to a rule like the convertibility principle and a fixed nominal anchor is too soon to tell.

We now turn from the general discussion of domestic and international monetary regimes to survey an important example of a domestic regime—the USA.

3. Episodes in US Central Banking History

3.1. Origins of US Central Banking

Before the passage of the Federal Reserve Act in 1913, the United States did not have a central bank, but it did adhere successfully to a specie standard from 1792 on, except for a brief wartime suspension at the end of the War of 1812 and the 17-year greenback episode from 1862 to 1879. From 1879 to 1914, the United States adhered to the gold standard without a central bank. With the exception of a period in the 1890s, when agitation for free coinage of silver led to capital flight and threats of speculative attacks on the dollar [Grilli (1990), Calomiris (1993)], US commitment to gold convertibility was as credible as that of the other core countries [Giovannini (1993)].

Although a formal central bank was not in place before 1914, other institutions performed some of its functions. The Independent Treasury, established in 1840, served as a depository for federal government tax receipts in specie. On a number of occasions, by transferring specie to commercial banks, by judicious timing of its debt management, and by disbursement of the budget surplus, the Treasury mitigated financial stress. It even engaged in primitive open market operations, according to Timberlake (1993, ch. 6). Clearing house associations in various financial centers, beginning with New York in 1857, provided lender of last resort services of a central bank by issuing emergency currency [Timberlake (1993), ch. 14], but often after rates became extremely high—100 percent in 1907.

The Federal Reserve system was established to deal more systematically than had the Treasury and the clearing houses with the perceived problems of the banking system, including periodic financial panics and seasonally volatile short-term interest rates. It came into existence at the end of the classical gold standard era, yet it was founded directly upon the precepts of central banking under the gold standard: use of discount rate policy to defend gold convertibility, and the importance of a lender of last resort [Meltzer (1995a), ch. 2]. In addition, the new institution was organized to smooth seasonal movements in short-term interest rates by providing an elastic money supply. By accommodating member bank demand for rediscounts, based on eligible, self-liquidating commercial bills, the reserve banks were designed to promote sufficient liquidity to finance economic activity over the business cycle [Meltzer (1996), ch. 3].

The remaining subsections cover episodes of the eighty-odd years of the Federal Reserve's existence within the broad regimes demarcated in Section 2: 1919–1941; 1946–1971; 1971–1995.[10] The environment in which the system operated in each of these episodes was vastly different from that envisioned by the founders. Monetary policy changes took place. The changes reflected the influence of three sets of players, who shaped the saga of the system: Congress, by legislation and oversight; the system's officials, by their efforts to fulfill its mission, as they understood it; and the research community, by its interpretation and evaluation of the system's performance. Our discussion comments on these sources of influence on the system.

To accompany the discussion, Figures 3.1A–F present annual series for six important macroeconomic aggregates, 1914–1995: CPI and real per capita income; M2 and the monetary base; the short-term commercial paper rate, and a long-term bond yield. Vertical lines on each plot mark the separate monetary policy episodes that distinguish the Federal Reserve era.

3.2. Federal Reserve 1914

In the 30 sections of the Federal Reserve Act that was signed into law on 13 December 1913 Congress sketched the outlines of the system it sought to create. Its structure included a board based in Washington, DC, of five (increased to six, June 1922) appointees of the President, one of whom he would designate as the Governor, plus the Comptroller of the Currency, and the Secretary of the Treasury as ex officio chairman; no fewer than eight and no more than twelve Federal Reserve banks, each located in a principal city, the final number and boundaries of the districts to be

FIGURE 3.1A   Real Per Capita Income, 1914–1995, USA. Regimes:
1. World War II; 2. 1920's; 3. Great Contraction; 4. the Recovery;
5. Interest Rate Peg; 6. Fed. Discretionary Regime; 7. Breakdown of
Convertibility Principle; 8. Shifting the Focus of Monetary Policy

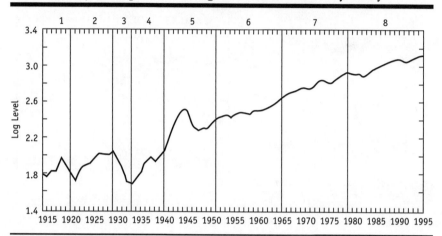

DATA SOURCES: See Appendix A.

FIGURE 3.1B   CPI, 1914–1995, USA. See Figure 3.1A for Legend

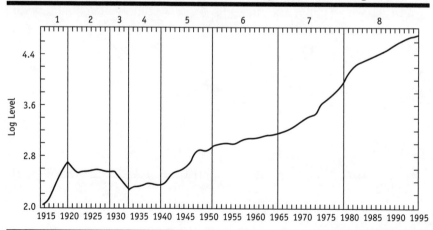

FIGURE 3.1C   Monetary Base, 1914–1995, USA. See Figure 3.1A for Legend

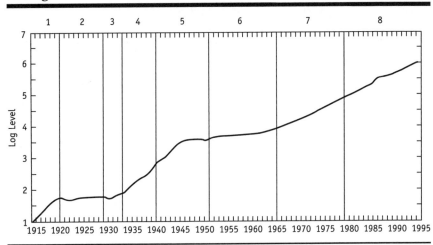

FIGURE 3.1D   M2, 1914–1995, USA. See Figure 3.1A for Legend

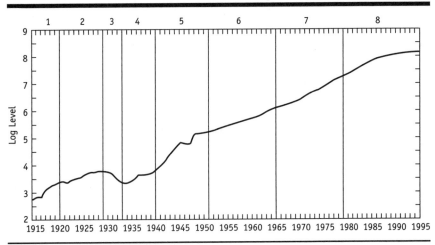

FIGURE 3.1E   Short-Term Interest Rate, 1914–1995, USA. See
Figure 3.1A for Legend

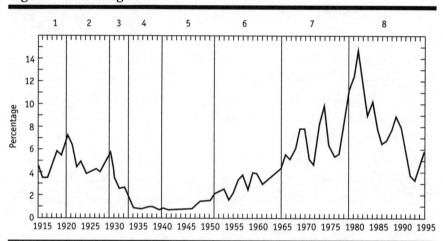

FIGURE 3.1F   Long-Term Interest Rate, 1914–1995, USA. See
Figure 3.1A for Legend

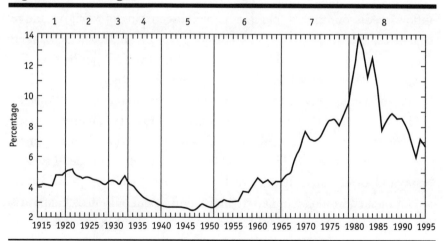

determined by a committee of the Secretaries of Treasury and Agriculture, and the Comptroller of the Currency; a Federal Advisory Council of one banker elected by each reserve bank.

By this structure Congress intended to create a system of semi-autonomous regional reserve banks, loosely subject to the supervision of the Washington board. Over the next two decades the board and the reserve banks and the reserve banks among themselves would be pitted against one another in a struggle to determine which one was dominant.

The principal change the Federal Reserve Act introduced was the provision of an "elastic currency", Federal Reserve notes (or, equivalently, member bank deposits at the reserve banks). "Elastic" meant that the new Federal Reserve money would be subject to substantial change in quantity over short periods, thus requiring some body to control the creation and retirement of the money, some means for creating and retiring the money, and some criteria to determine the amount to be created or retired [Friedman and Schwartz (1963)].

Both the board and the reserve banks, without clear lines of demarcation of their respective powers, were given joint control of the creation and retirement of Federal Reserve money. The means for creating it were gold inflows, rediscounting of "eligible" paper, discounting of foreign trade acceptances, and open market purchases of government securities, bankers' acceptances, and bills of exchange. Retirements involved the converse. The criteria for determining the amount of Federal Reserve money, on the one hand, was a gold standard rule, imposing the requirement of a 40 percent gold reserve against notes and a 35 percent gold reserve against deposits, and convertibility of Federal Reserve money in gold on demand at the Treasury Department or in gold and lawful money at any Federal Reserve bank; and, on the other hand, a real bills doctrine, according to which the amount issued would be linked to "notes, drafts, and bills of exchange arising out of actual commercial transactions" (section 13), offered for discount at rates to be established "with a view of accommodating commerce and business" (section 14d). In addition to gold backing, each dollar of Federal Reserve notes was also to be secured by a 60 percent commercial paper collateral requirement.

The two criteria were on the surface contradictory. While the gold standard rule requires the stock of notes and deposits to be whatever is necessary to balance international payments over the long run, in the short run, the stock of gold reserves and international capital market flows can accommodate temporary imbalances. However, the gold standard does not determine the division of the stock of money between currency and deposits, although facilitating shifts between the two forms of money was a crucial attribute of the new institution. The real bills criterion, by contrast, which was linked to this division, sets no limit to the quantity of money.

A basic monetary problem that the Federal Reserve Act was intended to solve was an attempt by the public to shift from holding deposits to holding currency. Such attempts had led to a series of banking crises before 1914 [Schwartz (1986a)]. The solution was to introduce a form of currency that could be rapidly expanded—the role of the Federal Reserve note—and to enable commercial banks readily to convert their assets into such currency—the role of rediscounting. By limiting the lender of last resort to rediscounting only such paper as arose from "actual commercial transactions" as opposed to paper arising from "speculative transactions" (i.e., loans backed by stock market collateral), the Federal Reserve Act sustained the real bills doctrine but, in so doing, it confused the elasticity of one component of the money stock relative to another and the elasticity of the total.

Systemwide open market operations were not contemplated in the Act. Each reserve bank had discretion to choose the amount of government securities to buy and sell and first claim on the earnings of its government securities portfolio.

The Federal Reserve Act gave the board and the reserve banks the right to regulate interest rates. As a result, the behavior of short-term interest rates changed. Before the Federal Reserve began operations, nominal interest rates displayed extreme seasonality, which was linked to financial crises [Kemmerer (1910), ch. 2; Macaulay (1938), chart 20; Shiller (1980), pp. 136–137; Clark (1986), Miron (1986), Mankiw, Miron and Weil (1987), Miron (1996)]. Once in operation, it apparently altered the process generating short-term interest rates. According to Barro (1989), the shifts in monetary policy involved changes in the process for monetary-base growth.

Federal Reserve policy did not completely eliminate seasonality in nominal interest rates, but substantially reduced its amplitude. Why the policy of smoothing was quickly effective in reducing seasonality and other transitory movements in nominal interest rates has been the subject of debate. Was it the founding of the Federal Reserve, as Miron (1986) and Goodfriend (1991) contend, or the abandonment of the gold standard by many countries in 1914 that led to diminished interest rate seasonality, as Truman Clark (1986) contends, or was there no regime change at all, as Fishe and Wohar (1990) maintain?

Whichever interpretation one adopts, if one regards the nominal interest rate as the implicit tax on holding real money balances, smoothing the nominal interest rate over the year is a benefit but only of small consequence in raising welfare. McCallum (1991) suggests, however, that seasonal interest rate smoothing encouraged Federal Reserve smoothing in nonseasonal ways also, which was probably detrimental to monetary policy more generally.

Goodfriend (1988) asks how the Federal Reserve was able to combine a commitment to a fixed dollar price of gold, on its founding, with interest rate smoothing. His answer is that, under a gold standard, the Federal Reserve could choose policy rules for both money and gold. It varied its stockpile of gold in supporting a fixed price of gold, and used monetary policy to target interest rates.

Semi-autonomous reserve banks, according to the Federal Reserve Act, would each establish discount rates in accordance with regional demand for and supply of rediscounts, subject to review and determination of the board (section 13). Discount rates were to vary by types of eligible paper and by different maturities. Where the power rested to initiate discount rate changes would become contentious. The example of the Bank of England in setting its rate above market rates influenced early reserve bank belief that discount rates should be penalty rates. This belief conflicted with the political interest to use the Act to achieve a low level of interest rates [Meltzer (1996), ch. 3].

The Federal Reserve Act also included a fiscal provision (section 7). Member banks own the reserve banks, and are paid a 6 percent cumulative dividend on their capital stock, as if the reserve banks were a public utility and the board were the regulatory body [Timberlake (1993)]. Expenses of both the reserve banks and the board were paid from earnings on assets. Timberlake finds a contradiction between regarding the reserve banks as both the income-earning utility and regulators of the commercial banking system.

The net earnings of the reserve banks, according to the law, after payment of dividends were to be divided between the surplus account and the Treasury. However, before they needed to turn over any part of their earnings to the government, the reserve banks could build up their surplus until the accounts equaled (originally 40 percent, changed in March 1919 to 100 percent of) their subscribed capital and, even then, 10 percent of net earnings would continue to be added to the surplus before the remainder was paid to the Treasury as a franchise tax on the note issue.

The objective of the Federal Reserve was to serve as a lender of last resort and thus eliminate financial crises, to be achieved by interest rate smoothing, according to the consensus view of writers on its founding. It would issue notes and deposits, based on real bills, and convertible into gold on demand.

Toma (1997) regards the foregoing specification of the intent of the Federal Reserve Act as misconceived. Based on a public choice approach, he describes the reserve banks as a network of competitive clearinghouses that were to provide liquidity for retail banks. Assigning money creation powers to the Federal Reserve was a way of funding the general government, which could indeed raise revenue for itself by granting monopoly status to a clearinghouse and taxing its profits. That strategy, however, would reduce the liquidity the clearinghouse were to offer banks. Greater government financing needs meant less liquidity supplied by the reserve industry and greater bank fragility. Hence, for Toma, the founding of the Federal Reserve reflected a tradeoff between government revenue needs and financial stability. Since prospective government seigniorage requirements were low in 1913, financial stability goals dominated.

Toma also disputes the role of interest rate smoothing. The solution to the financial crisis problem in his view did not rely on interest rate control. Instead, the Federal Reserve rebated earnings to large city banks through an in-kind payment of check-clearing services, and subsidized loans during the fall when discount rates were constant and market interest rates rose. Hence probability of a financial crisis was reduced. Manipulation of market interest rates was not required.

Toma's emphasis on government revenue needs as an important element in the thinking of the founders of the Federal Reserve would carry weight if he would cite evidence to this effect during the lengthy debate preceding the law's enactment. As it is, his evidence is that public finance considerations accounted for the creation of the national banking system and nineteenth-century central banks. These examples do not clinch his case. Similarly, Toma's argument that interest rate smoothing was not needed for financial stability because it was achieved by the alternative means he identifies does not challenge the fact that smoothing occurred.

3.3. Interwar Years, 1919–1941

3.3.1. 1919–1929. The system's experiences during World War I and the aftermath left the policy guidelines of the Federal Reserve Act of questionable value. The gold criterion had become operative only when inflation rose in 1919–1920, and the system's gold reserve ratio plunged. In the face of that decline, the system had contracted. However, when gold inflows followed, and the gold criterion signaled the need to lower interest rates, the real bills criterion signaled the opposite policy. The real bills criterion had been emasculated by wartime finance considerations, but in 1920 member bank indebtedness to the reserve banks and their large portfolios of government securities signaled a need for higher interest rates. Moreover, the steep discount rates in 1920–1921 were not penalty rates since they were lower than open market rates on commercial paper [Meltzer (1996), ch. 3]. In the deep contraction of 1920–1921 the system had no compass by which to steer to keep to a chosen course.

The violent swings of prices that marked the inflation of 1919 and deflation of 1920 was the background to Federal Reserve performance in the years before the Great Depression. No disputes exist about what the Federal Reserve's actions were, but a contentious literature has arisen about the interpretation of those actions. The issues concern the Federal Reserve's commitment to the gold standard criterion and the real bills doctrine, and whether stabilization of the business cycle became its goal.

With respect to the gold standard criterion, the problem for the Federal Reserve was that gold standard rules appeared to be inapplicable in a world where only the United States maintained gold payments. The flow of gold to the United States in 1921–1922 threatened monetary stability if the authorities responded with expansionary actions. But gold sterilization was incompatible with using the gold reserve ratio as a guide to Federal Reserve credit.

From 1923 on gold movements were largely offset by movements in Federal Reserve credit, so essentially no relation is observed between the gold movements and the monetary base [Friedman and Schwartz (1963), pp. 279–284]. The system justified sterilization of gold movements on three grounds: pending the return to gold standards by countries abroad, much of the gold was in this country only temporarily; gold movements could not serve their equilibrating role with most of the world not on the gold standard; sterilization of the inflow was desirable to increase the gold stock in view of increased short-term foreign balances here. Once other countries returned to the gold standard, however, these reasons were no longer valid, although the system still repeated them.

Wicker's (1965, pp. 338–339) objection to regarding gold sterilization as a significant indicator of monetary policy is that "Federal Reserve monetary policy may not have been at all times rationally conceived and administered" (p. 338). He sees a conflict between sterilization for domestic considerations and the commitment to fully convertible gold currencies abroad, but he concedes that the Federal Reserve rejected the reserve ratio as a guide, although only until the international gold standard would be fully restored.

To replace the gold reserve ratio, the *Tenth Annual Report* [Federal Reserve Board (1924)] of the Federal Reserve system maintained that credit would not be excessive "if restricted to productive uses". This seems to be a procyclical needs of trade doctrine. The Report distinguishes between "productive" and "speculative" use of credit, the latter referring to speculative accumulation of commodity stocks, not stock market speculation.

Wicker argues that the Report emphasized a quantitative as well as a qualitative criterion for the adequacy of bank credit, and that the system was not guilty of the real bills fallacy (1965, pp. 340–341). How the quantitative criterion was to be applied in practice Wicker does not explain. Strong in 1922 in a speech at Harvard showed that he understood that the qualitative criterion was ineffectual, noting that "the definition of eligibility does not affect the slightest control over the use to which the proceeds (of Federal Reserve credit) are put" [Chandler (1958), p. 198; Meltzer (1996), ch. 3].

A third issue that divides commentators on monetary policy during the 1920s is whether the system consciously pursued the goal of stabilizing the business cycle. After its unfortunate experience with the discount rate in 1919–1920 as the instrument to implement monetary policy, in the following years the system experimented with open market operations. They were initially regarded as a means to obtain earnings for the reserve banks. The banks individually bought government securities without apparent concern for the influence of those purchases on the money market, with the result that their uncoordinated operations disturbed the government securities market. The Treasury's dismay led the reserve banks in May 1922 to organize a committee of five governors from eastern reserve banks to execute joint purchases and sales and to avoid conflicts with Treasury plans for new issues or acquisitions for its investment accounts. The committee met for the first time on 16 May at the New York reserve bank and elected Strong as permanent chairman. Although the centralization of open market operations led to a recognition of the bearing of purchases and sales on monetary policy, it did not happen immediately.

Opposition to open market operations was voiced by Adolph Miller, an economist member of the reserve board. He argued that changes in member bank borrowing offset open market operations and therefore had no effect on credit conditions. In his view the reserve banks should limit provision of credit to rediscounting bills that member banks submitted.

Opposition to open market operations was related to a general view of monetary policy that distinguished sharply between discounts and bankers' acceptances, on the one hand, and government securities on the other as sources of credit expansion. Reserve creation by buying bills and discounting bills was regarded as financing a genuine business transaction, while reserve creation by buying government securities had no such direct connection with the needs of trade. Reserve creation in the latter case might filter into loans on Wall Street.

These conflicting domestic policy positions were intertwined with international considerations. The system attached great importance to the reestablishment of a worldwide gold standard, but official literature contained no discussion of the policy measures appropriate to achieve the objective. Strong played the leading role in the system's relations with other countries, promoting credit arrangements with countries that returned to the gold standard during the 1920s.

From Strong's standpoint, easing measures in 1927 served two purposes: overcoming slack business conditions, despite his concern about speculation in the stock market; and helping to strengthen European exchange rates. Recession in the United States reached a trough in November 1927, and European exchange rates strengthened.

Wicker (1965, p. 343) disputes that stabilization through skilful open market operations was Strong's objective. He contends that open market purchases in 1924 and 1927 were intended to reduce US interest rates relative to Britain's to encourage a gold flow to London. According to Wicker, for Strong it was through the restoration of the world gold standard that stabilization of national economies would automatically occur. Wicker concludes, "The error of assigning too much weight to domestic stability as a major determinant of monetary policy has arisen . . . out of a faulty and inadequate account of the nature of Benjamin Strong's influence on open market policy and a tendency to exaggerate the extent to which some Federal Reserve officials understood the use of open market policy to counteract domestic instability".

Wheelock (1991) models econometrically the Federal Reserve's open market policy from 1924 to 1929 with alternative explanatory variables. His results confirm that the Federal Reserve attempted "to limit fluctuations in economic activity, to control stock market speculation, and to assist Great Britain retain gold" (p. 29). He is unable, however, to discriminate between Wicker's approach and that of Friedman and Schwartz.

Toma (1997) disputes the Friedman and Schwartz view that the Federal Reserve in the 1920s discovered how to use open market policy to fine-tune the economy and that those years were the high tide of the system. He contends that the system had no such stabilization powers. Open market purchases tend to reduce the volume of discounting and open market sales to increase it—the so-called scissors effect—that Adolph Miller had earlier mentioned, for reasons different from Toma's. For Toma the private banking system eliminated any lasting effect these operations might have had on Federal Reserve credit (p. 80), and the relative stability of the 1920s cannot be attributed to fine-tuning by the Federal Reserve (p. 87). In his view the stability is associated with monetary restraint that competitive open market operations of profit-seeking reserve banks induced. The period of the 1920s, for him, was "one of reserve bank competition interrupted by occasional episodes of coordination" (p. 73).

Toma also contends that the Federal Reserve did not use centralized open market operations to smooth interest rates during the 1920s (p. 80). He reports that seasonal behavior of Federal credit during 1922–1928 was "driven by the demands of the private banking system (i.e., discount loans and bankers' acceptances) rather than by open market operations".

Two fallacies undermine Toma's positions. He treats the scissors effect as if it were a one-to-one offset of open market operations. The inverse relation between borrowing and open market operations was hardly that close [Meltzer (1995b), ch. 5]. In addition, Toma's insistence that open market operations continued to be decentralized after the OMIC was established is incorrect. His portrayal of the system in a public choice framework seems far removed from the facts.

3.3.2. The Great Depression of 1929–1933.

No period of Federal Reserve history has elicited as much discussion as the four years that set off the economic collapse that began in August 1929 and ended in March 1933. Since our subject is monetary regimes, we exclude the view that the contraction can be explained by real business cycle theory [Prescott (1996)].[11] Instead we deal with issues on which opinions are divided among students of the period for whom monetary policy is the central focus.

There are six principal issues: (1) Was there a significant change in Federal Reserve conduct of monetary policy between 1923–1929 and 1929–1933? (2) Were bank failures a significant contributor to the economic collapse?

(3) How was the monetary collapse transmitted to the real economy? (4) Did the stock market crash in October 1929 play an important role in initiating the economic decline? (5) Had the Federal Reserve not allowed the money stock to decline, would the depression have been attenuated? (6) Did gold standard policies transmit the depression to the rest of the world?

3.3.2.1. Policy continuity?   Friedman and Schwartz (1963) maintain that during the 1920s the Federal Reserve responded effectively to fluctuations in economic activity, but during the depression it did not. They attribute the change to the death of Benjamin Strong in 1928. It removed from the scene the dominant figure in the system who had the best understanding of its capabilities. No one with equal authority replaced Strong. Power within the system shifted from him to a leaderless conference of reserve bank governors and a board that had no stature.

Challenges to the foregoing position have been mounted by Wicker (1965), Brunner and Meltzer (1968), Temin (1989), Wheelock (1991), and Meltzer (1995b). They find no shift in Federal Reserve performance between the Strong years and the depression years.

For Wicker, who believes international considerations dominated open market operations in the 1920s, the reason the Federal Reserve saw no need for action in 1929–1931 was that those years posed no threat to the gold standard. When Britain abandoned the gold standard in 1931, however, the system raised discount rates in order to maintain convertibility. It was acting on the consistent principle that domestic stability was subordinate to the gold standard. Temin agrees with Wicker.

Brunner and Meltzer (1968, p. 341) do not accept the argument for continuity based on the primacy of international considerations. Rather, they trace the continuity to the Federal Reserve's mistaken monetary policy strategy, which they assert has been an unchanging characteristic of its performance. For the system, a low level of nominal interest rates and of member bank borrowing are indicators of monetary ease, a high level, of monetary tightness. In 1924 and 1927, interest rates and bank borrowing had declined only moderately, hence they indicated relative monetary tightness, justifying open market purchases. During the depression years, since interest rates and member bank borrowing were at exceptionally low levels, they signified to the Federal Reserve that there was monetary ease and that injections of reserves were unneeded.

Based on regression estimates of the demand for borrowed reserves for all member banks in the New York reserve district and for weekly reporting member banks in New York City, Wheelock (1991) also finds Federal Reserve behavior largely consistent throughout the 1920s and the depression.

Meltzer (1995b, ch. 5) disagrees with the view that, had Strong lived, policies would have differed. He describes Strong as an ardent upholder of market interest rates and borrowing as the main indicators of monetary policy. Since Strong approved of the deflationary policy of 1920–1921, he sees no reason to believe that Strong would have opposed deflation from 1929 to 1931.

Meltzer notes that, while the real bills doctrine and member bank borrowing as policy indicator were the prevailing principles of Federal Reserve officials, and some so-called liquidationists supported a more deflationary policy, support for expansionary policy was at best a future possibility, "much of the time" not under consideration during the depression years. For Friedman and Schwartz, Strong was not a slavish follower of the prevailing principles of the Federal Reserve, and there is enough evidence in his speeches and Congressional testimony to suggest that he would not have passively observed cataclysmic economic decline without championing policies he knew had succeeded in 1924 and 1927. Hetzel (1985) provides the evidence on Strong's views. The expansionist position taken by the New York reserve bank during 1930 is also persuasive evidence that policy would have been different had Strong then been alive.

3.3.2.2. Banking panics.

Friedman and Schwartz (1963) identified four banking panics between October 1930 and March 1933, and found them largely responsible for the steep contraction in the stock of money that took place. A bank failure not only eliminated its deposits from the money stock, but also diminished the public's confidence in other banks, with the result that holding currency became preferable to holding a bank's liabilities. A withdrawal of deposits in the form of currency reduced bank reserves. Given Federal Reserve policy to hold back on the provision of reserves, both the deposit–currency and the deposit–reserve ratios declined, contributing far more to the decline in the money stock than did a bank failure.

Recent research on banking panics has centered on whether it is accurate to designate the cluster of bank failures in November 1930–January 1931 as the first banking panic, as Friedman and Schwartz do; the geographical boundaries of each of the panics and whether they had a national impact; whether periods additional to those Friedman and Schwartz designated qualify as bona fide panics; whether panics during the Great Depression differed from pre-1914 examples; causes of bank suspensions.

Wicker (1996) is the author of the most substantial empirical work on the microeconomic level of banking panics during the Great Depression. He has combed old newspaper files to learn the names and locations of failed banks, and compiled data on currency inflows and outflows by Federal Reserve districts to track the fallout from a concentration of bank failures in panic subperiods.

Controversy over the validity of the assignment by Friedman and Schwartz of special significance to the failure of the Bank of United States in December 1930 dates back to Temin (1976). He asserted that failures were induced by the decline in agricultural income and in the prices of relatively risky long-term securities held by banks, and that the failure of the Bank of United States did not precipitate a liquidity crisis. In his Lionel Robbins lecture [Temin (1989)], he repeated the view that the first banking panic was a minor event.

White (1984), who found that balance sheets of failed banks in the 1930s did not differ from those of the 1920s, denied the characterization by Friedman and Schwartz of bank failures in 1930 as cases of illiquidity, unlike pre-1914 cases of insolvency. White overlooks the fact that runs on banks in distress in the 1920s were rare [Schwartz (1988)], but in the 1930s were common. Wicker (1980) called attention to the omission by Friedman and Schwartz of the failure in November 1930 of Caldwell and Company, the largest investment banking house in the South, that led to runs on 120 banks in four states. He concludes [Wicker (1996), p. 32] that, on the evidence of Temin, White, and his own research, "the 1930 crisis was a region specific crisis without noticeable national economic effects". He believes the second crisis from April to August 1931 perhaps is also region specific, and without clearly identifiable national effects (p. 18). Wicker also identifies a fifth panic in June 1932 in the city of Chicago, comparable in severity, he says, to the 1930 panic.

Measured by the deposit–currency ratio, however, and the money stock, which are national in coverage, their fall unmistakably records the incidence of the first two bank crises. Regional disparities are not incompatible with national effects. As for the absence of noticeable national economic effects, does Wicker suggest that economic activity did not deteriorate between October 1930 and August 1931?

Some attention has been given to the question whether banks that fail during panics are in the main illiquid or insolvent. Calomiris and Gorton (1991) find the answer depends on which of two rival theories applies. The random withdrawal theory associates bank suspensions with illiquidity induced by contagion of fear. The asymmetric information theory associates suspensions with insolvency due to malfeasance. Saunders and Wilson (1993) found contagion effects in a sample of national banks 1930–1932, but did not examine separately panic and nonpanic months. Wicker also notes contagion effects in the Caldwell collapse in November 1930.

Wicker (1996) highlights a difference between pre-1914 and Great Depression panics. In the former the New York money market was the center of the crisis. In 1930 and 1931, however, the crisis originated in the interior of the country, with minimal central money market involvement. Wicker credits the Federal Reserve with this result: "there were no spikes in the call money rate or other short-term interest rates" (p. 23). However, he faults the Federal Reserve for not attempting to restore depositor confidence through open market purchases.

3.3.2.3. Transmission of the monetary collapse to the real economy.   The literature on the propagation of the depression takes two different approaches. One stresses real wage and price rigidity as the propagator [on price setting in product markets and wage setting in labor markets, see Gordon (1990)]. The other approach stresses the consequences of price deflation, whether anticipated or unanticipated. The disruption of the process of financial intermediation owing to bank failures has also been studied as a nonmonetary link to output decline.

O'Brien (1989) provides empirical evidence on nominal wage rigidity in the late 1920s and thereafter. Manufacturing firms became convinced following the 1920–1922 steep wage and price decline that maintaining wage rates during a downturn was necessary if precipitous sales declines were to be avoided. They did so collectively and voluntarily. The puzzle is why firms adhered to the policy once the severity of the sales decline in 1929–1931 became evident. It took until the fall of 1931 for many firms to decide that wage cuts would not have adverse consequences for productivity.

Based on data for 22 countries, 1929–1936, Bernanke and Carey (1996) assess empirically whether slow adjustment of nominal wages was an important factor in the depression. They found a strong inverse relationship between output and real wages. They do not offer their own explanation of the failure of wages and other costs to fall along with prices that thus contributed to the rise in unemployment and the decline in sales. They cite conjectures by other researchers that coordination failures or politicization of wage and price setting as possible explanations.[12]

The issue whether the price deflation during the Great Depression was anticipated or not is important for choosing between the debt deflation hypothesis or high ex ante real interest rates as the explanation for the severity of the Great Depression. According to the debt deflation hypothesis, unanticipated deflation increases the real burden of nominal debt, curtails expenditures, and makes it more difficult for borrowers to repay bank loans. As a result bank balance sheets deteriorate, and banks ultimately may fail. Financial intermediation is reduced, with negative effects on economic activity. However, if deflation was anticipated, the debt explanation for the severity of the Great Depression turns on a collapse of consumption and investment expenditures driven by high real interest rates.

No conclusive evidence can be cited in support of deflation as either unanticipated or anticipated. Research findings diverge. Barsky (1987) and Cecchetti (1992) concluded that simple time series models predicted price changes. An opposite conclusion was reached by Dominguez, Fair and Shapiro (1988), on the basis of forecasts from VAR models using data ending at various dates between September 1929 and June 1930. Hamilton (1987, 1992) links unanticipated deflation to the Federal Reserve's tight monetary policy in 1928, and shows that deflation was not anticipated in selected commodities markets for which he examined the relationship between spot and futures prices. Nelson (1991) found in reviewing the contemporary business press that there was some expectation that prices would decline but not the degree or the duration of the decline.

Evans and Wachtel (1993) construct a test using data on inflation and interest rates that suggests that time series forecasts of price change, such as Cecchetti reported, are not accurate representations of what people expected prices would be. The prospect of future policy changes or knowledge of past changes of policy made them highly uncertain about the future behavior of prices. They expected little of the deflation that actually occurred. Evans and Wachtel indicate that, in 1930–1933, with anticipated deflation of no more than 2 percent and nominal interest rates ranging between 5 and 1 percent, the ex ante real rate of interest was unlikely to have exceeded 7 percent and was probably much smaller.

The foregoing studies focus on the United States. Bernanke and James (1991) in an examination of the experience of 24 countries find that the extent of the worldwide deflation was less than fully anticipated in view of two facts: the nominal interest rate floor was not binding in the deflating countries, and nominal returns on safe assets were similar whether countries did or did not remain on the gold standard.

The issue whether price deflation during the Great Depression was anticipated or unanticipated is still unresolved. Another nonmonetary channel that served to propagate the depression has also been studied. Bernanke (1983) introduced the decline in financial intermediation as a nonmonetary shock, operating as an independent force in producing real economic decline in the 1930s. The disruption of financial markets as a result of the reduction in banks' ability to lend engendered a fall in the net worth of households and firms holding nominally fixed debt. The ensuing debt crisis became an important propagator of economic contraction, increasing the number of bankruptcies [see also Bernanke (1995), Bernanke and Gertler (1989), Calomiris (1993)].

Brunner and Meltzer (1968, 1993) accept Bernanke's emphasis on the importance of the credit market in the transmission of shocks but not his treatment of it and the debt crisis as a separate and independent exogenous shock. They regard it as an induced response to the monetary authorities' failure to counter deflation.

3.3.2.4. The October 1929 stock market crash.

The Dow Jones Industrial Index was between 300 and 320 during the first half of 1929 until the end of June, when it stood at 333. It climbed during the following months and peaked at 381 on 2 September. By the end of September, the index had fallen to 343. On 23 October stock prices dropped to 305. The crash came on 24 October, "Black Thursday". By 6 November the index was down to 231. A week later the index had fallen to 199. This was the low following the crash [Wigmore (1985), pp. 4–26 and Table A-19].

It is commonly believed that the stock market crash reduced the willingness of consumers to spend. It is said to have caused "a collapse in domestic consumption spending" [Romer (1993), p. 29] because it created uncertainty, decreased wealth, and reduced the liquidity of households' balance sheets [Mishkin (1978)]. Temin (1976) specifically rejects an explanation of the fall in consumption as reflecting the effect on wealth of the stock market crash, on the ground that the wealth effect was too small. He regards the fall as autonomous and unexplained.

Yet econometric evidence in support of this proposition is far from convincing. In her recent paper Romer bases her regressions on her intuition that stock market variability made people temporarily uncertain about the level of their future income and thus caused them to postpone durable goods purchases and stimulate consumer spending on nondurables. Her model predicts a greater fall in 1930 in durables than actually occurred, does not predict the slight fall in perishables, and overpredicts a rise in semidurables.

Romer goes on to examine the estimated effect of stock market variability following the October 1987 crash and suggests that uncertainty was both more severe and more persistent in 1929–1930 than in 1987–1988, and that this explains why consumers began spending again in 1988 while they continued to defer purchases of durable goods in 1930. A key difference that Romer does not note is that the stock of money grew 4.9 percent (M1; 5.5 percent M2) in the year following the 1987 crash.

A policy issue that has not been addressed in recent research on the 1929 stock market crash is whether the Federal Reserve then should have made itself an "arbiter of security speculation" (in the words of the press statement released by the board on 9 February 1929). The board wrangled with the reserve banks by insisting that moral suasion rather than raising the discount rate would curb speculation. In the end the discount rate was raised. It broke the bull market but also sacrificed stable economic growth. The question of the system's responsibility for stock market valuations applies not only to 1929 but to 1987 and 1997.

3.3.2.5. Would stable money have attenuated the depression?   McCallum (1990) showed that his base rule (with feedback) would have avoided the severe decline in nominal income that occurred between 1929 and 1933. Following McCallum's methodology of using an empirical model of the economy based on interwar data to examine how a counterfactual policy would have performed, Bordo, Choudhri and Schwartz (1995) considered two variants of Milton Friedman's constant money growth rule and estimated separate relations for output and the price level.

Basic simulations of both variants yielded results consistent with claims that, had a stable money policy been followed, the depression would have been mitigated and shortened. The view that a k percent rule (constant money growth rule) is suboptimal [Eichenbaum (1992)] compares economic performance under constant money growth with alternative rules or discretion that yield a superior outcome. Focus on the constant money growth policy relative to actual performance during the depression shows that it was clearly preferable.

3.3.2.6. Gold standard policies in transmitting the Great Depression.   Recent research gives the gold standard a major role in the causation and transmission of the depression, but assigns no special significance to US monetary policy, although Bernanke and James (1991) note that US panics may have contributed to the severity of the world deflation. They stress the close connection between deflation and nations' adherence to the gold standard, but find the case for nominal wage stickiness or real interest rates as transmission mechanisms dubious. They favor financial crises as the mechanism by which deflation can induce depression.

Another view [Temin (1989, 1993)] is that gold standard ideology, which accorded external balance more weight than internal balance, produced the transmission, with financial crises constituting another transmission channel. According to Temin (1989, p. 84), dealing only with the United States, it is hard to explain how the initial downturn was spread and intensified to produce three or four years of contraction, much less the international propagation mechanism.[13]

The operation of the gold standard in interwar years was impaired by forced contraction in countries losing gold without producing expansion in countries gaining gold [Eichengreen (1992)]. Instead of gold standard ideology, Meltzer (1995b) emphasizes the hold of the belief that there had been a speculative situation between 1921 and 1929; he asks (1995b, ch. 5) why deficit countries chose to deflate rather than suspend convertibility, which happened many times in the nineteenth century. His answer is that policy makers in many of these countries believed that deflation was the corrective needed in response to previous speculative excesses. What was paramount in their minds was not so much the gold standard imperative as it was the real bills doctrine.

Similarly, with respect to Federal Reserve failure to purchase government securities in 1930 and most of 1931, when the system's reserve ratio was generally twice the required ratio, and subsequently when the "free gold problem"[14] was alleged to prevent such action, the explanation for Meltzer was the real bills doctrine, the belief that deflation was exacted by earlier speculative credit expansion. The board could have suspended reserve requirements in 1932–1933 rather than compel intensified contraction, but did not.[15]

Meltzer's perspective suggests that it was not an unyielding commitment to the gold standard that enforced deflation on the world. It was the failure of policy makers to exercise temporary release from the commitment, which was a well-established feature of the gold standard, in response to an internal or external drain [Bordo and Kydland (1995)]. And the failure can be traced to the hold of the real bills doctrine and unawareness of the distinction between nominal and real interest rates.

A subject that needs to be explored is whether it is true that expansionary monetary policy by the Federal Reserve would have been futile because it would have aroused suspicion that the United States intended to leave the gold standard, and consequently resulted in gold losses. For two reasons this scenario is hard to credit. In the first place, it does not acknowledge the enormous size of US gold reserves. In February 1933, when there was both an internal and external drain, reflecting lack of confidence in Roosevelt's commitment to gold, the gold loss was \$263 million. Gold reserves of \$4 billion remained. In the second place, had expansionary monetary policy been in place, it would have stabilized the money supply and propped up the banking system. A quantitative estimate of the gold loss coefficient under these conditions, we conjecture, would reveal it to be modest in size, and would dispose of the argument that the possibility of expansionary monetary policy was illusory.

3.3.3. 1933–1941. The passivity of the Federal Reserve during the depression continued after it ended but under wholly different circumstances. New Deal institutional changes transformed monetary policy.

Institutional changes that enhanced the authority of the board at the expense of the reserve banks ironically were the setting in which the Federal Reserve was overshadowed by the Treasury. The Treasury became the active monetary authority, while the Federal Reserve was passive.

The main source of growth in the base was gold imports, which surged as foreigners took advantage of the steadily higher price of gold in 1933 that was fixed at \$35 by the Gold Reserve Act. When the Treasury bought gold, it paid with a check at a reserve bank, which increased member bank reserves. The Treasury could print a corresponding amount of gold certificates, which it could deposit at the reserve bank to restore its deposits. These transactions accounted for the major movements in the monetary base.

However, as a result of the gold sterilization program the Treasury adopted in December 1936, in the first nine months of 1937 the monetary base did not reflect the growth of the gold stock. During that period, the Treasury paid for the gold it bought by borrowing rather than by using the cash balances it could create on the basis of the gold. This was similar to sterilization by the Federal Reserve in the 1920s, when it sold government securities to offset the effect on the monetary base of gold inflows.

The difference was that in the 1930s the Treasury rather than the Federal Reserve sold the bonds and took the initiative in sterilizing gold.

The Treasury's gold sterilization program became effective at a time when the Federal Reserve undertook its first monetary policy action since the New Deal was in place. The sharp rise in member bank excess reserves beginning after the banking panic of 1933 was seen as raising dangers of future inflation. Sales of securities would have been desirable but for the need for adequate earnings. The system's room for maneuver was further limited by the political context within which it had to operate, since the Treasury could nullify anything it wished to do. The one option the Federal Reserve thought it had was to reduce excess reserves by exercising the power to double reserve requirements that the Banking Act of 1935 gave it. It did so in three steps between August 1936 and May 1937. Given the banks' demand for prudential reserves, the action backfired and led to recession.

Reserve requirements were not reduced until April 1938 to a level that eliminated one-quarter of the combined effect of earlier rises.

A start toward Treasury desterilization was made in September 1937, when the board requested the Treasury to release $300 million from the inactive gold account. The board itself, of course, could have taken the economic equivalent by buying $300 million of government securities. On 19 April 1938 the Treasury discontinued the inactive gold account.

Romer (1992) highlights money growth in stimulating real output growth between 1933 and 1942. Three other studies examine Federal Reserve behavior during those years: Eichengreen and Garber (1991), Calomiris and Wheelock (1998), and Toma (1997).

Eichengreen and Garber regard monetary policy in 1933–1940 as foreshadowing wartime practices. The Federal Reserve acceded to Treasury requests in 1935 to moderate the rise in interest rates, and it purchased long-term government bonds for the first time in its history. In April 1937 after the second increase in reserve requirements the Federal Reserve again bought government bonds to moderate interest rate rises, acknowledging in 1938 its responsibility for "orderly conditions in the government securities market". The reason it did so, according to Eichengreen and Garber, was that changes in bond prices might endanger financial and economic security.

Calomiris and Wheelock attribute the Treasury's dominance to the increase in its resources generated by gold and silver purchase programs which enabled it to alter bank reserve positions and to intervene directly in financial markets. In fact, the Treasury always had these powers. It was the New Deal political environment which was hospitable to their use. That had not been the case in preceding administrations. A shift in the focus of monetary policy away from markets for commercial paper and bankers acceptances and toward the market for government securities seems to Calomiris and Wheelock less a result of economic conditions than of administration pressure.

With the gold standard constraint absent and Federal Reserve independence diminished, monetary policy was free to monetize government debt, Calomiris and Wheelock conclude. Of course, it was the continued growth of the monetary gold stock that freed the Federal Reserve from the gold reserve constraint, not the absence of a legal gold standard constraint.

In Toma's (1997) interpretation of the New Deal period, the government's financing requirements took center stage and induced changes in monetary institutions. In his view, New Deal legislation increased the seigniorage capacity of the monetary sector and fundamentally changed the Treasury's monetary authority. The Treasury took possession of the monetary gold stock and with the allowance for change in the dollar price of gold (the weight of the gold dollar at any level between 50 and 60 percent of its prior legal weight, of which the President specified 59.06 percent), a long-run constraint on the government's monetary powers was relaxed. A positive probability of future upward revaluation of the official gold price created the opportunity for future Treasury profits. The Treasury had money-creating powers equal to those of the Federal Reserve.

Neither the Federal Reserve nor the Treasury had to share with each other revenue from money creation. After 1933 the Federal Reserve could keep all its earnings and make no transfers to the Treasury. And only the Treasury benefited from gold inflows since the gold certificates the Federal Reserve received did not give it legal title to the gold.

Toma explains the Federal Reserve constant credit policy as a way of assigning monopoly rights to the Treasury as the money producer. The Treasury happened to be the least cost producer; it could provide the government's seigniorage requirement by the increase in the monetary base that was equal to or less than the value of gold inflows. In effect, the Federal Reserve paid the Treasury for the right to operate by forgoing its role as money producer.

The doubling of reserve requirements, on Toma's interpretation, occurred because of an increase in the government's financing needs. The legislative authorization of flexibility in reserve requirements provided not only for the government's needs but also for the Federal Reserve's earnings objective. Had reserve requirements not been increased, the government's seigniorage revenue would have been lower, and income tax rates would have been higher, damaging real economic activity. Higher reserve requirements imposed costs on retail banks, so policy makers established federal deposit insurance as one way to moderate adverse stability implications for the financial system.

Toma's version of events does not square with the record. The Federal Reserve was concerned with its own earnings needs, not with maximizing the government's seigniorage revenue. The reserve requirement increases led to government securities sales by member banks that raised interest rates for the Treasury, hardly the optimal principal agent relationship. Toma's linkage of the passage of federal deposit insurance with the reserve requirement increases rewrites the history of that act, which was a response to depression bank failures.

3.4. Bretton Woods, 1946–1971

3.4.1. 1946–1951.   As in World War I, Federal Reserve credit outstanding rather than gold accounted for the increase in the monetary base during World War II. The Federal Reserve again became the bond-selling window of the Treasury and used its powers almost entirely for that purpose. After World War II ended, as after World War I, the system continued the wartime policy of providing the reserves demanded at a fixed cost: through supporting the price of government securities at unchanged levels.

During the immediate postwar period and for some time thereafter, the Federal Reserve did not question the desirability of supporting the price of government obligations. On 10 July 1947, however, the posted 3/8 of 1 percent buying rate on Treasury bills and the repurchase option granted to sellers of bills were terminated. The Treasury, which had been reluctant to see any change in the pattern of rates, was reported to have consented to the rise in interest costs on its short-term debt owing to the offset created by the adoption on 23 April 1947 by the system of a policy of paying into the Treasury approximately 90 percent of the net earnings of the reserve banks.

The next step in the program of raising the support rates somewhat was the sharp narrowing of the difference between short and long rates as a result of a rise in rates on bills and certificates. This led to a shift to short-term securities by individual holders and to a reverse shift by the Federal Reserve. The $5 billion of bonds the system bought was offset by a reduction of some $6 billion in its holdings of short-term securities, so there was monetary contraction in 1948. It was not, however, recognized and inflation fears prevailed, when inflationary pressure in fact was waning. Banks were urged to avoid making nonessential loans, discount rates were raised to 1.5 percent in 1948, reserve requirements were raised in September after Congress authorized a temporary increase in the legal maximum, and consumer credit controls were reinstated.

The system was slow in reacting to the cyclical decline that began in November 1948. Not until March–April 1949 were credit controls eased. Between May and September, six successive reductions were made in reserve requirements. In June the system announced that it would not seek to prevent bond prices from rising. For the time being, the system regained some control over its credit outstanding. After the final reduction in reserve requirements in September 1949, the system held outstanding credit roughly constant for the balance of the year and early 1950, and hence refrained from offsetting the expansionary influence of the released reserves.

The outbreak of the Korean War in June 1950 unleashed a speculative boom. The accompanying rise in interest rates pushed up yields to levels at which the Federal Reserve was committed to support government security prices. Concern grew that the support program would become the engine for an uncontrollable expansion of the money stock. The system's desire to be freed from this commitment was, however, accomplished only after protracted negotiations with the President and the Treasury, which was fearful of losing the advantage of a ready residual buyer of government securities and of low interest rates. In March 1951 an agreement with the Treasury was finally reached, relieving the system of responsibility for supporting the government security market at pegged prices.

Eichengreen and Garber (1991) contend that the existing literature lacks a formal analysis of why investors were willing to hold Treasury securities at low interest rates in the 1940s, and why this willingness disappeared at the end of the decade. They build on the explanation by Friedman and Schwartz (1963) that expectations of deflation after the war induced the public to hold higher amounts of liquid assets than they otherwise would, and that expectations of inflation after 1948 induced the public to hold smaller amounts of liquid assets than they otherwise would. In 1946–1948, the implication of the target zone approach that they adopt is that the 1948 increases in reserve requirements and the 1949 bond sales by the Federal Reserve can be thought of as keeping the price level below the upper bound. Bank liquidity declined, and inflationary pressure subsided. Eventually the Federal Reserve reduced reserve requirements as if the price level was approaching the lower bound of the implicit price zone, and by the end of 1949 M1 began to rise. Interest rates rose with inflationary expectations and the cap on interest rates became inconsistent with Korean War imperatives. That is why the Accord with the Treasury was negotiated, if the Eichengreen and Garber analysis is accepted.

A question Eichengreen and Garber pose and answer is why the Federal Reserve was concerned about price and interest rate stability—referring to an interest rate peg, not a target—in the aftermath of World War II and not in other periods. They say it was not the system's subservience to the Treasury's pursuit of low debt-service costs that is the answer. Instead, it was fear that a rise in interest rates would cause capital losses on commercial bank portfolios and undermine the stability of the banking system. Despite the fact that by 1951 the banks' vulnerability to capital losses had been attenuated, the Federal Reserve was still concerned to minimize them, and the Treasury helped by offering at par nonmarketable bonds with 2.75 percent yields in exchange for 2.5 percent long-term bonds marketed in 1945.

Toma (1997) disagrees with Eichengreen and Garber that the Federal Reserve adopted the stable interest rate program for financial stability reasons. He assigns the seigniorage motive as the driving force with financial stability as at best a secondary consideration. According to Toma, coordination between the Treasury and the Federal Reserve as the two money producers substituted for the gold standard in limiting monetary growth.

It seems to us quixotic, however, to describe wartime inflationary monetary growth as a substitute for the gold standard.

3.4.2. Federal Reserve discretionary regime, 1951–1965. The Treasury–Federal Reserve Accord overthrew the dominance of Treasury financing needs over monetary policy. In 1951, after more than 20 years of depression and war, the Federal Reserve had to formulate the criteria by which it would operate as an independent central bank. At that date the Bretton Woods system was in a formative stage, but under its aegis the US commitment to the convertibility of the dollar into gold initially seemed impregnable. By the end of the 1950s, however, as the gold stock began to decline, preventing gold outflows became a major objective of the Treasury as well as the Federal Reserve.

A more immediate criterion for monetary policy than the convertibility principle was that the Federal Reserve should "lean against the wind", by taking restrictive action during periods of economic expansion, and expansionary action during periods of economic contraction. The countercyclical theme in the period ending 1965 was generally described in terms of avoiding either inflation or deflation, but full employment was also accepted as an equally important goal of monetary policy.

The specific operating strategy for implementing "leaning against the wind" that the Federal Reserve adopted was unchanged from its practice in the 1920s [Calomiris and Wheelock (1998)]. It used open market operations to affect the level of discount window borrowing and free reserves—excess reserves minus borrowings. The theory of bank borrowing the Federal Reserve developed was that a change in nonborrowed reserves, i.e., reserves provided by open market operations, forced banks to adjust the amount they borrowed. A tradition at the Federal Reserve against borrowing acted to restrain borrowing, even if it were profitable for banks to do so. According to the theory, when free or net reserves were high, market interest rates tended to fall, and bank credit and the money supply tended to grow. When free reserves were low or negative, i.e., net borrowed reserves, market rates tended to rise, bank credit and the money supply tended to contract [Brunner and Meltzer (1964)].

Because of this framework, the Federal Reserve has seen itself as exercising a dominant influence on the evolution of short-term market interest rates. In the 1951–1965 period, it targeted the Federal funds rate indirectly by using the discount rate and borrowed reserves target. This is now known as interest rate smoothing, a procedure that was earlier known as free reserves or net borrowed reserves targeting [Goodfriend (1991)]. The intention of indirect targeting is to avoid fluctuations and minimize surprise changes in interest rates. Removing seasonality in interest rates, however, is not the main aspect of smoothing under consideration here.

Goodfriend describes the modus operandi of indirect targeting in the 1950s as follows. The Federal Reserve estimated the banks' demand for reserves during a defined period and provided most of the reserves by open market purchases. The balance had to be obtained from the discount window where borrowing became a privilege not a right. The Federal Reserve thus targeted borrowed reserves. The amount the banks were willing to borrow, however, depended positively on the spread between the Federal funds rate and the discount rate. Accordingly, the Federal Reserve targeted the Federal funds rate indirectly. Because the demand for borrowed reserves was unstable, it could not target borrowing exactly. In the relation between borrowed reserves and a discount rate–Federal funds rate combination, there was no tight linkage between the Federal funds rate and the discount rate. As a result, the market could not readily determine precisely what the indirect Federal funds rate target was, but it could estimate the range in which the funds rate should fall.

Goodfriend's explanation for the Federal Reserve's preference for indirect targeting, even if the result was market misinterpretation of its intention, was that the procedure gave it the option to make changes quietly, keeping target changes out of the headlines. As we shall see, in 1994 it reversed the position it had held for decades and began to announce changes in the Federal funds rate, by that time a directly targeted rate, immediately after an FOMC decision. Capturing headlines did not have the adverse effects on monetary policy the Federal Reserve had for so long claimed would occur.

For monetarist criticism of interest rate smoothing one must turn to earlier studies [Brunner and Meltzer (1964), Meigs (1962)]. Essentially, the criticism of interest rate smoothing is that, if the Federal Reserve sets the price of bank reserves and lets the market determine the quantity demanded, it abdicates control over the quantity. Goodfriend does not pose the normative question whether the procedure is optimal. Poole (1991), the discussant, does. He tries to make the case for the Federal Reserve's implementation of policy through the Federal funds rate rather than through monetary aggregates control, the preferable alternative for him. The smoothing arguments for interest rate control—it smooths the flow of revenue from the inflation tax; it stabilizes unemployment and inflation; it stabilizes rates at all maturities—in Poole's analysis lack substance. The only argument that he finds plausible is the belief that asset prices under the alternative policy of steady money growth could differ significantly from full-employment equilibrium levels and that the Federal Reserve can anchor interest rates at approximately the correct level when the market cannot do as well.

Successful central banks, according to Poole, permit short-run fluctuations in monetary growth but adjust money market interest rates as necessary to constrain money aggregates in the long run from growing too fast or too slow. The Federal Reserve's performance since 1992 provides support for Poole's conclusion.

Interest rate smoothing by the Federal Reserve during the decade and a half from 1951 did not preclude a low average inflation rate, but it also yielded unstable industrial output, as contemporaries judged it. Whether this outcome could have been avoided had the Federal Reserve's objective been only the price level and not also output is a subject to which we return when we discuss the 1990s.

3.4.3. Breakdown of Bretton Woods, 1965–1971.   Money growth accelerated in the early 1960s and persisted through the 1970s. US inflation began to accelerate in 1964, with a pause in 1966–1967, and was not curbed until 1980. An inflationary monetary policy was inappropriate for the key reserve currency in the Bretton Woods system. US balance of payments deficits from the late 1950s threatened a convertibility crisis as outstanding dollar liabilities rose and the monetary gold stock dwindled. To prevent conversion of dollars into gold, the United States and other central banks formed the London Gold Pool in 1961 to peg the price of gold at $35 an ounce, established a network of currency swaps with the other central banks, and issued bonds denominated in foreign currencies. These measures fell short. If the link with the dollar was unbroken, US inflation condemned the rest of the world to inflate. The only way to restrain US policy was to convert dollars into gold. French and British intentions to do just that prompted US suspension of gold convertibility in August 1971. Generalized floating of exchange rates followed (see Section 2.4 above).

3.5. Post-Bretton Woods, 1971–1995

3.5.1. 1971–1980.   As tenuous as the convertibility obligation had become by the mid-1960s, its absence after the early 1970s totally removed the discipline of convertibility from domestic monetary policy. The Federal Reserve was freed of commitment to maintain a stable price level. To cope with inflation that they blamed on supply-side shocks or shifts in demand for money, policy makers turned to incomes policy which soon failed.

Peacetime inflationary episodes as a result came to be associated with discretionary monetary policy. The episode from 1965 to 1980 is commonly attributed to the willingness of the Federal Reserve to fund government expenditures for the Vietnam war and Great Society social programs and to the authority's belief that it could exploit short-run Phillips curve trade-offs. Raising monetary growth to provide employment was consonant with Federal Reserve discretion. When the inflation rate accelerated, the authority became ensnared in a trap it itself had set. Monetarist doctrine had convinced Federal Reserve officials that reducing monetary growth in order to curb inflation would produce a recession. They could not bring themselves to choose that option, because of the political costs. So they permitted continuance of high monetary growth rates and ever-rising inflation until Paul Volcker broke the spell in 1979.

Monetary policy in this period, as in earlier ones, was implemented by control over interest rates rather than control over money growth. The dangers of operating with an interest rate instrument became clear when rising interest rates from the mid-1960s on reflected growing fears of inflation, not restrictive monetary policy. Rising interest rates were accompanied by high money growth. In January 1970, in response to criticism of its policy making, the FOMC for the first time adopted a money growth target. In 1975 Congress passed Joint Congressional Resolution 133 requiring the Federal Reserve to adopt and announce 1-year money growth targets and, in October 1979, the reason for the change in Federal Reserve operating procedures was said to be more precise control of money growth.

The Federal Reserve announced the target growth range each year on a base equal to the actual level of the money stock in the fourth quarter of the previous year. In the late 1970s, above-target money growth in one year was built into the next year's target, and in 1981, below-target money growth was built into the 1982 target. The Federal Reserve thus permitted base drift, contributing to instability of money growth. These differences between targets and actual money growth were a consequence of the Federal Reserve's policy of maintaining a narrow, short-run target range for the Federal funds rate, unchanged from its operating procedures before monetary growth targets were adopted.[16]

One change in Federal Reserve operational procedure during the period was its gradual shift during the early 1970s from indirect targeting to direct targeting of the Federal funds rate within a narrow band specified by the FOMC each time it met [Goodfriend (1991)]. The range within which the rate was allowed to move was commonly 25 basis points. The Federal Reserve managed the rate within the band by open market operations, adding reserves to maintain the rate at the upper bound of the band, subtracting reserves to maintain the rate at the lower bound. A move of the band up or down signaled a change in the target, which the market readily perceived. The financial press usually reported a change the day after the Federal Reserve implemented it [Cook and Hahn (1989)].

To support the current target, the Federal Reserve had to accommodate changes in money demand. It had to supply the level of reserves that would keep the Federal funds target within the narrow band the FOMC set for periods between meetings. This is another way of explaining how it became an engine of inflation during the second half of the 1970s, given that it had no nominal anchor and that the current target could be too low. If the Federal Reserve was slow in raising the target and, when it did raise the target, did not raise it enough, as total nominal spending in the economy rose, rapid money growth resulted, and accordingly higher inflation.

Furthermore, interest rate smoothing could itself be a determinant of the inflation generating process. In Goodfriend's (1987) model, he shows that rate smoothing with a price level objective induces a nontrend-stationary process for the money stock and the price level. This contributes to both money stock trend and price level drift. Interest smoothing increases both the price level forecast error variance and the variability of expected inflation. So interest rate smoothing tends to create macroeconomic instability.[17]

3.5.2. Shifting the focus of monetary policy, 1980–1995.   In the period following the inflation episode of 1965–1980, operating procedures at the Federal Reserve underwent modifications.

The adoption by the FOMC on 6 October 1979 of targeting on nonborrowed reserves in place of direct Federal funds rate targeting represented an admission that earlier interest rate smoothing had failed to provide non-inflationary monetary growth. The new procedure was designed to supply banks with the average level of total reserves that would produce the rate of monetary growth the FOMC desired over the period from a month before a meeting to some future month, without regard for the accompanying possible movement of the Federal funds rate outside a widened range of 400 basis points.

At each FOMC meeting a decision was made and never kept not only about the desired growth rate of M1 and M2 but also about the average level of borrowed reserves that it was assumed the banks would desire over the intermeeting period. The staff then estimated a weekly total reserves path from which it subtracted the borrowing assumption to arrive at a nonborrowed reserves path on which the Open Market Desk targeted open market purchases. It sought to keep the average level of nonborrowed reserves between FOMC meetings equal to the nonborrowed reserves path.

Under this procedure an increase in the demand for reserves was not mechanically accommodated; in the event, to keep total reserves on its path, nonborrowed reserves might be decreased. When total reserves were above the path level, the level of the nonborrowed reserves path or the discount rate was adjusted to reduce deviations of the money aggregates from their desired rate of growth. When the nonborrowed reserves path was lowered, banks were compelled to increase their borrowings, as a result of which the Federal funds rate rose. A 3 percent surcharge on discount window borrowings by banks with deposits of $500 million or more that borrowed frequently that was first imposed by the Federal Reserve on 14 March 1980 was eliminated a few months later, then reimposed at a lower rate, which was subsequently raised, and later again lowered until finally eliminated on 17 November 1981.

Despite the official description of the operation of the nonborrowed reserves procedure, movements in the Federal funds rate were far from automatic [Cook (1989), Goodfriend (1993)]. There were judgmental adjustments to the nonborrowed reserve path at FOMC meetings and between FOMC meetings that changed what the reserves banks were expected to borrow at the discount rate, in effect changing the funds rate target. There were also changes in the discount rate and, as just noted, in the surcharge. Goodfriend concludes that the 1979–1982 period was one of aggressive Federal funds rate targeting rather than of nonborrowed reserve targeting.

At the 5 October 1982 FOMC meeting, it abandoned nonborrowed reserve targeting. The Federal Reserve interpreted its experience over the preceding three years as demonstrating that short-run control of monetary aggregates was inferior to interest rate smoothing for stabilization. The outcome of the experiment was that, although M1 growth slowed on average, its volatility tripled compared to the period preceding October 1979 [Friedman (1984)], the Federal funds rate became highly volatile [Gilbert (1994)], and both nominal and real GDP displayed exceptionally large fluctuations quarterly [Friedman (1984)].

Goodfriend (1983) attributed the Federal Reserve's difficulty with reserve targeting to the unreliability of the demand function for discount window borrowing on which its operating procedure critically depended. Pierce (1984) found that the flaw in the operating procedure was produced by lagged reserve accounting in effect at the time, under which required reserves were based on deposit liabilities two weeks earlier. Therefore, only free reserves could serve as a target and, hence, borrowing estimates, which were inaccurate, became crucial. The upshot was that open market operations destabilized money growth.

On 5 October 1982, when the Federal Reserve suspended the nonborrowed reserves procedure, it shifted to targeting borrowed reserves. In line with this change, the FOMC at each meeting stated its instruction to the Open Market Desk for open market operations to achieve either more or less reserve restraint. More restraint was equivalent to a higher level of borrowings, less, to a lower level. If the demand for total reserves increased, the Federal funds rate and borrowings would rise. In order to reduce borrowed reserves to their desired predetermined level, nonborrowed reserves had to increase, with the effect of reducing the Federal funds rate. No change in borrowed reserves or the funds rate would then occur. This amounted to indirect targeting of the Federal funds rate. To keep the total of reserves the banks borrowed near some desired level, the spread between the Federal funds rate and the discount rate had to be such that banks would have an incentive to borrow that level of reserves. An increase in the spread induced banks to increase their borrowings. It could be achieved by changing the discount rate or the Federal funds rate. The target level of borrowings was attained by providing the appropriate amount of nonborrowed reserves. The borrowed reserves target operated with loose control of the funds rate.

Sometime about 1992 the Federal Reserve began to target the Federal funds rate directly in a narrow band. Target changes were made in small steps of 25–50 basis points, usually separated by weeks or months, and not soon reversed. The FOMC directive has not, however, specified the target Federal funds rate, but refers to degrees of reserve restraint that would be acceptable. The model of this regime that Rudebusch (1995) sets up and simulates replicates Federal Reserve operations.

Nevertheless, since February 1994, the Federal Reserve during FOMC meetings has announced a change in the funds rate if one has been made. A further procedural change was made in mid-December 1996 in Federal Reserve daily money market operations, revealed at a press conference at the New York reserve bank. The system will announce when it enters the market the size of its open market operations, to be conducted from system accounts, rather than from its customer accounts. The objective is to inform the market about the amount of liquidity the open market operations provide to or withdraw from the banking system.

So, in the 1920s and since the 1950s, the Federal Reserve in one way or another has targeted the Federal funds rate, while simultaneously announcing a money growth target. In the years since 1992 it has apparently taken low inflation as its sole objective and has succeeded in adjusting the target rate. A side effect is that monetary volatility has been low, and the real economy has not been buffeted by monetary shocks, facilitating low unemployment and financial market stability. Only possible inflation of equity market prices seems troubling.

The Federal Reserve along with other central banks changed its policy goals during this period. The primary goal became resisting inflationary pressures. It did so aggressively in 1980–1982. Disinflation was largely accomplished by 1983, when the inflation rate declined to 4 percent per annum. Goodfriend (1993) interprets rising long-term rates in 1983 and 1987 as signaling expectations that the Federal Reserve might again allow inflation to increase. The Federal Reserve met the test by raising the Federal funds rate long enough to contain the inflation scare. Goodfriend remarks on the fragility of the credibility of the Federal Reserve and on how costly it is to maintain.

In 1996–1997 the long rate at 6.5–7 percent was high enough to suggest that Goodfriend's assessment of the Federal Reserve's credibility is accurate. The duration of a 30-year bond at an interest rate of 6.75 percent is 14.8 years. Who would confidently predict that the then current inflation rate of 2.5 percent would not increase over that horizon? So the expectations explanation for the success of monetary policy targeted on the funds rate seems questionable. The basic problem is that there are no institutional underpinnings of the low-inflation policy. There is no guarantee that the successor to the present chairman of the Federal Reserve will also have a strong aversion to inflation.

The durability of Federal Reserve commitment to price stability is a question that only the future will determine. Of the 82 years that the Federal Reserve has been in existence, only 18 can be termed years of stable (consumer) prices—1923–1929 (average per year change of 0.3 percent); 1960–1965 (average per year price change of 1.3 percent); 1992–1995 (average per year price change of 2.8 percent). The most recent episode is too brief to take for granted its staying power.

Arguments in favor of a stable price level in preference to a low inflation rate have been advanced by Feldstein (1996, 1997) and Svensson (1996a,b). Svensson compares price level and inflation targeting, when society (the principal) delegates the choice to a central bank (the agent), under the assumption that output and employment are at least moderately persistent. The decision rule the central bank follows under discretion for inflation targeting is a linear feedback rule for inflation on employment. The variance of inflation is proportional to the variance of employment. Under price level targeting, the decision rule is a linear feedback rule for the price level on employment. Inflation, the change in the price level, is a linear function of the change in employment. Based on a very special set of assumptions, Svensson concludes that society will be better off assigning a price level target rather than an inflation target to the central bank because the variance of inflation will be lower, there is no inflation bias, and employment variability will be the same as under inflation targeting.

Feldstein bases his argument on the interaction of taxes and inflation that bias the allocation of resources in favor of current consumption and in favor of owner-occupied housing. The higher the inflation rate, the bigger the bias. Reducing the inflation rate by 2 percent would raise the level of real GDP by 2/3 of 1 percent each year in the future as long as the inflation rate remained at the lower level. Feldstein maintains that the arguments against going from low inflation to price stability do not singly or collectively outweigh the tax–inflation case for going to price stability or even to a lower inflation rate.

One argument for inflation targeting is that reducing the permanent rate of inflation requires a loss of output. With a target price path, the monetary authority offsets past errors, creating more uncertainty about short-term inflation than with an inflation target [Fischer (1994), pp. 281–284]. Feldstein's response is that the output loss is temporary, a shortfall of GDP below what it would otherwise be of 2.5 percent for two years to reduce the inflation rate by 2 percentage points. That is why he compares the one-time loss of reducing the inflation rate with the permanent increase of real GDP from reducing the tax–inflation effect.

Another argument for inflation targeting has been made by Akerlof, Dickens and Perry (1996). They contend that a very low level of inflation may lead to higher unemployment than at a higher inflation level because workers are unwilling to accept nominal wage decreases. Feldstein's response is that, by reducing fringe benefits, it is possible to reduce a worker's compensation without reducing his money wage rate. They also assume that workers don't learn that falling prices raise real wages.

Whether the price level or inflation is the target, a central bank has to determine the pace at which to try to achieve either one. The question is whether it is optimal to move immediately to the target. One answer is that gradualism is acceptable in the absence of a cost in terms of growth foregone [Dornbusch (1996), p. 102]. The information and transactions costs of moving from the old to the new regime also argue for a gradual return to a noninflationary position. Long-term borrowing and lending contracts and employment contracts arranged under the old regime need to be unwound. Advance announcement of the gradualism policy would give the private sector time to adjust its expectations. The speed of adjustment of monetary policy should respond to the speed with which expectations adjust and the gradualist prescription is that expectations adjust slowly. Feldstein suggests that this view needs to be modified and disinflation should proceed forthwith when political support for the policy permits it to go forward, since political support is indispensable but is not always at hand.

A stronger argument for speedy adjustment than Feldstein's is the rational expectations approach that treats expectations as adjusting quickly, and hence finds shock treatment is preferable. Sargent's view (1986, p. 150) is that "gradualism invites speculation about future reversals, or U-turns in policy". A major consideration in the choice between gradualism and shock treatment is the initial position. With moderate inflation of 8–10 percent, as observed in advanced countries, gradualism may be the answer. With very high inflation rates of 1,000 percent per year, as recently experienced in Latin America, gradualism is meaningless. Only shock treatment will suffice.

Still another view, dubbed "opportunistic disinflation" [Orphanides and Wilcox (1996)], argues that the Federal Reserve should conduct contractionary monetary policy only during business expansions; during recessions, it should abstain, counting on recessionary tendencies themselves to produce further disinflation. McCallum (1996, p. 112] notes a confusion in this view between regime design, with which the paper advocating opportunistic disinflation is concerned, and the issue of managing the transition from one regime with higher inflation to a regime with a lower level of inflation. Opportunistic disinflation is not a contribution to the literature on the timing of disinflation during the transition.

If there is a temporary cost in bringing down inflation, how high is that cost? Unfortunately, no quantitative estimates exist of the cost in lost output and employment of a disinflation of a given magnitude pursued over a given period. Hypothetical scenarios based on differing models arrive at qualitatively different conclusions. The announcement of a perfectly credible disinflation will either entail no expected output loss [King (1996)] or, perhaps, an increase in cumulative output [Ball (1994)]. The cost depends on the speed of adjustment of anticipations, which in turn depends on the underlying price level performance of the monetary regime.

Alan Greenspan at the Tercentenary Symposium of the Bank of England [Greenspan (1994, p. 259)] remarked: ". . . the pressure towards reserving or rather focusing central bank activity to the equivalent of the gold standard will become increasingly evident". If this is a correct prediction that price stability will be the single goal of the Federal Reserve over the long term, and if it is achieved, price stability may well become a credible surrogate for convertibility. The system will then end up fulfilling a key element of the vision of its founders.

3.6. Conclusion

Three events stand out in our survey of monetary policy episodes and macroeconomic performance. One is the breakdown of the gold standard in stages over the period from 1914 to 1971. The second is the Great Depression of 1929–1933. The third is the Great Inflation of 1965–1980. To escape from the macroeconomic experience that marked the economy in each of these watershed happenings became the driving force for change. The change was intellectual, reflecting what was perceived as the problem and deduced as its solution. It also led to a change in the monetary policy episode that succeeded each of these events. The new episode in turn exhibited unforeseen deficiencies. To conclude the section, we comment on the way the triad of events unfolded.

3.6.1. Breakdown of the gold standard, 1914–1971.   After World War I, the discipline of the gold standard came to be regarded as an impediment to the management of the economy to achieve the objectives of growth and high employment. The deep depressions of the interwar years were the measure by which the economy under a gold standard was judged to be a failure. The loosening of the link to gold after World War I presaged its abandonment 50 years later. Although price stability was generally included among the goals of the post-World War II era, stability of employment took precedence.

The instability of the interwar years led to the creation of the Bretton Woods system, which had a good record of price and output stability until the mid-1960s. Nevertheless, the convertibility principle lost favor. Improving the real performance of the economy was given pride of place. To achieve the improvement, the task was assigned to government management of monetary and fiscal policy, not to impersonal market forces.

The simple rule for governments to maintain a fixed price of gold was set aside in 1971, but the seeds of the downfall of that rule were sown earlier in the postwar years as country after country opted for monetary independence, full employment, and economic growth. Countries rejected the restraints that the operation of a fixed exchange rate imposed on the pursuit of these widely supported national objectives. In the United States, where the share of international trade was a minor factor in aggregate national income, the view prevailed that the domestic economy should not be hostage to the balance of payments. Maintenance of the price of gold was not an objective of the Employment Act of 1946.

The growth of government itself has destroyed the viability of a gold standard. A real gold standard was feasible in a world in which government spent 10 percent of national income, as in Britain and the USA pre-

World War I. It is not feasible in a world in which governments spend half or more of national income.

3.6.2. The Great Depression, 1929–1933.
The Great Depression was *sui generis*. To explain it, it is necessary to examine policy errors and the weaknesses of the interwar gold standard.

It is a consensus view that monetary contraction began in the United States, and was transmitted to the rest of the world by fixed exchange rates. Monetary contraction began in 1928 to curb a boom on the New York Stock Exchange. Although the stock market crashed in October 1929, the policy of contraction was not then halted. Instead, it was pursued relentlessly by the Federal Reserve until the spring of 1932. The Federal Reserve mistakenly believed that monetary policy had been overexpansionary in the 1920s and that deflation was the proper remedy. In fact the system had achieved stable economic growth from 1922 to 1929 with falling wholesale prices.

The US gold stock rose during the first two years of the 1929–1933 contraction, but the Federal Reserve did not permit the inflow of gold to expand the US money stock. It not only sterilized the inflow, it went much further. The US quantity of money moved perversely, going down as the gold stock went up, contrary to gold standard rules.

Under a fixed exchange rate system, shocks in one country's income, employment, and prices tend to be transmitted to its trading partners' income, employment, and prices.

Absent policy changes in the USA, the only recourse for countries on the gold standard was to cut the fixed exchange rate link. The first major country to do so was Britain. After runs on sterling, it abandoned the gold standard in September 1931. The international monetary system split in two, one part following Britain to form the sterling area; the other part, the gold bloc, following the United States. The trough of the depression in Britain and in other countries that accompanied her in leaving gold was reached in the third quarter of 1932.

In the two weeks following Britain's departure from gold, central banks and private holders in foreign countries converted substantial amounts of their dollar assets in the New York money market to gold. The US gold stock declined by the end of October 1931 to about its level in 1929. The Federal Reserve, which had not responded to an internal drain from December 1930 to September 1931 as a series of runs on banks, bank failures, and shifts from bank deposits to currency by anxious depositors produced downward pressure on the US quantity of money, responded vigorously to the external drain. A sharp rise in discount rates ended the gold drain but intensified bank failures and runs on banks. In October 1931, unlike the situation in 1920, the system's reserve ratio was far above its legal minimum. The system overreacted to the gold outflow and magnified the internal drain.

Federal Reserve officials believed that purchases of government securities, which would have relieved monetary contraction, were inconsistent with the real bills doctrine that the Federal Reserve Act enshrined. They resisted engaging in such purchases until March 1932, when they undertook doing so, following which there was widespread revival in the real economy in the summer and fall. The termination of the purchase program during the summer was followed in the six months from October 1932 by mounting banking difficulties. States began to declare banking holidays. By February 1933, fears of a renewed foreign drain added to the general anxiety. For the first time also, the internal drain took the form of a specific demand by depositors for gold coin and gold certificates in place of Federal Reserve notes or other currency.

The Federal Reserve reacted as it had in September 1931, raising discount rates in February 1933 in reaction to the external drain but not seeking to counter either the external or internal drain by extensive open market purchases. The drains continued until 4 March, when the Federal Reserve banks and all the leading exchanges did not open for business. A nationwide banking holiday was proclaimed after midnight on 6 March by the incoming administration, which ushered in a new regime.

3.6.3. The Great Inflation, 1965–1980.   By the mid-1960s, the convertibility principle no longer dominated central bank policies. The goal of full employment supplanted it in the minds of central bank and government officials. The Phillips curve presented them with a course of action that promised higher employment at the cost of rising inflation, a cost that was typically dismissed as insignificant. An additional factor that nurtured an acceleration of inflation was central bank reliance on short-term interest rates as the instrument to control monetary growth.

Under noninflationary conditions, this practice produced a procyclical movement in monetary growth. Under the gathering inflationary conditions from the mid-1960s, the inflation premium that became imbedded in interest rates made the instrument unreliable as an indicator of restriction or ease. Reliance on it contributed to a rise in the rate of monetary growth.

It was not until the 1970s, when ever higher inflation was accompanied by a decline in economic activity and a rise in unemployment that pressure arose to reverse the policies and procedures that led to the Great Inflation. The upshot was a shift to a new regime in 1979, in which disinflation was the guiding principle. The regime since the last decade has focused on price stability, reviving the peacetime domestic objective of the classical gold standard.

4. Monetary Regimes and Economic Performance: The Evidence

4.1. Overview

Having surveyed the history of international monetary regimes and of the institutional arrangements and episodes in Federal Reserve history viewed as a domestic policy regime, we ask the question, under what conditions is one or another type of monetary regime best for economic performance? One based on convertibility into specie (gold and/or silver), in which the monetary authority defines its monetary unit in terms of a fixed weight of specie and ensures that paper money claims on the specie monetary unit are always interchangeable for specie? Or one based on government fiat? Alternatively, in the international monetary sphere, which international monetary regime is superior, one based on fixed exchange rates? One based on floating rates? Or some intermediate variant such as the adjustable peg that characterized the Bretton Woods system and the EMS? Or the managed float which prevails in the world today? Evidence on the performance of alternative monetary regimes is crucial in assessing which regime is best for welfare.

4.2. Theoretical Issues

Traditional theory posits that a convertible regime, such as the classical gold standard that prevailed 1880–1914, is characterized by a set of self-regulating market forces that tend to ensure long-run price level stability. These forces operate through the classical commodity theory of money [Bordo (1984)]. According to that theory, substitution between monetary and nonmonetary uses of gold and changes in production will eventually off-set any inflationary or deflationary price level movements.

The fixed nominal anchor also ensures long-run price predictability and hence protects long-term contracts. It also may foster investment in long-lived projects [Klein (1975), Leijonhufvud (1984), Flood and Mussa (1994)].

Adherence to the fixed nominal anchor by providing credibility to monetary policy contributes to low inflation both by restraining money growth and by enhancing money demand [Ghosh et al. (1996)].

However, while ensuring long-run price stability and predictability, a gold standard provided no immunity to unexpected shocks to the supply of or demand for gold. Such shocks could have significant short-run effects on the price level. In a world with nominal rigidities they would generate volatility in output and employment.[18] Indeed, because of the problem of wide swings in the price level around a stable mean under the gold standard, Fisher (1920), Marshall (1926), Wicksell (1898), and others advocated reforms such as the compensated dollar and the tabular standard that would preserve the fixed nominal anchor yet avoid swings in the price level [Cagan (1984)].

In an inconvertible fiat money regime, without a nominal anchor, monetary authorities in theory could use open market operations, or other policy tools, to avoid the types of shocks that may jar the price level under a specie standard and hence provide both short-run and long-run price stability. However, in the absence of a fixed nominal anchor, some other type of commitment would be required to prevent the monetary authority from using seigniorage to satisfy the government's fiscal demands, or to maintain full employment.

In its international dimension, the convertible regime was one of fixed exchange rates and a stable nominal anchor for the international monetary system. Stability, however, came at the expense of exposure to foreign shocks through the balance of payments. In the presence of wage and price stickiness, these shocks again could produce volatile output and employment. Adherence to the international convertible regime also implied a loss of monetary independence. Under such a regime the monetary authorities' prime commitment was to maintain convertibility of their currencies into the precious metal and not to stabilize the domestic economy.

In a fiat (inconvertible) money regime, adhering to a flexible exchange rate provides insulation against foreign shocks.[19] However, as in a convertible regime, countries in fiat money regimes can adopt fixed exchange rates with each other. The key advantage is that it avoids the transactions cost of exchange. However, a fixed rate system based on fiat money may not provide the stable nominal anchor of the specie convertibility regime unless all members define their currencies in terms of the currency of one dominant country (e.g., the USA under Bretton Woods or Germany in the EMS). The dominant country in turn must observe the rule of price stability [Giavazzi and Pagano (1988)].

The theoretical debate on the merits of fixed and flexible exchange rates stemming from Nurkse's (1944) classic indictment of flexible rates and Friedman's (1953) classic defense is inconclusive.[20] It is difficult to defend an unambiguous ranking of exchange rate arrangements.[21] Hence, evidence on the performance of alternative monetary regimes is crucial in assessing the condition under which one or another regime is best for welfare.[22]

4.3. Measures of Macroeconomic Performance, by Regime

In Table 3.1 we present annual data on two key measures of economic performance, the inflation rate (GNP deflator) and the growth rate of real per capita income (GNP) for the five largest industrial countries across four regimes over the period 1881–1995.[23] The regimes covered are: the classical gold standard (1881–1913); the interwar period (1919–1938); Bretton Woods (1946–1970); the present floating exchange rate regime (1973–1995).[24] We divide the Bretton Woods period into two subperiods: the preconvertible phase (1946–1958) and the convertible phase (1959–1970).[25] We divide

TABLE 3.1 Descriptive Statistics of Inflation and Real Per Capita Growth, the Group of Five Countries, 1881–1995[a]

| | Gold Standard (1881–1913) | | Interwar (1919–1938) | | Bretton Woods | | | | | | Floating Exchange Rate | | | | | | Postwar (1946–1995) | |
| | | | | | Total (1946–1970) | | Preconvertible (1946–1958) | | Convertible (1959–1970) | | Total (1974–1995) | | High Inflation (1974–1982) | | Low Inflation (1983–1995) | | | |
Country	Mean	S.D.	Mean	S.D.	Mean	S.D.	Mean	S.D.	Mean	S.D.	Mean	S.D.	Mean	S.D.	Mean	S.D.	Mean	S.D.
Inflation (GDP deflator)[b]																		
USA[c]	0.3	3.0	-1.8	8.4	2.5	3.5	2.8	4.6	2.8	1.5	5.0	2.4	7.8	1.3	3.6	1.0	4.4	3.0
	0.4	3.0	-1.4	6.5														
UK	0.3	3.1	-1.5	8.5	3.9	2.2	4.6	2.7	3.8	1.6	7.5	5.6	13.7	4.7	4.9	1.6	7.0	4.5
Germany	0.6	2.6	-2.1	4.7	2.7	4.0	2.1	6.2	3.2	1.8	3.2	1.3	4.1	1.1	2.7	0.9	3.7	2.9
France	-0.0	4.9	2.2	9.1	5.0	3.5	5.6	5.1	4.1	1.4	6.4	3.8	10.2	1.0	3.2	2.3	6.5	3.6
Japan	4.6	5.6	-1.7	8.7	4.7	4.5	4.7	7.3	5.4	1.2	2.3	4.0	4.8	4.9	1.3	0.8	4.9	4.4
Grand mean	1.2	3.8	-1.0	7.9	3.8	3.5	3.9	5.2	3.9	1.5	4.9	3.4	8.1	2.6	3.1	1.3	5.3	3.7
Real per capita growth[b]																		
USA[c]	1.8	4.9	0.0	8.1	2.0	4.6	1.8	6.0	2.8	1.7	1.5	2.3	1.3	2.8	1.5	1.7	1.8	3.6
	1.6	2.7	-0.2	7.1														
UK	1.1	2.4	1.2	5.3	2.1	1.8	2.1	2.2	2.4	1.2	1.8	2.3	1.2	2.3	1.8	2.2	2.0	2.1
Germany	1.7	2.8	2.6	8.5	5.0	3.3	7.3	3.9	3.5	2.6	1.1	4.9	2.3	2.3	-0.3	6.2	2.9	4.5
France	1.5	4.7	1.3	7.2	4.1	2.1	4.6	2.7	4.4	1.4	1.7	1.5	2.2	1.4	1.6	1.5	3.1	2.2
Japan	1.4	3.8	2.0	5.9	7.9	2.3	5.7	1.1	8.6	1.9	3.2	1.9	3.3	1.9	3.2	2.0	5.2	3.2
Grand mean	1.5.	3.7	1.4	7.0	4.2	2.8	4.3	3.2	4.3	1.8	1.9	2.6	2.1	2.2	1.6	2.7	3.0	3.1

[a] Annual data: Mean, Standard Deviation; see Appendix A for data sources.

[b] The mean growth rate was calculated as the time coefficient from a regression of the natural logarithm of the variable on a constant and a time trend.

[c] First line: data from Balke and Gordon (1986); second line: data from Romer (1989).

the recent float into two subperiods: high inflation (1973–1982) and low inflation (1983–1995).

For the United States over the period 1880–1929, we show data from two sources: Balke and Gordon (1986), and Romer (1989). All sources for the USA and other countries are shown in the Data Appendix. For each variable and each country we present two summary statistics: the mean and standard deviation. As a summary statistic for the countries taken as a group, we show the grand mean.[26] We comment on the statistical results for each variable.

4.4. Inflation and Output Levels and Variability

4.4.1. Inflation.   The rate of inflation was lowest during the classical gold standard period (Figure 3.2). This was true for every country except Japan which did not go on the gold standard until 1897. During the interwar period mild deflation prevailed. The rate of inflation during the Bretton Woods period was on average and for every country except Japan lower than during the subsequent floating exchange rate period.

During the Bretton Woods convertible period the inflation rate in the USA, the UK, and France was higher than in the preceding subperiod; the reverse was true for Germany and Japan but on average there was not much difference between the subperiods. During the floating regime inflation has been lower in the recent subperiod of low inflation than during the Bretton Woods convertible subperiod except in the USA and UK.[27]

The Bretton Woods period had the most stable inflation rate as judged by the standard deviation. The managed float and the gold standard periods were next. The interwar period was the most unstable. However, when subperiods of the regimes are distinguished, the recent decade of low inflation was the most stable, followed by the Bretton Woods convertible regime, then the inflation phase of the float, and last, the gold standard period.

In general, the descriptive evidence of lower inflation under the gold standard and the Bretton Woods convertible regime than is the case for the other regimes is consistent with the view that convertible regimes provide an effective nominal anchor. The marked low inflation of the recent decade suggests that the equivalent of the convertibility principle may be operating. At the same time, evidence that inflation variability on average was

FIGURE 3.2   Annual Inflation Rate, 1880–1995, Five Countries

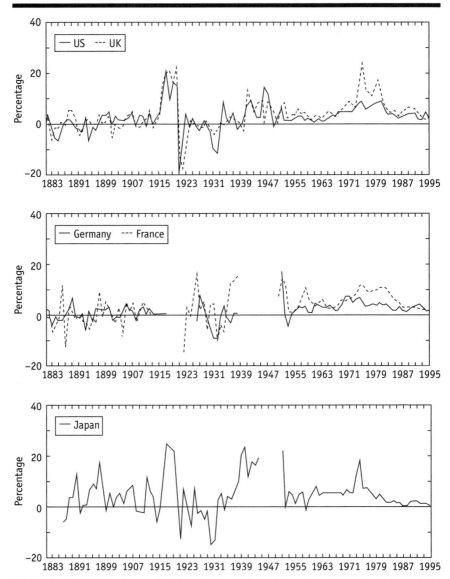

higher in the classical gold standard period than in most other regimes is consistent with the commodity theory of money and the price–specie flow mechanism which posits offsetting changes in the monetary gold stock.[28]

The evidence on inflation and inflation variability is also consistent with the behavior of two other nominal variables [Bordo (1993b)]. First, money growth was generally lowest under the gold standard across all countries, followed by the Bretton Woods convertible regime. It was most stable during the Bretton Woods convertible regime. Second, long-term nominal interest rates were lowest during the classical gold standard period. During Bretton Woods they were lower than in the recent float [see also McKinnon (1988)].

4.4.2. Real per capita income growth.   Generally, the Bretton Woods period, especially the convertible period, exhibited the most rapid output growth of any monetary regime, and, not surprisingly, the interwar period the lowest (Figure 3.3). Output variability was also lowest in the convertible subperiod of Bretton Woods, but because of higher variability in the preconvertibility period, the Bretton Woods system as a whole was more variable than the floating exchange rate period. Both pre-World War II regimes exhibit considerably higher variability than their post-World War II counterparts. The comparison does not apply to the USA based on the Romer data.[29,30,31]

To link rapid growth in the industrialized countries in the quarter century following World War II to the Bretton Woods international monetary system [Bretton Woods Commission (1994)], seems less compelling than for other aspects of macroeconomic performance. First, there is little conclusive evidence linking exchange rate volatility to either trade flows or the level of investment [Mussa et al. (1994)], avenues by which a stable exchange rate regime might have affected economic growth. Although Ghosh et al. (1996) find evidence linking real growth to the growth of investment and trade for pegged countries, they also find total factor productivity growth to be an important channel of growth for floaters.

Second, although trade liberalization may have played an important role in the acceleration of growth rates in the European economies during the Golden Age, most of the liberalization of trade, before nations declared

FIGURE 3.3   Annual Real Per Capita Income Growth, 1880–1995,
Five Countries

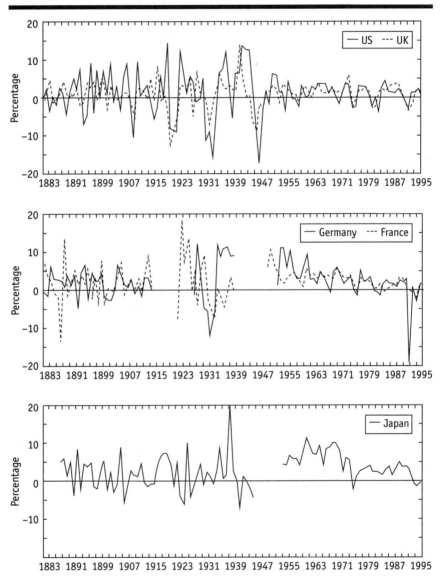

Article VIII current account convertibility in December 1958, was under the aegis of institutions developed outside of the Bretton Woods framework—the Marshall Plan, Organization for European Economic Cooperation (OEEC), European Payments Union (EPU), and European Coal and Steel Community (ECSC) [Eichengreen (1995)].

Finally, the Bretton Woods arrangements might have contributed to postwar growth by being part of the overall package creating political and economic stability—"the Pax Americana", that was a reaction to the chaos of the interwar and World War II periods. In this view, rapid postwar growth represented a "catch up" by the European nations and Japan from low levels of per capita output compared to that of the leading industrial country, the USA. The "catch up" by these nations was encouraged by the USA. They adopted the leader's best-practice technology and hence grew at a much more rapid rate than before [Abramovitz (1986)].[32]

Adherence to the convertibility rules of the Bretton Woods system by the USA and other industrialized countries may possibly explain the stability of real output in that regime. Money growth, but not the growth of real government spending, was less variable under Bretton Woods than under the succeeding float [Bordo (1993b), Eichengreen (1993a)]. Also temporary (aggregate demand) shocks, measured using the Blanchard–Quah (1989) procedure, presumably incorporating policy actions, were lowest under Bretton Woods of any regime [Bordo (1993b), Bayoumi and Eichengreen (1994a,b)]. According to Eichengreen (1993b), the credibility of commitment to the nominal anchor, as evidenced by the low degree of inflation persistence under Bretton Woods, made inflationary expectations mean reverting (see Table 3.2). This produced a flatter short-run aggregate supply curve than under the float where, in the absence of a nominal anchor, inflationary expectations became extrapolative. Under these conditions stabilization policy could be effective in stabilizing output.

That activist stabilization policy is in the main responsible for the low real output variability under Bretton Woods is doubtful. For the USA, activist Keynesian policies were a product of the late 1960s and 1970s and, for the other countries, the ongoing conflict between internal and external balance dominated policy making. A more likely explanation for

TABLE 3.2 Persistence of CPI Inflation: Group of Five Countries 1881–1995[a]

	USA			UK			Germany			France			Japan		
	AR1	S.E.	t-stat.[b]	AR1	S.E.	t-stat.[b]	AR1	S.E.	t-stat.[b]	AR1	S.E.	t-stat.[b]	AR1	S.E.	t-stat.[b]
Whole Period	0.65	0.07	4.87[c]	0.71	0.07	4.43[c]	0.53	0.09	5.54[c]	0.39	0.09	6.54[c]	0.57	0.08	5.17[c,d]
Gold standard	0.27	0.18	4.05[c]	0.30	0.17	4.03[c]	0.52	0.16	3.07[c]	−0.23	0.18	6.89[c]	0.13	0.19	4.52[c]
Interwar	0.45	0.18	3.08[c]	0.35	0.19	3.34[c]	0.62	0.25	1.51	0.48	0.23	2.29	0.35	0.19	3.42[c]
Bretton Woods (total)	0.49	0.19	2.77	0.33	0.20	3.38[c]	−0.16	0.20	5.68[c]	0.52	0.18	2.61	0.27	0.25	2.90
(preconvertible)	0.41	0.27	2.15	0.15	0.29	2.96	−0.24	0.30	4.15[c]	0.59	0.33	1.24	0.37	0.48	1.33
(convertible)	1.07	0.20	−0.33	0.57	0.34	1.28	0.44	0.31	1.79	0.55	0.30	1.49	0.06	0.33	2.88
Floating Exch (total)	0.78	0.15	1.48	0.77	0.15	1.52	0.79	0.12	1.81	0.93	0.07	1.05	0.57	0.07	6.28[c]
(high inflation)	0.44	0.39	1.44	0.23	0.45	1.70	0.52	0.26	1.84	0.51	0.30	1.66	0.41	0.14	4.28[c]
(low inflation)	0.44	0.29	1.92	0.60	0.26	1.54	0.67	0.23	1.44	0.63	0.10	3.57[c]	0.71	0.27	1.08
Postwar	0.66	0.11	3.17[c]	0.76	0.09	2.61	0.27	0.14	5.24[c]	0.73	0.10	2.64	0.64	0.12	2.93

[a] Annual data: AR1, coefficient of AR1 regression; S.E., Standard error; t-stat, t-statistic for unit root test; see Appendix A for data sources.
[b] The 5 percent significance level for a unit root test with 25 observations is 3.00.
[c] Statistically significant at the 5 percent level.
[d] The GDP deflator was used because of the unavailability of CPI data.

real output stability was the absence of serious permanent (aggregate supply) shocks. Bordo (1993b) and Bayoumi and Eichengreen (1994a,b) show permanent (supply) shocks—presumably independent of the monetary regime—to be the lowest under Bretton Woods of any regime.

In sum, there is compelling evidence linking convertible regimes to superior nominal performance. Whether such a connection can be made for the real side is less obvious. More evidence is required.

4.5. Stochastic Properties of Macrovariables

We investigated the stochastic properties (of the log) of the price level and (of the log) of real per capita GNP across monetary regimes.[33] Economic theory suggests that the stochastic properties of the price level and other nominal series would be sensitive to the regime. Under convertible regimes based on a nominal anchor, the price level should follow a trend-stationary process, whereas under a regime not so anchored, it should follow a difference-stationary process or a random walk. By contrast there are few predictions that can be made about the stochastic properties of real output under different regimes.

To ascertain the stochastic properties of the (log of) the price level and the (log of) real per capita GNP across monetary regime we follow the approach of Cochrane (1988) and Cogley (1990) and calculate the variance ratio. This statistic, defined as the ratio of $1/k$ times the variance of the series k differences divided by the variance of first differences, provides a point estimate of the size of the unit root, rather than a test for the existence or absence of a unit root, as in the earlier literature.

The variance ratio is the variance of the unit root component of a series relative to the variance of the trend-stationary component. If the ratio is above one, the series contains a substantial unit root and is clearly difference stationary. When it is below one, the unit root represents a much smaller fraction of the variance of the series; and when it is zero, the series is completely trend stationary.[34]

Figure 3.4 shows the variance ratio of the log of the price level for the five countries and their aggregate by regime.[35] From the figure there appears to be a marked difference between the gold standard, interwar, and Bretton Woods regimes on the one hand and the recent float on the other.

FIGURE 3.4   Variance Ratio for the Price Level by Regimes

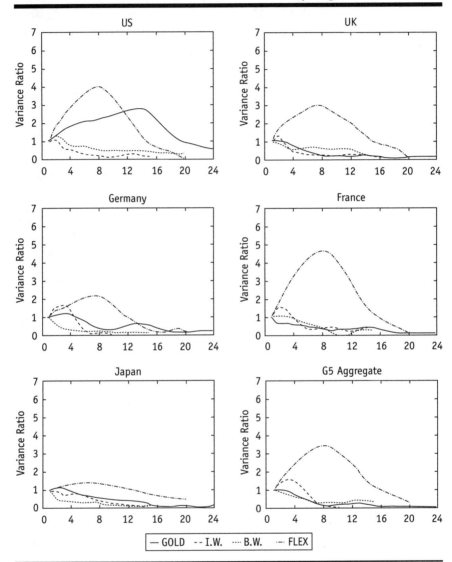

For the USA, the ratio rises above three during the float and then declines below one after eight years; under the gold standard it gradually rises above two for 13 years and then declines to zero. In the other regimes it declines to zero. For the other four countries and for the aggregate, for all regimes except the float, the ratio quickly declines below one. These results, which suggest that the price level is trend stationary under convertible regimes, but apparently not in the inconvertible fiat regime, generally are consistent with the evidence on persistence and price predictability described in the following subsection. The findings, however, are at best suggestive, since they are based on short samples of annual data for which it may not be possible to draw on asymptotic theory and perform tests of statistical significance.

In Figure 3.5 (overleaf), which shows the variance ratio of the log of real per capita GNP, it is difficult to detect a distinct pattern across countries by regimes. The only exception is a marked rise in the variance ratio in the interwar period in the USA and Germany, the two countries hardest hit by the Great Depression. For the aggregate, however, it appears as if the gold standard and interwar ratios decline quickly below one, whereas in both postwar regimes they do so only after three to five years. That shocks to output seem to be more long-lived in the post-World War II period than prewar is more likely consistent with explanations other than the nature of the monetary regime.

4.6. Inflation Persistence, Price Level Predictability, and Their Effects on Financial Markets

4.6.1. Inflation persistence. An important piece of evidence on regime performance is the persistence of inflation. Evidence of persistence in the inflation rate suggests that market agents expect that monetary authorities will continue to pursue an inflationary policy; its absence would be consistent with market agents' belief that the authorities will pursue a stable monetary rule such as the gold standard's convertibility rule.

Evidence of inflation persistence can be gleaned from an AR(1) regression on CPI inflation. Table 3.2 presents the inflation rate coefficient from such regressions for five countries over successive regimes since 1880, as well as the standard errors, and the Dickey–Fuller tests for a unit root.

FIGURE 3.5   Variance Ratio for Real Per Capita Income by Regimes

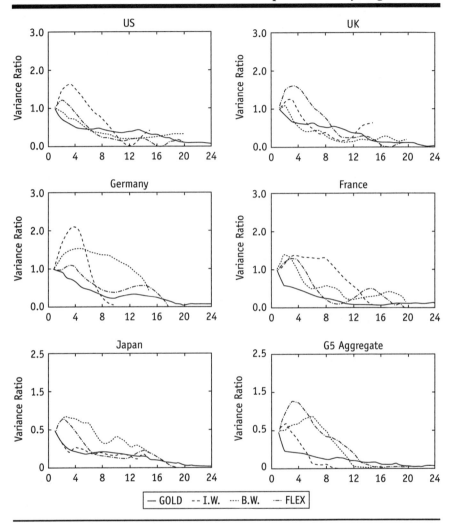

The results show an increase in inflation persistence for most countries between the classical gold standard and the interwar period, and also between the interwar period and the post-World War II period as a whole.[36] Within the post-World War II period, inflation persistence is generally lower (but not in France and Japan) in the preconvertible Bretton Woods than in the convertible period. This suggests that, though the immediate post-World War II period was characterized by rapid inflation, market agents might have expected a return to a stable price regime. The higher degree of persistence in the convertible regime suggests that this expectation lost credence. Persistence was generally highest during the float and it did not decline much between the high inflation and low inflation episodes.[37] This may mean that the public is aware of the absence of a stable nominal anchor.[38]

4.6.2. Price level uncertainty.   An important distinction between a convertible or fixed nominal anchor regime (or even one dedicated to price level stability) compared to an inconvertible regime (or one following an inflation target) is lower long-run price level uncertainty. This reflects the trend-stationary (mean reversion) process underlying a convertible regime, compared to the difference-stationary process of an inconvertible regime. Moreover, forecast errors should increase linearly as the time horizon is lengthened [Leijonhufvud (1984), Fischer (1994)].

Early evidence, by Klein (1975) for the USA, showing long-run price level uncertainty under the pre-1914 gold standard, the interwar period and the 1950s, compared to the 1960s and 1970s, is supported by stochastic simulations of hypothetical price level paths by Fischer (1994), Duguay (1993) and Lebow, Roberts and Stockton (1992).[39]

While a convertible regime (or one dedicated to price level stability) yields lower long-run price level uncertainty, short-run price level uncertainty may be higher as a consequence of the equilibrating changes in the monetary gold stock (or offsetting changes in money supply required to maintain price stability) than under an inconvertible (or inflation targeting) regime, where price level increases need not be reversed. In this regard, Klein (1975) using annual data for the USA, Meltzer (1986) using quarterly US data, and Meltzer and Robinson (1989) using annual data for seven countries observed higher short-run price level uncertainty for the gold standard than under subsequent regimes.[40]

4.6.3. Effects on financial markets.   Adherence or non-adherence to a nominal anchor also had implications for financial markets. Mean reversion in price level expectations anchored the term structure of interest rates.

Under the gold standard in the USA and the UK, the long-term–short-term interest rate spread predicted short-term rates according to the expectations theory. Under the subsequent fiat money regime, in which monetary authorities smoothed short-term interest rates, the relationship broke down. Similarly the response of long-term rates to shocks to short-term rates increased after 1914 as short-term rates exhibited more persistence [Mankiw and Miron (1986), Mankiw, Miron and Weil (1987), Miron (1996)]. Moreover, the Fisher effect—the correlation between nominal interest rates and expected inflation—is hard to detect before 1914 because inflation was a white noise process whereas, later in the twentieth century, when inflation became more persistent, it became more apparent [Barsky (1987), Mishkin (1992)].

4.7. Temporary and Permanent Shocks

An important issue is the extent to which the performance of alternative monetary regimes, as revealed by the data in Table 3.1, reflects the operation of the monetary regime in constraining policy actions or the presence or absence of shocks to the underlying environment. One way to shed light on this issue is to identify such shocks.

Authors have used structural VARs to calculate permanent and temporary output shocks to identify differences in behavior across regimes. In a number of recent papers Bayoumi and Eichengreen [e.g., Bayoumi and Eichengreen (1994a,b)] have extended the bivariate structural vector autoregression (VAR) methodology developed by Blanchard and Quah (1989) which identified permanent shocks as shocks to aggregate supply and temporary shocks as shocks to aggregate demand. According to Bayoumi and Eichengreen, aggregate supply shocks reflect shocks to the environment and are independent of the regime, but aggregate demand shocks likely reflect policy actions and are specific to the regime.[41]

The methodology developed by Blanchard and Quah (1989) raises econometric issues.[42] More controversial, however, is the labeling of the shocks as aggregate supply and demand shocks, as Bayoumi and Eichengreen (1994a,b) do. Interpreting shocks with a permanent impact on output as supply disturbances and shocks with a temporary impact on output as demand disturbances implies that one accepts the aggregate demand–aggregate supply model as correct. For our purpose, it is not necessary to take a stand on this issue. We reach no conclusion that depends on differentiating the two types of shocks, or whether one type predominates. It is enough to retain the more neutral descriptions of temporary and permanent shocks when relying on the VAR results to identify underlying disturbances across regimes.[43]

Figure 3.6 summarizes the results of this line of research.[44] It displays the permanent (aggregate supply) and temporary (aggregate demand) shocks for the five-country aggregate for the data underlying Table 3.1.[45] For these countries, both temporary and permanent shocks were considerably larger before World War II than afterwards. Both types of shocks, but especially permanent shocks, were much larger under the classical gold standard than during the two post-World War II regimes. There is not much difference in the size of both types of shocks between Bretton Woods and the subsequent float, although the Bretton Woods convertible regime was the most tranquil of all the regimes. Thus, this evidence suggests that the superior real performance of the Bretton Woods convertible period may have a lot to do with the lower incidence of shocks compared to the gold standard and interwar periods.

This raises an interesting question: why was the classical gold standard durable in the face of substantial shocks (it lasted approximately 35 years), whereas Bretton Woods was fragile (the convertible phase lasted only 12 years) in the face of the mildest shocks in the past century?

One possible answer is more rapid adjustment of prices and output to shocks under the gold standard than under the postwar regimes. Evidence in Bordo (1993b), based on calculations from the impulse response functions derived from the bivariate autoregressions underlying Figure 3.6, reveals that the response of both output and prices to both temporary and permanent shocks in the G-7 aggregate and in most of the individual countries was markedly more rapid under the gold standard than under the postwar regimes. Within the postwar regimes, the response was also more rapid under Bretton Woods than under the float [also see Bayoumi and Eichengreen (1994a)].

Perhaps countries under the gold standard were able to endure the greater shocks that they faced owing to both greater price flexibility and greater factor mobility before World War I [Bordo (1993b)]. Alternatively,

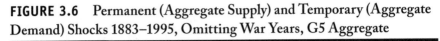

FIGURE 3.6 Permanent (Aggregate Supply) and Temporary (Aggregate Demand) Shocks 1883–1995, Omitting War Years, G5 Aggregate

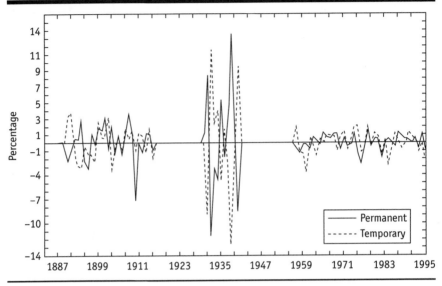

perhaps the gold standard was more durable than Bretton Woods because, before World War I the suffrage was limited, central banks were often privately owned and, before Keynes, there was less understanding of the link between monetary policy and the level of economic activity. Hence, there was less of an incentive for the monetary authorities to pursue full-employment policies which would threaten adherence to convertibility [Eichengreen (1992)].

Another explanation for the relative longevity of the international gold standard and the short life of Bretton Woods may be the design of the monetary regime and specifically the presence or absence of a credible commitment mechanism (or a monetary rule). As shown in Section 2, although Bretton Woods, like the gold standard, was a regime based on rules, the system did not provide a credible commitment mechanism, such as the gold standard contingent rule for the core countries. That outcome may in turn have reflected a shift in society's objectives away from convertibility and price stability towards domestic real stability.

5. Overall Assessment of Monetary Policy Regimes

The historical record and evidence on the performance of monetary policy regimes leave unanswered questions concerning the forces that predispose policy makers to adopt and then to abandon a regime. We do not know in detail why so many countries chose the gold standard before World War I as the monetary regime par excellence. Was it simply path dependence, since monetary systems evolved from specie-based regimes, and the success of England, the leading commercial power, which accidentally shifted to gold in the early eighteenth century, led many silver and bimetallic adherents as well as those on paper standards in turn to switch to gold? Was it the opinion of experts who testified before commissions regarding the choice that swayed the decision makers? Was it economic theory that convinced the leaders of public opinion? Was it the experience of inflationary fiat money in preceding regimes that carried the day? Finally, was the gold standard viable because the scope of government activity was limited?

In the case of the United States, we know that the combination of real bills and gold standard rules in the Federal Reserve Act reflected the influence of bankers and public servants as well as the testimony of representatives of foreign central banks. Yet the wartime departures from the arrangements that the Act prescribed were never undone.

The explanation of the abandonment of the gold standard under wartime conditions, in both wars, poses no problem. When financing government becomes the primary concern of the monetary and fiscal authorities, gold standard rules cannot be sustained. Peacetime limits on money creation give way to the requirement to provide the financial sinews of war in tandem with contributions from taxation and government debt issues.

Accounting for the monetary regime choices in postwar eras, however, raises many questions. Did the rise of the democracy and the power of the labor movement make adherence to the strictures of the gold standard less acceptable? Has the growth of government been inimical to the requirements of a real gold standard? Were the political disorders of the post-World War I decades so crippling—reparations, war debts, US isolationism, rearmament, fascist and communist dictatorships—that, after the brief restoration of the gold standard, no international monetary regime was viable? Was the brief restoration possible only because the American Benjamin Strong and the Englishman Montagu Norman willed it? Bretton Woods, post-World War II, again represented the will of an American Harry Dexter White and an Englishman Maynard Keynes, but this time, more so than in the 1920s, the economic weight of the US backing of its representative was overwhelming. Is that why countries fell into line to apply for membership in the system? Or, alternatively, was the Anglo-Saxon system imposed on other leading countries, which because they were either occupied or were enemies during the war, had no input in constructing Bretton Woods?

Post-Bretton Woods, the questions center on the commonality of the experience of stagflation in the 1970s and the switch since the 1980s to low inflation as the objective of domestic monetary policy regimes. We can observe the change in procedures that central banks adopted in order to achieve the low inflation result, but pinpointing the forces that led country after country to change its monetary policy objective is less apparent. We have learned much about the virtues and shortcomings of the monetary regimes that the world has experienced since 1880. Much more still has to be learned.

Appendix A. Data Sources

A.1. United States of America

(1) *Population.*
   1880–1975, Bordo and Jonung (1987).
   1976–1995, *International Financial Statistics Yearbook*, 1996, pp. 787–791, line 99z.
(2) *M2.*
   1880–1947, Bordo and Jonung (1987).
   1948–1989, Data supplied by Robert Rasche.
   1990–1995, *International Financial Statistics Yearbook*, 1996, pp. 787–791, line 59mb.
(3) *Real GNP.*
   1880–1945, Balke and Gordon (1986), pp. 781–783, col. 2.
   1946–1989, *The Economic Report of the President*, 1991, p. 288.

Real GDP.

1990–1995, *International Financial Statistics Yearbook,* 1996, pp. 787–791, line 99br.

(4) *Deflator.*

1880–1945, Balke and Gordon (1986), pp. 781–783, col. 2.

1946–1989, *The Economic Report of the President,* 1991, p. 290.

1990–1995, *International Financial Statistics Yearbook,* 1996, pp. 787–791, line 99bir.

(5) *Money Base.*

1880–1982, Balke and Gordon (1986), pp. 784–786, col. 4.

1946–1989, 1983–1995, *International Financial Statistics Yearbook,* 1996, line 14.

(6) *Consumer Price Index.*

1880–1970, US Bureau of the Census (1975), *Historical Statistics of the United States: Colonial Times to 1970: Bicentennial Edition* (Washington, DC), pp. 210–211 (hereafter cited as *Historical Statistics).*

1971–1995, *International Financial Statistics Yearbook,* 1996, pp. 787–791, line 64.

(7) *Short-Term Interest Rate.* Commercial paper rate.

1880–1986, Bordo and Jonung (1987).

1987–1995, *International Financial Statistics Yearbook,* 1996, pp. 787–791, line 60bc.

(8) *Long-Term Interest Rate.* Long-term government bond yield.

1880–1986, Bordo and Jonung (1987).

1987–1989, Bordo and Jonung (1990), pp. 165–197.

1990–1995, *International Financial Statistics Yearbook,* 1996, pp. 787–791, line 61.

A.2. United Kingdom

(1) *Population.*

1880–1975, Bordo and Jonung (1987).

1976–1995, *International Financial Statistics Yearbook,* 1996, pp. 782–785, line 99z.

(2) *Real GNP.*

1880–1985, Bordo and Jonung (1987).

1986–1989, Central Statistical Office, *Economic Trends* (various issues).

Real GDP.

1990–1995, *International Financial Statistics Yearbook*, 1996, pp. 782–785, line 99br.

(3) *Deflator.*

1880–1985, Bordo and Jonung (1987). 1986–1989, Central Statistical Office, *Economic Trends* (various issues).

1990–1995, *International Financial Statistics Yearbook*, 1996, pp. 782–785, line 99bir.

(4) *Consumer Price Index.*

1880–1965, Feinstein's retail price series [Capie and Webber (1985), vol. 1, table III.(12)].

1966–1995, *International Financial Statistics Yearbook*, 1996, pp. 782–785, line 64.

(5) *Exchange Rate.* US Dollar/Pound.

1880–1939, Friedman and Schwartz (1982), table 4.9, col. 8, pp. 130–135.

1947–1995, *International Financial Statistics* (various issues), pp. 782–785, line rh.

A.3. Germany

(1) *Population.*

1880–1979, Sommariva and Tullio (1987), pp. 234–236.

1980–1995, *International Financial Statistics Yearbook*, 1996, pp. 376–379, line 99z.

(2) *Real GNP.*

1880–1985, Data underlying Meltzer and Robinson (1989).

Real GDP.

1986–1995, *International Financial Statistics Yearbook*, 1996, pp. 376–379, line 99br.

(3) *Deflator.*

1880–1985, Meltzer and Robinson (1989).

1986–1995, *International Financial Statistics Yearbook,* 1996, pp. 376–379, line 99bir.
(4) *Consumer Price Index.*
   1880–1979, Sommariva and Tullio (1987), pp. 231–234. 1980–1995, *International Financial Statistics Yearbook,* 1996, pp. 376–79, line 64.
(5) *Exchange Rate.* Deutsche Mark/US Dollar.
   1880–1979, Sommariva and Tullio (1987), pp. 231–234.
   1990–1995, *International Financial Statistics Yearbook,* 1996, pp. 376–379, line rh.

A.4. France

(1) *Population.*
   1880–1949, Mitchell (1978), table Al.
   1950–1995, *International Financial Statistics Yearbook,* 1996, pp. 364–367, line 99z.
(2) *Real GDP.*
   1880–1900, Calculated from the Toutain Index [Saint Marc (1983), pp. 99–100].
   1901–1949, Sauvy (1954).
   1950–1988, INSEE, *Statistique annuaire de la France retrospectif* (1966) and *Statistique annuaire de la France* (various issues).
   1989–1995, *International Financial Statistics Yearbook,* 1996, pp. 364–367, line 99br.
(3) *Deflator.*
   Calculated as the ratio of nominal to real GDP. Nominal GDP, 1880–1913, Levy-Leboyer and Bourguignon (1990), table A-III.
   1914–1988, INSEE, *Statistique annuaire de la France retrospectif* (1966) and *Statistique annuaire de la France* (various issues).
   1989–1995, *International Financial Statistics Yearbook,* 1996, pp. 364–367, line 99bir.
(4) *Consumer Price Index.*
   1880–1969, Saint Marc (1983), p. 107.
   1970–1995, *International Financial Statistics Yearbook,* 1996, pp. 364–367, line 64.

(5) *Exchange Rate*. French Franc/US Dollar.

1880–1969, Saint Marc (1983), p. 107. 1970–1995, *International Financial Statistics Yearbook*, 1996, pp. 364–367, line rh.

A.5. Japan

(1) *Population*.

1880–1949, Bureau of Statistics (1957), *Japan Statistical Yearbook*.

1950–1995, *International Financial Statistics Yearbook* (various issues), pp. 458–461, line 99z.

(2) *Real GNP*.

1885–1988, Data supplied by Robert Rasche.

Real GDP.

1989–1995, *International Financial Statistics Yearbook*, 1996, pp. 458–461, line 99br.

(3) *Deflator*.

1885–1988, Data supplied by Robert Rasche.

1989–1995, *International Financial Statistics Yearbook*, 1996, pp. 458–461, line 99bir.

(4) *Consumer Price Index*.

1950–1995, *International Financial Statistics Yearbook* (various issues), pp. 458–461, line 64.

(5) *Exchange Rate*. Japan Yen/US Dollar.

1880–1989, Data Supplied by James Lothian.

1990–1995, *International Financial Statistics Yearbook*, 1996, pp. 458–461, line rh.

Notes

1. See Leijonhufvud (1984) and Bordo and Jonung (1996). Eichengreen (1991a, p. 1) defines "a regime as an equilibrium in which a set of rules or procedures governing the formulation of public policy generates stable expectations among market participants". He views a monetary regime "as a set of rules or procedures affecting money's ability to provide one or more of [the] three functions [of money]".

2. A moving nominal anchor is used by central banks today. The monetary authorities pursue an inflation target based on the desired growth rate of a nominal

variable, treating the inherited past as bygones. In this regime, although the inflation rate is anchored, the price level rises indefinitely [Flood and Mussa (1994)].

3. Gallarotti (1995) describes the shift of political power in favor of the gold standard in Germany. See Friedman and Schwartz (1963) and Friedman (1990b) for a discussion of the US switch de facto to gold in 1879.

4. The evidence on revenue smoothing is mixed. According to Mankiw (1987), both the inflation tax and conventional taxes should follow a Martingale process and a regression of the inflation rate on the average tax rate should have a positive and significant coefficient as the former as well as Poterba and Rotemberg (1990) and Trehan and Walsh (1990) found for the post-World War I United States.

However, Bordo and White (1993) for the Napoleonic War suspension of convertibility by Britain, Lazaretou (1995) for Greece in periods of inconvertibility in the nineteenth century, and Goff and Toma (1993) for the USA under the classical gold standard reject the hypothesis of revenue smoothing but not that of tax smoothing. As Goff and Toma (1993) argue, seigniorage smoothing would not be expected to prevail under a specie standard where the inflation rate does not exhibit persistence (which was the case during the British and during the Greek inconvertibility episodes). The Bordo and White, and Lazaretou results suggest that, although specie payments were suspended, the commitment to resume prevented the government from acting as it would under the pure fiat regime postulated by the theory.

5. A vociferous debate continues between the followers of Keynes who attribute the UK's weak economic performance and high unemployment in the 1920s to the decision to return to gold at an overvalued parity, and those who attribute the high unemployment to policies that raised the replacement ratio (the ratio of unemployment benefits to money wages), as well as other supply-side factors. See, e.g., Pollard (1970); Thomas (1981); and Benjamin and Kochin (1979, 1982). For a recent discussion of the economics of resumption in 1925, see Bayoumi and Bordo (1998).

6. According to Sargent (1984), because the reform package was credibly believed to signal a change in the monetary regime, the price level stabilized with no adverse real effects. Wicker (1986), by contrast, presents evidence of a substantial increase in unemployment in Austria, Hungary, and Poland, which persisted for several years.

7. According to Eichengreen (1992), a change in the statutes of the Banque de France following the Poincaré stabilization, prevented the Banque from using open market operations to expand the money supply. Meltzer (1995b, Ch. 5) disputes this interpretation, arguing that the Banque was not required to deflate the world economy by selling foreign exchange for gold.

8. Eichengreen (1990) contrasts two alternative explanations for the collapse of the gold exchange standard: it collapsed after the start of the Great Depression in

1929 because of a scramble by central banks for gold in the face of a loss of confidence in the reserve country currencies; it collapsed as a consequence of inappropriate policies followed by the USA and France in sterilizing gold inflows and thereby creating deflationary pressure on the international monetary system. Cross-country regressions for 24 countries over the period 1929–1935 explaining the demands for international reserves, gold and foreign exchange, including dummy variables for the USA and France, provide strong support for the latter hypothesis.

9. McKinnon (1993) also views Bretton Woods and the gold standard as regimes based on a set of rules.

10. We omit war years, 1915–1918 and 1941–1946. World War II for the USA began later than for the European countries, hence the difference between the dating of the Fed episodes and the broad international regimes in Sections 2 and 4.

11. Bernanke and Carey (1996) note that "any purely real theory" (p. 880) is unable to give a plausible explanation of the strong inverse relationship they find (across a panel of countries over the period 1931–1936) between output and real wages, and of their finding that countries that adhered to the gold standard typically had low output and high real wages, while countries that left the gold standard early had high output and low real wages. The dominant source of variation between the two sets of countries was differences in money stocks and hence in levels of aggregate demand.

Another view attributes the severity of the Great Depression to the collapse of world trade following the passage of the Smoot–Hawley tariff in 1930 [Meltzer (1977), Crucini and Kahn (1996)]. The importance of the tariff act and the retaliation it provoked are minimized as an important cause of the downturn in Eichengreen (1989) and Irwin (1996).

12. Bordo, Erceg and Evans (1997) simulate over the interwar period an equilibrium model of the business cycle with sticky wages embodied in Fischer (1977) and Taylor (1980) staggered contracts. They show that monetary contraction closely replicates the downturn in output until early 1933. Thereafter, their monetary model produces a much faster recovery than actually occurred. Other forces, such as Roosevelt's NIRA policy [Weinstein (1981)] and technology shocks may be important in accounting for the recovery.

13. A response to this view was made by Haberler (1976, p. 8):

Given the dominant position of the US economy and the monetary arrangements and policy maxims of the time—fixed exchanges under the new gold standard—the depression that came about in the United States was bound to spread to the four corners of the world. This does not mean that there were no other focal points of depression elsewhere in the world, for example in Central Europe; but the American infection clearly was the most virulent and the United States was in the strongest position to stop the slide.

14. Eichengreen (1992) argues that low free gold reserves prevented the system from conducting expansionary policy after 1931. Friedman and Schwartz (1963) and Meltzer (1995b, Ch. 5) regard free gold reserves as a pretext for the system's inaction that is explained by totally different reasons.

15. On 3 March 1933, when the New York reserve bank's reserve percentage fell below its legal limit, the board suspended reserve requirements for thirty days, too late to alter the imminent collapse of the system.

16. Differences between an aggregate selected for monetary control and a stable relationship with prices and nominal income that existed before the adoption of the targeted aggregate are said to arise because of financial innovations. The breakdown of the relationship has come to be known as Goodhart's Law [Goodhart (1989)]. It is true that financial innovation does occur and affects the definition of any monetary aggregate and the predictability of its velocity. There is no evidence, however, that links monetary targeting to innovation.

17. An empirical study of UK monetary policy, 1976–1985, by Bordo, Choudhri and Schwartz (1990) suggests that rate smoothing by the Bank of England allowed money stock base drift to reduce the predictability of the trend price level. Had the Bank of England followed a trend-stationary money supply rule, it would have reduced the variance of the trend in prices by more than one-half. Ireland (1993) extends this analysis to the US case. He shows that the Friedman rule would have reduced long-run price uncertainty by 82 percent over the 1915–1990 period.

18. According to Fischer (1994), in a comparison of price level stability versus low inflation, these volatility costs outweigh the benefits of long-run price level predictability.

19. Theoretical developments in recent years have complicated the simple distinction between fixed and floating rates. In the presence of capital mobility, currency substitution, policy reactions, and policy interdependence, floating rates no longer necessarily provide insulation from either real or monetary shocks [Bordo and Schwartz (1989)]. Moreover, according to recent real business cycle approaches, no relationship may exist between the international monetary regime and transmission of real shocks [Baxter and Stockman (1989)].

20. For surveys, see Frenkel and Mussa (1985) and Bordo and Schwartz (1989). Also see McCallum (1997, 15).

21. See, for example, Helpman and Razin (1979) and Helpman (1981).

22. Meltzer (1990) argues the need for empirical measures of the excess burdens associated with flexible and fixed exchange rates—the costs of increased volatility, on the one hand, compared to the output costs of sticky prices on the other hand. His comparison between EMS and non-EMS countries in the postwar period, however, does not yield clear-cut results.

23. For similar comparisons for the G-7 see Bordo (1993b). For 21 countries including advanced and developing countries see Bordo and Schwartz (1996b). Other

studies comparing historical regime performance include: Bordo (1981); Cooper (1982); Meltzer (1986); Schwartz (1986b); Meltzer and Robinson (1989); Eichengreen (1993b); and Mills and Wood (1993).

24. One important caveat is that the historical regimes presented here do not represent clear-cut examples of fixed and floating exchange rate regimes. The interwar period is not an example of either a fixed or floating rate regime. It comprises three regimes: a general floating rate system from 1919 to 1925, the gold exchange standard from 1926 to 1931, and a managed float to 1939. For a detailed comparison of the performances of these three regimes in the interwar period, see Eichengreen (1991b). We include this regime as a comparison to the other three more clear-cut cases. The Bretton Woods regime cannot be characterized as a fixed exchange rate regime throughout its history. The preconvertibility period was close to the adjustable peg envisioned by its architects, and the convertible period was close to a de facto fixed dollar standard. Finally, although the period since 1973 has been characterized as a floating exchange rate regime, at various times it has been subject to varying degrees of management.

25. We also examined the period (1946–1973), which includes the three years of transition from the Bretton Woods adjustable peg to the present floating regime. The results are similar to those of the 1946–1970 period.

26. Bordo (1993b) also presents data on seven other variables: money growth, nominal and real short-term and long-term interest rates, and nominal and real exchange rates. Bordo and Schwartz (1996b) show the same data plus the government budget deficit relative to GDP for fourteen additional countries.

27. The dispersion of inflation rates between countries was lowest during the classical gold standard and to a lesser extent during the Bretton Woods convertible subperiod compared to the floating rate period and the mixed interwar regime [Bordo (1993b)]. This evidence is consistent with the traditional view of the operation of the classical price–specie–flow mechanism and commodity arbitrage under fixed rates and insulation and greater monetary independence under floating rates.

28. Supporting evidence is provided in a recent study by Ghosh et al. (1996). Classifying the exchange rate systems for 136 countries over the period 1960 to 1990 into pegged, intermediate, and floating, they adopt a methodology similar to that of Table 3.1. They find that the unconditional mean inflation rate for countries on pegged exchange rates was significantly lower than for those that did not peg. This result holds up, controlling for the 1960s during which most countries adhered to Bretton Woods. The only exception was high-income floating countries which had lower than average inflation rates. Their results are unchanged when conditioned on a set of determinants of inflation, and when account is taken of possible endogeneity of the exchange rate regime. With respect to the volatility of inflation, they found it to be highest among floaters, again with the exception of high-income countries. For them, it was the lowest.

29. The Bretton Woods regime also exhibited the lowest dispersion of output variability between countries of any regime, with the interwar regime the highest [Bordo (1993b)]. The lower dispersion of output variability under Bretton Woods may reflect conformity between countries' business fluctuations, created by the operation of the fixed exchange rate regime [Bordo and Schwartz (1989)].

30. The Hodrick–Prescott filter alternative to the first differences used in Table 3.1, yields basically the same rankings of regimes.

31. In their 1960–1990 sample, Ghosh et al. (1996) find little connection between adherence to a pegged exchange rate and growth, once account is taken of the 1960s experience. High-income floaters generally had more rapid growth than low-income floaters. There was little correlation between output volatility and the regime.

32. In an institutional vein, it has been argued that the Bretton Woods framework (plus GATT) contributed to growth by providing an overall framework of rules. Within them Western European nations solved a hierarchy of coordination problems, allowing them to encourage investment in growth-generating export sectors [Eichengreen (1995)]. Without the Bretton Woods framework it might not have been possible to solve prisoner's dilemma games between labor and capital within each country taken in isolation and, for the OEEC, EPU, Marshall Plan, and ECSC to liberalize trade on comparative advantage lines between the members. Given that the European regional arrangements occurred outside of, and because of, shortcomings in the Bretton Woods arrangements, one wonders if institutional developments would have been much different if the European countries were not party to Bretton Woods at all.

33. A controversial literature has centered on whether real GNP and other time series are trend stationary or difference stationary [Nelson and Plosser (1982)] or, alternatively, whether GNP and other series contain a substantial unit root. This debate pertains to different theories of the business cycle: those emphasizing real factors positing a unit root (the primacy of real shocks), and those emphasizing monetary and other actions in the face of price rigidities positing reversion to a long-run trend (the primacy of transitory shocks).

34. Initially we tested for a unit root in both series in the different regimes using the Dickey–Fuller test (1979) and the Kwiatkowski–Phillips–Schmidt–Shin (KPSS) test (1992). The results detecting the presence or absence of a unit root were inconclusive. The Dickey–Fuller test rejected the hypothesis of a unit root for the price level for the USA only during the Bretton Woods period. For real output, the unit root is rejected only for the USA and France during Bretton Woods. These results are generally in accordance with the original Nelson and Plosser (1982) findings. On the other hand, the KPSS test could not reject the hypothesis that both series are trend stationary universally across regimes at the 5 percent level.

35. To calculate the aggregates we used current GNP weights in current US dollars.

36. Alogoskoufis and Smith (1991) also show, based on AR (1) regressions of the inflation rate, that inflation persistence in the USA and the UK increased between the classical gold standard period and the interwar period and between the interwar period and the post-World War II period. Also see Alogoskoufis (1992), who attributes the increase in persistence to the accommodation of shocks by the monetary authorities.

37. However, Emery (1994), using quarterly data, finds that inflation persistence in the USA declined significantly between 1973–1981 and 1981–1990.

38. Supportive evidence, based on autocorrelations and time series models of CPI and WPI inflation for the USA, UK, France, and Italy in the nineteenth and twentieth centuries, shows that inflation under the gold standard was very nearly a white noise process, whereas in the post-World War II period it exhibited considerable persistence [Klein (1975), Barsky (1987), Bordo and Kydland (1996)].

39. Bordo and Jonung (1996), using the univariate Multi-State Kalman Filter methodology, measured forecast errors in inflation at one-, five-, and ten-year horizons for sixteen countries over the period 1880–1990, across regimes. They found that forecast errors at the one-year horizon were lowest on average for the advanced G-11 countries during the Bretton Woods convertible regime, followed by the gold standard and the floating rate period. Also they found that the inflation forecast error increased with time across all regimes, but much more so under the recent float, as Leijonhufvud (1984) predicted.

40. Klein (1975) based his conclusions on a 6-year moving standard deviation of the annual rate of price change; Meltzer (1986) and Meltzer and Robinson (1989) calculated 1-period ahead forecast errors, using a univariate Multi-State Kalman Filter. Simulations by Fischer (1994) of univariate models showed higher short-run forecast errors under a price level target than under a low inflation target.

41. Restrictions on the VAR identify an aggregate demand disturbance, which is assumed to have only a temporary impact on output and a permanent impact on the price level, and an aggregate supply disturbance, which is assumed to have a permanent impact on both prices and output. Overidentifying restrictions, namely, that demand shocks are positively correlated and supply shocks are negatively correlated with prices, are tested by examining the impulse response functions to the shocks.

42. Lippi and Reichlin (1993) point out that the Blanchard–Quah procedure assumes that the error terms in the model are fundamental, whereas results are different with nonfundamental representations. This comment, however, applies to all dynamic econometric analyses, not the Blanchard–Quah procedure in particular [Blanchard and Quah (1993)]. Likewise, the comment by Faust and Leeper (1994) that using finite-horizon data and problems of time aggregation cast doubt on the identification of the shocks applies also to other strategies for isolating shocks from responses, and analyzing the speed of adjustment.

43. For two reasons Bayoumi and Eichengreen (1994b) strongly defend use of the aggregate demand–aggregate supply framework. First, it allows attributing the difference in macroeconomic behavior between fixed and floating exchange rate regimes to a change in the slope of the aggregate demand curve. Second, the model implies that demand shocks should raise prices, supply shocks lower them. These responses are not imposed, hence can be thought of as "over-identifying restrictions" that the data satisfy. However, they acknowledge that the shocks could be misidentified as supply, when they are temporary, and demand, when they are permanent.

Finally, a limitation of this approach is that it is difficult to identify the historical events in each monetary regime that correspond to the statistical results. Some authors have conjectured what these events might be.

44. Meltzer (1986) and Meltzer and Robinson (1989) use the univariate Multi-State Kalman Filter methodology to distinguish between permanent and transitory shocks to the price level and real output for cross-regime comparisons.

Authors who use the bivariate structural VAR methodology to identify underlying shocks to demand and supply include Bordo (1993b), who extends the approach to historical regime comparisons over the 1880–1990 period for G-7 countries. Bordo and Schwartz (1996a) and Bordo and Jonung (1996) apply the methodology for comparisons over a larger set of countries. Cecchetti and Karras (1994) and Betts, Bordo and Redish (1996) follow Galí (1992) in decomposing the aggregate demand shock into an LM (money) shock and an IS (rest of aggregate demand) shock, applying it to historical data over the interwar period for the USA and Canada, respectively. A different labeling has been adopted by Robinson and Wickens (1992) who refer to shocks with a temporary impact on output as nominal shocks, and those with a permanent effect on output as real shocks.

45. The shocks were calculated from a two variable vector autoregression in the rate of change of the price level and real output.

The VARs are based on three separate sets of data: 1880–1913, 1919–1939, and 1946–1995, omitting the war years because complete data are available for only two of the countries. The VARs have two lags. We derived the number of lags using the Akaike (1974) procedure. We rendered the two series stationary by first differencing.

The aggregate income growth and inflation rates are a weighted average of the rates in the different countries. The weights for each year are the share of each country's nominal national income in the total income in the five countries, where the national income data are converted to US dollars using current exchange rates.

References

Abramovitz, M. (1986), "Catching up, forging ahead, and falling behind", Journal of Economic History 46(2, June):385–406.

Akaike, H. (1974), "A new look at the statistical model identification", IEEE Transactions on Automatic Control A619:716–723.

Akerlof, G.A., W.T. Dickens and G.L. Perry (1996), "The macroeconomics of low inflation", Brookings Papers on Economic Activity 1996(1):1–76.

Alesina, A., and A. Drazen (1991), "Why are stabilizations delayed?", American Economic Review 81(5):1170–1188.

Alogoskoufis, G.S. (1992), "Monetary accommodation, exchange rate regimes and inflation persistence", Economic Journal 102(412, May):461–480.

Alogoskoufis, G.S., and R. Smith (1991), "The Phillips curve, the persistence of inflation and the Lucas critique: evidence from exchange-rate regimes", American Economic Review 81(2):1254–1273.

Bagehot, W. (1873), Lombard Street. Reprint of the 1915 edition (Arno Press, New York, 1969).

Balke, N.S., and R.J. Gordon (1986), "Appendix B: Historical data", in: R.J. Gordon, ed., The American Business Cycle: Continuity and Change (University of Chicago Press, Chicago, IL).

Ball, L. (1994), "Credible disinflation with staggered price-setting", American Economic Review 84(March):282–289.

Barro, R.J. (1979), "Money and the price level under the gold standard", Economic Journal 89:12–33.

Barro, R.J. (1989), "Interest-rate targeting", Journal of Monetary Economics 23(January):3–30.

Barro, R.J., and D.B. Gordon (1983), "Rules, discretion and reputation in a model of monetary policy", Journal of Monetary Economics 12:101–121.

Barsky, R.B. (1987), "The Fisher hypothesis and the forecastability and persistence of inflation", Journal of Monetary Economics 19(1, January):3–24.

Baxter, M., and A.C. Stockman (1989), "Business cycles and the exchange-rate regime: some international evidence", Journal of Monetary Economics 23(May):377–400.

Bayoumi, T., and M.D. Bordo (1998), "Getting pegged: comparing the 1879 and 1925 gold resumptions", Oxford Economic Papers 50:122–149.

Bayoumi, T., and B. Eichengreen (1994a), "Economic performance under alternative exchange rate regimes: some historical evidence", in: P. Kenen, F. Papadia and F. Saccomani, eds., The International Monetary System (Cambridge University Press, Cambridge) 257–297.

Bayoumi, T., and B. Eichengreen (1994b), "Macroeconomic adjustment under Bretton Woods and the post-Bretton Woods float: an impulse-response analysis", Economic Journal 104(July):813–827.

Benjamin, D., and L. Kochin (1979), "Searching for an explanation of unemployment in interwar Britain", Journal of Political Economy 87:441–478.

Benjamin, D., and L. Kochin (1982), "Unemployment and unemployment benefits in 20th Century Britain: a reply to our critics". Journal of Political Economy 90:410–436.

Bernanke, B.S. (1983), "Non-monetary effects of the financial crisis in the propagation of the great depression", American Economic Review 73(June):257–276.

Bernanke, B.S. (1995), "The macroeconomics of the great depression: a comparative approach", Journal of Money, Credit and Banking 27(February):1–28.

Bernanke, B.S., and K. Carey (1996), "Nominal wage stickiness and aggregate supply in the great depression", Quarterly Journal of Economics 111(August):853–883.

Bernanke, B.S., and M. Gertler (1989), "Agency costs, net worth, and business fluctuations", American Economic Review 79(March):14–31.

Bernanke, B.S., and H. James (1991), "The Gold Standard, deflation and financial crisis in the great depression: an international comparison", in: R.G. Hubbard, ed., Financial Markets and Financial Crisis (University of Chicago Press, Chicago, IL) 33–68.

Betts, C.M., M.D. Bordo and A. Redish (1996), "A small open economy in depression: lessons from Canada in the 1930s", Canadian Journal of Economics 29(February):1–36.

Blanchard, O.J., and D.T. Quah (1989), "The dynamic effects of aggregate demand and aggregate supply disturbances", American Economic Review 79(September): 655–673.

Blanchard, O.J., and D.T. Quah (1993), "The dynamic effects of aggregate demand and supply disturbances: reply", American Economic Review 88(June):653–658.

Bloomfield, A. (1959), Monetary Policy under the International Gold Standard, 1880–1914 (Federal Reserve Bank of New York, New York).

Bordo, M.D. (1981), "The Classical Gold Standard: some lessons for today", Federal Reserve Bank of St. Louis Review 63(May):2–17.

Bordo, M.D. (1984), "The Gold Standard: the traditional approach", in: M.D. Bordo and A.J. Schwartz, eds., A Retrospective on the Classical Gold Standard, 1821–1931 (University of Chicago Press, Chicago, IL) 23–119.

Bordo, M.D. (1993a), "The Bretton Woods international monetary system. A historical overview", in: M.D. Bordo and B. Eichengreen, eds., A Retrospective on the Bretton Woods System: Lessons for International Monetary Reform (University of Chicago Press, Chicago, IL) 3–108.

Bordo, M.D. (1993b), "The Gold Standard, Bretton Woods and other monetary regimes: an historical appraisal", in: Dimensions of Monetary Policy: Essays in Honor of Anatole B. Balbach. Federal Reserve Bank of St. Louis Review, Special Issue, April–May.

Bordo, M.D. (1995), "Is there a good case for a new Bretton Woods International Monetary System?", AEA Papers and Proceedings (May):317–322.

Bordo, M.D., and B. Eichengreen (1998), "Implications of the Great Depression for the development of the International Monetary System", in: M.D. Bordo, C. Goldin and E.N. White, eds., The Defining Moment: The Great Depression and the American Economy in the 20th Century (University of Chicago Press, Chicago, IL).

Bordo, M.D., and R.E. Ellson (1985), "A model of the Classical Gold Standard with depletion", Journal of Monetary Economics 16(1, July): 109–120.

Bordo, M.D., and L. Jonung (1987), The Long-Run Behavior of Velocity of Circulation: The International Evidence (Cambridge University Press, New York).

Bordo, M.D., and L. Jonung (1990), "The long-run behavior of velocity: the institutional approach revisited", Journal of Policy Modeling 12(Summer):165–197.

Bordo, M.D., and L. Jonung (1996), "Monetary regimes, inflation and monetary reform", in: D. Vaz and K. Velupillai, eds., Inflation, Institutions and Information, Essays in Honor of Axel Leijonhufvud (Macmillan Press, London).

Bordo, M.D., and F.E. Kydland (1995), "The Gold Standard as a rule: an essay in exploration", Explorations in Economic History 32(4 October):423–464.

Bordo, M.D., and F.E. Kydland (1996), "The Gold Standard as a commitment mechanism", in: T. Bayoumi, B. Eichengreen and M. Taylor, eds., Modern Perspectives on the Gold Standard (Cambridge University Press, Cambridge).

Bordo, M.D., and R. MacDonald (1997), "Violations of the 'Rules of the Game' and the credibility of the Classical Gold Standard, 1880–1914", Working Paper (NBER, July).

Bordo, M.D., and H. Rockoff (1996), "The Gold Standard as a 'Good Housekeeping Seal of Approval'", Journal of Economic History 56(2, June):384–428.

Bordo, M.D., and A.J. Schwartz (1989), "Transmission of real and monetary disturbances under fixed and floating rates", in: J.A. Dom and W.A. Niskanen, eds., Dollars, Deficits and Trade (Kluwer, Boston) 237–258.

Bordo, M.D., and A.J. Schwartz (1996a), "Why clashes between internal and external stability goals end in currency crises, 1797–1994", Open Economies Review 7(Suppl. 1):437–468.

Bordo, M.D., and A.J. Schwartz (1996b), "The operation of the Specie Standard: evidence for core and peripheral countries, 1880–1990, in: J. Braga de Macedo, B. Eichengreen and J. Reis, eds., Currency Convertibility: The Gold Standard and Beyond (Rutledge, New York) 11–83.

Bordo, M.D., and C.A. Végh (1998), "What if Alexander Hamilton had been Argentinean: a comparison of the early monetary experiences of Argentina and the United States", Working Paper No. 6862 (NBER).

Bordo, M.D., and E. White (1993), "British and French finance during the Napoleonic Wars", in: M.D. Bordo and F. Capie, eds., Monetary Regimes in Transition (Cambridge University Press, Cambridge).

Bordo, M.D., E.U. Choudhri and A.J. Schwartz (1990), "Money stock targeting, base drift, and price-level predictability: lessons from the U.K. experience", Journal of Monetary Economics 25(March): 253–272.

Bordo, M.D., E.U. Choudhri and A.J. Schwartz (1995), "Could stable money have averted the great contraction?", Economic Inquiry 33(July):484–505.

Bordo, M.D., C.J. Erceg and C.L. Evans (1997), "Money, sticky wages and the Great Depression", Working Paper No. 6071 (NBER, June).

Bretton Woods Commission (1994), "Bretton Woods: looking to the future" (Bretton Woods Commission, Washington, DC).

Brunner, K., and A.H. Meltzer (1964), An Analysis of Federal Reserve Monetary Policymaking. House Committee on Banking and Currency (Government Printing Office, Washington, DC).

Brunner, K., and A.H. Meltzer (1968), "What did we learn from the monetary experience of the United States in the Great Depression?", Canadian Journal of Economics 1(May):334–348.

Brunner, K., and A.H. Meltzer (1993), Money in the Economy: Issues in Monetary Analysis. Raffaele Mattioli Lectures (Cambridge University Press, Cambridge).

Cagan, P. (1965), Determinants and Effects of Changes in the Stock of Money 1875–1960 (Columbia University Press, New York).

Cagan, P. (1984), "On the Report of the Gold Commission 1982 and convertible monetary systems", Carnegie-Rochester Conference Series on Public Policy 21(Spring):247–267.

Calomiris, C.W. (1993), "Greenback resumption and silver risk: the economics and politics of monetary regime change in the United States, 1862–1900", in: M.D. Bordo and F. Capie, eds., Monetary Regimes in Transition (Cambridge University Press, Cambridge).

Calomiris, C.W., and G. Gorton (1991), "The origin of banking panics: models, facts, and bank regulation", in: R.G. Hubbard, ed., Financial Markets and Financial Crises (Chicago University Press, Chicago, IL) 109–173.

Calomiris, C.W., and D.C. Wheelock (1998), "Was the Great Depression a watershed for American monetary policy?", In: M.D. Bordo, C. Goldin and E.N. White, eds., The Defining Moment: The Great Depression and the American Economy in the 20th Century (University of Chicago Press, Chicago, IL) 23–65.

Canzoneri, M.B. (1985), "Monetary policy games and the role of private information", American Economic Review 75(December):1056–1070.

Canzoneri, M.B., and D.W. Henderson (1991), Monetary Policy in Interdependent Economies (MIT Press, Cambridge, MA).

Capie, F., and A. Webber (1985), A Monetary History of the United Kingdom (Allen & Unwin, London).

Capie, F., C. Goodhart and N. Schnadt (1994), "The development of central banking", in: F. Capie, C. Goodhart, S. Fischer and N. Schnadt, The Future of Central Banking (Cambridge University Press, Cambridge) 1–231.

Capie, F., T.C. Mills and G.E. Wood (1986), "What Happened in 1931?", in: F. Capie
and G.E. Wood, eds., Financial Crises and the World Banking System (Macmillan, London) 120–148.

Cecchetti, S.G. (1992), "Prices during the Great Depression: was the deflation of
1930–1932 really unanticipated?", American Economic Review 92(March):
141–156.

Cecchetti, S.G., and G. Karras (1994), "Sources of output fluctuations during the
interwar period: further evidence on the causes of the Great Depression",
Review of Economics and Statistics 76(February): 80–102.

Chandler, L.V. (1958), Benjamin Strong: Central Banker (Brookings, Washington,
DC).

Clark, T.A. (1986), "Interest rate seasonals and the Federal Reserve", Journal of
Political Economy 94(February):76–125.

Cochrane, J.H. (1988), "How big is the random walk in GNP?", Journal of Political
Economy 96(October): 893–920.

Cogley, T. (1990), "International evidence on the size of the random walk in output", Journal of Political Economy 98(June):501–518.

Cook, T. (1989), "Determinants of the Federal Funds rate:1979–1982", Federal Reserve Bank of Richmond Economic Review 75(January–February):3–19.

Cook, T., and T. Hahn (1989), "The effect of changes in the Federal Funds rate target on market interest rates in the 1970s", Journal of Monetary Economics
24(November) 331–351.

Cooper, R. (1982), "The gold standard: historical facts and future prospects", Brookings Papers on Economic Activity 1982(1):1–45.

Crucini, M.J., and J. Kahn (1996), "Tariffs and aggregate economic activity: lessons
from the Great Depression", Journal of Monetary Economics 38(December):
427–467.

Cunliffe Report (1918), First Interim Report of the Committee on Currency and
Foreign Exchanges after the War. Cmnd 9182. Reprinted 1979 (Arno Press,
New York).

Darby, M.R., J.R. Lothian, A.E. Gandolfi, A.J. Schwartz and A.C. Stockman (1983),
The International Transmission of Inflation (University of Chicago Press, Chicago, IL).

Davutyan, N., and W.R. Parke (1995), "The operations of the Bank of England,
1890–1908: a dynamic probit approach", Journal of Money, Credit and Banking
27(4, November Part I):1099–1112.

DeCecco, M. (1974), Money and Empire: The International Gold Standard: 1890–
1914 (Rowman and Littlefield, London).

DeKock, G., and V. Grilli (1989), "Endogenous exchange rate regime switches", Working Paper No. 3066 (NBER, August).

Dickey, D.A., and W.A. Fuller (1979), "Distribution of the estimators for autoregressive time series with a unit root", Journal of the American Statistical Association, Part I, 74(June):427–431.

Dominguez, K. (1993), "The role of international organizations in the Bretton Woods system", in: M.D. Bordo and B. Eichengreen, eds., A Retrospective on the Bretton Woods System (University of Chicago Press, Chicago, IL) 357–404.

Dominguez, K., R.C. Fair and M.D. Shapiro (1988), "Forecasting the Depression: Harvard versus Yale", American Economic Review 78(September):595–612.

Dornbusch, R. (1996), "Commentary: How should central banks reduce inflation?— Conceptual issues", in: Achieving Price Stability (Federal Reserve Bank of Kansas City, August) 93–103.

Duguay, P. (1993), "Some thoughts on price stability versus zero inflation", mimeograph (Bank of Canada).

Dutton, J. (1984), "The Bank of England and the rules of the game under the international Gold Standard: new evidence", in: M.D. Bordo and A.J. Schwartz, eds., A Retrospective on the Classical Gold Standard (University of Chicago Press, Chicago, IL) 173–202.

Eichenbaum, M. (1992), "Comment on 'Central bank behavior and the strategy of monetary policy: observations from six industrialized countries'", in: O.J. Blanchard and S. Fischer, eds., NBER Macroeconomics Annual 1992 (MIT Press, Cambridge) 228–234.

Eichengreen, B. (1985), "Editor's introduction", in: B. Eichengreen, ed., The Gold Standard in Theory and History (Methuen, London).

Eichengreen, B. (1987), "Conducting the international orchestra: Bank of England leadership under the Classical Gold Standard", Journal of International Money and Finance 6:5–29.

Eichengreen, B. (1989), "The political economy of the Smoot–Hawley Tariff", in: R.L. Ransom, P.H. Lindert and R. Sutch, eds., Research in Economic History, vol. 12 (JAI Press, Greenwich, CT) 1–43.

Eichengreen, B. (1990), Elusive Stability (Cambridge University Press, New York).

Eichengreen, B. (1991a), "Editor's introduction", in: B. Eichengreen, ed., Monetary Regime Transformations (Edward Elgar, Cheltenham).

Eichengreen, B. (1991b), "Comparative performance of fixed and flexible exchange rate regimes: interwar evidence", in: N. Thygesen, K. Velupillai and S. Zambelli, eds., Business Cycles: Theories, Evidence and Analysis (Macmillan, London) 229–272.

Eichengreen, B. (1992), Golden Fetters: The Gold Standard and the Great Depression, 1919–1939 (Oxford University Press, New York).

Eichengreen, B. (1993a), "History of the international monetary system: implications for research in international macroeconomics and finance", in: F. van der Ploeg, ed., Handbook of International Macroeconomics (Blackwell, Oxford).

Eichengreen, B. (1993b), "Three perspectives on the Bretton Woods System", in: M.D. Bordo and B. Eichengreen, eds., A Retrospective on the Bretton Woods System (University of Chicago Press/ NBER, Chicago/New York).

Eichengreen, B. (1995), "Institutions and economic growth: Europe after World War II", in: N.F.R. Crafts and G. Toniolo, eds., Comparative Economic Growth of Postwar Europe (Cambridge University Press, Cambridge).

Eichengreen, B. (1996), Globalizing Capital: A History of the International Monetary System (Princeton University Press, Princeton, NJ).

Eichengreen, B., and P.M. Garber (1991), "Before the U.S. Accord: U.S. monetary-financial policy, 1945–51", in: R.G. Hubbard, ed., Financial Markets and Financial Crises (University of Chicago Press, Chicago, IL) 175–205.

Eichengreen, B., and I. McLean (1994), "The supply of gold under the pre-1914 Gold Standard", Economic History Review 48:288–309.

Eichengreen, B., J. Tobin and C. Wyplosz (1995), "Two cases for sand in the wheels of international finance", Economic Journal 105(January):162–172.

Emery, K.M. (1994), "Inflation persistence and Fisher effects: evidence of a regime change", Journal of Economics and Business 46(August):141–152.

Evans, M., and P. Wachtel (1993), "Were price changes during the great depression anticipated?: evidence from nominal interest rates", Journal of Monetary Economics 32(August):3–34.

Faust, J., and E.M. Leeper (1994), "When do long-run identifying restrictions give reliable results?", Working Paper 94–2 (Federal Reserve Bank of Atlanta).

Federal Reserve Board (1924), Tenth Annual Report (Government Printing Office, Washington, DC).

Feldstein, M. (1996), "Overview", in: Achieving Price Stability (Federal Reserve Bank of Kansas City) 319–329.

Feldstein, M. (1997), "The costs and benefits of going from low inflation to price stability", in: C. Romer and D. Romer, eds., Reducing Inflation (University of Chicago Press, Chicago, IL).

Fischer, S. (1977), "Long-term contracts, rational expectations, and the optimal money supply rule", Journal of Political Economy 85(February):191–205.

Fischer, S. (1994), "Modern central banking", in: F. Capie, C. Goodhart, S. Fischer and N. Schnadt, The Future of Central Banking (Cambridge University Press, Cambridge) 262–308.

Fishe, R.P.H., and M.E. Wohar (1990), "The adjustment of expectations to a change in regime: comment", American Economic Review 80(September): 968–976.

Fisher, I. (1920), Stabilizing the Dollar (Macmillan, New York).

Fisher, I. (1922), The Purchasing Power of Money (Augustus M. Kelley Reprint, New York, 1965).

Fishlow, A. (1985), "Lessons from the past: capital markets during the 19th Century and the interwar period", International Organization 39:383–439.

Flandreau, M. (1996), "The French Crime of 1873: an essay on the Emergence of the international Gold Standard, 1870–1880", Journal of Economic History 51(4, December):862–897.

Flood, R.P., and P. Isard (1989), "Simple rules, discretion and monetary policy, Working Paper No. 2934 (NBER).

Flood, R.P., and M. Mussa (1994), "Issues concerning nominal anchors for monetary policy", in: T.J.T. Balino and C. Cottarelli, eds., Framework for Monetary Stability: Policy Issues and Country Experiences (International Monetary Fund, Washington, DC).

Ford, A.G. (1962), The Gold Standard 1880–1914: Britain and Argentina (Clarendon Press, Oxford).

Frenkel, J.A., and M.L. Mussa (1985), "Asset markets, exchange rates, and the balance of payments", in: R.W. Jones and P.B. Kenen, eds., Handbook of International Economics, vol. 2 (North-Holland, Amsterdam) Chapter 14.

Friedman, M. (1953), "The case for flexible exchange rates", in: Essays in Positive Economics (University of Chicago Press, Chicago, IL) 157–203.

Friedman, M. (1968), "The role of monetary policy", American Economic Review 58(March):1–17.

Friedman, M. (1984), "Lessons from the 1979–82 monetary policy experiment", American Economic Review 74(May):397–400.

Friedman, M. (1990a), "Bimetallism revisited", Journal of Economic Perspectives 4(4):85–104.

Friedman, M. (1990b), "The Crime of 1873", Journal of Political Economy 98(December):1159–1194.

Friedman, M., and A.J. Schwartz (1963), A Monetary History of the United States 1867 to 1960 (Princeton University Press, Princeton, NJ).

Friedman, M., and A.J. Schwartz (1982), Monetary Trends in the United States and the United Kingdom (University of Chicago Press, Chicago, IL).

Galí, J. (1992), "How well does the IS-LM model fit postwar U.S. data?", Quarterly Journal of Economics 107(May):709–738.

Gallarotti, G.M. (1995), The Anatomy of an International Monetary Regime: The Classical Gold Standard 1880–1904 (Oxford University Press, New York).

Garber, P.M. (1993), "The collapse of the Bretton Woods fixed exchange rate system", in: M.D. Bordo and B. Eichengreen, eds., A Retrospective on the Bretton Woods System (University of Chicago Press, Chicago, IL).

Garber, P.M., and R.P. Flood (1984), "Gold monctization and gold discipline", Journal of Political Economy 92(February):90–107.

Genberg, H., and A. Swoboda (1993), "The provision of liquidity in the Bretton Woods system", in: M.D. Bordo and B. Eichengreen, eds., A Retrospective on the Bretton Woods System (University of Chicago Press, Chicago, IL) 269–306.

Ghosh, A.R., A.M. Gulde, J.D. Ostry and H. Wolf (1996), "Does the nominal exchange rate regime matter?", Working Paper 121 (IMF, November).

Giavazzi, F., and A. Giovannini (1989), Limiting Exchange Rate Flexibility (MIT Press, Cambridge, MA).

Giavazzi, F., and M. Pagano (1988), "The advantage of tying one's hands: EMS discipline and central bank credibility", European Economic Review 32:1055–1082.

Gilbert, R.A. (1994), "A Case Study in Monetary Control: 1980–82", Federal Reserve Bank of St. Louis Review (September/October):35–55.

Giovannini, A. (1986), "'Rules of the Game' during the International Gold Standard: England and Germany", Journal of International Money and Finance 5:467–483.

Giovannini, A. (1993), "Bretton Woods and its precursors: rules versus discretion in the history of international monetary regimes", in: M.D. Bordo and B. Eichengreen, eds., A Retrospective on the Bretton Woods System: Lessons for International Monetary Reform (University of Chicago Press, Chicago, IL).

Goff, B.L., and M. Toma (1993), "Optimal seigniorage, the Gold Standard, and central banking financing", Journal of Money, Credit and Banking 25(February): 79–95.

Goodfriend, M. (1983), "Discount window borrowing, monetary policy, and the post-October 6, 1979 Federal Reserve operating procedure", Journal of Monetary Economics 12(3, September):343–356.

Goodfriend, M. (1987), "Interest rate smoothing and price level trend-stationarity", Journal of Monetary Economics 19(May):335–348.

Goodfriend, M. (1988), "Central banking under the Gold Standard", Carnegie-Rochester Conference Series on Public Policy 19:85–124.

Goodfriend, M. (1991), "Interest rates and the conduct of monetary policy", Carnegie-Rochester Conference Series on Public Policy 34:7–30.

Goodfriend, M. (1993), "Interest rate policy and the inflation scare problem: 1979–1992", Federal Reserve Bank of Richmond Economic Quarterly 79(Winter):1–24.

Goodhart, C.A.E. (1989), "The conduct of monetary policy", Economic Journal 99 (June):293–346.

Gordon, R.J. (1990), "What is new-Keynesian economics?", Journal of Economic Literature 28(September):1115–1171.

Greenspan, A. (1994), "Open session: The development of central banking", in: F. Capie, C. Goodhart, S. Fischer and N. Schnadt, eds., The Future of Central Banking: The Tercentenary Symposium of the Bank of England (Cambridge University Press, Cambridge) 259.

Grilli, V.U. (1990), "Managing exchange rate crises: evidence from the 1890s", Journal of International Money and Finance 9(September):258–275.

Grossman, H.J., and J.B. Van Huyck (1988), "Sovereign debt as a contingent claim: excusable default, repudiation, and reputation", American Economic Review 78:1088–1097.

Haberler, G. (1976), The World Economy, Money, and the Great Depression 1919–1939 (American Enterprise Institute for Public Policy Research, Washington, DC).

Hamilton, J.D. (1987), "Monetary factors in the Great Depression", Journal of Monetary Economics 19(March) 145–170.

Hamilton, J.D. (1992), "Was the deflation during the Great Depression anticipated?, Evidence from the commodity futures market", American Economic Review 82(March): 157–178.

Helpman, E. (1981), "An exploration in the theory of exchange rate regimes", Journal of Political Economy 89(5):865–890.

Helpman, E., and A. Razin (1979), "Toward a consistent comparison of alternative exchange-rate regimes", Canadian Journal of Economics 12:394–409.

Hetzel, R.L. (1985), "The rules versus discretion debate over monetary policy in the 1920s", Federal Reserve Bank of Richmond Economic Quarterly 71(November/December):3–14.

Ikenberry, G.J. (1993), "The political origins of Bretton Woods", in: M.D. Bordo and B. Eichengreen, eds., A Retrospective on the Bretton Woods System: Lessons for International Monetary Reform (University of Chicago Press, Chicago, IL) 155–182.

Ireland, P.N. (1993), "Price stability under long-run monetary targeting", Federal Reserve Bank of Richmond Economic Quarterly 79(1, Winter):25–45.

Irwin, D.A. (1996), Against the Tide: An Intellectual History of Free Trade (Princeton University Press, Princeton).

Jeanne, O. (1995), "Monetary policy in England 1893–1914: a structural VAR analysis", Explorations in Economic History 32:302–326.

Jonung, L. (1984), "Swedish experience under the Classical Gold Standard, 1873–1914", in: M.D. Bordo and A.J. Schwartz, eds., A Retrospective on the Classical Gold Standard, 1821–1931 (University of Chicago Press, Chicago, IL).

Kemmerer, E.W. (1910), Seasonal Variations in the Demand for Currency and Capital in the United States, National Monetary Commission (Government Printing Office, Washington, DC).

Kenen, P.B. (1960), "International liquidity and the balance of payments of a reserve-currency country", Quarterly Journal of Economics (November):572–586.

Keynes, J.M. (1925), "The economic consequences of Mr. Churchill", in: The Collected Writings of John Maynard Keynes, vol. IX, Essays in Persuasion (1972, Macmillan, London).

Keynes, J.M. (1930), The Applied Theory of Money: A Treatise on Money. Volume 1 of The Collected Writings (1971, Cambridge University Press, Cambridge).

Kindleberger, C.P. (1973), The World in Depression, 1929–1939 (University of California Press, Berkeley, CA).

King, M. (1996), "How should central banks reduce inflation?—Conceptual issues", in: Achieving Price Stability (Federal Reserve Bank of Kansas City, August) 53–91.

Klein, B. (1975), "Our new monetary standard: measurement and effects of price uncertainty, 1880–1973", Economic Inquiry 13:461–484.

Kwiatkowski, D., P.C.B. Phillips, P. Schmidt and Y. Shin (1992), "Testing the null hypothesis of stationarity against the alternative of a unit root: how sure are we that economic time series have a unit root?", Journal of Econometrics 54(October/December):159–78.

Kydland, F.E., and E.C. Prescott (1977), "Rules rather than discretion: the inconsistency of optimal plans", Journal of Political Economy 85:473–491.

Lazaretou, S. (1995), "Government spending, monetary policies and exchange rate regime switches: the Drachma in the Gold Standard period", Explorations in Economic History 32(1, January):28–50.

League of Nations (1930), "First Interim Report of the Gold Delegation of the Financial Committee" (Geneva).

Lebow, D.E., J.O. Roberts and D.J. Stockton (1992), "Economic performance under price stability", Working Paper No. 125 (Board of Governors Federal Reserve System, Division of Research and Statistics, April).

Leijonhufvud, A. (1984), "Constitutional constraints on the monetary power of government", in: R.B. McKenzie, ed., Constitutional Economics (Lexington Books, Lexington, MA) 95–107.

Levy-Leboyer, M., and F. Bourguignon (1990), The French Economy in the Nineteenth Century (Cambridge University Press, New York).

Lindert, P. (1969), Key Currencies and Gold, 1900–1913. Princeton Studies in International Finance (Princeton University Press, Princeton).

Lippi, M., and L. Reichlin (1993), "The dynamic effects of aggregate demand and supply disturbances: comment", American Economic Review 83(June):644–653.

Lucas Jr, R.E., and N.L. Stokey (1983), "Optimal fiscal and monetary policy in an economy without capital", Journal of Monetary Economics 12:55–93.

Macaulay, F.R. (1938), Some Theoretical Problems Suggested in the Movements of Interest Rates, Bond Yields, and Stock Prices in the United States since 1856 (National Bureau of Economic Research, New York).

Mankiw, N.G. (1987), "The optimal collection of seigniorage: theory and evidence", Journal of Monetary Economics 20:327–342.

Mankiw, N.G., and J.A. Miron (1986), "The changing behavior of the term structure of interest rates", Quarterly Journal of Economics 101(May):211–228.

Mankiw, N.G., J.A. Miron and D.N. Weil (1987), "The adjustment of expectations to a change in regime: a study of the founding of the Federal Reserve", American Economic Review 77(June):358–374.

Marshall, A. (1926), Official Papers (Macmillan, London).

Marston, R.C. (1993), "Interest differentials under Bretton Woods and the post Bretton Woods float: the effects of capital controls and exchange risk", in: M.D. Bordo and B. Eichengreen, eds., A Retrospective on the Bretton Woods System: Lessons for International Monetary Reform (University of Chicago Press, Chicago, IL) 515–540.

McCallum, B.T. (1990), "Could a monetary base rule have prevented the Great Depression?", Journal of Monetary Economics 26(1):3–26.

McCallum, B.T. (1991), "Seasonality and monetary policy: a comment", Carnegie-Rochester Conference Series on Public Policy 34:71–76.

McCallum, B.T. (1996), "Commentary: how should central banks reduce inflation?— Conceptual issues", in: Achieving Price Stability (Federal Reserve Bank of Kansas City) 105–114.

McCallum, B.T. (1997), "Issues in the design of monetary policy rules", Working Paper No. 6016 (NBER, April).

McKinnon, R.I. (1988), "An international Gold Standard without gold", Cato Journal 8(Fall):351–373.

McKinnon, R.I. (1993), "International money in historical perspective", Journal of Economic Literature 31(1, March): 1–44.

Meigs, A.J. (1962), Free Reserves and the Money Supply (University of Chicago Press, Chicago, IL).

Meltzer, A.H. (1977), "Monetary and other explanations of the start of the Great Depression", Journal of Monetary Economics 2:455–471.

Meltzer, A.H. (1986), "Some evidence on the comparative uncertainty experienced under different monetary regimes", in: C.D. Campbell and W.R. Dougan, eds., Alternative Monetary Regimes (Johns Hopkins University Press, Baltimore, MD) 122–153.

Meltzer, A.H. (1990), "Some empirical findings on differences between EMS and non-EMS regimes: implications for currency blocs", Cato Journal 10(2): 455–483.

Meltzer, A.H. (1995a), "The development of central banking, theory and practice", mimeograph, in: A History of the Federal Reserve (Carnegie-Mellon University) Chapter 2.

Meltzer, A.H. (1995b), "Why did monetary policy fail in the Thirties?", mimeograph, in: A History of the Federal Reserve (Carnegie-Mellon University) Chapter 5.

Meltzer, A.H. (1996), "In the beginning", mimeograph, in: A History of the Federal Reserve (Carnegie-Mellon University) Chapter 3.

Meltzer, A.H., and S. Robinson (1989), "Stability under the Gold Standard in practice", in: M.D. Bordo, ed., Monetary History and International Finance: Essays in Honor of Anna J. Schwartz (University of Chicago Press, Chicago, IL) 163–195.

Mills, T.C., and G.E. Wood (1993), "Does the exchange rate regime affect the economy?", Federal Reserve Bank of St. Louis Review (July/August):3–20.

Miron, J.A. (1986), "Financial panics, the seasonality of the nominal interest rate, and the founding of the Fed", American Economic Review 76(March):125–140.

Miron, J.A. (1996), The Economics of Seasonal Cycles (MIT Press, Cambridge, MA).

Mishkin, F.S. (1978), "The household balance sheet and the Great Depression", Journal of Economic History 38(December):918–937.

Mishkin, F.S. (1992), "Is the Fisher effect for real?", Journal of Monetary Economics 30(2):195–215.

Mitchell, B.R. (1978), European Historical Statistics, 1750–1970 (Columbia University Press, New York).

Mussa, M., M. Goldstein, P.B. Clark, D. Matthieson and T. Bayoumi (1994), "Improving the International Monetary System: constraints and possibilities", Occasional Paper 116 (International Monetary Fund, Washington, DC, December).

Nelson, C.R., and C.I. Plosser (1982), "Trends and random walks in macroeconomic time series: some evidence and implications", Journal of Monetary Economics 10(September):139–62.

Nelson, D.B. (1991), "Was the deflation of 1929–1930 anticipated? The monetary regime as viewed by the business press", in: R.L. Ransom and R. Sutch, eds., Research in Economic History, vol. 13 (JAI Press, Greenwich, CT) 1–65.

Nurkse, R. (1944), International Currency Experience (League of Nations, Geneva).

O'Brien, A.P. (1989), "A behavioral explanation for nominal wage rigidity during the Great Depression", Quarterly Journal of Economics 104(November):719–735.

Obstfeld, M. (1991), "Destabilizing effects of exchange rate escape clauses", Working Paper No. 3603 (NBER).

Obstfeld, M. (1993), "The adjustment process", in: M.D. Bordo and B. Eichengreen, eds., A Retrospective on the Bretton Woods System (University of Chicago Press, Chicago, IL).

Obstfeld, M., and A. Taylor (1998), "The Great Depression as a watershed: international capital mobility over the long run", in: M.D. Bordo, C. Goldin and E.N. White, eds., The Defining Moment: The Great Depression and the American Economy in the Twentieth Century (University of Chicago Press, Chicago, IL).

Officer, L. (1986), "The efficiency of the Dollar–Sterling Gold Standard, 1890–1908", Journal of Political Economy 94(October):1038–1073.

Officer, L. (1996), Between the Dollar–Sterling Gold Points: Exchange Rates, Parity and Market Behavior (Cambridge University Press, New York).

Oppers, S. (1996), "Was the worldwide shift to gold inevitable? An analysis of the end of Bimetallism", Journal of Monetary Economics 37:143–162.

Orphanides, A., and D.W. Wilcox (1996), "The opportunistic approach to disinflation", Discussion Paper 96–24, mimeograph (Federal Reserve Board).

Phelps, E.S. (1968), "Money–wage dynamics and labor market equilibrium", Journal of Political Economy 76(July–August):678–711.

Pierce, J.L. (1984), "Did financial innovation hurt the Great Monetarist Experiment?", American Economic Review 74(May):392–396.

Pippenger, J. (1984), "Bank of England operations, 1893–1913", in: M.D. Bordo and A.J. Schwartz, eds., A Retrospective on the Classical Gold Standard, 1821–1931 (University of Chicago Press, Chicago, IL).

Pollard, S., ed. (1970), The Gold Standard and Employment Policies Between the Wars (Methuen, London).

Poole, W (1991), "Interest rates and the conduct of monetary policy", Carnegie-Rochester Conference Series on Public Policy 34:31–40.

Poterba, J.M., and J.J. Rotemberg (1990), "Inflation and taxation with optimizing government", Journal of Money, Credit and Banking 22:1–18.

Prati, A. (1991), "Poincaré's stabilization: stopping a run on government debt", Journal of Monetary Economics 27(2, April):213–240.

Prescott, E.C. (1996), Profile. The Region (Federal Reserve Bank of Minneapolis).

Redish, A. (1990), "The evolution of the Gold Standard in England", Journal of Economic History (December):789–806.

Redish, A. (1993), "Anchors aweigh: the transition from commodity money to fiat money in Western economies", Canadian Journal of Economics 26(4, November):777–795.

Redmond, J. (1984), "The Sterling overvaluation in 1925: a multilateral approach", Economic History Review 2nd ser. 37:520–532.

Robinson, D., and M.R. Wickens (1992), "Measuring real and nominal macroeconomic shocks and their international transmission under different monetary systems", Discussion Paper (London Business School, Center for Economic Forecasting).

Rockoff, H. (1984), "Some evidence on the real price of gold, its cost of production, and commodity prices", in: M.D. Bordo and A.J. Schwartz, eds., A Retrospective on the Classical Gold Standard, 1821–1931 (University of Chicago Press, Chicago, IL).

Rockoff, H. (1986), "Walter Bagehot and the theory of central banking", in: F. Capie and G.E. Wood, eds., Financial Crises and the World Banking System (Macmillan, London) 160–180.

Romer, C.D. (1989), "The prewar business cycle reconsidered: new estimates of gross national product, 1869–1908", Journal of Political Economy 97(1, February):1–37.

Romer, C.D. (1992), "What ended the Great Depression?", Journal of Economic History 52(December): 757–784.

Romer, C.D. (1993), "The Nation in Depression", Journal of Economic Perspectives 7(Spring):19–39.

Rudebusch, G.D. (1995), "Federal Reserve interest rate targeting, rational expectations, and the term structure", Journal of Monetary Economics (April):245–274.

Saint Marc, M. (1983), Histoire Monetaire de la France, 1800–1980 (Presses Universitaires de la France, Paris).

Sargent, T. (1984), "Stopping moderate inflations: the methods of Poincaré and Thatcher", in: R. Dornbusch and M.H. Simonsen, eds., Inflation, Debt and Indexation (MIT Press, Cambridge, MA).

Sargent, T. (1986), Rational Expectations and Inflation (Harper & Row, New York).

Saunders, A., and B. Wilson (1993), "Contagious bank runs: evidence from the 1929–1933 period", mimeograph (New York University Salomon Center).

Sauvy, A. (1954), Rapport sur le Revenu National Presente (Conseil Economique, Paris, March).

Sayers, R.S. (1957), Central Banking After Bagehot (Clarendon Press, Oxford).

Scammell, W.M. (1965), "The working of the Gold Standard", Yorkshire Bulletin of Economic and Social Research 12(May):32–45.

Schwartz, A.J. (1984), "Introduction", in: M.D. Bordo and A.J. Schwartz, eds., A Retrospective on the Classical Gold Standard, 1821–1931 (University of Chicago Press, Chicago, IL).

Schwartz, A.J. (1986a), "Real and pseudo-financial crises", in: F. Capie and G.E. Wood, eds., Financial Crises and the World Banking System (Macmillan, London) 10–31.

Schwartz, A.J. (1986b), "Alternative monetary regimes: the Gold Standard", in: C.D. Campbell and W.R. Dougan, eds., Alternative Monetary Regimes (Johns Hopkins University Press, Baltimore, MD) 44–72.

Schwartz, A.J. (1988), "Financial stability and the federal safety net", in: W.S. Haraf and R.M. Kushmeider, eds., Restructuring Banking Financial Services in America (American Enterprise Institute, Washington, DC) 34–62.

Shiller, R.J. (1980), "Can the Fed control real interest rates?", in: S. Fischer, ed., Rational Expectations and Economic Policy (University of Chicago Press, Chicago, IL) 117–156; 165–167.

Simmons, B. (1994), Who Adjusts: Domestic Sources of Foreign Economic Policy During the Interwar Years (Princeton University Press, Princeton).

Sommariva, A., and G. Tullio (1987), German Macroeconomic History, 1880–1979 (St. Martin's Press, New York).

Svensson, L.E.O. (1994), "Why exchange rate bands?: Monetary independence in spite of fixed exchange rates", Journal of Monetary Economics 33(1):157–199.

Svensson, L.E.O. (1996a), "Commentary: how should monetary policy respond to shocks while maintaining long-run price stability?—Conceptual issues", in: Achieving Price Stability (Federal Reserve Bank of Kansas City) 209–219.

Svensson, L.E.O. (1996b), "Price level targeting vs inflation targeting: a free lunch?", Working Paper No. 5719 (NBER, August).

Taylor, J.B. (1980), "Aggregative dynamics and staggered contracts", Journal of Political Economy 88(1, February):1–23.

Temin, P. (1976), Did Monetary Forces Cause the Great Depression? (W.W. Norton, New York).

Temin, P. (1989), Lessons from the Great Depression (MIT Press, Cambridge, MA).

Temin, P. (1993), "Transmission of the Great Depression", Journal of Economic Perspectives 7(Spring): 87–102.

Thomas, T.J. (1981), "Aggregate demand in the United Kingdom 1918–45", in: R. Floud and D.N. McCloskey, eds., The Economic History of Britain since 1700, vol. 2 (Cambridge University Press, Cambridge).

Timberlake, R.H. (1993), Monetary Policy in the United States: An Intellectual and Institutional History (University of Chicago Press, Chicago, IL).

Toma, M. (1997), Competition and Monopoly in the Federal Reserve System, 1914–1951 (Cambridge University Press, Cambridge).

Trehan, B., and C.E. Walsh (1990), "Seigniorage and tax smoothing in the United States:1914–1986", Journal of Monetary Economics 25:97–112.

Triffin, R. (1960), Gold and the Dollar Crisis (Yale University Press, New Haven, CT).

Tullio, G., and J. Wolters (1996), "Was London the conductor of the international orchestra or just the triangle player? An empirical analysis of asymmetries in interest rate behaviour during the Classical Gold Standard, 1876–1913", Scottish Journal of Political Economy 43(September):419–443.

Weinstein, M.M. (1981), "Some macroeconomic impacts of the National Industrial Recovery Act, 1933–1935", in: K. Brunner, ed., The Great Depression Revisited (Martinus Nijhoff, Boston) 262–281.

Wheelock, D.C. (1991), The Strategy and Consistency of Federal Reserve Monetary Policy 1924–1933 (Cambridge University Press, Cambridge).

White, E.N. (1984), "A reinterpretation of the banking crisis of 1930", Journal of Economic History 44(March):119–138.

Wicker, E. (1965), "Federal Reserve monetary policy, 1922–33: a reinterpretation", Journal of Political Economy 73(August):325–343.

Wicker, E. (1980), "A reconsideration of the causes of the banking panic of 1980", Journal of Economic History 40(September):571–583.

Wicker, E. (1986), "Terminating hyperinflation in the dismembered Habsburg Monarchy", American Economic Review 76(June):350–364.

Wicker, E. (1996), The Banking Panics of the Great Depression (Cambridge University Press, Cambridge).

Wicksell, K. (1898), Interest and Prices: A Study of the Causes Regulating the Value of Money [Translated from the original German by R.F. Kahn] (Macmillan, London, 1936)].

Wigmore, B.A. (1985), The Crash and Its Aftermath: A History of Securities Markets in the United States, 1929–1933 (Greenwood Press, Westport, CT).

Wigmore, B.A. (1987), "Was the Bank Holiday of 1933 caused by a run on the Dollar?", Journal of Economic History 47(3, September):739–756.

CHAPTER 4

Introduction to
"The Great Inflation: The Rebirth
of Modern Central Banking"

MICHAEL D. BORDO AND ATHANASIOS ORPHANIDES

For eight years economic policy and the news about the economy have
been dominated by inflation. . . . Many programs have been launched
to stop it—without success. Inflation seemed a Hydra-headed monster,
growing two new heads each time one was cut off.
            —Council of Economic Advisers (1974, 21)

Overview

Maintaining an environment of low and stable inflation is widely regarded
as one of the most important objectives of economic policy, in general, and
the single most important objective for monetary policy, in particular. The
reasons are clear. An environment of price stability reduces uncertainty, im-
proves the transparency of the price mechanism, and facilitates better planning and the efficient allocation of resources, thereby raising productivity.

Originally published in "Introduction to *The Great Inflation*" in *The Great Inflation: The Rebirth
of Modern Central Banking*, ed. Michael D. Bordo and Athanasios Orphanides (Chicago: University of Chicago Press, 2013), 1–22. This chapter is a selection from a published volume from
the National Bureau of Economic Research.

The Great Inflation from 1965 to 1982 caused significant damage to the US economy and to the economies of many other countries and was a serious policy concern. Inflation in the United States rose from below 2 percent in 1962 to above 15 percent by 1979. Attempts to control it in the early 1970s included the Nixon administration's imposition of wage and price controls, which were largely ineffective but that added to distortions in the US economy and likely contributed to the deep slump of 1974. The inflation rate in the 1970s also contributed to a marked decline in the US stock market and volatility in the US dollar, including a serious exchange rate crisis in 1978 and 1979. The period was also coincident with a marked decline in productivity growth, which by the end of the 1970s was only a fraction of its performance during the 1960s.

Since the early 1980s, the United States, as well as other industrialized and some emerging countries, has been highly successful in controlling inflation. This is evident in the ability of the monetary authorities to stick to their basic low inflation objectives in the face of significant recent oil price shocks and other supply shocks.

By the end of the twentieth century, a consensus view had developed that the Great Inflation represented the most costly deviation from a period of stable prices and output growth in the period between the Great Depression and the recent financial crisis in the United States, as well as many other developed countries. It would appear self-evident that understanding the fundamental causes of this event, and avoiding its repetition, should be viewed as an important issue for macroeconomists. Many attempts to understand what happened can be identified, but over the past three decades there have been substantial disagreements, misconceptions, and misunderstandings of the period, which makes it quite hard to compare even seemingly reasonable and plausible alternatives and to draw useful lessons. In addition, recent research has produced new useful perspectives on what might have led to the unprecedented peacetime run-up in inflation.

The objective of the conference was to bring together this research, helping put the pieces together and to draw the important policy lessons necessary to help avoid the repetition of the Great Inflation. Because of the likelihood that once the present recession is past, inflationary pressure may return, this would seem an opportune time to revisit the Great Inflation. The findings of the research in this volume could have lasting influence on policy.

This introduction briefly describes the dimensions of the Great Inflation. The next section surveys the themes that have dominated the research on the Great Inflation from the 1970s to the present.

The Dimensions of the Great Inflation

The Great Inflation was a worldwide phenomenon, experienced throughout the developed world. As can be seen from a plot of inflation in the G7 countries (Figure 4.1), inflation started to trend upwards in the second half of the 1960s, although the defining decade when its virulence was better understood was the 1970s. Two sharp increases resulting in two peaks, one in the middle of the 1970s and the second around 1980, are evident in all countries. The second peak was followed by disinflation, sharp in some cases, during the first half of the 1980s. Though the contours of inflation were similar, there were significant differences in the extent of the problem. Inflation exceeded 20 percent in the United Kingdom and Italy, reached double digits rather briefly in the United States, but did not exceed single digits in Germany.

In addition to the adverse developments in inflation, the 1970s saw increases in unemployment and a notable slowdown in growth, relative to what had been experienced earlier in the post–World War II period (Figures 4.2 and 4.3). Unemployment levels were historically low in the 1950s and 1960s and productivity increased rapidly. In this light, the relative stagnation of the 1970s, together with the increases in inflation, raised alarms that the worst of both outcomes was being observed, popularizing a description of the period with one word—stagflation.[1] Following a long period of relative stability, the Great Inflation developments surprised policy makers and academics alike. Inflation ran higher than anticipated for long stretches. In the United States, survey data indicate that business economists were notably biased in their forecasts, expecting lower inflation than materialized for several years. Similarly, policy forecasts proved over optimistic. For example, at the Federal Reserve,

FIGURE 4.1   Inflation

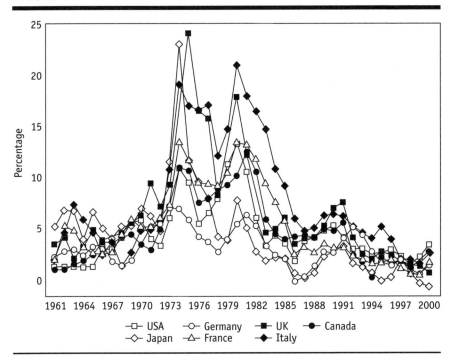

the staff forecasts prepared for Federal Open Market Committee (FOMC) meetings and shown in the Green Book were on average predicting lower inflation.

The surprises did not end with developments in inflation. Another area where a deterioration was slowly recognized was in productivity. In the 1950s and 1960s rapid productivity growth in much of the developed world raised expectations of the prospects for sustained increases in prosperity. In this environment, estimates of potential output growth—the natural rate of growth that could be expected to be achieved with price stability— were increased. But, as was noted in an Organization for Economic Co-operation and Development (OECD) report by a group of independent experts headed by Paul McCracken (OECD 1977), throughout the developed world subsequent developments disappointed and potential output prospects were marked down as the 1970s progressed. In the United States, suspicions that productivity was slowing down were already expressed by

FIGURE 4.2   Unemployment Rate

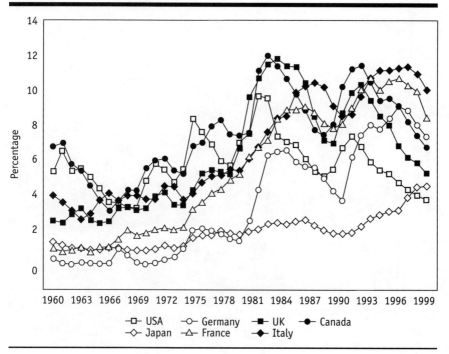

some before the end of the 1960s but the degree of deterioration and successively more pessimistic assessments of productivity and potential output became common as the 1970s progressed.

The malaise was also evident in deteriorating outcomes on employment during the period. During the 1970s, a secular upward trend in the rate of unemployment became evident. In the United States, whereas during the 1950s and 1960s it was increasingly accepted that an unemployment rate of 4 percent or so corresponded to the economy's full employment potential, by the end of the Great Inflation 6 percent or even higher unemployment rates were considered more appropriate reflections of the natural rate. Similar developments were observed elsewhere, and in Europe, in particular, the deterioration in what constituted full employment was even more dramatic.

The deterioration in both inflation stability and economic growth and employment prospects experienced during the Great Inflation were

FIGURE 4.3   Real Output Growth

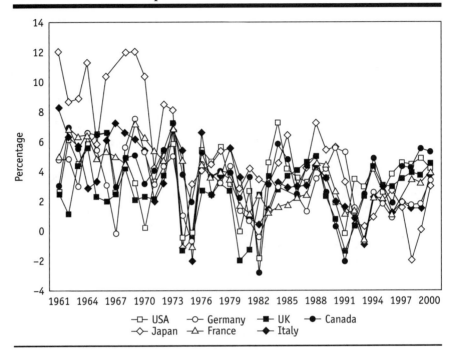

disappointing but also perplexing as they challenged the view prevailing during the 1960s regarding advances in the understanding of the workings of the economy and associated improvements in policy conduct. The timing of the deterioration was especially disheartening to policy economists as it came following a period of what was thought to be a great advance in doctrine. In the United States, the "New Economics" that guided economic policy starting with the Kennedy administration was seen as a period of great promise. (See the accounts of some of the protagonists: Heller 1966; Tobin 1966, 1972; and Okun 1970.) Whereas before the 1960s, policy makers appeared content to ensure that the economy was growing satisfactorily and recessions were avoided, starting with the 1960s, active management of aggregate demand counteracting any shortfall or excess relative to the economy's potential was pursued. As Arthur Okun, whose work on the measurement of potential was critical for the implementation of this strategy explained: "The revised strategy emphasized, as the standard for judging economic performance, whether the economy was living up to its potential rather than merely whether it was advancing" (Okun 1970, 40). Following many years of growth and declining unemployment with relative price stability, the Great Inflation proved a tremendous letdown. Characteristic of the sentiment were the titles of some postmortems written after the destructive forces of the Great Inflation were fully recognized. Arthur Burns titled his 1979 Per Jacobson lecture delivered shortly after he stepped down as Federal Reserve chairman, *The Anguish of Central Banking*. The title of an essay written in 1980 by Robert Solow (1982) in honor of Walter Heller was an apt question: "Where Have All the Flowers Gone?"

The Debate over the Causes of the Great Inflation

The Great Inflation posed a major intellectual challenge because considerable disagreement prevailed as to its immediate causes in both policy and academic circles, both while it was happening and in the decades since.

A number of hypotheses have been advanced as possible explanations, or at least as contributing answers to some of the questions that must be addressed on the way to providing a thorough understanding of the possible causes. Questions such as: What went wrong? What started the Great Inflation? What stopped it? Why did the inflation start in the mid-1960s and accelerate in the 1970s? What accounts for the disinflation of the 1980s? Was the increase in inflation intentional or was it an unavoidable consequence of exogenous factors against which policy was helpless? Were exogenous factors ("bad luck") or endogenous decisions ("bad policy") or a deficient institutional structure ("bad institutions") to blame? To what extent was the initial realization of higher inflation a surprise to policy makers? When was the threat of persistently higher inflation recognized by policy makers? How did households' and businesses' perceptions and attitudes regarding inflation evolve? Did policy makers try to contain inflation and fail or did they decide to let it continue once they understood its persistence? Alternatively, did policy makers perceive constraints that discouraged or rendered infeasible the adoption of policies that could have stopped it? To what extent was the inflation a conscious policy choice responding to the sociopolitical environment of the times? Was it pre-ordained by the institutional environment that evolved following the world wars? Or was it the outcome of the prevalent economic reasoning during the period?

Price changes arise from imbalances in demand and supply and either supply or demand shocks can have influence. In the aggregate, inflation could arise from either source. Identifying the relative importance of "demand" and "supply" shocks as drivers of inflationary developments is a perennial issue, and, unsurprisingly, a matter of controversy with regard to the Great Inflation. In the post–World War II era, including during the Great Inflation, the identification of "cost push" versus "demand pull" inflation occupied many discussions but perceptions varied with schools of thought. Among the economists identified as "monetarists," overexpansionary monetary conditions and excessive nominal aggregate demand, virtually axiomatically, were given prominence in explaining inflation outcomes. Among those identified as "Keynesians," the adverse inflationary outcomes were more often than not identified as due to adverse supply.

During the 1970s in the United States, a common explanation of the inflationary developments was that it resulted from a series of adverse supply shocks. Based on the analysis by Gordon (1975, 1977), Eckstein (1978), and Blinder (1979, 1982), one could argue that the bulk of the two sharp increases in inflation during the 1970s, in 1973 to 1975 and in 1978 to 1980, could be explained due to the unusual developments in food, energy, and other commodities were taken into account to supply shocks in food and energy. In addition to the oil-cartel–induced increases in energy prices, reference was made to agricultural shortages due to unusual weather phenomena, and price increases in other commodities. In his 1977 analysis, Gordon found that structural wage and price equations that were developed to fit the 1954 to 1971 sample, prior to the realization of the unusual supply shocks observed during the first half of the 1970s, tracked the inflation developments well. According to this view, the 1970s experience represented a break from earlier history as a result of the unique supply shocks that hit the economy. The state of aggregate demand and macroeconomic policy did not need to be invoked as an important part of the explanation, and policy directed toward managing aggregate demand—either fiscal or monetary—did not play a major role in determining the adverse inflationary outcomes of the period.

Perhaps the Great Inflation would not have been characterized as such if it were not for the spikes in inflation experienced during the 1970s. While the supply shock hypothesis makes contact with the sharp increases in inflation associated in time with the two sharp increases in oil prices during the 1970s, it does not address the upward drift in inflation evident already from the mid-1960s and through the end of the 1970s. Thus, other factors must have contributed to an underlying aggregate demand pressure that may have persisted for over a decade and could have played a role over and above the supply shock explanation. Further, Barsky and Kilian (2001) suggest skepticism regarding the exogeneity of the commodity shocks of the 1970s and argue that the oil shocks, in particular, were largely the endogenous outcome of accumulated worldwide aggregate demand pressures. If this interpretation is correct, then at least some—if not all—of what is attributed to temporary supply factors should also be attributed to inflationary demand developments and the understanding of the Great Inflation must center on explaining the causes of what may have been a persistently inflationary aggregate demand imbalance.

An underlying element in a number of explanations of the Great Inflation is that policy makers accepted the increase in inflation as an unavoidable choice, necessary to advance overall economic welfare. One such mechanism is based on the time-inconsistency problem of discretionary monetary policy advanced by Kydland and Prescott (1977) and Barro and Gordon (1983). In that model, the time-consistent inflation rate that arises from the monetary policy maker's decisions increases with the economy's natural rate of unemployment. Parkin (1993) and Ireland (1999) use this link to argue that the upward drift in inflation was due to a corresponding drift in the natural rate of unemployment. Indeed, exogenous factors, including demographic changes and a productivity slowdown, seem to have caused an upward drift in the natural rate of unemployment during the late 1960s and 1970s so the time-inconsistency problem could serve as an explanation if policy makers recognized the upward drift in the natural rate at that time and set policy accordingly. The disinflation of the 1980s is harder to reconcile with this explanation alone, however, as it does not similarly coincide with a downward drift in the natural rate.

Another mechanism relating to the time-inconsistency issue that potentially explains episodes of high inflation is the presence of expectations traps, as argued by Chari, Christiano, and Eichenbaum (1998) and Christiano and Gust (2000). An expectations trap arises when an increase in private agents' inflation expectations in the economy pressures the monetary authority to accommodate those expectations to meet other objectives, for example, to avoid a costly recession. A key element in the story is the presence of multiple expectational equilibria. While under commitment a unique equilibrium with low inflation obtains, episodes of high and low inflation can arise in the absence of commitment in monetary policy. The expectations traps provide a mechanism for translating temporary shocks that influence adversely inflation expectations to permanent changes in the inflation tolerated by discretionary policy makers. Thus, it can explain the Great Inflation as due to the combination of adverse shocks and the policy makers' decision to accommodate their inflation consequences permanently. Although policy makers did not seek higher inflation in this story, they decided to accept it as they considered the costs associated with pursuing disinflation too high. Under these circumstances, the disinflation started once policy makers became unwilling to continue to tolerate high inflation.

The willingness of policy makers to accept high inflation is also a feature of the monetary neglect hypothesis advanced in Hetzel (1998, 2008), Nelson and Nikolov (2004), and Nelson (2005a). In this story, monetary policy makers appear unwilling to push for a disinflation once inflation starts because they doubt the effectiveness of monetary policy to tackle inflation relative to alternative policies. The story emphasizes the role of nonmonetary explanations of inflation, such as the belief that inflation can be a purely cost-push phenomenon. The prevalence of such beliefs is thus identified as culprit for the neglect toward achieving price stability. Disinflation started once the dominance of such beliefs receded.

Tolerance for inflation and an aversion to the monetary policy actions needed to end it is also at the heart of political explanations of the Great

Inflation. Politics are always an unavoidable part of economic policy design and this was not different during the Great Inflation period (see Mayer 1999 and Stein 1984). Even if fiscal policy is politically motivated, however, price stability should prevail if the monetary authority can independently decide and implement its policies. The question is whether independent central banks tolerated inflation or whether central banks lacked the necessary independence to do so. Documenting several episodes of political pressure at the Federal Reserve, Meltzer (2005, 2010) argues that politics was an important part for the start, the continuation, and the end of the Great Inflation. The unprecedented public bashing by both the administration and the Congress of Chairman Martin following a policy-tightening with which the administration disagreed in December 1965 marked the start of the episode. According to Meltzer, monetary policy in the second half of the 1960s became more accommodative of the administration's policy objectives. As inflation rose, lack of political consensus for incurring the costs that disinflation would induce tied Chairman Burns's hands. Inflation was ended only when the high costs of inflation were recognized and sufficient political support for disinflation mustered.

An alternative set of explanations, dubbed the "Berkeley story" by Sargent (2002), gives prominence to the rise of views during the 1960s regarding the policy trade-offs implied by a downward sloping Phillips curve. Samuelson and Solow (1960) presented a menu of choices between unemployment and inflation that could be available to policy makers, according to the statistical relationship between inflation and unemployment following World War II. Although they were careful to qualify the stability of this relationship, the policy menu was interpreted as suggesting that if unemployment was deemed intolerably high (as it was in the early 1960s), it could be reduced by pursuing expansionary policies that corresponded to a higher level of inflation. According to DeLong (1997) and Romer and Romer (2002), following Kennedy's election as president in the 1960s, economic policy in the United States was guided by this reasoning and higher inflation was sought and tolerated during the 1960s in an attempt to achieve full employment. DeLong argues that in light of the erroneous beliefs regarding the Phillips curve, the Great Inflation of the 1970s was an accident waiting to happen as policy makers aimed to reduce unemployment toward 4 percent or lower throughout the 1960s. At some point in time, such a policy would trigger accelerating inflation, as implied by the natural rate hypothesis. By the time policy makers accepted the natural rate hypothesis, and adopted an accelerationist view of the Phillips curve (during the Nixon administration), inflation was already embedded in the economy and was difficult to reverse as that would require raising unemployment above the natural rate. Thus, inflation persisted.

Sargent (1999) embeds the discretionary policy of Kydland and Prescott and doubts regarding the natural rate hypothesis in an adaptive model where the policy maker relies on adaptive estimation of the Phillips curve to learn about the policy trade-off. He demonstrates that policy formulated based on the evolving views that arise from the changing statistical relationships between inflation and unemployment in the data gives rise to endogenously determined episodes of high inflation. Using quarterly US data, Cogley and Sargent (2002) confirm that the pattern of evolving statistical relationships is consistent with the story where policy makers could be misled by the data into exploiting a Phillips curve, resulting in higher inflation. In a related model of learning dynamics, Primiceri (2006) shows that the combination of changing beliefs about the persistence of inflation and the inflation–unemployment trade-offs can account for the evolution of policy during the rise of inflation and also the disinflation that followed.

A different theoretical error is involved in yet another explanation of what might have caused monetary policy to be overly expansionary during the period. The starting point for this explanation is the characterization of monetary policy in terms of a simple policy rule that captures the response of the nominal short-term interest rate to developments in the economy and real economy. As Taylor (1993) suggested, if correctly specified, such policy rules can capture desirable elements of systematic monetary policy and deliver good outcomes with respect to both price stability and economic stability. Taylor (1999) and Clarida, Galí, and Gertler (2000) suggested that a policy rule responding to inflation and the output gap provided a good characterization of the period of monetary stability that followed the Great Inflation and argued that had a similar policy rule been followed during the Great Inflation, that episode would have been avoided. Instead, their analysis suggests that in the late 1960s and 1970s the Federal Reserve failed to increase the nominal rate enough to offset the negative effect of inflation on real interest rates. In this explanation, the Federal Reserve inadvertently eased monetary conditions with inflation, causing a rise in inflation during the period. The episode ended when this error was recognized and policy became more responsive to inflation. Supporting this explanation is the fact that ex post real short-term rates remained quite low or were even negative for much of the 1970s. This view, however, rests on the hypothesis of widespread policy confusion of real and nominal interest rates. The validity of this hypothesis was doubted in work by Orphanides (2003a, 2004), who argued that the empirical results presented by Taylor (1999) and Clarida, Galí, and Gertler (2000) were statistical artifacts of the use by these authors of retrospectively revised data for characterizing policy decisions. If, instead, real-time data and forecasts available to the FOMC when decisions were taken were used to characterize policy decisions, the evidence of insufficient responsiveness of policy to inflation was overturned.

Examining the information available to the FOMC during the Great Inflation reveals misinformation as another potential explanation of the Great Inflation. Orphanides (2003b) points to substantial misperceptions regarding the measurement of full employment as the cause of overly expansionary monetary policy. Using a model with an accelerationist Phillips curve, Orphanides compares the results of counterfactual simulations with policy following the Taylor (1993) policy rule. He shows that while the Great Inflation would have been avoided had the output gap been properly measured, when the mismeasurement of the output gap observed during the late 1960s and 1970s is introduced then policy following the Taylor rule delivers inflation outcomes similar to the Great Inflation. Alternative policy rules that deemphasize the output gap are more robust to misperceptions. According to this story, the reliance on the output gap (and related unemployment gap) as a guide for stabilization policy was responsible for the inflationary outcomes. A significant lag of recognition of the productivity slowdown and increase in the natural rate of unemployment implied that estimates of potential output in the late 1960s and throughout the 1970s proved overly optimistic. Although monetary policy was properly responding to inflation it was deliberately easy to counter what were perceived as substantial output gaps and unemployment gaps. The perceived gaps were consistent with projected declining paths of inflation, as suggested by the historical record of policy discussions and the Green Book. Thus, policy was not deliberately inflationary. A persistent overestimation of potential output, an activist policy toward closing output or unemployment gaps, and a significant lag of recognition of its implications on inflation during the 1970s are necessary elements for this hypothesis. Narrative evidence confirms the prominence of the output gap following the rise of activist monetary policy during the 1960s and the delayed recognition of the over optimism reflected in real-time estimates. (See, e.g., Solow 1982, who attributes most of the error to the unexpected unfavorable shift in trend productivity that started in the 1960s.)

Whether an activist policy responding to the output gap like the Taylor (1993) rule can explain the large increase in inflation observed in the 1970s in the presence of misperceptions about the natural rate of unemployment or the output gap alone depends on the persistence of inflation dynamics. Since inflation was not very persistent before the Great Inflation, part of the explanation for the episode must account for the increase in the persistence of inflation during the 1970s. Orphanides and Williams (2005) introduce learning dynamics to examine the evolution of inflation expectations and show that the combination of activist policies and natural rate misperceptions could explain the slow rise of inflation persistence and disanchoring of inflation expectations during the 1970s. Had policy been less activist, inflation expectations would have remained well anchored throughout the 1970s and the Great Inflation would have been avoided. Once Paul Volcker became chairman of the Federal Reserve, the destabilizing role of activist policies on inflation expectations was recognized and less activist policies adopted, ending the inflation episode.

The Great Inflation was an international phenomenon. Inflation was elevated in all advanced countries in the late 1960s and 1970s. Until 1973 most advanced countries were part of the Bretton Woods international monetary system, which operated as a gold dollar standard. The Bretton

Woods articles required that member countries' exchange rates be pegged to the dollar and the dollar be pegged to gold at the official parity of $35 per ounce. Member countries also used the dollar as their international reserve. Like the gold standard that preceded it, monetary shocks would be transmitted between countries in the pegged exchange rate regime through the balance of payments.

There was considerable research in the 1970s and 1980s on the global transmission of inflation under Bretton Woods (see Bordo 1993). Expansionary US monetary policy beginning in 1965 was transmitted through a rising balance of payments deficit that led to dollar flows to the surplus countries of continental Europe and Japan. The central banks in these countries attempted to sterilize the dollar inflows but most led to increases in their money supplies and rising prices. Transmission occurred mainly through the traditional price specie flow plus capital flows channel, less so through commodity market arbitrage (Darby et al. 1983). An alternative, global monetarist view posited that US monetary growth raised the global money supply and global prices and individual country prices converged to global prices via commodity market arbitrage (Genberg and Swoboda 1977).

In the face of this inflationary pressure, the Europeans, beginning in 1968, staged a series of runs on US gold reserves, converting their outstanding dollar liabilities into gold. The runs ended when President Nixon closed the US gold window on August 15, 1971. An attempt to restart Bretton Woods at different parities at the Smithsonian Agreement in Washington, DC, in December 1971 was unsuccessful. Following a series of currency crises and devaluations in the next two years, all of the advanced countries dropped their pegs by 1973 and began floating their currencies.

The run-up of inflation after the collapse of Bretton Woods was attributed by some to the termination of the Bretton Woods nominal anchor to gold and the departure of the last vestiges of the gold standard. In the 1970s the central banks of other advanced countries followed similar expansionary policies to the Fed. Like the Fed, they were influenced by Keynesian doctrine and many attributed the rise in inflation to nonmonetary cost push forces that could only be contained by incomes policies (see DiCecio and Nelson 2013 for the United Kingdom, and Nelson 2005b for the cases of Australia, Canada, and New Zealand). Moreover, these countries (like the

United States) accommodated the oil price shocks of 1974 and 1979. Germany and Switzerland were notable exceptions to this pattern. Policy makers there did not hold Keynesian views nor did they believe in cost push inflation. They viewed inflation to be a monetary phenomenon (see Beyer et al. 2013). The central banks also appeared to enjoy greater independence. Unlike the other countries, they did not accommodate the oil price shocks. Japan also, after accommodating the first oil price shock in 1974, resisted doing so for the second one (see Ito 2013).

Note

1. See Nelson and Nikolov (2004) for the origin of the word in the United Kingdom.

References

Barro, Robert, and David Gordon. 1983. "A Positive Theory of Monetary Policy in a Natural Rate Model." *Journal of Political Economy* 91:589–610.

Barsky, Robert, and Lutz Kilian. 2001. "Do We Really Know Oil Caused the Great Stagflation? A Monetary Alternative." In *NBER Macroeconomics Annual 2001*, edited by Ben Bernanke and Kenneth Rogoff, 137–83. Cambridge, MA: MIT Press.

Beyer, Andreas, Vitor Gaspar, Christina Gerberding, and Otmar Issing. 2013. "Opting Out of the Great Inflation: German Monetary Policy after the Breakdown of Bretton Woods." In *The Great Inflation: The Rebirth of Modern Central Banking*, edited by Michael D Bordo and Athanasios Orphanides, 301–46. Chicago: University of Chicago Press.

Blinder, Alan. 1979. *Economic Policy and the Great Stagflation*. New York: Academic Press.

———. 1982. "The Anatomy of Double-Digit Inflation in the 1970s." In *Inflation: Causes and Effects*, edited by Robert Hall, 261–82. Chicago: University of Chicago Press.

Bordo, Michael D. 1993. "The Bretton Woods International Monetary System: An Historical Overview." In *A Retrospective on the Bretton Woods System: Lessons for Monetary Reform*, edited by Michael D. Bordo and Barry Eichengreen, Chapter 1. Chicago: University of Chicago Press.

Chari, V. V., Lawrence Christiano, and Martin Eichenbaum. 1998. "Expectations Traps and Discretion." *Journal of Economic Theory* 81:462–92.

Christiano, Lawrence J., and Christopher Gust. 2000. "The Expectations Trap Hypothesis." *Federal Reserve Bank of Chicago—Economic Perspectives* 24 (2): 21–39.

Clarida, Richard, Jordi Galí, and Mark Gertler. 2000. "Monetary Policy Rules and Macroeconomic Stability: Evidence and Some Theory." *Quarterly Journal of Economics* 115:147–80.

Cogley, Timothy, and Thomas Sargent. 2002. "Evolving Post-World War II US. Inflation Dynamics." *NBER Macroeconomics Annual 2001*, edited by Ben S. Bernanke and Kenneth Rogoff, 331–73. Cambridge, MA: MIT Press.

Council of Economic Advisers. 1974. *Economic Report of the President*. Washington, DC: United States Printing Office.

Darby, Michael R., James R. Lothian, Artur Gandolfi, Anna J. Schwartz, and Alan Stockman. 1983. *The International Transmission of Inflation*. Chicago: University of Chicago Press.

DeLong, J. Bradford. 1997. "America's Peacetime Inflation: The 1970s." In *Reducing Inflation: Motivation and Strategy*, edited by Christina Romer and David Romer, 247–80. Chicago: University of Chicago Press.

DiCecio, Riccardo, and Edward Nelson. 2013. "The Great Inflation in the United States and the United Kingdom: Reconciling Policy Decisions and Data Outcomes." In *The Great Inflation: The Rebirth of Modern Central Banking*, edited by Michael D. Bordo and Athanasios Orphanides, 393–445. Chicago: University of Chicago Press.

Eckstein, Otto. 1978. *The Great Recession with a Postscript on Stagflation*. Amsterdam: North-Holland.

Genberg, Hans, and Alexander Swoboda. 1977. "Causes and Origins of the Current Worldwide Inflation." In *Inflation Theory and Anti-Inflation Policy*, edited by Erik Lundberg, 72–93. London: Macmillan.

Gordon, Robert. 1975. "Alternative Response of Policy to External Supply Shocks." *Brookings Papers on Economic Activity* 1:183–205.

———. 1977. "Can the Inflation of the 1970s Be Explained?" *Brookings Papers on Economic Activity*: 253–79. Washington, DC: Brookings Institution.

Heller, W. W. 1966. *New Dimensions in Political Economy*. Cambridge, MA: Harvard University Press.

Hetzel, Robert. 1998. "Arthur Burns and Inflation." *Federal Reserve Bank of Richmond Economic Quarterly* 84:21–44.

———. 2008. *The Monetary Policy of the Federal Reserve: A History*. New York: Cambridge University Press.

Ireland, Peter. 1999. "Does the Time-Consistency Problem Explain the Behaviour of Inflation in the United States?" *Journal of Monetary Economics* 44:279–91.

Ito, Takatoshi. 2013. "Great Inflation and Central Bank Independence." In *The Great Inflation: The Rebirth of Modern Central Banking*, edited by Michael D. Bordo and Athanasios Orphanides, 359–87. Chicago: University of Chicago Press.

Kydland, Finn, and Edward Prescott. 1977. "Rules Rather Than Discretion: The Inconsistency of Optimal Plans." *Journal of Political Economy* 85 (3): 473–91.

Mayer, T. 1999. *Monetary Policy and the Great Inflation in the United States: The Federal Reserve and the Failure of Macroeconomic Policy, 1965–1979.* Cheltenham, UK: Edward Elgar.

Meltzer, Allan. 2005. "Origins of the Great Inflation." *Federal Reserve Bank of St. Louis Review* 87 (2, part 2): 145–75.

———. 2010. *A History of the Federal Reserve,* vol. 2. Chicago: University of Chicago Press.

Nelson, Edward. 2005a. "The Great Inflation of the 1970s: What Really Happened?" *Advances in Macroeconomics* 3: Article 3.

———. 2005b. "Monetary Policy Neglect and the Great Inflation in Canada, Australia and New Zealand." *International Journal of Central Banking* 1 (1): 133–79.

Nelson, Edward, and Kalin Nikolov. 2004. "Monetary Policy and Stagflation in the UK." *Journal of Money, Credit and Banking* 36 (3, part 1): 293–318.

OECD. 1977. *Toward Full Employment and Price Stability.* Paris: Organization for Economic Cooperation and Development.

Okun, Arthur. 1970. *The Political Economy of Prosperity.* Washington, DC: Brookings Institution.

Orphanides, Athanasios. 2003a. "Historical Monetary Policy and the Taylor Rule." *Journal of Monetary Economics* 50:983–1022.

———. 2003b. "The Quest for Prosperity without Inflation." *Journal of Monetary Economics* 50 (3): 633–63.

———. 2004. "Monetary Policy Rules, Macroeconomic Stability and Inflation: A View from the Trenches." *Journal of Money, Credit and Banking* 36 (2): 151–75.

Orphanides, Athanasios, and John C. Williams. 2005. "The Decline of Activist Stabilization Policy: Natural Rate Misperceptions, Learning and Expectations." *Journal of Economic Dynamics and Control* 29:1927–50.

Parkin, Michael. 1993. "Inflation in North America." In *Price Stabilization in the 1990s: Domestic and International Policy Requirements,* edited by K. Shigehara, 47–83. Bank of Japan.

Primiceri, Giorgio. 2006. "Why Inflation Rose and Fell: Policymaker's Beliefs and US Postwar Stabilization Policy." *Quarterly Journal of Economics* 121 (3): 867.

Romer, Christina D., and David H. Romer. 1989. "Does Monetary Policy Matter? A New Test in the Spirit of Friedman and Schwartz." In *NBER Macroeconomics Annual 1989,* edited by O. J. Blanchard and S. Fisher, 121–69. Cambridge, MA: MIT Press.

Romer, Christina, and David Romer. 2002. "The Evolution of Economic Understanding and Postwar Stabilization Policy." In *Rethinking Stabilization Policy,* Federal Reserve Bank of Kansas City, 11–78.

Samuelson, Paul, and Robert M. Solow. 1960. "Analytical Aspects of Anti-Inflation Policy." *American Economic Review* 50 (2): 177–94.

Sargent, Thomas. 1999. *The Conquest of American Inflation.* Princeton, NJ: Princeton University Press.

————. 2002. "Commentary: The Evolution of Economic Understanding and Postwar Stabilization Policy." Federal Reserve Bank of Kansas City, *Proceedings* 2002:79–94.

Solow, Robert M. 1982. "Where Have All the Flowers Gone? Economic Growth in the 1960s." In *Economics in the Public Service: Essays in Honor of Walter W. Heller,* edited by Joseph A Pechman and N. J. Simler, 46–74. New York: Norton.

Stein, Herbert. 1984. *Presidential Economics.* New York: Simon and Schuster.

Stock, James W., and Mark W. Watson. 2007. "Why Has Inflation Become Harder to Forecast?" *Journal of Money, Credit, and Banking* 29 (1 suppl.): 3–33.

Taylor, John. 1993. "Discretion versus Policy Rules in Practice." *Carnegie-Rochester Series on Public Policy* 39, pp. 195–214.

————. 1999. "A Historical Analysis of Monetary Policy Rules." In *Monetary Policy Rules,* edited by John Taylor, Chapter 7. Chicago: University of Chicago Press.

Tobin, James. 1966. *National Economic Policy.* New Haven, CT: Yale University.

————. 1972. *New Economics One Decade Older.* Princeton, NJ: Princeton University Press.

PART THREE

MONETARY POLICY PERFORMANCE

CHAPTER 5

Exits from Recessions
The US Experience, 1920–2007

MICHAEL D. BORDO AND JOHN S. LANDON-LANE

Introduction

THE RECESSION OF 2007–2009 ended in June 2009, and the US economy has been recovering slowly ever since. Monetary policy has been expansionary since fall 2008 (as has fiscal policy). The Federal Reserve reduced the funds rate from 5.25 percent in August 2007 to close to zero by January 2009, and the Fed has followed two rounds of quantitative easing. There is considerable interest in when the Fed should turn its policy toward one consistent with long-run growth and low inflation—the exit strategy. This involves switching from expansionary to neutral monetary policy, reducing the Fed's balance sheet, and, for fiscal policy, reducing the large fiscal deficits and reducing the national debt.

The key question is when this should happen. A leading view on the issue argues that because of the financial crisis, the credit crunch, and the large overhang of nonperforming loans and toxic assets, the recovery will be slow and the need to tighten will not occur for quite some time. This

Originally published in "Exits from Recessions: The US Experience, 1920–2007," chap. 8 in *No Way Out: Persistent Government Interventions in the Great Contraction*, ed. Vincent R. Reinhart (Washington, DC: AEI Press), 117–62. Copyright 2013 by the American Enterprise Institute for Public Policy Research, Washington DC.

view is backed up by cross-country evidence, which demonstrates that recessions accompanied by financial turmoil tend to be deeper and longer (Claessens, Kose, and Terrones 2008; Reinhart and Rogoff 2009). An alternative view argues that in US history, deep recessions (including those accompanied by financial crises) have been followed by rapid recoveries (Mussa 2009) and that this recovery may be slow in reflecting deep-seated structural factors (Stock and Watson 2012) and the collapse of the housing sector (Bordo and Haubrich 2012). These factors may not be easily overcome by continued expansionary monetary policy.

The risks facing monetary policy with respect to the exit strategy are twofold: tightening too soon and creating a double-dip recession, and tightening too late leading to a run-up of inflation. There are a number of famous historical examples of each type of error. Tightening too soon after the Great Contraction led to the recession of 1937–38. Tightening too late in the recessions of the 1960s and 1970s contributed to the Great Inflation.

In this chapter, we examine the historical record of US business cycles from 1920 to 2007. First we provide a brief historical narrative on each of the cycles. Then we present descriptive evidence on the timing of policy change from ease to tightness and on the changes of macro aggregates around the lower turning point of each cycle, based on the work of the National Bureau for Economic Research (NBER). We divide the sample in two: cycles before World War II from 1920 to 1938, and cycles from 1948 to the present.

To supplement the descriptive analysis, we then run some simple regressions of the timing of policy changes relative to the trough of the real variables (real gross national product [GNP], industrial production, the output gap, and unemployment) and price variables (inflation and the price level pre-1960). We also use the coefficients of the effects of the timing of the indicator in the postwar period to predict the possible exits from the current recession.

We can discern some basic patterns from history. In general, in the post–World War II period, the Fed tends to tighten when inflation (the price level) is rising and postpones tightening when the output gap and unemployment have yet to turn. However, the decision to wait until unemployment (the output gap) turns dominates the decision to tighten when inflation rises. The timing of tightening differs somewhat before and after

World War II. In the prewar era, the Fed generally tightened when the price level turned up. This policy sometimes caused it to tighten too soon. In the postwar era, the Fed, by focusing on unemployment, tends to err on the side of tightening too late—that is, after inflation resurges.

We also find that there are a few cycles when the Fed got the timing just right and followed a countercyclical policy.[1] These were in the 1920s and 1950s, as discussed by Friedman and Schwartz (1963) and Meltzer (2003, 2010). In most cycles, Fed actions were procyclical.

We further note a significant difference between the cycles before 1965, when the Fed adhered to some form of gold-standard convertibility rule and attached the highest priority to price stability (Bordo and Eichengreen 2008), and the cycles since, when the gold standard became a less important consideration and then did not matter at all. In the late 1960s and 1970s, the Fed generally waited until unemployment and the output gap declined before tightening and placed little emphasis on the pace of inflation. Since the Volcker shock in the early 1980s, the Fed has placed more emphasis on reducing inflation in determining its exit strategy. A memorable episode in which the Fed tightened when unemployment was high and rising was in 1981, when Fed chairman Paul Volcker was determined to break the back of inflation.

In the early 1990s and early 2000s, the Fed, concerned with persistent unemployment ("a jobless recovery"), waited too long. In the first case, significant tightening occurred close to three years after the trough following the inflation scare of 1994. In the second case, the Fed, concerned with the risk of deflation, waited four years after the trough and accordingly may have ignited the housing-price boom that burst in 2006 leading to the 2007–2009 recession.

Historical Narrative: 1920–38

Peak January 1920; Trough July 1921

The recession of 1920–21 was one of the three worst recessions of the twentieth century. Friedman and Schwartz (1963) viewed it as the Fed's first policy failure. They indicted the Fed for waiting too long to raise rates to

stem the inflationary boom that followed World War I, and then for waiting too long to reverse the ensuing recession. The Fed waited until November 1919 to begin tightening because the Treasury pressured the Fed
to keep the prices of its wartime bond issues high. During the recession
that followed, real GNP fell by 15 percent, industrial production (IP) fell
by 23 percent, the GNP deflator fell by 20 percent, and the unemployment
rate increased by 8 percent.

The cause of the recession was the Fed's decision (triggered by a decline in its gold reserves) to implement a rapid deflation to roll back the
run-up in prices that had occurred since the United States entered World
War I. The Fed raised the discount rate from 4.75 percent in January 1920
to 7 percent in June and kept it at that level until May 1921. The highly
persistent rise in nominal interest rates in the face of a shift in expectations from inflation to deflation represented a much tighter policy stance
than agents anticipated (Bordo et al. 2007). In the face of mounting political pressure, the Fed reversed course four months after the recession
ended. IP recovered in August and by March 1922 had increased 20 percent
above the previous year.

Peak May 1923; Trough July 1924

The recession of 1923–24 was relatively brief and, by pre–World War II
standards, mild: real GNP fell by 4 percent. The recession followed a
tightening of monetary policy beginning in May 1922, which reflected
concern that the rapid recovery from the previous recession was becoming
inflationary. In contrast to the previous recession, the Fed began reversing
course soon after the recession became apparent in December 1923, with
open market operations and then cuts in the discount rate in May 1924
(Meltzer 2003). Friedman and Schwartz (1963) gave the Fed high marks
for conducting a successful countercyclical policy.

Peak October 1926; Trough November 1927

Similar to the recession of 1923–24, the Fed began tightening, reflecting
fears of inflation, in January 1925, with open market sales and then a rise
in the discount rate in February. As in the preceding recession, the Fed

reversed course and began open market purchases in May 1927, halfway through the mild recession (Meltzer 2003).

Peak August 1929; Trough March 1933

The Great Contraction of 1929–33, during which prices, real GNP, and the money stock (M2) declined by about a third, was the worst recession in US history. Since Friedman and Schwartz (1963), it is widely attributed to policy failures at the Federal Reserve. Beginning in 1927, the Federal Reserve Board became increasingly concerned over stock market speculation and the growing boom on Wall Street. Based on the real bills doctrine, many officials believed that stock market speculation was inflationary. The Fed began monetary restraint with open market sales in February 1928 and continued this policy through 1929, with a rise in the discount rate from 5 to 6 percent in August 1929.

The tightening, while insufficient to halt the stock market boom, was sufficient to induce a downturn beginning in August 1929. The stock market crash in October 1929 exacerbated the downturn but did not cause the depression. The failure of the Fed to follow its mandate from the Federal Reserve Act of 1913 to act as a lender of last resort and to allay a series of four banking panics beginning in October 1930 led to the serious downturn that followed. A major hike in the discount rate in October 1931 designed to protect the dollar after sterling's exit from the gold standard added fuel to the fire. Despite short-lived expansionary open market purchases in spring 1932, which, if continued, could have ended the recession (Friedman and Schwartz 1963), the recovery in March 1933 was not precipitated by Fed policy.

Recovery began in March 1933 with President Franklin D. Roosevelt's banking holiday, ending the fourth banking panic. The country's banks were closed for a week, during which an army of bank inspectors separated the insolvent banks from the rest. Insolvent banks were closed, ending the uncertainty driving the panic. This action was quickly followed by Roosevelt taking the United States off the gold standard in April 1933, Treasury gold (and silver) purchases designed to raise gold prices and prices in general, and formal devaluation of the dollar by close to 60 percent in January 1934. These policies produced a big reflationary impulse from gold inflows, which were passing unsterilized directly into the money supply. They also helped convert deflationary expectations into inflationary ones (Eggertsson 2008).

The recovery of 1933 to 1941 was largely driven by gold inflows, initially reflecting Treasury policies and the devaluation, later reflecting capital flight from Europe as war loomed. Expansionary fiscal policy played only a minor role in the recovery of the 1930s (Romer 1992). Recovery was impeded somewhat by New Deal cartelization policies like the National Industrial Recovery Act, which artificially reduced labor supply and aggregate supply in an attempt to raise wages and prices (Cole and Ohanian 2004). Over the period 1933–37, output increased by 33 percent.

Peak May 1937; Trough June 1938

The 1937–38 recession, which cut short the rapid recovery from the Great Contraction of 1929–33, was the third-worst recession in the twentieth century: real GNP declined by 10 percent, and unemployment, which had declined considerably after 1933, increased to 20 percent. The recession was primarily a consequence of a serious policy mistake by the Fed. Mounting concern by the Fed over the inflationary consequences of the buildup in excess reserves in member banks (held as a precaution against a repeat of the banking panics of the early 1930s) led the Board of Governors to double reserve requirements in three steps between August 1936 and May 1937. Fed officials were concerned that these reserves would lead to an explosion of lending and would foster a reoccurrence of the asset-price speculation of the 1920s. They also believed that reducing excess reserves would encourage member banks to borrow at the discount window. The Burgess-Riefler doctrine that prevailed at the time argued that the Fed could exert monetary control by using open market operations to affect member bank borrowing and hence to alter bank lending (Meltzer 2003).

The consequence of doubling reserve requirements was that banks sold off their earning assets and cut their lending to restore their desired cushion of precautionary reserves. The Fed's contractionary policy action was complemented by the Treasury's decision in late 1936 to sterilize gold inflows in order to reduce excess reserves. These policy actions led to a spike in short-term interest rates and a severe decline in money supply.

The recession ended in April 1938 after Roosevelt pressured the Fed to roll back reserve requirements, the Treasury stopped sterilizing gold inflows and desterilized all the remaining gold sterilized since December 1936, and the administration began pursuing expansionary fiscal policy. The recovery from 1938 to 1942 was spectacular; output grew by 49 percent, fueled by gold inflows from Europe and a major defense buildup.

Peak November 1948; Trough October 1949

After the war, inflation increased to 15 percent per year by 1948. Tightening by both the Treasury and the Fed began in October 1947. A mild recession ensued beginning in November 1948. Real GNP fell by less than 2 percent, IP by 9 percent, and Consumer Price Index (CPI) prices by 2 percent. Fed policy was slow to change during the recession because the Fed viewed low nominal interest rates (T bills) at close to 1 percent as evidence of ease and did not realize that real rates were elevated in the face of recession. The board reduced reserve requirements by 2 percent in May 1949. According to Meltzer (2003, chapter 7), 1948–49 was similar to 1920–21 in that deflation—by both encouraging gold inflows and increasing the real value of the monetary base—helped to reinflate the economy.

Peak July 1953; Trough May 1954

After the Federal Reserve–Treasury Accord of March 1951, the Fed was again free to use its policy rates to pursue its policy aims. One of the first occasions was at the end of the Korean War, when both monetary and fiscal policy tightened to prevent an increase in inflation. In January 1953, the Fed raised its discount rate and the real money base declined, leading to a recession beginning in July. The real economy declined by 3.2 percent, IP declined by 9.4 percent, and unemployment rose to 6.1 percent. However, unlike earlier recessions, the Fed eased policy in June 1953 to offset a spike in long-term Treasury bond rates. Ease continued with a decline in reserve requirements in July 1953; a decline in the discount rate in February, April, and May 1954; and declines in reserve requirements in June and July. By October 1954, with recovery well underway, the Fed began to tighten in December in the face of incipient inflationary pressure. The Fed raised the discount rate in seven steps from the end of 1954 to 1957. This was evident in a rise in ex post interest rates (Meltzer 2010, chapter 2; Friedman and Schwartz 1963, chapter 11).

Peak August 1957; Trough April 1958

Growing concern over the pace of recovery from the previous recession and a run-up in inflation in 1955 led the Fed to begin tightening in April by raising the discount rate. Further increases followed in 1956. The ensuing recession was relatively mild, with real GNP falling by 3 percent and unemployment rising to 7.5 percent. The Fed was slow to respond to the recession because of continuing concern over inflation (Meltzer 2010, chapter 2). It began easing in November 1957 by reducing the discount rate and reserve requirements and conducting open market purchases in March and April 1958. The recovery was vigorous, and the Fed, again worried about inflation, began tightening (raising the discount rate) in August, four months after the trough. It was also concerned for the first time in the postwar period with gold outflows (Friedman and Schwartz 1963, 618).

Peak April 1960; Trough February 1961

The Fed began tightening in spring 1959 in the face of rising inflation and gold outflows. By early 1960, the Federal Reserve Board's policy-setting group, the Federal Open Market Committee (FOMC), recognized that the economy had slowed and began to ease two months before the April business-cycle peak, as it had done in 1953. The ensuing recession was mild and lasted ten months. Real GNP fell by less than 1 percent, and unemployment increased to 7 percent. Fed policy continued to be loose throughout the downturn: the discount rate was cut in March and August and reserve requirements were cut in August. The recession ended in February. After the trough, the policy directive for ease was moderated in April (Meltzer 2010, chapter 3). The real federal funds rate began to rise one quarter after the trough, and the growth of the real base slowed at the trough. Unemployment peaked in May.

Peak November 1969; Trough November 1970

The period from 1961 to 1964 exhibited rapid growth with low inflation. Inflation began to rise in 1965. The Fed tightened in December 1965 against President Lyndon B. Johnson's wishes, but not enough to stem rising inflation. Further tightening in spring and summer 1966 led to the credit crunch of 1966, a growth slowdown but not a recession (Bordo and Haubrich 2009). The Fed began tightening again in summer 1969, seen in a decline in real base growth and a rise in real interest rates leading to the mild recession that began in July 1969. Real GNP fell less than half a percent, unemployment increased to 5.9 percent, and inflation only slowed moderately. Policy began to ease after January 1970, seen in a flattening of real base growth.

In April 1970, Fed chairman Arthur Bums abandoned the antiinflationary policy that had been pursued by his predecessor, William McChesney Martin, because of the slowing economy. By June 1970, real base growth was positive and real interest rates declined. The easy policies continued until after the trough. Recovery in real GNP was relatively sluggish, and unemployment did not peak until summer 1971. Policy shifted to less ease after the trough, seen in a rise in the real funds rate and a flattening of real growth. This recession was the first during the Great Inflation episode in which the Fed revealed its unwillingness to stem inflation at the expense of unemployment (Meltzer 2010, chapter 3).

Peak November 1973; Trough March 1975

The Nixon administration imposed wage-price controls in August 1971 to fight unemployment, but the policy was unsuccessful. CPI inflation increased to 10 percent by 1974. In the face of rising inflation from December to August 1972, the Fed tightened, but not enough (Meltzer 2010, chapter 6). Further tightening occurred in summer 1973, seen in a decline in real base growth. The recession, which began in November, was one of the worst in the postwar period: real GNP declined by 4.7 percent and unemployment increased to 8.6 percent. The recession was greatly aggravated by the first oil price shock, which doubled the price of oil and, by the price controls, prevented the necessary adjustment. Beginning in July 1974, the Fed shifted to easier policy in the face of rising unemployment, seen in a reversal in the federal funds rate (both nominal and real). Monetary ease continued in the first quarter of 1975 when the Fed cut the funds rate, the discount rate, and reserve requirements. The recovery began in April 1975, but according to Meltzer (2010, chapter 7), the Fed did not recognize it until August. The Fed, still concerned with inflation, began increasing the funds rate in the quarter after the recession ended, and real base growth flattened in the same quarter.

Peak January 1980; Trough July 1980

By 1979, inflation had reached double-digit levels. In August 1979, President Jimmy Carter appointed a well-known inflation hawk, Paul Volcker, as chairman of the Federal Reserve. Two months after taking office, Volcker announced a major shift in policy aimed at rapidly lowering the inflation rate. He desired the policy change to be interpreted as a decisive break from past policies that had allowed the run-up in inflation. The announcement was followed by a series of sizable hikes in the federal funds rate. The roughly 7 percentage point rise in the nominal funds rate between October 1979 and April 1980 was the largest increase over a six-month period in the history of the Federal Reserve System. The tight monetary stance was temporarily abandoned in mid-1980 as interest rates spiked and economic activity decelerated sharply. The FOMC then imposed credit controls (March to July 1980) and let the funds rate decline—moves that the Carter administration had politically supported. The controls led to a marked decline in consumer credit, personal consumption, and economic activity, leading to an increase in unemployment from 6.3 to 7.5 percent. In July 1980, the Fed shifted to an expansionary monetary policy, seen in cuts in the federal funds rate and increases in real base growth. The recession ended in July 1980, followed by a rapid recovery. Fed policy started to tighten again in May 1981 in the face of a jump in inflation, seen in a sharp reversal in real base growth and then successive rises in the discount rate beginning in September. The FOMC policy reversal and acquiescence to political pressure in 1980 were widely viewed as a signal that it was not committed to achieving a sustained fall in inflation. Having failed to convince price and wage setters that inflation was going to fall, the GNP deflator rose almost 10 percent in 1980.

Peak July 1981; Trough November 1982

The Fed embarked on a new round of tightening in spring 1981. It raised the federal funds rate from 14.7 percent in March to 19.1 percent in June. This second and more durable round of tightening succeeded in reducing the inflation rate from about 10 percent in early 1981 to about 4 percent in 1983, but at the cost of a sharp and prolonged recession. Real GNP fell by close to 5 percent, and unemployment increased from 7.2 percent to 10.8 percent. The Fed's tightening during a recession was initially supported by both President Ronald Reagan and Congress. However, by spring 1982, the Fed faced increasing pressure from Congress and the administration to loosen policy. There was also concern over the solvency of the money center banks hit by the Latin American debt defaults and over the effects of high interest rates on other countries. The Fed shifted to a looser policy in June 1982, with a decline in the discount rate and the federal funds rate and a rise in the growth rate of the real monetary base. After the trough, real output, the output gap, and IP rose rapidly. Unemployment peaked quickly. Policy tightened somewhat in terms of both the real funds rate and the real base soon after the trough, reflecting the FOMC's determination to continue to reduce inflation (Meltzer 2010, chapter 8).

Peak July 1990; Trough March 1991

The recession of 1991 was preceded by Fed tightening beginning in December 1988 (Romer and Romer 1994). The FOMC wanted to reduce inflation from the 4–4.5 percent range. The federal funds rate rose from 6.5 percent to 9.9 percent between March 1988 and May 1989. The recession began in July 1990 and was aggravated by an oil price shock after Iraq invaded Kuwait in August 1990. The recession was mild. Real GNP fell by only 1.4 percent. The FOMC only began cutting the federal funds rate in November because its primary concern was to reduce inflation, which had reached 6.1 percent in the first half of 1990 (Hetzel 2008, chapter 15).

The recovery from the trough in March 1991 was considered tepid (real output grew at 3.6 percent for the three years following the trough, compared to the postwar average of 5 percent), and it was referred to as a jobless recovery—unemployment peaked at 7.7 percent in June 1992.The recession is also viewed as a credit crunch (Bernanke and Lown 1991). Evidence in Bordo and Haubrich (2009) and the International Monetary Fund *World Economic Outlook* (2008) suggests that recessions involving credit events tend to last longer. The federal funds rate declined until October 1992. Inflation began to pick up in the first quarter of 1993, and by early 1994 the Fed shifted to a tighter policy, the inflation scare of 1994 (Hetzel 2008, 202).

Peak March 2001; Trough November 2001

In 2000, the Fed loosened monetary policy because of the fear of Y2K. The tech boom, which had elevated the NASDAQ to unsustainable levels, burst, leading to a decline in wealth and consumption. The FOMC did not forecast a recession and was slow to respond because of tightness in the labor market (Hetzel 2008, 241). Although real growth began decelerating in mid-2000, the FOMC began reducing the funds rate in January 2001 and lowered the rate from 6.5 to 1 percent by June 2003. Real short-term rates fell from 5 percent in mid-2001 to zero percent in mid-2002, but not rapidly enough to prevent policy from being contractionary (Hetzel 2008, 242). Although real growth had picked up after the trough in November, employment had not, and like the previous recession, there was talk about a jobless recovery. By March 2004, the unemployment rate was at 5.7 percent, still near its cyclical peak. Moreover, the Fed worried about deflation and the zero-lower-bound problem in 2003. Consequently, the federal funds rate was maintained at its recession low until June 2004, when alarm caused by an increase in inflationary expectations led the Fed to begin raising the federal funds rate in 0.25 percent increments until late summer 2007.

Peak December 2007; Trough June 2009

The recent recession is familiar in some respects and novel in others. It is familiar in that the recession, although somewhat longer in duration and somewhat deeper than the postwar average, is within the realm of the postwar experience. It is novel in that it was precipitated by a financial crisis caused by the end of a major housing boom. It has been argued by many that a key contributing factor to the asset boom, along with lax regulatory oversight and a relaxation of normal standards of prudent lending, was an extended period of loose monetary policy from 2002 to 2004 in reaction to slow employment growth, fears of incipient crises, and deflation. Contributing factors to the asset bust include a return to tighter monetary policy in 2005, the collapse of the subprime mortgage market, and the debunking of the securitization model by which derivatives, including toxic mortgages, were bundled. The severity of the resultant recession, from December 2007 to summer 2009, reflected both a credit crunch and tight Federal Reserve policies in 2008, seen in high real federal funds rates (Hetzel 2008). The recession is in some respects the most severe event in the postwar period (real GNP declined by close to 4 percent and unemployment reached 10 percent), and the financial crisis is without doubt the most serious event since the Great Depression (the quality spread, as measured by the spread between the yield on BAA-rated commercial debt and the yield on long-term Treasury debt, increased by 342 basis points by April 2009, which was higher than in 1929–33).

Both the crisis and the recession were dealt with by vigorous policy responses (expansionary monetary policy cutting the funds rate from 5.25 percent in early fall 2007 to close to zero by January 2009 and a massive fiscal stimulus package), by unorthodox quantitative easing (the purchase of mortgage-backed securities and long-term Treasuries since January 2009), and by an extensive network of facilities (such as the Term Auction Facility) created to support the credit market directly and reduce spreads (involving a tripling of the Fed's balance sheet). It is too soon to analyze the recovery or the exit strategy, but in a subsequent section we use our econometric analysis to estimate when tightening will occur.

Using historical narratives allowed us to determine those exits in which the Fed was deemed to have exited too early, too late, or at the right time. We next turn to a more descriptive analysis, where we analyze the patterns between the turning points of the policy variables and the turning points of the real and nominal variables that we follow.

Turning Point Analysis

For all the business cycles since 1920 (excluding the two cycles that bracketed World War II), we ascertained the turning points in the quarterly values of several policy variables: before 1954, the discount rate (nominal and real); since 1954, the federal funds rate (nominal and real); the growth rate of the monetary base (nominal and real); and the growth rate of M2 money stock (nominal and real). We did the same for several real macro aggregates: real GNP, industrial production, the unemployment rate, the output gap, and two measures of the price level and inflation (the GNP deflator and the CPI).[2] For data sources and definitions, see appendix Table 5.A1.

In the period before 1960, when inflation was generally low and the United States adhered to some form of the gold standard (under which prices are mean reverting), we focus on the price level as a policy target. Since 1960, inflation has been continuously positive, so we focus on measures of inflation as our policy target.

Determining the Turning Points

The turning points of each of the series, reported in Tables 5.1 and 5.2 below, were determined as follows: for each of the macroeconomic aggregate variables (two measures of the price level and inflation, real output, industrial production, the output gap, and unemployment), the date at which the variable started to improve after the start of the recession was chosen by visual inspection of the time series figures for each variable as shown in the appendix.

For the price level and inflation, this was the first date after the start of the recession when the price level or inflation rate changed from having a negative slope to a positive slope. Similarly, for real output, industrial production, and the output gap, we looked for the first quarter after the start of the recession in which the slope of the series changed from being negative to positive. The rule for unemployment was the opposite, with the turning point being the first quarter after the start of the recession in which the derivative of the unemployment series changed from positive to negative.

TABLE 5.1A Descriptive Evidence Policy Variables, 1920–1937

Cycle	Narratives	Discount Rate	Real Discount Rate	Base Growth	Real Base Growth	M2 Growth	Real M2 Growth
1. 1920Q1–1923Q1 (1921Q3)[a]	3[b]	5	—	5	1	2	2
2. 1923Q2–1926Q2 (1924Q3)	3	1	2	0	2	−1	2
3. 1926Q3–1929Q2 (1927Q4)	1	0	0	1	0	0	0
4. 1929Q3–1937Q1 (1933Q1)	14	—	—	3	3	−2	4

Source: Authors' calculations.

[a] Numbers in parentheses are the NBER trough dates for each cycle.

[b] Numbers in cells represent number of quarters after official NBER trough date that the series was determined to have turned. In the case of the policy variables, this was the date of initial tightening. Missing values represent a cycle in which no definitive turning point was identified.

TABLE 5.1B Descriptive Evidence Macro Aggregates, 1920–1937

Cycle	Price Level (GNP defl.)	Price Level (CPI)	Real GNP	Industrial Production	Output Gap	Unemployment
1. 1920Q1–1923Q1 (1921Q3)[a]	3[b]	2	−2	−2	−2	−2
2. 1923Q2–1926Q2 (1924Q3)	0	−2	0	−1	0	−2
3. 1926Q3–1929Q2 (1927Q4)	−2	1	0	0	0	1
4. 1929Q3–1937Q1 (1933Q1)	0	0	0	0	0	−4

Source: Authors' calculations.

[a] Numbers in parentheses are the NBER trough dates for each cycle.

[b] Numbers in cells represent number of quarters after official NBER trough date that the series was determined to have turned. In the case of the policy variables, this was the date of initial tightening.

TABLE 5.2A   Descriptive Evidence Policy Variables, 1948–2007

Cycle	Narratives	Federal Funds Rate (Discount Rate)	Real Federal Funds Rate (Real Discount Rate)	Base Growth	Real Base Growth	M2 Growth	Real M2 Growth
1. 1948Q4–1953Q1 (1949Q4)[a]	−2[b]	(2)	(6)	−2	−2	1	0
2. 1953Q2–1957Q2 (1954Q2)	3	2	1	1	1	0	0
3. 1957Q3–1960Q1 (1958Q2)	1	0	0	−1	−1	−1	−1
4. 1960Q2–1969Q3 (1961Q1)	1	1	2	2	2	0	−1
5. 1969Q4–1973Q3 (1970Q4)	1	1	1	0	−2	1	1
6. 1973Q4–1979Q4 (1975Q1)	0	1	0	0	0	0	0
7. 1980Q1–1981Q2 (1980Q3)	3	0	0	−1	−1	−1	−1
8. 1981Q3–1990Q2 (1982Q4)	3	1	−1	0	1	0	0
9. 1990Q3–2000Q4 (1991Q1)	12	9	9	5	5	−1	0
10. 2001Q1–2007Q3 (2001Q4)	10	10	5	0	0	3	−1

SOURCE: Authors' calculations.

  [a] Numbers in parentheses are the NBER trough dates for each cycle.

  [b] Numbers in cells represent number of quarters after official NBER trough date that the series was determined to have turned. In the case of the policy variables, this was the date of initial tightening.

For the policy variables, the decision rule was to look for the first period in which there is evidence of monetary tightening. For the various interest rate series, this meant looking for the first quarter after the start of the recession in which interest rates started to increase from a period of falling or relatively level rates. For the monetary aggregate growth variables, we looked for the first quarter after the start of the recession in which the aggregate growth rates started to fall from a time of increasing growth rates or relatively constant growth rates.

Obviously this approach of visual inspection is a subjective approach to selecting turning points of time series, but in almost all cases, there was a clear-cut choice. In some cases, there seemed to be multiple periods close together that could be considered a turning point of a series. In these cases, we made sure to pick a turning point where there were at least two quarters on each side of the turning point where the time series was either always above or always below the level of the series, depending on the type of series being inspected. In the rare cases where there were multiple turning points that did not meet these criteria, we chose the turning point that was the highest or lowest point depending on the type of series. In the case of the policy variables, if there was any doubt about the turning point, we chose the turning point closest to the date of the turning point inferred by our reading of the historical narratives above.

Descriptive Evidence

Appendix Tables 5.A2A and 5.A2B display the dates of the turning points. In Tables 5.1 and 5.2, we present the timing of turning points of a data series as the number of quarters the turning point of the series occurred after the NBER trough (a minus sign indicates number of quarters before the trough).

Table 5.1 shows the timing of the turning points relative to the NBER trough of the policy variables and the macro aggregates for each cycle in the pre–World War II period (1920–1937). Table 5.2 shows the timing of the turning points relative to the NBER trough from the cycles from 1948 to 2007. In both tables, we also show the timing of tightening as discerned from the historical narratives above.

Pre–World War II: 1920–1937

In this narrative, we briefly describe the salient patterns of the policy indicators and the real aggregates and prices.

- *1920Q1–1923Q1; Trough 1921Q3.* In this cycle, the official discount rate tightened well after the trough, after the real aggregates, and after the

TABLE 5.2B   Descriptive Evidence Macro Aggregates, 1948–2007

Cycle	Inflation (GNP) (Price Level)	Inflation (CPI) (Price Level)	Real GNP	Industrial Production	Output Gap	Unemployment
1. 1948Q4–1953Q1 (1949Q4)[a]	0(1)[b]	−2(1)	0	−2	0	0
2. 1953Q2–1957Q2 (1954Q2)	0(−2)	1(2)	−1	−1	0	1
3. 1957Q3–1960Q1 (1958Q2)	−1	0	−1	−1	0	0
4. 1960Q2–1969Q3 (1961Q1)	−1	0	−1	−1	0	1
5. 1969Q4–1973Q3 (1970Q4)	−2	0	0	0	0	3
6. 1973Q4–1979Q4 (1975Q1)	0	0	0	0	0	1
7. 1980Q1–1981Q2 (1980Q3)	−1	−1	0	−1	0	0
8. 1981Q3–1990Q2 (1982Q4)	1	0	−1	0	0	0
9. 1990Q3–2000Q4 (1991Q1)	5	0	0	0	2	6
10. 2001Q1–2007Q3 (2001Q4)	−1	−1	−1	0	5	7

SOURCE: Authors' calculations.
  [a] Numbers in parentheses are the NBER trough dates for each cycle.
  [b] Numbers in cells represent number of quarters after official NBER trough date that the series was determined to have turned. In the case of the policy variables, this was the date of initial tightening.

price level turned up. Policy measured by the growth in the real monetary base and by real M2 also tightened after the NBER trough and after the real aggregates (real GNP, IP, the output gap, and unemployment) turned but before the price level increased. Thus, in this cycle, policy measured by real base growth was relatively well timed to prevent rising prices, but measured by the discount rate, the Fed was too late.

- *1923Q2–1926Q2; Trough 1924Q3.* In this cycle, monetary policy (both the official discount rate and the real rate in addition to real base growth) tightened after the real economy turned up and after the price level turned up. This suggests that policy was too late to prevent prices from rising.

- *1926Q3–1929Q2; Trough 1927Q4.* Monetary policy (with the exception of base growth) tightened when the real economy turned up and before the CPI price level (but after the GNP deflator) turned. This suggests that policy was more or less on time.
- *1929Q3–1937Q1; Trough 1933Q1.* The Great Contraction ended in March 1933. Policy tightened long after recovery began, based on the monetary aggregates. The Fed rarely changed its policy rates from 1934 to 1951, since it was subservient to the Treasury for most of this period and was committed to maintaining a low interest rate peg. This suggests that the nominal discount rate is not a good measure of the stance of policy. Significant tightening after this trough occurred in 1936, according to the narratives, when the Fed began doubling reserve requirements (although the monetary aggregates in Table 5.1 show minor slowdowns in 1933–34). The doubling of reserve requirements occurred after real economic activity and prices turned up, but well before output reached full capacity and while unemployment was still high. This episode is generally viewed as one where policy tightened too soon.

Post–World War II, 1948–2007

We omitted the two cycles containing the war years from the analysis. In these cycles—1937Q2–1944Q4; Trough 1938Q2 and 1945Q1–1948Q3; Trough 1945Q4—the timing of monetary policy changes seemed unconnected to the business cycle and occurred many years after the troughs. This made it difficult to analyze the timing of the exit from recession comparable to the peacetime cycles.

- *1948Q4–1953Q1; Trough 1949Q4.* In this first postwar cycle, the discount rate (nominal and real) tightened after the real economy recovered and after inflation (prices) turned up. Real and nominal base growth turned up before the real economy, with CPI, and before GNP inflation.
- *1953Q2–1957Q2; Trough 1954Q2.* Monetary policy measured by the federal funds rate (nominal and real) began tightening, not immediately after real GNP began to recover but when unemployment peaked.

Policy tightened after GNP inflation (prices) picked up but before the CPI. As measured by real base growth, monetary policy was too late for GNP inflation (prices) but just about on time for CPI inflation (prices). This suggests that, on average, monetary policy was close to being timely.

- *1957Q3–1960Q1; Trough 1958Q2.* Monetary policy measured by the federal funds rate (real and nominal) suggests that tightening occurred after the real economy turned but at the same time as unemployment and the output gap turned and before GNP inflation turned up. By this measure, policy was just right. Moreover, real base growth turned close to the real economy and before GNP inflation increased. Again, as in the preceding cycle, the timing of policy was, on average, close to being just right.

- *1960Q2–1969Q3; Trough 1961Q1.* Policy measured by the federal funds rate (nominal and real) turned up close to or after the real economy recovered. The case is similar for inflation. Real base growth turned up after the real economy troughed and after inflation turned up. This was the cycle in which inflation began to rise persistently as discussed above.

- *1969Q4–1973Q3; Trough 1970Q4.* Policy, using both rates and aggregates, tightened after the real economy recovered but was closer to the turning point in unemployment. Moreover, as has been the case in most cycles, policy was procyclical. In addition, policy using both rates and aggregates tightened after GNP inflation picked up. Monetary policy was clearly too late.

- *1973Q4–1979Q4; Trough 1975Q3.* Both measures of policy (the real and nominal funds rate and the nominal and real monetary base) tightened approximately when the real economy began to recover and when inflation turned up. Although the Fed timed its exit well, inflation was not substantially reduced.

- *1980Q1–1981Q2; Trough 1980Q3.* In this cycle, both measures of policy tightened close to when the economy began to recover and shortly after GNP inflation picked up. In this episode, as mentioned above, Fed tightening focusing on monetary aggregates was designed to break the back of inflationary expectations.

- *1981Q3–1990Q2; Trough 1982Q4.* Monetary policy measured by the real and nominal federal funds rate tightened about the time the real economy began to recover and when inflation turned up. A similar pattern holds for nominal and real base growth. Thus, on average, policy was well timed.
- *1990Q3–2000Q4; Trough 1991Q1.* Using the federal funds rate shows that policy tightened after unemployment peaked—six quarters after real activity began recovering. It also tightened after inflation resurged. Using real base growth as a policy measure leads to a similar outcome. Both policy indicators suggest that the Fed was focused on unemployment (the jobless recovery). With respect to stemming inflationary pressure, the Fed was too late.
- *2001Q1–2007Q3; Trough 2001Q4.* Using the nominal funds rate suggests that policy tightened well after GNP recovered and closer to when unemployment began recovering. Both measures tightened long after inflation picked up. These actions suggest that policy tightened too late. The timing of real base growth suggests that the Fed tightened after the real recovery and well before the peak in unemployment but after the turning point in inflation. Using this measure, policy was also too late.

Lessons from the Timing Exercise

The Pre–World War II Evidence

The first lesson is that the pre–World War II evidence suggests that the Fed was too late in tightening to offset incipient inflation more often than not. However, in two episodes (after the recessions of 1921 and 1927), the timing of the policy exit was much better. Second, the verdict on timing often differs between focusing on nominal and real base growth and focusing on the nominal and real discount rates. Meltzer (2003) provides evidence that real base growth is generally more closely lined up with the turning points in the business cycle than is the real discount rate. He also points out that Fed officials did not understand the distinction between nominal and real interest rates.

The Post–World War II Evidence

The first lesson is that, in the postwar cycles, the descriptive evidence suggests that policy was often too late by one measure or another to prevent inflation from rising. The Fed generally tightened when unemployment peaked and when the other real indicators troughed at roughly the same time. However, the recessions of the 1950s stand out as ones where the exit timing was favorable. Second, during the Great Inflation cycles of the 1960s and 1970s, the problem of mistiming the exits was less serious than the unwillingness to tighten sufficiently to stem inflationary pressures. This was not the case after the 1980 recession. Third, in the subsequent Great Moderation period from the mid-1980s to 2007, policy was too late in exiting in the last two cycles of the early 1990s and early 2000s. In each case, monetary policy only tightened when unemployment and the output gap declined, long after the recovery of real activity and a recovery in inflation. However, the Fed's actions in these cycles may reflect the fact that it felt it had achieved credibility for low inflation after its success in stemming inflationary expectations in the 1980s; hence, it felt it could afford to wait. In the last cycle, the Fed was concerned with deflation from 2002 to 2004, and for that reason was reluctant to tighten. The recent recession, with unemployment high, may be similar to the last two episodes in the timing of the exit from monetary ease.

Figure 5.1 summarizes the evidence on tightening in the post–World War II cycles. In each subfigure, the vertical axis shows the number of quarters that the two principal recession variables (unemployment and inflation) turned before the particular policy variable tightened. On the horizontal axis of each subfigure is the year in which the recession ended. A value of –1, for example, means that the recession variable turned one quarter before the Federal Reserve tightened. A positive number means that the variables turned after the policy variable tightened. In all subfigures the 0 line represents the quarter that the tightening occurred for the variable represented in the figure.

In Figure 5.1, we report the turning points of unemployment and inflation relative to the tightening dates of five important policy variables: a) the historical narratives, b) the nominal federal funds rate, c) the real

FIGURE 5.1 Comparison of Turning Points for Unemployment and Inflation with Tightening Dates

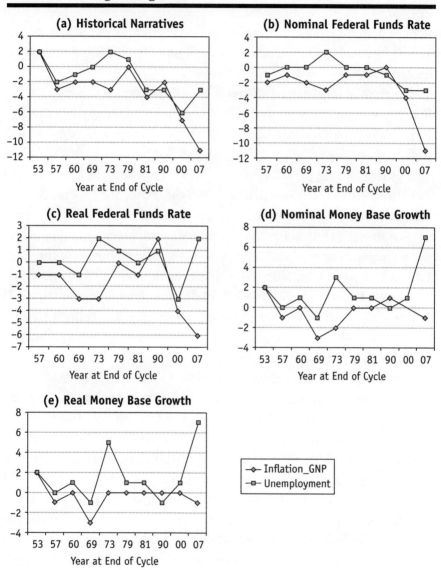

Source: Authors' calculations.

federal funds rate, d) the growth rate of the nominal money base, and e) the growth rate of the real money base. Except for the recession ending in 1990, the unemployment line is always above the inflation line, which implies that, except for that one recession, unemployment always turned after inflation. However, the relative position of the turning points to the date of tightening varies by policy variable.

For the historical narratives and the nominal federal funds rate (see the first two subfigures on the first row of Figure 5.1), the lines lie almost always below or on the zero line (the date that the policy variable tightened). According to the historical narratives, the Fed tightened after or on the date of the turning point of inflation for all but the recession ending in 1953. In the two recessions that ended in the 1970s, the Federal Reserve tightened before unemployment turned. Other than that, the narratives suggest that the Federal Reserve waited for unemployment to turn before tightening monetary policy. The second subfigure, which looks at the nominal federal funds rate, tells a similar story. The Federal Reserve waited until inflation and unemployment turned before tightening monetary policy. In one case, the most recent complete recession, the Federal Reserve waited a long time for unemployment to turn before tightening monetary policy. In only one case, the recession ending in 1973, did the federal funds rate increase before unemployment turned.

Using the real federal funds rate to identify the tightening date, we observe that, for the early cycles (that is, up until the cycle ending in 1969), the Fed waited for unemployment to turn. During the 1970s, the real federal funds rate tightened before unemployment and after inflation and again during the last complete post–World War II cycle.

For the other nominal policy variable—the growth rate of the monetary base—the pattern is not as obvious. It appears that, with respect to the monetary base, the Fed typically did not wait for unemployment to peak before tightening, but still often tightened after inflation turned up. This is most apparent for the last complete post–World War II recession, in which the tightening occurred seven quarters before unemployment turned, but one quarter after inflation turned.

Finally, looking at the growth rate of the real monetary base series, the pattern shows some similarity to that of the nominal monetary base, but there are two cycles (the cycles ending in 1973 and 2007) for which the real monetary base tightened well before unemployment turned. Also, policy usually tightened close to when unemployment turned, but before inflation turned, and tightening for inflation was often closer to the business cycle trough.

Figure 5.1 shows that across the different policy measures, policy typically tightened close to when unemployment peaked and close to when, but more often after, inflation turned up. This was most evident when we used either the tightening dates suggested by the historical narratives or ones suggested by the key policy variable (the federal funds rate). This highlights the conclusion that policy tightening was often too late to prevent inflation from rising.

Evidence from Simple Regression Analysis

The evidence presented in the section above relied on informally sifting through each recession and the historical narratives to categorize the recessions in our sample. In this section, we aim to use regression analysis to see if there are any systematic relationships between the turning points of the policy variables and the turning points of the recession variables.[3] There have been sixteen full recessions since 1920. As explained above, we do not include the two recessions between 1937Q2 and 1948Q3. Thus, we are left with fourteen recessions. Furthermore, we suspect that the post–World War II recessions may be different from the pre–World War II recessions, so for the postwar sample we are left with only ten recessions. Clearly, there are not enough observations to perform an extensive regression analysis. However, we believe there are enough observations to allow for any systematic relationships between the turning points in the policy variables and the turning points in the recession variables to appear in simple regression models.

In our analysis, we perform two types of regressions. The first is a simple linear regression that aims to see if there is a systematic relationship between the turning point of a policy variable and the turning point of an explanatory variable. For example, we would like to see if there is a relationship between the turning point in unemployment and the turning point in the main policy interest rate—the federal funds rate after 1954 and the nominal discount rate before 1954. For the policy variables, we measure the turning point as the first quarter after the start of the recession in which the Federal Reserve began to pursue tighter monetary policy. For the recession variables—that is, the variables that reflect the current state of the economy—we record the turning point as the first quarter after the start of the recession in which that variable started to improve. For example, in the case of unemployment, this would be the quarter in which the unemployment rate started to decline.

The regression analysis aims to see if there are systematic patterns between the turning points in the recession variables—the variables that reflect the current state of the economy—and the turning points (or the period of first tightening) of the policy variables. To do this, we estimate an equation like that presented in (1).

$$tp\_policy_i = \beta_0 + \beta_1 tp\_recession_i + \varepsilon_i. \tag{1}$$

In (1), the variable *tp_policy* consists of the turning (tightening) points for a policy variable of interest, such as the federal funds rate, for each recession in our sample. The explanatory variable *tp_recession* consists of the turning point of a recession variable. For both variables, the tightening and turning points are measured in the number of quarters after the official NBER trough date for that cycle.

If the recession variable does not influence the Federal Reserve's decision to tighten monetary policy, then we would not expect a relationship between the turning point of the recession variable and the turning point of the policy variable. In this case, we would expect an estimate of β_1 that was close to 0 and insignificant. If the Federal Reserve always waited for the recession variable to turn before tightening, then we would expect an estimate of β_1 that was positive and significant. An estimate of β_1 close to 1 would suggest that the Federal Reserve always tightened on or about the same quarter in which the recession variable turned. An estimate of β_1 much larger than 1 would suggest that the Federal Reserve always waited until after the recession variable had turned before it tightened the policy variable, and an estimate of 1 that was positive and less than 1 would suggest that the Federal Reserve would be influenced by the turning point of the recession variable, but would not always wait for that variable to turn before tightening the policy variable.

Obviously there may be more than one recession variable that the Federal Reserve watches, but given our small sample size, we are not able to estimate a fully specified model. Instead we estimate a number of versions of (1) with each policy variable regressed on each recession variable. Only if a recession variable is significant and positive for a majority of the policy variables do we suggest there is evidence of a systematic relationship between the recession variable and the Federal Reserve's decision to tighten. Tables 5.3 and 5.4 report the estimates of β_1 for each regression for each sample. Table 5.3 reports the estimates of β_1 from (1) for the post–World

TABLE 5.3   Estimates for Slope Coefficient in Equation (1) (Post–World War II Sample)

			Policy Variables				
Explanatory Variables	Narratives	Federal Funds	Real Federal Funds	Base Growth	Real Base Growth	M2 Growth	Real M2 Growth
Inflation (GNP)	1.480	1.240	−0.710	0.730	1.000	−0.190	0.080
	(0.610)	(0.400)	(0.340)	(0.270)	(0.120)	(0.200)	(0.120)
	[0.04]	[0.02]	[0.07]	[0.03]	[0.00]	[0.36]	[0.53]
Inflation (CPI)	1.200	1.000	−0.810	1.000	0.930	−0.500	0.190
	(1.210)	(1.290)	(1.770)	(0.390)	(0.720)	(0.500)	(0.310)
	[0.35]	[0.47]	[0.66]	[0.03]	[0.23]	[0.34]	[0.56]
Real GNP	−2.060	−0.330	−0.710	−1.100	−1.210	−0.260	0.620
	(2.590)	(1.610)	(1.650)	(0.980)	(1.220)	(0.820)	(0.460)
	[0.45]	[0.84]	[0.68]	[0.30]	[0.35]	[0.76]	[0.22]
Ind. prod.	2.180	3.510	−0.100	1.000	0.890	0.200	0.280
	(1.980)	(2.570)	(1.590)	(0.470)	(1.040)	(0.630)	(0.360)
	[0.30]	[0.21]	[0.95]	[0.07]	[0.42]	[0.75]	[0.46]
Output gap	2.190	2.100	1.370	0.350	0.340	0.480	−0.120
	(0.690)	(0.340)	(0.430)	(0.510)	(0.480)	(0.230)	(0.160)
	[0.01]	[0.00]	[0.02]	[0.51]	[0.50]	[0.07]	[0.47]
Unemployment	1.440	1.430	0.710	0.530	0.320	0.480	0.010
	(0.330)	(0.120)	(0.160)	(0.250)	(0.280)	(0.100)	(0.100)
	[0.00]	[0.00]	[0.00]	[0.07]	[0.30]	[0.00]	[0.91]

Source: Authors' calculations.

TABLE 5.4 Estimates for Slope Coefficient in Equation (1) (Full Sample)

Explanatory Variables		Policy Variables					
	Narratives	Policy Rate[a]	Real Policy Rate	Base Growth	Real Base Growth	M2 Growth	Real M2 Growth
Price level/ inflation[b] (GNP)	0.100 (0.40) [0.81]	0.840 (0.33) [0.03]	1.120 (0.45) [0.03]	0.660 (0.26) [0.03]	0.560 (0.25) [0.04]	−0.020 (0.20) [0.93]	0.150 (0.20) [0.45]
Price level/inflation (CPI)	−0.560 (1.02) [0.59]	0.630 (0.62) [0.33]	−0.160 (1.04) [0.88]	0.580 (0.57) [0.33]	−0.120 (0.54) [0.83]	0.460 (0.30) [0.15]	0.120 (0.37) [0.74]
Real GNP	−0.940 (1.22) [0.46]	−0.480 (1.03) [0.65]	1.990 (2.46) [0.44]	−1.070 (0.94) [0.28]	−0.240 (0.89) [0.79]	−0.850 (0.63) [0.20]	0.280 (0.62) [0.66]
Ind. prod.	1.020 (1.22) [0.42]	−0.370 (0.81) [0.65]	−0.500 (1.37) [0.72]	−0.340 (0.72) [0.65]	−0.180 (0.65) [0.79]	0.250 (0.45) [0.59]	−0.710 (0.43) [0.12]
Output gap	1.480 (0.54) [0.02]	1.930 (0.40) [0.00]	4.170 (0.50) [0.00]	−0.140 (0.41) [0.74]	0.090 (0.38) [0.82]	−0.750 (0.19) [0.00]	−0.300 (0.23) [0.21]
Unemployment	1.030 (0.34) [0.01]	0.990 (0.29) [0.01]	0.690 (0.32) [0.06]	−0.070 (0.21) [0.76]	−0.100 (0.19) [0.62]	0.450 (0.07) [0.00]	−0.270 (0.12) [0.05]

SOURCE: Authors' calculations.

[a] The policy rate is the federal funds rate after 1954 and the discount rate before 1954.

[b] For cycles up to and including the one ending in 1957Q2, the turning point used is for the price level. For recessions after 1957Q2, the turning point for inflation is used.

War II sample. Table 5.4 reports the estimates of β_1 from (1) for the whole sample excluding the two cycles around World War II.[4]

Because of the small samples (ten observations for the post–World War II sample and fourteen for the whole sample), the least squares estimates of (1) are likely to be highly sensitive to outliers and influential observations. To mitigate this problem, a robust estimator was used to estimate (1). The robust estimator used was an iteratively reweighted least squares procedure found in Holland and Welsch (1977).[5] This estimator is robust to those observations whose ordinary least squares (OLS) residuals are large.

As discussed above, we do not have enough observations to estimate a fully specified version of (1). The second approach we take is to estimate (1) for different policy variables in a system. The utility of the system estimator is to increase the effective sample size, which will allow the inclusion of more than one recession variable in the estimation of (1). To get the increase in effective sample size, we impose equality constraints on the slope coefficients while allowing the constants to differ across equations. We also take into account any correlation between the errors of the equations by estimating the system using a one-step feasible generalized least squares (GLS) estimator. The system estimated is:

$$y_{1i} = \beta_{10} + \beta_1 X_{1i} + \cdots + \beta_{ki} X_{ki} + \varepsilon_{1i}$$
$$\vdots \tag{2}$$
$$y_{ni} = \beta_{n0} + \beta_1 X_{1i} + \cdots + \beta_{ki} X_{ki} + \varepsilon_{ni},$$

where $E(\varepsilon\varepsilon') = \begin{bmatrix} \sigma_1^2 \cdots \sigma_{1n} \\ \vdots \ddots \vdots \\ \sigma_{n1} \cdots \sigma_n^2 \end{bmatrix}$ and $\sigma_{ij} \neq 0$ for all i and j. In (2) the variable y_i

is the tightening point of policy variable i, and the variable x_i is the turning point of the recession variable j.

The systems estimates are reported for post–World War II samples and for the whole sample in Tables 5.5 and 5.6. The systems are chosen so the dependent variables are similar in nature. Thus, nominal policy variables such as the growth rate of the nominal money base would be included with the growth rate of nominal M2 and the nominal policy interest rate (the federal funds rate after 1954 and the nominal discount rate before 1954). Real variables will be included with other real variables.

We must emphasize that the aim of this exercise is not to identify any causal relationships between any of the recession variables and the decision to tighten; rather we aim to find evidence of any systematic relationship between when the Federal Reserve tightened and when some or all of the recession variables turned. Our hope is that this exercise will sharpen our analysis and give us the ability to predict when the Federal Reserve will start to tighten during the current business cycle.

Lessons from the Individual Regressions

The Post–World War II Period

Table 5.3 reports the results for the estimation of equation (1) using a robust estimator. The point estimates, the standard errors (in round brackets), and the p-values (in square brackets) are reported for all the combinations of policy and recession variables used in our analysis.[6] The slope coefficients reported in Tables 5.3 and 5.4 can be interpreted as the expected change in the time it takes for the Fed to tighten the particular dependent variable, given a one-quarter increase in the turning point of the explanatory variable from the NBER recession trough. The results suggest that three variables—GNP inflation, the output gap, and unemployment—appear to affect the decision to tighten.

Unemployment appears to delay the date at which the Fed tightens when we use the dates extracted from the narratives, the main policy rate (the federal funds rate), the real policy rate, and the rate of growth of the money base. The coefficients on unemployment are all positive, suggesting that the longer it takes for unemployment to start declining, the longer it takes the Fed to tighten.

TABLE 5.5   Estimates for Slope Coefficient in Equation (2) (Post–World War II)

Variable	{Narr, FFR}		{FFR, Base}		{Real FFR, Real Base}	
Inflation (GNP)	0.89	0.60	0.71	0.51	0.87	0.74
	(0.1)	(0.1)	(0.1)	(0.0)	(0.1)	(0.1)
	[0.0]	[0.0]	[0.0]	[0.0]	[0.0]	[0.0]
Output gap	1.85	0.76	0.99	−0.18	0.58	−0.65
	(0.1)	(0.3)	(0.1)	(0.4)	(0.1)	(0.6)
	[0.0]	[0.05]	[0.00]	[0.70]	[0.00]	[0.32]
Unemployment	1.20	0.94	0.72	0.97	0.46	1.03
	(0.14)	(0.22)	(0.08)	(0.30)	(0.12)	(0.41)
	[0.00]	[0.00]	[0.00]	[0.00]	[0.00]	[0.02]

Source: Author's calculations.

The other macroeconomic aggregate that consistently affects policy variables is the output gap. The slope coefficient of equation (1), when output gap is used as the explanatory variable, is significant and positive for the turning points identified from the narratives, the policy rate, and the real policy rate. Unlike unemployment, however, the output gap does not significantly affect money base growth. Both the output gap and unemployment also positively affect M2 growth.

The other real macroeconomic aggregates, real GNP and industrial production, do not affect the policy variables except that industrial production does have a significant effect on the rate of growth of the money base. Thus, it appears that the only real variables that consistently affect a majority of the policy variables are unemployment and the output gap.

We also looked at the effect the price level and inflation had on the decision to tighten. From Table 5.3 we see that inflation constructed from the GNP deflator has a significant and positive effect on all the policy variables except for M2 growth and real M2 growth. GNP inflation is the only variable that significantly affects growth of the real money base. While inflation is significant, it presents troubling results. The slope coefficient for inflation when the real federal funds rate is used as the dependent

TABLE 5.6 Estimates for Slope Coefficient in Equation (2) (Full Sample)

Variable	{Narr, Policy Rate}		{Policy Rate, Base}		{Real Policy Rate, Real Base}	
Price level/	0.90	0.85	0.78	0.76	0.85	0.95
inflation (GNP)	(0.46)	(0.54)	(0.26)	(0.23)	(0.25)	(0.25)
	[0.06]	[0.13]	[0.00]	[0.00]	[0.00]	[0.00]
Output gap	1.48	2.80	0.61	1.14	0.33	1.46
	(0.59)	(0.99)	(0.34)	(0.70)	(0.33)	(0.64)
	[0.02]	[0.01]	[0.08]	[0.11]	[0.32]	[0.03]
Unemployment	0.22	−0.90	0.06	−0.37	−0.16	−0.58
	(0.37)	(0.62)	(0.15)	(0.37)	(0.16)	(0.31)
	[0.56]	[0.13]	[0.68]	[0.32]	[0.32]	[0.08]

Source: Authors' calculations.

variable in equation (1) is negative. Further inspection of the data used to estimate equation (1) shows that there is one observation that is treated by the robust estimator as an outlier. Unfortunately, this observation, while statistically an outlier, is actually a useful piece of information. The observation taken during the recession from 1990Q3 to 2000Q4 causes this problem. In this recession, inflation turned five quarters after the NBER trough date, and the real federal funds rate turned eight quarters after the NBER trough date. This observation falls in line with our previous belief that the Fed would wait to tighten after it observes inflation starting to increase. Taking this observation out of the regression leads to a negative coefficient, while leaving it in and giving it equal weight (that is, using OLS) gives us a positive and significant coefficient. This suggests that the negative coefficient we have estimated is more a function of our statistical procedure and the fact that we have small samples than an actual relationship.

Thus, from the post–World War II sample, there appears to be a systematic, positive relationship between the length of time it takes for inflation to increase, for the output gap to increase, or for the unemployment rate to decrease and the length of time the Fed waits to tighten. However, it is difficult to draw any inferences from the actual size of the coefficients as reported, as our sample sizes are small. We are not able to include these variables in a regression equation at the same time. Clearly the estimates are going to suffer from omitted variable bias, so at present we do not know which variables are more important than others. We attempt to find a solution for this problem by using the system estimator given in equation (2). Before reporting the system estimates for the post–World War II period, we first need to check if the relationship we found extends back to the interwar period.

Full Sample

Table 5.4 reports the estimates of the slope coefficients for equation (1) using the larger sample that includes the business cycles from the interwar period. There is a problem in that the main policy rate used after World War II—the federal funds rate—did not exist before 1954. Before 1954, the Fed used the discount rate. However, the discount rate did not change much during the 1930s and was not the main instrument for monetary policy then. To estimate a model for the whole period, we needed to construct a number of composite variables.

The first variable constructed was a composite policy rate variable. This variable was made up of the turning points for the federal funds rate after 1954 and the turning points for the discount rate before 1954. However, after the recession of 1929Q3–1937Q1, the discount rate became ineffective in the face of expected deflation and was not changed after 1933. For that period, we used the turning point from the narratives. The second composite variable that we constructed was the composite price level/inflation variable. This reflects the fact that, before the 1960s, inflation in the United States was not persistent and the Fed was primarily concerned with monitoring the price level. It was only after the recession ending in 1957Q2 that inflation became important. Thus, the composite price level/inflation variable consists of turning points for the price level up to the recession ending in 1957Q2, and thereafter consists of the turning points of inflation.

The results are strikingly similar to the results we obtained for the post–World War II period. The output gap and the unemployment rate are significant and positive for the whole period, and the only change is that now these two variables no longer significantly affect the growth of the money base. The composite price level/inflation variable significantly and positively affects the policy rate, the real policy rate, the growth of the money base, and the growth of the real money base. It is interesting to note that when the sample is slightly increased, the effect of the price level/ inflation rate is no longer negative on the real policy rate. This further strengthens our contention that the inflation rate also has a positive and significant effect on the real policy rate in the post–World War II period.

The conclusion of all these individual regressions is that there is a significant and positive relationship between the output gap, unemployment, and the price level/inflation rate and the length of time it takes for the Fed to tighten after a recession. As noted earlier, however, the sample size and the fact that all these results are from simple linear regressions did not allow us to judge the relative importance of each variable. In the next section, we report system estimates that allowed us to include more than one variable at a time in our regression. We also must note that the output gap variable and the unemployment rate variable are highly correlated, so the results we obtained in Table 5.3 for either variable may be picking up the same effect. The only way we can check which variable is important is to include them both in the same regression. We do that using the system estimator described in (2).

Lessons from the System Regressions

Tables 5.5 and 5.6 report the results for equation (2), where a system of seemingly unrelated equations is estimated. The tables report results for a number of different systems: the turning points from the narratives, the turning points from the federal funds rate, the nominal variables (the federal funds rate and the rate of growth of the money base), and the real variables (the real federal funds rate and the rate of growth of the real money base).

Post–World War II Sample

For each system, three separate equations are estimated: one with inflation and the output gap, one with inflation and unemployment, and one with the output gap and unemployment. The first thing to notice from Table 5.5 is that the estimate on inflation ranges from 0.51 to 0.89 with the median value of 0.73. The estimates on the other variable in the equation with inflation included are significant and significantly higher than the estimates for inflation for the systems based on the nominal variables, suggesting that more emphasis is placed on the real side of the economy in the post–World War II period when setting the nominal variables. Given that the output gap and unemployment are highly correlated (a correlation of 0.88 in the postwar sample), it is uncertain whether these variables are picking up the same information. To find out, a third regression is run with both unemployment and output gap included. We see that unemployment is always significant in these regressions, with output gap only significant in the system with the turning point constructed from the narratives and the federal funds rate. Even in this system, the coefficient on the output gap is smaller than unemployment. These results together suggest that unemployment and inflation were the important variables that the Fed watched in the postwar period.

The Full Sample

Table 5.6 contains the results for the full sample using the composite variables used in the individual analysis. The results for the output gap and unemployment in the full sample are not as robust as in the post–World War II sample. One striking result is that, for the full sample, the coefficients on the price level/inflation variable are now higher than in the postwar sample. The estimates range from 0.76 to 0.95 with a median estimate of 0.85. This suggests that if we had enough data to estimate the interwar period separately from the postwar period, the coefficient on price level/inflation would be higher than in the postwar period. A tentative conclusion is that the Fed was more sensitive to the aggregate price level during the interwar period than in the postwar period.

However, the results for the output gap and the unemployment rate are not as consistent as in the postwar period. Again, a tentative conclusion is that the Fed has emphasized the real side of the economy more after World War II than it did before or during the interwar period. There is evidence that the Fed did take into account the real side before World War II, but that it was the output gap and not the unemployment rate that was important.

Thus, our results suggest that the real side played a more significant role after World War II. Our results also indicate that inflation (or price level before the war) is important for both periods, with some evidence suggesting that there is less emphasis on prices after World War II than during the interwar period.

Predictions for the Most Recent Recession

Given our estimates for (1) and (2), we are now interested in predicting, based on current data, the dates of tightening for each of the important policy variables. The policy variables we make predictions for are the tightening date based on the historical narratives, the tightening date for the federal funds rate, the tightening date for the real federal funds rate, the tightening date for the growth rate of the money base, and the tightening date for the rate of growth of the real money base. Table 5.7 contains the predictions based on our estimate of the tightening dates using inflation, output gap,

TABLE 5.7   Predicted Tightening Dates (Quarters after 2009Q2)

Variable	Narratives	Federal Funds Rate	Real Federal Funds Rate	Base Growth	Real Base Growth
Inflation (GNP)	4.52	2.94	−0.44	1.37	1.00
Output gap	1.78	1.02	0.41	0.38	0.27
Unemployment	3.65	2.99	1.25	0.35	0.43
{Inf, Out Gap}	3.22	2.23			
{Inf, Unemp.}	4.24	3.24			
{Out Gap, Unemp.}	3.08	2.08			
{Inf, Out Gap}		2.71		0.60	
{Inf, Unemp.}		3.21		1.10	
{Out Gap, Unemp.}		2.81		0.70	
{Inf, Out Gap}			2.31		0.98
{Inf, Unemp.}			2.58		1.25
{Out Gap, Unemp.}			2.28		0.95

Source: Authors' calculations.
Notes: These predictions are based on predicted turning points for inflation, the output gap, and unemployment of 1, 0, and 2, respectively.

and unemployment as our predictors. The National Bureau of Economic Research has determined that the most recent recession ended in June of 2009, so we use 2009Q2 as the trough date of the current business cycle.

To predict the tightening dates, we need predictions of the turning points for these three predictor series. Figures 5.2 through 5.4 show the values of these three variables for the most recent cycle. Figure 5.2 reports the value for the inflation rate based on the GNP deflator. It is quite clear from this figure that inflation, measured using the GNP deflator, turned during the third quarter of 2009. Thus, we will use 2009Q3 as the turning point for inflation. We label this one quarter after the trough date. Figure 5.3 shows the output gap measured as the percentage deviation from the Hodrick-Prescott filter trend of log real output. It appears that the output gap turned in the second quarter of 2009, so we use 0 as the turning point for the output gap (measured relative to the business cycle trough date). Figure 5.4 shows the unemployment rate for the most recent cycle.

FIGURE 5.2 Inflation Rate for 2007–2011

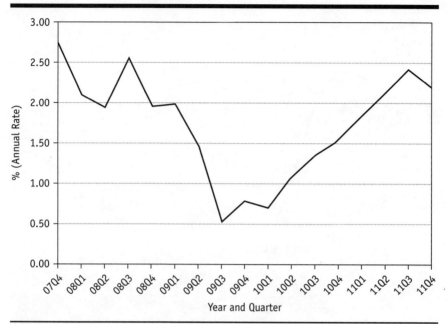

Source: Federal Reserve Economic Database.

Unemployment appears to have peaked in the fourth quarter of 2009, although the decline from the peak appears to be slow. For unemployment we use Figure 5.2 for our prediction. Unemployment is the only variable of the three that we follow for which the recovery after the turning point is not sharp. Thus there may be some doubt as to whether unemployment has indeed turned or instead has plateaued. This may lead to some policy uncertainty if, as we showed above, policy makers have put more emphasis on unemployment in the more recent exits.

These turning points were used to generate the predicted tightening dates for the various policy variables. The predicted tightening dates for the federal funds rate using the individual regressions reflect the differences in turning points in the predictors. Using inflation or unemployment, we get predicted tightening dates for the nominal federal funds rate or the narrative rate between three and four and a half quarters after the trough date, suggesting Fed tightening sometime in late 2010. Using the systems

FIGURE 5.3   Output Gap for 2007–2011

SOURCE: Federal Reserve Economic Database.

estimates, a similar and consistent picture emerges. The predicted tightening dates for these models range from two quarters after the trough date to just over four quarters after the trough date. The predicted tightening dates for the growth of the monetary base and real monetary base are slightly earlier, with tightening predicted to occur approximately two quarters after the trough date (2009Q2). This reflects the observation that the monetary base has typically tightened earlier than the nominal policy rates over the post–World War II sample.

Obviously our predictions, which are based on past observations, have not turned out to be accurate. As of May 2012, the Fed has not officially tightened. One reason for this might be that unemployment has not declined enough for the Fed to be comfortable enough to start tightening. The experience of the previous two exits suggests that the Fed has waited for unemployment to fall before moving to tighten. Another reason could be that the optimum value of the federal funds rate is negative so that we

FIGURE 5.4   Unemployment Rate for 2007–2011

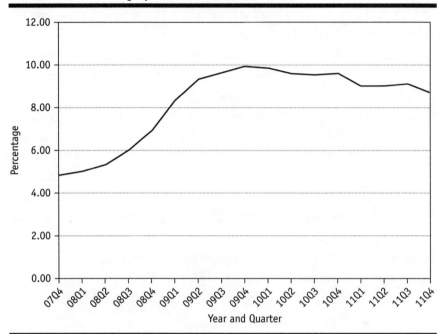

SOURCE: Federal Reserve Economic Database.

cannot observe a tightening of this variable yet; we have to wait for the optimal federal funds rate to become positive before we will see evidence of tightening. In fact, the nonstandard monetary policy that the Fed has pursued since 2007 can be viewed as being equivalent to cutting the federal funds rate. The lack of a third round of quantitative easing and the rolling back of positions may, as some Fed officials have argued, constitute a tightening of the implicit federal funds rate. In time we may look back at the narratives of this period and see that tightening may already have begun, just that tightening did not manifest itself as an increase in the federal funds rate.

Conclusion

This chapter presents historical narrative, descriptive, and econometric evidence on the timing of monetary policy in the United States over fourteen business cycles from 1920 to 2007. We evaluate the monetary exits with respect to the turning points of principal macro aggregates (especially unemployment and inflation).

In general, we found that monetary policy tightens close to when unemployment peaks and when inflation troughs, but that the timing is usually dominated by unemployment. We also find that, on a number of occasions, monetary policy measured by the monetary base (real and nominal) shows a different pattern than the official policy interest rates.

We found that the timing evidence differed between the interwar period (and in some ways the 1950s) and the postwar period in a number of respects: First, inflation was not persistent in the interwar period (or until the 1960s), so the measure of price stability that mattered most was the price level. In the 1920s and 1950s, policy tightened when the price level began to rise. Second, in the 1920s and 1950s, tightening occurred when prices rose and before unemployment peaked. We found a few episodes where tightening occurred before recessions ended, suggesting that the Fed was following countercyclical policy.

Beginning in the mid-1960s, inflation increased and became persistent for close to twenty years. In those cycles, the timing of the tightening does not show that the pace of tightening was not sufficient to reduce the rising trend in inflation. Although inflation was reduced significantly beginning with the Great Moderation, the timing of policy tightening still favored unemployment.

There are several possible reasons for these patterns: First, in the interwar period, the Fed followed gold-standard orthodoxy, which placed primary importance on price stability. Second, after World War II and the Employment Act of 1945, the Fed followed a dual mandate for price stability and high employment. Third, beginning in the 1960s, the Fed adhered to Keynesian theories and the Phillips Curve, which attached primary importance to low unemployment over low inflation. Fourth, the dominance of unemployment in the timing of tightening in the postwar era reflects, in addition to the influence of Keynesian theory, political pressure by Congress and the administration not to tighten while unemployment was unacceptably high. Fifth, even in the Great Moderation, when inflation had been significantly reduced and considerable emphasis had been placed on the importance of a credible nominal anchor, the timing of exits favored unemployment. This was evident in the last two cycles. In both cases of jobless recoveries, political pressure may have been important.

How will the exit strategy play out for the current cycle? The evidence suggests that were the timing patterns of the postwar era followed in the current cycle, with unemployment peaking in the fourth quarter of 2009, then we should have seen a tightening in the first half of 2010. This did not happen, and there is little evidence that policy will change any time soon. The experience since 2010 is consistent with the view that the Fed has attached top priority to the unemployment part of the dual mandate. It has felt justified in doing so because measures of the core inflation rate have been below their 2 percent implicit target rate. It also may be responding to political pressure to fight unemployment. If, as some have argued, incipient inflationary pressure observant in global commodity markets and reflecting past monetary expansion leads to a run-up in headline inflation and in inflationary expectations, then the Fed will have waited too late to tighten. Only the future will tell if its current strategy is correct.

Appendix

TABLE 5.A1   Data Definitions

Variable	Source
Discount rate	Obtained from the Board of Governors database (H.15). Before 1954, the discount rate is the Federal Reserve Bank of New York discount rate. The discount rate series is discounted after 2002, and the discount window primary credit rate is used after 2002. Monthly data converted to quarterly data using quarterly averages.
Federal funds rate	Effective federal funds rate (FEDFUNDS): Obtained from Federal Reserve Bank of St. Louis database (FRED).[a] Monthly data converted to quarterly data using quarterly averages. Real rate obtained by subtracting inflation rate (computed using GNP deflator).

(continued)

TABLE 5.A1 (*continued*)

Money base	St. Louis Adjusted Monetary Base (AMBSL seasonally adjusted): obtained from FRED. Monthly data converted to quarterly data using quarterly averages. Real rate obtained by dividing by GNP deflator. Growth rates are one-quarter growth rates expressed as an annualized rate.
M2	M2 from Balke and Gordon (1986) until 1983. After 1983 used M2 series from FRED database (seasonally adjusted, M2SL). Monthly data converted to quarterly data using quarterly averages. The two series were spliced at join. Real data obtained by dividing by GNP deflator. Growth rates are one-quarter growth rates expressed as an annualized rate.
Price level (GNP)	GNP deflator obtained from Balke and Gordon (1986) until 1983. After that, used GNP deflator from FRED database (seasonally adjusted, GNPDEF). The two series were spliced at join.
Price level (CPI)	Consumer price index for all urban consumers: all items. Obtained from FRED database (CPIAUCNS). Monthly data converted to quarterly data using quarterly averages.
Inflation (GNP)	Percentage one-quarter change in GNP deflator expressed at an annualized rate.
Inflation (CPI)	Percentage one-quarter change in CPI expressed at an annualized rate.
Real GNP	Real gross national product obtained from Balke and Gordon (1986) for periods until 1983. After that, used quarterly GNP data from FRED database (GNP). GNP price deflator from FRED spliced with Balke and Gordon (1986) price deflator. Real GNP after 1983 is nominal GNP divided by spliced GNP deflator series.
Industrial production	Obtained from FRED database (INDPRO). Monthly series converted to quarterly series using quarterly averages.
Unemployment	Obtained from Bureau of Labor Statistics. Unemployment rate: civilian labor force (LNS14000000, seasonally adjusted). Monthly data converted to quarterly data using quarterly averages.
Output gap	Proportional deviation of real GNP from long-run trend. Computed as the deviations of the logarithm of real GNP from its long-run trend as computed using Hodrick-Prescott filter with smoothing parameter $\lambda = 1600$.

[a] http://research.stlouisfed.org/fred2/

TABLE 5.A2A Turning Dates: Policy Variables, 1920–1937

Cycle	Narratives	Discount Rate	Real Discount Rate	Base Growth	Real Base Growth	M2 Growth	Real M2 Growth
1. 20Q1–23Q1 (1921Q3)[a]	1922Q2	1922Q4	—	1922Q4	1921Q4	1922Q1	1922Q1
2. 23Q2–26Q2 (1924Q3)	1925Q2	1924Q4	1925Q1	1924Q3	1925Q1	1924Q2	1925Q1
3. 26Q3–29Q2 (1927Q4)	1928Q1	1927Q4	1927Q4	1928Q1	1927Q4	1927Q4	1927Q4
4. 29Q3–37Q1 (1933Q1)	1936Q3	—	—	1933Q4	1933Q4	1932Q3	1934Q1

[a] Dates in parentheses are the NBER trough dates for each cycle. Missing values represent a cycle in which no definitive turning point was identified.

TABLE 5.A2B Turning Dates: Macro Aggregates, 1920–1937

Cycle	Price Level (GNP Deflator)	Price Level (CPI)	Real GNP	Industrial Production	Output Gap	Unemployment
1. 20Q1–23Q1 (1921Q3)[a]	1922Q2	1922Q1	1921Q1	1921Q1	1921Q1	1921Q1
2. 23Q2–26Q2 (1924Q3)	1924Q3	1924Q1	1924Q3	1924Q2	1924Q3	1924Q1
3. 26Q3–29Q2 (1927Q4)	1927Q2	1928Q1	1927Q4	1927Q4	1927Q4	1928Q1
4. 29Q3–37Q1 (1933Q1)	1933Q1	1933Q1	1933Q1	1933Q1	1933Q1	1932Q1

[a] Dates in parentheses are the NBER trough dates for each cycle.

TABLE 5.A3A   Turning Dates: Policy Variables, 1948–2007

Cycle	Narratives	Federal Funds Rate (Discount Rate)	Real Federal Funds Rate (Real Discount Rate)	Base Growth	Real Base Growth	M2 Growth	Real M2 Growth
1. 48Q4–53Q1 (1949Q4)[a]	1949Q2	(1950Q2)	(1951Q1)	1949Q2	1949Q2	1950Q1	1949Q4
2. 53Q2–57Q2 (1954Q2)	1955Q1	1954Q4	1954Q3	1954Q3	1954Q3	1954Q2	1954Q2
3. 57Q3–60Q1 (1958Q2)	1958Q3	1958Q2	1958Q2	1958Q1	1958Q1	1958Q1	1958Q1
4. 60Q2–69Q3 (1961Q1)	1961Q2	1961Q2	1961Q3	1961Q3	1961Q3	1961Q1	1960Q4
5. 69Q4–73Q3 (1970Q4)	1971Q1	1971Q1	1971Q1	1970Q4	1970Q2	1971Q1	1971Q1
6. 73Q4–79Q4 (1975Q1)	1975Q1	1975Q2	1975Q1	1975Q1	1975Q1	1975Q1	1975Q1
7. 80Q1–81Q2 (1980Q3)	1981Q2	1980Q3	1980Q3	1980Q2	1980Q2	1980Q2	1980Q2
8. 81Q3–90Q2 (1982Q4)	1983Q3	1983Q1	1982Q3	1982Q4	1983Q1	1982Q4	1982Q4
9. 90Q3–00Q4 (1991Q1)	1994Q1	1993Q2	1993Q2	1992Q2	1992Q2	1990Q4	1991Q1
10. 01Q1–07Q3 (2001Q4)	2004Q2	2004Q2	2003Q1	2001Q4	2001Q4	2002Q3	2001Q3

[a] Dates in parentheses are the NBER trough dates for each cyle.

TABLE 5.A3B   Turning Dates: Macro Aggregates, 1948–2007

Cycle	Inflation (GNP) (Price Level)	Inflation (CPI) (Price Level)	Real GNP	Industrial Production	Output Gap	Unemployment
1. 48Q4–53Q1 (1949Q4)[a]	1949Q4 (1950Q1)	1949Q2 (1950Q1)	1949Q4	1949Q2	1949Q4	1949Q4
2. 53Q2–57Q2 (1954Q2)	1954Q2 (1953Q4)	1954Q3 (1954Q4)	1954Q1	1954Q1	1954Q2	1954Q3

TABLE 5.A3B (*continued*)

Cycle	Inflation (GNP) (Price Level)	Inflation (CPI) (Price Level)	Real GNP	Industrial Production	Output Gap	Unemployment
3. 57Q3–60Q1 (1958Q2)	1958Q1	1958Q2	1958Q1	1958Q1	1958Q2	1958Q2
4. 60Q2–69Q3 (1961Q1)	1960Q4	1961Q1	1960Q4	1960Q4	1961Q1	1961Q2
5. 69Q4–73Q3 (1970Q4)	1970Q2	1970Q4	1970Q4	1970Q4	1970Q4	1971Q3
6. 73Q4–79Q4 (1975Q1)	1975Q1	1975Q1	1975Q1	1975Q1	1975Q1	1975Q2
7. 80Q1–81Q2 (1980Q3)	1980Q2	1980Q2	1980Q3	1980Q2	1980Q3	1980Q3
8. 81Q3–90Q2 (1982Q4)	1983Q1	1982Q4	1982Q3	1982Q4	1982Q4	1982Q4
9. 90Q3–00Q4 (1991Q1)	1984Q1	1991Q1	1991Q1	1991Q1	1991Q3	1984Q2
10. 01Q1–07Q3 (2001Q4)	2001Q3	2001Q3	2001Q3	2001Q4	2003Q1	2003Q7

[a] Dates in parentheses are the NBER trough dates for each cycle.

Notes

1. Friedman (1953) was the first to analyze the difficulty of achieving the pace and timing for successful countercyclical policy.

2. The Fed did not have GNP or unemployment data during the interwar period (these data were constructed after World War II). Moreover, it did not think about recessions in terms of output gaps. It did, however, have data on industrial production. Nevertheless, we use the available modern data on GNP and unemployment to make comparisons between the post–World War II era and the interwar period.

3. By recession variables, we mean those variables that depict the turning point of the recession to expansions. These variables are the real variables (output, industrial production, unemployment, output gap) and the price/inflation variables.

4. The omitted cycles are 1937Q2–1944Q4 and 1945Q1–1948Q3.

5. The weight function used in the iteratively reweighted least squares procedure was the "biweight" weight function. The *robustfit* command of Matlab's Statistics Toolbox was used to implement the robust estimation procedure used in this chapter.

6. We also looked at financial variables such as the term spread, the quality spread, and the return to the S&P500 but did not find any systematic relationship between the policy variable turning points and the financial variables. We do not report these results here, for the sake of brevity. These results are available from the authors upon request.

References

Balke, Nathan S., and Robert J. Gordon. 1986. "Historical Data (Appendix B)." Vol. 25 of *The American Business Cycle: Continuity and Change*, edited by Robert J. Gordon. Chicago: University of Chicago Press.

Bernanke, Ben S., and Cara S. Lown. 1991. "The Credit Crunch." *Brookings Papers on Economic Activity*, no. 2: 205–247.

Bordo, Michael, and Barry Eichengreen. 2008. "Bretton Woods and the Great Inflation." NBER Working Paper 14532.

Bordo, Michael, Christopher Erceg, Andrew Levin, and Ryan Michaels. 2007. "Three Great American Disinflations." NBER Working Paper 12982.

Bordo, Michael, and Joseph Haubrich. 2009. "Credit Crises, Money, and Contractions: An Historical View." NBER Working Paper 15389.

———. 2012. "Deep Recessions, Fast Recoveries, and Financial Crises: Evidence from the American Record." Rutgers University (mimeo). May.

Claessens, Stijn, M. Ayhan Kose, and Marco Terrones. 2008. "What Happens during Recessions, Crunches, and Busts?" IMF Working Paper 08/274.

Cole, Hal, and Lee Ohanian. 2004. "New Deal Policies and the Persistence of the Great Depression: A General Equilibrium Analysis." *Journal of Political Economy* 112(4): 779–816.

Eggertsson, Gautti. 2008. "Great Expectations and the End of the Depression." *American Economic Review* 94(4): 1476–1516.

Friedman, Milton. 1953. "The Effects of a Full Employment Policy on Economic Stability: A Formal Analysis." In *Essays in Positive Economics*. Chicago: University of Chicago Press.

Friedman, Milton, and Anna J. Schwartz. 1963. *A Monetary History of the United States: 1867 to 1960*. Princeton: Princeton University Press.

Hetzel, Robert. 2008. *The Monetary Policy of the Federal Reserve: A History*. New York: Cambridge University Press.

Holland, Paul W., and Roy E. Welsch. 1977. "Robust Regression Using Iteratively Reweighted Least-Squares." *Communications in Statistics: Theory and Methods*, A6, 813–827.

International Monetary Fund. 2008. *World Economic Outlook.*

Meltzer, Allan H. 2003. *A History of the Federal Reserve, Volume I: 1913–1951.* Chicago: University of Chicago Press.

———. 2010. *A History of the Federal Reserve, Volume II: 1951–1987.* Chicago: University of Chicago Press.

Mussa, Michael. 2009. "Global Economic Prospects as of September 2009: Onward to Global Recovery." Washington, DC: Peterson Institute. September.

Reinhart, Carmen, and Kenneth S. Rogoff. 2009. *This Time Is Different: Eight Centuries of Financial Folly.* Princeton: Princeton University Press.

Romer, Christina. 1992. "What Ended the Great Depression?" *Journal of Economic History* 52 (December): 757–784.

Romer, Christina, and David Romer. 1994. "Monetary Policy Matters." *Journal of Monetary Economics* 34 (August): 75–88.

Stock, James, and Mark Watson. 2012. "Disentangling the Channels of the 2007–2009 Recession." NBER Working Paper 18094. May.

CHAPTER 6

Deep Recessions, Fast Recoveries, and Financial Crises

Evidence from the American Record

MICHAEL D. BORDO AND JOSEPH G. HAUBRICH

I. Introduction

THE RECOVERY FROM THE RECENT recession has now been proceeding for over 7 years. Many argue that this recovery is unusually sluggish and that this reflects the severity of the financial crisis of 2007–2008 (Reinhart and Rogoff 2009; Roubini 2009). Yet if this is the case, it appears to fly in the face of the record of U.S. business cycles in the past century and a half. Indeed, Milton Friedman noted as far back as 1964 that in the American historical record "A large contraction in output tends to be followed on the average by a large business expansion; a mild contraction, by a mild expansion" (Friedman 1969, 273). Much work since then has confirmed this stylized fact but has also begun to make distinctions between cycles, particularly between those that include a financial crisis. Zarnowitz (1992) documented that pre-World War II recessions accompanied by banking panics tended to be more severe than average recessions and that they tended to be followed by rapid recoveries.

Originally published in "Deep Recessions, Fast Recoveries, and Financial Crises: Evidence from the American Record," *Economic Inquiry* 55, no. 1 (January 2016): 527–41.

In this chapter, we revisit the issue of whether business cycles with financial crises are different. We use the evidence we gather to shed some light on the recent recovery. A full exploration of this question benefits from an historical perspective, not only to provide a statistically valid number of crises but also to gain perspective from the differing regulatory and monetary regimes in place. We restrict ourselves to the United States, where we have a better grasp and can take a closer focus on the monetary regimes and institutional environment. This also avoids comparability problems with other countries, which often have very different stochastic structures of output (Cogley 1990), but of course this means that our data contains many fewer crises and business cycles than is the case with studies based on multicountry panels. We look at 27 cycles starting in 1882 and use several measures of financial crises. We compare the change in real output (real gross domestic product [RGDP]) over the contraction with the growth in real output in the recovery, and test for differences between cycles with and without a financial crisis. We check for robustness to various definitions of financial crises, output, and business cycles. Finally, we suggest residential investment as a possible explanation for a slow recovery after a recession that involves a housing bust, as the United States is currently experiencing.

Abbreviations
FDIC: Federal Deposit Insurance Corporation
FOMC: Federal Open Market Committee
NBER: National Bureau of Economic Research
RGDP: Real Gross Domestic Product

Our analysis of the data shows that steep expansions tend to follow deep contractions, though this depends heavily on how the recovery is measured. In contrast to much conventional wisdom, the stylized fact that deep contractions breed strong recoveries is particularly true when there is a financial crisis. In fact, on average, it is cycles without a financial crisis that show the weakest relation between contraction depth and recovery strength. This is our key finding. For many configurations, the evidence for a robust bounceback is stronger for cycles with financial crises than those without. The results depend somewhat on the time period, with cycles before the Federal Reserve looking different from cycles after the Second World War.

Until quite recently, the extensive literature on business cycle dynamics rarely combined a long data series with a focus on financial crises. Friedman (1969, 1993) has a long series but does not consider the effect of financial crises, in addition to using data and empirical techniques that are somewhat different than ours. In contrast to most subsequent work, Friedman looks at growth over the entire expansion. Wynne and Balke (1992, 1993) include only cycles since 1919 and do not consider the effect of financial crises. They measure growth four quarters into the expansion. Kahn and Rich (2007) have a neoclassical growth model with regime shifts in permanent and transitory components, but their focus is on identifying post-World War II productivity trends, not business cycles or financial crises. Among more recent papers, the first major split is between papers like ours that focus on one country, and those that use international data. Lopez-Salido and Nelson (2010) explicitly look at the connection between financial crises and recovery strength but look only at post-World War II cycles in the United States. Bordo and Haubrich (2010) find that contractions associated with a financial crisis tend to be more severe but do not gauge the speed of the resulting recovery. Stock and Watson (2012) use a 198-variable dynamic factor model on data since World War II, attributing recent slow recoveries to demographic factors in the labor market. Galí, Smets, and Wouters (2012) estimate a structural new Keynesian model and attribute the current slow recovery to adverse demand shocks stemming from the zero lower bound and wage markups. Hall (2011) defines a related concept of slump, when employment is below 95.5% of the labor force. On the international side, Howard, Martin, and Wilson (2011) look at the relationship between recoveries and crises for 59 countries since 1970 and reach conclusions similar to ours. Benati (2012), in a paper that originated as a conference discussion of our paper, looks at impulse response functions for five countries and the euro area since 1970 and does not find different dynamics after crises. A recent paper by Romer and Romer (2015) looks at the impact of financial distress on advanced countries in the post-World War II period and find results similar to ours.

The second major split is over the definition of recovery. Most of the literature follows Friedman and considers a recovery or expansion as starting at the cyclical trough. Several important papers, however, measure a recovery from peak to peak, that is, how long it takes the economy to return to the cyclical peak. These are important differences, and seemingly divergent results often stem from differing formulations of the question. Reinhart and Rogoff (2009) concentrate on major international financial crises and document long and severe recessions but make few direct comparisons of the recovery speed with noncrisis cycles. They also measure speed by how long it takes to get back to the previous business cycle peak and not how fast the economy grows once the recovery has started. Jordà, Schularick, and Taylor (2011) find slow growth after a credit boom but say little about the patterns after a recovery has started, again making peak-to-peak comparisons. Cerra and Saxena (2008) look at data for 190 countries and find that output losses in disasters are in general not recovered, in the sense of returning to the pre-crisis trend line. Gourio (2008) finds strong recoveries after disasters, in the sense of exceptionally high growth rates.

The remainder of the chapter is as follows: Section II presents an historical narrative on U.S. recoveries; Section III examines the amplitude, duration, and shape of business cycles since 1882, testing whether strong recoveries follow deep contractions, and whether financial crises alter that pattern; and Section IV concludes.

II. Narrative

The relation between a contraction, a recovery, and an associated financial crisis can in principle depend on the monetary regime, banking system, and macroeconomic environment. To provide some context for the econometric results, and offer some justification (and skepticism) for treating over a century of financial crises and business cycles in a coherent fashion, we present some descriptive evidence and historical narratives on economic recoveries following recessions associated with a financial crisis in the United States, from 1880 to the present. For example, financial crises before the advent of the Federal Deposit Insurance Corporation (FDIC) in 1934 were banking panics reflecting a scramble for liquidity, fast-moving events that lasted at most a matter of months. Since 1934, financial crises have been mostly insolvency events, not liquidity events, resolved by fiscal rescues by the FDIC and Treasury. They often lasted for years. We do not aim to establish causality, particularly about the extent to which contractions and crises influence each other, but rather to foster a broader appreciation of the idiosyncracies of the timing, policy, and environment that surround each cycle and crisis.

Table 6.1 shows some metrics on the salient characteristics of the recessions and recoveries. Columns 1 and 2 report the date of the cyclical peak and trough, as determined by the National Bureau of Economic Research (NBER). Column 3 lists the date of the onset of the financial crisis, if any, associated with the cycle. Column 4 shows the total change (usually a drop) in GDP during the contraction, and column 5 shows the total change (usually an increase) during the recovery going out the same number of quarters as the contraction lasted (so if the contraction lasted five quarters, five quarters of the recovery will be counted). Columns 6 and 7 show the percentage changes.

A. 1880–1913: The Pre-Federal Reserve Period

During this era, the United States was on the gold standard and did not have a central bank. The NBER demarcates 11 business cycles, of which three, 1882(I) to 1887(II), 1893(I) to 1894(II), and 1907(II) to 1908(II), had associated financial crises. All of the recessions associated with financial crises were followed by recoveries at least as rapid as the downturns.

The recession of 1882–1885 featured a banking panic in May 1884 following the collapse of the brokerage firm, Grant and Ward, and a stock market crash (Wicker 2000, 35). The banking panic ended with the issuance of clearinghouse loan certificates and U.S. Treasury quasicentral banking operations. The recovery of 1885(II) to 1887(II) was driven by capital and gold inflows. The recovery was interrupted by a brief 1-year mild contraction.[1]

The decade of the 1890s was shadowed by silver uncertainty and falling global gold prices, which produced persistent deflationary pressure. The recovery from the 1890–1891 recession ended early in the first quarter of 1893. A stock market crash on May 3, 1893, was followed by a banking

TABLE 6.1   Output Change in Business Cycles, 1880–2011

			RGDP Change		Percent Change	
Peak	Trough	Crisis Date	Contraction	Recovery	Contraction	Recovery
March 1882	May 1885	June 1884	2.59	5.14	3.15	6.25
March 1887	April 1888	No	−3.36	2.32	−3.75	2.70
July 1890	May 1891	No	−1.03	13.27	−1.05	13.72
January 1893	June 1894	May 1893	−12.38	17.21	−11.09	17.33
December 1895	June 1897	October 1896	1.67	4.86	1.41	4.04
June 1899	December 1900	No	2.92	15.39	2.10	10.88
September 1902	August 1904	No	3.34	31.37	2.09	19.23
May 1907	June 1908	October 1907	−24.13	23.54	−11.82	13.08
January 1910	January 1912	No	7.71	11.55	3.61	5.22
January 1913	December 1914	August 1914	−19.38	24.28	−8.33	11.39
August 1918	March 1919	No	−23.86	−43.67	−8.34	−16.66
January 1920	July 1921	No	−7.66	33.28	−3.42	15.39
May 1923	July 1924	No	13.99	12.32	5.43	4.54
October 1926	November 1927	No	−3.78	26.84	−1.26	9.08
August 1929	March 1933	October 1930[a]	−99.95	87.64	−31.60	40.51
May 1937	June 1938	No	−21.96	27.52	−6.96	9.37
February 1945	October 1945	No	−122.94	−49.97	−19.25	−9.69
November 1948	October 1949	No	3.86	40.02	0.81	8.36
July 1953	May 1954	No	−15.96	48.43	−2.53	7.88
August 1957	April 1958	No	−21.95	46.31	−3.15	6.86
April 1960	February 1961	No	−4.04	42.22	−0.54	5.62
December 1969	November 1970	No	−1.80	50.50	−0.16	4.45
November 1973	March 1975	1973–1975	−42.00	88.90	−3.18	6.96
January 1980	July 1980	No	−35.10	61.00	−2.23	3.96
July 1981	November 1982	1982–1984	−42.40	153.42	−2.64	9.81
July 1990	March 1991	1988–1991	−29.09	23.25	−1.36	1.10
March 2001	November 2001	No	21.92	57.71	0.73	1.90
December 2007	June 2009	September 2008	−182.49	153.21	−5.14	4.55

NOTES: Recoveries are measured by the duration of contraction after the trough; RGDP in 1972 dollars.
    [a] Additional crises in March to June 1931 and January to March 1933.
SOURCE: Authors' calculations based on Bordo and Haubrich (2010), Balke and Gordon (1986), and NIPA accounts. Crisis dates from Eichengreen and Bordo (2002) and Lopez-Salido and Nelson (2010) with monthly dating from Gorton and Tallman (2016).

panic which spread from New York to the interior and back. The panic, which ran in waves from May to July, led to many bank failures across the country (Friedman and Schwartz 1963, chapter 3; Wicker 2000, chapter 4). The issuance of clearinghouse loan certificates and the suspension of convertibility of deposits into currency eventually ended the panic by the fall of 1893. The subsequent recovery from 1894(II) to 1895(III) was aided by the Belmont Morgan syndicate, which was created in early 1895 to rescue the U.S. Treasury's gold reserves from a silver-induced run.

In 1906, the Bank of England reacted to declining gold reserves by raising its discount rate and rationed lending based on U.S. securities. This created a serious shock to U.S. financial markets, triggering a stock market crash and a major banking panic in October 1907. The banking panic led to many bank failures, a steep drop in the money supply, and a serious recession, which ended in May 1908. The recession of 1907–1908 was followed by a vigorous recovery from 1908(II) to 1910(I). Friedman and Schwartz attribute this to gold inflows reflecting a decline in U.S. prices relative to those in Britain stemming from the crisis. The onset of World War I in 1914 led to a recession and a global banking crisis (Silber 2007). The recession was then followed by a major boom, driven by the demand for U.S. goods by the European belligerents and then by the United States as it prepared for war.

B. The World Wars and Between: 1914–1945

The Federal Reserve was established in 1914 in part to solve the problem of the absence of a lender of last resort in the crises of the pre-1914 national banking era. In the Fed's first 31 years, there were three very severe business cycle downturns and several minor cycles. Most of the recoveries in this period were at least as rapid as the downturns that preceded them with one important exception: the recovery from the Great Contraction of 1929 to 1933.

Recovery 1933(I) to 1937(II). A recession began in August 1929 with a major stock market crash in October. A series of banking panics beginning in October 1930 ensued. The Fed did little to offset them, turning a recession into the Great Contraction. The recovery began after Roosevelt's inauguration in March 1933 with the Banking Holiday. The recovery, although rapid (output grew by 33%), was not sufficient to completely reverse the preceding downturn. The recovery may have been impeded somewhat by New Deal cartelization policies like the National Industrial Recovery Act, which, in an attempt to raise wages and prices, artificially reduced labor supply and aggregate supply (Cole and Ohanian 2004).

C. Post-World War II: 1945–2014

In the post-World War II era, with only two exceptions, recoveries were at least as rapid as the downturns. In general, recessions were shorter and recoveries longer than before World War II (Zarnowitz 1992). There also were fewer stock market crashes. There were only four events demarcated as financial crises in the period. This may have reflected the presence of deposit insurance and the financial safety net.

1975(I) to 1980(I). The recession that began in November was one of the worst in the postwar period. RGDP fell by 3.4% and unemployment increased to 8.6%. The recession was greatly aggravated by the first oil price shock, which quadrupled the price of oil, and by wage price controls which prevented the necessary adjustment. The United States experienced a minor banking crisis with the failure of Franklin National in October 1974 and other significant banks, as market conditions were made more stressful by the payments problems stemming from the Herstatt failure in June 1974 (Lopez-Salido and Nelson 2010). Faced with inflation and rising unemployment the Federal Open Market Committee (FOMC) sought moderate growth in monetary aggregates (Roesch 1975). The recovery began in April 1975. As in most of the postwar recessions, the pace of the recovery exceeded the pace of the downturn.

1982(IV) to 1990(III). Fed policy began to tighten in May 1981 in the face of a jump in inflation. It raised the federal funds rate from 14.7% in March to 19.1% in June. This second and more durable round of tightening induced by Chairman Volcker succeeded in reducing the inflation rate from 10% in early 1981 to 4% in 1983 but at the cost of a sharp and very prolonged recession. RGDP fell by close to 3% and unemployment increased from 7.2% to 10.8%. During this period there were two banking crises. The first, between 1982 and 1984, involved the failure and bail-out of Penn Square Bank in 1982 and Continental Illinois in 1984. Both banks were hit hard by the collapse in global oil prices. The money center banks were hard hit by the Latin American debt crisis in 1982, and the Volcker Fed eased policy as part of a complicated plan to avoid extensive defaults (Meltzer 2010, book 2). The second was the Savings and Loan Crisis from 1988 to 1991: Thrift resolutions spiked from 47 in 1987 to 205 in 1988 as the loan charge-off ratio for commercial banks increased and in 1991 reached a postwar peak not equaled until 2009 (Lopez-Salido and Nelson 2010).

1991(I) to 2001(I). The FOMC only began cutting the funds rate in November 1990 because its primary concern was to reduce inflation, which had reached 6.1% in the first half of 1990 (Hetzel 2008, chapter 15). The recovery from the trough in March 1991 was considered tepid, and it was referred to as a jobless recovery. Unemployment peaked at 7.75% in June 1992. The recession was also viewed as a credit crunch (Bordo and Haubrich 2010), and real housing prices declined by 13%, suggesting a minor housing bust. This is the first recovery in the postwar era where the pace of expansion was less than that in the downturn. The recovery continued into a lengthy expansion, however.

2009(II)–? The last recession which began in December 2007 was preceded by a crisis in the shadow banking sector after the collapse of the housing market reduced the value of mortgage-backed securities. This later affected the balance sheets of the banking system. The fact that the Fed had supported the insolvent investment bank Bear Stearns in March 2008, but to prevent moral hazard did not do so for Lehman Brothers in September, even though it was in similar shape, many believe triggered a global liquidity panic (Bordo 2014). According to Hetzel (2014), the recession was not caused by the financial crisis but by the Fed following tight monetary policy in the fall of 2007 and early 2008. The recession was the most severe in the postwar period (RGDP fell by more than 5% and unemployment increased to 10.8%). The financial crisis in the fall of 2008 was without doubt the most serious event since the Great Contraction.

Both the crisis and the recession were dealt with by vigorous policy responses: on the monetary policy side, the Federal Reserve cut the funds rate from 5.25% in early fall 2007 to close to zero by January 2009 and created a variety of programs that tripled the Federal Reserve's balance sheet, on top of a massive fiscal stimulus package. The recovery since 2009 has been tepid, with real growth expanding at slightly above 2%. The pace of recovery is well below the pace of the decline in output.

III. The Relationship between Recessions and Recoveries

In this section, we take a more statistical view of the relationship between the depth of the contraction and the strength of the following expansion. We make no claims about causality: we do not consider here whether financial crises contribute to recessions or recessions create financial crises. That is, we examine recoveries that occur against the backdrop of a recent financial crisis; the analysis does not require attributing the preceding recession to the crisis.

Our data is based on Bordo and Haubrich (2010), where we provide a more detailed description. Business cycle turning points (in quarters) come from the NBER. RGDP, again at a quarterly frequency, is based on Balke and Gordon (1986) and Gordon and Krenn (2010), extended via the NIPA accounts. This gives us quarterly RGDP for 27 business cycles, starting with the peak in 1882 and ending with the recovery from the 2007 recession.

We measure the amplitude of the contraction by the percentage drop (from the peak to the trough) of quarterly RGDP. We measure the recovery strength as the percentage change from the trough at two horizons: four quarters after the cyclical trough and after a time equal to the duration of the contraction. Figure 6.1 plots the strength of the recovery against the depth of the contraction, for both recovery conventions. Going out the length of the contraction, while it appeals to symmetry, appears to be new, as most papers restrict their attention to four quarters (or 12 months if they use monthly data). Friedman (1993) is the exception, looking at growth to

FIGURE 6.1   Expansion Growth against Contraction Depth: All Cycles

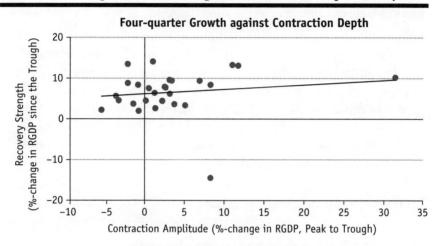

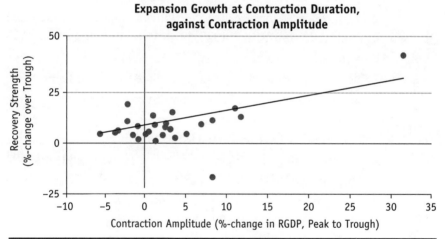

the next cyclical peak. Morley and Piger (2012) in their discussion of bounceback models, consider recoveries of up to six quarters after a trough, while Howard, Martin, and Wilson (2011) look out 3 years after a trough. Papell and Prodan (2012) look at when growth rates return to trend and when both levels and growth return to trend.

Exactly what constitutes a financial crisis depends on how it is defined, and the question has been answered several ways. In this section, for the pre-World War II years we use the chronology from Eichengreen and

Bordo (2002) and also add 1914, a year in which the bond markets closed. Eichengreen and Bordo describe their definition as follows (15–16):

> For an episode to qualify as a banking crisis, we must observe either bank runs, widespread bank failures and the suspension of convertibility of deposits into currency such that the latter circulates at a premium relative to deposits (a banking panic), or significant banking sector problems (including but not limited to bank failures) resulting in the erosion of most or all of banking system collateral that are resolved by a fiscally underwritten bank restructuring.[2]

For the postwar period, we use the chronology of Lopez-Salido and Nelson. This gives us crisis periods of 1884–1885, 1892–1893, 1907, 1914, 1930–1933, 1973–1975, 1982–1984, 1988–1991, and 2007 (Table 6.1).

Consequently, the recessions we associate with a financial crisis are those that start in 1882, 1893, 1907, 1913, 1929, 1973, 1981, 1990, and 2007. (We drop the 1945 recession from our sample. This is reasonable, but it matters, as it was the deepest recession of the century outside the Great Depression, with an extremely weak recovery.) It is perhaps interesting to note that the five GDP "disasters" picked out by Barro and Jin (2011) correspond to the cycles with troughs in 1914, 1921, 1933, and 1947, with two of those five being associated with a financial crisis. (With our data, we would add 1894 as a disaster where RGDP fell by 10% or more.) Interestingly, of our 27 business cycles, only 4 did not have some form of financial crisis, according to the reckoning of Reinhart and Rogoff[3] (1899, 1923, 1953, and 1960).

A. Are Deep Recessions Followed by Steep Recoveries?

The visual evidence (Figure 6.1) definitely suggests that deep recessions are followed by strong recoveries, though a few outliers, particularly the Great Depression, may have a disproportionate impact. Regressing growth four quarters after the trough against contraction amplitude shows a positive but small and statistically insignificant relationship. The relationship is tighter, and stronger, if we examine more of the recovery, measuring growth out to the duration of the contraction after the trough. Looking out only four quarters can give a misleading picture, particularly for longer recessions. Much of the difference is in fact driven by the Great Depression, and it should not be surprising that the drop in output from 1929 to 1933 was not fully reversed by 1934, since monetary policy (using M2) only became expansionary in early 1934 with the devaluation of the dollar and resulting gold inflows (Friedman and Schwartz 1963, chapter 8). By 1936 though, output was much closer to its pre-crisis level.

Do financial crises affect the bounceback? Or more precisely, since we cannot assess causality without a carefully identified model, do the recoveries from recessions with a financial crisis look different than those without? Figure 6.2 plots the strength of the recovery against the depth of the recession, separately identifying crisis and noncrisis cycles. The scatterplot suggests a difference, but for reasons contrary to the conventional wisdom. In crisis times, strong recoveries follow deep recessions, but outside of a crisis, they do not. The relation is in fact negative, though not statistically significant.

To get a more formal view of the difference, we run a set of regressions based on the following specification:

$$\%\Delta Y_{T+k} = a_1 + a_2 D_F + \beta_1 \left[\%\Delta Y_{P-T}\right] + \beta_2 D_F \left[\%\Delta Y_{P-T}\right]. \tag{1}$$

Here, $\%\Delta Y_{T+k}$ is the percentage increase in RGDP from the cyclical trough (T) to quarter $T+k$; as mentioned above, k is either 4 or equals the number of quarters in the recession. D_F is a dummy for financial crises, $\%\Delta Y_{P-T}$ is the percentage change in RGDP from peak to trough (peak [RGDP] minus trough [RGDP] over trough [RGDP], so in typical contractions this will be a positive number). Thus the strength of the expansion is regressed against a constant, a dummy for financial crises, a measure of the depth of the contraction and an interaction between the financial crisis dummy and the depth of the contraction, in effect a slope dummy. An F-test then determines the significance of excluding the dummy and the interaction term. This specification is meant to capture two separate ways that a crisis may affect the bounceback. On average, such contractions may have a slower recovery, but the relationship between contraction depth and recovery strength may also be affected.

FIGURE 6.2   Recovery Strength versus Contract Amplitude, Crisis and Noncrisis Cycles

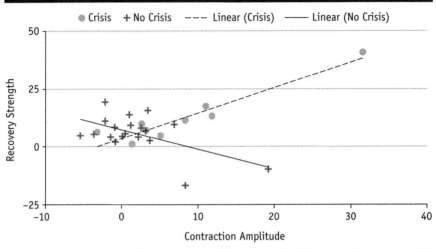

It may not be proper to lump all crises and all cycles together, given the very different monetary standards and regulatory regimes in place over time. We split the data several ways, dropping the Great Depression, and separately examine the years after the founding of the Federal Reserve and after World War II. Table 6.2 reports the results out to the first four quarters of the expansion, and Table 6.3 looks at the expansion going out the duration of the contraction.

Looking only at four quarters of the recovery, there is little evidence that recoveries following financial crises are much different. At a formal level, the F-test does not show a significant difference. Informally, the coefficient on the financial dummy is uniformly negative, indicating that recoveries following financial crises are on average somewhat smaller, though the coefficient is significant in only one case. The interaction term, also insignificant, is split between negative and positive values: in the one significant case the depth of the recession has a greater impact on the strength of recoveries when there is a crisis.

The differences are more striking once more of the recovery is considered, as Table 6.3 shows (Figure 6.2 plots the data). The interaction term and the F-test are significant in all but the post-World War II samples.

TABLE 6.2 Regressions of Four Quarter Expansion Growth on Contraction Amplitude

Variable	All	No 29	Post-Fed	Post-WWII
Constant	6.434***	6.434***	5.658***	5.539***
	(1.044)	(1.044)	(1.301)	(1.242)
FinDum	−0.5864	−2.360*	−1.254	−0.404
	(1.293)	(1.381)	(1.536)	(1.917)
C_{Amp}	−0.565	−0.565	−0.510	0.756
	(0.556)	(0.556)	(0.705)	(0.541)
$FinDum * C_{Amp}$	0.796	1.219**	0.692	−0.816
	(0.593)	(0.559)	(0.704)	(0.740)
R^2	0.16	0.20	0.12	0.20
F-Test $\chi^2(2)$	2.18	8.13**	1.574	2.605
Sig level	0.34	0.02	0.46	0.27
N	27	26	17	11

NOTE: HAC robust standard errors in parentheses.
*Significant at 10%; **significant at 5%; ***significant at 1%.

TABLE 6.3 Regressions of Expansion Growth on Contraction Amplitude

Variable	All	No 29	Post-Fed	Post-WWII
Constant	7.229***	7.229***	6.281***	5.159****
	(1.875)	(1.090)	(1.026)	(1.251)
FinDum	−3.663*	−2.251	−4.376**	−1.168
	(2.246)	(1.820)	(1.776)	(2.538)
C_{Amp}	−0.790	−0.790	−0.677	0.415
	(0.573)	(0.573)	(0.738)	(0.488)
$FinDum * C_{Amp}$	1.886***	1.549**	1.893**	0.109
	(0.552)	(0.603)	(0.735)	(0.849)
R^2	0.51	0.23	0.67	0.06
Chow Test $\chi^2(2)$	15.51***	7.48**	11.95***	0.303
Sig level	0.004	0.02	0.003	0.86
N	27	26	17	11

NOTE: HAC robust standard errors in parentheses.
*Significant at 10%; **significant at 5%; ***significant at 1%.

The dummy for financial crises is always negative, but it is significant only half the time. The post-World War II sample shows no significant difference between crisis and noncrisis recoveries (perhaps because crises were less severe, and the intercept dummy dominates the slope dummy), but for the other samples a clear pattern emerges: the dummy for financial crises is negative, but the interaction term is positive. This means that relatively mild recessions with a crisis have slower-than-average recoveries, but the deeper the recession, the stronger the recovery. For the entire sample, the crossover point is about 3.25%, met by most crisis contractions except 1882, 1973, 1981, and 1990, which perhaps contributes to the impression that the crisis recoveries are weaker. The numbers have economic heft: a 1% deeper recession with a crisis will lead to greater than an extra 1.5% of growth in the quarters following the trough.

As a check on the robustness of the results, we look at alternative measures of crises. Bordo and Landon-Lane (2012) find the world has had five global financial crises since 1880 (1890–1891, 1907–1908, 1913–1914, 1930–1933, and 2007–2008). Figure 6.3 plots recovery amplitude (four quarters) against contraction amplitude for these crises and all post-World War II contractions, including 2007–2008. The Appendix conducts further robustness tests with alternate measures of output and of business cycles.

Like the previous figures, Figure 6.3 shows a positive relationship between contraction amplitude and recovery strength, though the coefficient is relatively small. In part, this arises from the three most recent cycles, which appear different, with both a lower intercept and a lower slope. Some speculation suggests that this results from changes in labor market behavior since the 1980s (Beauchemin 2010; Jaimovich and Siu 2012).

Another classification of financial crises comes from Reinhart and Rogoff (2009), and using their measure also lets us make distinctions between financial crises based on their severity. Replacing the crisis dummy in the interaction term with the Reinhart and Rogoff index of crisis severity (which essentially adds up the number of different crises occurring during particular years, which we sum over contractions), provides yet another robustness check. The results looking out either four quarters from the

FIGURE 6.3   Bordo–Landon-Lane Crises. Severity of Recession and
Strength of Recovery, BLL Crisis

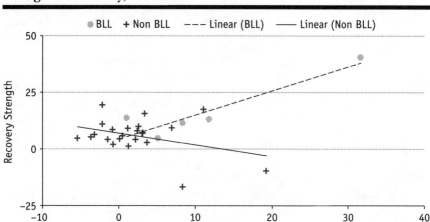

trough or the duration of the contraction into the expansion were quite
similar, so in Table 6.4 we report only the results for duration. Again the
results are somewhat mixed. The financial crisis dummy is usually positive, but insignificant. The interaction term is significant in all four cases,
and positive except for the post-World War II period. Thus, for most time
periods, a more severe crisis means a stronger recovery.

Yet another approach to measure financial stress uses the spread between CD spreads and 3-month Treasury bills (see Figure 6.4). Using the
spread removes 1990 as a crisis event. As the Appendix shows, the results
that recoveries are generally more rapid from financial recessions are robust to this change.

IV. Prospects for the Current Recovery

Recessions that accompany a financial crisis tend to be long and severe
(Bordo and Haubrich 2010; Reinhart and Rogoff 2009). What that por-
tends for economic growth once a recovery has started is less certain,
however. On the one hand, there is the feeling that "growth is sometimes

TABLE 6.4 Regressions of Expansion Growth on Contraction
Amplitude and RNR Crises Severity

Variable	All	No 29	Post-Fed	Post-WWII
Constant	6.839***	7.207***	6.215***	4.811***
	(1.144)	(1.098)	(1.036)	(1.388)
FinDum	1.708	−0.755	0.111	0.764
	(2.703)	(1.884)	(2.305)	(2.109)
C_{Amp}	−0.382	−0.767	−0.640	0.761
	(0.462)	(0.566)	(0.727)	(0.60605)
$RnRDum * C_{Amp}$	0.103***	0.316***	0.123**	−0.227**
	(0.031)	(0.122)	(0.048)	(0.124)
R^2	0.55	0.23	0.66	0.14
Chow Test $\chi^2(2)$	18.23***	7.86**	13.70***	4.43
Sig level	0.000	0.020	0.001	0.109
N	27	26	17	11

NOTE: HAC robust standard errors in parentheses.
  *Significant at 10%; **significant at 5%; ***significant at 1%.

quite modest in the aftermath as the financial system resets" (Reinhart
and Rogoff 2009, 235). On the other hand, there is the stylized fact behind
Friedman's plucking model, that "a large contraction in output tends to be
followed on the average by a large business expansion" (Friedman 1969,
273). One popular measure of recovery strength, the time required to return output to the pre-crisis level, confounds the depth of the recession
with the strength of recovery. For many purposes, it is important to separate the notions of contraction depth and recovery strength. Our results
show that if there is a difference between recoveries, it is because the recoveries following a financial crisis tend to be steeper, and far from being
an exception to the plucking rule, are the major evidence for it.

Where does that leave the current recovery? It remains an outlier, as
one of the few cases where output did not return to the level of the previous peak after the duration of the recession. In this, it resembled two very
different recessions, the Great Depression and 1990. Significantly, both
of those combined financial problems and (real) housing price declines,
albeit of strikingly different magnitudes. In Bordo and Haubrich (2012),
we provide suggestive evidence that supports housing as at least a partial

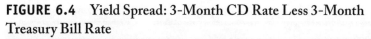

FIGURE 6.4   Yield Spread: 3-Month CD Rate Less 3-Month
Treasury Bill Rate

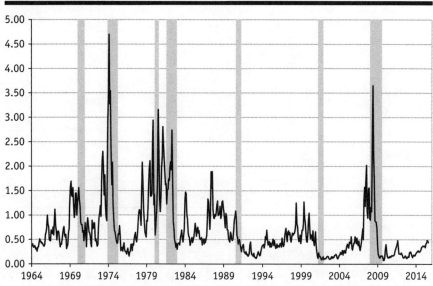

factor. Others point to policy uncertainty as having a role (Baker, Bloom, and Davis 2015), but at this point the evidence does not provide a definite resolution. The unanswered question, of course, relates to causality; tracing out the exact shocks, and their transmission, remains key. Must housing recover for the recovery to take off, or will the economy pull the industry along? Would monetary policy, credit policy, or fiscal policy be an appropriate response? These are questions for another day.

Appendix: Data

Construction of the Quarterly Bank Loan Numbers

We started with the annual numbers for all commercial banks, *Millennial Statistics,* table Cj253 "commercial banks-number and assets," Total Loans. After 1914Q4 these are made quarterly by interpolation using the RATS *disaggregate* (linear, ar1) procedure using total loans for all member banks, from the Fed's *Banking and Monetary Statistics, 1914–1941* No. 18, All

FIGURE 6.A1   Bank Lending, on a Log Scale

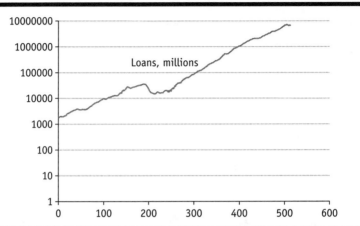

Member banks-Principal assets, "Loans" p. 72–74. The data were pushed forward to 1955 Q4 using the data from Banking and Monetary Statistics 1941–1970 table 2.1, All Member Banks. Total assets and number of bank loans. There were several missing quarters, which we interpolated using No. 48, Weekly Reporting Banks in 101 Leading Cities-Principal Assets and Liabilities, weekly and monthly.

To go back further, we again began with the Millennial statistics, and interpolated again, this time using national and state bank data. The national bank data came from the NBER series, adding up NBER 14016, Loans and Discounts, national banks, country districts, NBER 14018, Loans and discounts, national banks, Reserve cities other than central, and NBER 14019, Loans and Discounts, National Banks, Central Reserve cities. Some judgment was used to apportion the data into quarters.

Annual State bank data comes from Millennial Statistics, Cj151, State banks, Loans, and discounts. It was made quarterly by linear interpolation. The state and national bank numbers were added together and used to interpolate the Millennial statistics annual number. This let us interpolate from 1896 to 1913. Then we attached the series for state and national banks, discounting by the ratio for that series to the Millennial series in 1914. This gave us a series from 1882 to 1955. Figure 6.A1 shows the series.

TABLE 6.A1   Bry-Boschan Cycles: Expansion Growth on
Contraction Amplitude

Variable	All	No 29	Post-Fed
Constant	4.841**	4.841**	6.139***
	(2.151)	(0.215)	(2.204)
FinDum	−5.536**	−2.546	−6.924***
	(2.665)	(0.300)	(2.649)
C_{stp}	0.286***	0.286**	0.225**
	(0.104)	(0.104)	(0.104)
FinDum $* C_{stp}$	0.950***	0.432*	1.081***
	(0.158)	(0.2.30)	(0.115)
R^2	0.85	0.34	0.95
Chow Test χ^2 (2)	176.3***	1126***	13.52***
Sig level	0.000	0.000	0.000
N	17	16	11

NOTE: HAC robust standard errors in parentheses.
*Significant at 10%; **significant at 5%; ***significant at 1%.

TABLE 6.A2   Regressions of Four Quarter Expansion Steepness
on Contraction Steepness

Variable	All	No 29	Post-Fed	Post-WWII
Constant	1.833***	1.833***	1.713***	1.430***
	(0.252)	(0.252)	(0.363)	(0.310)
FinDum	−0.906***	−0.916***	−0.923*	2.096***
	(0.298)	(0.300)	(0.473)	(0.593)
C_{stp}	−0.776**	−0.776**	−0.771**	0.366
	(0.346)	(0.346)	(0.390)	(0.453)
FinDum $* C_{stp}$	1.585***	1.617***	1.487***	−3.787***
	(0.368)	(0.366)	(0.405)	(0.764)
R^2	0.42	0.41	0.39	0.30
Chow Test $\chi^2(2)$	22.77***	23.48***	13.52***	25.61
Sig level	0.000	0.000	0.001	0.000
N	27	26	17	11

NOTE: HAC robust standard errors in parentheses.
*Significant at 10%; **significant at 5%; ***significant at 1%.

Further Robustness Results

The next step is to check whether the results depend on using RGDP as an output measure. One approach is to use per capita income (population taken from Millennial Statistics): the cycles with a financial crisis show a positive correlation between contraction depth and recovery strength. Though not reported here, the regression analysis for per capita RGDP follow along the same lines as RGDP; going out only four quarters into the expansion shows no significant difference between crisis and noncrisis cycles. Going out further into the recovery, the difference is highly significant, again with the intercept dummy negative and the slope dummy positive.

Industrial production is a less compehensive measure of output, but it is also available monthly and so makes another natural comparison point. We use two data sets (both taken from Mark Watson's website) used in Watson (1994). For January 1884 to December 1940, we use the Miron and Romer (1990) IP numbers. For January 1947 to December 1990, we use Watson's postwar approximation of the Miron-Romer numbers, which re-weights the postwar index to approximate the Miron-Romer pre-war

TABLE 6.A3   Regressions of Expansion Steepness on Contraction Steepness

Variable	All	No 29	Post-Fed	Post-WWII
Constant	1.965***	1.965***	2.068***	1.467***
	(0.361)	(0.361)	(0.487)	(0.269)
FinDum	−1.3741***	−1.371***	−1.513***	2.126***
	(0.381)	(0.382)	(0.540)	(0.717)
C_{stp}	−1.475**	−1.475**	−1.652**	0.655**
	(0.627)	(0.627)	(0.641)	(0.3050)
FinDum $*$ C_{stp}	2.475***	2.468***	2.616***	−4.253***
	(0.639)	(0.643)	(0.649)	(1.037)
R^2	0.48	0.47	0.54	0.56
Chow Test χ^2 (2)	123.45***	22.972***	17.615***	38.90
Sig level	0.000	0.000	0.000	0.000
N	27	26	17	11

Note: HAC robust standard errors in parentheses.
*Significant at 10%; **significant at 5%; ***significant at 1%.

TABLE 6.A4 Regressions of Expansion on Contraction Depth, Controlling for Changes in Stock Price, and Bank Loans, 1887–2007

Variable	All (4Q)	No 29 (4Q)	All (Dur)	No 29 (Dur)
Constant	3.206	3.563***	3.723***	3.031**
	(1.084)	(1.168)	(1.206)	(1.252)
FinDum	−0.400	−2.908	−5.158***	−1.025
	(1.112)	(1.793)	(1.746)	(1.762)
C_{Amp}	−0.535	−0.535	−0.719	−0.652
	(0.567)	(0.557)	(0.588)	(0.573)
FinDum * C_{Amp}	0.853	1.219**	1.909***	1.243**
	(0.558)	(0.573)	(0.560)	(0.532)
Loan	0.307***	0.200	0.199***	0.361***
	(0.093)	(0.131)	(0.071)	(0.110)
Stock	0.127***	0.143***	0.146***	0.108***
	(0.041)	(0.042)	(0.044)	(0.041)
R^2	0.32	0.33	0.68	0.41
Chow Test $\chi^2(2)$	2.35	5.45*	18.48***	5.62*
Sig level	0.309	0.066	0.000	0.060
N	26	25	26	25

Note: HAC robust standard errors in parentheses.
*Significant at 10%; **significant at 5%; ***significant at 1%.

index. The gap means we cannot calculate statistics for the 1945 contraction, but as discussed above, we drop that from the results for other reasons. With these data, strong recoveries follow steep recessions in both crisis and noncrisis cycles. The response looks similar, and indeed is not significantly different in a statistical sense, but we wish to stress that it certainly is not the case that crisis recoveries look weaker.

A third check for robustness is with different definitions of the business cycle. This is perhaps particularly important in our case because the early NBER cycles were determined before the development of the GDP concept, much less its implementation. As a result, cyclical troughs do not always coincide with troughs of RGDP. We use the Bry and Boschan (1971) approach to finding cyclical turning points, as implemented by the RATS program bry-boschan.src. This results in a smaller number of business cycles (18 as opposed to 27) and a somewhat different distribution of crisis cycles—10 instead of 9.

Table 6.A1 reports the regression results. The striking change is that Bry-Boschan cycles show that a deep recession is followed by a strong recovery, regardless of whether or not there is a financial crisis. It remains true, however, that the response of the two groups is (statistically and economically) different: as before, crisis cycles have a lower intercept but a higher slope. Again the bounceback is stronger for a good sized crisis cycle.

Another possible relationship between contractions and expansions concerns their shape. One obvious measure of shape is steepness, or change in output divided by duration. Tables 6.A2 and 6.A3 report the results of regressing the steepness of the recovery against the steepness of the contraction, again dropping 1929 and looking at post-Fed and post-World War II periods.

Steepness does pick out differences between recoveries with and without financial crises. The financial crisis dummy is significantly negative in six of eight cases, turning positive for the post-World War II period both times. So everything else equal, crisis recoveries are smaller. But everything else is not equal, for the interaction term is significantly positive in the same six cases, while the coefficient on contraction depth is insignificant, small, and generally negative. The conclusion is that crisis recoveries show a strong relationship between contraction depth and recovery strength, but the noncrisis recoveries do not. Far from overturning the stylized fact, crisis recoveries account for it!

Steepness is not the only measure of shape. For example, the contraction might be "L" shaped, that is, dropping quickly at first, but then only slowly reaching a trough (Macroeconomic Advisers 2009). The recovery might be slow, with a "U" shape as opposed to a quicker recovery yielding a "V" shape. Some even described the 2007 cycle as having a "square root sign" shape. Quantifying shape appears a daunting task, but Harding and Pagan (2002) have a measure of how much the change in output deviates from a straight line. The specifications we have considered, however, have not uncovered any meaningful relationship between the shape of the contraction and the shape of the recovery.

Another approach preserves the interaction between the simple dummy for financial crises but adds controls for financial conditions during the recovery. To capture both the market-based and the intermediary-based

TABLE 6.A5 Regressions of Expansion Growth on Contraction
Amplitude, Excluding 1990

Variable	All	No 29	Post-Fed	Post-WWII
Constant	7.229***	7.229***	6.281***	5.159***
	(1.089)	(1.089)	(1.025)	(1.251)
FinDum	−2.825	−0.860	−3.351	8.798***
	(1.988)	(1.482)	(2.314)	(1.787)
C_{Amp}	−0.790	−0.790	−0.677	0.415
	(0.573)	(0.573)	(0.737)	(0.488)
$FinDum * C_{Amp}$	1.847	1.425**	1.854**	−2.290***
	(0.550)	(0.587)	(0.735)	(0.531)
R^2	0.58	0.23	0.66	0.39
F-Test $\chi^2(2)$	13.00***	6.23**	7.87**	24.31***
Sig level	0.001	0.04	0.02	0.00
N	26	25	16	10

NOTE: HAC robust standard errors in parentheses.
*Significant at 10%; **significant at 5%; ***significant at 1%.

aspects of finance, we include stock prices and bank loans. While certainly
the price of credit should matter, some authors (Owens and Schreft 1995)
define a "credit crunch" as nonprice rationing of credit, and thus observable
mostly from the quantity side. Schularick and Taylor (2012) use (annual)
bank lending as a measure of credit conditions. The stock price index for
1875–1917 is the Cowles commission index, releveled to match the Standard and Poor's index which begins in 1917. For bank lending, we construct
a new quarterly series from 1882 to 2010 for all commercial banks, detailed
in the Appendix.

Table 6.A4 reports the results of regressing the expansion strength
against contraction depth, the change in real loans over the expansion
and the change in the stock index over the expansion. It is meant to un-
cover whether financing problems held back the recovery. Because adding dependent variables reduces the degrees of freedom, we only report
results for the entire sample and for a subsample that excludes the 1929
cycle. The interaction term is positive in the entire sample, both at four quarters and duration, and positive, statistically significant and quantitatively
large in three of the four cases considered. Again it appears that if there is a

difference between cycles with and without a crisis, the rebound from a financial crisis is particularly strong if the recession was deep.

Looking at the controls, however, shows that financing matters for the recovery, though the results do depend on the horizon, particularly for bank lending. Loans are quantitatively and statistically significant except when 1929 is dropped from the four-quarter specification. Higher bank lending is associated with a stronger recovery. The effect on the stock index is more consistent across horizons. There is a positive relationship between changes in the stock index and the strength of recovery, both with and without the Great Depression. Of course, particularly with the stock market, causality is hard to determine, and the results may only be telling us that strong recoveries have bull markets.

It is perhaps more common to measure financial conditions via some sort of credit spread, and in our earlier work we followed that tradition and looked at the spread between Baa and safe bonds, or between different grades of railroad bonds for the nineteenth century. As mentioned in the main text, using a risk spread to define banking crisis makes 1990 look less compelling. Table 6.A5 drops 1990 as a crisis, and results are similar to the steepness results.

Notes

1. The November 1890 Baring crisis in London led to a sudden stop of capital flows to all emerging markets, including the United States. The issuance of clearinghouse loan certificates (Wicker 2000, chapter 3) quickly stemmed a local banking panic in New York in November. Because it was averted we do not include it in the narrative.

2. The demarcation of banking panics in Eichengreen and Bordo (2002) is based on Sprague (1912) and Friedman and Schwartz (1963). Kemmerer (1912), Wicker (1991), and more recently Jalil (2015) consider a broader range including 1890, 1896, and 1902.

3. Reinhart and Rogoff have a more liberal definition of financial crisis than do Eichengreen and Bordo (2002), whose chronology we follow. See Bordo and Meissner (2016) for a comparison of the dating of financial crises across databases. There is likewise considerable debate over measuring crisis severity. On the one hand, the Friedman and Schwartz view is that the banking panics pre-1934 had serious consequences because they led to bank failures and declines in the money supply. On the other hand, others measure the capitalized losses of the banking sector in the earlier period, adding bailout costs in the later period. The IMF (Laeven and Valencia 2012)

measures losses by the decline in real output from the crisis to the recovery. And of course there is the tradition stemming from Bernanke (1983) which looks at increases in the cost of credit intermediation.

References

Baker, S. R., N. Bloom, and S. J. Davis. "Measuring Policy Uncertainty." NBER Working Paper No. 21633, 2015.

Balke, N. S., and R. J. Gordon. "Appendix B: Historical Data," in *The American Business Cycle: Continuity and Change,* edited by R. J. Gordon. NBER Studies in Business Cycles, Vol. 25. Chicago: University of Chicago Press, 1986, 781–850.

Barro, R. J., and T. Jin. "On the Size Distribution of Macroeconomic Disasters." *Econometrica,* 79(5), 2011, 1567–89.

Beauchemin, K. R. "Not Your Father's Recovery?" FRB Cleveland Economic Commentary, September 9, 2010.

Benati, L. "Why Are Recessions Associated with Financial Crises Different?" University of Bern Working Paper, 2012.

Bernanke, B. S. "Nonmonetary Effects of the Financial Crisis in the Propagation of the Great Depression." *American Economic Review,* 73, 1983, 257–76.

Bordo, M. D. "The Federal Reserve's Role: Actions Before, During, and After the Panic in the Historical Context of the Great Contraction," in *Across the Great Divide; New Perspectives on the Financial Crisis,* Chapter 6, edited by M. N. Bailey and J. Taylor. Stanford, CA: Hoover Institution Press, 2014.

Bordo, M. D., and J. G. Haubrich. "Credit Crises, Money and Contractions: An Historical View." *Journal of Monetary Economics,* 57(1), 2010, 1–18.

———. "Deep Recessions, Fast Recoveries, and Financial Crises: Evidence from the American Record." NBER Working Paper No. 18194, 2012.

Bordo, M. D., and J. S. Landon-Lane. "The Global Financial Crisis of 2007–2008: Is It Unprecedented?" in *Global Economic Crisis: Impact, Transmission and Recovery,* Chapter 2, edited by M. Obsfeld, D. Cho, and A. Mason. Cheltenham, UK: Edward Elgar, 2012, 19–56.

Bordo, M. D., and C. M. Meissner. "Fiscal and Financial Crises." NBER Working Paper No. 22059, 2016.

Bry, G., and C. Boschan. "Cyclical Analysis of Time Series: Selected Procedures and Computer Programs." NBER Technical Paper No. 20, National Bureau of Economic Research, Columbia University Press, New York, 1971.

Cerra, V., and S. C. Saxena. "Growth Dynamics: The Myth of Recovery." *American Economic Review,* 98(1), 2008, 439–57.

Cogley, T. "International Evidence on the Size of the Random Walk in Output." *Journal of Political Economy,* 98(3), 1990, 501–18.

Cole, H. L., and L. E. Ohanian. "New Deal Policies and the Persistence of the Great Depression: A General Equilibrium Analysis." *Journal of Political Economy*, 112(4), 2004, 779–816.

Eichengreen, B., and M. D. Bordo. "Crises Now and Then: What Lessons from the Last Era of Financial Globalization?" NBER Working Paper No. 8716, 2002.

Friedman, M. "The Monetary Studies of the National Bureau," in *The Optimum Quantity of Money and Other Essays*, Chapter 12, by M. Friedman. Chicago: Aldine Publishing Company, 1969, 262–85. (Originally from "The National Bureau Enters Its 45th Year," 44th Annual Report, New York, 1964.)

Friedman, M. "The 'Plucking Model' of Business Fluctuations Revisited." *Economic Inquiry*, 31, 1993, 171–77.

Friedman, M., and A. J. Schwartz. *A Monetary History of the United States, 1867–1960*. Princeton, NJ: NBER and Princeton University Press, 1963.

Galí, J., F. Smets, and R. Wouters. "Slow Recoveries: A Structural Interpretation." NBER Working Paper No. 18085, 2012.

Gordon, R. J., and R. Krenn. "The End of the Great Depression 1939–41: Policy Contributions and Fiscal Multipliers." NBER Working Paper No. 16380, 2010.

Gorton, G. B., and E. Tallman. "How Did Pre-Fed Banking Panics End?" Federal Reserve Bank of Cleveland Working Paper No. 16-03, 2016.

Gourio, F. "Disaster and Recoveries." *American Economic Review*, 98(2), 2008, 68–73.

Hall, R. E. "The Long Slump." *American Economic Review*, 101(2), 2011, 431–69.

Harding, D., and A. Pagan. "Dissecting the Cycle: A Methodological Investigation." *Journal of Monetary Economics*, 29(2), 2002, 365–81.

Hetzel, R. L. *The Monetary Policy of the Federal Reserve: A History*. Cambridge: Cambridge University Press, 2008.

———. *The Great Recession Market Failure or Policy Failure?* Cambridge: Cambridge University Press, 2014.

Howard, G., R. F. Martin, and B. A. Wilson. "Are Recoveries from Banking and Financial Crises Really So Different?" International Finance Discussion Papers No. 1037, Board of Governors of the Federal Reserve System, 2011.

Jaimovich, N., and H. E. Siu. "The Trend Is the Cycle: Job Polarization and Jobless Recoveries." NBER Working Paper No. 18334, 2012.

Jalil, A. J. "A New History of Banking Panics in the United States, 1825–1929: Construction and Implications." *American Economic Journal: Macroeconomics*, 7(3), 2015, 295–330.

Jordà, O., M. Schularick, and A. M. Taylor. "When Credit Bites Back: Leverage, Business Cycles, and Crises." FRBSF Working Paper No. 2011–27, 2011.

Kahn, J. A., and R. W. Rich. "Tracking the New Economy: Using Growth Theory to Detect Changes in Trend Productivity." *Journal of Monetary Economics*, 54, 2007, 1670–1701.

Laeven, L., and F. Valencia. "Systemic Banking Crises Database: An Update." IMF Working Paper No. 12/163, 2012.

Lopez-Salido, D., and E. Nelson. "Postwar Financial Crises and Economic Recoveries in the United States." Working Paper, May 21, 2010.

Macroeconomic Advisers. "The Shape of Things to Come." *MA Macro Focus*, 4(6), 2009, 1–11.

Meltzer, A. H. *A History of the Federal Reserve, Volume 2, Book 1: 1951–1969.* Chicago: University of Chicago Press, 2010.

Miron, J. A., and C. D. Romer. "A New Monthly Index of Industrial Production, 1884–1940." *Journal of Economic History*, 50(2), 1990, 321–37.

Morley, J., and J. Piger. "The Asymmetric Business Cycle." *Review of Economics and Statistics*, 94(1), 2012, 208–21.

Owens, R. E., and S. L. Schreft. "Identifying Credit Crunches." *Contemporary Economic Policy*, 13(2), 1995, 63–76.

Papell, D. H., and R. Prodan. "The Statistical Behavior of GDP after Financial Crises and Severe Recessions." *The B.E. Journal of Macroeconomics, Special Issue: Long-Term Effects of the Great Recession*, Article 2, 2012, 1–29.

Reinhart, C. S., and K. S. Rogoff. *This Time Is Different: Eight Centuries of Financial Folly.* Princeton, NJ: Princeton University Press, 2009.

Roesch, S. R. "The FOMC in 1974: Monetary Policy during Economic Uncertainty." *Federal Reserve Bank of St. Louis Review*, 57(4), 1975, 2–13.

Romer, C. D., and D. H. Romer. "New Evidence on the Impact of Financial Crises in Advanced Countries." NBER Working Paper No. 21021, 2015.

Roubini, N. "A Phantom Recovery?" Project Syndicate No. 14, August 2009.

Schularick, M., and A. M. Taylor. "Credit Booms Gone Bust: Monetary Policy, Leverage Cycles, and Financial Crises, 1870–2008." *American Economic Review*, 102(2), 2012, 1029–61.

Silber, W. L. *When Washington Shut Down Wall Street: The Great Financial Crisis of 1914 and the Origin of America's Monetary Supremacy.* Princeton, NJ: Princeton University Press, 2007.

Stock, J. H., and M. W. Watson. "Disentangling the Channels of the 2007–2009 Recession," NBER Working Paper No. 18094, 2012.

Watson, M. W. "Business-Cycle Durations and Postwar Stabilization of the U.S. Economy." *American Economic Review*, 84(1), 1994, 24–46.

Wicker, E. R. *Banking Panics of the Gilded Age.* Cambridge: Cambridge University Press, 2000.

Wynne, M. A., and N. S. Balke. "Are Deep Recessions Followed by Strong Recoveries?" *Economics Letters*, 39, 1992, 183–89.

———. "Recessions and Recoveries." *Economic Review*, Q1, 1993, 1–17.

Zarnowitz, V. *Business Cycles: Theory, History, Indicators, and Forecasting.* Chicago: University of Chicago Press, 1992.

CHAPTER 7

Credit Crises, Money and Contractions
An Historical View

MICHAEL D. BORDO AND JOSEPH G. HAUBRICH

1. Introduction

CREDIT MARKET DISTRESS ARISES in its more virulent form only in certain monetary environments, and has its most extreme effects when it exacerbates a business cycle downturn. Policy questions about a central bank's role as lender of last resort or regulator must be seen in the context of monetary policy.

The relatively infrequent nature of major credit distress events makes an historical approach to these issues particularly useful. Using a combination of historical narrative and econometric techniques, we identify major periods of credit distress from 1875 to 2007, examine the extent to which credit distress arises as part of the transmission of monetary policy, and document the subsequent effect on output.

These issues involve relationships between policy rates (monetary aggregates), credit spreads, and GDP growth. Using turning points defined by the Harding–Pagan algorithm, we compare the timing, duration, amplitude

Originally published in "Credit Crises, Money and Contractions: An Historical View," *Journal of Monetary Economics* 57, no. 1 (March 2010): 1–18. © 2009 Elsevier B.V. All rights reserved.

and co-movement of cycles in money, credit and output. For the period since the 1920s, this is most easily done with a risk spread between corporate and Treasury bonds, the discount rate, and real GDP. This allows us to pick out and compare periods of tight credit that result from tight monetary policy and those that have a more exogenous cause. For the period from 1875 to 1920, credit spreads are measured by differences between yields on different railroad bonds, and the conditions in the money market are measured by commercial paper yields. We also examine the patterns for real stock prices since stock market crashes also can act as an exacerbating factor in credit turmoil.

1.1. Literature Review

The effect of credit on the broader economy has been of concern to economists since the early days of the profession. Nineteenth-century authors often spoke of "discredit," a term Kindleberger (2000) adopts for the later phase of a financial crisis. Mitchell (1913) was an early expositor of the credit channel as was Hansen (1927), and J. Laurence Laughlin (1913) testified that "the organization of credit is more important than the question of bank notes." Disentangling the impact of credit supply from changes in demand as well as from the myriad channels of monetary policy remains a challenging empirical (and theoretical!) exercise even today. The importance of expectations in forward-looking financial markets—indeed for economic behavior in general—further compounds the problem.

Much work has focused on isolating the "credit channel" of monetary policy from other transmission mechanisms. Bernanke and Gertler (1995) review the ways monetary policy can affect the "external finance premium" and the cost and amount of credit obtained by firms. The balance sheet (or broad lending) channel affects firm (and individual) credit worthiness by changing the value of available collateral (Bernanke and Gertler, 1989; Mishkin, 1978). The bank lending (or narrow lending) channel works by restricting banks' ability to borrow and subsequently lend to smaller firms (Bernanke and Blinder, 1988). Earlier, of course, Brunner and Meltzer (1972) emphasized the importance of distinguishing between money and bank credit.

Though agency problems, credit rationing, and other deviations from the Modigliani–Miller paradigm provide a basis for financial accelerator models that transmit the effects of monetary policy, such frictions also mean that credit markets can produce as well as transmit shocks. Rajan (1994) shows how banks can transmit business cycle shocks independently of monetary policy, as reputational concerns induce herding in credit availability. Gorton and Ping (2008) view credit tightening as an increase in monitoring by banks resulting from the need to enforce collusive behavior over time.

Empirically there have been several approaches to identifying credit effects. One looks at particular historical episodes for evidence, and our historical narrative takes a closer look at this section of the literature. A second strand uses microeconomic data of particular industries, often looking at regulatory or other changes that shift bank portfolios (Haubrich and Wachtel, 1993; Beatty and Gron, 2001) or demonstrate that financial constraints affect firm investment (Fazzari et al., 1988; Lamont, 1997). A third strand examines the relationship between bank lending standards as a measure of the credit cycle. See e.g., Asea and Blomberg (1998), Lown and Morgan (2006), and Dell'Ariccia and Marquez (2006). And a fourth strand has worked to calibrate general equilibrium models with explicit financial frictions, looking to obtain tighter bounds of credit effects (Carlstrom and Fuerst, 1997; Christiano et al., 2008), building on the earlier work of Bernanke et al. (1996). This fourth strand builds upon the real business cycle work that emphasizes the importance of technology shocks as a driver of business cycles (Kydland and Prescott, 1982; Long and Plosser, 1983). This literature also suggests that the historical record of money and credit shocks may be endogenous responses to more fundamental technology shocks (Cole and Ohanian, 1999). We attempt to address these concerns by examining historical values of total factor productivity in our examination of cycles.

More recently, there has been renewed interest in observing correlations between macro-variables across broad ranges of countries and time periods, as in Reinhart and Rogoff (2009) and Claessens et al. (2008). Our work is closer to these latter papers and the related work of Mishkin (1990). Relative to Mishkin and Reinhart and Rogoff, we give greater attention to all business cycles, not just those associated with crises, giving a broader picture of the relations between money, credit and output. Relative to

Claessens, Kose and Terrones and Reinhart and Rogoff, we look at one country, and are able to give greater detail on the institutional and historical factors at work in the economy. For example, we can compare how contemporary accounts of credit conditions compare with empirical measures of credit tightness.

Section 2 presents an historical narrative, providing descriptive evidence on the incidence of policy tightening, banking and stock market crashes, and credit market turmoil across 27 U.S. business cycles. This narrative is designed to complement the empirical evidence in the rest of the paper where we use empirical methods to discern significant patterns in the data. We focus on the relationship between monetary policy, credit cycles, asset busts and real GDP. Section 3 discusses our methodology. We use the Harding and Pagan (2002) algorithm to identify cycles in money credit, stock prices and real GDP and then examine the concordance of these cycles.

Section 4 presents the empirical results, first comparing the duration, timing, and amplitude of cycles in money, credit, and output. Several sets of regressions then compare the depth of recessions to the cyclical movements in other variables. Section 5 concludes.

2. Historical Narrative

Table 7.1 presents some salient qualitative features of the 29 U.S. business cycle recessions from 1875 to the present. We show evidence on the incidence of banking crises, stock market crashes, real estate busts, tight monetary policy, credit crunches. We also provide brief comments on the underlying events. Figure 7.1 shows related data on real GDP, the price level, money supply (M2), short-term interest rates, the quality spread, the Standard and Poor's stock price index, and Shiller's (2005) index of real house prices.

2.1. Classical Gold Standard Period 1875–1914

From 1875 to 1914[1] the U.S. was an open economy on the gold standard and had significant capital inflows from Europe, especially the U.K. There was no central bank but the Treasury on occasion performed central banking functions. The country had frequent business recessions and also frequent banking panics which greatly worsened the contractions. Banking

TABLE 7.1 Descriptive Data 1873–2008

	NBER Business Cycle Peak	Banking Crises	Stock Market Crash	Real Estate Bust	Tight Monetary Policy	Credit Crunch	Comments
1	October 1873	September 1873	September 1873	No	Bank of England tightens	?	International Financial Crisis; real estate bust in Germany, Austria; Railroad scandal stock market crisis and serious recession focused on railroads. Panic ends with suspension of convertibility
2	March 1882	June 1884	February 1884	No	No	Yes[a]	Minor panic consequent upon failure of Grant and Ward, attenuated by NY clearing house
3	March 1887	No	No	No	No	No	Minor recession
4	July 1890	November 1890	November 1890	No	Bank of England tightens	No	Baring crisis in London caused by Argentine defaults. Bank of England tightening leads to sudden stop, minor banking panic attenuated by NY clearing house
5	January 1893	May 1893	May 1893	No	Silver risk	Yes[a]	Major U.S. banking panic related to fears U.S. would be found off gold standard after passage of Sherman Silver Purchase Act. Panic ends with suspension of convertibility

(continued)

TABLE 7.1 Descriptive Data 1873–2008 (*continued*)

	NBER Business Cycle Peak	Banking Crises	Stock Market Crash	Real Estate Bust	Tight Monetary Policy	Credit Crunch	Comments
6	December 1895	October 1896[b]	No	No	Silver risk	No	Gorton (1988) identifies a banking panic but Sprague and Friedman and Schwartz (1963) do not. Silver risk induced run on U.S. Treasury gold reserves stemmed by Belmont Morgan Syndicate (Friedman and Schwartz, 1963)
7	June 1899	No	No	No	No	No	Minor recession
8	September 1902	No	October 1903	No	No	No	Minor recession. Rich man's panic (Friedman and Schwartz, 1963, p. 151)
9	May 1907	October 1907	October 1907	No	Bank of England tightens	Yes[a]	Major recession and banking panic, rescue by JPMorgan, suspension of convertibility. Contemporaries discuss credit squeeze
10	January 1910	No	No	No	No	No	Minor recession
11	January 1913	August 1914 (incipient)	August 1914 (incipient)	No	No	No	Outbreak of World War I

12	August 1918	No	Fall 1917	No	No	No	Mild recession, Mishkin and White (2002) attribute stock market crisis to rising interest rates and controls on new issues
13	January 1920	No	Fall 1920	No	Yes	No	Major recession induced by Fed tight money to roll back wartime inflation
14	May 1923	No	No	No	Yes	No	Minor recession. Fed followed policy of moderate restraint (Friedman and Schwartz, 1963, p. 287) to offset incipient inflation
15	October 1926	No	No	No[c]	Yes	No	Minor recession. Fed takes "moderate restraining measures" (Friedman and Schwartz, 1963, p. 288)
16	August 1929	October 1930 April 1931 September/ October 1931 January/ February 1933	October 1929	Yes[d]	Yes	Yes[e]	Great contraction. Tight Fed policy 1928–1929 to stem stock market speculation for Banking crises. Contraction in net worth, debt deflation, bank capital crunch
17	May 1937	No	February 1937 May 1940	No	Yes	Yes[f]	Major recession. Fed doubles reserve requirements in 1936, Contraction in net worth, bank capital crunch

(continued)

TABLE 7.1 Descriptive Data 1873–2008 (*continued*)

	NBER Business Cycle Peak	Banking Crises	Stock Market Crash	Real Estate Bust	Tight Monetary Policy	Credit Crunch	Comments
18	February 1945	No	September 1946	No	No	No	End of World War II. Sharp decreases in government expenditures. Adjustment from war to peace
19	November 1948	No	No	No	Yes[g]	No	Fed tightens to offset post-war inflation
20	July 1953	No	No	No	Yes	Yes[h]	Mild recession. Moderate tightening reflecting Fed concern of inflation. Bond crisis raises rates
21	August 1957	No	No	No	Yes[i]	Yes[j]	Significant recession induced by Fed tightening. Evidence of credit rationing
22	April 1960	No	Spring 1902[k]	No	Yes	Yes[l]	Mild recession induced by Fed tightening. Disintermediation as market rates pierced Regulation Q ceilings leads to reduced bank lending
						August–September 1966[m]	"Credit crunch" of 1966 background of Fed tightening monetary policy end of 1965. Fed bank regulators urged restraint on bank lending. Disintermediation Regulation Q ceilings bound

#							
23	December 1969	No[n]	May 1970	No	Yes[o]	Yes[p]	Mild recession. Fed tightening and jawboning by Fed and government to restrain lending. Disintermediation as market rates exceed Regulation Q ceilings
24	November 1973	No[q]	November 1973[r]	No	Yes	Yes[p]	Fed tightening. OPEC shock. Significant recession. Arthur Burns (May 1974) urges banks to allocate credit through non-price rationing
25	January 1980	No	No[s]	No[t]	Yes	Yes[p]	Significant Fed tightening begins October 1979 (Volcker shock). March 1980 Fed at Carter's administration request imposes selective consumer credit controls. Controls lifted July 1980
26	July 1981	No[u]	No	No	Yes	Yes[p]	Tight Fed policy induces serious recession
27	July 1990	No	August 1990	No[v]	Yes[w]	Yes[x]	Fed tightening. Gulf war. Mild recession. Evidence of non-price credit rationing and a capital crunch
28	March 2001	No	Spring 2001	No	Yes	No	Fed restraint leads to mild recession, tech bust

(continued)

TABLE 7.1 Descriptive Data 1873–2008 (*continued*)

	NBER Business Cycle Peak	Banking Crises	Stock Market Crash	Real Estate Bust	Tight Monetary Policy	Credit Crunch	Comments
29	December 2007	September	October[y]	Yes[z]	Yes[aa]	Yes	Fed tightening beginning in June 2004 may have helped trigger a real estate bust, Lehman Brothers failure, credit crunch, stock market slide, and severe recession

SOURCES: *Banking Crises:* Bordo (1986), Friedman and Schwartz (1963), Gorton (1988). *Stock Market Crashes:* Bordo (1986), Bordo et al. (2008), Friedman and Schwartz (1963), Mishkin and White (2002), Sprague (1910). *Real Estate Busts:* Shiller (2005), White (2008). *Tight Monetary Policy:* Friedman and Schwartz (1963), Meltzer (2003), Romer and Romer (1989). *Credit Crunch:* Bernanke (1983), Bernanke and Lown (1991), Calomiris and Hubbard (1989), Calomiris and Mason (2003), Calomiris and Wilson (2004), Eckstein and Sinai (1986), Owens and Schreft (1993), Wojnilower (1980, 1985, 1992).

[a] Calomiris and Hubbard (1989), citing Sprague and others.

[b] Gorton (1988).

[c] Florida land bust, White (2008).

[d] White (2008).

[e] Bernanke (1983), Calomiris and Mason (2003), Calomiris and Wilson (2004).

[f] Bernanke (1983), Calomiris and Wilson (2004).

[g] Romer and Romer (1989) pick October 1947 as the start of Fed tightening.

[h] Wojnilower (1992) states that bank lending was impaired by the collapse in Treasury bond prices.

[i] Romer and Romer (1989) date tightening as beginning September 1955.

[j] Wojnilower (1980, 1985, 1992), Eckstein and Sinai (1986) discuss credit rationing as leading to the 1957–1958 recession.

[k] Real stock prices decline by 29% January 1966 to October 1966 (Bordo et al., 2008).

[l] According to Wojnilower (1980, 1992), Fed tightening pushed T-bill rates above the Regulation Q ceiling leading to disintermediation.

[m] Wojnilower (1980), Owens and Schreft (1993).

[n] Penn Central collapse in July 1970. The Fed averted a crisis by backstopping the money center banks' support of the commercial paper market.

[o] Romer and Romer (1989) date Fed tightening as beginning in December 1968.

[p] Owens and Schreft (1993).

[q] Failures of Franklin National Bank October 1974 and Germany's Herstatt Bank June 1974.

[r] Romer and Romer (1989) date monetary tightening as beginning in April 1974.

[s] Real stock prices decline by 20%, November 1980 to July 1982 (Bordo et al., 2008).

[t] Shiller (2005) Fig. 2.1 shows a 13% decline in real house prices 1979–1993.

[u] Failures of Continental Illinois and Penn Square banks in 1984. Also savings and loan crisis in 1984.

[v] Shiller (2005) Fig. 2.1 shows a 13% decline in real house prices 1989–1993.

[w] Romer and Romer (1989) give December 1988 as the beginning of tight policy.

[x] Bernanke and Lown (1991) provide evidence of a capital crunch in New England. Bonds reduced lending to replenish their capital to meet regulatory standard. Owens and Schreft (1993) document non-price credit rationing in the real estate sector.

[y] The Standard and Poor's stock price index declined 55% from July 2007 to March 2009.

[z] The Case and Shiller real home price index declined 33% from December 2006 to October 2008.

[aa] The Federal Funds rate increased from a trough in May 2004 at 1.00% to a peak of 5.26% in July 2007.

panics were endemic in a banking system characterized by unit banking (with prohibitions against branching or interstate banking) and the absence of an effective lender of last resort. Foreign interest rate shocks as the Bank of England periodically raised its discount rate led to sudden stops in capital inflows, gold outflows, declines in the money supply, bank lending and declines in real output and prices (Bordo, 2006).

These events were associated with stock market crashes and banking panics. The stock market was closely linked to the national banking system through the inverted pyramid of credit whereby national bank reserves in the country and reserve city national banks were concentrated in the New York banks. These reserves were held as call loans and were invested in the New York Stock exchange. Consequently shocks to the stock market would spread to the banking system and vice versa (Bordo et al., 1992).

Contemporaries such as Sprague (1910) discussed the tightening of bank credit during these events. Calomiris and Hubbard (1989) present evidence of equilibrium credit rationing reflecting asymmetric information in the context of the Stiglitz and Weiss (1981) model.[2]

Of the 10 business cycles for this period covered in Table 7.1, three had serious banking panics, with mild or incipient panics in another four. Deep recessions were associated with the banking panics. Seven downturns were associated with stock market crashes. There is no evidence of national real estate busts in this period although there were some famous regional busts, e.g., California in the 1890s. In three of the recessions associated with panics, Bank of England tightening leading to a sudden stop of capital inflows was likely the source of the shock. In addition monetary tightening contingent on the fear that legislation associated with the Free Silver movement (Bland Allison Act of 1878 and the Sherman Silver Purchase Act of 1893) likely led to the panic of 1893 and the currency (and minor banking) crisis of 1896 (Friedman and Schwartz, 1963; Gorton, 1988). According to Calomiris and Hubbard (1989) citing Sprague and others, credit crunches occurred in the major recessions.

2.2. Important Episodes

2.2.1. 1873.   A serious international crisis with origins in a real estate bust in Vienna and Berlin was in the U.S. associated with corporate malfeasance

FIGURE 7.1   Plot of Selected Macro-and Financial Variables. Shaded
Bars Are NBER Recessions

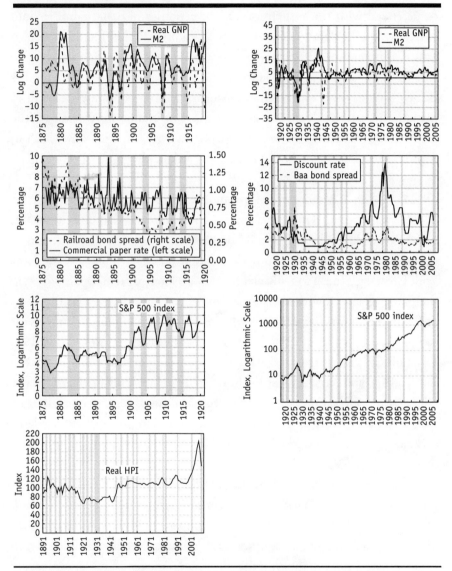

SOURCES: Standard and Poor's; Balke and Gordon (1986), NBER, Federal Reserve Board,
Friedman and Schwartz (1963), Macaulay (1938), and authors' calculations.

in the dominant railroad sector (Benmelech and Bordo, 2008), a stock market crash and a banking panic with widespread banking failures. The panic ended with the suspension of convertibility of bank liabilities into currency. The evidence of fraud in railroads precipitated a sudden stop in capital inflows from England. The resultant recession lasted until 1879. Mishkin (1990) provides evidence that a quality spread between Moody's Baa corporate bond rate and the long-term Treasury bond rate spiked after the banking panic and stock market crash. This is cited as evidence for the presence of declining net worth and asymmetric information, which in turn increased agency costs and reduced bank lending.

2.2.2. 1893.   A serious banking and stock market crash in the summer of 1893 was triggered by the passage of the Sherman Silver Purchase Act, which led to fears the U.S. would be forced off the gold standard and to capital flight. In the crisis hundreds of banks failed. Attempts by the New York Clearing House to issue clearing house loan certificates did not stop the panic. It ended with the suspension of convertibility. As in the crisis of 1873, Calomiris and Hubbard cite evidence of equilibrium credit rationing, e.g., Stevens (1894) ". . . wholesale transactions [are] usually done on credit. [New] general business was . . . being done almost on a cash basis" (p. 141), and Mishkin (1990) shows the quality spread peaks with the crisis. "The contraction of lending by the banking system as a result of its trouble reduced its role in solving adverse selection and agency problems and clearly made these problems worse in the financial markets" (p. 19).

2.2.3. 1907.   This serious recession was also accompanied by a banking panic and stock market crash. It may have been triggered by Bank of England tightening in 1906 in reaction to a gold outflow to the U.S. to cover insurance claims from the San Francisco earthquake (Odell and Weidenmeir, 2004). In the U.S. the collapse of a corner of the copper market in October led to the failure of 8 banks, followed by the failure of the Knickerbocker Trust Company. This led to a run on the other trust companies and then a general panic. The issue of clearing house loan certificates, the transfer of funds from the Treasury to key New York banks and a rescue by a syndicate organized by J.P. Morgan alleviated the pressure, but the panic only ended with the suspension of convertibility. The panic was associated with hundreds of bank failures, a significant drop in money supply and a deep recession. As in other panic episodes, Calomiris and Hubbard cite contemporary evidence for a credit crunch. Persons (1920) discusses "a halt in further credit expansion" (p. 147); Sprague (1910): "It would seem, then, past business distress from lack of credit facilities was due at least to three influences: the restriction of cash payments by the banks increased the requirements of borrowers; the supply of loans was reduced by a moderate amount of contraction; and the shifting of loans involved considerable uncertainty and inconveniences" (p. 303). Mishkin (1990), as in the previous crisis shows a spike in the quality spread. According to him "the decline in the valuation of firms [in the stock market crash] raises adverse selection and agency problems for borrowing firms because it has in effect lowered their net worth. The resulting increases in asymmetric information problems even before the October banking panic, should raise the spread between interest rates for high and low quality borrowers. . . . The process of severe asymmetric problems even before the banking panic suggests that they were . . . potentially important factors in creating a severe business cycle contraction" (pp. 21–27).

2.2.4. 1914. The outbreak of World War I led to a massive capital outflow from U.S. financial markets to the belligerents. This massive sudden stop threatened the New York stock market, the banking system and U.S. gold reserves. Treasury Secretary McAdoo invoked the Aldrich Vreeland Act to issue emergency currency to allay the banking panic, closed the NYSE and pooled U.S. gold reserves. The crisis was largely averted. There is no narrative evidence of a credit crunch.

2.3. The Interwar Years: 1918–1945

The Federal Reserve was established in 1914 in part to solve the absence of a lender of last resort in the crises of the pre-1914 National Banking era. In its first 25 years there were three very severe business cycle downturns: 1920–1921, 1929–1933 and 1937–1938. All three were associated with very tight money. The 1929–1933 recession had four banking panics producing the Great Contraction. The stock market crashed in 1920, 1929,

1930–1932 and 1937. According to White (2008) there was a real estate boom and bust in the 1920s and another in 1929–1933. There is considerable evidence for collapse of bank lending (a credit crunch) in 1930–1933 and 1937–1938. According to Bernanke (1983) both the numerous bank failures that occurred and the collapse in net worth brought about by bankruptcies, falling asset prices and deflation, increased the cost of credit intermediation and reduced real output over and above the efforts of a decline in money supply posited by Friedman and Schwartz (1963).

2.3.1. 1920–1921. The Fed tightened dramatically raising its discount rate in late 1919 to roll back the inflation that had built up during World War I and to restore effective adherence to the gold standard. This followed a severe but brief recession (industrial production fell 23%, wholesale prices fell 37% and unemployment increased from 4% to 12%) possibly because Fed actions were not anticipated (Bordo et al., 2007). No banking crises occurred but there was a stock market crash, according to Mishkin and White (2002). Also there is no narrative evidence for a credit crunch; the transmission of tight money occurred through a rise in real interest rates (Meltzer, 2003, p. 118).

2.3.2. 1929–1933. The Fed tightened beginning in early 1928 to stem the stock market boom which began in 1926. This tightening led to a recession in August 1929 and a stock market crash in October. The New York Fed initially followed expansionary policy to prevent a money market panic in October. It then stopped easing by the end of the year. Despite demands from New York, the Federal Reserve Board in Washington, following the real bills doctrine, was concerned about rekindling stock market speculation. A series of banking panics beginning in October 1930 ensued. The Fed did little to offset them, hence allowing the recession to become a depression. According to Friedman and Schwartz (1963), the banking panics reduced the money stock by a third and led to similar declines in real output and prices. The process was aggravated by debt and asset price deflation. According to Bernanke (1983) the bank failures and the collapse of net worth (Mishkin, 1978) raised the cost of credit intermediation seen in an increase in quality spreads. In addition, Calomiris and Mason (2003) and Calomiris and Wilson (2004) identify the shocks to bank lending (credit crunch) using, respectively, a panel of bank data by states and by New York City national banks.

2.3.3. 1937–1938.

Recovery from the Great Contraction began with Roosevelt's Banking Holiday in early March 1933 and Treasury gold purchases (Romer, 1992). It was slowed somewhat by the supply shocks of the NIRA (Cole and Ohanian, 2004). A second severe recession in 1937–1938 was produced by a major Fed policy error. It doubled reserve requirements in 1936 to sop up banks' excess reserves. This led to another collapse in money supply and a return to severe recession. Both Bernanke (1983) and Calomiris and Wilson (2004) see evidence for a decline in the supply of bank loans (a crunch) in response to deflation and declining net worth.

2.4. The Post-War Period: 1945–1980

The Fed emerged from World War II still pegging Treasury bond prices. This policy led to high inflation which ended with tightening in October 1947 (Romer and Romer, 1989) that led to a recession in 1948. The famous Federal Reserve Treasury accord of 1951 restored Fed independence. The next 15 years were characterized by relatively stable monetary policy (Meltzer, 2003). The Fed under William McChesney Martin in the 1950s viewed price stability as its primary objective. On several occasions, when facing incipient inflation, the Fed tightened, precipitating a recession.

In the post-war period there were no banking panics and no serious stock market crashes. However, according to Wojnilower (1980, 1985, 1992), credit crunches occurred when the Fed tightened, raising short-term interest rates. As rates increased above the Regulation Q ceiling on time deposits (and later on CDs) this led to disintermediation of funds from the banking system and a decline in bank lending. Such disintermediation crunches were said to have occurred in 1953, 1957 and 1960.

The term "credit crunch" was coined in 1966. The Fed tightened in December 1965 at the beginning of the Great Inflation by raising the discount rate by 50 basis points to 4½%. Disintermediation, as rates rose above the Regulation Q ceiling, was prevented by the Fed raising the ceiling rate to 5½%. Continued concern by the FOMC over inflationary pressure coming from higher rates led the Fed's bank regulating agencies to issue a statement in March urging lending restraint by the banks (Owens and Schreft, 1993, p. 8).

Further statements urging non-price credit rationing came from the House Banking and Currency Committee. This was echoed in a report by the American Banking Association. Then in July 1966 in the face of rising prime rates, the FOMC allowed Regulation Q to bind and banks experienced an outflow of funds. On September 1, the Fed sent a letter to all member banks urging them to slow the growth of their business loan portfolios (Owens and Schreft, 1993, p. 15). The credit crunch led to a slowdown in bank lending and economic growth and on September 21 the Congress passed a law (which the Fed endorsed) urging it to "reduce interest rates as much as possible given prevailing economic conditions" (Owens and Schreft, 1993, p. 16). The crunch ended.

A similar sequence of events occurred in 1969. In early 1969, the Fed began tightening to stem inflationary pressure. Disintermediation occurred as market rates exceeded the Regulation Q ceilings. To discourage banks from raising their rates (which was deemed to be inflationary) the Fed and the administration urged the banks in the spring to restrict their lending. Jawboning accelerated as the summer began. "Bowing to political pressure the major banks refrained from raising their prime rates further in the latter half of 1969 despite strong loan demand and rising loan rates. [The banks] instead relied more heavily on non-price credit allocation methods" (Owens and Schreft, 1993, p. 22). Loan demand slowed by the end of 1969 as the economy slipped into recession, ending the credit crunch.

In 1973, the Fed again tightened to fight inflation. To insure against a credit crunch the Fed in May suspended Regulation Q ceilings on large CDs and raised ceilings on other deposit categories. At the same time it raised marginal reserve requirements: apparently it had shifted to a policy based on the price mechanism rather than credit availability (Owens and Schreft, 1993, p. 26).[3] Yet on May 22, Chairman Burns wrote a letter to bankers asking them to allocate credit through non-price rationing instead of raising rates further (Owens and Schreft, 1993). The Fed continued to tighten through 1974 by repeated hikes in the discount rate but ceased pressuring the banks with non-price allocation techniques (Owens and Schreft, 1993, p. 28).

2.5. Disinflation and Beyond: 1980–2007

Inflation continued unabated through the 1970s. Debate swirls over the causes of the Great Inflation, 1965–1982. Some observers attribute it to the accommodation of expansionary fiscal policy, others to the Phillips Curve tradeoff and an unwillingness driven by political pressure to raise unemployment at the expense of inflation, and others to measurement errors in estimating potential output (Bordo and Orphanides, 2009). Finally, in the face of an exchange rate crisis and growing popular discontent, President Carter in October 1979 appointed Paul Volcker as chairman of the Federal Reserve. Monetary policy tightened significantly as Volcker effectively targeted monetary aggregates instead of interest rates, and produced a series of sizeable hikes in the federal funds rate. However, the tight monetary stance was temporarily abandoned in mid-1980 as economic activity decelerated sharply.

In March 1980 at the request of the Carter administration, as a signal to the public in an election year of its willingness to fight inflation, the Fed imposed selective consumer credit controls. The controls involved direct restrictions on bank loan growth. The Fed provided broad guidelines for credit allocation suggesting for example that banks avoid making unsecured consumer loans (Owens and Schreft, 1993, p. 30). The program led to a marked decline in consumer credit as lending rates hit binding usury law ceilings. This reduced personal consumption, contributing to a very sharp decline in economic activity. The controls were lifted in July 1980.

The Federal Reserve embarked on a new round of monetary tightening in late 1980. The federal funds rate rose to 20% in late December, implying an ex post real rate of about 10% (Bordo et al., 2007). Newly elected President Reagan's support of Volcker's policy was significant in giving the Federal Reserve the mandate it needed to keep interest rates elevated for a prolonged period, and provided some shield from growing opposition in Congress (Feldstein, 1993). This second and more durable round of tightening succeeded in reducing the inflation rate from about 10% in early 1981 to about 4% in 1983, but at the cost of a very sharp and very prolonged recession. In this episode there is no narrative evidence of a credit crunch.

The recession of 1990–1991 was preceded by Fed tightening beginning in December 1988 (Romer and Romer, 1994). It coincided with the first Gulf War. There was no banking crisis but there was a stock market crash in August 1990. There also was not a real estate bust, although real house prices declined 13% 1989–1993. According to Bernanke and Lown (1991) there was a credit crunch which they define as "a significant leftward shift in the supply of bank loans holding constant the safe real interest rate and the quality of potential borrowers." According to them a collapse in New England real estate reduced their equity capital and forced banks to scale back their lending. This reduced aggregate demand via the lending channel (Bernanke and Blinder, 1988) and contributed to the recession.

Owens and Schreft (1993), who define a credit crunch as "non-price credit rationing," also posit that there was a credit crunch in the commercial real estate market, a "sector specific credit crunch that prevented commercial real estate developers and business borrowers using real estate as collateral from getting credit at any price" (p. 50).

The recession of 2001 was preceded by a mild tightening of monetary policy (the funds rate was raised from 4½% in November 1998 to 6% in May), and the collapse of the tech boom in the stock market in the spring of 2001. There is no narrative evidence of a real estate bust or a credit crunch.

Finally, the recession which began in December 2007 was preceded by Fed tightening beginning in June 2004 following 3 years of excessively low rates. The low policy rates as well as a global savings glut helped fund a housing boom which began deflating at the end of 2006. The ensuing housing bust initially centered on the U.S. subprime mortgage market in the spring of 2007. Factors behind the boom in addition to low interest rates include U.S. government initiatives to extend home ownership, changes in financial regulation, lax oversight and the relaxing of prudent standards (Bordo, 2008).

The default on subprime mortgages produced spillover effects around the world via the securitized mortgage derivatives into which these mortgages were bundled, to the balance sheets of investment banks, hedge funds and conduits which intermediate between mortgage and other asset-backed commercial paper and long-term securities. The uncertainty about the value of the securities collateralized by these mortgages led to the freezing of the interbank lending market in August 2007 and subsequently to a massive credit crunch. The collapse in credit reflected a severe drop in asset prices which eroded net worth and collateral, greatly increasing agency costs and quality spreads. In addition the weakening of major banks' balance sheets has impaired their lending. This has been greatly aggravated by a more than 50% drop in stock prices. Despite extensive central bank liquidity injections and the creation of a number of facilities at the Fed to rejuvenate the credit markets, the crunch still prevails. The credit crunch has produced a serious recession in the U.S. which has spread to the rest of the world.

3. Empirical Methodology

With an aim of examining cycles in money, credit and output since 1875, data availability and consistency become key issues. For business cycles, we use the NBER chronology (at a quarterly frequency). For Real Gross National Product (note it is GNP, not GDP) we use the numbers from Balke and Gordon (1986), extended via the NIPA accounts. Likewise for the money supply, we use the M2 numbers from Balke and Gordon, spliced and updated with the M2 numbers from the Board of Governors. For many other series, 1919 becomes a natural break point. For the interest rate (risk) spread in 1919 and after, we use Moody's Seasoned Baa Corporate Bond Yield (% p.a.) less Long-Term Treasury Composite, Over 10 Years (% p.a.). For the earlier period, we construct a difference between averages of the high yielding and low yielding railroad bond yields taken from Macaulay (1938).[4] Macaulay is also the source for early values of commercial paper. The discount rate since 1945 is the rate from the Board of Governors and prior to that is the rate at the Federal Reserve Bank of New York, from Banking and Monetary Statistics (1943). The stock price index for 1875–1917 is the Cowles Commission index, its level adjusted to match the Standard and Poor's index, which begins in 1917. Real estate prices are from Shiller (2005). Before 1954, our measure of total factor productivity is taken from Kendrick (1961) and since then calculated from standard BLS series.[5]

3.1. Methods

A focus on recessions and contractions, credit crunches, and monetary policy makes it natural that the empirical techniques should be consistent with such a cyclical focus. Fortunately, the suite of techniques developed by Harding and Pagan (2002, 2006) provides a ready fit with the classical NBER discussion of business cycles. In this paper we will use the methods of Harding and Pagan to extract turning points in the series for money, credit spreads, and stock prices and compare the characteristics of those cycles to the NBER cycle, concentrating on contractions.

The first step must be to identify cycles via their turning points. The NBER does this via the business cycle dating committee, but Bry and Boschan (1971) develop an algorithm that closely mimics the committee's decisions at a monthly frequency. Harding and Pagan (2002) extend the algorithm to a quarterly frequency, which matches the frequency of our data.

Any such algorithm needs three components. First, a way to identify turning points, essentially choosing local maximums and minimums. For a quarterly frequency, Harding and Pagan look for a data point that is a local max or min for two quarters on either side, that is, y_t is a cyclical peak if $y_t = \max\{y_{t-2}, y_{t-1}, y_{t+1}, y_{t+2}\}$.

Secondly, the procedure must make sure peaks and troughs alternate. Finally, it should impose censoring rules to obtain cycles of the appropriate length (for example, without these an algorithm may pick out seasonal cycles, though this is less likely in quarterly data). We use the RATS quarterly implementation (bryboschan.src).

Once defined, it becomes possible to measure cycle characteristics. Primarily, these are

(i) *Duration:* The length of the cycle and its phases (along with noting the asymmetry between phases)

(ii) *Amplitude:* Change in value between turning points
(iii) Shape, sometimes called cumulative movement, to distinguish how steeply the economy contracts or recovers.

To measure co-movement in what are often non-stationary series, Harding and Pagan propose a measure of synchronization between cycles which they term *concordance,* essentially a measure of how often two series are in the same phase of the cycle. Denote the periods that series Y_t spends in an expansion as $S_{yt} = 1$ and the time spent in contraction as $S_{yt} = 0$. Then the concordance C_{xy} between series x and series y is defined as $C_{xy} = (1/n)[\#\{S_{xt} = 1, S_{yt} = 1\} + \#\{S_{xt} = 0, S_{yt} = 0\}]$.

Two perfectly procyclical series would have a concordance of 1, with perfect countercyclicality having a concordance of 0. Such perfect alignment is never seen in economic time series, so it is more useful to compare the series to the standard of independence, or what Harding and Pagan term strong non-synchronization. The concordance associated with non-synchronization depends strongly on the asymmetry of the phases; if both series were in contractions 99% of the time, they would show a high concordance even if they were independent. The most useful comparison is then with the expected concordance $E[C_{xy}] = E[S_{xt}]E[S_{yt}] + (1 - E[S_{xt}])(1 - E[S_{yt}])$ where of course $E[S_{xt}] = \text{prob}(S_{xt} = 1)$. A higher concordance indicates procyclicality and a lower concordance indicates countercyclicality. Harding and Pagan (2006) also provide a regression-based test of independence that we report below.

Two cycles may be strongly non-synchonized and still influence each other; for example, an overlapping contraction might influence the depth of the recession.

Looking at the cycle overlaps provides more information about the empirical linkages between money, credit, and the business cycle over the years from 1875 to 2007. We explore how money, credit, and asset prices behave in recessions and look at how recessions differ according to whether or not they are associated with credit crunches, tight money, and asset price drops. In this we are broadly following the methods of Reinhart and Rogoff (2009) and Claessens et al. (2008). By also incorporating total factor productivity, our regressions attempt to separate out the effects of technology shocks (Long and Plosser, 1983; Cole and Ohanian, 1999) from financial turbulence in business cycles.

We present two sets of regressions.

The first set regresses the amplitude of the percentage peak-to-trough change in Real GNP against the changes in credit spreads, measures of money, and the stock index between the same NBER turning points.

The second set of regressions looks at how monetary, credit, and asset cycles affect the business cycle. For example, do recessions that start during a credit crunch look different than those that do not? Each NBER contraction is associated with the money, credit, or asset cycle phase that it starts in. The amplitude of the contraction is then regressed against the amplitude of the other cycle phases. For example, a recession that starts in a period of tightening credit and tightening monetary policy is associated with the amplitudes of those two "contraction" phases.

4. Empirical Results

Cycles can be described both by their individual characteristics and by their relation to each other. In our sample, from 1875:I to 2007:III, we have 27 (NBER) recessions, counted as complete peak-to-trough episodes.

4.1. Cycle Characteristics

Tables 7.2 and 7.3 report the mean amplitude and duration of cycles for the 1875:I–1918:IV period, and Tables 7.4 and 7.5 report the amplitude and durations for 1919:I–2007:IV, calculated for the peak-to-trough and trough-to-peak. If the beginning quarters belong to a contraction that started before our sample, those are not counted. Likewise for an expansion that continues beyond our sample.

The average duration of a recession (peak to trough) is 15.4 months, that of an expansion 39 months. Because of data limitations, we separately look at two subsamples, from 1875:I to 1918:IV and from 1919:I to 2007:IV, the period for which we have Federal Reserve discount rate data. For the later period, recessions have shortened and expansions lengthened. For the early period, the average duration of a recession is 6 quarters

TABLE 7.2 Cycle Amplitudes, 1875:1–1918:4, Quarterly

Amplitude	Peak–Trough	P–T%	Trough–Peak	T–P%
RGNP (NBER cycles)	−11.13	−7.8	36.37	34.1
Railroad spread	−0.28		0.27	
CP	−2.63		2.51	
M2 growth	10.4%		12.1%	

TABLE 7.3 Cycle Durations, 1875: 1–1918:4, Quarterly

Duration (quarters) 19th	Peak–Trough		Trough–Peak
RGNP (NBER cycles)	Mean	6	8.3
	Max	13	12
	Min	3	5
Railroad spread	Mean	8.25	9.89
	Max	18	36
	Min	2	2
CP	Mean	5.54	6.75
	Max	11	14
	Min	3	3
M2 growth	Mean	7.45	6.91
	Max	18	12
	Min	4	3

TABLE 7.4 Cycle Amplitudes, 1920:1 to 2007:4

Amplitude	Peak–Trough	P–T%	Trough–Peak	T–P%
RGNP (NBER cycles)	−28.69	−5.9%	238.52	29.0%
Baa spread	−1.18		1.14	
Discount rate	−2.18		2.18	
M2 growth	−2.9%		3.1%	

TABLE 7.5 Cycle Durations, 1920:1 to 2007:4

Duration 20th	Peak–Trough		Trough–Peak
RGNP (NBER cycles)	Mean	4.5	17.7
	Max	14	40
	Min	2	4
Baa spread	Mean	11.1	8.4
	Max	30	21
	Min	4	2
Discount rate	Mean	8.8125	20.8
	Max	18	66
	Min	2	9
M2 growth	Mean	11	6
	Max	65	15
	Min	3	2

TABLE 7.6 Concordances, Expected Concordances, and Probability of Independence (Regression Method) for Twentieth Century Series: 1920:1 to 2007:4, Quarterly, M2 Is Annual Log Difference, Using Data from 1919: 1 Calculated from Balke-Gordon, Spliced with Board of Governors M2 Data

	NBER	Baa	Discount	M2 (log diff)
NBER cycle concordance	1	34.4%	61.6	50.3
Expected concordance		45.5%	54.6	48.0
Prob. of independence		0.005%	0.9%	35.4%
Baa spread		1	54.0%	40.3
			48.8%	50.5
			26%	0.5%
Discount rate			1	38.1
				49.5
				0.4%
M2 (log difference)				1

Moody's Seasoned Baa Corporate Bond Yield (% p.a.) less Long-Term Treasury Composite, over 10 years (% p.a.)
Discount rate: Pre-1945, FRB NY rate, then BOG rate.

(8.3 for expansions). For the later period, the durations are 4.5 for contractions, 17.7 quarters for expansions.[6]

Credit shows a longer cycle. For the earlier sample, our measure of credit is the spread between different railroad bonds. These show a mean peak-to-trough duration of 8.25 quarters, and a trough-to-peak duration of nearly 10 quarters, as well as showing noticeably longer maximum cycles. Also note the greater symmetry between expansions and contractions in the credit spread series. For consistency, the P–T of rates and spreads should be compared to the T–P of RGNP. For the later sample, using the spread between Moody's seasoned Baa corporate bond yield less the long-term treasury composite, "contractions," or periods of generally falling spreads, last an average of 11.1 quarters, longer than the NBER contractions, but the periods of "expansion" or rising spreads, last only 8.4 quarters, significantly shorter than the 17.7 of NBER expansions.

What about monetary policy? For the earlier period, we use two measures. The first is Balke and Gordon's measure of M2, taken as the year-over-year log difference. Mean peak-to-trough duration is 7.5 quarters, measuring 9.9 quarters for the trough-to-peak expansions. This indicates a cycle length similar to the NBER cycle and a bit shorter than the credit cycle. We also use the commercial paper rate as a measure of monetary tightness. This seems to exhibit a shorter and less variable cycle, with expansions and contractions of 6.75 and 5.5 quarters. For the later period, we continue with the Balke and Gordon M2 series, splicing in the Board of Governors M2 when it becomes available. Like the NBER cycle, it is rather asymmetric, and perhaps not surprisingly, with contractions nearly twice as long as expansions. The discount rate, our other measure of policy, exhibits even more asymmetry, with mean peak-to-trough duration of nine quarters and mean trough-to-peak duration of over 20 (again note that a "contraction" in the money supply probably corresponds to an "expansion" in the discount rate). Overall it is noticeably longer than the business cycle.

In the later period, recessions tend to occur in an environment of monetary tightening and tighter credit. Of the 17 NBER business cycle peaks in the subsample, 4 occurred in the same quarter as the peak in the monetary policy (discount rate) cycle, another 9 occurred during the tightening phase of policy, and 2 occurred in the quarter immediately after a peak in the discount rate cycle. Fourteen of the 17 occurred in periods of credit tightening.

In the earlier period, the pattern repeats. Recessions tended to occur in time of monetary tightening, with all 11 NBER recessions occurring in a contractionary phase of M2 growth, and 10 of the 11 occurring in an environment of rising commercial paper rates. These were also generally periods of tightening credit, though the pattern is not quite so obvious: in 7 of the 11 cases railroad spreads were increasing.

Table 7.6 reports the concordances and tests of synchronicity for the twentieth century. Recall that an actual concordance above expected concordance indicates series that move procyclically. Most interesting for our purposes is concordance with the NBER cycle, though we find it gratifying that the discount rate moves countercyclically with M2. For the nineteenth century, we find evidence for the importance of credit in that the Baa spread moves countercyclically to the business cycle: increasing risk spreads are associated with recessions. The evidence for money is mixed, with the discount rate showing procyclical concordance, but we cannot reject independence for the log difference of M2.

Table 7.7 reports on concordance and synchronicity tests for the nineteenth century. The risk spread (on railroad bonds) is again procyclical, but significant only at the 10% level. Money is again mixed, with short rates showing procyclicality but quantity showing independence.

4.2. Regressions

The questions of whether larger changes in money, credit or asset prices are somehow associated with different amplitudes of contractions can be addressed in several ways. Following Claessens, Kose and Terrones, Tables 7.8 and 7.9 report regressions of recession amplitude against changes in the risk spread, money measures, and stock prices over the same dates as the NBER peak-to-trough phase. Such a regression of course does not determine causality, but to attempt to partially control for other factors, we also include the change in total factor productivity over the cycle. For both time periods, the coefficient on the risk spread is generally negative, though not always significant, indicating that larger changes in risk spreads are associated with larger amplitudes. (To be clear, a rise in the spread from

TABLE 7.7 Same as Above, for Nineteenth-Century Data, 1875:1 to 1918:4 (Quarterly)

	NBER	Rail Spread	CP rate	M2 (log dif)
NBER cycle concordance	1	59.7%	63.6	50.6%
Expected concordance		50.1%	51.0	49.8%
Prob. of independence		8.1%	1.3%	80.9%
Railroad spread		1	54.0	50.0
			50.1	50.0
			37.9%	84.3%
Commercial paper rate			1	39.2
				49.7
				6.4%
M2 (log difference)				1
Real GNP				67.0
				54.1%
				0.000%

the business cycle peak to trough comes in as negative, while for RGNP, measured as peak minus trough, is positive.) The positive (and often significant) coefficient on the change in the stock index indicates larger stock price drops are associated with larger contraction amplitudes, that is, deeper recessions. Of further interest are the two interaction terms, one for the risk spread and the money growth, and the second for risk and the short-term interest rate. Both are significant only for the later period. The coefficient on Interaction 1 indicates that times of rising risk spreads and tight money are particularly associated with high amplitudes. Interaction 2 confirms that, when tight money is measured by high discount rates.

Another approach is to relate the amplitude not to changes over the NBER contraction, but over the cycle phases for money, credit and stock prices that the Harding–Pagan algorithm identifies. Claessens, Kose and Terrones compare the depth of recessions with large and small credit crunches. With fewer recessions, we take a more multivariate approach, and regress recession amplitude against cycle amplitude for the risk spread, the money measure (either quantity or short-term interest rate) and the

TABLE 7.8 NBER 19 Recession Amplitude, Nineteenth Century

Independent Variables	1	2	3	4
Constant	0.518*** (3.89)	-0.032 (1.19)	-0.038 (-1.18)	0.041 (1.43)
RR spread	-0.145 (-1.18)	-0.884*** (-7.65)	-1.43* (-1.67)	-0.340* (-0.611)
Commercial paper	0.624*** (5.65)			0.616*** (5.69)
Stock index	0.083 (0.563)	0.412** (2.49)	0.352* (1.73)	0.178 (0.58)
M2 growth		0.044 (5.43)	0.053*** (3.01)	
TFP growth	0.558** (2.46)	0.088 (0.47)		0.349 (0.516)
Interaction 1			0.317 (0.632)	
Interaction 2				-1.61 (-0.41)
Observations	8	8	8	8
R^2	0.887	0.791	0.800	0.888
$R\text{-bar}^2$	0.736	0.513	0.301	0.609

Recession amplitude (peak–trough real GNP as a fraction of peak RGNP) for NBER contractions, regressed against the peak–trough change in other variables. Money supply and stock index are also measured as fractional changes.

Dependent variable: RNGP.

Data is for the NBER recessions starting in 1893, 1895, 1899, 1902, 1907, 1910, and 1913.

With heteroscedasticity-consistent (Eicker–White) standard errors (t-statistics in parentheses).

* 10% significance level; **5% significance level; ***1% significance level.

TABLE 7.9 NBER 20 Recession Amplitude, Twentieth Century

Independent Variables	1	2	3	4
Constant	0.077*** (2.54)	0.064*** (4.35)	0.025 (1.58)	0.081*** (3.74)
Baa spread	0.045** (2.39)	−0.003 (−0.156)	−0.051* (−1.84)	0.048** (2.21)
Discount rate	−0.011 (−1.36)			−0.033** (−2.56)
Stock index	0.209*** (3.78)	0.014 (0.28)	−0.074 (−0.81)	0.178*** (3.26)
M2 growth		0.590*** (4.34)	−0.001 (−0.001)	
TFP growth	1.57*** (4.59)	0.487 (1.43)	−0.918 (−1.39)	0.841 (2.40)**
Interaction 1				
Interaction 2			−0.4738** (−2.01)	−0.029** (−2.41)
Observations	16	16	16	16
R^2	0.719	0.752	0.8534	0.803
R-bar²	0.616	0.662	0.779	0.705

Recession amplitude (peak–trough Real GNP is a fraction of peak RGNP) for NBER contractions, regressed against the peak–trough change in other variables.
Money supply and stock index are also measured as fractional changes.
  Dependent variable: RNGP.
  Data is for the NBER recessions starting in 1920, 1923, 1926, 1929, 1937, 1945, 1948, 1953, 1957, 1960, 1969, 1973, 1980, 1981, 1990, 2001.
  Dependent variable: RNGP.
With heteroscedasticity-consistent (Eicker–White) standard errors (t-statistics in parentheses).
* 10% significant level; ** 5% significance level; *** 1% significance level.

stock price. For example, if a recession begins (e.g., a peak occurs) when the money supply is in a contraction phase, we associate the amplitude of the NBER recession with the amplitude of that monetary contraction (which will rarely have the same turning points or duration). Tables 7.10 and 7.11 report the results for the nineteenth and twentieth centuries. The results are broadly similar to those in the NBER focused regression of Tables 7.9 and 7.10, but there are some differences. The coefficient on the risk spread shows up as positive in the twentieth century. Few coefficients are significant in the twentieth century, except when the risk-spread–money–growth interaction is included. TFP growth tends to be negatively associated with recessions.

Both the historical narrative and the empirical results suggest that a confluence of financial shocks—in risk spreads, assets prices and money supply—will exacerbate a contraction, or at least be associated with deeper contractions. A closer look that the deeper recessions in our sample bears

TABLE 7.10 PAGAN 19 Recession Amplitude Associated with Cycles in Other Variables

Independent Variables	1	2	3	4
Constant	−0.175 (−1.32)	−0.004 (−0.04)	0.007 (0.087)	1.88** (1.99)
RR spread	0.038 (0.16)	−0.209 (−1.23)	−0.045 (−0.155)	−2.62*** (−6.63)
Commercial paper	0.029* (1.78)			−0.202*** (5.95)
Stock index	0.553** (2.42)	0.400 (1.32)	0.210 (0.663)	0.539*** (5.43)
M2 growth		−0.137 (−0.516)	−1.28 (−0.95)	
TFP growth	−0.097 (−0.27)	0.217 (0.98)	0.17 (0.71)	−0.567*** (3.05)
Interaction 1			3.74 (0.86)	
Interaction 2				1.44*** (7.39)
Observations	7	7	7	7
R^2	0.701	0.648	0.663	0.941
R-bar^2	0.104	−0.05	−1.0	0.649

This shows the results of regression of RGNP percent amplitude in an NBER contraction (P–T) against the change over other variables over their individual Harding–Pagan cycle.

Dependent variable: RNGP.

For the recessions of the nineteenth century.

With heteroscedasticity-consistent (Eicker–White) standard errors (t-statistics in parentheses).

* 10% significance level; ** 5% significance level; *** 1% significance level.

this out, even though the correspondence between financial shocks and depth of recession is not one-to-one. Figures 7.2 and 7.3 provide scatterplots of recession amplitude against the risk spread, short-term rates, money supply, and stock movements.

Since the First World War, four recessions are particularly deep (measured as percentage change in real GNP from peak to trough): those of 1929, 1945, 1920, and 1937. These were at least triple the size of any other contraction (with a possible exception of the combined 1980–1981 drop). 1945 stands out as an anomaly, but the other three stand out as having the three largest percentage drops in the money supply and stock prices, and two of the three largest increases in the risk spread. Contemporary accounts of the 1920 contraction do not mention a credit crunch in line with the only moderate increase in the risk spread in that contraction. While the 1929 contraction also shows the largest drop in total factor productivity, TFP actually grew in the contractions of '45, '20, and '37.

TABLE 7.11   PAGAN 20 Recession Amplitude Associated with Cycles in Other Variables

Independent Variables	1	2	3	4
Constant	0.070* (1.84)	0.056*** (2.64)	0.021* (1.77)	0.029 (0.68)
Baa spread	0.019 (0.88)	0.013 (0.82)	0.029*** (6.56)	0.040 (1.40)
Discount rate	−0.011* (−1.74)			0.021 (1.19)
Stock index	0.013* (1.88)	0.005 (1.55)	0.001 (0.61)	−0.003 (−0.28)
M2 growth		0.096 (0.45)	0.094* (1.77)	
TFP growth	−0.039 (−0.53)	−0.096 (−1.56)	−0.186*** (−8.46)	−0.032 (−0.52)
Interaction 1			0.146*** (22.41)	
Interaction 2				−0.015 (−1.58)
Observations	15	15	15	15
R^2	0.297	0.192	0.952	0.403
R-bar^2	0.015	−0.131	0.924	0.071

This shows the results of regression of RGNP percent amplitude in an NBER contraction (P–T) against the change other variables over their individual Harding–Pagan cycle.
   Dependent variable: RNGP.
   With heteroscedasticity-consistent (Eicker–White) standard errors (*t*-statistics in parentheses).
   * 10% significance level; ** 5% significance level; *** 1% significance level.

FIGURE 7.2   Scatterplots of NBER Recession Amplitude Sand Risk
Spread, Short-Term Rate, Money Supply, and Stock Price. Post-World
War I Sample. Amplitudes Are Peak Minus Trough Values of the
Variables.

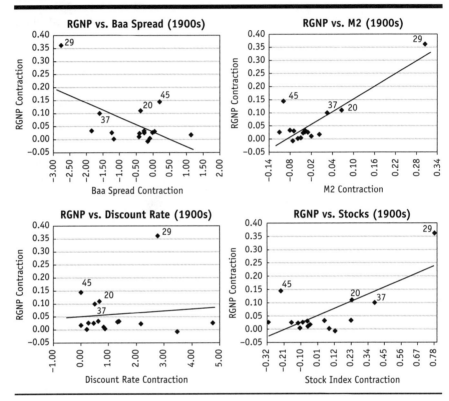

Prior to the First World War, three contractions stand out, all over
twice as deep as the others: 1907, 1893, and 1913. The connections with
financial shocks are perhaps not as striking as for the later period, but still
strong. The three contractions have two of the top three declines in stock
prices, and the top two changes in money and bond spread. These contractions also show three of the top four declines in TFP. Contemporary
accounts noted a credit crunch in 1893 despite only a small movement in
the risk spread.

An alternative approach is to sort on the size of movements in risk
spreads, money and stock prices, looking to see if larger movements in these

FIGURE 7.3   Scatterplots of NBER Recession Amplitudes and Risk Spread, Short-Term Rate, Money Supply, and Stock Price. Pre-World War I Sample. Amplitudes Are Peak Minus Trough Values of the Variables.

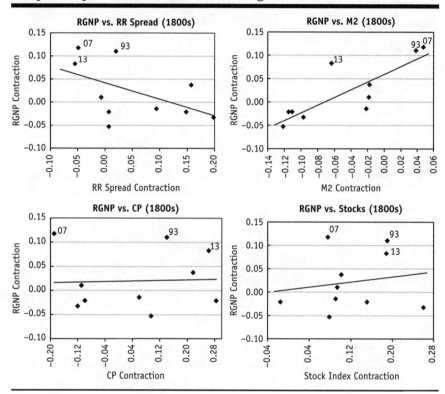

variables lead to larger recessions. Since World War I, four contractions had particularly large increases in the Baa spread, four had particularly large drops in M2 (in fact only four saw actual drops) and four had particularly large drops in stock prices. Table 7.12 compares the mean recession amplitude for these extreme events with recession amplitudes without those events. If you will, it picks out the credit crunches and the stock crashes from the mere corrections. It makes a similar comparison between the three largest events in each category for the pre-WWI cycles. In every case, the contractions associated with a large crunch or crash are noticeably larger than those without, though this difference is statistically significant only for the pre-WWI years.

TABLE 7.12   Recession Amplitudes with and without
Large Financial Events

P–T RGNP Amplitude, 20th	Credit	M2	Stock
With crunch (%)	10.4	14.8	15.2
Without crunch (%)	3.8	2.9	2.8
t-Statistic	0.98	1.57	1.34
P–T RGNP amplitude, 19th	credit	M2	Stock
With crunch (%)	7.1	6.9	5.4
Without crunch (%)	0.1	−0.7	0.8
t-Statistic	1.83**	3.12**	0.94

t-tests for equal mean with unequal variances.
  **Significant at 5% level.

5. Conclusions

The evidence, though not conclusive, indicates both that more severe financial events are associated with more severe recessions, and that a confluence of such events also indicates increased severity.

The empirical results complement the cross country evidence of Claessens Kose and Terrones, and Reinhart and Rogoff. Causality is of course always hard to determine, but the narrative evidence strongly suggests, and the empirical work is at least consistent with, the claim that credit turmoil worsens recessions. The timing of cycles is likewise consistent with the work of Gilchrist et al. (2008) and others on the ability of corporate bond spreads to predict recession in more recent periods.

The results are consistent with work, such as Barro and Ursúa (2009), who find a high association between stock market crashes and large contractions, and Claessens, Kose, and Terrones (2008), who find an interaction between stock market crashes and tight money and credit.

Somewhat paradoxically, the cycles in the quantity of money appear not to be synchronized with business cycles, but when the cycles do coincide, monetary tightening has a significant effect, and seems implicated in major recessions. Money market measures, such as the discount rate, show greater synchronicity, but not more significant correlations. The historical evidence of banking panics associated with credit turmoil makes a case for the central bank acting as a lender of last resort.

The current episode combines elements of a credit crunch, asset price bust and banking crisis. It is consistent with the patterns we find using 140 years of U.S. data. How does the current crisis measure up? Between August 2007 and April 2009, the difference between the yield on Baa bonds and long-term Treasuries has moved up 342 basis points, a larger increase than seen in the 1929 contraction, and approaching the combined increase of 436 bp over both the Depression contractions. The percentage drop in the $S \& P$ index of 42% is second only to the 78% of the Great Contraction. Money supply, however, is a different matter, with an increase of 13% in the current period, the largest increase of M2 seen in any contraction. This should not be particularly surprising, however. As Friedman and Schwartz (1963) point out, prior to deposit insurance banking panics would cause a collapse in the money multiplier, driving M2 down. Zarnowitz (1992) shows that business cycle downturns with panics are much more severe than others. Today because of deposit insurance, financial turmoil does not lead to panics and collapses in the money multiplier, and credit turmoil is less likely to feed into the money supply. The credit disturbance thus becomes relatively more important, given that disturbances on the asset side of the balance sheet no longer have as strong an influence on the money supply.

Notes

1. From 1875 to January 1, 1879 the U.S. was still on the floating Greenback Standard. However, the Resumption Act of 1875 anchored expectations on the announced return to gold parity and the dollar pound exchange rate was very close to parity (Bordo et al., 2007).

2. Bordo et al. (1992) provide evidence doubting the presence of credit rationing in the National Banking era. They argue that it is difficult to distinguish credit shocks from shocks to the money supply. They explain most of the variation in national bank lending by the movement of stock prices held as collateral.

3. According to Owens and Schreft (1993) the 1973–1974 episode was not a true credit crunch which they define as non-price credit rationing because bank lending rates were permitted to rise.

4. For 1914 quarter 3, the markets were closed, and we entered a judgmental value of 1% for the spread. As this was a time of turmoil in the markets, it is not an innocuous assumption.

5. Quarterly data is a linear interpolation from the annual data in Table A-XIX in Kendrick (1961), re-indexed. TFP since then is calculated using $\log(\text{TFP}) = \log(Y) - 0.3\log(K) - 0.7\log(L)$, with Y the BLS measure of "Nonfarm Business Sector: Output," L the "Nonfarm Business Sector: Hours of All Persons," and K the "Net Capital Stock of Private Fixed Nonresidential Assets" from the Bureau of Economic Analysis, linearly interpolated to obtain a quarterly series. See Levy and Chen (1994) or Cooley and Prescott (1995) for comparisons of construction techniques.

6. Total factor productivity also shows an asymmetric cycle, with mean peak-to-trough time for the two periods of 5.1 and 5.2 quarters, with a trough-to-peak means of 8 and 16 quarters. It shows a concordance with the NBER cycle of only 45% in the early period, but 82% for the later.

References

Asea, P.K., Blomberg, S.B., 1998. Lending cycles. Journal of Econometrics 83, 89–128.

Balke, N.S., Gordon, R.J., 1986. Appendix B: historical data, The American Business Cycle: Continuity and Change. NBER Studies in Business Cycles. University of Chicago Press, Chicago.

Barro, R.J., Ursúa, J.F., 2009. Stock-market crashes and depressions. NBER Working Paper 14769.

Beatty, A.L., Gron, A., 2001. Capital, portfolio, and growth: bank behavior under risk-based capital guidelines. Journal of Financial Services Research 20, 5–31.

Benmelech, E., Bordo, M., 2008. The financial crisis of 1873 and 19th century American corporate governance. Mimeo, Harvard University.

Bernanke, B., 1983. Non monetary effects of the financial crisis in the propagation of the great depression. American Economic Review LXXIII, 217–276.

Bernanke, B., Blinder, A., 1988. Credit, money, and aggregate demand. American Economic Review Papers and Proceedings 78 (4), 435–439.

Bernanke, B.S., Gertler, M., 1995. Inside the Black Box: the credit channel of monetary policy. The Journal of Economic Perspectives 9 (4), 27–48.

Bernanke, B., Gertler, M., 1989. Agency costs, net worth and business fluctuations. American Economic Review 79, 14–31.

Bernanke, B., Gertler, M., Gilchrist, S., 1996. The financial accelerator and the flight to quality. The Review of Economics and Statistics 78, 1–15.

Bernanke, B., Lown, C., 1991. The credit crunch. Brookings Papers on Economic Activity 2 (1991), 205–239.

Board of Governors of the Federal Reserve System, 1943. Banking and Monetary Statistics, 1914–1941, Washington, DC.

Bordo, M.D., 1986. Financial crises, banking crises, stock market crashes and the money supply: some international evidence, 1870–1933. In: Capie, Forrest, Wood, Geoffrey E. (Eds.), Financial Crises and the World Banking System. Macmillan, London, pp. 190–248.

Bordo, M.D., 2006. Sudden stops, financial crises, and original sin in emerging countries: Déjà vu? NBER Working Paper No. 12397, July.

Bordo, M.D., 2008. An historical perspective on the crisis of 2007–2008. NBER Working Paper No. 14569, December.

Bordo, M.D., Dueker, M., Wheelock, D.C., 2008. Inflation monetary policy and stock market conditions. NBER Working Paper No. 14019, May.

Bordo, M.D., Erceg, C., Levin, A., Michaels, R., 2007. Three great American disinflations. NBER Working Paper No. 12982, March.

Bordo, M.D., Orphanides, A., 2009. NBER conference on the great inflation. NBER Conference Website.

Bordo, M.D., Rappoport, P., Schwartz, A., 1992. Money vs credit rationing: evidence for the national banking era, 1880–1914. In: Goldin, Claudia, Rockoff, Hugh (Eds.), Strategic Factors in Nineteenth Century American History. University of Chicago Press, Chicago.

Brunner, K., Meltzer, A.H., 1972. Money, debt, and economic activity. The Journal of Political Economy 80 (5), 951–977.

Bry, G., Boschan, C., 1971. Cyclical analysis of time series: selected procedures and computer programs. NBER, New York.

Calomiris, C., Hubbard, R.G., 1989. Price flexibility, credit availability and economic fluctuation: evidence from the United States, 1894–1919. Quarterly Journal of Economics 104 (3), 429–453.

Calomiris, C., Mason, J.R., 2003. Fundamentals, panics and bank distress during the depression. American Economic Review 93 (December), 1615–1647.

Calomiris, C., Wilson, B., 2004. Bank capital and portfolio management: the 1930s "Capital Crunch" and the scramble to shed risk. Journal of Business 77 (3), 421–455.

Carlstrom, C.T., Fuerst, T.S., 1997. Agency costs, net work and business fluctuations: a computable general equilibrium analysis. American Economic Review 87, 893–910.

Christiano, L., Motto, R., Rostagno, M., 2008. Shocks, structures or monetary policies? The Euro area and U.S. after 2001. Journal of Economic Dynamics and Control 32 (8), 2476–2506.

Claessens, S., Kose, M.A., Terrones, M.E., 2008. What happens during recessions, crunches and busts? IMF Working Paper, WP/08/274.

Cole, H.L., Ohanian, L.E., 1999. The great depression in the United States from a neoclassical perspective. Federal Reserve Bank of Minneapolis Quarterly Review 23, 2–24.

Cole, H.L., Ohanian, L.E., 2004. New deal policies and the persistence of the great depression: a general equilibrium analysis. Journal of Political Economy 112 (4), 779–816.

Cooley, T.F., Prescott, E.C., 1995. Economic growth and business cycles. In: Cooley, Thomas F. (Ed.), Frontiers of Business Cycle Research. Princeton University Press, Princeton, NJ (Chapter 1).

Dell'Ariccia, G., Marquez, R., 2006. Lending booms and lending standards. Journal of Finance 61 (5), 2511–2546.

Eckstein, O., Sinai, A., 1986. The mechanisms of the business cycle in the postwar era. In: In: Robert J., Gordon (Ed.), The American Business Cycle: Continuity and Change. National Bureau of Economic Research Studies in Business Cycles, vol. 25. University of Chicago Press, Chicago.

Fazzari, M., Hubbard, R.G., Petersen, B.C., 1988. Financing constraints and corporate investment. Brookings Papers on Economic Activity 1988 (1), 141–206.

Feldstein, M., 1993. Monetary Policy and Inflation in the 1980s: A Personal View. NBER Working Papers 4322.

Friedman, M., Schwartz, A.J., 1963. In: A Monetary History of the United States 1867–1960. Princeton University Press, Princeton.

Gilchrist, S., Yankov, V., Zakrajsek, E., 2008. Credit market shocks and economic fluctuations: evidence from corporate bond and stock markets. Working Paper.

Gorton, G.B., 1988. Banking panics and business cycles? Oxford Economic Papers New Series 40, pp. 751–781.

Gorton, G.B., Ping, H., 2008. Bank Credit Cycles.

Hansen, A.H., 1927. In: Business Cycle Theory. Ginn, Boston.

Harding, D., Pagan, A.R., 2006. Synchronization of cycles. Journal of Econometrics 132, 59–79.

Harding, D., Pagan, A., 2002. Dissecting the cycle: a methodological investigation. Journal of Monetary Economics 49, 365–381.

Haubrich, J.G., Wachtel, P., 1993. Capital requirements and shifts in commercial bank portfolios. Economic Review (Federal Reserve Bank of Cleveland) 29, 2–15.

Kendrick, J.W., 1961. Productivity Trends in the United States, Princeton University Press for the NBER.

Kindleberger, C.P., 2000. Manias, Panics and Crashes, fourth edition, Wiley, New York.

Kydland, F., Prescott, E., 1982. Time to build and aggregate fluctuations. Econometrica 50, 1345–1371.

Lamont, O., 1997. Cash flow and investment: evidence from internal capital markets. The Journal of Finance 52, 83–109.

Laughlin, Laurence J., 1913. Banking and Currency Reform, hearings before a subcommittee of the House Banking and Currency Committee, Washington, DC.

Levy, D., Chen, H., 1994. Estimates of the aggregate quarterly capital stock for the post-war U.S. economy. Review of Income and Wealth 40 (3), 317–349.

Long, J.B., Plosser, C., 1983. Real business cycles. Journal of Political Economy 91, 39–69.

Lown, C., Morgan, D.P., 2006. The credit cycle and the business cycle: new findings using the survey of senior loan officers. Journal of Money, Credit and Banking 38, 1575–1598.

Macaulay, F.R., 1938. Some theoretical problems suggested by the movements of interest rates, bond yields and stock prices in the United States since 1856. NBER.

Meltzer, A.H., 2003. In: A History of the Federal Reserve, vol. 1, 1913–1951. University of Chicago Press, Chicago.

Mishkin, F.S., 1978. The household balance sheet and the great depression. Journal of Economic History 38 (December), 918–937.

Mishkin, F.S., 1990. Asymmetric information and financial crises: a historical perspective. NBER Working Paper No. 3400, July.

Mishkin, F.S., White, E.N., 2002. U.S. stock market crashes and their aftermath: implications for monetary policy. NBER Working Paper No. 8992, June.

Mitchell, W.C., 1913. In: Business Cycles. University of California Press, Berkeley.

Odell, K., Weidenmeir, M., 2004. Real shock, monetary aftershock: the 1906 San Francisco earthquake and the panic of 1907. Journal of Economic History 52 (December), 757–784.

Owens, R.E., Schreft, S.L., 1993. Identifying credit crunches. Federal Reserve Bank of Richmond Working Paper 93-2.

Persons, W.M., 1920. A nontechnical explanation of the index of general business conditions. Review of Economics and Statistics 3, 39–55.

Rajan, R.G., 1994. Why bank credit policies fluctuate: a theory and some evidence. Quarterly Journal of Economics 109, 399–441.

Reinhart, C.M., Rogoff, K.S., 2009. The aftermath of financial crises. American Economic Review 99 (2), 466–472.

Romer, C.S., 1992. What ended the great depression? Journal of Economic History 52 (December), 757–784.

Romer, C.S., Romer, D.H., 1989. Does monetary policy matter? A test in the spirit of Friedman and Schwartz. In: Blanchard, Olivier, Fischer, Stanley (Eds.), NBER Macroeconomics Annual 1989. MIT, Cambridge.

Romer, C.S., Romer, D.H., 1994. Monetary policy matters. Journal of Monetary Economics 34 (August), 75–88.

Shiller, R.J., 2005. In: Irrational Exuberance, second edition. Princeton University Press, Princeton.

Sprague, O.M.W., 1910. History of crises under the national banking system. National Monetary Commission. Senate Document No. 538, 61st Congress, 2nd Session.

Stevens, A.C., 1894. Analysis of the phenomenon of the panic in the U.S. in 1893. Quarterly Journal of Economics IX, 117–145.

Stiglitz, J.E., Weiss, A., 1981. Credit rationing in markets with perfect information. American Economic Review 71, 393–410.

White, E.N., 2008. The great American real estate bubble of the 1920s: causes and consequences. Mimeo, Rutgers University.

Wojnilower, A.M., 1980. The central role of credit crunches in recent financial history. Brookings Papers on Economic Activity 2, 277–326.

Wojnilower, A.M., 1985. Private credit demand, supply and crunches, how different are the 1980s. American Economic Review 75 (2), 351–356.

Wojnilower, A.M., 1992. In: Credit Crunches in the New Palgrave Dictionary of Money and Finance. Macmillan, London.

Zarnowitz, V., 1992. Business cycles: Theory, history, indicators and forecasting, NBER Studies in Business Cycles, vol. 27, University of Chicago Press, Chicago.

CHAPTER 8

Three Great American Disinflations

MICHAEL D. BORDO, CHRISTOPHER ERCEG,
ANDREW LEVIN, AND RYAN MICHAELS

1. Introduction

SINCE AT LEAST THE TIME of David Hume (1752) in the mid-eighteenth century, it has been recognized that episodes of deflation or disinflation may have costly implications for the real economy, and much attention has been devoted to assessing how policy should be conducted to reduce such costs. The interest of prominent classical economists in these questions, including Hume, Thornton, and Ricardo, was spurred by practical policy debates about how to return to the gold standard following episodes of pronounced wartime inflation.[1] Drawing on limited empirical evidence, these authors tried to identify factors that contributed to the real cost of deflation, including those factors controlled by policy. They advocated that a deflation should be implemented gradually, if at all; in a similar vein a century later, Keynes (1923) and Irving Fisher (1920) discussed the dangers of trying to quickly reverse the large run-up in prices that occurred during World War I and its aftermath.

While the modern literature has provided substantial empirical evidence to support the case that deflations or disinflations are often quite costly, there is less agreement about the underlying factors that may have

Originally published in "Three Great American Disinflations," NBER Working Paper (2008).

contributed to high real costs in some episodes, or that might explain pronounced differences in costs across episodes.[2] Indeed, disagreement about the factors principally responsible for influencing the costs of disinflation helped fuel contentious debates about the appropriate way to reduce inflation during the 1970s and early 1980s. Many policy makers and academics recommended a policy of gradualism—reflecting the view that the costs of disinflation were largely due to structural persistence in wage and price setting—while others recommended aggressive monetary tightening on the grounds that the credibility of monetary policy in the 1970s had sunk too low for gradualism to be a viable approach.

In this chapter, we examine three notable episodes of *deliberate* monetary contraction: the post-Civil War deflation, the post-WWI deflation, and the Volcker disinflation. One goal of our chapter is to use these episodes to illuminate the factors that influence the costs of monetary contractions. These episodes provide a fascinating laboratory for this analysis, insofar as they exhibit sharp differences in the policy actions undertaken, in the credibility and transparency of the policies, and in the ultimate effects on inflation and output. Our second objective is to evaluate the ability of a variant of the New Keynesian model that has performed well in fitting certain features of post-war U.S. data to account for these historical episodes.

Our chapter begins by providing a historical overview of each of these episodes. In the decade following the Public Credit Act of 1869, which set a 10-year timetable for returning to the gold standard, the price level declined gradually by 30 percent, while real output grew at a robust 4–5 percent per year. We argue that the highly transparent policy objective, the credible nature of the authorities' commitment, and gradual implementation of the policy helped minimize disruptive effects on the real economy. By contrast, while prices fell by a similar magnitude during the deflation that began in 1920, the price decline was very rapid, and accompanied by a sharp fall in real activity. We interpret the large output contraction as attributable to the Federal Reserve's abrupt departure from the expansionary policies that had prevailed until that time; fortunately, because the ultimate policy objective was clear (reducing prices enough to raise gold reserves), the downturn was fairly short-lived. Finally, the Volcker disinflation succeeded in reducing inflation from double digit rates in the late 1970s to a steady 4 percent by 1983, though at the cost of a severe and prolonged recession. We argue that the substantial costs of this episode on the real economy reflected the interplay both of nominal rigidities, and the lack of policy credibility following the unstable monetary environment of the previous 15 years.

We next attempt to measure policy predictability during each of the three episodes in order to quantify the extent to which each deflation was anticipated by economic agents. For the two earlier periods, we construct a proxy for price level forecast errors by using commodity futures data and realized spot prices. While these commodity price forecast errors provide very imperfect measures of errors in forecasting the general price level, we believe that they provide useful characterizations of the level of policy uncertainty during each period: in particular, the commodity price forecast errors in the early 1920s were much larger and more persistent than in the 1870s. This pattern confirms other evidence on policy predictability during each episode taken from bond yields, contemporary narrative accounts, and informal surveys. Finally, for the Volcker period, we utilize direct measures of survey expectations on inflation to construct inflation forecast errors, and show that forecast errors were large and extremely persistent, suggesting a high degree of uncertainty about the Federal Reserve's policy objectives.

We then examine whether a relatively standard DGSE model is capable of accounting for these different episodes. The model that we employ is a slightly simplified version of the models used by Christiano, Eichenbaum, and Evans (2005) and Smets and Wouters (2003). Thus, our model incorporates staggered nominal wage and price contracts with random duration, as in Calvo (1983) and Yun (1996), and incorporates various real rigidities including investment adjustment costs and habit persistence in consumption. The structure of the model is identical across periods, aside from the characterization of monetary policy. In particular, we assume that the monetary authority targets the price level in the two earlier episodes, consistent with the authorities desire to reinstate or support the gold standard; by contrast, we assume that the Federal Reserve followed a

Taylor-style interest rate reaction function in the Volcker period, responding to the difference between inflation and its target value. Moreover, we assume that agents had imperfect information about the Federal Reserve's inflation target during the Volcker episode, and had to infer the underlying target through solving a signal extraction problem.

We find that our simple model performs remarkably well in accounting for each of the three episodes. Notably, the model is able to track the sharp but transient decline in output during the 1920s, as well as generate a substantial recession in response to the monetary tightening under Volcker. More generally, we interpret the overall success of our model in fitting these disparate episodes as reflecting favorably on the ability of the New Keynesian model—augmented with some of the dynamic complications suggested in the recent literature—to fit important business cycle facts. However, one important twist is our emphasis on the role of incomplete information in accounting for the range of outcomes.

Finally, we use counterfactual simulations of our model to evaluate the consequences of alternative strategies for implementing a new nominal target (i.e., either a lower price level, or a lower inflation rate). We find that under a highly transparent policy regime, a new nominal target can be achieved with minimal fallout on the real economy, provided the implementation occurs over a period of at least 3–4 years. In this vein, we use model simulations to show that a more predictable policy of gradual deflation—as occurred in the 1870s—could have helped avoid the sharp post-WWI downturn. However, our analysis of the Volcker period emphasizes that the strong argument for gradualism under a transparent and credible monetary regime becomes less persuasive if the monetary regime lacks credibility. In this lower credibility case, an aggressive policy stance can play an important signalling role insofar as it makes a policy shift—such as a reduction in the inflation target—more apparent to private agents. Because inflation expectations adjust more rapidly than under a gradualist policy stance, output can rebound more quickly.

The rest of the chapter proceeds as follows. Section 2 describes the three episodes, while Section 3 examines empirical evidence on the evolution of expectations during each episode. Section 4 outlines the model, and

Section 5 describes the calibration. Section 6 matches the model to the salient features of the three episodes, and considers counterfactual policy experiments. Section 8 concludes.

2. Historical Background

2.1. The Post-Civil War Episode

Given the high cost of financing the Civil War, the U.S. government suspended gold convertibility in 1862 and issued fiat money ("greenbacks"). The monetary base expanded dramatically in the subsequent two years, precipitating a sharp decline in the value of greenbacks relative to gold. The dollar price of a standard ounce of gold rose from its official price of $20.67 that had prevailed since 1834 to over $40 by 1864 (the lower panel of Figure 8.1 shows an index of the greenback price of gold relative to its official price of $20.67). Despite some retracing in the late stages of the war, the dollar price of gold remained about 50 percent above its official price by the cessation of hostilities in mid-1865.

Following the war, there was widespread support for reverting to a specie standard at the pre-war parity. In the parlance of the period, this meant eliminating the "gold premium," the difference between the market price of gold and the official price. Using simple quantity theory reasoning, policy makers regarded monetary tightening as the appropriate instrument for achieving this objective: if the overall price level fell sufficiently, the dollar price of gold would drop, and the gold premium eventually disappear. Accordingly, Congress passed the Contraction Act in April 1866, with the backing of President Johnson. This act instructed the U.S. Treasury—the effective monetary authority during that period—to retire the supply of greenbacks. Given initial public support for a quick return to convertibility, the Treasury proceeded aggressively, reducing the monetary base about 20 percent between 1865 and 1867. However, the sharp price deflation that ensued had a contractionary impact on the economy, with certain sectors experiencing disproportionate effects (e.g., heavily leveraged farmers). Thus, Congress and President Johnson were forced

FIGURE 8.1   The Post-Civil War Deflation

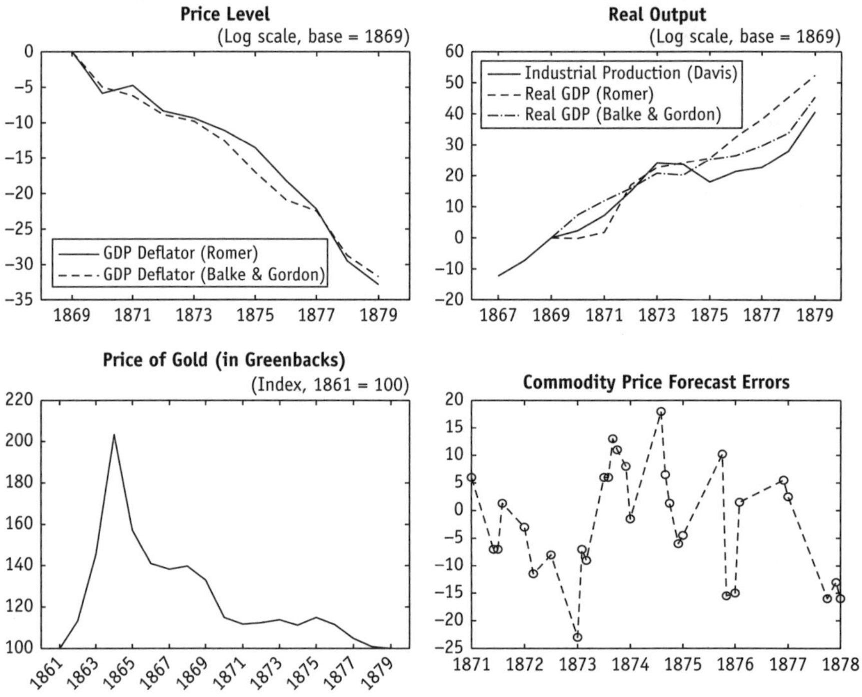

to temporarily suspend monetary tightening in the face of strong public protest (Friedman and Schwartz, 1963).

President Grant promised to renew the march toward resumption when he delivered his first inaugural in March 1869, but with the important difference that the deflation would be gradual. The president received key legislative support with the passage of the Public Credit Act of 1869, which pledged that the Federal Government would repay its debt in specie within ten years. The long time frame reflected the new political imperative of a gradualist approach. With further monetary contraction deemed infeasible, supporters of resumption planned to keep the money stock roughly constant, and allow prices to fall slowly as the economy expanded. This philosophy helped guide legislation, and in turn the U.S. Treasury's operational procedures for conducting monetary policy. Thus, Treasury policy kept the monetary base fairly constant through most of the 1870s, offsetting the issuance of National Bank notes with the retirement of greenbacks. The Treasury's ability to adhere to this policy was facilitated by the passage of the Resumption Act in 1875, which sealed January 1, 1879, as the date of resumption of convertibility, and by the election of the hard-money Republican candidate Rutherford Hayes in the 1876 election.

As seen in the upper-left panel of Figure 8.1, these policies succeeded in producing a fairly smooth and continuous decline in the aggregate price level, and allowed the authorities to comfortably meet the January 1879 deadline for the resumption of specie payments. Furthermore, as shown in the upper-right panel, all three of the available measures of real output grew at a fairly rapid and steady pace over the period from 1869 to 1872. Of course, the worldwide financial panic of 1873 had marked consequences for U.S. markets and economic activity; nevertheless, real output growth over the decade of the 1870s was remarkably strong, averaging about 4 to 5 percent per year.[3]

This strong economic growth in the face of persistent deflation seems to have been made possible because of the slow and fairly predictable nature of the price decline between the passage of the Public Credit Act in 1869 and resumption a decade later. Two factors played an important role in making the price decline predictable. First, the ultimate objective of restoring the gold price to its official (pre-war) level was highly credible. This served to anchor expectations about the long-run expected price level within a fairly narrow range, so that uncertainty about the future price level mainly reflected uncertainty about the path of the real value of gold (in terms of goods). Second, it was clear after 1868 that the target of restoring convertibility would be achieved gradually. As discussed above, there was little support in Congress for returning to the rapid pace of monetary contraction that followed the Civil War.

Our contention that the policy of restoring gold convertibility at the official pre-war price was highly credible may seem difficult to reconcile with the political agitation in favor of greenbacks that seemed a salient feature of the 1870s. But support for the gold standard—both within the U.S. government, and the public at large—remained extremely strong in the post-Civil War period, so that the net effect of the political agitation was simply to graduate progress towards convertibility.[4] This support for resumption stemmed in part from historical precedent: the United States had been on a specie standard for almost its entire history, dating to the passage of the Coinage Act of 1792. It also reflected deeply-seated views about how a specie standard protected private property rights against unjust seizure, which was regarded as a moral and political imperative.

Overall, this analysis suggests that it is appropriate to characterize the U.S. deflation experience over at least the 1869–1879 period as one in which both the final objective of policy was transparent and credible, and which implied a fairly clear path for the overall price level. Moreover, the authorities appeared to place a large weight on minimizing the adverse consequences to the real economy, and hence were content to achieve convertibility gradually in an environment of predictable deflation.[5]

2.2. The Post-WWI Episode

The U.S. government suspended the gold standard de facto shortly after it entered World War I and began an enormous arms build-up that fueled inflation. President Wilson ordered the suspension and placed an embargo on the export of gold in order to protect the country's stock. In the absence of the embargo, high inflation likely would have triggered large outflows of gold: GNP prices rose almost 40 percent while the U.S. was at war, which was equal to the cumulative increase in prices over the previous 15-year period. Wartime inflation had its roots in a roughly twenty-fold increase in federal government expenditure from the time the U.S. entered the war in April 1917 to the armistice in November 1918 (see Firestone, 1960, Table A3).[6]

When the war ended, the embargo was lifted, and the Treasury and the Federal Reserve had to negotiate monetary policy in order to protect the gold standard.[7] The Federal Reserve's Board of Governors included five appointees and two ex-officio members, the Secretary of Treasury and the Comptroller of the Currency. This governance structure gave the Secretary of the Treasury a disproportionate influence over monetary policy, since the five appointees to the Board were reluctant to cross the Treasury. Faced with a 25-fold increase in gross public debt after the War (Meltzer 2003), the Secretary refused to support an increase in discount

FIGURE 8.2 The Deflation of 1920–1921

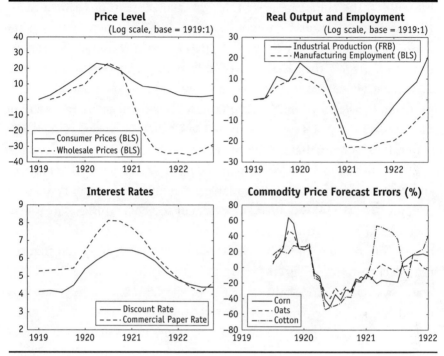

rates despite an acceleration in inflation into double digits in 1919.[8] However, the Treasury's reputation was strongly linked to the success of the gold standard. In particular, U.S. law required the Federal Reserve to ensure a stock of monetary gold equal to at least 40 percent of the supply of base money. By November 1919, sizeable gold outflows put the legal minimum in sight, and the Treasury finally supported Board action to raise the discount rate.

Once freed to act, the Board raised the System-wide average discount rate over 2 percentage points between late 1919 and mid-1920 (see Figure 8.2). Although an eventual tightening of policy was anticipated insofar as private agents believed that the government was committed to defending the gold standard, both the timing and severity of the contraction were a surprise. The highly persistent rise in nominal rates in the face of rapidly shifting expectations about inflation (i.e., towards deflation) represented a much tighter policy stance than agents had anticipated. As seen in Figure 8.2, the aggregate price level plunged 20 percent between mid-1920 and mid-1921, and commodity prices declined much more precipitously. Output also declined very abruptly, especially in manufacturing. As seen in Figure 8.2, the FRB's index of industrial production fell more than 30 percent between mid-1920 and early 1921, while manufacturing employment showed a commensurate decline. But the short-lived nature of the depression appears equally striking, as a robust expansion pushed output back to its pre-deflation level by early 1922.

The deflation of 1920 was recognized both by contemporary observers and by later historians as a dramatic event in U.S. monetary history. Irving Fisher (1934) was strongly critical of the Federal Reserve's role in engineering a "disastrous deflation" for which "millions of workers were thrown out of work." Friedman and Schwartz (1963) observed that the price decline was "perhaps the sharpest in the entire history of the United States" and characterized the output contraction as "one of the severest on record."

The industrial production and employment measures shown in Figure 8.2 indicate a much more severe recession than would be suggested from annual data for the aggregate economy.[9] First, the magnitude of the downturn is obscured by its relatively transitory nature, particularly since the decline in output and employment began in mid-1920 and ended partway through the following year; indeed, Friedman and Schwartz argued that this recession was so abrupt that "annual data provide a misleading indicator of its severity." Second, the fluctuations in real GNP were dampened by the stability of real agricultural output (which comprised a substantial fraction of aggregate output) and hence this measure is somewhat less relevant for gauging the effects of monetary policy during this period.[10]

As in the post-Civil War episode, the authorities' commitment to supporting the gold standard after WWI seems beyond doubt. By the 1920s, the gold standard was entrenched as both a national and international norm, and even countries that had experienced much larger wartime inflations expected to return to gold. The high credibility of the monetary regime ultimately served an important role in allowing the economy to recover quickly once it was clear that prices had fallen enough. But clearly, the major difference between the episodes was in the Federal Reserve's decision to implement a very rapid deflation in the early 1920s, which contrasted starkly with the gradualist policy of 1869–1879. Influential Federal Reserve policy makers including Benjamin Strong believed that it was of foremost importance to reverse quickly most of the price level increase that had occurred since the U.S. entry into the war; while they acknowledged this might cause a substantial output contraction, they believed the recessionary effects would be transient and did not warrant dragging out the deflation (Meltzer 2003). Thus, policy makers kept nominal interest rates at elevated levels even as prices fell dramatically. This departure from traditional gold standard rules—which would have prescribed cutting interest rates in the face of a massive deflation and sizeable gold inflows—helped create a depression in activity through its effect on real interest rates.

2.3. The Volcker Disinflation

As of 1979, the Federal Reserve had been in operational control of U.S. monetary policy for about 25 years, even if it remained sensitive to the political climate. The Accord of 1951 between the central bank and the Treasury had ceded monetary policy to the Federal Reserve. For a dozen years after the Accord, the Federal Reserve generally maintained a low and steady inflation rate. But beginning in the mid-1960s, the Federal Reserve permitted inflation to rise to progressively higher levels. By the time President Carter appointed in 1979 a well-known inflation "hawk," Paul Volcker, to run the Federal Reserve, (GNP) price inflation had reached 9 percent.

Two months after taking office in August 1979, Volcker announced a major shift in policy aimed at rapidly lowering the inflation rate. Volcker desired the policy change to be interpreted as a decisive break from past policies that had allowed the inflation rate to rise to double digit levels (Figure 8.3). The announcement was followed by a series of sizeable hikes in the federal funds rate: the roughly 7 percentage point rise in the nominal federal funds rate between October 1979 and April 1980 represented the largest increase over a six-month period in the history of the Federal Reserve System. However, this tight monetary stance was temporarily abandoned in mid-1980 as economic activity decelerated sharply. Reluctantly,

FIGURE 8.3   The Volcker Disinflation

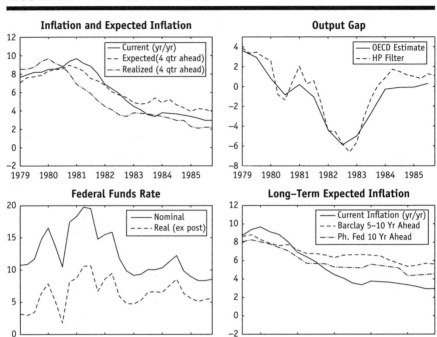

the FOMC imposed credit controls and let the funds rate decline—
moves that the Carter administration had publically supported. The
FOMC's policy reversal and acquiesence to political pressure was widely
viewed as a signal that it was not committed to achieving a sustained fall
in inflation (Blanchard, 1984). Having failed to convince price and wage
setters that inflation was going to fall, GNP prices rose almost 10 percent
in 1980.

The Federal Reserve embarked on a new round of monetary tightening in late 1980. The federal funds rate rose to 20 percent in late December, implying an ex post real interest rate of about 10 percent. Real ex post
rates were allowed to fall only slightly from this extraordinarily high level
over the following two years. Newly elected President Reagan's support
of Volcker's policy was significant in giving the Federal Reserve the political mandate it needed to keep interest rates elevated for a prolonged

period, and provided some shield from growing opposition in Congress; cf. Feldstein (1993). This second and more durable round of tightening succeeded in reducing the inflation rate from about 10 percent in early 1981 to about 4 percent in 1983, but at the cost of a sharp and very prolonged recession. The OECD's measure of the output gap expanded by 6 percent between mid-1980 and mid-1982, and the unemployment rate (not shown) hovered at 10 percent until mid-1983.

While policy makers in the gold standard environment examined in the earlier episodes had the advantage of a transparent and credible long-run nominal anchor, the Volcker disinflation was conducted in a setting in which there was a high degree of uncertainty about whether policy makers had the desire and ability to maintain low inflation rates. But notwithstanding that Federal Reserve policy during the 1970s and early 1980s merits some criticism for a lack of transparent objectives, it seems unlikely that simple announcements about long-run policy goals (e.g., an inflation target of 3 percent) would have carried much weight given the poor track record of the preceding two decades. Thus, it seems arguable that Volcker's FOMC had little hope of harnessing inflation expectations in a way that could facilitate lower inflation without sizeable output costs.

3. Policy Predictability: Empirical Evidence

Empirical evidence about the predictability of price decline that preceded Resumption in 1879 appears fairly limited. However, as argued by Friedman and Schwartz (1963) and later Calomiris (1985 and 1993), the behavior of longer term bond yields seems at least consistent with the view that private agents expected the dollar to appreciate (and prices to fall) by enough to support an eventual return to gold. As seen in Figure 8.4, the nominal yields on high-quality greenback-denominated railroad bonds were actually somewhat lower than the yield on gold-denominated U.S. treasury bonds at the passage of the Public Credit Act in 1869. By that time, confidence was very high that the government would satisfy its obligation to repay its bonds in gold. Thus, drawing on uncovered interest parity, Friedman and Schwartz interpreted the lower interest rate on privately issued railroad bonds as suggesting that private agents on balance

FIGURE 8.4   The Evolution of Long-Term Bond Yields, 1867–1870

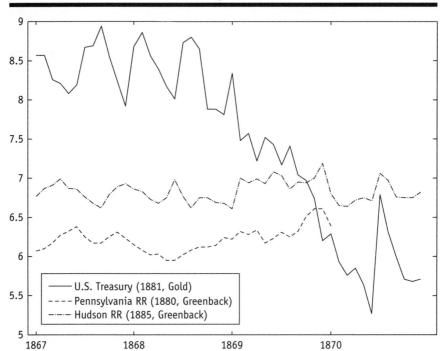

expected some appreciation of the greenback relative to gold. Of course, the simple difference between the interest rate series would understate expected appreciation of the greenback to the extent that the interest rate on the railroad bonds included a premium for default risk.[11]

Some evidence from commodity futures markets also appears consistent with our interpretation that the gradual price decline prior to Resumption was largely anticipated. Taking the futures price as a proxy for the expected price of a given commodity at a date K months ahead, we constructed a series of forecast errors as the difference between the realized commodity price and the (futures-based) forecast. The futures prices are on 4–5 month contracts (the longest maturities regularly available during that period) on pork, corn, wheat, and lard.[12] Given the paucity of observations on each individual commodity, Figure 8.1 pools forecast errors for all four of the commodities (yielding 30 observations over our 1871–78 sample period). The forecast errors seem relatively small, especially given the substantial volatility in spot prices of the underlying commodities: the average absolute error using these pooled observations is around 10 percent. Moreover, realized prices do not appear consistently lower than forecast (i.e., the forecast errors are not consistently negative). Despite obvious limitations of our data—including the short duration of futures contracts, and small number of observations—they are at least suggestive that agents were not surprised by declining prices.

There is considerably more evidence about the predictability of policy in the case of the deflationary episode following WWI. One very useful source is Harvard's Monthly Survey of General Business Conditions, which appeared as a monthly supplement to the *Review of Economics and Statistics* beginning in 1919. Harvard's Monthly Survey (HMS) interpreted recent financial and macroeconomic developments, and also made projections about the future evolution of output, prices, and short-term interest rates. While projections about individual macroeconomic series were primarily qualitative, the HMS did make some explicit forecasts about the likely duration of the business downturn during the course of 1920–1921.

Drawing on the surveys from the first half of 1920, the HMS forecasters correctly predicted that the post-war inflation would be followed by a period of monetary retrenchment, and appeared to have a fairly clear understanding of the channels through which the monetary tightening would operate. In particular, they argued that the Federal Reserve's imposition of higher discount rates beginning in late 1919 would precipitate a fall in commodity prices, followed by a decline in consumer prices, wages, and business activity; but drawing on historical experience, they expected that lower prices would allow monetary easing, and promote a vigorous recovery within about a year.

The HMS forecasters turned out to be surprised by the severity of the monetary tightening, and by the associated magnitude of price and output decline. At the onset of the tightening, the HMS commented that "both the Treasury and the Federal Reserve Board have embarked on a policy of orderly deflation," and projected in April 1920 that "it does not seem probable . . . that liquidation in the near future will cause prices to fall below the level of a year ago and perhaps not below the level of

November 1918," suggesting an anticipated fall in commodity prices of only 15–20 percent.[13] But in the wake of a 40 percent decline in commodity prices by early 1921 and depression in business activity, Bullock (1921) observed that he and the other HMS forecasters "had not expected a (monetary) reaction of such acute severity. We had looked for a return [of commodity prices] to some such level as had prevailed in the few months following the armistice, and as late as July expected nothing so drastic as the events of the last half of the year." Moreover, the HMS forecasters were forced to revise their optimistic initial predictions (made in the spring of 1920) that recovery would occur within a year as the sharp nature of the downturn became more apparent. The HMS attributed the severity of the downturn in part to persistently high interest rates, as interest rates remained elevated for a longer duration than in previous cyclical downturns dating back to the 1890s.[14] Nevertheless, given the enormous price contraction by early 1921, the HMS forecasters were confident that prices would soon stabilize (as in fact occurred by late 1921), and that an eventual easing of monetary conditions would facilitate a rebound in real activity.

Commodity price forecast errors provide complementary evidence that prices fell more quickly and by a greater magnitude than expected by private agents. Figure 8.2 shows commodity price forecast errors for three individual commodities—corn, oats, and cotton—measured again as the realized price of each commodity minus the "forecast" implied by the futures price.[15] In the post-World War I deflation, commodity price forecast errors turned consistently negative shortly after monetary policy was tightened in early 1920, and reached 50 percentage points or higher in absolute value terms. The average forecast errors over the 1920–1921 tightening period are several times as large as the commodity price forecast errors derived from the post-Civil War data. But interestingly, forecast errors are generally much smaller after early 1921. This seems consistent with our intepretation that after a markedly lower price level was achieved, the policy environment became much more predictable, as agents expected the aggregate price level to remain roughly stable.

Lastly, we turn to the Volcker disinflation, for which there is considerable survey data available on inflation expectations at different horizons. Figure 8.3 plots the median projection of four-quarter-ahead GNP price inflation from the Survey of Professional Forecasters. The average inflation forecast error at a one-year horizon (the gap between realized inflation over the subsequent year, the dash-dotted line, and the forecast, the dashed line) averaged about 2 percentage points over the 1981–84 period. Importantly, the inflation forecast errors show little tendency to die out, reflecting that inflation was consistently lower than what agents projected. The lower right panel of Figure 8.3 also contrasts the relatively quick decline in current inflation with the much more sluggish adjustment of long-run inflation expectations (as proxied by Barclay's projection of inflation 5–10 years ahead, and by the 10-year-ahead inflation projection of the Philadephia Federal Reserve Bank). Taken together, the survey data suggests that inflation expectations were very slow to react to the decline in realized inflation, which we interpret as strong evidence that private agents doubted the ability or desire of policy makers to maintain low inflation rates. This interpretation is consistent with that of Goodfriend (1993) and Goodfriend and King (2005), who argued that the slow adjustment of inflation expectations was a primary factor accounting for the high nominal interest rates on long-term bonds that prevailed through most of the 1980s.

4. The Model

We utilize the same basic model to analyze each of the three historical episodes, aside from differences in the characterization of monetary policy. The model can be regarded as a slightly simplified version of the model utilized by Christiano, Eichenbaum, and Evans (2005), and Smets and Wouters (2003). Thus, our model incorporates nominal rigidities by assuming that labor and product markets each exhibit monopolistic competition, and that wages and prices are determined by staggered nominal contracts of random duration (following Calvo (1983) and Yun (1996)). We also include various real rigidities emphasized in the recent literature, including habit persistence in consumption, and costs of changing the rate of investment. Given that our characterization of monetary policy differs across episodes, we defer this discussion to Section 6 (when we present simulation results for each episode).

4.1. Firms and Price Setting

Final Goods Production. As in Chari, Kehoe, and McGratten (2000), we assume that there is a single final output good Y_t that is produced using a continuum of differentiated intermediate goods $Y_t(f)$. The technology for transforming these intermediate goods into the final output good is constant returns to scale, and is of the Dixit-Stiglitz form:

$$Y_t = \left[\int_0^1 Y_t(f)^{\frac{1}{1+\theta_p}} df \right]^{1+\theta_p},$$ (1)

where $\theta_p > 0$.

Firms that produce the final output good are perfectly competitive in both product and factor markets. Thus, final goods producers minimize the cost of producing a given quantity of the output index Y_t, taking as given the price $P_t(f)$ of each intermediate good $Y_t(f)$. Moreover, final goods producers sell units of the final output good at a price P_t that is equal to the marginal cost of production:

$$P_t = \left[\int_0^1 P_t(f)^{\frac{-1}{\theta_p}} df \right]^{-\theta_p}.$$ (2)

It is natural to interpret P_t as the aggregate price index.

Intermediate Goods Production. A continuum of intermediate goods $Y_t(f)$ for $f \in [0, 1]$ is produced by monopolistically competitive firms, each of which produces a single differentiated good. Each intermediate goods producer faces a demand function for its output good that varies inversely with its output price $P_t(f)$, and directly with aggregate demand Y_t:

$$Y_t(f) = \left[\frac{P_t(f)}{P_t} \right]^{\frac{-(1+\theta_p)}{\theta_p}} Y_t.$$ (3)

Each intermediate goods producer utilizes capital services $K_t(f)$ and a labor index $L_t(f)$ (defined below) to produce its respective output good. The form of the production function is Cobb-Douglas:

$$Y_t\,(f) = K_t\,(f)^a\,L_t\,(f)^{1-a}.$$ (4)

Firms face perfectly competitive factor markets for hiring capital and the labor index. Thus, each firm chooses $K_t\,(f)$ and $L_t\,(f)$, taking as given both the rental price of capital R_{Kt} and the aggregate wage index W_t (defined below). Firms can costlessly adjust either factor of production. Thus, the standard static first-order conditions for cost minimization imply that all firms have identical marginal cost per unit of output. By implication, aggregate marginal cost MC_t can be expressed as a function of the wage index W_t, the aggregate labor index L_t, and the aggregate capital stock Kt, or equivalently, as the ratio of the wage index to the marginal product of labor MPL_t:

$$MC_t = \frac{W_t\,L_t^a}{(1-a)K_t^a} = \frac{W_t}{MPL_t}.$$ (5)

We assume that the prices of the intermediate goods are determined by Calvo-Yun style staggered nominal contracts. In each period, each firm f faces a constant probability, $1-\xi_p$, of being able to reoptimize its price $P_t(f)$. The probability that any firm receives a signal to reset its price is assumed to be independent of the time that it last reset its price. If a firm is not allowed to optimize its price in a given period, we follow Yun (1996) by assuming that it simply adjusts its price by the steady-state rate of inflation Π (i.e., $P_t\,(f) = \pi P_{t-1}(f)$). Finally, the firm's output is subsidized at a fixed rate τ_p (this allows us to eliminate the monopolistic competition wedge in prices by setting $\tau_p = \theta_p$).

4.2. Households and Wage-Setting

We assume a continuum of monopolistically competitive households (indexed on the unit interval), each of which supplies a differentiated labor service to the production sector; that is, goods-producing firms regard each household's labor services $N_t\,(h)$, $h \in [0, 1]$, as an imperfect substitute for the labor services of other households. It is convenient to assume that a representative labor aggregator (or "employment agency") combines households' labor hours in the same proportions as firms would choose.

Thus, the aggregator's demand for each household's labor is equal to the sum of firms' demands. The labor index L_t has the Dixit-Stiglitz form:

$$L_t = \left[\int_0^1 N_t(h)^{\frac{1}{1+\theta_w}} dh \right]^{1+\theta_w} \tag{6}$$

where $\theta_w > 0$. The aggregator minimizes the cost of producing a given amount of the aggregate labor index, taking each household's wage rate $W_t(h)$ as given, and then sells units of the labor index to the production sector at their unit cost W_t:

$$W_t = \left[\int_0^1 W_t(h)^{\frac{-1}{\theta_w}} dh \right]^{-\theta_w}. \tag{7}$$

It is natural to interpret W_t as the aggregate wage index. The aggregator's demand for the labor hours of household h—or equivalently, the total demand for this household's labor by all goods-producing firms—is given by

$$N_t(h) = \left[\frac{W_t(h)}{W_t} \right]^{-\frac{1+\theta_w}{\theta_w}} L_t. \tag{8}$$

The utility functional of a typical member of household h is

$$\mathbb{E}_t \sum_{j=0}^{\infty} \beta^j \left\{ \frac{1}{1-\sigma} (C_{t+j}(h) - \kappa C_{t+j-1}(h))^{1-\sigma} + \right. \tag{9}$$

$$\left. \frac{\chi_0}{1-\chi} (1 - N_{t+j}(h))^{1-\chi} + \frac{\mu_0}{1-\mu} \left(\frac{M_{t+j}(h)}{P_{t+j}} \right)^{1-\mu} \right\}, \tag{10}$$

where the discount factor β satisfies $0 < \beta < 1$. The dependence of the period utility function on consumption in both the current and previous period allows for the possibility of external habit persistence in consumption spending (e.g., Smet and Wouters, 2003). In addition, the period utility function depends on current leisure $1 - N_t(h)$, and current real money balances $\frac{M_t(h)}{P_t}$.

Household h's budget constraint in period t states that its expenditure on goods and net purchases of financial assets must equal its disposable income:

$$P_t C_t(h) + P_t I_t(h) + \frac{1}{2}\varphi_I P_t \frac{(I_t(h) - I_{t-1}(h))^2}{I_{t-1}(h)} M_{t+1}(h) - M_t(h)$$

$$+ \int_s \xi_{t,t+1} B_{D,t+1}(h) - B_{D,t}(h) = (1 + \tau_W) W_t(h) N_t(h) + R_{Kt} K_t(h) + \Gamma_t(h) - T_t(h) \tag{11}$$

Thus, the household purchases the final output good (at a price of P_t), which it chooses either to consume C_t (h) or invest I_t (h) in physical capital. The total cost of investment to each household h is assumed to depend on how rapidly the household changes its rate of investment (as well as on the purchase price). Our specification of such investment adjustment costs as depending on the square of the change in the household's gross investment rate follows Christiano, Eichenbaum, and Evans (2005). Investment in physical capital augments the household's (end-of-period) capital stock $K_{t+1}(h)$ according to a linear transition law of the form:

$$K_{t+1}(h) = (1 - \delta) K_t(h) + I_t(h). \tag{12}$$

In addition to accumulating physical capital, households may augment their financial assets through increasing their nominal money holdings $(M_{t+1}(h) - M_t(h))$, and through the net acquisition of bonds. We assume that agents can engage in frictionless trading of a complete set of contingent claims. The term $\int_s \xi_{t,t+1} B_{D,t+1}(h) - B_{D,t}(h)$ represents net purchases of state-contingent domestic bonds, with $\xi_{t,t+1}$ denoting the state price, and $B_{D,t+1}$ (h) the quantity of such claims purchased at time t. Each member of household h earns labor income $(1 + \tau_W) W_t$ (h) N_t (h) (where τ_W is a subsidy that allows us to offset monopolistic distortions in wage-setting), and receives gross rental income of $R_{Kt} K_t(h)$ from renting its capital stock to firms. Each member also receives an aliquot share Γ_t (h) of the profits of all firms, and pays a lump-sum tax of T_t (h) (this may be regarded as taxes net of any transfers).

In every period t, each member of household h maximizes the utility functional (9) with respect to its consumption, investment, (end-of-period) capital stock, money balances, and holdings of contingent claims, subject to its labor demand function (8), budget constraint (11), and transition equation for capital (12). Households also set nominal wages in Calvo-style staggered contracts that are generally similar to the price contracts described above. Thus, the probability that a household receives a signal to reoptimize its wage contract in a given period is denoted by $1 - \xi_w$, and as in the case of price contracts this probability is independent of the date at which the household last reset its wage. However, we specify a dynamic indexation scheme for the adjustment of the wages of those households that do not get a signal to reoptimize, i.e., $W_t(h) = \omega_t W_{t-1}(h)$, in contrast to the static indexing assumed for prices. As discussed by Christiano, Eichenbaum, and Evans (2005), dynamic indexation of this form introduces some element of structural persistence into the wage-setting process. Our asymmetric treatment is motivated by the empirical analysis of Levin, Onatski, Williams, and Williams (2005). These authors estimated a similar model using U.S. data over the 1955:1–2001:4 period, and found evidence in favor of nearly full indexation of wages, but not of prices (hence our specification of prices as purely forward-looking).

4.3. Fiscal Policy and the Aggregate Resource Constraint

The government's budget is balanced every period, so that total lump-sum taxes plus seignorage revenue are equal to output and labor subsidies plus the cost of government purchases:

$$M_t - M_{t-1} + \int_0^1 T_t(h)\, dh = \int_0^1 \tau_p P_t(f)\, Y_t(f)\, df + \int_0^1 \tau_w W_t(h)\, N_t(h)\, dh + P_t G_t, \tag{13}$$

where G_t indicates real government purchases. We assume that government spending is a fixed share of output in our analysis. Finally, the total output of the service sector is subject to the following resource constraint:

$$Y_t = C_t + I_t + G_t. \tag{14}$$

5. Solution and Calibration

To analyze the behavior of the model, we log-linearize the model's equations around the nonstochastic steady state. Nominal variables, such as the contract price and wage, are rendered stationary by suitable transformations. We then compute the reduced-form solution of the model for a given set of parameters using the numerical algorithm of Anderson and Moore (1985), which provides an efficient implementation of the solution method proposed by Blanchard and Kahn (1980).

5.1. Parameters of Private Sector Behavioral Equations

The model is calibrated at a quarterly frequency. Thus, we assume that the discount factor $\beta = .9925$, consistent with a steady-state annualized real interest rate $\bar{r}$ of about 3 percent. We assume that the subutility function over consumption is logarithmic, so that $\sigma = 1$, while we set the parameter determining the degree of habit persistence in consumption $\kappa = 0.6$ (similar to the empirical estimate of Smets and Wouters 2003). The parameter χ, which determines the curvature of the subutility function over leisure, is set equal to 10, implying a Frisch elasticity of labor supply of 1/5. This is considerably lower than if preferences were logarithmic in leisure, but within the range of most estimates from the empirical labor supply literature. The scaling parameter χ_0 is set so that employment comprises one-third of the household's time endowment, while the parameter μ_0 on the subutility function for real balances is set an arbitrarily low value (so that variation in real balances has a negligible impact on other variables). The share of government spending of total expenditure is set equal to 12 percent.

The capital share parameters $\alpha = 1/3$. The quarterly depreciation rate of the capital stock $\delta = 0.02$, implying an annual depreciation rate of 8 percent. The price and wage markup parameters $\theta_P = \theta_W = 1/5$. We set the cost of adjusting investment parameter $\varphi_I = 2$, which is somewhat smaller than the value estimated by Christiano, Eichenbaum, and Evans (2001) using a limited information approach; however, the analysis of Erceg, Guerrieri, and Gust (2005) suggests that a lower value in the range of unity may be better able to capture the unconditional volatility of investment within a similar modeling framework. We assume that price contracts last three quarters, while nominal wage contracts last four quarters. The calibration of contract duration is in the range typically estimated in the literature.

6. Model Simulations

6.1. The Post-Civil War Deflation

While we will attempt to use our model to account for the evolution of real activity during the latter two episodes—on the premise that monetary changes played a principal role in driving the output fluctuations that occurred—our objective in applying the model to the post-Civil War deflation is narrower in scope. In particular, while a more complicated model with a richer set of shocks would be required to account for output behavior over the long period prior to Resumption, our focus here is simply to rationalize why the "secular" deflation of 2–3 percent per year appeared to exert little drag on output growth in the decade following the Public Credit Act of 1869.

In this vein, we characterize the monetary authorities in the 1869–1879 period as following a simple targeting rule derived from minimizing a loss function that depends on the gap between the price level p_t and its target value p_t^* (which we call the price level gap), and on the output gap g_t. Under a quadratic period loss function in each of these gaps, the targeting rule is derived by minimizing a discounted conditional loss function of the form:

$$\mathbb{E}_t \sum_{j=0}^{\infty} \beta^j \left\{ (p_{t+j} - p_{t+j}^*)^2 + \lambda_G g_{t+j}^2 \right\} \tag{15}$$

subject to the behavioral constraints implied by household and firm optimization from the model of Section 4.[16]

The solid line in Figure 8.5 presents our benchmark characterization of the post-Civil War deflation period in response to a permanent reduction in p_t^* of 30 percent. The weight on the output gap in the loss function is chosen to stretch out the price decline over the course of a decade, so that the simulated price level decline appears quite similar to the historical experience (this is achieved by setting $\lambda_G = 5000$ in (15)). It is evident from the figure that the large cumulative decline in prices has little impact on real activity: in fact, output never falls more than 0.1 percent below

FIGURE 8.5   Simulations of the Post-Civil War Episode

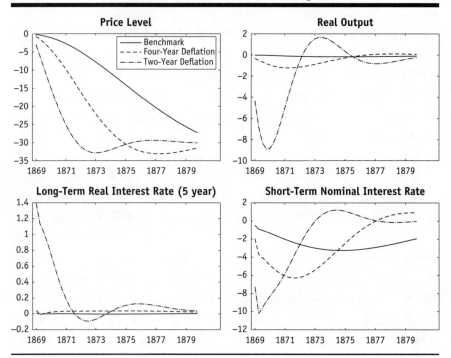

potential. The optimal policy achieves this sizeable price decline at mini-mal output cost by relying heavily on an "expectations channel": current price-setters are willing to lower prices today in the expectation that future prices will be lower (and hence deflation does not require a recession). A notable characteristic of the optimal policy is that it implies a persistent decline in short-term nominal interest rates, which is consistent with the policy shift exerting little effect on long-term real interest rates.

We believe that this simple characterization of policy captures many of the relevant features of the historical environment following the passage of the Public Credit Act in 1869 that were recounted in Section 2. These features included: first, the mandate to effect a substantial reduction in the general price level, subject to the proviso that the deflation would be gradual enough to avoid a reprise of the post-war monetary recession; and second, the ability of the authorities to commit to such a policy. Admittedly, our characterization abstracts from some aspects of implementation that were discussed in Section 2, including the operational procedure of controlling the monetary base. However, taking account of such features would require significant complications to our model, and would seem highly unlikely to change our basic message that a very gradual and predictable deflation exerts small effects on real activity under a reasonable and well-understood rule (specified either in terms of the money stock or nominal interest rate).[17]

Given the negligible output losses under the ten-year implementation window, it is also natural to inquire whether the 1869–1879 price level decline could have occurred more rapidly without significantly exacerbating the effects on the real economy: did the authorities perhaps become overly cautious in response to the public acrimony that followed their first attempts to deflate? This rather general question about how quickly a deflation can be implemented without causing substantial fallout on the real economy has close parallel in earlier work by Taylor (1983) and Ball (1994b, 1995), but with the important difference that the latter authors assessed how the real costs depended on the horizon over which the *inflation rate* was changed, rather than the *price level*. While these authors found that a disinflation could be implemented over a short horizon of roughly two years or less with minimal output costs, our results suggest that a considerably longer horizon is required to implement a change in the price level; the difference reflects that while the staggered contracts framework implies little endogenous persistence in the inflation rate—so that it is relatively easy for inflation to jump—it implies considerably more price level persistence. Under our baseline calibration, the implied tradeoff between a shorter horizon for implementing the disinflation and higher output losses can be derived by varying the relative weight on the output gap (λ_G) in the targeting rule (15). Two alternative cases are shown in Figure 8.5. The dashed line shows that a value of λ_G which causes the 30 percent price decline to occur over only four years causes the output loss to rise to about 1 percent, which still seems quite modest. However, while our benchmark model allows an inflation target to be reduced over a narrow 2-year window with minimal output losses (as verified below, consistent with the earlier literature cited), implementing a new price level target over such an abbreviated time frame causes a pronounced recession (as depicted by the red dash-dotted line).

These results suggest that the ten-year window for phasing in the deflation might have been reduced considerably without much of an adverse effect on output. Moreover, to the extent that wages and prices may have been somewhat more flexible in this episode than implied by our benchmark calibration, the output losses associated with shortening the implementation horizon would be mitigated relative to those indicated in Figure 8.5. Nevertheless, provided there is some sluggishness in prices and wages—even if less than embedded in our benchmark—real interest rates must rise sharply to implement a discrete downward shift in the price level over a short horizon. Thus, it is arguable that a short implementation window in the neighborhood of a year or two might have risked a substantial recession.

6.2. The Post-WWI Deflation

We now turn to using our model to characterize the severe monetary recession that began in 1920. As discussed above, the salient feature was a precipitous and largely unexpected decline in the price level of about 20 percent over a period of less than two years, and a sharp but fairly short-lived contraction in activity. Our model simulations in Figure 8.5 suggest that attempting to achieve a new price level objective so quickly would precipitate a severe recession even under a well-designed policy derived in an optimization-based setting. But given that monetary policy seemed far from optimal during the 1920s, it remains of interest to assess the implications of a large shift in the price level target under an alternative monetary rule that may better account for the nature of policy.

Despite obvious difficulties in characterizing policy during this turbulent period, we believe that many of the prominent features of the policy-making framework can be summarized in a simple instrument rule of the form:

$$i_t = \gamma_i i_{t-1} + \gamma P(p_t - p_t^*). \tag{16}$$

This rule posits the nominal interest rate i_t as responding to the price level gap $(p_t - p_t^*)$, as well as to its own lag (a constant term is suppressed for simplicity). This specification has two salient features. First, policy rates are driven exclusively by the difference between the current price level and its target p_t^*. This specification is intended to capture the belief of key Federal Reserve policy makers that continued adherence to the gold standard hinged on rolling back the rise in the U.S. price level that had occurred following the U.S. entry into the war. While it was recognized that real activity might suffer in the short run, it was regarded of paramount importance to reduce prices enough to faciliate an adequate build-up of gold reserves. The second key feature of (16) is that nominal rates do not respond to inflation (either ex post or ex ante). As shown below, this helps account for the empirical observation that nominal rates remained high despite an enormous decline in the price level in 1920–21. This feature of the instrument rule evidently contrasts with the behavior of nominal rates under the optimal rule shown in Figure 8.5, in which declining inflation exerts sizeable downward pressure on nominal rates.

The price level target is assumed to follow an exogenous random walk, so that any shift in the target is perceived as permanent. The shock we consider involves a 20 percent cumulative reduction in p_t^* that begins in 1920q1. While private agents are assumed to observe the underlying price level target, we assume that the shock is phased in over three quarters, in part to match the modest persistence suggested by the commodity price forecast errors discussed in Section 3. Finally, we set $\gamma_i = .5$ to allow for a bit of interest rate smoothing, and $\gamma_p = .12$ in order to allow our model to do reasonably well in matching the rise in nominal interest rates that occurred in the historical episode.

Simulation results for our benchmark case are shown by the solid lines in Figure 8.6. The model simulation generates a large decline in the price level beginning in 1920 that is similar in magnitude to that observed. The sharpness of this price decline is well captured by our modelling framework, in which prices are determined by Calvo-style contracts with no dynamic indexation. The speed of the price decline would be much more difficult to rationalize in a model that incorporated dynamic indexation or other forms of intrinsic inflation persistence.

The model implies a pronounced output decline that is followed by a rapid recovery, which is similar to the pattern observed historically. The

FIGURE 8.6 Simulations of the Post-WWI Episode

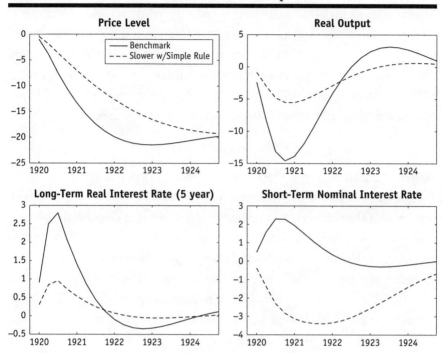

output decline in our model simulation is attributable to a sizeable and fairly persistent rise in the real interest rate. The substantial rise in real long-term interest rates despite little movement in the nominal interest rate reflects both that agents came to expect large price declines, and that policy would maintain high nominal rates even in a deflationary environment.[18]

Thus, our simulation results suggest that the high costs of the 1920–21 deflation reflect that the Federal Reserve attempted to engineer an extremely rapid deflation, and that it was perceived as following a monetary policy stance in which future nominal rates were expected to remain high (at least for a few quarters) in the face of deflation: in effect, consistent with our historical analysis, the Federal Reserve used the blunt instrument of a severe recession to push down prices, rather than operating through an expectations channel. Accordingly, it is of interest to consider the counterfactual simulation depicted by the dotted lines, which shows a case in which the central bank is assumed to change its target path level incrementally, and to follow a rule in which the nominal interest rate also responds to ex post inflation (but is otherwise identical to equation (16)). Clearly, while allowing for nominal rates to decline with inflation would have induced a more gradual convergence in prices to target, it would have greatly ameliorated the output costs. Obviously, even more favorable outcomes could be derived to the extent that policy could better approximate the optimal targeting rules discussed in the previous section rather than a simple ad hoc instrument rule.

6.3. The Volcker Disinflation

A striking feature of the Volcker disinflation period was the fact that inflation forecast errors were extremely persistent. Erceg and Levin (2003) argued that the persistence in the forecast errors—and associated high persistence in realized inflation—may have reflected a high level of uncertainty about the central bank's inflation target.[19] In this chapter, we take a similar stylized approach to characterizing uncertainty about the inflation target of the central bank by assuming that agents cannot differentiate permanent shocks to the inflation target from transient shocks to the monetary policy reaction function.

We specify the central bank's reaction function over the Volcker period as a slightly modified version of the Taylor rule:

$$i_t = \gamma_i i_{t-1} + (1 - \gamma_i)(\bar{r} + \pi_t) + \gamma_\pi(\pi_t - \pi_t^*) + \gamma_y(\Delta y t - \bar{g}) + e_t, \tag{17}$$

where i_t is the short-term nominal interest rate, π_t is the four-quarter change in the GDP price deflator, π_t^* is the central bank's inflation target, Δy_t is the four-quarter change in real GDP, and e_t denotes the shock to the policy reaction function, where all variables are expressed at annual rates in percentage points.[20]

In estimating this policy reaction function, we utilize the sample period 1980:4 through 1986:4, thereby excluding the policy reversals that occurred during the first year of Volcker's tenure (as discussed in Section 2.3).[21] Least squares estimation over this sample period yields $\gamma_i = 0.65, \gamma_\pi = 0.59$, and $\gamma_y = 0.30$. As seen in Figure 8.7, this simple form of the reaction function accounts reasonably well for the evolution of the funds rate over the sample period.

FIGURE 8.7 The Estimated Policy Reaction Function during
the Volcker Disinflation

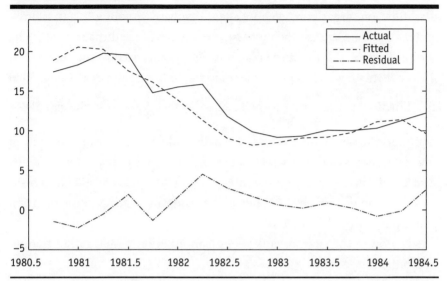

Agents cannot directly observe the long-run inflation target π_t^*, or the
monetary shock e_{qt}; but given that agents observe interest rates, inflation,
and output growth (as well as all of the structural parameters of the model),
they can infer a composite shock ϕ_t which is a hybrid of the inflation target
shock and the monetary policy shock:

$$\phi_t = -\gamma_6 \pi_t^* + e_t. \tag{18}$$

The unobserved components in turn are perceived to follow a first-order
vector autoregression:

$$\begin{bmatrix} \pi_t^* \\ e_t \end{bmatrix} = \begin{bmatrix} \rho_p & 0 \\ 0 & \rho_q \end{bmatrix} \begin{bmatrix} \pi_{t-1}^* \\ e_{t-1} \end{bmatrix} + \begin{bmatrix} \upsilon_1 & 0 \\ 0 & \upsilon_2 \end{bmatrix} \begin{bmatrix} \varepsilon_{pt} \\ \varepsilon_{pt} \end{bmatrix}. \tag{19}$$

The inflation target π_t^*, is highly persistent, and has an autoregressive root
ρ_p arbitrarily close to unity. For simplicity, we assume that the random
policy shock e_t is white noise (so $\rho_q = 0$). The innovations associated with
each shock, ε_{pt} and ε_{qt}, are mutually uncorrelated with unit variance.

Given this linear structure, we assume that agents use the Kalman filter to make optimal projections about the unobserved inflation target π_t^*. The inflation target perceived by agents evolves according to a first order autoregression. Agents update their assessment of the inflation target by the product of the forecast error innovation and a constant coefficient. This coefficient, which is proportional to the Kalman gain, can be expressed as a function of the signal-to-noise ratio $\left(\gamma \pi \dfrac{v_1}{v_2} \right)$. Clearly, the signal-to-noise ratio depends on the relative magnitude of innovations to each of the components of the observed shock θ_t; but importantly, it also depends directly on the weight γ_π on the inflation target in the central bank's reaction function. Intuitively, if policy is aggressive in reacting to the inflation gap, agents will attribute more of any unexplained rise in interest rates to a reduction in the central bank's long-run inflation target, rather than to random policy shocks.

As argued by Erceg and Levin (2003) in the context of a somewhat simpler dynamic model, the signal-to-noise ratio plays a crucial role in affecting model responses to a shock to the inflation target. Following their approach, we estimate this composite parameter (i.e., $\dfrac{v_1}{v_2}$, using the estimated value of γ_π) by choosing the value that minimizes the difference between historical four-quarter-ahead expected inflation (taken from survey data) and the corresponding expected inflation path implied by our model.[22]) In particular, we minimize the loss function:

$$Loss = \sum_{j=0}^{20} \left[\mathbb{E}_{t+j}(\pi_{t+3+j}^4 (survey\ data)) - \mathbb{E}_{t+j}(\pi_{t+3+j}^4 (model)) \right]^2 \tag{20}$$

The estimation period is 1980:4 through 1985:4. The model expectation in (20) is the expected rate of four-quarter-ahead inflation that agents project at each date, given an assumed one-time shift in the inflation target of 6 percentage points that occurs in 1980:4. Our estimation routine yields a point estimate of $\left(\dfrac{v_1}{v_2} \right)$ that implies a Kalman gain coefficient on the forecast error innovation of about 0.10.

FIGURE 8.8   Benchmark Simulation of the Volcker Disinflation

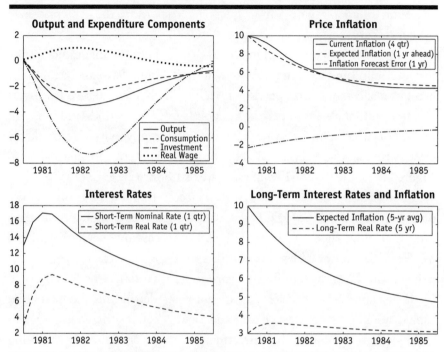

Figure 8.8 shows the effects of a 6 percentage point immediate reduction in the Federal Reserve's inflation target in our benchmark model. The learning problem about the inflation target plays a critical role in allowing our model to account for the main features of the Volcker disinflation episode discussed above, including sluggish inflation adjustment, a persistently negative output gap, and an initial rise in the nominal interest rate. The inflation rate declines in roughly exponential fashion in our model simulation, with about half of the eventual 6 percentage point fall occurring after four quarters, and most of it after ten quarters. Our model's predicted path for inflation is very similar to that observed during the actual episode. Moreover, long-run expected inflation in our model (see the lower right panel) declines much more slowly than current inflation, which is also consistent with the historical experience. This pattern in our simulation reflects that long-run inflation is largely determined by expectations about

the future course of the inflation target, which evolve very slowly, while short-run inflation can drop more quickly in response to the depressed state of real activity.

Our model does quite well in accounting for both the magnitude of the output decline and its timing. As shown in the upper-left panel, real GDP exhibits a substantial and persistent decline, with a cumulative loss (relative to trend) of about 10 percentage points over the period 1981 through 1984. This loss is consistent with a sacrifice ratio of about 1.7, remarkably close to the sacrifice ratio implied by the OECD output gap data shown in Figure 8.3 and to Ball's (1994a) estimate of 1.8 for this episode.

Interestingly, the model does well in accounting for the timing of the output trough: as in the OECD data, the trough occurs about six quarters after the initial shock. Our model's ability to capture the timing of the Volcker recession provides support for specifying adjustment costs as dependent on the change in investment, rather than following a traditional Q-theory approach in which adjustment costs depend on the change in capital stock.[23] By contrast, Erceg and Levin (2003) utilized a Q-theory specification, and found that investment dropped precipitously following the initial rise in interest rates, so that the peak decline in both output and the expenditure components occurred roughly one quarter after the shock.

The ability of our model to account for the Volcker period is enhanced by allowing for the dynamic indexation of nominal wage contracts. In the absence of dynamic wage indexation, real interest rates exhibit a smaller and less persistent increase, and output contracts much less than under our benchmark specification. It might be supposed that the additional inclusion of dynamic price indexation would produce an even larger output decline, and hence improve on our benchmark model's ability to account for the output contraction under Volcker. We found, however, that incorporating this form of structural persistence in the inflation rate produced only a marginally larger output decline in our model simulation, while implying a much slower drop in inflation than occurred in the historical episode.

While we think that the ability of a relatively simple model to account for the broad features of the Volcker recession is impressive, we suspect

FIGURE 8.9   Counterfactual Simulation of Volcker Disinflation under
Complete Information

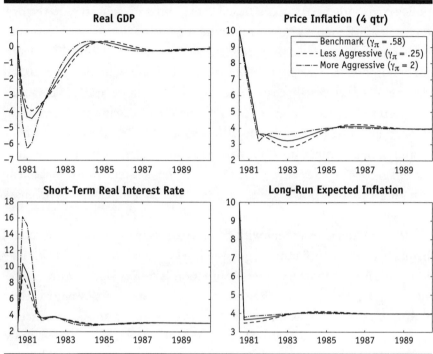

that the inclusion of credit market imperfections and sectoral differentia-
tion in production could enhance the model's ability to account for the
depth of the Volcker recession. In particular, a model that could account
for the massive increase in default spreads that occurred in the early 1980s,
such as the financial accelerator framework of Bernanke, Gertler, and
Gilchrist (1999), might well provide an even closer quantitative match to
the actual experience.

We next turn to applying our model to evaluate some of the criticism
levelled at the rapid pace of the Volcker disinflation and the highly aggressive policy stance required to support it. Our analysis indicates that
this critique would have been justified if the Federal Reserve's policies
were regarded as highly credible. In particular, Figure 8.9 reconsiders
our benchmark scenario under the assumption that agents have complete

information about the shift in the inflation target π_t^*. We interpret this setting as approximating the case of a highly credible and transparent policy environment. As might be expected, inflation converges to the new target in a little more than a year while the output decline is correspondingly much shorter-lived. Nevertheless, a policymaker placing a sufficiently high weight on the output gap relative to inflation might view this output decline as unnecessarily costly. Accordingly, the figure also depicts a rule that responds much less aggressively to the inflation gap; that is, $\gamma_\pi = 0.25$ rather than 0.58 as in our benchmark rule. In this case, the output decline is a bit smaller while inflation declines almost as rapidly. Conversely, a more aggressive rule with a coefficient of $\gamma_\pi = 2$ would only succeed in bringing inflation down a bit more quickly than under the benchmark rule but at the cost of a significantly larger output decline.

Thus, in an environment with complete information about the central bank's underlying inflation target, the level of inflation comes down rapidly even if the monetary reaction function is fairly nonaggressive in responding to inflation. This is because the expectation of slower growth in future prices and wages immediately exerts a strong restraining effect on current inflation. Nevertheless, because there is some structural persistence in inflation due to dynamic wage indexation, attempting to disinflate too quickly—meaning faster than in roughly five or six quarters—can still produce a sizeable contraction in activity. Given these tradeoffs, a more gradualist course would seem preferable unless the policymaker placed virtually no weight on output gap stabilization.

However, this argument in favor of a gradualist policy is predicated on high credibility and transparency of the underlying inflation target, assumptions which seem implausible in the environment faced by Volcker. Our benchmark model with imperfect information appears well suited to examining some of the benefits that might be derived from an aggressive policy stance that accrue through a signalling channel. A given-sized change in the inflation target induces a sharper rise in interest rates if γ_π is large: thus, in an environment where agents must infer policy actions rather than observe them directly, an aggressive policy stance can help them disentangle policy shifts from "discretionary" departures from the perceived policy rule.

FIGURE 8.10   Counterfactual Simulation of Volcker Disinflation under Incomplete Information

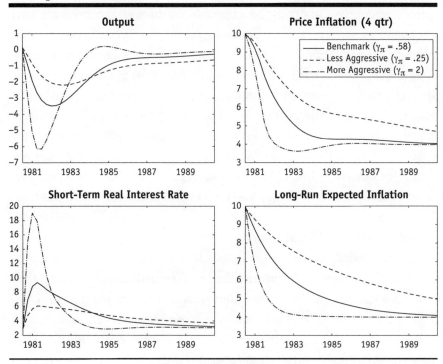

In this vein, Figure 8.10 compares the implications of our benchmark policy rule under incomplete information (repeating the analysis of Figure 8.8) to two alternative rules that vary the weight on the inflation gap in the same way as just considered above: thus, we consider a less aggressive response with $\gamma_\pi = 0.25$, and a more aggressive response with $\gamma_\pi = 2$. We model the signalling value associated with an aggressive policy response by assuming that the innovations υ_1 and υ_2 of the observable ϕ_t are constant in our experiments, which has the effect of reducing the Kalman gain coefficient as γ_π falls. Thus, the Kalman gain coefficient falls from 0.10 in our benchmark to 0.04 in the alternative with a coefficient of $\gamma_\pi = 0.25$; conversely, the Kalman gain rises to 0.3 with the aggressive coefficient of $\gamma_\pi = 2$.

Considering the same 6 percentage point shock to the inflation target, it is evident in the lower right panel that long-term expected inflation declines much more gradually for the lower value of γ_π. In particular, long-run expected inflation is still close to 5 percent even at the end of the decade; in contrast, under the benchmark rule, these expectations approach very close to the 4 percent target within about five years. Unsurprisingly, output exhibits a smaller short-run contraction under the alternative policy rules compared with the benchmark rule, reflecting less pronounced increases in both short-term and long-term real interest rates. But importantly, because private agents learn more slowly about the new inflation target under this alternative, output shows a less rapid recovery in these cases than under the benchmark rule, and real interest rates remain persistently above baseline. Conversely, while a policy that responded even more aggressively to inflation than under the benchmark would produce a larger initial downturn, it causes inflation to fall even more quickly, and hence generates a faster recovery.

Overall, while the less aggressive rules succeed in reducing the severity of the initial output downturn relative to our benchmark scenario, these rules also lead to a somewhat more protracted recession, and markedly prolong the period over which inflation remains above target. Thus, even if gradualism might seem highly attractive under policy credibility for a wide range of policy maker preferences (provided preferences aren't tilted toward reducing inflation at all cost), a much more aggressive response might be warranted in cases of low policy credibility.

7. Conclusions

In this chapter, we have examined three famous episodes of deflation (or disinflation) in U.S. history, including episodes following the Civil War, World War I, and the Volcker disinflation of the early 1980s. Our model simulations suggest that the relatively robust output growth that occurred during the post-Civil war deflation of the 1870s was facilitated by the highly predictable nature of the price decline. By analogy, a more predictable policy of gradual deflation could have helped avoid the sharp post-WWI downturn. However, our analysis of the Volcker period emphasizes that the strong argument for gradualism that is apparent under a transparent and credible monetary regime becomes less persuasive if the monetary regime lacks credibility: in the latter case, gradualism may simply serve to prolong the suffering associated with a disinflationary episode.

Notes

1. Humphrey (2004) provides an excellent survey of the views of leading classical economists regarding the macroeconomic effects of deflation and the associated challenges for policy makers.

2. For example, see Gordon (1982), Taylor (1983), and Ball (1994a).

3. As seen in Figure 8.1, available output measures suggest that growth was relatively strong throughout the period surrounding the passage of the Public Credit Act in 1869. In particular, Davis's (2004) industrial production series (which is available prior to 1869, the year the GDP series begin) grows at about 6 percent per year between 1867 and 1873, notwithstanding about a 25 percent appreciation of the dollar relative to gold and major foreign currencies.

4. The restoration of specie convertibility was supported by all three branches of government. It had the enthusiastic backing of the three successive Republican presidents who held office during the period (Johnson, Grant, and Hayes), and, through its decisions, the indirect support of the Supreme Court. While there was less unanimity in Congress, especially after the 1873 Panic, the debate hinged more on the appropriate speed of restoring convertibility at the official price, rather than on the ultimate goal.

5. There was admittedly some uncertainty about what the target for the dollar price of gold implied for the long-run price level, i.e., for how much price deflation would ultimately have to take place. However, while the real price of gold rose through the 1870s, it seems unlikely that this slow and steady rise significantly exacerbated the problem faced by private agents of making price-level forecasts to set the terms of multiperiod contracts.

6. While the war was primarily financed through higher taxes and the issuance of government bonds, money creation by the Federal Reserve System also played a significant role (Rockoff, 2005).

7. Unlike the Civil war period, in which the dollar was allowed to float, the official price of gold remained fixed during WWI. Thus, the task facing policy makers was to ensure that gold reserves were sufficient to support free convertibility after the lifting of the embargo.

8. The System's most potent policy instrument was the discount rate charged by the System's Reserve Banks to its member commercial banks on short-term loans. The Reserve Banks could request an adjustment in its discount rate, but the Board had to approve.

9. While government statistics indicate a very sharp recession—with real GNP in 1921 nearly 15 percent lower than in the previous year—the analysis of Romer

(1988) and Balke and Gordon (1989) indicates that real output declined by roughly 3 to 6 percent over the period from 1919 through 1921.

10. For example, the National Industrial Conference Board estimated that non-agricultural employment contracted nearly 10 percent from 1919 through 1921.

11. It is difficult to assess the magnitude of this premium, which presumably fluctuated considerably with the business cycle. However, for some quantitative guidance, it is useful to consider the period after Resumption in 1879, when both railroad bond interest rates and U.S. treasury bond rates were denominated in gold. In 1880, the risk spread on high quality railroad bonds appeared to be in the range of 100–150 basis points. For example, the average yield on the Chicago and Alton Railroad 7's maturing in 1893 was about 5.3 percent in 1880 (Macaulay Table A51), compared with a yield on U.S. treasury bonds (4-1/2s of 1891) of 4.1 percent (Homer and Sylla, 1996).

12. Futures prices were obtained from various issues of the Chicago Tribune. Realized prices were taken from the NBER's macro history database, and from annual reports of the Chicago Board of Trade.

13. The HMS drew on two different measures of commodity prices: a Bureau of Labor Statistics index of wholesale commodity prices, and an alternative index produced by the trade publication Bradstreet's. Using the BLS measure apparently favored by HMS researchers, commodity prices were about 19 percent higher in March 1920 than in March 1919, and about 15 percent higher than in November 1918 (using Bradstreet's, commodity prices were 15 percent higher than in March 1919, and 9 percent higher than in November 1918).

14. Given that the HMS forecasters saw the adjustment of retail prices to lag that of commodity prices, retail prices were expected to fall through much of 1921 (e.g., Bullock, 1921), suggesting that ex ante real interest rates were expected to remain at very elevated levels.

15. The futures data on corn and oats are from the Annual Reports of the Chicago Board of Trade, as in Hamilton (1992). Cotton futures traded on the New York commodity futures exchange, with the data recorded in the Commercial and Financial Chronicle.

16. See Svensson (2003) and Woodford (2003) for extensive discussions of the use of targeting rules to characterize monetary policy.

17. It is worth noting that the optimal targeting rule implies a complicated underlying interest rate reaction function (see Woodford and Gianonni 2005). But at least for our baseline case of a very slow deflation, the targeting rule can be approximated fairly well by a simple instrument rule in which the ex post real interest rate responds to the price level gap and output gap.

18. In an earlier version of this chapter, we attempted to account for the effects of the massive decline in government spending following the November 1918 armistice by including a sequence of contractionary government spending shocks. We found that the inclusion of these shocks markedly dampened the effects of the

post-war monetary expansion on output. However, given that the government spending declines were concentrated in 1919, they had a small effect on the behavior of output and prices thereafter. Hence, given our focus on the period following the monetary contraction of early 1920, we have confined our attention to monetary shocks.

19. These authors argued that inflation persistence was not structural, but due to uncertainty about the conduct of monetary policy. Cogley and Sargent (2001) present econometric evidence that inflation persistence is regime-dependent using a time-varying coefficients model.

20. For simplicity, the constant terms have been suppressed in equation 17.

21. In this regression, the short-term nominal interest rate is measured by the federal funds rate, the steady-state real interest rate $\bar{r}$ is set to 3 percent (consistent with our specification of the discount factor β), steady-state output growth $\bar{g}$ is set to 2.5 percent, and the inflation target π^* is specified as 4 percent over this sample period.

22. We use the median of four-quarter-ahead inflation forecasts taken from the Survey of Professional Forecasters; this series is plotted in Figure 8.4).

23. Christiano, Eichenbaum, and Evans (2005) argued that such a specification provides a much better account of investment dynamics in response to a monetary policy shock.

References

Anderson, G.S., and G. Moore, 1985, A linear algebraic procedure for solving linear perfect foresight models, *Economic Letters* 17, 247–252.

Balke, Nathan S., and Robert J. Gordon, 1986, Data Appendix B in Robert J. Gordon (ed.) *The American Business Cycle: Continuity and Change*, Chicago: University of Chicago Press.

Balke, Nathan S., and Robert J. Gordon, 1989, The Estimation of Prewar Gross National Product: Methodology and New Evidence, *Journal of Political Economy*, vol. 97, no. 1, 38–92.

Ball, Lawrence, 1994a, What determines the sacrifice ratio? in N.G. Mankiw (ed.), *Monetary Policy*, Chicago: University of Chicago Press.

Ball, Lawrence, 1994b, Credible disinflation with staggered price-setting, *American Economic Review*, 84, 282–289.

Ball, Lawrence, 1995, Disinflation and Imperfect Credibility, *Journal of Monetary Economics*, 35, 5–24.

Beney, Ada, 1936, *Wages, Hours, and Employment in the United States, 1914–1936*, New York: National Industrial Conference Board, Inc.

Bernanke, Ben, Mark Gertler, and Simon Gilchrist, 1999, The Financial Accelerator in a Quantitative Business Cycle Framework, in J. Taylor and M. Woodford (eds.), *Handbook of Macroeconomics*, Amsterdam: Elsevier.

Blanchard, Olivier, 1984, The Lucas Critique and the Volcker Disinflation, NBER Working paper 1326.

Blanchard, Olivier, and Charles Kahn, 1980, The Solution of Linear Difference Models under Rational Expectations, *Econometrica* 48, 1305–1311.

Bullock, Charles J., 1921, Review of the Year 1920, *Review of Economics and Statistics*, vol. 3 issue 1, 7–10.

Calomiris, Charles, 1985, "Understanding Greenback Inflation and Deflation: An Asset-Pricing Approach," Ph.D. dissertation.

Calomiris, Charles, 1993, "Greenback Resumption and Silver Risk: The Economics and Politics of Monetary Regime Change in the United States, 1862–1900," in Michael D. Bordo and Forrest Capie (eds.), *Monetary Regimes in Transition*, Cambridge: Cambridge University Press.

Calvo, Guillermo, 1983, Staggered Prices in a Utility Maximizing Framework, *Journal of Monetary Economics*, 12, 383–398.

Christiano, Lawrence, Martin Eichenbaum, and Charles Evans, 1999, Monetary Policy Shocks: What Have We Learned, and to What End? in Taylor, John and Michael Woodford (eds.), *Handbook of Macroeconomics* Vol. 1A, 65–148.

Christiano, Lawrence, Martin Eichenbaum, and Charles Evans, 2001, Nominal Rigidities and the Dynamic Effects of Shocks to Monetary Policy, National Bureau of Economic Research Working Paper no. 8403.

Cogley, Timothy, and Thomas Sargent, 2001, "Evolving Post WWII Inflation Dynamics," in Bernanke, Benjamin and Kenneth Rogoff (eds.), *Macroeconomics Annual.*

Commercial and Financial Chronicle, 1919–1922, various issues.

Davis, Joseph, 2004, An Annual Index of U.S. Industrial Production, 1790–1915, *The Quarterly Journal of Economics*, vol. 99, issue 4, 1177–1215.

Erceg, Christopher, Luca Guerrieri, and Christopher Gust, 2005, Can Long Run Restrictions Identify Technology Shocks? *Journal of the European Economic Association*, forthcoming.

Erceg, Christopher, Dale Henderson, and Andrew Levin, 2000, Optimal Monetary Policy with Staggered Wage and Price Contracts, *Journal of Monetary Economics*, 46, 281–313.

Erceg, Christopher, and Andrew Levin, 2003, Imperfect Credibility and Inflation Persistence, *Journal of Monetary Economics* 50, 915–944.

Feldstein, Martin, 1993, American Economic Policy in the 1980s: A Personal View, in M. Feldstein (ed.), *American Economic Policy in the 1980s*, Chicago: University of Chicago Press.

Firestone, John, 1960, *Federal Receipts and Expenditures during Business Cycles, 1879–1958,* Princeton: Princeton University Press.

Fisher, Irving, 1920, *Stabilizing the Dollar,* New York: The Macmillan Company.

Fisher, Irving, 1934, *Stable Money,* New York: Adelphi Company Publishers.

Friedman, Milton, and Anna Schwartz, 1963, *A Monetary History of the United States, 1867–1960,* Princeton: Princeton University Press.

Fuhrer, Jeffrey, 2000, Habit Formation in Consumption and Its Implications for Monetary-Policy Models, *American Economic Review,* 90, 367–390.

Giannoni, Mark, and Michael Woodford, 2005, *Optimal Inflation Targeting Rules,* in Bernanke, Ben and Woodford, Michael (eds)., Inflation Targeting, Chicago: University of Chicago Press.

Goodfriend, Marvin, 1993, Interest Rate Policy and the Inflation Scare Problem: 1979–1992, *Federal Reserve Bank of Richmond Economic Quarterly 79* vol. 1, 2–23.

Goodfriend, Marvin, 1997, Monetary Policy Comes of Age: A 20th Century Odyssey, *Federal Reserve Bank of Richmond Economic Quarterly* 83, 1–24.

Goodfriend, Marvin, and Robert King, 1997, The New Neoclassical Synthesis and the Role of Monetary Policy, in Bernanke, B.S., Rotemberg, J.J. (eds.), *NBER Macroeconomics Annual 1997* (MIT Press: Cambridge), 231–283.

Goodfriend, Marvin, and Robert King, 2005, The Incredible Volcker Disinflation, *Journal of Monetary Economics* vol. 52 issue 5, 981–1015.

Gordon, Robert, 1982, Why Stopping Inflation May Be Costly: Evidence from Fourteen Historical Episodes, in Hall, Robert E. (ed.), *Inflation: Causes and Effects,* Chicago: University of Chicago Press, 11–40.

Homer, Sidney, and Richard Sylla, 1996, *A History of Interest Rates,* 3rd edition, New Brunswick, NJ: Rutgers University Press.

Humphrey, Thomas, 2004, "Classical Deflation Theory," Federal Bank of Richmond Economic Quarterly, 90, 11–32.

Macaulay, Frederick R., 1938, *The Movements of Interest Rates, Stock Prices, and Bond Yields in the United States since 1856,* New York: National Bureau of Economic Research, Inc.

Meltzer, Allan, 2003, *A History of the Federal Reserve,* Volume 1, 1913–1951, Chicago: University of Chicago Press.

Miller, Adolph, 1921, Federal Reserve Policy, *American Economic Review,* 11, no. 2, 177–206.

Miron, Jeffrey and Christina Romer, 1990, A New Monthly Index of Industrial Production, 1884–1940, *The Journal of Economic History,* vol. 50, issue 2, 321–337.

Mitchell, Wesley, 1903, *A History of the Greenbacks, with Special Reference to the Economic Consequences of their Issue: 1862–1865,* Chicago: University of Chicago Press.

Mitchell, Wesley, 1908, *Gold, Prices, and Wages under the Greenback Standard,* Berkeley: The University Press.

Review of Economics and Statistics, 1919–1921, Monthly Survey of General Business Conditions, vol. 1–3, various issues.

Rockoff, Hugh, 2005, Monetary Statistics before the National Banking Era, in *Historical Statistics of the United States, Millenial Edition, Colonial Times to the Present,* Cambridge: Cambridge University Press.

Roll, Richard, 1972, Interest Rates and Price Expectations during the Civil War, *The Journal of Economic History*, vol. 32, issue 2, 476–498.

Romer, Christina, 1988, World War I and the Postwar Depression: A Reinterpretation Based on Alternative Estimates of GNP, *Journal of Monetary Economics* vol. 22, 91–115.

Romer, Christina, 1989, The Prewar Business Cycle Reconsidered: New Estimates of Gross National Product, 1869–1908, *Journal of Political Economy*, vol. 97, no. 1, 1–37.

Rotemberg, Julio, and Michael Woodford, An Optimization-Based Econometric Framework for the Evaluation of Monetary Policy, in Bernanke, Ben and Julio Rotemberg (eds.), *NBER Macroeconomics Annual 1997*, Cambridge: MIT Press, 297–346.

Sargent, Thomas, 1982, The Ends of Four Big Inflations, in Hall, Robert (ed.), *Inflation: Causes and Effects*, Chicago: University of Chicago Press, 41–97.

Sargent, Thomas, 1999, *The Conquest of American Inflation*, Princeton: Princeton University Press.

Smets, F., and R. Wouters, 2003. An Estimated Dynamic Stochastic General Equilibrium Model of the Euro Area, *Journal of the European Economic Association*, vol. 1, 1124–1175.

Svensson, Lars, 2003. "What Is Wrong with Taylor Rules: Using Judgement in Monetary Policy through Targeting Rules," *Journal of Economic Literature*, vol. 41, 426–477.

Taylor, John, 1980, Aggregate Dynamics and Staggered Contracts, *Journal of Political Economy*, 88, 1–24.

Taylor, John, 1983, "Union Wage Settlements during a Disinflation," *The American Economic Review*, 73, no. 5, 981–994.

Timberlake, Richard H., 1975, The Resumption Act and the Money Supply, *Journal of Economic History*, 43, no. 3, 729–739.

Woodford, Michael, 2003, *Interest and Prices*, Princeton: Princeton University Press.

Yun, Tack. 1996, Nominal Price Rigidity, Money Supply Endogeneity, and Business Cycles. *Journal of Monetary Economics* 37, 345–370.

CHAPTER 9

Aggregate Price Shocks and Financial Instability

A Historical Analysis

MICHAEL D. BORDO, MICHAEL J. DUEKER,

AND DAVID C. WHEELOCK

I. Introduction

THE NOTION THAT CENTRAL BANKS should act as lenders of last resort is not controversial. How best to carry out that responsibility is, however, not widely agreed on. One view holds that the financial system is inherently fragile, and a central bank should forgo other objectives, such as preventing inflation, when financial instability threatens. An alternative view argues that by controlling inflation a central bank will in fact promote financial stability. Anna Schwartz (1988, 1995), for example, contends that financial instability has often been caused by monetary policies that cause fluctuations in the rate of inflation. She argues that monetary policy should focus exclusively on maintaining price stability.

A few countries, for example, Canada and New Zealand, have recently made inflation control the paramount objective of their central bank's

Originally published in "Aggregate Price Shocks and Financial Instability: A Historical Analysis," *Economic Inquiry* 40, no. 4 (2002): 521–38.

monetary policy, and the Maastricht Treaty, which established monetary union among 11 European Community countries, specifies control of inflation as the principal objective for the European Central Bank. Most countries, including the United States, assign their central banks multiple objectives, such as full employment and financial stability, as well as inflation control. Implicitly, the specification of multiple objectives for monetary policy assumes trade-offs between those goals—that a country might have to accept higher inflation, at least temporarily, to maintain financial stability, for example.

This chapter investigates the historical association between aggregate price and financial stability to shed light on the question of whether a commitment to price stability is likely to enhance or lessen financial stability. Specifically, we use data for the United States from 1790 to 1997 to test the hypothesis that aggregate price disturbances cause or worsen financial instability. Unanticipated aggregate price declines might increase financial distress by leaving some borrowers with insufficient income to repay contracted nominal debt. Thus unanticipated aggregate price declines would increase insolvency and default rates. Positive aggregate price shocks, on the other hand, might cause default rates to fall below expectations and could encourage financial expansion if borrowers and lenders are unable to distinguish changes in relative prices from changes in the aggregate price level. Financial expansion based on aggregate price misperceptions can lead to resource misallocation, however, and thereby worsen financial distress associated with subsequent unanticipated aggregate price declines.

During 1790–1933, unanticipated movements in the price level best represent price shocks, whereas the persistence of inflation since 1933 led us to examine the impact of unanticipated inflation on financial conditions during 1934–97. We use the phrase "aggregate price shock" to refer to unanticipated movements in either the price level or the inflation rate.

In the absence of consistent time-series measures of aggregate financial conditions over a long period, we construct an annual index of financial conditions from both quantitative and narrative sources. We use a dynamic time-series probit model to estimate the impact of aggregate price shocks on financial conditions, as reflected in the index. We also regress four series used to construct the index on aggregate price shocks to confirm that the relationship between aggregate price shocks and the index is present in its constituent series. We control for liquidity, real output growth, and supply shocks and test whether relationships changed with changes in monetary or financial regime. Our objective is to shed light on the extent that aggregate price disturbances exacerbate financial instability, and whether the relationship between such disturbances and financial conditions is affected by the institutional environment.

We begin by outlining why aggregate price shocks might cause or worsen financial instability. We then discuss how one might identify the impact of price or inflation disturbances on financial conditions empirically and describe the construction of an annual index of financial conditions. Next, we describe the dynamic time-series probit model used in the estimation and present empirical estimates of the impact of price level and inflation shocks on financial variability, as reflected in the index. We conclude by summarizing and discussing implications of our findings.

II. Aggregate Price Shocks and Financial Instability

Financial instability can have either monetary or non-monetary causes and may be solely domestic or spread among countries. In the United States, the nineteenth and early twentieth centuries were punctuated by banking panics—episodes of widespread panic among depositors leading to bank runs. Banking panics were a principal cause of monetary contraction, deflation, and declines in real economic activity, as Friedman and Schwartz (1963) have shown.

Whereas the impact of banking panics on the price level and economic activity is well understood, a falling price level (or inflation rate) can also be a source of financial distress. Because debt contracts typically are written in nominal, fixed-rate terms, a decline in the price level increases the real cost of servicing outstanding debt. In the presence of positive recontracting costs, loan defaults and bankruptcies increase, which in turn puts pressure on lenders. Even a decline in the rate of inflation can cause distress if the decline is unexpected and not hedged, because some borrowers will have insufficient revenue to service debt that could have been repaid in the absence of disinflation.

Fisher (1932, 1933) was among the first to describe the impact of a falling price level on financial conditions in a business cycle framework. According to Fisher, business cycle upturns are triggered by exogenous factors that provide new profit opportunities. Rising prices and profits encourage more investment and also speculation for capital gains. Debt finance through bank loans increases deposits and the money supply and raises the price level. A general optimism or euphoria takes hold, which increases monetary velocity and further fuels the expansion, and rising prices encourage further borrowing by reducing the real value of outstanding debt.

The process continues until a general state of "overindebtedness" is reached, that is, the point at which individuals, firms, and banks generate insufficient cash flow to service their liabilities. Any shortfall in the price level from its expected value, regardless of cause, will then leave borrowers unable to service their debts and lead to distress selling. As loans are extinguished, bank deposits and the money supply decline, further lowering the price level. Deflation increases the real burden of remaining debt, leading to further bankruptcies and declining economic activity—a process referred to as debt-deflation. The process continues until either widespread bankruptcy has eliminated the overindebtedness or a reflationary monetary policy has been adopted. Once recovery begins, however, the whole process will repeat itself.

Schwartz (1988, 1995, 1997) offers an alternative explanation, focused explicitly on monetary policy, of how aggregate price instability can lead to financial instability. Schwartz contends that when monetary policy produces fluctuations in the inflation rate, information problems associated with evaluating alternative investments are made worse, which in turn increases financial instability:

> Both [borrowers and lenders] evaluate the prospects of projects by extrapolating the prevailing price level or inflation rate. Borrowers default on loans not because they have misled uninformed lenders but because, subsequent to the initiation of the project, authorities have altered monetary policy in a contractionary direction. The original price level and inflation rate assumptions are no longer valid. The change in monetary policy makes rate-of-return calculations on the yield of proj-

ects, based on the initial price assumptions of both lenders and borrowers, unrealizable. (Schwartz, 1995, 24)

Schwartz does not formally model how changes in the inflation rate can lead to financial instability, but her description fits well with the monetary misperceptions model of Lucas (1972, 1973). In that model, individuals are unable to distinguish with certainty shifts in relative prices from changes in the aggregate price level. This uncertainty can lead to resource misallocation, which is corrected only once the true nature of a price change becomes known.

This model is easily extended to incorporate financial decisions. Uncertainty about the nature of price changes can lead to bad forecasts of real returns to investment projects and, hence, to unprofitable borrowing and lending decisions. Because of misperceptions regarding the nature of individual price changes, inflation tends to encourage overly optimistic forecasts of real returns and thus can lead to "lending booms." By the same token, disinflation and, especially, deflation may lead to overly pessimistic forecasts and hence discourage the financing of projects that might otherwise be funded.[1]

When not fully anticipated or hedged, a change in the inflation rate can cause the net realized real return to investment to deviate from what had been expected. Default rates in debt markets can thus be affected. An unanticipated disinflation, for example, can increase default rates by causing realized borrower incomes to fall below expectations. Although disinflation causes the real income to lenders on loans that do not default to exceed expectations, an increase in default rates could more than offset this gain and result in significant distress for lenders. In the aggregate, financial distress is likely to be associated with disinflation because some projects will generate sufficient nominal income to repay loans only if the rate of inflation equals or exceeds the rate that had been expected when the loans were made. Similarly, higher than anticipated inflation can result in lower than expected default rates.[2]

A country's institutional environment can affect the form and possibly the severity of financial instability associated with either a real or an aggregate price shock. Banking panics, for example, are much less likely to occur in the presence of an effective lender of last resort. Similarly, high bank failure rates are less likely in systems dominated by large, branching banks, than in unit banking systems. Nevertheless, regardless of the institutional environment, aggregate price instability can still increase borrower defaults and thereby reduce banking system profits.

Similarly, the contribution of aggregate price stability to stability of the financial system depends neither on the cause of specific price-level movements nor on the nature of the monetary regime, except insofar as they affect the extent that changes in aggregate prices are anticipated. For example, an abrupt decline in inflation following a sustained price-level increase will likely contribute to financial distress regardless of whether a country has a gold standard or a fiat monetary system.

Throughout much of the nineteenth and twentieth centuries, the United States was on either a bimetallic or gold standard.[3] Under a commodity standard, real shocks to the demand or supply of the commodity cause changes in the money stock and, over the long term, the price level. The underlying shock might be an adverse movement in the trade balance, for example, leading to a gold outflow, monetary contraction, and, if sustained, a decline in the price level. There may well be theoretical reasons to not offset real shocks of this sort—the classical "rules of the game," for example, held that gold flows should not be offset and that the price level should be permitted to adjust to restore equilibrium in the international gold market. Nevertheless, an unstable price level may well increase financial instability.

Even if there are reasons to permit some movement in aggregate prices, a finding that financial distress is worsened by aggregate price instability would suggest that financial instability could be lessened by limiting aggregate price disturbances, and that price and financial stability should be considered complementary rather than competing policy objectives. We now turn to the historical record to gauge whether there may be support for the proposition that aggregate price instability exacerbates financial instability in general.

III. Empirical Analysis

Our conjecture is that unanticipated movements in the aggregate price level or inflation rate destabilize financial conditions. Negative aggregate price shocks will cause financial distress by increasing insolvency and default rates above "normal" levels. Positive aggregate price shocks, on the other hand, will temporarily reduce insolvency and default rates.

The nature of aggregate price disturbances depends on whether the monetary regime is based on a commodity (such as gold) or a fiat regime. Bordo and Schwartz (1999) show that under the gold and bimetallic standards, the U.S. price level had a persistent stochastic trend because real shocks to the demand or supply of gold and silver caused changes in the money stock and, over the long term, the price level. Before 1933, therefore, we identify aggregate price shocks in terms of the price level.

Inflation has become increasingly persistent since the establishment of the Federal Reserve System in 1914, as Barsky (1987) shows. This period witnessed the decline and eventual abandonment of the gold standard in favor of a government-managed fiat standard. A substantial shift in regime occurred in 1933 with suspension of the gold standard, as Calomiris and Wheelock (1998) describe. Since then, the price level has risen almost continuously, and aggregate price shocks are best measured in terms of unanticipated inflation.

Measuring Financial Conditions

We use a discrete-valued index to measure financial conditions, following Eichengreen et al. (1996), Kaminsky and Reinhart (1999), and other literature on currency crises. Much of the sample variance of continuous measures of financial conditions is generated by variation within the range where financial conditions might be considered normal. Because our goal is to identify variables that cause financial conditions to move from normal conditions to distress or to euphoria, we are unconcerned with explaining financial conditions within the normal range.

Table 9.1 presents our index of financial conditions, in which each year is placed into one of five categories, from severe distress to financial euphoria. The number of years in each category is noted in parentheses. For

TABLE 9.1   Index of Financial Conditions, 1790–1997

Severe Distress (12)[a]	Moderate Distress (46)	Normal (107)	Moderate Expansion (30)	Euphoria (13)
1797	1796	1790	1791	1795
1819	1798	1792–94	1804	1805
1837	1808–09	1799–1803	1806	1824
1857	1812	1807	1813	1917–19
1878	1814–16	1810–11	1823	1943–48
1931–32	1818	1817	1835–36	1951
1982–86	1820	1821	1847	
	1822	1827–28	1850	
	1825–26	1830–32	1852	
	1829	1834	1862–64	
	1833	1843–45	1903–07	
	1838–42	1849	1909–13	
	1846	1851	1916	
	1848	1853	1920	
	1854	1855–56	1942	
	1858	1859–60	1950	
	1861	1865–68	1952–55	
	1869	1870–72		
	1873–77	1879–83		
	1884	1885–92		
	1893	1894–1902		
	1921–22	1908		
	1930	1914–15		
	1933–34	1923–29		
	1938	1935–37		
	1981	1939–41		
	1987–92	1949		
		1956–80		
		1993–97		

Source: See text and appendix.

[a] Numbers of observations in each category are indicated in parentheses.

1790–1869, the index is derived from narrative sources, as described. For 1870–1933, the index is based on annual observations on business and bank failure rates, an ex post real interest rate, and an interest rate quality spread.[4] Because of the minimal number of bank failures after the Great Depression, for 1934–97 we dropped the bank failure rate in favor of a series on bank loan charge-offs. Charge-off data are not available prior to 1934. Data sources and definitions are provided in the appendix. The index provides a means of capturing in a single variable the different aspects of financial conditions reflected in the four variables that make up the index. For example, it treats a year with severe banking distress and a high business failure rate as having more severe financial distress than a year with severe banking distress but few business failures.

In general, business failure rates, measures of banking conditions, and various financial market indicators are likely to reflect financial conditions well. High rates of firm or bank failures reflect unrealized income expectations and borrower defaults. Bank failure rates, in particular, however, can be affected by regulation and market structure. For example, the Canadian banking system's oligopolistic structure and close ties to the government probably explain why Canada had no bank failures during the Great Depression, despite suffering severe financial distress in the form of firm and household bankruptcies. Similarly, in the United States, the introduction of federal deposit insurance and imposition of barriers to entry and other regulations in the 1930s probably lowered the number of bank failures that would result from a given macroeconomic shock. By including multiple measures of financial conditions in our index, we reduce the influence of such structural breaks on the observed relationship between aggregate price shocks and financial conditions.

In addition to business and bank failure rates, we include an ex post real interest rate and an interest rate quality spread in our index. The disinflationary period of the early 1980s witnessed unusually high real interest rates and interest rate quality spreads. High real interest rates increase the burden of debt on borrowers and may increase the likelihood of loan defaults.

Increases in observed real interest rates during disinflationary periods may reflect expectations that disinflation is only temporary. After some

15 years of rising inflation before 1980, it might have been reasonable to expect that inflation would also be high during the 1980s—that is, to doubt the credibility of the Federal Reserve's pledge to reduce inflation. Hence, lenders demanded high nominal interest rates to compensate for expected inflation, and (some) borrowers were willing to pay those rates, such that equilibrium nominal rates were high relative to current inflation. Because inflation did come down and stayed down, ex post real interest rates were high, and consequently default rates were unusually high. If observed high real rates reflected similar expectational errors in other periods, we would expect the real rate to be a reasonable proxy of financial conditions.[5]

The difference in yields on low- and high-quality bonds is another possible measure of financial conditions. Friedman and Schwartz (1963) and Mishkin (1991) found that quality spreads historically have reflected financial turbulence. More recently, in the unsettled period following the Russian government's debt default and devaluation in August 1998, spreads between yields on corporate bonds (especially those issued by low-rated firms) and U.S. Treasury securities increased sharply. This was widely interpreted as reflecting a flight to quality in the wake of increased uncertainty about foreign economies generally and ultimately about the continued strength of the U.S. economic expansion. Quality spreads tend to increase during recessions, reflecting the higher default rates of firms during business cycle downturns. Similarly, by redistributing wealth from debtors to creditors, unexpected deflation (or disinflation) reduces the net worth of borrowers and thereby causes markets to demand higher yields on risky debt than on low-risk securities.[6]

We aggregate the four series on business failures, banking conditions, the real interest rate, and the quality spread to produce our index for 1870–1997 as follows. For each series, we computed the differences between annual observations and the series median for the subperiod, divided by the subperiod standard deviation. These standardized differences were summed across the four series for each year. We classify years in which the summed differences exceed ±1.5 standard deviations from the overall mean as years of "euphoria" ("severe distress"); we classify years in which the summed differences are between ±0.75 and ±1.5 standard deviations from the mean as years of "moderate" expansion (distress); and we classify years in which the summed differences fall between −0.75 and +0.75 standard deviations from the mean as "normal."

In constructing the index, we treated the two periods 1870–1933 and 1934–97 entirely separately. Observations in one period have no influence on the classification of years in the other period; thus, one cannot directly compare index classifications in one period with those in the other. In estimating the probit model, we estimate separate coefficients for each independent variable in each subperiod. Hence, consistency in the index between the subperiods is not important. The appendix presents additional detail on the construction of the index.

Index for 1790–1869

Except for short periods, continuous, consistent time series data on bank and business conditions for the period of U.S. history before 1870 are unavailable. Thus, to extend the analysis before 1870, we constructed an index of financial conditions from narrative sources, principally Thorp (1926), who prepared annual summaries of economic and financial conditions for several countries. By comparing Thorp's descriptions of financial conditions across years, supplemented by other historical accounts, such as Smith and Cole (1935), we place each year into one of five categories of financial conditions.

For example, 1797 is the first year we assign to the severe distress category. Thorp (1926, 114) describes the year as one of "depression; panic; . . . falling prices; many failures, foreign trade restricted. Money tight; little speculation; financial panic, autumn." For 1798, which we classify as a year of moderate distress, Thorp (1926, 114) writes: "Continued depression in the North with failures; . . . prosperity in the South; collapse of land speculation . . . money very tight." For 1799, which we classify as normal, Thorp (1926, 114) writes: "Revival. Marked improvement in Northern activity; continued prosperity, South . . . money eases somewhat."

We classify 1824 as a year of financial euphoria. Thorp (1926, 119) describes this year as one of "prosperity; widespread activity; excited speculation . . . bank mania; many new banks chartered . . . money easy." For 1850, a year we classify as one of moderate financial expansion, Thorp (1926, 125) writes: "Money easy; revival of stock market . . . influx of gold from California." By contrast, for 1855 Thorp (1926, 125) writes: "Money eases, but tightens, autumn; railroad securities reach low point and recover somewhat." We classify the year as normal.

We also classify 1853 as normal. For that year, Thorp (1926, 125) writes: "Continued activity and expansion, slackening last quarter . . . very active railroad construction; extensive speculation . . . money tightens severely; panics and distress in interior cities; decline in railroad stock prices." The Year 1853 illustrates the difficulty of assigning some years to a single category because financial conditions can change markedly within a year.

For the Antebellum era, we also relied on narrative and quantitative information provided by Smith and Cole (1935). Smith and Cole (1935, 20) refer to the financial distress of 1818–19 as America's first major banking crisis and describe how a decline in commodity prices "meant serious losses to merchants who had speculated in commodities. . . . Banks with extended loans to speculators were now confronted with a demand for specie . . . and the curtailment of bank loans made the position of the American merchant even more difficult." This description seems consistent with later financial crises in which sudden declines in commodity prices resulted in financial losses, especially for speculators who had bet on continued price increases and the bankers who supported them. More severe price declines were associated with widespread bank and business failures and recessions.

Figures 9.1–9.3 plot our index against price level (inflation) shocks. Index categories are ordered from 1 (severe distress) to 5 (financial euphoria), with 3 assigned to normal years. We use a trend-cycle decomposition to identify aggregate price shocks in terms of the price level for 1795–1933 and inflation rate for 1934–97, as described in the appendix.

During 1795–1869, price-level shocks were large in comparison with those of later years, and the index varies considerably from year to year. Moderate or severe financial distress occurred in several years that had deflationary shocks, though deflationary shocks also occurred in a few years, for example, 1823–24, in which our narrative sources indicate that financial conditions were strong. Moreover, a few years of moderate or severe financial distress, for instance, 1819, 1837, and 1857, were not characterized by large deflationary shocks. Our narrative sources place a great deal of emphasis on financial panics, which often occurred at the beginning of major declines in prices. Our concern here, however, is with financial distress characterized by bank and other commercial failures and losses, which tended to occur during the deflationary periods that followed panics.

Figure 9.2 plots our index against price-level shocks for 1870–1933. Price-level shocks are plotted on the same scale as in Figure 9.1, and it is readily apparent that price shocks were considerably smaller on average in the later period. Only the deflationary shock of 1921 rivals the worst shocks of 1795–1869. Nevertheless, considerable financial distress was associated with deflation during the 1870s and during 1930–33. Financial euphoria, characterized by unusually low business and bank failure rates and low real interest rates and quality spreads, occurred during the highly inflationary years of World War I (1916–18).

Figure 9.3 plots the index against inflation rate shocks for 1934–97. The later years of World War II and the immediate postwar years were the most financially expansive or euphoric. Most of the 1950s–70s fall into the normal category, whereas much of the early 1980s are classified as years of moderate or severe financial distress. The 1980s had the highest rates of

FIGURE 9.1   Index of Financial Conditions and Price-Level Shocks

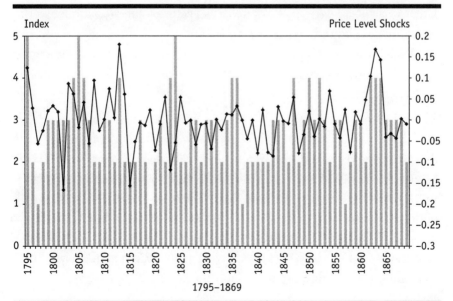

bank loan charge-offs and business failures since the Great Depression, alongside unusually high real interest rates and quality spreads.

IV. Model and Estimation Results

We gauge the impact of aggregate price shocks on U.S. financial conditions historically by estimating both a dynamic probit model in which our categorical index of financial conditions is the dependent variable, and ordinary least squares regressions for the individual series used to construct the index for 1870–1997. In estimating the impact of aggregate price shocks, we control for real output, supply side, and liquidity shocks.

Dynamic Probit Model

The dynamic ordered probit model is designed explicitly for discretely valued time-series data in which pressure for a discrete change can build over time. The model also can account for features of time-series data, such as serial correlation and heteroscedasticity. The general set-up is that an observed variable, y, takes on one of J different discrete values. A continuous latent level, y^*, follows a standard time-series process and determines the discrete level of y. The discrete variable $y_t \in$ category j if the continuous latent variable $y_t^* \in (c_{j-1}, c_j)$, where c is a vector of cut-off parameters that determine the boundaries of the categories.

A basic time-series probit model of y^* includes at least one autoregressive term on the right-hand side of the equation for the latent variable:

$$y_t^* = \rho y_{t-1}^* + X_t \beta + \varepsilon_t. \tag{1}$$

The dynamic ordered probit model of Eichengreen et al. (1985) serves as a time-series probit because it allows the continuous latent variable to move gradually toward the boundary with another category over several periods. The maximum-likelihood estimation procedure of Eichengreen et al. (1985) requires numerical evaluation of an integral for each observation to obtain the density, h, of y_t^*, where ϕ is the standard normal density, and I_t is the information available up to time t:

$$h(y_t^* \mid I_t) = 1/\sigma_\varepsilon \int_{l_{t-1}}^{u_{t-1}} \phi(y_t^*/\sigma_\varepsilon) h(y_{t-1}^* \mid I_t) dy_{t-1}^* \qquad (2)$$

where $\{l_t, u_t\} = \{c_{j-1}, c_j\}$ if $y_t \in$ category j. Because numerical evaluation of these integrals is time-consuming and approximate, it is not tractable under direct maximum-likelihood estimation to extend the model to include additional features, such as regime-switching parameters.

Gibbs sampling offers a tractable method of estimating the dynamic probit model, as well as other models where the joint density of y_t^* and y_{t-1}^* is difficult to evaluate. Gibbs sampling involves generating a sample of draws from a joint distribution through a sequence of draws from the respective conditional distributions. In the present context, such data augmentation allows one to treat augmented values of $y_s^*, s \neq t$, as observed data when evaluating the conditional density of y_t^*. Thus, one conditions the density of y_t^* on a value, instead of a density, of y_{t-1}^*, making the problem much simpler than recursive evaluation of the integral in

FIGURE 9.2   Index of Financial Conditions and Price-Level Shocks

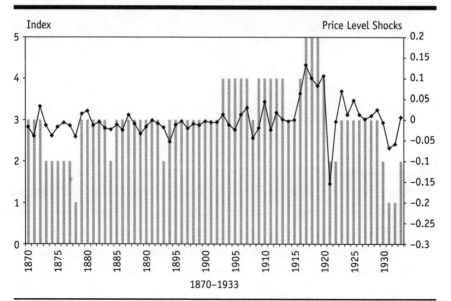

1870–1933

FIGURE 9.3   Index of Financial Conditions and Inflation Shocks

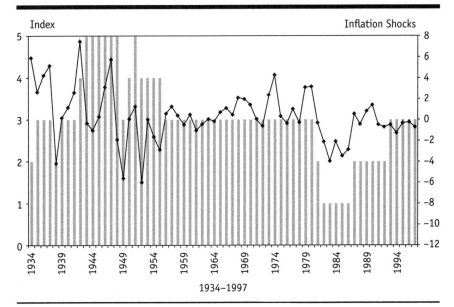

equation (2). Furthermore, once the latent variable has been augmented, it becomes straightforward to model any regime switching, such as conditional heteroscedasticity.

Markov Regime Switching

We include two forms of regime switching in the latent variable for the time-series probit. First, our model allows for heteroscedasticity by way of Markov-switching variances. Both the explanatory variables and the data that went into the construction of the quantitative index contain outliers that should be downweighted when estimating the regression coefficients. Therefore we introduce switching between a high and low variance level governed by a binary variable, $S1 : \sigma^2_{S1t} \in \{\sigma^2_0, \sigma^2_1\}$.

The model also includes Markov switching in the intercept, β_0, to allow for shifts in the unconditional level of the financial conditions index. The binary variable that governs drift switching is $S2$:

$$y_t^* = \rho y_{t-1}^* + \beta_0(S2_t) + X_t'\beta + \varepsilon_t, \tag{3}$$

where $\beta_0(S2_t) \in \{\beta_{0l}, \beta_{0h}\}$, $\varepsilon_t = \sigma_{S1t}e_t$ and $e_t \sim N(0, 1)$. The transition probabilities for the state variables, $S1$ and $S2$, are: $\text{Prob}(S1_t = 0 \mid S1_{t-1} = 0) = p1$; $\text{Prob}(S1_t = 1 \mid S1_{t-1} = 1) = q1$; $\text{Prob}(S2_t = 0 \mid S2_{t-1} = 0) = p2$; $\text{Prob}(S2_t = 1 \mid S2_{t-1} = 1) = q2$. Additional details of the Gibbs sampling framework as applied to the dynamic ordered probit are presented in Bordo et al. (2000). The main result of interest is the conditional distribution of the latent variable, y^*:

$$y_t^* \sim N[\rho y_{t-1}^* + X_t'\beta + \rho r_0 \sigma_{S1t}^2 / (\rho^2 \sigma_{S1t}^2 + \sigma_{S1t+1}^2), \sigma_{S1t+1}^2 \sigma_{S1t}^2 / (\rho^2 \sigma_{S1t}^2 + \sigma_{S1t+1}^2)] \tag{4}$$

where $r_0 = \rho\varepsilon_t + \varepsilon_{t+1}$.

Explanatory Variables

We use the unanticipated components of the price level and inflation described to estimate the effects of aggregate price shocks on financial conditions. We control for the possible impacts of both real and liquidity shocks on financial conditions. All data are annual and, except for a lagged dependent variable, contemporaneously timed.

We control for real output fluctuations using available data on gross domestic product (GDP). We expect that negative shocks to GDP growth increase financial distress.[7] We also include the growth rates of potential GDP and labor productivity to control for the effects of possible supply side and natural rate disturbances on the estimated relationship between aggregate price shocks and financial conditions. Gray and Spencer (1990) find that the estimated impact of price surprises on real activity is sensitive to the inclusion of such disturbances in their empirical model. The same might be true for financial conditions. For example, a negative productivity shock might generate both a positive price shock and an increase in financial distress which, unless controlled for, would make it appear as though a positive price surprise worsened financial distress. We test whether supply side effects are important by reporting one specification that includes potential GDP growth and productivity growth and one that does not.

Finally, we also include the growth rate of the monetary base as an independent variable. Over time, nominal money supply shocks will affect inflation. In the short run, however, liquidity shocks might contribute to financial distress independent of their impact on the price level or inflation. We expect that declines in base growth, for example, will increase financial distress.

Dynamic Probit Model Results

As in Figures 9.1–9.3, we assign values to the index categories listed in Table 9.1, from 1 for severe distress to 5 for financial euphoria. Hence, in the ordered probit model, a positive coefficient on an independent variable would indicate that an increase in the value of that variable would lower financial distress or, equivalently, encourage financial expansion or euphoria. We expect to find positive coefficients on the price level and inflation shock variables, indicating, for example, that an unanticipated decline in the price level worsens financial distress.

Table 9.2 reports coefficient estimates and corresponding probability values for statistical significance for two specifications of the dynamic probit model.[8] To produce reliable estimates of the cut-off parameters—which provide an indication of how much the values of the independent variables must change to move from one category of financial distress to another—we need reasonably large numbers of observations in each category. Hence, we estimated the models over the entire 1795–1997 period, allowing for the coefficients on the independent variables to differ between subperiods. In addition to the parameters reported in Table 9.2, each specification included individual dummy variables for major war periods.[9]

We investigate whether the impact of price level shocks differed between 1792–1869 and 1870–1933 because the price level was more stable after the Civil War and because 1870 marks the point at which our index of financial conditions is based purely on quantitative information.[10] We estimate the impact of inflation rate shocks for 1934–97, with a break at 1979/80 to test whether inflation shocks had a different impact during the recent era of financial deregulation. Furthermore, we include various coefficient breaks for the growth rates of GDP, potential GDP, labor productivity, and the monetary base at points where there are changes in data sources or definitions (see appendix).[11]

For 1795–1933, the results reported in Table 9.2 support the hypothesis that shocks to the price level affected financial conditions. The positive coefficients on the price-level shock variables for 1795–1869 and 1870–1933 indicate that deflationary price-level shocks worsened financial distress (or, equivalently, that positive price-level shocks lessened financial distress). For 1795–1869, the coefficients on aggregate price shocks for the two specifications are statistically significant at 90% or better (p value of 0.10 or less). For 1870–1933, the coefficient on price shocks is significant at better than 95% in both specifications. We also estimate a high degree of persistence in financial conditions, as reflected in a large positive and statistically significant coefficient on the lagged index. Finally, for 1795–1933, we estimate positive coefficients for the growth rates of GDP, potential GDP, labor productivity, and the monetary base, though for the most part they are not statistically significant at conventional levels. Comparison of the two specifications reported reveals that controlling for the growth of potential output and productivity has little impact on the estimated relationship between aggregate price shocks and financial conditions, raising the price shock coefficient estimate for 1870–1933 only slightly.

The impact of aggregate price shocks on financial conditions can be measured by the average size shock required to move financial conditions from one state to another. In standard probit estimation, the mean of the latent variable is not recovered. Because the Gibbs sampler used here provides inferred values (draws) of the latent variable, y^*, however, we can calculate $\beta\sigma_x/\sigma_{y^*}$ and $\bar{y}^*/\sigma_{y^*}$. The former indicates the immediate change in y^* caused by a one-standard-deviation size price shock (impact effect), and the latter indicates the average distance that y^* lies from the boundary between the moderate distress and normal states (average distance). Here we have normalized distances between categories of financial conditions by defining $y^*=0$ at the boundary between the normal and moderate distress states.

For 1795–1869, the impact effect is 0.188 and the average distance is 0.369. Thus, on average, a two-standard-deviation negative price shock was necessary to cause financial conditions to deteriorate immediately from the average level (which was in the normal state) to moderate distress, all else equal. The dynamic probit also captures the long-run effects of changes in

TABLE 9.2　Probit Model Coefficient Estimates

Independent Variable	Specification 1	Specification 2
P^{ue}, 1795–1869	1.73	1.59
(p value for significance)	(0.08)	(0.10)
P^{ue}, 1870–1933	5.97	6.14
(p value)	(0.00)	(0.00)
π^{ue}, 1934–1979	0.02	0.00
(p value)	(0.20)	(0.22)
π^{ue}, 1980–1997	0.22	0.24
(p value)	(0.01)	(0.01)
Δ ln GDP, 1795–1874	0.01	0.01
(p value)	(0.20)	(0.17)
Δ ln GDP, 1875–1933	0.02	0.02
(p value)	(0.10)	(0.17)
Δ ln GDP, 1934–1997	0.01	0.03
(p value)	(0.17)	(0.12)
Δ ln Base, 1795–1833	0.00	0.00
(p value)	(0.19)	(0.18)
Δ ln Base, 1834–1933	0.02	0.01
(p value)	(0.18)	(0.16)
Δ ln Base, 1934–1997	0.01	0.01
(p value)	(0.13)	(0.17)
Δ ln Potential GDP, 1875–1933		0.01
(p value)		(0.22)
Δ ln Potential GDP, 1934–1997		0.04
(p value)		(0.16)
Δ ln Labor Prod., 1875–1933		0.01
(p value)		(0.21)
Δ ln Labor Prod., 1934–1997		−0.04
(p value)		(0.13)
Lagged index	0.52	0.50
(p value)	(0.00)	(0.00)
Dependent variable: index of financial conditions		
Cut-off Constants for Category Boundaries		
Severe/moderate distress (c_1)	−0.66	−0.70
Moderate distress/Normal	Fixed at 0	Fixed at 0

TABLE 9.2   (*continued*)

Independent Variable	Specification 1	Specification 2
Normal/expansion (c_2)	0.76	0.77
Expansion/euphoria (c_3)	1.22	1.22
Transition Probabilities for Markov Switching		
Transition probability p_1	0.76	0.77
Transition probability q_1	0.30	0.30
Transition probability p_2	0.66	0.66
Transition probability q_2	0.36	0.36
Intercept $S2 = 0$	0.06	0.01
Intercept $S1 = 1$	0.13	0.10

NOTES: The variances are fixed at 0.10 when $S1 = 0$ and 0.50 when $S1 = 1$.
Variable definitions:
P^{ue} = price-level shock.
π^{ue} = inflation rate shock.
Δ In GDP = log change in GDP.
Δ In Base = log change in the monetary base.
Δ In Potential GDP = log change in potential GDP.
Δ In Labor Prod. = log change in labor productivity.
Lagged index = autoregressive coefficient.

the explanatory variables. With a coefficient of approximately 0.50 on the lagged dependent variable, the long-run impact of an aggregate price shock is roughly double the initial impact. Hence, a one-standard-deviation aggregate price shock is sufficient to move financial conditions to the moderate distress state in the long run.

We estimate that aggregate price shocks had a larger impact on financial conditions during 1870–1933. For that period, the impact effect is 0.449 and the average distance 0.625. Thus, on average, a negative price shock of approximately 1.4 standard deviations was required to produce immediate deterioration in financial conditions from average to moderate distress. A 0.7 standard deviation shock would produce a similar effect in the long run.

One also can calculate the contribution of aggregate price shocks (or any independent variable) to the probability that financial conditions are in a particular state. The marginal impact of an independent variable on the probability of being in a particular state is often evaluated at the mean of the data. Here it is meaningful to calculate the marginal effect of aggregate price shocks at the boundary between the moderate distress and normal states, that is, where $y^* = 0$. At this point the probability that a random disturbance will tip financial conditions into a distress state is 0.50. Moreover, evaluating the marginal effect at $y^* = 0$ in each subperiod, rather than at subperiod-specific mean values of y^*, facilitates comparison of the marginal effects across subperiods.

In our model, the probability of not being in one of the two states of financial distress is $1 - \Phi(-X_t'\beta/\sigma_t)$, where Φ is the normal cumulative density function and φ is its derivative. Hence, the marginal effect of a change in X at $y^* = 0$ is

$$[\partial\text{Pr(no distress)}/\partial x_i]\sigma_{xi} = \varphi(y^* = 0)\beta\sigma_{xi}. \tag{5}$$

The partial derivative is multiplied by the standard deviation of x_i to reflect the size of the shocks. Assuming the normal density for φ, the marginal impact effect is 0.04 for 1795–1869 and 0.10 for 1870–1933, indicating that a one-standard-deviation negative price shock increases the probability of distress from 50% to 54% during 1795–1869 and to 60% during 1870–1933.[12]

Whereas we find a statistically close relationship between aggregate price shocks and financial conditions before 1933, our coefficient estimates for the impact of inflation rate shocks during 1934–79 are small and not statistically significant. We test, however, whether aggregate price shocks had a stronger impact during the 1980s and 1990s when Depression-era financial regulations were being dismantled. Indeed, we estimate a strong, statistically significant impact of inflation rate shocks for 1980–97. For this period, we estimate that the marginal effect of inflation shocks on the probability of being in a particular state is 0.17. Hence, a one-standard-deviation negative shock to inflation would increase the probability of financial conditions being in a state of distress from 50% to 67%. At the mean level of financial conditions for the period, located in the region of moderate distress, we calculate that a positive inflation shock of size 0.84 standard deviations would lift financial conditions into the normal state immediately. A shock of size 0.42 standard deviations would have a similar impact in the long run. In sum, we find that aggregate price shocks were an important contributor to financial instability historically, except during 1934–79, but that their impact on financial conditions varied somewhat over time in magnitude.

Boundary and Markov Switching Parameter Estimates

The cut-off coefficients reported in the second panel of Table 9.2 provide information on the extent to which the category boundaries around the normal financial conditions category are symmetrical. We look for symmetry by comparing the distance between the upper bound of the normal category and the lower bound of the financial euphoria category with the distance between the lower bound of the normal category and the upper bound of the severe distress category. That is, we ask whether shocks of a given magnitude will move financial conditions from normal to either extreme, or whether a larger shock is needed in one direction. The comparison is between $0 - c_1$ and $c_3 - c_2$.

For the full specification, we estimate that the moderate distress category is wider than the moderate expansion category: c_1 is greater in absolute value (0.7) than $c_3 - c_2$ (0.45). Hence, the magnitude of the shock required to move financial conditions from the bottom boundary of the normal range to the upper boundary of the severe distress range is greater than the magnitude of the shock needed to move financial conditions from the upper boundary of normal to the lower boundary of financial euphoria. This asymmetry could occur simply because the moderate distress region contains more observations than the moderate expansion region.

The bottom panel of Table 9.2 reports the transition probabilities for Markov switching. These probabilities sum to little more than one $(p+q)$ in both specifications, indicating that the states are not strongly serially correlated. Episodes of high volatility are not clustered in a way that make it valuable to estimate two transition probabilities instead of setting $q = (1 - p)$. In this way the latent variable for financial conditions does not act like most other financial data, where volatility clustering is prevalent.

Estimation for Individual Time Series

For additional insight into the impact of aggregate price shocks on financial conditions historically, we estimated separate regressions for each of the series used to construct the index for 1870–1997. Doing so provides an indication of whether the individual series underlying the quantitative index are themselves associated with aggregate price shocks.

Table 9.3 reports regression estimates for 1875–1933 (1932 in the case of the bank failure rate).[13] We find support for the hypothesis that price-level disturbances affect financial conditions in the behavior of the business failure rate, real interest rate, and interest rate quality spread. Unanticipated deflation, for example, increased the rate of business failures and drove up the real interest rate and quality spread.[14] The coefficient on price-level shocks is, however, not significant for the bank failure rate, which seems to have been driven more by fluctuations in the growth of real output.[15]

Table 9.4 reports similar regressions for 1934–97. Again we estimate a statistically significant impact of aggregate price shocks on the business failure rate and real interest rate. As before 1933, a negative aggregate price shock increased the business failure rate and real interest rate. In contrast with 1875–1933, we estimate a positive impact of aggregate price shocks on the interest rate quality spread during 1934–97. Similar to the earlier period, however, we find that banking conditions were affected more by the growth of real output than by aggregate price disturbances.

V. Conclusion

Our investigation finds that unanticipated movements in the price level and inflation rate have contributed historically to financial instability in the United States. Negative aggregate price shocks have tended to worsen financial distress, whereas positive price shocks have tended to encourage financial expansion.

Our evidence for the impact of price-level shocks is strongest for the period 1870–1933, during most of which the United States was anchored to the gold standard. Because of this anchor, the price level was expected to change little over the long run, with price-level declines expected to follow increases of similar magnitude. Indeed, except during World War I, the price level changed little between 1870 and 1929 in comparison with either the Antebellum or post–World War II periods. Serious financial distress accompanied severe deflation during the Great Depression of 1930–33,

TABLE 9.3   Regression Estimates for Alternative Measures of Financial Conditions, 1875–1933

Dependent Variable	Business Failure Rate	Bank Failure Rate	Real Interest Rate	Interest Rate Quality Spread
Intercept	38.08	0.01	4.58	0.09
(p value)	(0.01)	(0.43)	(0.00)[a]	(0.74)
P^{ue}	−124.35	0.01	−87.12	−2.62
(p value)	(0.04)	(0.88)	(0.00)[a]	(0.11)
Δ ln GDP	−159.89	−0.13	−1.46	−3.03
(p value)	(0.00)	(0.02)	(0.71)[a]	(0.04)
Δ ln Base	−96.75	0.02	−10.65	2.72
(p value)	(0.02)	(0.61)	(0.01)[a]	(0.00)
Δ ln Potential GDP	397.71	−0.04	−17.67	5.54
(p value)	(0.18)	(0.88)	(0.45)[a]	(0.45)
Δ ln Labor Prod.	77.72	0.14	−0.97	2.72
(p value)	(0.41)	(0.11)	(0.92)[a]	(0.25)
Lag Dep. Var.	0.66	0.57	0.33	0.82
(p value)	(0.00)	(0.00)	(0.00)[a]	(0.00)
Lag2 Dep. Var.	−0.09	0.28	−0.02	−0.31
(p value)	(0.41)	(0.24)	(0.59)[a]	(0.05)
1919 dummy				1.18
(p value)				(0.00)
Adjusted R^2	0.69	0.61	0.96	0.94
Q-statistic	1.50	0.15	5.72	0.64

NOTES: Variable definitions:

P^{ue} = price-level shock.

Δ ln GDP = log change in GDP.

Δ ln Base = log change in the monetary base.

Δ ln Potential GDP = log change in potential GDP.

Δ ln Labor Prod. = log change in labor productivity.

Lag Dep. Var. = lagged dependent variable.

Lag2 Dep. Var. = second lag of dependent variable.

1919 dummy = dummy set equal to 1 in 1919 and subsequent years.

[a] p value based on robust standard errors (Newey-West correction for autocorrelation).

TABLE 9.4 Regression Estimates for Alternative Measures of Financial Conditions, 1934–1997

Dependent Variable	Business Failure Rate	Bank Loan Charge-Off Rate	Real Interest Rate	Interest Rate Quality Spread
Intercept	22.65	0.07	1.02	0.47
(p value)	(0.01)	(0.16)[a]	(0.39)[a]	(0.11)
π^{ue}	−1.24	0.00	−0.69	0.04
(p value)	(0.06)	(0.75)[a]	(0.00)[a]	(0.10)
Δ In GDP	−88.45	−0.60	4.48	−7.10
(p value)	(0.07)	(0.12)[a]	(0.68)[a]	(0.00)
Δ In Base	13.41	0.02	2.13	0.66
(p value)	(0.63)	(0.93)[a]	(0.71)[a]	(0.63)
Δ In Potential GDP	−346.73	−1.25	−26.70	−1.01
(p value)	(0.09)	(0.29)[a]	(0.49)[a]	(0.89)
Δ In Labor Prod.	62.76	0.60	7.60	5.91
(p value)	(0.30)	(0.21)[a]	(0.49)[a]	(0.02)
Lag Dep. Var.	1.10	1.31	0.77	0.93
(p value)	(0.00)	(0.00)[a]	(0.00)[a]	(0.00)
Lag2 Dep. Var.	−0.27	−0.39	−0.22	−0.14
(p value)	(0.01)	(0.00)[a]	(0.00)[a]	(0.20)
Adjusted R^2	0.89	0.92	0.76	0.78
Q-statistic	0.97	5.33	8.77	0.24

Notes: Variable definitions:
π^{ue} = inflation rate shock.
Δ In GDP = log change in GDP.
Δ In Base = log change in the monetary base.
Δ In Potential GDP = log change in potential GDP.
Δ In Labor Prod. = log change in labor productivity.
Lag Dep. Var. = lagged dependent variable.
Lag2 Dep. Var. = second lag of dependent variable.
[a] p value based on robust standard errors (Newey-West correction for autocorrelation).

however, paving the way for fundamental reforms to protect the financial system from macroeconomic shocks while partially insulating the U.S. money stock from gold shocks.

For 1934–97, we find that inflation shocks had a statistically significant impact on financial conditions, as reflected in business failures. Our results suggest, however, that aggregate price shocks did not have as strong an impact on financial conditions after 1933 as price-level shocks had in the years before. The New Deal introduced several institutional changes, including construction of a safety net for the financial sector, especially for the banking system, and reorganization of the Federal Reserve into an effective lender of last resort that appear to have insulated the financial system somewhat from macroeconomic shocks. Under the new regime, financial response to macroeconomic shocks, including inflation shocks, appears to have been slower and perhaps less severe than it had been to similar shocks before 1934.

Environmental changes in the late 1970s and 1980s made the financial system more vulnerable to macroeconomic shocks, even though key features of the safety net, such as deposit insurance and "too big to fail" closure policies, remained in place and partly insulated and certainly delayed the impact of disinflation on financial intermediaries. Considerable financial instability accompanied high inflation during the 1970s and, especially, sharp disinflation during the 1980s. Our dynamic probit model estimates indicate that financial conditions were more affected by inflation shocks during the 1980s and 1990s than they had been during 1934–79. These results suggest the need for further research to investigate the specific channels by which macroeconomic shocks and environmental changes interacted to increase financial stresses. Despite the influence of regulation and other institutional factors at various times, however, our results indicate that a monetary regime that produces aggregate price stability will, as a by-product, tend to promote stability of the financial system.

Appendix

DATA SOURCES AND DEFINITIONS

Bank Failure Rate

Failed banks divided by number of operating banks. Failed banks, 1865–91, from Federal Deposit Insurance Corporation (1934, 92); 1892–1933, from Federal Reserve Board (1943, 283); 1934–97, from FDIC Website: https://www.fdic.org. Number of operating banks, 1865–96, from White (1983, table 1.1); 1896–1997, from Federal Reserve Board (1943, various years).

Bank Loan Charge-off Rate

Net loan charge-offs at commercial banks divided by total commercial bank assets, 1934–97, from FDIC Website: https://www.fdic.org.

Business Cycle Reference Dates

1790–1854, from Economic Cycle Research Institute Website, https://www.businesscycle.com; 1854–1997, from National Bureau of Economic Research Website, https://www.nber.org.

Business Failure Rate

1870–1970, from United States Bureau of the Census (1976, Series V-23); 1971–97, from *Economic Report of the President* (1999, table B-96).

Gross Domestic Product

1789–1874, from Berry (1988); 1875–1959, from Gordon (2000, table A-1); 1959–97, from U.S. Department of Commerce.

Labor Productivity

1875–1997, from Gordon (2000, table A-1).

Monetary Base

1790–1866, from Friedman and Schwartz (1970); 1867–1935, from Friedman and Schwartz (1963, table B-3); 1936–97, from Federal Reserve Bank of St. Louis (adjusted monetary base).

Potential GDP

1875–1997, from Gordon (2000, table A-1).

Price Level

1789–1947, from David and Solar (1977); 1948–97, from Bureau of Labor Statistics (Consumer Price Index).

Real Interest Rate

Commercial paper rate minus current year's inflation rate. Commercial paper rate, 1831–1900, from Homer and Sylla (1996, table 44); 1901–97, from Federal Reserve Board (various).

Quality Spread

1857–1918, spread between low- and high-quality railroad bond yields from Macaulay (1938, aa34–aa90) (three lowest and three highest bonds, 1857–66; five lowest and five highest bonds, 1867–81; eight lowest and eight highest, 1882–87; ten lowest and ten highest, 1888–1918); 1919–97, spread between average yield on Moody's Baa-rated corporate bonds and U.S. long-term treasury composite bond, from Federal Reserve Board (various).

Construction of Index of Financial Conditions for 1870–1997

The index is derived from four series for each of two subperiods. For 1870–1933, these series are the bank failure rate (except for 1933), the business failure rate, the real interest rate, and the quality spread. For 1934–97, the series are the bank loan charge-off rate, the business failure rate, the real interest rate, and the quality spread.

For each variable in each subperiod, we compute the distances between each observation and the subperiod median for that variable. We measure distances from the median, rather than mean, because the distributions of the variables tend to be skewed. Because of skewness, we also evaluate the distances for observations that are below the median separately from those above the median. Distances for those observations that are below the median are divided by the standard deviation of a series consisting of all observations below the median and an equal number of generated observations of equal distances above the median. Similarly, distances for observations that are above the median are divided by the standard deviation of a series consisting of all observations above the median and an equal number of generated observations of equal distance below the median. The generated observations are then discarded, leaving a series of observations for each variable consisting of standardized distances from the median.

For each year, we compute a simple unweighted average (Z_t) of these standardized distances across the four variables. Next, we compute an overall subperiod mean and standard deviation of these average distances. Following the approach of Kaminsky and Reinhart (1999), we assign Z_t larger than 1.5 standard deviations above the subperiod mean to the severe distress category; Z_t larger than 0.75 standard deviations above the subperiod mean to the moderate distress category; Z_t falling between ±0.75 standard deviations of the mean to the normal category; Z_t between -0.75 and -1.5 standard deviations of the mean to the moderate expansion category; and Z_t below -1.5 standard deviations of the mean to the euphoria category.

Expected/Unexpected Aggregate Price Decomposition

We use a trend/cycle decomposition of inflation as the basis for our calculation of the inflation/price level explanatory variables. The following unobserved-components model is estimated via the Kalman filter: $y_t = y_{1t} + y_{2t}$, where $y_{1t} = \mu + y_{1,t-1} + \eta_t$ represents the trend; $y_{2t} = \phi_1 y_{2,t-1} + \phi y_{2,t-2} + \varepsilon_t$ represents the cyclical component; and $\sigma_\eta^2, \sigma_\varepsilon^2$, and $\sigma_{\eta,\varepsilon}$ are variance parameters. The expected price level (inflation rate) is then $y_{1,t-1} + \mu + \phi_1 y_{2,t-1} + \phi y_{2,t-2}$.

Notes

1. In addition to causing mistakes that increase default rates, uncertainty about future inflation can add to the cost of finance because lenders may require an inflation risk premium on interest rates that would not exist in the absence of inflation uncertainty.

2. Although Schwartz emphasizes how inflation increases the difficulty of projecting real returns for both borrowers and lenders, variability in the price level, according to Schwartz (1988, 49), can also worsen problems associated with asymmetric information between borrowers and lenders because "fraud and mismanagement are more likely to gain ground in conditions of price variability, and institutions of unimpeachable standards of risk management may make judgments that later turn out to be mistaken, if not disastrous."

3. The regime changed considerably over time. The Mint Act of 1792 put the United States on a bimetallic (gold and silver) standard, which prevailed until the Civil War, when convertibility was suspended. When convertibility was restored in 1879, the dollar was made officially convertible only into gold. Convertibility was suspended in 1933, and under the Gold Reserve Act of 1934 convertibility was restored only for international payments. The dollar remained convertible into gold for official international transactions under the postwar Bretton Woods System until 1971, when the last ties to gold were broken.

4. Because of the bank holiday, data on bank failures for 1933 are not comparable with those for other years. For 1933, therefore, our quantitative index is based only on the business failure rate, the real interest rate, and the quality spread.

5. The observed real rate is simply the nominal interest rate minus the current inflation rate, so a negative correlation between the measured real rate and inflation is not surprising. The nominal interest rate does not fully adjust to changes in the inflation rate simply because some changes are unanticipated or (especially before 1933) because of mean reversion in the inflation rate. Hence, we would be quite surprised not to find a highly negative coefficient on price or inflation shocks in a regression of the real interest rate.

6. As Mishkin (1991) notes, asymmetric information between borrowers and lenders implies that a decline in borrower net worth will increase adverse selection and agency problems inherent in credit markets.

7. We experimented with using NBER business cycle dates instead of GDP and found no substantive differences in our results for the effects of aggregate price shocks on financial conditions.

8. The p values are posterior means of the 5000 values calculated at each iteration of the Gibbs sampler: one p value per iteration.

9. The following years were treated as war (and postwar) years, and thus were assigned dummy variables: 1813–15, 1861–67, 1917–21, and 1942–49. The inclusion of dummy variables for war years is not crucial for our results with respect to the impact of aggregate price shocks on financial conditions. See Bordo et al. (2000) for probit model estimates that exclude war year dummies.

10. Bordo et al. (2000) extend the narrative-based index forward to 1997 and find that the estimated impact of aggregate price shocks on financial conditions is not qualitatively different using the narrative-based index to measure financial conditions from the results presented here.

11. Consistent annual data on potential GDP and labor productivity are not available before 1875.

12. One caveat regarding these results is that with Markov switching the actual density is not normal but a mixture of normals. The distortion from using the normal

density is not large, however. For example, we can bound the marginal effect of 0.10 during 1870–1933 to the interval (0.096, 0.1175). Details are available from the authors.

13. We begin with 1875, rather than 1870, because of the absence of data on potential GDP and labor productivity before 1875. In addition, the bank failure rate regression ends at 1932 because the bank holiday and subsequent government licensing procedures for reopening banks make the computation of a bank failure rate for 1933 on a basis that is consistent with other years impossible.

14. The quality spread regressions also include a dummy variable to account for a change in the series' measure in 1919. See the appendix for details.

15. Our results contrast with those of Weber (1986) who, using Granger causality analysis, finds a statistically significant impact of price shocks on the bank failure rate in this period.

References

Barsky, Robert B. "The Fisher Hypothesis and the Forecastability and Persistence of Inflation." *Journal of Monetary Economics*, 19(1), 1987, 3–24.

Berry, Thomas S. "Production and Population since 1789: Revised GNP Series in Constant Dollars." *Bostwick Paper*, no. 6, 1988.

Bordo, Michael D., Michael J. Dueker, and David C. Wheelock. "Aggregate Price Shocks and Financial Instability: An Historical Analysis." NBER Working Paper 7652, April 2000.

Bordo, Michael D., and Anna J. Schwartz. "Monetary Policy Regimes and Economic Performance: The Historical Record." *Handbook of Macroeconomics*. Amsterdam: North-Holland, 1999.

Calomiris, Charles W., and David C. Wheelock. "Was the Great Depression a Watershed for American Monetary Policy?" in *The Defining Moment: The Great Depression and the American Economy in the Twentieth Century*, edited by M. D. Bordo, C. Goldin, and E. White. Chicago: University of Chicago Press, 1998, 23–66.

David, Paul A., and Peter Solar. "A Bicentenary Contribution to the History of the Cost of Living in America." *Research in Economic History*, 2, 1977, 1–80.

Economic Report of the President. Washington, DC, 1999.

Eichengreen, Barry, Andrew Rose, and Charles Wyplosz. "Contagious Currency Crises: First Tests." *Scandinavian Journal of Economics*, 98(4), 1996, 463–84.

Eichengreen, Barry, Mark W. Watson, and Richard S. Grossman. "Bank Rate Policy under the Interwar Gold Standard: A Dynamic Probit Model." *Economic Journal*, 95(379), 1985, 725–45.

Federal Deposit Insurance Corporation. *Annual Report.* Washington, DC, 1934.

Federal Reserve Board. *Annual Statistical Digest.* Washington, DC, various issues.

———. *Banking and Monetary Statistics, 1914–1941.* Washington, DC, 1943.

Fisher, Irving. *Booms and Depressions: Some First Principles.* New York: Adelphi, 1932.

———. "The Debt-Deflation Theory of Great Depressions." *Econometrica,* 1, 1933, 337–57.

Friedman, Milton, and Anna J. Schwartz. *A Monetary History of the United States, 1867–1960.* Princeton: Princeton University Press, 1963.

———. *Monetary Statistics of the United States: Estimates, Sources, and Methods.* New York: Columbia University Press, 1970.

Gordon, Robert J. *Macroeconomics.* Reading, MA: Addison-Wesley, 2000.

Gray, Jo Anna, and David E. Spencer. "Price Prediction Errors and Real Activity: A Reassessment." *Economic Inquiry,* 28(4), 1990, 658–81.

Homer, Sidney, and Richard E. Sylla. *A History of Interest Rates.* New Brunswick: Rutgers University Press, 1996.

Kaminsky, Graciela L., and Carmen M. Reinhart. "The Twin Crises: The Causes of Banking and Balance of Payments Problems." *American Economic Review,* 89(3), 1999, 473–500.

Lucas, Robert E., Jr. "Expectations and the Neutrality of Money." *Journal of Economic Theory,* 4(2), 1972, 103–24.

———. "Some International Evidence on Output-Inflation Tradeoffs." *American Economic Review,* 63(3), 1973, 326–34.

Macaulay, Frederick R. *Some Theoretical Problems Suggested by the Movement of Interest Rates, Bond Yields and Stock Prices in the United States since 1856.* New York: National Bureau of Economic Research, 1938.

Mishkin, Frederick S. "Asymmetric Information and Financial Crises: A Historical Perspective," in *Financial Markets and Financial Crises,* edited by R. G. Hubbard. Chicago: University of Chicago Press, 1991, 69–108.

Schwartz, A. J. "Financial Stability and the Federal Safety Net," in *Restructuring Banking and Financial Services in America,* edited by W. S. Haraf and R. M. Kushneider. Washington, DC: American Enterprise Institute, 1988, 34–62.

———. "Why Financial Stability Depends on Price Stability." *Economic Affairs,* 15(4), 1995, 21–25.

———. "Comment on 'Debt-Deflation and Financial Instability: Two Historical Explorations' by Barry Eichengreen and Richard S. Grossman," in *Asset Prices and the Real Economy,* edited by F. Capie and G. E. Wood. New York: St. Martin's Press, 1997, 100–105.

Smith, Walter B., and Arthur H. Cole. *Fluctuations in American Business, 1790–1860.* Cambridge: Harvard University Press, 1935.

Thorp, Willard L. *Business Annals.* New York: National Bureau of Economic Research, 1926.

United States Bureau of the Census. *Historical Statistics of the United States, Colonial Times to 1970, Bicentennial Edition.* Washington, DC: Department of Commerce, 1976.

Weber, Ernst J. "The Causes of Bank Failures: Deflationary Spells." *Economics Letters,* 20(4), 1986, 359–62.

White, Eugene N. *The Regulation and Reform of the American Banking System, 1900–1929.* Princeton: Princeton University Press, 1983.

CHAPTER 10

Does Expansionary Monetary Policy Cause Asset Price Booms?

Some Historical and Empirical Evidence

MICHAEL D. BORDO AND JOHN LANDON-LANE

D OES EXPANSIONARY MONETARY POLICY lead to asset price booms? There is some extensive theoretical, empirical and policy literature on this topic. The traditional view sees expansionary monetary policy as raising asset prices as part of the transmission mechanism of monetary policy. It works through the adjustment of the community's portfolio as agents replace cash with government securities and then by corporate instruments, immediately followed by stocks, real estate, paintings of the Old Masters and natural resources—eventually leading to global inflation. Another view attributed to the Austrian economists in the 1920s, and more recently the BIS, sees an environment of low inflation and accommodative monetary policy as creating an environment conducive to asset booms and consequent busts.[1]

Asset booms (especially those leading to bubbles) are often followed by busts, which can have serious economic effects. There is a long historical incidence of infamous boom busts ranging from the South Sea bubble in

Originally published in "Does Expansionary Monetary Policy Cause Asset Price Booms: Some Historical and Empirical Evidence," in *Macroeconomic and Financial Stability: Challenges for Monetary Policy*, ed. Sofía Bauducco, Lawrence Christiano, and Claudio Raddatz (Central Bank of Chile: Santiago, Chile). © 2014. Central Bank of Chile.

the early eighteenth century, to many famous stock market crashes in the nineteenth century, to the 1929 Wall Street Crash, to the U.K. housing boom bust of 1973, to the Nordic crises of the 1980s, to the Japanese housing and equity bubble and crash of 1990, and to the more recent dot-com and subprime mortgage boom busts. This history keeps repeating itself.

The policy implications of asset booms are significant, especially since asset busts have often led to banking crises and serious, prolonged recessions. To the extent monetary policy is a contributing factor, the question arises whether or not the monetary authorities should use their policy tools to defuse booms before they turn into busts. A vociferous debate raged in the early 2000s until the aftermath of the recent financial crisis over the subject of preemptive policy action. Central banks were unwilling to divert much attention away from their traditional concern over price and overall macro stability. However the tide has recently turned and the new emphasis on macro prudential monetary policy suggests that asset price booms have been elevated to the top level of interest.

Finally, the issue still remains that asset price booms, in addition to sometimes ending with damaging busts, can be the precursors to a future run-up in inflation. This leads to the question of when central banks should tighten their policies to prevent inflation from becoming embedded in expectations.

In this chapter we develop a method to demarcate asset price booms. We focus on house price booms, stock market booms and commodity booms for 18 OECD countries from 1920 to the present. We then ascertain whether or not our set of boom events can be related to different measures of expansionary monetary policy, deviations from Taylor rules, and monetary aggregate growth. Finally, we use panel regression techniques to control for other determinants of asset booms, including inflation, credit growth, output growth, financial liberalization, and the current account deficit.

Section 1 discusses the debate over the link between monetary policy and asset price booms. Section 2 contains historical narratives on some of the salient asset price booms throughout history. We discuss some booms in nineteenth-century Great Britain, the Wall Street stock market boom and the U.S. housing boom of the 1920s, the commodity price boom of the 1970s, the U.K. housing booms in the 1970s and 1980s, the Nordic asset booms in the 1980s, the Japanese boom of the late 1980s, the dot-com boom of the 1990s, and the recent subprime mortgage boom bust. Section 3 discusses our methodology of identifying asset price booms and presents a chronology from 1920 to the present booms so identified. Controlling for other factors, section 4 uses econometrics to isolate the links between expansionary monetary policy and asset price booms. Section 5 concludes with the implications of our findings for monetary policy.

1. The Issues

Debate swirls over the causes of the subprime Mortgage Crisis of 2007–2008 and the Great Recession of 2007–2009, and the subsequent slow recovery. Two views predominate. The first is that it was caused by global imbalances, an excess of global savings in Asia, which financed a consumption boom, and persistent budget deficits and current account deficits in the U.S and other advanced countries. The second is that it reflected domestic imbalances in the U.S., leading to an unprecedented nationwide housing boom, which burst in 2006 precipitating the crisis. This chapter focuses on the second view.[2]

A key element of the domestic U.S. story is that the Federal Reserve kept monetary policy too loose from the 2002–2006 period, which fueled a housing boom that had its origins in a long tradition of policies to encourage home ownership in succeeding administrations, financial innovation, lax regulatory supervision and oversight, and corporate malfeasance. John Taylor (2007, 2009) has led to the indictment of the Fed for fueling the housing boom in the early 2000s. Based on the Taylor rule (1993) showing that the Federal Funds rate was as low as 3 percentage points below what a simple Taylor rule would generate for the 2002–2005 period, Taylor then simulated the path of housing starts if the Fed had followed the Taylor rule over the 2000–2006 period. His calculations suggest that most of the run-up in housing starts from the 2002–2005 period would not have occurred.

An earlier OECD study by Ahrend et al. (2008) found a close relationship between negative deviations of the Taylor rule, and several measures of housing market buoyancy (mortgage lending, housing investment, construction investment and real house prices) for a number of OECD countries in the early 2000s. The principal examples are the U.S. (2000–2006), Canada (2001–2007), Denmark (2001–2004) and Australia (2000–2003) periods. For the euro area as a whole, they find that ECB policy rates are not far below the Taylor rule, but for a number of individual members (Portugal, Spain, Greece, Netherlands, Italy, Ireland and Finland), they are well below it. This evidence, as well as evidence in several other papers (Hott and Jokipii, 2012; Gerlach and Assenmacher-Wesche, 2008a), suggests that expansionary monetary policy had a key role to play in fostering recent housing booms, some of which led to devastating busts. Other literature finds evidence linking expansionary monetary policy to equity booms and commodity price booms (Gerlach and Assenmacher-Weshe, 2008b; Pagano, Lombardi, Anzuini, 2010).

Expansionary monetary policy can also generate booms in commodity prices, which can presage a run-up in global inflation. The Great Inflation of the 1970s was first manifested in commodity prices before feeding into overall inflation. This reflected the basic distinction, first pointed out by Okun (1975), between goods that are traded in auction markets and those whose prices react quickly to both nominal and real shocks, and goods traded in customer markets (manufactured goods and services) whose prices are relatively sticky. In the long run, the paths of prices for both types of goods are determined by the long-run growth of the money supply (reflecting monetary neutrality). What happens in episodes of expansionary monetary policy, characterized by falling real interest rates, is that real commodity prices rise much more quickly than the prices of other goods, and according to Frankel (2008), they overshoot the long-run equilibrium price level. At the same time the prices of other goods react slowly to the monetary pressure. Frankel (2008) finds that commodity prices are a good predictor of future inflation. Browne and Cronin (2007) use time series techniques for the U.S. (1959–2005) period to show that the growth of M2 and headline inflation are cointegrated, but that the adjustment mechanism to the long-run equilibrium involves considerable overshooting by commodity prices. Moreover the deviation of commodity prices from their long-run equilibrium values explains the subsequent path of the CPI.

There is some extensive, earlier literature on the relationship between monetary policy and asset prices. Asset prices are viewed as a key link in the transmission mechanism of monetary policy. The traditional view argues that added liquidity causes asset prices to rise as a link in the transmission mechanism of monetary policy actions to the economy as a whole. Another view, the Austrian/BIS's, argues that asset price booms are more likely to arise in environments of low and stable inflation and, thus, asset price booms can arise because monetary policy is geared to credibly stabilizing prices.

The traditional view has a long history. Early Keynesian models like Metzler (1951) showed central bank operations affecting the stock market directly. Friedman and Schwartz (1963a) and later Tobin (1969) and Brunner and Meltzer (1973) spelled out the transmission mechanism following an expansionary Fed open market purchase. It would first affect the prices (rate of return) on short-term government securities, then via a portfolio balance substitution mechanism, the price (rate of return) of long-term government securities, then corporate securities, equities, real estate, paintings of the Old Masters and commodities, including gold, would be bid up (their returns lowered). Thus substitution from more to less liquid assets would occur as returns on the former decline, relative to the latter. Thus the impact of expansionary monetary policy will impact securities, assets, commodities, and finally the overall price level. This view sees asset prices as possible harbingers of future inflation.

The Austrian BIS view which goes back to Hayek, von Mises, Robbins[3] and others in the 1920s posits that an asset price boom, whatever its fundamental cause, can degenerate into a bubble if accommodative monetary policy allows bank credit to rise to fuel the boom. This view argues that unless policy makers act to defuse the boom, a crash will inevitably follow that, in turn, may cause a serious recession. The Austrians equated rising asset prices with a rise in the overall price level. Although the level of U.S. consumer prices was virtually unchanged between 1923 and 1929, the Austrians viewed the period as one of rapid inflation, fueled by loose Federal Reserve policy and excessive growth of bank credit (Rothbard 1983).

The Austrian view has carried forward into the modern discussion of asset price booms. It has been incorporated into the BIS view of Borio and

Lowe (2002), Borio and White (2004) and others. They focus on the problem of "financial imbalances," defined as rapid growth of credit in conjunction with rapid increases in asset prices and, possibly, investment. Borio and Lowe (2002) argue that a build-up of such imbalances can increase the risk of a financial crisis and macroeconomic instability. They construct an index of imbalances, based on a credit gap (deviations of credit growth from trend), an equity gap, and an output gap, to identify incipient asset price declines that can lead to significant real output losses and advocate its use as a guide for proactive action. In this vein, Borio (2012) discusses a financial cycle based on property prices and credit growth that has much greater amplitude than the business cycle, and when its peak coincides with a business cycle peak, a housing bust, banking crisis and deep protracted recession can follow, as occurred in 2007.

Borio and Lowe argue that low inflation can promote financial imbalances regardless of the cause of an asset price boom. For example, by generating optimism about the macroeconomic environment, low inflation might cause asset prices to rise more in response to an increase in productivity than they would otherwise. Similarly, an increase in demand is more likely to cause asset prices to rise if the central bank is credibly committed to price stability. A commitment to price stability that is viewed as credible, Borio and Lowe (2002) argue will make product prices less sensitive, and output and profits more sensitive to an increase in demand in the short-run. At the same time, the absence of inflation may cause policy makers to delay tightening as demand pressures build up.[4] Thus, they contend (pp. 30–31) "these endogenous responses to credible monetary policy (can) increase the probability that the latent inflation pressures manifest themselves in the development of imbalances in the financial system, rather than immediate upward pressure in higher goods and service price inflation."[5]

Christiano et al. (2010) present historical evidence showing that stock price booms in the U.S. and Japan often occurred in periods of low inflation. Productivity shocks, which raise the natural rate of interest, are accommodated by expansion in bank credit, which pushes up stock prices. According to their analysis based on a DSGE model, following a Taylor type rule, in the face of low inflation, it will lead to lower interest rates that will further fuel the asset boom.

In section 5 below we present some evidence consistent with the loose monetary policy explanation for asset price booms and the Austrian BIS view that regards monetary policy, dedicated to low inflation and bank credit expansion, as creating an environment conducive to an asset boom.

2. Historical Narrative

2.1. The Nineteenth Century

Asset booms and busts have been a major part of the economic landscape since the early eighteenth century. Classic stock market booms followed by wrenching busts were the South Sea Bubble in England and John Law's Mississippi scheme in France (see Neal, 2011 and Velde, 2003). In the nineteenth century there were major stock market boom busts across the world that accompanied the advent of equities to finance the rapid economic development that followed the industrial revolution. Two famous stock market booms and busts in England occurred in the 1820s and the 1840s.

The earliest and probably most famous stock market boom bust in the modern era ended with the 1824–1825 stock market crash (Bordo, 1998; Bordo, 2003; Neal, 1998). After the Napoleonic wars and the successful resumption of the gold standard in 1821, the British economy enjoyed a period of rapid expansion stimulated by an export boom to the newly independent states of Latin America, and investment in infrastructure projects (e.g., gas lighting, canals and railroads). The sale of stocks to finance those ventures, in addition to gold and silver mines (some real, some fictitious) in Latin America, propelled a stock market boom fueled by the Bank of England's easy monetary policy. Prices rose by 78% in the boom. Indications are that the April 1825 collapse in stock prices was related to the prior tightening of the Bank of England's monetary policy stance in response to a decline in its gold reserves. The collapse, in which stock prices fell by 34%, triggered bank failures which, once they reached important City of London banks, precipitated a full-fledged panic in early December. Only then did the Bank of England begin to act as a lender of last resort, but it was too late to prevent massive bank failures, contraction of loans, and a serious recession.

The 1840s railroad mania was a precedent to the 1990s dot-com boom. After the first successful railroad was established in 1830, optimistic expectations about potential profits, which later turned out to be overly optimistic, led to massive investment in rails and rolling stock that extended the network across the country. The boom was accommodated by expansionary monetary policy in response to gold inflows. The end of the railroad boom was associated with the banking panic of 1847—one of the worst in British history. The crash, in which stock prices fell by 30%, and tightening of the Bank of England's monetary policy stance may have triggered the panic, as in earlier episodes, reflecting its concern over declining gold reserves (Dornbusch and Frenkel, 1984). The panic led to many bank failures and a serious recession.

The U.S. had many stock market booms and busts in its history. Several of them were associated with banking panics and serious recessions. One of the classic boom busts was the railroad boom in the 1870s, which opened up the west. The post-Civil War era experienced one of the most rapid growth rates in U.S. history. Much of the financing of railroad investment came from British capital inflows, which, in turn, accompanied by gold inflows, permitted monetary expansion. The boom was also accompanied by corporate malfeasance and corruption (Bordo and Benmelech, 2008). The boom ended with a stock market crash in 1873, once the extent of the corporate fraud was revealed. The stock market crash was followed by a banking panic and a recession that ended in 1879.

2.2. The 1920s

The most famous episode of an asset price boom is the Wall Street Boom beginning in 1923 and ending with the crash in October 1929. During the boom, stock prices rose by over 200%; the collapse from 1929 to 1932 had prices decline by 66%. The boom was associated with massive investment that brought the major inventions of the late nineteenth century (e.g., electricity and the automobile) to fruition. In addition, major innovations profoundly changed industrial organization and the financial sector, including the increased use of equity as a financial instrument. The economy of the 1920s, following the sharp recession of 1920–1921, was characterized by rapid real growth, rapid productivity advance and slightly declining prices punctuated by two minor recessions. Irving Fisher and other contemporaries believed that the stock market boom reflected the fundamentals of future profits from the high growth industries that were coming on stream, and that it was not a bubble. Recent work by McGrattan and Prescott (2003) concurs with that view; although, many others regard it as a bubble (Galbraith, 1955 and Rappoport and White, 1994).

Debate continues over the role of expansionary Federal Reserve policy in fueling the boom. In 1932, Adolph Miller, a member of the Federal Reserve Board, blamed the New York Fed and its President, Benjamin Strong, for pursuing expansionary open market purchases to help Britain restore the pound to its prewar parity in 1924, and again in 1927, to protect sterling from a speculative attack. In both occasions, the U.S. economy was in recession, justifying expansionary policy (Friedman and Schwartz, 1963b). Miller indicted Strong (who died in 1928) for fueling the stock market boom and the resultant crash. His views were instrumental in legislation in 1933, which prohibited Reserve banks from engaging in international monetary policy actions.

As mentioned in section 2 above, the Austrian economists, later followed by economists at the BIS, saw the 1920s as a credit boom accommodated by monetary policy. Eichengreen and Mitchener (2004) present evidence for the BIS view for the 1920s as a credit boom gone wild, based on their measures of a credit boom (deviations from trend of the ratio of broad money to GDP, the investment ratio and real stock prices) for a panel of 9 countries.

The 1920s also witnessed a major house price boom in the U.S. from 1923 to 1925. White (2009) argues that the boom was, in part, triggered by expansionary monetary policy. He finds that deviation from a Taylor rule has some explanatory power for the run-up in real housing prices. He also argues that the Fed, established in 1914 to act as a lender of last resort and to reduce the seasonal instability in financial markets, created some elements of a "Greenspan Put"—the view that emerged after Chairman Greenspan engineered a massive liquidity support for the New York money center banks during the October 1987 Wall Street Crash—in which the Fed would bail out the financial sector in the event of a crash. Unlike the Wall Street stock market boom, the housing boom bust in the 1920s had little impact on the financial system or the economy as a whole.

2.3. Post-World War II

The post-war period has exhibited a large number of housing and stock market boom busts. Many of these episodes occurred in an environment of loose monetary policy. In addition, expansionary monetary policy across the world in the 1960s and 1970s led to a global commodities boom that presaged the Great Inflation. We briefly discuss a number of salient episodes.

2.3.1 Asset booms in the U.K. The U.K. had a massive house price and stock market boom in the 1971–1974 period, referred to by Congdon (2005) as the Heath Barber Boom. Named after the (then) Prime Minister and Chancellor of the Exchequer, Congdon documents the rapid growth in broad money (M4) after the passage of the Competition and Credit Control Bill in 1971, which liberalized the U.K. financial system and ended the rate-setting cartel of the London clearing banks. He shows both rapid growth in M4 and a shift in its composition towards balances held by the corporate and financial sectors away from the household sectors. Following the Friedman and Schwartz (1963b) transmission story, the excess cash balances went into equities first, and properties second, greatly pushing up their prices. The big asset price booms were soon followed by an unprecedented rise in inflation to close to 20% per year by the end of the 1970s. Congdon also shows a tight connection between expansion in broad money supply in the 1986–1987 period and subsequent asset price booms, which he calls the Lawson boom after the Chancellor of the Exchequer. As in the 1970s boom, rapid growth in M4 and in its holdings by the corporate and financial sectors fueled a stock market boom which burst in 1987, and a housing boom that burst in 1989. Finally, he attributes a big run-up in financial sector real broad money holdings in 1997–1998 to an equities boom in the late 90s and a housing boom that peaked in 2006.

2.3.2 Nordic asset booms in the 1980s. The Nordic countries, Norway, Sweden and Finland, all experienced major asset booms and busts in the 1980s. In each country, the run-up in asset prices followed liberalization of their financial sectors after 5 decades of extensive controls on lending rates and government control over the sectoral allocation of bank lending. Asset booms were accommodated by expansionary monetary policy as each country adhered to pegged exchange rates, which tended to make monetary policy pro-cyclical.

In the case of Norway, quantitative restrictions on bank lending were lifted in 1984 without allowing interest rates to rise. Real interest rates were low and sometimes negative. Banks used their newborn freedom to expand lending on a large scale: all of them with a firm desire to increase their market shares. This stimulated a massive real estate boom until 1986. The boom ended with tighter monetary policy in 1986. The legacy of the collapse of the real estate boom and the buildup in bad assets in the commercial banks was a banking crisis in 1991 and a recession (Steigum, 2009).

Similar stories occurred in Finland and Sweden (Jonung et al., 2009). Their crises and recessions were much worse than in Norway, largely because their currencies were pegged to the DM in the EMS system, and they were hard hit by tight German monetary policy in reaction to the high fiscal costs of German reunification.

2.3.3 Japan in the 1980s.   The Japanese boom-bust cycle began in the mid-1980s with a run-up of real estate prices fueled by an increase in bank lending and easy monetary policy. The Bank of Japan began following a looser monetary policy after the Plaza Accord of 1985 to attempt to devalue the yen and ease the upward pressure on the dollar. The property price boom, in turn, led to a stock market boom as the increased value of property owned by firms raised future profits and, hence, stock prices (Iwaisako and Ito, 1995). Both rising land prices and stock prices, in turn, increased firms' collateral, encouraging further bank loans and more fuel for the boom. The bust may have been triggered by the Bank of Japan's pursuit of a tight monetary policy in 1989 to stem the asset market boom.

The subsequent asset price collapse in the next five years led to a collapse in bank lending with a decline in the collateral backing corporate loans. The decline in asset prices further impinged on the banking system's capital, making many banks insolvent. This occurred because the collapse in asset prices reduced the value of their capital. Lender of last resort policy prevented a classic banking panic, but regulatory forbearance propped up insolvent banks. It took over a decade to resolve the banking crisis and Japan is still mired in slow growth.

2.3.4 The 1994–2000 U.S. dot-com stock market boom. The stock market of the 1990s in the U.S. (and other countries) had many of the elements of the railroad boom in England in the 1840s and the Wall Street Boom of the 1920s, including rapid productivity growth and the dissemination and marketing of technologies that had been developed earlier. Massive funds flowed from IPOs and the stock market to finance companies using the new high tech personal computer and internet based technologies. Significant run-ups in the market value of leaders like AOL and Microsoft (even before they reported profits) led others to join in the game. The investment boom in the IT industry led to a stock price boom in the late 1990s, which burst in 2000.

As in earlier booms, easy bank (and non-bank credit) finance was crucial, as well as accommodative monetary policy. As in the 1920s boom, the question arose whether the rise in stock prices reflected underlying fundamentals (referred to as the "New Economy") or a speculative bubble. The BIS view attributed the boom to the environment of low inflation and credibility for low inflation produced by the Federal Reserve and other central banks during the Great Moderation of the 1980s and 1990s. In this opinion, central banks, focused on low inflation, did not see the risks that the benign environment had for fostering an asset boom.

2.4. Commodity Price Booms

2.4.1 The 1930s. The recovery from the Great Contraction after 1933 witnessed a global commodity boom. Friedman and Schwartz (1963a) document the policies of Franklin Roosevelt and his Secretary of the Treasury, Henry Morgenthau, to purchase gold and silver in the London market to reflate the U.S. economy. They were following the approach suggested by Warren and Pearson (1935). The Treasury's gold and silver purchases succeeded in pushing up gold and silver prices in the London commodity market and may have also helped produce the general commodity boom of the mid-1930s. Other factors would have been global recovery and the looming threat of World War II.

2.4.2 The 1970s.   The massive commodities boom in the 1970s has been viewed as a precursor to the Great Inflation. Following the monetarist transmission mechanism, expansionary monetary policy pushed up highly inelastic raw materials prices, which later fed into the prices of intermediate goods and final goods (Bordo, 1980). An alternative, widely held view at the time was that there were a series of negative supply shocks in the 1970s, which accounted for the boom (Blinder and Rudd, 2008). The most memorable events of the time were the two OPEC oil price shocks of 1974 and 1978. However, Barsky and Killian (2001) present evidence that what led to the formation of the OPEC cartel and its constriction of supply was an attempt to compensate the oil producers for a decline in the real value of oil prices in terms of dollars. This reflected global inflation aided by expansionary U.S. (and other countries) monetary policies beginning in the mid-1960s.

2.4.3 The 2000s.   A run-up in commodity prices in the 2000s has popularly been attributed to globalization and the rapid growth of emerging market economies, especially China, which pushed up the prices of commodities, like copper, crucial to their economic development. However, there is also an argument that the boom reflected expansionary monetary policy in the U.S. and other advanced countries concerned over the threat of deflation after the dot-com boom burst (Frankel, 2008). The rise in commodity prices then fed into global inflation (Browne and Cronin, 2007; Ciccarelli and Mojon, 2010).

2.5. Summary

The wide history of asset price booms displays evidence of a connection between monetary expansion and booms. However, the circumstances of the different episodes varied considerably. In the case of some famous stock price booms (e.g., the 1840s, 1870s, 1920s and 1990s), the fundamental drivers were productivity shocks, such as the advent of the railroads, consumer durables and the internet. The run-up in asset prices was fueled by bank credit in an environment of accommodative monetary policy.

House price booms reflected real shocks on some occasions, such as rapid immigration, financial liberalization, as well as expansionary monetary policy. Commodity price booms also reflected both real shocks and highly expansionary monetary policy. In the rest of the chapter we provide some empirical evidence on the contribution of monetary policy and several other factors in a large sample of asset price booms.

3. Identifying Asset Price Booms

Before outlining our econometric approach, we first identify asset price booms for real house prices, real stock prices and real commodity prices. Our approach to identifying boom/bust periods is a mixture of the formal and informal. We first use a well-known dating algorithm to find turning points in our asset price series, and then use our discretion to select those expansions/contraction pairs that meet our criteria. We do this to avoid some well-known problems that dating algorithms can have in identifying cycles when the underlying data are purely random (see, for example, Cogley and Nason, 1995).

The first step of the process is to date the turning points of our asset price series. We do this using the method described in Harding and Pagan (2002) and Pagan and Sossounov (2003). In these two related papers, the authors use the method of Bry and Boschan (1971) to date turning points of time series. The dating algorithm of Bry and Boschan (1971) was formulated to mimic the NBER dating process and is successful in dating turning points in time series. For real house prices and real commodity prices, we look for peaks (troughs) that are higher (lower) than the two nearest observations on each side of the turning point under the constraint that peaks and troughs must alternate. For real stock prices, because of the higher volatility of stock prices and the lower duration that is found for cycles in stock prices, we use a modified rule where a turning point is declared if the observation on each side of the peak (trough) is lower (higher) than the candidate turning point. Note that this is the first stage of our process. It is possible that the rule for the stock price series may identify expansion/

contraction pairs that are nothing more than short-term "blips." This is the reason why in the second stage of the process we inspect the cycles found by the algorithm and reject those that do not meet our criteria.

For the second stage of our process we do the following, once turning points are identified: we inspect each expansion (defined as the period from a trough to the next peak) to see if it fits our definition of an asset price boom. To identify asset price booms, we take a "holistic" approach. That is, we first look for expansions that meet our criteria and then we visually inspect each prospective boom to check whether the dates for the boom should be corrected. For example, starting dates are moved to the point where the gradient of the asset price series first significantly picks up if the initial periods of the expansion are relatively flat.

The definition of a boom that we use is that a boom is a sustained expansion in asset prices that ends in a significant correction. The expansion is such that the rate of growth is higher than what would be considered usual based on previous cycles. For an expansion to meet the definition of a sustained expansion, the expansion must last at least two years and average at least 5% per year for real house and commodity prices, and average at least 10% per year for real stock prices. This is similar to the criteria used in Bordo and Wheelock (2009). The second screening that we use is that the price correction that follows the expansion in prices must be greater than 25% of the expansion in price that occurred during the expansion. We believe that this definition rules out secular trends where there can be large increases in asset prices followed by small corrections, followed by another large expansion. The booms that we identify are all followed by significant price corrections which suggest that the price expansion was not sustainable and, hence, a boom/bust period

The identified asset price booms are reported in Tables 10.1, 10.2 and 10.3 and are depicted in figures in the appendix. We have annual data on real house prices and real stock prices for 18 countries from 1920 to 2010. We also have a single, real global commodity price index for that period.[6] The approach we follow is similar to that used in IMF WEO (2003), Helbling and Terrones (2004), and Bordo and Wheelock (2009). All of these studies used monthly data for a smaller set of countries. Only the Bordo and Wheelock study covered the pre-World War II period. As in

TABLE 10.1 Identified Real House Price Booms

	Booms			Corrections			
Period	Duration	% Δ	APC[a]	Period	Duration	% Δ	APC[a]
Belgium							
1971–1979	8	58.9	7.36	1979–1985	6	−37.06	−6.18
Canada							
1984–1989	5	57.52	11.5	1989–1998	9	−14.39	−1.6
Denmark							
1982–1986	4	53.08	13.27	1986–1990	4	−25.72	−6.43
2003–2007	4	53.49	13.37	2007–2009	2	−19.24	−9.62
Finland							
1947–1955	8	50.77	6.35	1955–1958	3	−19.81	−6.6
1971–1974	3	14.42	4.81	1974–1979	5	−26.82	−5.36
1986–1989	3	61.85	20.62	1989–1993	4	−45.79	−11.45
France							
1930–1935	5	37.69	7.54	1935–1941	6	−47.15	−7.86
1971–1980	9	36.74	4.08	1980–1984	4	−16.76	−4.19
1985–1991	6	30.84	5.14	1991–1997	6	−16.03	−2.67
U.K.							
1971–1973	2	59.27	29.64	1973–1977	4	−30.91	−10.30
1977–1980	3	26.18	8.73	1980–1982	2	−10.17	−5.08
1985–1989	4	67.18	16.8	1989–1993	4	−26.83	−6.71
Ireland							
1976–1979	3	40.58	13.53	1979–1987	8	−21.54	−2.69
1996–2007	11	194.53	17.68	2007–2011	4	−40.52	−10.13
Italy							
1980–1981	1	24.02	24.02	1981–1985	4	−30.65	−7.66
1988–1992	4	49.63	12.41	1992–1997	5	−27.58	−5.52
Japan							
1986–1991	5	34.16	6.83	1991–1994	3	−12.98	−4.33
Netherlands							
1958–1964	6	51.11	8.52	1964–1966	2	−27.51	−13.75
1976–1978	2	36.09	18.05	1978–1985	7	−47.75	−6.82
New Zealand							
1971–1974	3	66.96	22.32	1974–1980	6	−38.19	−6.37
Norway							
1983–1986	3	50.29	16.76	1986–1992	6	−35.2	−5.87
Sweden							
1974–1979	5	22.02	4.4	1979–1985	6	−36.92	−6.15
1985–1990	5	36.71	7.34	1990–1993	3	−28.58	−9.53

TABLE 10.1   (*continued*)

	Booms				Corrections		
Period	Duration	% Δ	APC[a]	Period	Duration	% Δ	APC[a]
Switzerland							
1971–1973	2	21.2	10.6	1973–1976	3	−26.01	−8.67
1983–1989	6	43.31	7.22	1989–1997	8	−36.61	−4.58
United States							
1921–1925	4	19.12	4.78	1925–1932	7	−12.57	−1.8
1976–1979	3	14.47	4.82	1979–1982	3	−12.74	−4.25
1984–1989	5	18.76	3.75	1989–1993	4	−13.01	−3.25
1997–2006	9	79.38	8.82	2006–2009	3	−33.09	−11.03

SOURCE: Authors' calculations.
[a] APC = annualized percentage change.

the earlier studies we identify many more stock price booms than house price booms.

3.1. Housing Booms

With the exception of France in the 1930s and the U.S. in the 1920s, in Table 10.1, we did not identify any house price booms before World War II. In the post-World War II period, most countries had house price booms in the 1970s and 1980s. The literature at the time associated them with the liberalization of financial markets that occurred after the breakdown of the Bretton Woods system. Many of the boom busts were dramatic, especially in Japan, the Scandinavian countries, the Netherlands and Switzerland. The U.S. only experienced mild booms and corrections in that period. Several dramatic episodes occurred in the late 1990s and early 2000s. The U.S. housing boom of 1997–2006, when real prices rose by 79% and fell by 33%, and the Irish boom of 1996–2007, when real prices rose by 195% and then fell by 40%, really stands out.

3.2. Stock Price Booms

Stock prices show considerably more volatility than house prices, and many more booms and busts (Table 10.2). In the pre-World War II period, most countries had major stock market booms and busts. In the 1920s, many

TABLE 10.2   Identified Real Stock Price Booms

	Booms				Corrections		
Period	Duration	% Δ	APC[a]	Period	Duration	% Δ	APC[a]
Australia							
1920–1928	8	128.67	16.08	1928–1930	2	−35.73	−17.87
1930–1936	6	154.21	25.7	1935–1941	5	−30.93	−6.19
1956–1959	3	65.71	21.9	1959–1960	1	−15.02	−15.02
1966–1969	3	79.3	26.43	1969–1971	2	−31.71	−15.85
1978–1980	2	61.93	30.96	1980–1982	2	−44.92	−22.46
2002–2007	5	88.03	17.61	2007–2008	1	−45.04	−45.04
Belgium							
1987–1989	2	58.41	29.2	1989–1990	1	−28.21	−28.21
1994–1998	4	141.32	35.33	1998–2002	4	−44.69	−11.17
2002–2006	4	115.02	28.75	2006–2008	2	−53.95	−26.97
Canada							
1920–1928	8	269.07	33.63	1928–1932	4	−64.99	−16.25
1932–1936	4	146.19	36.55	1936–1937	1	−23.19	−23.19
1953–1956	3	67.9	22.63	1956–1957	1	−24.81	−24.81
1977–1980	3	61.95	20.65	1980–1982	2	−29.57	−14.79
1998–2000	2	30.08	15.04	2000–2002	2	−29.22	−14.61
2002–2007	5	88.93	17.79	2007–2008	1	−35.77	−35.77
Denmark							
1932–1936	4	43.24	10.81	1936–1940	4	−42.37	−10.59
1952–1956	4	32.81	8.2	1956–1957	1	−13.46	−13.46
1957–1960	3	33.99	11.33	1960–1962	2	−11.88	−5.94
1987–1989	2	81.72	40.86	1989–1992	3	−31.93	−10.64
1998–2000	6	127.32	21.22	2000–2002	2	−35.79	−17.9
2002–2007	5	145.41	29.08	2007–2008	1	−50.17	−50.17
Finland							
1924–1927	3	154.64	51.55	1927–1929	2	−30.12	−15.06
1932–1936	4	115.41	28.85	1936–1940	4	−35.82	−8.96
1952–1956	4	87.27	21.82	1956–1958	2	−40.76	−20.38
1969–1973	4	1531.34	382.83	1973–1977	4	−68.6	−17.15
1985–1988	3	176.55	58.85	1988–1991	3	−63.41	−21.14
1995–1999	4	704.66	176.17	1999–2002	3	−62.93	−20.98
2004–2007	3	75.7	25.23	2007–2008	1	−54.95	−54.95
France							
1920–1923	3	82.56	27.52	1923–1926	3	−28.59	−9.53
1926–1928	2	109.19	54.59	1928–1931	3	−51.04	−17.01
1950–1957	7	241.61	34.52	1957–1958	1	−21.13	−21.13
1958–1962	4	76.66	19.17	1962–1967	5	−44.34	−8.87

TABLE 10.2 (*continued*)

	Booms			Corrections			
Period	Duration	% Δ	APC[a]	Period	Duration	% Δ	APC[a]
1977–1979	2	39.84	19.92	1979–1982	3	−31.33	−10.44
1982–1986	4	218.43	54.61	1986–1987	1	−31.57	−31.57
1987–1989	2	84.78	42.39	1989–1990	1	−27.72	−27.72
1995–1999	4	195.91	48.98	1999–2002	3	−48.85	−16.28
2002–2007	4	78.47	19.62	2007–2009	2	−44.86	−22.43
United Kingdom							
1920–1928	8	41.11	5.14	1928–1931	3	−35.11	−11.7
1931–1936	5	73.77	14.75	1936–1940	4	−53.24	−13.31
1952–1954	2	47.91	23.96	1954–1857	3	−21.08	−7.03
1957–1959	2	87.9	43.95	1959–1962	3	−16.48	−5.49
1966–1968	2	70.35	35.17	1968–1970	2	−30.58	−15.29
1970–1972	2	36.77	18.38	1972–1974	2	−76.72	−38.36
1990–1999	9	143.86	15.98	1999–2002	3	−45.25	−15.08
2002–2006	4	49.8	12.45	2006–2008	2	−34.7	−17.35
Germany							
1956–1960	4	231.36	57.84	1960–1968	2	−34.69	−17.34
1966–1969	3	64.14	21.38	1969–1971	2	−27.79	−13.9
1981–1986	5	180.19	36.04	1986–1987	1	−37.81	−37.81
1987–1989	2	65.88	32.94	1989–1992	3	−29.3	−9.77
1992–1999	7	189.94	27.12	1999–2002	3	−59.73	−19.91
2002–2007	5	130.96	26.19	2007–2008	1	−44.98	−44.98
Ireland							
1957–1968	11	248.42	22.58	1968–1970	2	−33.05	−16.52
1976–1978	2	106.51	53.25	1978–1982	4	−58.36	−14.59
1982–1989	7	303.94	43.42	1989–1990	1	−33.33	−33.33
1992–2000	8	279.45	34.93	2000–2002	2	−36.21	−18.11
2002–2006	4	109.43	27.36	2006–2008	2	−76.48	−38.24
Italy							
1922–1924	2	59.29	29.64	1924–1926	2	−44.26	−22.13
1926–1928	2	65.13	32.57	1928–1932	4	−50.07	−12.52
1956–1960	4	140.27	35.07	1960–1964	4	−53.85	−13.46
1977–1980	3	92.61	30.87	1980–1982	2	−29.77	−14.89
1982–1986	4	212.07	53.02	1986–1987	1	−35.78	−35.78
1987–1989	2	25.67	12.84	1989–1992	3	−45	−15.00
1995–2000	5	190.82	38.16	2000–2002	2	−46.2	−23.10
2002–2006	4	68.33	17.08	2006–2008	2	−55	−27.50

(continued)

TABLE 10.2 (*continued*)

	Booms				Corrections		
Period	Duration	% Δ	APCᵃ	Period	Duration	% Δ	APCᵃ
Japan							
1923–1926	3	43.2	14.40	1926–1930	4	−16.49	−4.12
1931–1933	2	89.73	44.87	1933–1938	5	−30.73	−6.15
1957–1960	3	169.68	56.56	1960–1963	3	−25.68	−8.56
1967–1969	2	66.51	33.26	1969–1970	1	−22.05	−22.05
1970–1972	2	136.21	68.10	1972–1974	2	−48.76	−24.38
1977–1989	12	479.01	39.92	1989–1992	3	−59.64	−19.88
2001–2006	4	101.39	25.35	2006–2008	2	−49.13	−24.56
Netherlands							
1924–1928	4	41.18	10.30	1928–1931	3	−62.06	−20.69
1951–1955	4	119.73	29.93	1955–1956	1	−18.80	−18.80
1956–1959	3	71.87	23.96	1959–1961	2	−14.00	−7.00
1965–1967	2	56.05	28.02	1967–1970	3	−38.24	−12.75
1993–1998	5	203.19	40.64	1998–2001	3	−54.89	−18.3
2001–2006	5	57.64	11.53	2006–2007	1	−52.68	−52.68
New Zealand							
1931–1934	3	52.51	17.50	1934–1938	4	−28.15	−7.04
1958–1964	6	117.6	19.60	1964–1966	2	−16.12	−8.06
1967–1969	2	47.54	23.77	1969–1971	2	−27.91	−13.95
1979–1981	2	45.44	22.72	1981–1982	1	−28.34	−28.34
1982–1986	4	324.35	81.09	1986–1988	2	−61.76	−30.88
Norway							
1921–1929	8	70.84	8.85	1929–1937	8	−41.47	5.18
1953–1956	3	36.23	12.08	1956–1958	2	−26.25	−13.12
1967–1970	3	69.70	23.23	1971–1971	1	−28.42	−28.42
1971–1973	2	37.59	18.79	1973–1975	2	−54.25	−27.12
2002–2007	5	231.3	46.26	2007–2008	1	−55.44	−55.44
2008–2010	2	76.58	38.29	2010–2011	1	−15.49	−15.49
Spain							
1950–1956	6	163.74	27.29	1956–1959	3	−48.60	−16.20
1961–1963	2	31.47	15.73	1963–1964	1	−13.87	−13.87
1967–1972	5	112.35	22.47	1972–1982	10	−91.31	−9.13
1982–1989	7	294.4	42.06	1989–1992	3	−38.81	−12.94
1994–1999	5	208.7	41.74	1999–2002	3	−43.39	−14.46
2002–2007	5	120.31	24.06	2007–2008	1	−41.40	−41.40
Sweden							
1923–1928	5	177.56	35.51	1928–1932	4	−62.81	−15.70
1932–1936	4	102.71	25.68	1926–1941	5	−35.40	−7.08

TABLE 10.2   (*continued*)

	Booms				Corrections		
Period	Duration	% Δ	APC[a]	Period	Duration	% Δ	APC[a]
1958–1950	2	29.61	14.8	1950–1952	2	−19.58	−9.79
1952–1954	2	47.97	23.98	1954–1957	3	−17.92	−5.97
1957–1959	2	58.37	29.18	1959–1962	3	−17.90	−5.97
1962–1965	3	36.16	12.05	1965–1966	1	−26.52	−26.52
1970–1972	2	17.60	8.80	1972–1974	2	−18.40	−9.20
1979–1989	10	503.68	50.37	1989–1990	1	−37.86	−37.86
1992–1999	7	443.67	63.38	1999–2002	3	−56.63	−18.88
2002–2006	4	141.66	35.42	2006–2008	2	−48.28	−24.14
2008–2010	2	74.64	37.32	2010–2011	1	−18.09	−18.09
Switzerland							
1920–1928	8	214.08	26.76	1928–1931	3	−46.72	−15.57
1935–1938	3	88.88	29.63	1938–1940	2	−35.94	−17.97
1957–1961	4	187.92	46.98	1961–1966	5	−67.27	−13.45
1990–2000	10	342.77	34.28	2000–2002	2	−44.58	−22.29
2002–2006	4	91.21	22.8	2006–2008	2	−38.88	−19.44
United States							
1923–1928	5	182.59	36.52	1928–1932	4	−63.07	−15.77
1934–1936	2	73.15	36.57	1936–1937	1	−40.34	−40.34
1953–1956	3	83.34	27.78	1956–1957	1	−16.73	−16.73
1962–1965	3	40.03	13.34	1965–1966	1	−16.00	−16.00
1966–1968	2	19.82	9.91	1968–1970	2	−20.86	−10.43
1970–1972	2	19.97	9.98	1972–1974	2	−52.44	−26.22
1994–1999	5	184.55	36.91	1999–2002	3	−44.29	−14.76

Source: Authors' calculations.
[a] APC = annualized percentage change.

countries had booms similar to that of Wall Street. The Wall Street Boom saw real prices rising by 183% between 1923–1928, and collapsing by 63% between 1928–1932. The U.S. was surpassed by Canada and Switzerland, but Australia, Finland and Sweden were not far behind. This pattern of international concordance of stock prices is well known (Goetzmann, Li and Rouwenhorst, 2005). The recovery from the Great Contraction in the mid-1930s also displayed some major booms, especially in Australia, Canada, Finland, the U.K., Sweden, Switzerland and the U.S.

TABLE 10.3 Identified Real Commodity Price Booms

Booms				Corrections			
Period	Duration	% Δ	APC[a]	Period	Duration	% Δ	APC[a]
1933–1938	5	88.86	17.77	1938–1940	2	−17.7	−8.85
1950–1952	2	38.11	19.06	1952–1954	2	−22.98	−11.49
1963–1967	4	27.52	6.88	1967–1969	2	−19.56	−9.78
1972–1975	3	141.94	47.31	1975–1976	1	−13.23	−13.23
1976–1981	5	113.44	22.69	1981–1983	2	−24.74	−12.37
1986–1989	3	53.3	17.77	1989–1992	3	−24.96	−8.32
1994–1996	2	35.62	17.81	1996–2000	4	−28.96	−7.24
2002–2009	7	139.08	19.87	2009–2010	1	−19.71	−19.71

Source: Authors' calculations.

[a] APC = annualized percentage change.

In the post-World War II era, booms reflecting Europe's recovery and catch up in the 1950s occurred in France, Italy and Switzerland. Japan also had a major boom in the 1950s. The Marshall Plan and the Dodge Plan may have been keen drivers of both rapid real growth and the rise in asset values in those years (Bordo and Wheelock, 2009).

The next big wave of stock market booms occurred in the 1980s and especially, the 1990s. The growth of the high tech industry led to dramatic booms in the U.S., U.K., Germany, Ireland, Italy, Spain, Sweden and Switzerland.

3.3. Commodity Price Booms

As discussed in section 3 above, Table 10.3 shows the post-Great Contraction commodity price boom in the mid-1930s. The boom in the 1970s associated with the oil price shocks and the Great Inflation is also evident. The last big boom in the 2000s associated with the rapid growth of emerging markets and expansionary monetary policy is also very visible in the table.

4. Empirical Analysis

In this analysis, we pool data from across the 18 countries in our data set to investigate the impact of loose monetary policy and low inflation on asset prices.[7] By pooling the data across the twentieth century, we are in a sense calculating the impact each of our control variables has on asset prices averaged across all the boom periods that we have identified. Low inflation could reflect the credibility for low inflation that occurred in the 1980s, 1990s and 1920s, according to Borio and Lowe (2002) and Eichengreen and Mitchener (2004). In this environment, endogenous asset price booms could arise, financed by easy credit accommodated by the central bank. Loose monetary policy refers to deliberately expansionary monetary policy (as evidenced in the policy rate being below the Taylor rule rate) made, for example, to prevent deflation as in the 2000s, or to stimulate recovery from a recession.

The asset price data that we use in the analysis are real house prices, real stock prices, and real commodity prices. We include two different measures of monetary policy: the deviation of a short-term interest rate from the optimal Taylor rule rate, and the deviation of the money growth rate from 3%. The optimal Taylor rule rate is given by the following equation:

$$r^{Taylor} = \pi_t + r^* + 0.5(y_t - y_t^*) + 0.5(\pi_t - \pi^*), \tag{1}$$

where the output gap term is given by the deviation in logging real GDP from its long-run trend (as determined by the Hodrick-Prescott filter with a smoothing parameter equal to 100, since the data are annual time series) and the inflation target is 2%. It should be noted that we do not use policy rates in this analysis and that we use, for all countries, a target interest rate (r^*) of 2% with coefficients of 0.5 and 0.5 as in Taylor (1993). Thus the optimal Taylor rule rate that we use is a very rough measure of the optimal policy rate for each country.[8] The same goes for our measure of monetary policy using the growth rate of broad money. We use the deviation of the growth rate of money from 3% as a simple measure of the stance of monetary policy present at the time. It also represents Milton Friedman's original (1960) monetary rule—to set money growth equal to the underlying trend growth rate of real output.[9] If we assume the trend growth rate in velocity is constant, this rule would give stable prices.[10] Money growth is also a useful measure of the stance of monetary policy in earlier periods when central banks engaged in monetary targeting or in episodes when it is more difficult to estimate a Taylor rule.

The three main controls that we use in our regressions are the deviation of monetary policy from the "optimal" policy rule, either the Taylor rule or the Friedman money growth rule, a measure of the inflationary state of the economy—a measure of the deviation of inflation from its long-run trend, and a measure of the credit conditions present as measured by the deviation of the share of bank loans to GDP from its long-run mean.

The deviation of the short-term interest rate (money growth rate) from the optimal rate is included to control for possible correlations between "loose" monetary policy and asset booms. The inflation control is included to control for possible correlations between low inflation policy and booms, and the credit control variable is included to determine if loose or "easy" credit has a role in asset booms. These variables are consistent with the Austrian BIS story, as well as recent papers by Schularick and Taylor (2012), Jorda, Schularick and Taylor (2012) and Christiano et al. (2010).

These are the three main alternative variables that have been argued to play a role in asset booms, and the aim of this chapter is to use data over the whole twentieth century to shed light on their roles. Of course these are not the only determinants of asset prices, so we also include other controls, such as the growth rate of GDP, a measure of current account imbalances and a measure of financial liberalization.[11]

The data in their raw form are non-stationary, either through the presence of a unit root or a time trend. In this chapter we are mainly interested in the role that our three main controls play in boom/bust periods. These periods are identified earlier as periods where there were sustained run-ups in asset prices followed by significant corrections. That is, these asset price booms are periods in which asset prices move away from their long-run trend. Our interest is to see whether or not there is a systematic relationship between deviations of our three main variables from their long-run trend, or in the case of the policy variable, the optimal rate, and the deviation of asset prices from its long-run trend. Thus, we are not focusing on secular movements and the relationship between asset price levels and the rate of inflation, interest rates, or the amount of credit available in the economy, but rather we are focusing on examining the departures from the norm.

Because of this, we convert all variables to deviations from a long-run trend. The policy variables, the short-term interest rate and the growth rate of M2 are deviated from the "optimal" rate. We do this using the Hodrick-Prescott (HP) filter with a smoothing parameter set to 100, since our data are collected at the annual frequency.[12]

Therefore, the variables used in our regression analysis are negative when the value is below the long-run trend, and positive when the variable is above the long-run trend. Our regression analysis then investigates the relationship between the deviation from the long-run trend of asset prices, the deviation of inflation and credit from their long-term trend, and the deviation of the short-term interest rate from the "optimal" Taylor rule rate (or deviation of the growth rate of money from 3% in the case where we use money growth rates in our regression). When the short-term rate is below the "optimal" Taylor rule rate or the money growth rate is above 3%, then the monetary policy conditions are "loose."

The model that is used is an autoregressive distributed lag (ARDL) model given by

$$\hat{p}_t = a + \sum_{j=1}^{p} \beta_j\, \hat{p}_{t-j} + \sum_{k=1}^{3} \sum_{j=0}^{q} \gamma_{kj}\, \hat{x}_{kt-j} + \varepsilon_t. \tag{2}$$

Here, variables in "hats" refer to deviations from trend, or in the case of the monetary policy variables, the "hats" refer to deviations from the optimal policy—the Taylor rule for interest rates and the Friedman rule for money growth. We include the three main control variables into the regression with lags in order to investigate the dynamic structure of low inflation, "loose" monetary policy, and relatively abundant or "easy" credit on asset prices. In determining the number of lags to include from each variable in our regression equation, sequential likelihood ratio tests are used. For simplicity we do not allow for different numbers of lags for each of the right hand side control variables.

Tables 10.4, 10.5 and 10.6 show the results for real house prices, real stock prices and real commodity prices for each of the monetary variables, respectively. The first two sets of regressions—the ones with house and stock prices as dependent variables—are panel regressions, and in these two regression equations country specific fixed effects are included. For the regression for real commodity prices, because the market for commodities is a global market, lacking measures of global monetary policy, we use U.S. data as covariates.

4.1. Real House Prices

Tables 10.4A and 10.4B report the results from our panel regressions where real house prices are the dependent variable. In all tables the numbers in parentheses are p-values. Country specific fixed effects are included, but their estimates are not reported for space considerations. There are four regressions reported in each table. The first regression is the basic ARDL model with only current and lagged deviations of trend of the three main control variables included. In Table 10.4A the "policy" variable that is included is the deviation of the short-term interest rate from the "optimal" rate given by the Taylor rule in (1). Table 10.4B includes the deviation of the growth rate of M2 from 3%. In both regressions it was determined that one lag of the dependent variable, the current value and two lags of the control variables should be included. In order to allow for the possibility that the three main covariates are only important during the boom periods, we include interactions between a dummy variable (D), that for each country takes a value of 0 if period t is not in a boom, and a value of 1 if period t is in a boom. Thus, we are able to tell if there are any nonlinearities present in the relationship between the controls and asset price deviations.

Regression (1) reported in Table 10.4A reports the estimates of (2) when we include the policy variable, the inflation variable, and the credit variable. For the policy variable, which is the deviation of the short-term interest rate from the Taylor rule rate, the coefficient on the first lag is significant and negative. This means that for every 1 percentage point you lower the short-term interest rate below the implied Taylor rule rate, real house prices would increase by 0.40% in the next period.[13] This is obviously a very small impact and given that the second lag is significant and positive the overall impact of a sustained period with the short-term interest rate below its target would not have a large initial impact on house prices.

As for the deviation of inflation from its long-run trend, again, the first lag is significant and negative. Thus a negative deviation of 1 percentage point in the inflation from its long-run trend would lead to an increase in house prices of 0.85%. Again, this initial impact is small. As for the variable that measures the deviation of credit from its long-run trend, there are no significant terms.

The results above are what you would expect in "normal" situations, that is, when $D=0$. During boom periods, when $D=1$, the impacts of deviations from trend are more striking. For the policy deviation variable, $(r^s - r^{Taylor})_t$, there is a significant and large negative coefficient on the second lag. Thus, when in a boom period the initial impact of a negative deviation from the Taylor-rule rate of 1 percentage point leads to a 2.15 percent increase in house prices two periods later. This large and significantly negative estimate is consistent across all specifications of our regression models and indicates that "loose" monetary policy is associated with increases in house prices during the identified boom periods.

The same results are apparent for the inflation deviation and the credit deviation. For inflation during boom periods, there are significant and negative coefficients on the current period and the second lag. The first lag is also significant but is positive, which means that the impact of a sustained 1 percentage point fall in inflation will be negative and in the range of 2.5%, initially.

The credit variable showed little impact during normal periods, but during the identified boom periods the coefficients are significant and positive for the current period and significant and negative for the second lag. This suggests that a 1 percent increase in loans, as a proportion of GDP, would lead house prices increasing in the short term but that this increase would be small and to the order of 0.25% to 0.5%. It should be noted that the modest size of this effect is in contrast to results reported in Jorda et al. (2012) and Christiano et al. (2010). Our estimates are based on panel estimates using evidence for booms across most of the twentieth century and so the estimates we report are essentially averages of the impact of credit expansion for each of the booms. It could be that the credit expansion story is appropriate for the most recent boom but not for earlier booms. The fact that we get a lower impact, on average, does not necessarily contradict the results from these authors.

As in the case of the policy variable, the evidence points to there being a bigger effect during booms than in calmer periods. This result that "loose"

TABLE 10.4A Panel Regression Results for Real House Prices
(Taylor Rule)[a]

Regressors	Dependent Variable: Deviation of log Real House Prices from long-run trend (HP trend)			
	(1)	*(2)*	*(3)*	*(4)*
$(p - \bar{p})_{t-1}$	0.77***	0.80***	0.80***	0.79***
	(0.00)	(0.00)	(0.00)	(0.00)
$(r^s - r^{Taylor})_t$	0.04	0.10	−0.02	−0.16
	(0.77)	(0.42)	(0.90)	(0.35)
$(r^s - r^{Taylor})_{t-1}$	−0.40**	−0.24	−0.06	−0.05
	(0.02)	(0.16)	(0.78)	(0.80)
$(r^s - r^{Taylor})_{t-2}$	0.26**	0.05	0.03	0.02
	(0.03)	(0.66)	(0.87)	(0.88)
$(\pi - \bar{\pi})_t$	0.17	0.26	−0.06	−0.17
	(0.43)	(0.21)	(0.84)	(0.59)
$(\pi - \bar{\pi})_{t-1}$	−0.85***	−0.55**	−0.07	−0.07
	(0.00)	(0.04)	(0.83)	(0.85)
$(\pi - \bar{\pi})_{t-2}$	0.12	−0.15	−0.35	−0.44
	(0.57)	(0.50)	(0.26)	(0.17)
$(L/Y - \overline{L/Y})_t$	−0.07	0.01	−0.12	−0.11
	(0.17)	(0.89)	(0.12)	(0.15)
$(L/Y - \overline{L/Y})_{t-1}$	−0.03	−0.08	−0.06	−0.05
	(0.67)	(0.21)	(0.49)	(0.56)
$(L/Y - \overline{L/Y})_{t-2}$	0.01	0.03	0.08	0.14**
	(0.89)	(0.57)	(0.23)	(0.05)
$D^*(p - \bar{p})_{t-1}$	0.17**	0.14*	0.10	0.00
	(0.02)	(0.09)	(0.29)	(1.00)
$D^*(r^s - r^{Taylor})_t$	0.22	0.26	0.15	1.01
	(0.48)	(0.42)	(0.68)	(0.06)
$D^*(r^s - r^{Taylor})_{t-1}$	0.47	0.49	0.68	0.24
	(0.27)	(0.26)	(0.16)	(0.75)
$D^*(r^s - r^{Taylor})_{t-2}$	−1.30***	−1.19***	−1.33***	−1.69***
	(0.00)	(0.00)	(0.00)	(0.00)
$D^*(\pi - \bar{\pi})_t$	−0.80*	−0.71	−0.75	−0.13
	(0.09)	(0.14)	(0.19)	(0.85)
$D^*(\pi - \bar{\pi})_{t-1}$	1.11*	1.16*	1.27	0.79
	(0.10)	(0.09)	(0.11)	(0.38)
$D^*(\pi - \bar{\pi})_{t-2}$	−2.32***	−2.17***	−2.16***	−2.13***
	(0.00)	(0.00)	(0.00)	(0.01)
$D^*(L/Y - \overline{L/Y})_t$	0.51***	0.44***	0.55***	0.56***
	(0.00)	(0.00)	(0.00)	(0.00)

TABLE 10.4A   (*continued*)

Regressors	Dependent Variable: Deviation of log Real House Prices from long-run trend (HP trend)			
	(1)	(2)	(3)	(4)
$D^*(L/Y - \overline{L/Y})_{t-1}$	−0.11	−0.18	−0.19	−0.20
	(0.58)	(0.38)	(0.41)	(0.43)
$D^*(L/Y - \overline{L/Y})_{t-2}$	−0.35	−0.31	−0.35	−0.39
	(0.02)	(0.03)	(0.04)	(0.03)
GDP growth		0.01	0.01	0.01
		(0.00)	(0.00)	(0.00)
Current account			−0.01	−0.01
			(0.00)	(0.00)
				0.00
Change in financial innovation				(0.65)
R^2	0.69	0.72	0.75	0.75
$\overline{R}^2$	0.67	0.70	0.73	0.72

SOURCE: Authors' calculations.
  [a] Fixed effects included in regression but not reported. Numbers in parentheses are *p*-values.

monetary policy, low inflation, and "easy" credit are associated with increases in house prices during boom periods is consistent across the other specifications and the impact of these variables is higher in magnitude than GDP growth and the measure of current account imbalance. The financial liberalization variable does not have any impact.[14]

Thus, there is evidence that during boom periods the relationship between interest rates, low inflation, credit conditions and house prices is heightened and conducive to fueling even higher prices.

Table 10.4B reports the same regression results as above, except this time the deviation of money growth (M2) is used as our measure of expansionary monetary policy instead of the deviation of the short-term interest rate from the optimal Taylor-rule rate. The results are reasonably consistent with the one reported above. A "loose" monetary condition which, in this case, means having a growth rate of money larger than the Friedman rule rate of 3%, is associated with an increase in house prices and this impact is greater during the identified boom periods than during

TABLE 10.4B   Panel Regression Results for Real House Prices (Money Growth Rate Rule)[a]

Regressors	Dependent Variable: Deviation of log Real House Prices from long-run trend (HP trend)			
	(1)	(2)	(3)	(4)
$(p - \bar{p})_{t-1}$	0.72	0.73	0.80	0.78
	(0.00)	(0.00)	(0.00)	(0.00)
$(\Delta\log(m) - 0.03)_t$	0.01	0.07	0.13	0.12
	(0.86)	(0.29)	(0.11)	(0.17)
$(\Delta\log(m) - 0.03)_{t-1}$	0.14	0.13	0.01	0.06
	(0.01)	(0.08)	(0.88)	(0.51)
$(\Delta\log(m) - 0.03)_{t-2}$	−0.04	−0.06	−0.13	−0.12
	(0.45)	(0.33)	(0.09)	(0.15)
$(\pi - \bar{\pi})_t$	−0.12	−0.12	0.06	0.14
	(0.26)	(0.26)	(0.77)	(0.52)
$(\pi - \bar{\pi})_{t-1}$	−0.08	0.00	−0.06	−0.04
	(0.41)	(0.98)	(0.74)	(0.85)
$(\pi - \bar{\pi})_{t-2}$	−0.51	−0.45	−0.33	−0.44
	(0.00)	(0.00)	(0.08)	(0.04)
$(L/Y - \overline{L/Y})_t$	−0.05	0.00	−0.14	−0.14
	(0.33)	(0.92)	(0.06)	(0.08)
$(L/Y - \overline{L/Y})_{t-1}$	0.03	0.01	−0.02	−0.02
	(0.60)	(0.86)	(0.83)	(0.83)
$(L/Y - \overline{L/Y})_{t-2}$	−0.02	−0.03	0.07	0.12
	(0.62)	(0.58)	(0.32)	(0.08)
$D^\star(p - \bar{p})_{t-1}$	0.29	0.30	0.19	0.17
	(0.00)	(0.00)	(0.04)	(0.10)
$D^\star(\Delta\log(m) - 0.03)_t$	0.17	0.17	0.32	0.26
	(0.16)	(0.24)	(0.05)	(0.15)
$D^\star(\Delta\log(m) - 0.03)_{t-1}$	0.30	0.07	−0.02	−0.14
	(0.02)	(0.67)	(0.93)	(0.49)
$D^\star(\Delta\log(m) - 0.03)_{t-2}$	0.23	0.29	0.25	0.32
	(0.06)	(0.06)	(0.15)	(0.09)
$D^\star(\pi - \bar{\pi})_t$	−0.18	−0.40	−0.55	−0.75
	(0.55)	(0.26)	(0.17)	(0.14)
$D^\star(\pi - \bar{\pi})_{t-1}$	0.17	0.31	0.27	0.67
	(0.63)	(0.46)	(0.54)	(0.29)
$D^\star(\pi - \bar{\pi})_{t-2}$	0.06	−0.24	−0.24	−0.25
	(0.82)	(0.43)	(0.48)	(0.61)
$D^\star(L/Y - \overline{L/Y})_t$	0.27	0.22	0.33	0.32
	(0.04)	(0.14)	(0.04)	(0.06)

TABLE 10.4B   (*continued*)

Regressors	Dependent Variable: Deviation of log Real House Prices from long-run trend (HP trend)			
	(1)	*(2)*	*(3)*	*(4)*
$D*(L/Y - \overline{L/Y})_{t-1}$	−0.09	−0.07	−0.05	−0.06
	(0.66)	(0.76)	(0.83)	(0.80)
$D*(L/Y - \overline{L/Y})_{t-2}$	−0.15	−0.21	−0.28	−0.32
	(0.28)	(0.18)	(0.10)	(0.07)
GDP growth		0.00	0.01	0.01
		(0.00)	(0.00)	(0.00)
Current account			−0.01	−0.01
			(0.00)	(0.00)
				0.00
Change in financial innovation				(0.50)
R^2	0.69	0.72	0.75	0.75
$\overline{R}^2$	0.67	0.70	0.73	0.72

SOURCE: Authors' calculations.

[a] Fixed effects included in regression but not reported. Numbers in parentheses are *p*-values.

normal periods. The same goes for credit, in that "easy" credit is associated with higher house prices; again, this is heightened during boom periods.

However, the one result that is different from the results reported in Table 10.4A for the interest rate variable is that low inflation does not appear to have a heightened impact during boom periods. Low inflation does have a significant and negative effect in normal times, but the interaction term where the boom dummy is interacted with the deviation of inflation from its long-run trend is not significant. Our conjecture is that money growth and inflation have been correlated in the past, for example during the 1960's and 1970's, and this is why the impact of inflation in the money growth regressions is reduced.

Overall, the results reported in Table 10.4B do indicate that the impact of the three variables is to increase house prices, and this impact is heightened during the identified boom periods. Again, the results are reasonably consistent across the different specifications.

Another reason why there might be differences between the two approaches is that some of the bigger booms occurred in the late 1980s and early 1990s in a period when the use of interest rates became more prevalent than money growth rates as policy instruments for the countries in our sample. This is obviously only speculation but does warrant further investigation.

4.2. Real Stock Prices

Tables 10.5a and 10.5b repeat the analysis for real stock prices. The specification used in his regression was to include one lag of the dependent variable and the current value, and one lag of the three control variables. The results for the case, when the interest rate deviation is used as a measure of the looseness of monetary policy, are reported in Table 10.5A.

For the "normal" periods, that is, for periods that are not designated to be boom periods, the interest rate deviation and the inflation deviation variables have significant coefficients. For the interest rate deviation, the results are mixed, in that while the coefficient on the current value of the interest rate deviation is negative and highly significant, the coefficient on the first lag of the interest rate deviation is equally large and positive. In fact, the sum of the two estimates is slightly positive. The same qualitative result also occurs for the inflation deviation, but this time the sum of the two estimates is negative. For the normal period, at least, "easy" credit does not appear to be associated with increases in stock prices.

As in the case of house prices there is evidence of nonlinearity in the results, in that there are significant coefficients on the interaction terms. In fact, the coefficient on the lag of the interest rate deviation is very negative and significant. Given that the regular coefficients on the interest rate deviation "wash out," there only appears to be a relationship between "loose" monetary policy and higher stock prices during the identified boom periods. The initial impact of the interest rate being 1 percentage point below the optimal rate is between 1.5% and 1.75% on stock prices. This negative and significant result is not consistent across all specifications. Once the current account variable is added, the significance disappears, but we must be careful to point out that the data for the current account variable is limited, and only goes back to the 1950's. Because of these data's limitations, not all the stock market booms before World War II are included in regression (3) or (4).

TABLE 10.5A Panel Regression Results for Real Stock Prices (Taylor Rule)[a]

Regressors	Dependent Variable: Deviation of log Real Stock Prices from long-run trend (HP trend)			
	(1)	(2)	(3)	(4)
$(p - \bar{p})_{t-1}$	0.32	0.27	0.25	0.30
	(0.00)	(0.00)	(0.00)	(0.00)
$(r^s - r^{Taylor})_t$	−2.02	−1.94	−1.76	−1.99
	(0.00)	(0.00)	(0.01)	(0.01)
$(r^s - r^{Taylor})_{t-1}$	2.33	2.29	2.14	2.22
	(0.00)	(0.00)	(0.00)	(0.01)
$(\pi - \bar{\pi})_t$	−3.45	−3.08	−2.90	−3.59
	(0.00)	(0.00)	(0.01)	(0.01)
$(\pi - \bar{\pi})_{t-1}$	2.48	2.49	2.60	3.16
	(0.00)	(0.00)	(0.03)	(0.03)
$(L/Y - \overline{L/Y})_t$	0.14	0.25	0.40	0.52
	(0.47)	(0.24)	(0.22)	(0.14)
$(L/Y - \overline{L/Y})_{t-1}$	−0.20	−0.29	−0.26	−0.30
	(0.29)	(0.16)	(0.37)	(0.35)
$D^*(p - \bar{p})_{t-1}$	0.35	0.38	0.43	0.31
	(0.00)	(0.00)	(0.00)	(0.01)
$D^*(r^s - r^{Taylor})_t$	0.61	0.92	0.80	1.31
	(0.44)	(0.27)	(0.46)	(0.28)
$D^*(r^s - r^{Taylor})_{t-1}$	−1.45	−1.74	−1.49	−1.54
	(0.06)	(0.03)	(0.17)	(0.19)
$D^*(\pi - \bar{\pi})_t$	−0.36	−0.10	0.05	1.01
	(0.77)	(0.94)	(0.98)	(0.62)
$D^*(\pi - \bar{\pi})_{t-1}$	−2.19	−2.49	−3.04	−4.72
	(0.11)	(0.08)	(0.13)	(0.04)
$D^*(L/Y - \overline{L/Y})_t$	0.65	0.44	0.39	0.12
	(0.03)	(0.16)	(0.38)	(0.79)
$D^*(L/Y - \overline{L/Y})_{t-1}$	−0.30	−0.13	−0.30	−0.11
	(0.30)	(0.67)	(0.48)	(0.81)
GDP growth		0.01	0.01	0.01
		(0.01)	(0.06)	(0.06)
Current account			0.02	0.01
			(0.04)	(0.08)
Change in financial innovation				0.00
				(0.89)
R^2	0.38	0.38	0.39	0.39
$\bar{R}^2$	0.35	0.35	0.34	0.33

SOURCE: Authors' calculations.

[a] Fixed effects included in regression but not reported. Numbers in parentheses are p-values.

TABLE 10.5B Panel Regression Results for Real Stock Prices (Money Growth Rate Rule)[a]

Regressors	Dependent Variable: Deviation of log Real House Prices from long-run trend (HP trend)			
	(1)	*(2)*	*(3)*	*(4)*
$(p - \bar{p})_{t-1}$	0.36	0.32	0.25	0.30
	(0.00)	(0.00)	(0.00)	(0.00)
$(\Delta \log(m) - 0.03)_t$	0.28	0.42	0.46	0.20
	(0.06)	(0.05)	(0.16)	(0.58)
$(\Delta \log(m) - 0.03)_{t-1}$	−0.34	−0.66	−1.01	−0.75
	(0.02)	(0.00)	(0.00)	(0.03)
$(\pi - \bar{\pi})_t$	−0.66	−0.43	−1.21	−1.78
	(0.06)	(0.25)	(0.09)	(0.07)
$(\pi - \bar{\pi})_{t-1}$	−0.73	−0.60	−0.40	0.22
	(0.04)	(0.11)	(0.58)	(0.82)
$(L/Y - \overline{L/Y})_t$	0.30	0.48	0.59	0.61
	(0.06)	(0.01)	(0.06)	(0.08)
$(L/Y - \overline{L/Y})_{t-1}$	−0.23	−0.39	−0.32	−0.33
	(0.16)	(0.03)	(0.27)	(0.31)
$D^*(p - \bar{p})_{t-1}$	0.32	0.35	0.42	0.29
	(0.00)	(0.00)	(0.00)	(0.01)
$D^*(\Delta \log(m) - 0.03)_t$	1.07	1.02	0.22	0.27
	(0.00)	(0.00)	(0.66)	(0.64)
$D^*(\Delta \log(m) - 0.03)_{t-1}$	−0.38	−0.32	0.22	−0.14
	(0.17)	(0.35)	(0.67)	(0.80)
$D^*(\pi - \bar{\pi})_t$	−0.58	−0.80	−0.29	0.14
	(0.29)	(0.18)	(0.81)	(0.92)
$D^*(\pi - \bar{\pi})_{t-1}$	−0.17	0.14	−1.01	−2.80
	(0.75)	(0.80)	(0.41)	(0.06)
$D^*(L/Y - \overline{L/Y})_t$	0.23	−0.01	0.09	−0.05
	(0.36)	(0.96)	(0.83)	(0.92)
$D^*(L/Y - \overline{L/Y})_{t-1}$	0.00	0.25	−0.07	0.08
	(1.00)	(0.35)	(0.87)	(0.86)
GDP growth		0.01	0.01	0.01
		(0.00)	(0.03)	(0.04)
Current account			0.02	0.02
			(0.03)	(0.06)
Change in financial innovation				0.00
				(0.74)
R^2	0.37	0.39	0.39	0.39
$\bar{R}^2$	0.35	0.36	0.35	0.33

SOURCE: Authors' calculations.
[a] Fixed effects included in regression but not reported. Numbers in parentheses are *p*-values.

For the inflation variable, there is some evidence of an extra kick during the booms. The impact is quite large—to the order of +2.5% in the case of regression (2)—but the significance is marginal. As for the credit variable—except for regression (1), where the coefficient is significant and positive for the interaction term—there is little evidence that "easy" credit has any impact on stock price booms.

Overall, there is, again, evidence that "loose" monetary policy and low inflation acts to boost stock prices and that this boost was heightened during the identified boom periods.

Next we re-estimate our model using the other measure of monetary policy; namely, the deviation of the growth rate of M2 from the Friedman 3% rule. The results are reported in Table 10.5B. The results are qualitatively similar to the ones reported in Table 10.5A. The monetary variable has inconsistent signs during "normal" periods, but it is large and, in this case, positive during the boom periods. This, again, suggests a relationship between "loose" monetary policy and increases in stock prices, especially during boom periods.

Interestingly, just as in the house price regressions, the impact of low inflation is only significant during the "normal" periods and there is no added "boost" during the boom periods. What is different however is that credit is not significant and positive. As in the case with the inflation variable, this positive impact on prices from "easy" credit—a value of the loans to GDP ratio that is above trend—is only evident during the "normal" periods. Again, there is no heightened effect during the booms.

This is an interesting result and one conjecture could be that the results, when we use the money growth variable, are being driven by the early periods where it is more likely that there is a strong relationship between credit conditions and the growth rate of money (Schularick and Taylor, 2012). It may be that the low inflation and credit story is more relevant during the latter part of twentieth century than in the early part.

4.3. Real Commodity Prices

Tables 10.6A and 10.6B report our estimated results for real commodity prices. Because of the global nature of the commodity price market, in lieu

TABLE 10.6A   Panel Regression Results for Real Commodity Prices (Taylor Rule)[a]

Regressors	Dependent Variable: Deviation of log Real Commodity Prices from long-run trend (HP trend)			
	(1)	(2)	(3)	(4)
$(p - \bar{p})_{t-1}$	0.71***	0.66***	0.38***	0.35***
	(0.00)	(0.00)	(0.27)	(0.53)
$(r^s - r^{Taylor})_t$	5.40**	7.78***	6.15	7.01
	(0.02)	(0.00)	(0.35)	(0.64)
$(r^s - r^{Taylor})_{t-1}$	−6.36*	−7.94**	−5.49	−5.74
	(0.07)	(0.02)	(0.51)	(0.62)
$(r^s - r^{Taylor})_{t-2}$	2.30	1.64	−0.08	−0.46
	(0.28)	(0.42)	(0.99)	(0.96)
$(\pi - \bar{\pi})_t$	4.62**	6.32**	10.02*	10.66
	(0.07)	(0.01)	(0.09)	(0.45)
$(\pi - \bar{\pi})_{t-1}$	−7.68**	−7.21**	−6.25	−6.10
	(0.02)	(0.02)	(0.52)	(0.67)
$(\pi - \bar{\pi})_{t-2}$	2.07	0.26	−1.03	−2.14
	(0.52)	(0.93)	(0.89)	(0.90)
$(L/Y - \overline{L/Y})_t$	−0.72	−1.11	−0.62	−1.33
	(0.47)	(0.24)	(0.75)	(0.78)
$(L/Y - \overline{L/Y})_{t-1}$	0.88	0.86	1.46	1.64
	(0.35)	(0.32)	(0.44)	(0.67)
$(L/Y - \overline{L/Y})_{t-2}$	−0.73	−0.14	−2.57	−2.27
	(0.49)	(0.89)	(0.27)	(0.46)
$D^*(p - \bar{p})_{t-1}$	−0.22	−0.28	−0.44	−0.53
	(0.42)	(0.28)	(0.31)	(0.52)
$D^*(r^s - r^{Taylor})_t$	−5.64*	−7.05**	−7.19	−10.12
	(0.10)	(0.03)	(0.37)	(0.55)
$D^*(r^s - r^{Taylor})_{t-1}$	6.95	7.80	16.52	22.90
	(0.16)	(0.09)	(0.14)	(0.26)
$D^*(r^s - r^{Taylor})_{t-2}$	−4.31	−3.30	−12.08	−16.41
	(0.15)	(0.25)	(0.11)	(0.43)
$D^*(\pi - \bar{\pi})_t$	−3.21	−2.52	−10.08	−14.06
	(0.43)	(0.51)	(0.14)	(0.34)
$D^*(\pi - \bar{\pi})_{t-1}$	6.50	5.70	16.67	24.70
	(0.32)	(0.35)	(0.20)	(0.30)
$D^*(\pi - \bar{\pi})_{t-2}$	−4.53	−2.28	−15.81	−20.25
	(0.38)	(0.64)	(0.14)	(0.52)
$D^*(L/Y - \overline{L/Y})_t$	1.40	2.13	2.99	4.57
	(0.33)	(0.13)	(0.30)	(0.48)

TABLE 10.6A   *(continued)*

	Dependent Variable: Deviation of log Real Commodity Prices from long-run trend (HP trend)			
Regressors	*(1)*	*(2)*	*(3)*	*(4)*
$D^*(L/Y - \overline{L/Y})_{t-1}$	−1.08	−1.51	−5.12	−6.44
	(0.54)	(0.36)	(0.15)	(0.27)
$D^*(L/Y - \overline{L/Y})_{t-2}$	0.49	0.22	5.46	5.67
	(0.73)	(0.87)	(0.07)	(0.17)
GDP growth		0.02**	0.03	0.03
		(0.02)	(0.22)	(0.53)
Current account			0.08	0.05
			(0.17)	(0.64)
Change in financial innovation				0.02
				(0.75)
R^2	0.70	0.74	0.84	0.81
$\bar{R}^2$	0.53	0.59	0.60	0.28

Source: Authors' calculations.
ª Numbers in parentheses are *p*-values.

of global monetary policy measures, we use U.S. data in these regressions. This means that we are unable to use a panel for this estimation; therefore, the number of observations available to us for these regressions is quite small.

For the interest rate deviation there are mixed results for the "normal" period in that the coefficient on the current period is significant and positive, while the coefficient on the first lag is negative and significant. Thus, during normal periods, the cumulative impact of a sustained decrease in the interest rate below the Taylor-rule rate would have a positive—but small—impact on commodity prices. However, during the boom periods, the impact of the interest rate deviation is significant and negative. Again, there appears to be a heightened impact on commodity prices of "loose" monetary policy during boom periods.

There is some evidence that low inflation also has a positive impact on commodity prices, but there is no "boost" during the boom periods, while

TABLE 10.6B Panel Regression Results for Real Commodity Prices
(Money growth rate rule)[a]

Regressors	Dependent Variable: Deviation of log Real House Prices from long-run trend (HP trend)			
	(1)	(2)	(3)	(4)
$(p - \bar{p})_{t-1}$	0.62***	0.66***	0.68**	1.07
	(0.00)	(0.00)	(0.03)	(0.17)
$(\Delta \log(m) - 0.03)_t$	−0.72	−0.64	−0.88	−0.71
	(0.45)	(0.50)	(0.54)	(0.76)
$(\Delta \log(m) - 0.03)_{t-1}$	−1.84	−2.22	−2.82	−5.90
	(0.22)	(0.14)	(0.23)	(0.24)
$(\Delta \log(m) - 0.03)_{t-2}$	0.31	0.80	1.33	4.29
	(0.76)	(0.46)	(0.39)	(0.44)
$(\pi - \bar{\pi})_t$	−0.36	0.38	6.15	11.13
	(0.89)	(0.88)	(0.22)	(0.36)
$(\pi - \bar{\pi})_{t-1}$	−2.35	−1.79	−0.11	−5.31
	(0.36)	(0.48)	(0.98)	(0.57)
$(\pi - \bar{\pi})_{t-2}$	0.90	1.02	2.50	4.76
	(0.56)	(0.50)	(0.37)	(0.34)
$(L/Y - \overline{L/Y})_t$	0.55	0.39	0.14	−1.48
	(0.54)	(0.66)	(0.92)	(0.64)
$(L/Y - \overline{L/Y})_{t-1}$	0.22	−0.07	1.24	2.49
	(0.76)	(0.92)	(0.34)	(0.38)
$(L/Y - \overline{L/Y})_{t-2}$	−0.54	−0.31	−4.13	−5.55
	(0.55)	(0.74)	(0.07)	(0.26)
$D^\star(p - \bar{p})_{t-1}$	−0.13	−0.23	−0.36	0.66
	(0.57)	(0.34)	(0.30)	(0.43)
$D^\star(\Delta \log(m) - 0.03)_t$	1.69	1.52	2.32	2.25
	(0.18)	(0.22)	(0.23)	(0.48)
$D^\star(\Delta \log(m) - 0.03)_{t-1}$	1.24	1.45	0.70	3.34
	(0.46)	(0.39)	(0.79)	(0.50)
$D^\star(\Delta \log(m) - 0.03)_{t-2}$	−0.10	−0.37	−0.86	−3.68
	(0.93)	(0.76)	(0.64)	(0.51)
$D^\star(\pi - \bar{\pi})_t$	3.96	3.61	−0.37	−6.05
	(0.17)	(0.20)	(0.95)	(0.62)
$D^\star(\pi - \bar{\pi})_{t-1}$	−0.27	−0.04	−2.74	2.34
	(0.92)	(0.99)	(0.64)	(0.81)
$D^\star(\pi - \bar{\pi})_{t-2}$	−0.21	−0.19	−1.45	−3.94
	(0.91)	(0.92)	(0.72)	(0.62)
$D^\star(L/Y - \overline{L/Y})_t$	0.50	0.81	1.76	3.46
	(0.67)	(0.49)	(0.41)	(0.49)

TABLE 10.6B   *(continued)*

Regressors	Dependent Variable: Deviation of log Real House Prices from long-run trend (HP trend)			
	(1)	*(2)*	*(3)*	*(4)*
$D*(L/Y - L/Y)_{t-1}$	−1.34	−1.06	−3.34	−5.32
	(0.31)	(0.42)	(0.18)	(0.19)
$D*(L/Y - \overline{L/Y})_{t-2}$	0.64	0.38	5.32**	7.35
	(0.59)	(0.74)	(0.05)	(0.16)
GDP growth		0.01	0.04**	0.03
		(0.12)	(0.05)	(0.38)
Current account			0.03	0.01
			(0.46)	(0.88)
Change in financial innovation				0.04
				(0.58)
R^2				
$\overline{R}^2$				

SOURCE: Authors' calculations.
    [a] Fixed effects included in regression but not reported. Numbers in parentheses are *p*-values.

there is no evidence that "easy" credit has a positive impact on commodity prices.

Table 10.6B reports the results for the regression when money growth rate deviations are used in place of interest rate deviations, but for this case, the results are poor. Almost all coefficients are insignificant, and except for the "credit" impact during booms, there is no difference between "normal" periods and "boom" periods.

4.4. Discussion

The results presented above show that "loose" monetary policy, that is, having an interest rate below the target rate or having a growth rate of money above the target growth rate positively impacts asset prices, and this correspondence is heightened during periods when asset prices grew quickly and then subsequently suffered a significant correction. This result was robust across multiple asset prices and different specifications and was present even when we controlled for other alternative explanations, such as low inflation or "easy" credit. The initial impacts are relatively small, especially when you consider that the run-up of asset prices in the boom periods are almost all greater than 5% per year, with some much higher than that.

It should also be noted that in alternative specifications not reported here, for reasons of brevity but available upon request, the result that "loose" monetary policy is associated with increases in asset prices was found in different sub-periods of the data and when the first difference of the variables was used instead of the deviations from trend. The size and significance of the estimates were very similar across all specifications.

We also found that low inflation and, to a lesser degree, "easy" credit are also associated with increases in asset prices. There does not appear to be one variable that is associated with increases in asset prices more than another. The monetary variable was consistently important during the boom periods; whereas, the other two controls were not always important. Again, the initial impacts were quite small relative to the sizes of the overall price increases during the booms.

Before moving to our policy lessons that we draw from this exercise, we must note the limitations of the empirical exercise we undertook. The regression model that we estimated is not a structural model, and so we cannot draw any conclusions about causality from these results. In fact, we try very hard to only say that we found associations between asset prices and the three control variables we use. The model, because of its atheoretical nature, does not have any explicit statement of the channel with which the three control variables impact asset prices. We do find evidence of nonlinear effects, but that is as far as we go. We also do not model the feedback of each of the three variables upon each other. This is obviously very important if we were to try to contrast the magnitudes of the effects these three controls had on asset prices during the identified boom periods. This last point is an important consideration and it is part of our ongoing and future research on this topic.

5. Policy Lessons

Our evidence that loose monetary policy (along with low inflation and credit expansion) does contribute significantly to booms in house prices, stock prices and commodity prices, leads to the question about what central banks should do about it. Should they use their policy tools to target housing prices, stock prices or commodity prices directly? Or, should they give important weight to asset prices when setting their policy instruments as a possible contingency to depart from their central goals (high employment) of low inflation? This subject received considerable attention during the tech boom of the late 1990s and again during the housing boom in the mid-2000s (Bordo and Wheelock, 2009). Since periods of explosive growth in asset prices have often preceded financial crises and contractions in economic activity, some economists have argued that by defusing asset price booms, monetary policy can limit the adverse impact of financial instability on economic activity.

However, the likelihood of a price collapse and subsequent macro-economic decline might depend on why asset prices are rising in the first place. Many analysts believe that asset booms do not pose a threat to economic activity or the outlook for inflation, as long as they can be justified by realistic prospects of future earnings growth, in the case of stock prices; or reflect real fundamentals such as population growth, in the case of housing booms; or real side shocks or changing conditions of supply, like natural disasters or demand (like the growth of China), in the case of commodity price booms.

On the other hand, if rising stock prices reflect "irrational exuberance," or rising house prices reflect a bubble, they may pose a threat to economic stability and justify a monetary policy response to encourage market participants to revalue equities more realistically or to deter speculation in real estate. In the case of commodity prices, to the extent a boom does not reflect fundamentals, policy tightening could defuse the real effects of a sudden bust.

The traditional view holds that monetary policy should react to asset price movements only to the extent that they provide information about future inflation. This view holds that monetary policy will contribute to financial stability by maintaining stability of the price level (Bordo et al., 2002, 2003; Schwartz, 1995), and that financial imbalances or crises should be dealt with separately by regulatory policies or lenders of last resort policies (Schwartz, 2002). Bernanke and Gertler (1999, 2001) presented the traditional view in the context of a Taylor rule.

Many economists do not accept the traditional view, at least not entirely. Smets (1997), for example, argued that monetary policy tightening is optimal in response to "irrational exuberance" in financial markets. Similarly, Cecchetti et al. (2000) contended that monetary policy should react when asset prices become misaligned with fundamentals. Bernanke and Gertler (2001) expressed doubts that policy makers can judge reliably whether asset prices are being driven by "irrational exuberance," or if an asset price collapse is imminent. However, Cecchetti (2003) replied that asset price misalignments are no more difficult to identify than other components of the Taylor rule, such as potential output.[15]

Bordo and Jeanne (2002a, 2002b) offered a different argument in support of a monetary policy response to asset price booms. They argued that preemptive actions to defuse an asset price boom can be regarded as insurance against the high cost of lost output should a bust occur. They contended that policy makers should attempt to contain asset price misalignments when the risk of a bust (or the consequences of a bust) is large, or when the cost of defusing a boom is low in terms of foregone output. Bordo and Jeanne showed that a tension exists between these two conditions. As investors become more exuberant, the risks associated with a reversal in market sentiment increases; however, leaning into the wind of investor optimism requires more costly monetary actions. Thus, the monetary authorities must evaluate both the probability of a costly crisis and the extent to which they can reduce this probability.

Since this earlier debate, where the warnings of Bordo and Jeanne and others were not largely heeded, the housing bust of 2006 in the U.S. and the subsequent financial crisis and Great Recession led many policy makers to decide that financial stability should be an important goal of central banks along with low inflation (and overall macro stability). The new view argued that central banks should be closely monitoring asset price developments and the state of the financial system (including non-banks and banks) and be willing to use policy to defuse threatening imbalances. This became known as the case for macro prudential regulation, which promoted the use of policy tools such as countercyclical capital requirements and liquidity ratios (Kashyap, Rajan and Stein, 2008). This case, fostered by the BIS and many others, has led to important changes in the central banking and financial regulatory landscape, including the 2010 Dodd Frank Bill in the U.S., which has given the Federal Reserve greatly expanded powers over the financial system as a whole, and in the U.K. where the Bank of England has taken over some of the responsibilities of the Financial Stability Authority.

The question arises if the new financial stability powers of central banks will work to prevent the next crisis, also whether or not the new impetus has gone too far in encroaching on the traditional role of central banks to maintain price stability, acting as lenders of last resort to the banking system and protectors of the integrity of the payments system. The history of financial regulation after big financial crises (e.g., the Great Depression) suggests that the government often overreacts and, in the name of safety, suppresses financial development and the price discovery mechanism of financial markets. The regime of the 1930s through the 1970s gave us financial stability at the expense of unworkable firewalls between complementary financial functions (Glass-Steagall) and price controls and ceilings like regulation Q in the U.S. and the prohibition of the payment of interest on demand deposits. Similar regulations were put in place across the world. These regulations and controls broke down in the face of the Great Inflation, financial market arbitrage, and financial innovation. In addition, in this immediate post-World War II period, central banks lost their independence to the fiscal authorities that had other politically driven objectives in mind. It would not be surprising if that happened again.

More fundamentally, many of the recent institutional changes pose threats to the independence of central banks and their ability to perform their core mission, which is to maintain the value of money (Bordo, 2010; Svennson, 2010). Central banks were also supposed to act as lenders of last resort to provide emergency liquidity to the banking system. They were not responsible for the solvency of banks or any other entities, or the financing of government deficits (except in wartime) (Bordo, 2012).

The bottom line is that asset price booms (stock market and housing market) are important and potentially dangerous to the real economy and should be closely monitored and possibly defused. However, the policy tools to do this should not be the traditional tools of monetary policy. Other tools, such as margin requirements for stock prices, minimum down payments for housing, and risk and bank-size weighted capital requirements for banks could be used. Authorities other than central banks could perform these tasks to prevent central banks from being diverted from their main functions.

To the extent that asset price booms—including commodity price booms—do not reflect real fundamentals, they should also be viewed as harbingers of future inflation, and as part of the normal transmission mechanism of monetary policy as has occurred in earlier historical episodes. In this case, they serve as a signal for tighter monetary policy.

Finally, our evidence—for the close to a century, for many countries, and for three types of asset booms—that expansionary monetary policy is a significant trigger, makes the case that central banks should follow stable monetary policies. These should be based on well understood and credible monetary rules.

Appendix A

Identified Boom/Busts

FIGURE 10.A1   Identified Housing Price Booms

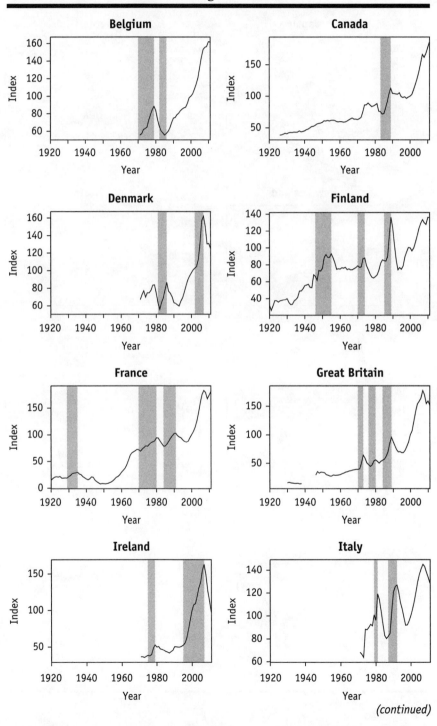

(continued)

FIGURE 10.A1   (continued)

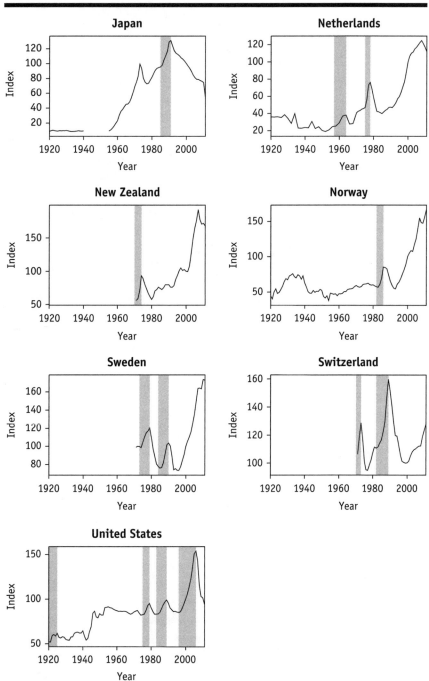

SOURCE: Authors' elaboration.

FIGURE 10.A2   Identified Stock Price Booms

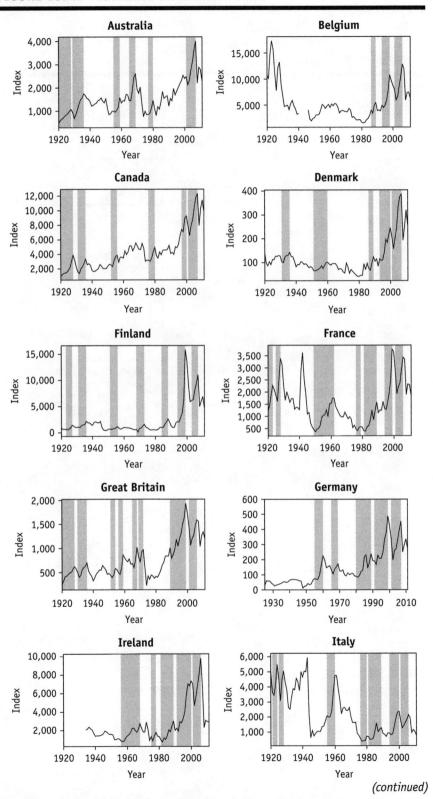

(continued)

FIGURE 10.A2 (continued)

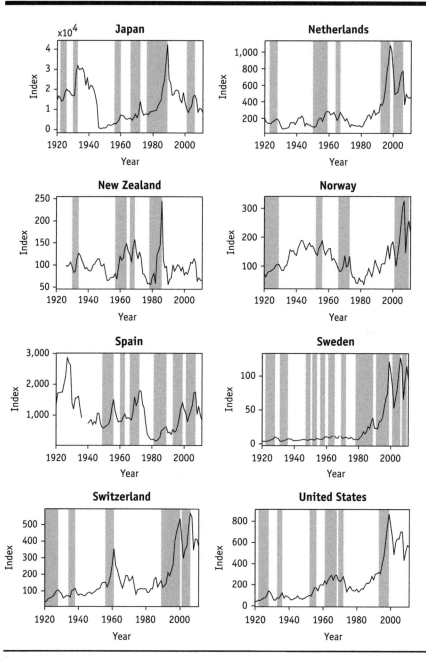

Source: Authors' elaboration.

FIGURE 10.A3   Identified Commodity Price Booms

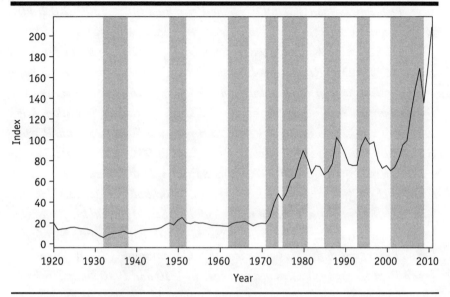

SOURCE: Authors' elaboration.

Appendix B

Data Sources

Real GDP:

See Michael D. Bordo and Christopher M. Meissner, "Does Inequality Lead to a Financial Crisis?" NBER Working Paper No. 17896.

Real house price index, 2000 = 100:

Detailed description: U.S. [*Robert J. Shiller, Irrational Exuberance, 2nd. Edition, Princeton University Press, 2005, 2009, Broadway Books 2006, also Subprime Solution, 2008, as updated by author*], Norway [*Norges Bank; Eitrheim, Ø. og Erlandsen, S. "Monetary aggregates in Norway 1819–2003," 349–376 Chapter 9 in Eitrheim, Ø., J.T. Klovland and J.F. Qvigstad (eds.), Historical Monetary Statistics for Norway 1819–2003, Norges Bank Occasional Papers No. 35, Oslo, 2004*], U.K. [*Department for Communities and Local*

Government, Housing statistics], France [*conseil général de l'Environnement et du Développement (CGEDD), Home Prices in France, 1200–2012: Historical French Property Price Trends, home price index of Paris*], Netherlands [*Piet M.A. Eichholtz, 1997, "The long run house price index: The Herengracht index, 1628–1973," Real Estate Economics, (25), 175–192, this index is based on the transactions of the buildings on the Herengracht, one of the canals in Amsterdam; for recent data the source is OECD*], Australia [*Stapledon, Nigel David, "Long-term housing prices in Australia and Some Economic Perspectives," The University of New South Wales, Sept. 2007; Australian median city house prices*], Spain [*before 1970 source: Prados de la Escosura; after 1970 source: OECD*]; Finland [*Hjerppe, Riitta, Finland's Historical National Accounts 1860–1994: Calculation Methods and Statistical Tables, Jyvaskylan Yliopisto Historian Laitos Suomen Historian Julkaisuja, 24, pp. 158–160; and OECD for recent data*], Canada [*Statistics Canada and OECD*], Japan [*The Japan Real Estate Institute, for data between 1910 and 1940 Nanjo, Takashi, "Developments in Land Prices and Bank Lending in Interwar Japan: Effects of the Real Estate Finance Problem on the Banking Industry," IMES Discussion Paper Series, 2002-E-10, Bank of Japan, 2002*]. For the cases of Denmark, Germany, Ireland, Italy, Sweden, Belgium, Switzerland and New Zealand, the OECD house price index was used.

Short-term interest rate:

See Michael D. Bordo, Christopher M. Meissner "Does Inequality Lead to a Financial Crisis?" NBER Working Paper No. 17896

Money:

M2 or M3—depending on the country. Source: Moritz Schularick and Alan M. Taylor. "Credit Booms Gone Bust: Monetary Policy, Leverage Cycles, and Financial Crises, 1870–2008" *American Economic Review* 2012, 102(2): 1029–1061

Stock market index (close, end of December):

The source is Global Financial Data.com.

Real commodity prices:

The Economist All-Commodity Dollar Index (close, end of December). The source is Global Financial Data.com.

Financial liberalization index, 0 to 21:

Sum of seven components [creditcontrols, intratecontrols, entry-barriers, bankingsuperv, privatization, intlcapital, securitymarkets]. Abdul Abiad, Enrica Detragiache, and Thierry Tressel "A New Database of Financial Reforms" IMF WP/08/275.

Credit:

Loans to GDP ratio.   Total lending, or bank loans, is defined as the end-of-year amount of outstanding domestic currency lending by domestic banks to domestic households and nonfinancial corporations (excluding lending within the financial system). Banks are defined broadly as monetary financial institutions and include: savings banks, postal banks, credit unions, mortgage associations, and building societies, whenever the data are available. We excluded brokerage houses, finance companies, insurance firms, and other financial institutions. See Michael D. Bordo, Christopher M. Meissner "Does Inequality Lead to a Financial Crisis?" NBER Working Paper No. 17896.

Current account:

Current account to GDP ratio.   See Michael D. Bordo, Christopher M. Meissner "Does Inequality Lead to a Financial Crisis?" NBER Working Paper No. 17896.

Notes

1. Related approaches emphasize financial liberalization and innovation accommodated by loose monetary policy as conducive to creating booms.

2. The possibility that monetary policy can produce asset price bubbles has also been studied extensively in rational expectations equilibrium models. In such models, poorly designed monetary policies, such as the use of interest rate rules without commitment to a steady long-run inflation rate, can lead to self-fulfilling prophecies and asset price bubbles. Such outcomes are less likely, argues Woodford (2003), if

monetary policy makers follow a clear rule in which the interest rate target is adjusted sufficiently to stabilize inflation. Thus, the theoretical literature suggests that consideration of the monetary policy environment may be crucial to understanding why asset booms come about.

3. See Laidler (2003).

4. A related issue to the impact of expansionary monetary policy on asset prices is whether or not the price index targeted by the central bank should include asset prices. Alchian and Klein (1973) contend that a theoretically correct measure of inflation is the change in the price of a given level of utility, which includes the present value of future consumption. An accurate estimate of inflation, they argue, requires a broader price index than one consisting only of the prices of current consumption goods and services. To capture the price of future consumption, Alchian and Klein (1973) contend that monetary authorities should target a price index that includes asset prices. Bryan et al. (2002) concur, arguing that because it omits asset prices (especially housing prices), the CPI seriously understated inflation during the 1990s.

5. For evidence that low inflation contributed to the housing booms of the 1990s and 2000s, see Frappa and Mesonnier (2010).

6. For definitions of the data that we use, see the data appendix.

7. The countries in our sample are Australia, Belgium, Canada, Denmark, Finland, France, Germany, Great Britain, Ireland, Italy, Japan, Netherlands, New Zealand, Norway, Spain, Sweden, Switzerland and the U.S. Countries are included in our regressions if data are available. When the number of countries reported for a regression is less than 18, it is because data for a country is missing.

8. As we collect more data, in particular data on policy rates, we will check the sensitivity of our results to this rough measure of the optimal policy rate.

9. The trend growth rate of real output would roughly hold for the U.S. 1920–2010 but may be too high for some countries like the U.K., and too low for others.

10. Over the 1920–2010 period, the trend growth rate of velocity was close to zero, averaging a decline to the 1960s and an increase since Bordo and Jonung (1987).

11. See the Data Appendix for a description of the sources for the data used in this analysis.

12. In order to make the current account variable stationary, we use deviations from its long-run (HP) trend. Thus, if the deviation is negative, the current account has worsened relative to its recent past; and if the value of this gap is positive, the current account has improved relative to its recent past. A positive value does not necessarily mean the current account is in surplus, and a negative value does not necessarily mean the current account is in deficit.

13. Note that all variables are in decimals, so that a 1 percentage point change is equivalent to a change of 0.01. Also note that the presence of a lagged dependent variable means that the long-run cumulative impact of this change can be higher than

the initial impacts, but for the purposes of this discussion we will discuss only the initial impacts.

14. Data for the financial liberalization variable are only available from 1970 onwards; so this regression only includes data after 1970.

15. For the debate within the FOMC over the 1990s stock market boom, see Bordo and Wheelock (2004).

References

Ahrend, R., B. Cournede, and R. Price. 2008. "Monetary Policy, Market Excesses and Financial Turmoil." Working Paper 597, OECD Economics Department.

Alchian, A. and B. Klein. 1973. "On a Correct Measure of Inflation." *Journal of Money, Credit and Banking* 5(1): 173–91.

Barsky, R. and L. Killian. 2001. "Do We Really Know that Oil Caused the Great Stagflation? A Monetary Alternative." In *NBER Macroeconomics Annual 2001* 16: 137–198.

Bernanke, B. and M. Gertler. 1999. "Monetary Policy and Asset Volatility." *Economic Review, Federal Reserve Bank of Kansas City* 84(4): 17–52.

———. 2001. "Should Central Banks Respond to Movements in Asset Prices?" *American Economic Review* 91(2): 253–57

Blinder, A. and J. Rudd. 2008. "The Supply Shock Explanation of the Great Stagflation Revisited." Working Paper 14568, National Bureau of Economic Research.

Bordo, M. 1980. "The Effects of Monetary Change on Relative Commodity Prices and the Role of Long-term Contracts." *Journal of Political Economy* 88(6): 1088–109.

———. 1998. "Commentary on Larry Neal, 'The Financial Crisis of 1825 and the Reconstruction of the British Financial System.'" *Federal Reserve Bank of St. Louis Review* May /June.

———. 2003. "Stock Market Crashes, Productivity Boom/Busts and Recessions: some Historical Evidence." *IMF World Economic Outlook,* Chapter III, April.

———. 2010. "Long Term Perspectives on Central Banking." *Norges Bank Symposium,* What is a Useful Central Bank? November.

———. 2012. "Under What Circumstances Can Inflation Be a Solution to Excessive National Debt?: Some Lessons from History." *Conference on Paper Money— State financing—Inflation.* Deutsche Bundesbank, November.

Bordo, M. and E. Benmelech. 2008. "The Crisis of 1873 and the Failure of Corporate Governance." NBER DAE Summer Institute.

Bordo, M., M. Dueker, and D. Wheelock. 2002. "Aggregate Price Shocks and Financial Stability: A Historical Analysis." *Economic Inquiry* 40(4): 521–38.

———. 2003. "Aggregate Price Shocks and Financial Stability: The United Kingdom 1796–1999." *Explorations in Economic History April,* 40 (4): 143–169.

Bordo, M. and O. Jeanne. 2002a. "Boom Bust in Asset Prices, Economic Instability, and Monetary Policy." Working Paper 8996, National Bureau of Economic Research.

——. 2002b. "Monetary Policy and Asset Prices: Does 'Benign Neglect' Make Sense?" *International Finance* 5(2): 139–64.

Bordo, M. and L. Jonung. 1987. *The Long-run Behavior of the Velocity of Circulation: The International Evidence.* New York, NY: Cambridge University Press.

Bordo, M. and D. Wheelock. 2004. "Monetary Policy and Asset Prices: A Look Back at Past U.S. Stock Market Booms." Working Capital 10704, National Bureau of Economic Research.

——. 2009. "When Do Stock Market Booms Occur? The Macroeconomic and Policy of Twentieth Century Booms." In Atack, J. and L. Neal (eds) *The Origins and Development of Financial Markets and Institutions.* Cambridge University Press

Borio, C. 2012. "The Financial Cycle and Macroeconomics: What have We Learnt?" Working Paper 395, Bank for International Settlements.

Borio, C. and P. Lowe. 2002. "Asset Prices, Financial and Monetary Stability: Exploring the Nexus." Working Paper 114, Bank for International Settlements.

Borio, C. and W. White. 2004. "Whither Monetary and Financial Stability? The Implications of Evolving Policy Regimes." Working Paper 147, Bank for International Settlements.

Browne, F. and D. Cronin. 2007. "Commodity Prices and Inflation." Working Paper 738, European Central Bank.

Brunner, K. and A. Meltzer. 1973. "Mr. Hicks and the 'Monetarists.'" *Economica* 40(157): 44–59.

Bry, G. and C. Boschan. 1971. *Cyclical Analysis of Time Series: Selected Procedures and Computer Programs.* New York, NY: National Bureau of Economic Research.

Bryan, M., S.G. Cecchetti, and R. O'Sullivan. 2002. "Asset Prices in the Measurement of Inflation." Working Paper 8700, National Bureau of Economic Research.

Cecchetti, S.G. 2003. "What the FOMC Says and Does When the Stock Market Booms." Conference on Asset Prices and Monetary Policy. Reserve Bank of Australia, Sydney, August.

Cecchetti, S.G., H. Genberg, J. Lipsky, and S. Wadhwami. 2000. "Asset Prices and Central Bank Policy." Geneva Reports on the World Economy 2, International Center for Banking Studies and Centre for Economic Policy Research.

Christiano, L., C. Ilut, R. Motto, and M. Rostagno. 2010. "Monetary Policy and Stock Market Booms." In Macroeconomic Challenges: The Decade Ahead. A Symposium Sponsored by the Federal Reserve Bank of Kansas City. Jackson Hole, Wyoming.

Ciccarelli, M. and B. Mojon. 2010. "Global Inflation." *Review of Economics and Statistics* 92(3): 524–35.

Cogley, T. and J. Nason. 1995. "Effects of the Hodrick-Prescott Filter on Trend and Difference Stationary Time Series: Implications for Business Cycle Research." *Journal of Economic Dynamics and Control* 19(1–2): 253–78.

Congdon, T. 2005. *Money and Asset Prices in Boom and Bust.* Institute of Economic Affairs, London.

Dornbusch, R. and J. Frenkel. 1984. "The Gold Standard and the Bank of England in the Crisis of 1847." In *A Retrospective on the Classical Gold Standard 1821–1931,* edited by M. Bordo and A. Schwartz. Chicago, Ill.: University of Chicago Press for the NBER.

Eichengreen, B. and K. Mitchener. 2004. "The Great Depression as a Credit Boom Gone Wrong." *Research in Economic History* 22: 183–237.

Frankel, J. 2008. "The Effect of Monetary Policy on Real Commodity Prices." *Asset Prices and Monetary Policy,* edited by J. Campbell. Chicago, Ill:. University of Chicago Press.

Frappa, S. and J.S. Mesonnier. 2010. "The Housing Boom of the Late 1990s: Did Inflation Targeting Matter?" *Journal of Financial Stability* 6(4): 243–54.

Friedman, M. 1960. *A Program for Monetary Stability.* New York, NY: Fordham University Press.

Friedman, M. and A.J. Schwartz. 1963a. "Money and Business Cycles." *Review of Economics and Statistics* 45B: 32–64.

———. 1963b. *A Monetary History of the United States, 1867–1960.* Princeton, NJ: Princeton University Press.

Galbraith, J.K. 1955. *The Great Crash, 1929.* Boston, Mass.: Houghton Mifflin.

Gerlach, S. and K. Assenmacher-Wesche. 2008a. "Financial Structure and the Impact of Monetary Policy on Asset Prices." Working Paper 2008–16, Swiss National Bank.

———. 2008b. "Monetary Policy, Asset Prices and Macroeconomic Conditions: A Panel VAR Study." Working Paper 149, National Bank of Belgium.

Goetzmann, W., L. Li, and G. Rouwenhorst. 2005. "Long-term Global Market Correlations." *The Journal of Business* 78(1): 1–38.

Harding, D. and A. Pagan. 2002. "Dissecting the Cycle: A Methodological Investigation." *Journal of Monetary Economics* 49(2): 365–381.

Helbling, T. and M. Terrones. 2004. "Asset Price Booms and Busts - Stylized Facts from the Last Three Decades of the 20th Century." Working Paper, International Monetary Fund.

Hott, C. and T. Jokipii. 2012. "Housing Bubbles and Interest Rates." Working Paper 2012–07, Swiss National Bank.

Iwaisako, T. and T. Ito. 1995. "Explaining Asset Bubbles in Japan." Working Paper 5350, National Bureau of Economic Research.

Jonung, L., J. Kiander, and P. Vartia. 2009. *The Great Financial Crisis in Finland and Sweden.* Northampton, Mass.: Edward Elgar publishers.

Jorda, O., M. Schularick, and A. Taylor. 2012. "When Credit Bites Back: Leverage, Business Cycles and Crises." Working Paper 1224, Department of Economics, University of California, Davis.

Kashyap, A., R. Rajan, and J. Stein. 2008. "Rethinking Capital Regulations." Presented at the Federal Reserve Bank of Kansas City Symposium on Maintaining Stability in a Changing Financial System. Jackson Hole, Wyoming, U.S. 21–23 August.

Laidler, D. 2003. "The Price Level, Relative Prices, and Economic Stability: Aspects of the Interwar Debate." Presented at the BIS Conference on Monetary Stability, Financial Stability and the Business Cycle. Basel, Switzerland, 28–29 March.

McGrattan, E. and E. Prescott. 2003. "The 1929 Stock Market: Irving Fisher Was Right." *Federal Reserve Bank of Minneapolis Research Department Staff Report* 294, May.

Metzler, L. 1951. "Wealth, Saving and the Rate of Interest." *Journal of Political Economy* 59(2): 93–116.

Neal, L. 1998. "The Financial Crisis of 1825 and the Reconstruction of the British Financial System." *Federal Reserve Bank of St. Louis Review* May/June.

———. 2011. "I am Not Master of Events." *The Speculations of John Law and Lord Londonderry in the Mississippi and South Sea Bubbles*. New Haven. Yale University Press.

Okun, A. 1975. "Inflation: Its Mechanics and Welfare Costs." *Brookings Papers on Economic Activity* 2: 351–401.

Pagan, A. and K. Sossounov. 2003. "A Simple Framework for Analysing Bull and Bear Markets." *Journal of Applied Econometrics* 18(1):23–46.

Pagano, P., M. Lombardi, and A. Anzuini. 2010. "The Impact of Monetary Policy on Commodity prices." Working Paper 1232, European Central Bank.

Rappoport, P. and E. White. 1994. "Was the Crash of 1929 Expected?" *American Economic Review* 84(1): 271–81.

Rothbard, M. 1983. *America's Great Depression (fourth edition)*. New York, NY: Richardson and Snyder.

Schularick, M. and A. Taylor. 2012. "Credit Booms Gone Bust: Monetary Policy, Leverage Cycles and Financial Crises, 1870–2008." *American Economic Review* 102(2): 1029–61.

Schwartz, A.J. 1995. "Why Financial Stability Depends on Price Stability." *Economic Affairs* 15(4): 21–25.

———. 2002. "Asset Price Inflation and Monetary Policy." Working Paper 9321, National Bureau of Economic Research.

Steigum, E. 2009. "The Boom and Bust Cycle in Norway." In *The Great Financial Crisis in Finland and Sweden,* edited by L. Jonung, J. Kiander, and P. Vartia. Northhampton, Mass.: Edward Elgar publishers.

Smets, F. 1997. "Financial Asset Prices and Monetary Policy: Theory and Evidence." Working Paper 47, Bank for International Settlements.

Svennson, L.E.O. 2010. "Where Do Central Banks Go from Here?" *Norges Bank Symposium,* What is a Useful Central Bank? November.

Taylor, J.B. 1993. "Discretion versus Policy Rules in Practice." *Carnegie-Rochester Conference Series on Public Policy* 39: 195–214.

———. 1999. "A Historical Analysis of Monetary Policy Rules." In *Monetary Policy Rules,* edited by J.B. Taylor. Chicago, Ill.: University of Chicago Press for the NBER.

———. 2007. "Housing and Monetary Policy." In *Housing, Housing Finance and Monetary Policy.* Federal Reserve Bank of Kansas City.

———. 2009. *Getting Off Track.* Stanford, Ca.: Hoover Press.

Tobin, J. 1969. "A General Equilibrium Approach to Monetary Theory." *Journal of Money, Credit and Banking* 1(1): 15–29.

Velde, F. 2003. "Government Equity and Money: John Law's System in 1720." Working Paper 2003–31, Federal Reserve Bank of Chicago.

Warren, G.F. and F.A. Pearson. 1935. *Gold and Prices.* New York, NY: Wiley.

White, E. 2009. "Lessons from the Great American Real Estate Boom and Bust of the 1920s." Working Paper 15573, National Bureau of Economic Research.

Woodford, M. 2003. *Interest and Prices: Foundations of a Theory of Monetary Policy.* Princeton, NJ: Princeton University Press.

PART FOUR

MONETARY HISTORY

CHAPTER 11

The History of Monetary Policy

MICHAEL D. BORDO

TODAY MONETARY POLICY is the principal way in which governments influence the macroeconomy. To implement monetary policy the monetary authority uses its policy instruments (short-term interest rates or the monetary base) to achieve its desired goals of low inflation and real output close to potential. Monetary policy has evolved over the centuries, along with the development of the money economy.

The Origins

Debate swirls between historians, economists, anthropologists and numismatists over the origins of money. In the West it is commonly believed that coins first appeared in ancient Lydia in the eighth century BC. Some date the origins to ancient China.

Money evolved as a medium of exchange, a store of value and unit of account. According to one authority—Hicks (1969), following Menger (1892)—its rise was associated with the growth of commerce. Traders would hold stocks of another good, in addition to the goods they traded in, which was easily stored, widely recognized, and divisible, with precious

Originally published in "The History of Monetary Policy," in *New Palgrave Dictionary of Economics*, 2nd ed., ed. Steven N. Durlauf and Lawrence E. Blume (New York: Palgrave Macmillan, 2008), 205–15.

metals evolving as the best example. This good would serve as the unit of account and then as a medium of exchange. According to this story, money first emerged from market activity.

Governments became involved when the monarch realized that it was easier to pay his soldiers in terms of generalized purchasing power than with particular goods. This led to the origin of seigniorage or the government's prerogative in the coining of money. Seigniorage originally represented the fee that the royal mint collected from the public to convert their holdings of bullion into coin. Governments generally since ancient times had a monopoly over the issue of coins (either licensing their production or producing them themselves).

The earliest predecessors to monetary policy seem to be those of debasement, where the government would call in the coins, melt them down and mix them with cheaper metals. They would alter either the weight or the quality of the coins (fineness). An alternative method used was to alter the unit of account (see Redish, 2000; Sussman, 1993; Sargent and Velde, 2002). The practice of debasement was widespread in the later years of the Roman Empire (Schwartz, 1973), but reached its perfection in western Europe in the late Middle Ages. Sussman (1993) describes how the French monarchs of the 15th century, unable to collect more normal forms of taxes, used debasement as a form of inflation tax to finance the ongoing Hundred Years War with the English. Debasement was really a form of fiscal rather than monetary policy, but it set the stage for the later development of monetary policy using fiduciary money.

Fiduciary or paper money evolved from the operations of early commercial banks in Italy (Cipolla, 1967) to economize on the precious metals used in coins (although there is evidence that paper money was issued by imperial decree in China centuries earlier; see Chown, 1994). This development has its origins in the practice of goldsmiths who would issue warehouse receipts as evidence of their storing gold coins and bullion for their clients. Eventually these certificates circulated as media of exchange. Once the goldsmiths learned that not all the claims were redeemed at the same time, they were able to circulate claims of value greater than their specie reserves. Thus was borne fiduciary money (money not fully backed by specie) and fractional reserve banking. The goldsmiths and early commercial bankers learned by experience to hold a precautionary reserve sufficient to meet the demands for redemption in the normal course of business.

Governments began issuing paper money in Europe only in the eighteenth century. An early example was Sweden's note issue, initiated to finance its participation in the Seven Years War (Eagly, 1969). Fiat money reached its maturity during the American Revolutionary Wars when the Congress issued continentals to finance military expenditures. These were promissory notes to be convertible into specie; but the promise was not kept. They were issued in massive quantities. However, the rate of issue and the average inflation rate of 65 per cent per annum (Rockoff, 1984) were not far removed from the revenue-maximizing rate of issue by a monopoly fiat money issuing central bank of the twentieth century (Bailey, 1956). During the French Revolution the overissue of paper money, the *assignats*, which were based initially on the value of seized Church lands, led to hyperinflation (White, 1995).

An early predecessor of monetary policy was John Law's system. In 1719 Law persuaded the Regent of France to convert the French national debt into stock in his Compagnie des Indes. He then used the stock as backing for the issue of notes in his Banque Royale. Note issue could then support and finance the issue of further shares. Law then conducted a proto typical form of monetary policy in 1720 to save his system when he attempted both to peg the exchange rate of notes in terms of specie and provide a support price to stem the collapse in the price of shares (Bordo, 1987; Velde, 2007).

Central Banks

Monetary policy is conducted by the monetary authority. It is the issuer of national currency and the source of the monetary base. Usually we think of central banks as fulfilling these functions, but in many countries, until well into the twentieth century, in the absence of a central bank, these were performed by the Treasury or in some cases (Australia, Canada, New Zealand) by a large commercial bank entrusted with the government's tax revenues (Goodhart, 1989). The earliest central banks were established in the 17th century (the Swedish Riksbank founded in 1664, the Bank of England founded in 1694, the Banque de France founded in 1800, and the Netherlands Bank in 1814) to aid the fisc of the newly emerging nation states.

In the case of the Bank of England a group of private investors was granted a royal charter to set up a bank to purchase and help market government debt. The establishment of the bank helped ensure the creation of a deep and liquid government debt market which served as the base of growing financial system (Dickson, 1969; Rousseau and Sylla, 2003). The bank eventually evolved into a bankers' bank by taking deposits from other nascent commercial banks. Its large gold reserves and monopoly privilege eventually allowed it to become a lender of last resort, that is, to provide liquidity to its correspondents in the face of a banking panic—a scramble by the public for liquidity.

Monetary policy as we know it today began by the bank discounting the paper of other financial institutions, both government debt and commercial paper. The interest rate at which the bank would lend, based on this collateral, became known as bank rate (in other countries as the discount rate). By altering this rate the bank could influence credit conditions in the British economy. It could also influence credit conditions in the rest of the world by attracting or repelling short-term funds (Sayers, 1957).

A second wave of central banks was initiated at the end of the nineteenth century. This was not based explicitly on the fiscal revenue motive as had been the case with the first wave, but on following the rules of the gold standard and ironing out swings in interest rates induced by seasonal forces and by the business cycle. Included in this group are the Swiss National Bank founded in 1907 (Bordo and James, 2007) and the Federal Reserve founded in 1913 (Meltzer, 2003). Subsequent waves of new central banks followed in the interwar period as countries in the British Empire, the new states of central Europe and Latin America attempted to emulate the experiences of the advanced countries (Capie et al., 1994).

Central Bank Independence

Although the early central banks had public charters, they were privately owned and they had policy independence. A problem that plagued the Bank of England in its early years was that it placed primary weight on its commercial activities and on several occasions of financial distress was criticized for neglecting the public good. Walter Bagehot formulated the responsibility doctrine in 1873 according to which the bank was to place primary importance on its public role as lender of last resort (Bagehot, 1873).

From the First World War onwards central banks focused entirely on public objectives, and many fell under public control. Their objectives also changed from emphasis on maintaining specie convertibility towards shielding the domestic economy from external shocks and stabilizing real output and prices. This trend continued in the 1930s and after the Second World War. Moreover, the Great Depression led to a major reaction against central banks, which were accused of creating and exacerbating the depression. In virtually every country monetary policy was placed under the control of the Treasury and fiscal policy became dominant. In every country central banks followed a low interest peg to both stimulate the economy and aid the Treasury in marketing its debt.

Monetary policy was restored to the central banks in the 1950s (for example, in the United States, after the Treasury–Federal Reserve Accord of 1951), and there followed a brief period of price stability until the mid-1960s. This was followed by a significant run up in inflation worldwide. The inflation was broken in the early 1980s by concerted tight monetary policies in the United States, the United Kingdom and other countries and a new emphasis placed on the importance of low inflation based on credible monetary policies. Central banks in many countries were granted goal independence and were given a mandate to keep inflation low.

Classical Monetary Policy

The true origin of modern monetary policy occurred under the classical gold standard, which prevailed from 1880 to 1914. The gold standard evolved from the earlier bimetallic regime. Under the gold standard all countries would define their currencies in terms of a fixed weight of gold and then all fiduciary money would be convertible into gold. The key role of central banks was to maintain gold convertibility. Central banks were also supposed to use their discount rates to speed up the adjustment to external shocks to the balance of payments, that is, they were supposed to follow the 'rules of the game' (Keynes, 1930). In the case of a balance of payments deficit, gold would tend to flow abroad and reduce a central bank's gold reserves. According to the rules, the central bank would raise its discount rate. This would serve to depress aggregate demand and offset the deficit. At the same time the rise in rates would stimulate a capital inflow. The opposite set of policies was to be followed in the case of a surplus.

There is considerable debate on whether the rules were actually followed (Bordo and MacDonald, 2005). There is evidence that central banks sterilized gold flows and prevented the adjustment mechanism from working (Bloomfield, 1959). Others paid attention to the domestic objectives of price stability or stable interest rates or stabilizing output (Goodfriend, 1988). There is also evidence that because the major central banks were credibly committed to maintaining gold convertibility they had some policy independence to let their interest rates depart from interest rate parity and to pursue domestic objectives (Bordo and MacDonald, 2005).

After the First World War the gold standard was restored, but in the face of a changing political economy—the extension of suffrage and organized labour (Eichengreen, 1992)—greater emphasis was placed by central banks on the domestic objectives of price stability and stable output and employment than on external convertibility. Thus for example the newly created Federal Reserve sterilized gold flows and followed countercyclical policies to offset two recessions in the 1920s (Meltzer, 2003).

The depression beginning in 1929 was probably caused by inappropriate monetary policy. The Federal Reserve followed the flawed real bills doctrine, which exacerbated the downturn, and the gold sterilization policies followed by the Fed and the Banque de France greatly weakened the adjustment mechanism of the gold standard. As mentioned above, the central banks were blamed for the depression and monetary policy was downgraded until the mid-1950s.

The Goals of Monetary Policy

The goals of monetary policy have changed across monetary regimes. Until 1914, the dominant monetary regime was the gold standard. Since then the world has gradually shifted to a fiat money regime. Under the classical gold standard the key goal was gold convertibility with limited focus on the domestic economy. By the interwar period gold convertibility was being overshadowed by emphasis on domestic price level and output stability, and the regime shifted towards fiat money. This continued after the Second World War. Under the 1944 Bretton Woods Articles of Agreement, member countries were to maintain pegged exchange rates and central banks were to intervene in the foreign exchange market to do this, but the goal of domestic full employment was also given predominance. The Bretton Woods system evolved into a dollar gold exchange standard in which member currencies were convertible on a current account basis into dollars and the dollar was convertible into gold (Bordo, 1993). A continued conflict between the dictates of internal and external balance was a dominant theme from 1959 to 1971 as was the concern over global imbalance because the United States, as centre country of the system, would provide through its balance of payments deficits and its role as a financial intermediary more dollars than could be safely backed by its gold reserves (Triffin, 1960).

The collapse of Bretton Woods between 1971 and 1973 was brought about largely because the United States followed an inflationary policy to finance both the Vietnam War and expanded social welfare programmes like Medicare under President Johnson's Great Society, thus ending any connection of the monetary regime to gold and propelling the world to a pure fiat regime. In this new environment the balance was largely tipped in favour of domestic stability and was coupled with the now dominant belief by central bankers in the Phillips curve trade-off between unemployment and inflation (Phillips, 1958): this led to a focus on maintaining full employment at the expense of inflation.

The resulting 'great inflation' of the 1970s finally came to an end in the early 1980s by central banks following tight monetary policies. Since then the pendulum has again swung towards the goal of low inflation and the belief that central banks should eschew control of real variables (Friedman, 1968; Phelps, 1968).

The Instruments of Monetary Policy

The original policy instrument was the use of the discount rate and rediscounting. Open market operations (the buying and selling of government securities) was first developed in the 1870s and 1880s by the Bank of England in order to make bank rate effective, that is to force financial institutions to borrow (Sayers, 1957). Other countries with less developed money markets than those of Britain used credit rationing (France) and gold policy operations to alter the gold points and impede the normal flow of gold (Sayers, 1936).

In the interwar period the newly established Federal Reserve initially used the discount rate as its principal tool, but after heavy criticism for its use in rolling back the post-First World War inflation and thereby creating one of the worst recessions of the twentieth century in 1920-1 (Meltzer, 2003), the Fed shifted to open market policy, its principal tool ever since. In the 1930s it also began changing reserve requirements. Its policy of doubling reserve requirements in 1936 was later blamed as the cause for the recession of 1937-8 (Friedman and Schwartz, 1963). In the 1930s and 1940s, along with the downgrading of monetary policy, came an increased use of various types of controls and regulations such as margin requirements on stock purchases, selective credit controls on consumer durables and interest rate ceilings. Similar policies were adopted elsewhere. The return to traditional monetary policy in the 1950s restored open market operations to the position of predominance.

Intermediate Targets

Traditionally, central banks altered interest rates as the mechanism to influence aggregate spending, prices and output. In the 1950s, the monetarists revived the quantity theory of money and posited the case for using money supply as the intermediate target (Friedman, 1956; Brunner and Meltzer, 1993). The case for money was based on evidence of a stable relationship between the growth of money supply, on the one hand, and nominal income and the price level, on the other hand, and the evidence that, by focusing on interest rates, the Fed and other central banks aggravated the business cycle, and then—in part because of their inability to distinguish between real and nominal rates—generated the great inflation of the 1970s (Brunner and Meltzer, 1993).

By the 1970s most central banks had monetary aggregate targets. However, the rise in inflation in the 1970s (which was followed by disinflation) as well as continuous financial innovation (which was in turn exacerbated by inflation uncertainty) made the demand for money function less predictable (Laidler, 1980; Judd and Scadding, 1982). This meant that central banks had difficulty in meeting their money growth targets. In addition, the issue was raised as to which monetary aggregate to target (Goodhart, 1984). By the late 1980s most countries had abandoned monetary aggregates and returned to interest rates. But since the early 1990s monetary policy in many countries has been based on pursuing an inflation target (implicit or explicit) with the policy rate set to allow inflation to hit the target, a policy which seems to be successful.

Theories of Monetary Policy

The development of the practice of monetary policy described above was embedded in major advances in monetary theory that began in the first quarter of the nineteenth century. A major controversy in England, the Currency Banking School debate, has shaped subsequent thinking on monetary policy ever since. That debate evolved out of the Bullionist debate during the Napoleonic wars over whether inflation in Britain was caused by monetary or real forces (Viner, 1937). In a later debate, Currency School advocates emphasized the importance for the Bank of England to change its monetary liabilities in accordance with changes in its gold reserves—that is, according to the currency principle, which advocated a rule tying money supply to the balance of payments. The opposing Banking School emphasized the importance of disturbances in the domestic economy and the domestic financial system as the key variables the Bank of England should react to. They advocated that the bank directors should use their discretion rather than being constrained by a rigid rule. The controversy still rages.

Later in the nineteenth century, the two principles became embedded in central banking lore (Meltzer, 2003, ch. 2). The Federal Reserve and other central banks (including the Swiss National Bank) were founded on two pillars that evolved from this debate—the gold standard and the real bills doctrine.

The latter evolved from nineteenth century practice and the Banking School theory. The basic premise of real bills is that as long as commercial banks lend on the basis of self-liquidating short-term real bills they will be sound. Moreover, as long as central banks discount only eligible real bills the economy will always have the correct amount of money and credit. Adherence to real bills sometimes clashed with the first pillar, gold adherence, for example when the economy was expanding and real bills dictated ease while the balance of payments was deteriorating, which dictated tightening. This conflict erupted in the United States on a number of occasions in the 1920s (Friedman and Schwartz, 1963).

Adherence to the two pillars led to disaster in the 1930s. The Fed made a serious policy error by following real bills. A corollary of that theory urged the Fed to defuse the stock market boom because it was believed that speculation would lead to inflation, which would ultimately lead to deflation (Meltzer, 2003). According to Friedman and Schwartz, Meltzer and others, the Fed's tight policy triggered a recession in 1929 and its inability to stem the banking panics that followed in the early 1930s led to the Great Depression. The depression was spread globally by the fixed exchange rate gold standard. In addition, the gold standard served as 'golden fetters' for most countries because, lacking the credibility they had before 1914, they could not use monetary policy to allay banking panics or stimulate the economy lest it trigger a speculative attack (Eichengreen, 1992).

The Great Depression gave rise to the Keynesian view that monetary policy was impotent. This led to the dominance of fiscal policy over monetary policy for the next two decades. The return to traditional monetary policy in the 1950s was influenced by Keynesian monetary theory. According to this approach monetary policy should influence short-term rates and then by a substitution process across the financial portfolio would affect the real rate of return on capital. This money market approach dominated policy until the 1960s.

The monetarists criticized the Fed for failing to stabilize the business cycle, for still adhering to vestiges of real bills (for example, free reserves;

Calomiris and Wheelock, 1998), and for its belief in a stable Phillips curve—that unemployment could be permanently reduced at the expense of inflation. This, they argued, led to an acceleration of inflation as market agents' expectations adjusted to the higher inflation rate, which produced the great inflation of the 1970s. As mentioned above, the subsequent adoption of monetary aggregate targeting was short lived because of unpredictable shifts in velocity.

The approach to monetary policy followed since the early 1990s has learned the basic lesson from the monetarists of the primacy of price stability. It also learned about the distinction between nominal and real interest rates (Fisher, 1922). Moreover, it has adopted a principle from the earlier gold standard literature, Wicksell's (1898) distinction between the natural rate of interest and the bank rate (Woodford, 2003). In Wicksell's theory, central banks should gear their lending rate to the natural rate (the real rate of return on capital). If it keeps bank rate too low, inflation will ensue, which under the gold standard will lead to gold outflows and upward market pressure on the bank rate. Today's central banks, dedicated to low inflation, can be viewed as following the Taylor rule, according to which they set the nominal policy interest rate relative to the natural interest rate as a function of the deviation of inflation forecasts from their targets and real output from its potential (Taylor, 1999).

Rules versus Discretion

A key theme in the monetary policy debate is the issue of rules versus discretion. The question that followed the Currency Banking School debate was whether monetary policy should be entrusted to well-meaning authorities with limited knowledge or to a rule that cannot be designed to deal with unknown shocks (Simons, 1936; Friedman, 1960).

A more recent approach focuses on the role of time inconsistency. According to this approach a rule is a credible commitment mechanism that ties the hands of policy makers and prevents them from following time-inconsistent policies—policies that take past policy commitments as given and react to the present circumstances by changing policy (Kydland and Prescott, 1977; Barro and Gordon, 1983). In this vein, today's central bankers place great emphasis on accountability and transparency to support the credibility of their commitments to maintain interest rates geared towards low inflation (Svensson, 1999).

Conclusion

Monetary policy has evolved since the early nineteenth century. It played a relatively minor role before 1914, although it was then that many of its tools and principles were developed. The role of monetary policy in stabilizing prices and output came to fruition in the 1920s, but for the Federal Reserve, which used a flawed model—the real bills doctrine—and adhered to a less than credible gold standard, the policy was a recipe for disaster and led to the great contraction of 1929–33. When monetary policy was restored in the 1950s in the United States, it still was influenced by real bills (Calomiris and Wheelock, 1998), which may have led to the policy mistakes that created the great inflation. The rest of the world was tied to the United States by the pegged exchange rates of Bretton Woods. Since the early 1990s monetary policy in many countries has returned back to a key principle of the gold standard era—price stability based on a credible nominal anchor (Bordo and Schwartz, 1999) and to Wicksell's distinction between real and nominal interest rates. Yet it is based on a fiat regime and the commitment of central banks to follow credible and predictable policies.

Bibliography

Bagehot, W. 1873. *Lombard Street: A Description of the Money Market.* Reprint edn. London: John Murray, 1917.

Bailey, M.J. 1956. The welfare costs of inflationary finance. *Journal of Political Economy* 64, 93–110.

Barro, R.I. and Gordon, D.B. 1983. Rules, discretion and reputation in a model of monetary policy. *Journal of Monetary Economics* 12, 101–21.

Bloomfield, A.I. 1959. *Monetary Policy under the International Gold Standard.* New York: Federal Reserve Bank of New York.

Bordo, M.D. 1987. John Law. In *The New Palgrave: A Dictionary of Economic Theory and Doctrine*, ed. J. Eatwell and M. Milgate. London: Macmillan.

Bordo, M.D. 1993. The Bretton Woods international monetary system: a historical overview. In *A Retrospective on the Bretton Woods System: Lessons for International Monetary Reform*, ed. M.D. Bordo and B. Eichengreen. Chicago: University of Chicago Press.

Bordo, M.D. and James, H. 2007. The SNB 1907–1946: a happy childhood or a troubled adolescence? In Swiss National Bank. Centenary Conference volume, Zurich.

Bordo, M.D. and MacDonald, R. 2005. Interest rate interactions in the classical gold standard: 1880–1914: was there monetary independence? *Journal of Monetary Economics* 52, 307–27.

Bordo, M.D. and Schwartz, A.J. 1999. Monetary policy regimes and economic performance: the historical record. In *Handbook of Macroeconomics*, ed. J.B. Taylor and M. Woolford. New York: North-Holland.

Brunner, K. and Meltzer, A.H. 1993. *Money and the Economy: Issues in Monetary Analysis*. Cambridge: Cambridge University Press.

Calomiris, C.W. and Wheelock, D.C. 1998. Was the great depression a watershed for American monetary policy? In *The Defining Moment: The Great Depression and the American Economy in the Twentieth Century*, ed. M.D. Bordo, C. Goldin and E.N. White. Chicago: University of Chicago Press.

Capie, F., Goodhart, C., Fischer, S. and Schnadt, N. 1994. *The Future of Central Banking*. Cambridge: Cambridge University Press.

Chown, J.F. 1994. *The History of Money from AD 800*. London: Routledge.

Cipolla, C.M. 1967. *Money, Prices, and Civilization in the Mediterranean World, Fifth to Seventeenth Century*. New York: Gordian Press.

Dickson, P.M. 1969. *The Financial Revolution in England: A Study in the Development of Public Credit, 1688–1756*. London: Macmillan.

Eagly, R.U. 1969. Monetary policy and politics in mid-eighteenth century Sweden. *Journal of Economic History* 29, 739–57.

Eichengreen, B. 1992. *Golden Fetters*. New York: Oxford University Press.

Fisher, I. 1922. *The Purchasing Power of Money*. New York: Augustus M. Kelley, 1965.

Friedman, M. 1956. Quantity theory of money: a restatement. In *Studies in the Quality Theory of Money*, ed. M. Friedman. Chicago: University of Chicago Press.

Friedman, M. 1960. *A Program for Monetary Stability*. New York: Fordham University Press.

Friedman, M. 1968. The role of monetary policy. *American Economic Review* 58, 1–17.

Friedman, M. and Schwartz, A.J. 1963. *A Monetary History of the United States, 1867–1960*. Princeton: Princeton University Press.

Goodfriend, M. 1988. Central banking under the gold standard. *Carnegie Rochester Conference Series on Public Policy* 19, 85–124.

Goodhart, C.A.E. 1984. Chapter 3 problems of monetary management. In *Monetary Theory and Practice. The UK Experience*. London: Macmillan.

Goodhart, C. 1989. *The Evolution of Central Banks*. Cambridge, MA: MIT Press.

Hicks, J.R. 1969. *A Theory of Economic History*. Oxford: Clarendon Press.

Judd, J.P. and Scadding, J.L. 1982. The search for a stable money demand function: a survey of the post-1973 literature. *Journal of Economic Literature* 20, 993–1023.

Keynes, J.M. 1930. *A Treatise on Money*, vol. 2: *The Applied Theory of Money*. Repr. in *The Collected Writings of John Maynard Keynes*. 30 vols, ed. A. Robinson and D. Moggridge, vol. 6. London: Macmillan for the Royal Economic Society, 1971.

Kydland, F.E. and Prescott, E.C. 1977. Rules rather than discretion: the inconsistency of optimal plans. *Journal of Political Economy* 85, 473–92.

Laidler, D. 1980. The demand for money in the United States—yet again. In *The State of Macro-Economics, Carnegie-Rochester Conference Series on Public Policy*, vol. 12, ed. K. Brunner and A.H. Meltzer. New York: North-Holland.

Meltzer, A.H. 2003. *A History of the Federal Reserve*, vol. 1. Chicago: University of Chicago Press.

Menger, K. 1892. On the origins of money. *Economic Journal* 2, 238–58.

Phelps, E.S. 1968. Money-wage dynamics and labor market equilibrium. *Journal of Political Economy* 76, 678–711.

Phillips, A.W. 1958. The relation between unemployment and the rate of change of money wage rates in the United Kingdom 1861–1957. *Economica* 25, 283–99.

Redish, A. 2000. *Bimetallism: An Economic and Historical Analysis*. Cambridge: Cambridge University Press.

Ricardo, D. 1811. High price of bullion: a proof of the depreciation of bank notes. In *The Works and Correspondence of David Ricardo*, ed. P. Sraffa. Cambridge: Cambridge University Press.

Rockoff, H. 1984. *Drastic Measures: A History of Wage and Price Controls in the United States*. New York: Cambridge University Press.

Rousseau, P. and Sylla, R. 2003. Financial systems, economic growth and globalization. In *Globalization in Historical Perspective*, ed. M.D. Bordo, A. Taylor and J. Williamson. Chicago: University of Chicago Press.

Sargent, T. and Velde, F. 2002. *The Big Problem of Small Change*. Princeton: Princeton University Press.

Sayers, R.S. 1936. *Bank of England Operations, 1890–1914*. London: P.S. King & Son.

Sayers, R.S. 1957. *Central Banking after Bagehot*. Oxford: Oxford University Press.

Schwartz, A.J. 1973. Secular price change in historical perspective. *Journal of Money, Credit and Banking* 5, 243–69.

Simons, H.C. 1936. Rule versus authorities in monetary policy. *Journal of Political Economy* 44, 1–30.

Sussman, N. 1993. Debasement, royal reviews and inflation in France during the second stage of the Hundred Years War. *Journal of Economic History* 56, 789–808.

Svensson, L.E.O. 1999. Inflation targeting as a monetary policy rule. *Journal of Monetary Economics* 43, 607–54.

Taylor, J.B. 1999. A historical analysis of monetary policy rules. In *Monetary Policy Rule*, ed. J.B. Taylor. Chicago: University of Chicago Press.

Thornton, H. 1802. *An Inquiry into the National Effects of the Paper Credit of Great Britain.* Fairfield, NJ: Augustus M. Kelley, 1978.

Triffin, R. 1960. *Gold and the Dollar Crisis.* New Haven: Yale University Press.

Velde, F. 2007. *Government Equity and Money: John Laws System in 1720 France.* Princeton: Princeton University Press.

Viner, J. 1937. *Studies in the Theory of International Trade.* New York: Augustus M. Kelley, 1975.

White, E.N. 1995. The French Revolution and the politics of government finance, 1770–1815. *Journal of Economic History* 55, 227–55.

Wicksell, K. 1898. *Interest and Prices.* New York: Augustus M. Kelley, 1965.

Woodford, M. 2003. *Interest and Prices: Foundations of a Theory of Monetary Policy.* Princeton: Princeton University Press.

CHAPTER 12

The Banking Panics in the United States in the 1930s

Some Lessons for Today

MICHAEL D. BORDO AND JOHN LANDON-LANE

I. Introduction: The Friedman and Schwartz Hypothesis and the Subsequent Debate

IN THIS CHAPTER we raise and answer some questions about the recent financial crisis in light of the experience of the Great Depression of the 1930s. We ask what was similar and what was different between now and then, and examine the implications of the 1930s banking panics for policy towards recent banking crises.

The Great Depression was by far the greatest economic event of the twentieth century and comparisons to it were rife during the recent Great Recession. Milton Friedman and Anna Schwartz's *A Monetary History of the United States 1867 to 1960* (1963) has long been viewed as the classic treatment of the Great Depression in the United States.[1] They labelled the downturn in the United States from August 1929 to March 1933 the Great

Originally published in "The Banking Panics in the United States in the 1930s: Some Lessons for Today," *Oxford Review of Economic Policy* 26, no. 3 (2010): 486–509. © The Authors 2010. Published by Oxford University Press. For permissions please email: journals.permissions@ oxfordjournals.org.

Contraction. Since that event a voluminous literature has debated its causes in the United States and its transmission around the world.

Friedman and Schwartz (1963) challenged the prevailing Keynesian view and attributed the Great Contraction from 1929 to 1933 to a collapse of the money supply by one-third, brought about by a failure of Federal Reserve policy. The story they tell begins with the Fed tightening policy in early 1928 to stem the Wall Street boom. Fed officials believing in the real bills doctrine were concerned that the asset-price boom would lead to inflation. The subsequent downturn beginning in August 1929 was soon followed by the stock-market crash in October. Friedman and Schwartz, unlike Galbraith (1955), did not view the crash as the cause of the subsequent depression. They saw it as an exacerbating factor (whereby adverse expectations led the public to attempt to increase their liquidity) in the decline in activity in the first year of the Contraction.

The real problem arose with a series of four banking panics beginning in October 1930 and ending with Roosevelt's national banking holiday in March 1933. According to Friedman and Schwartz, the banking panics worked through the money multiplier to reduce the money stock (via a decrease in the public's deposit-to-currency ratio). The panic in turn reflected what Friedman and Schwartz called a 'contagion of fear' as the public, fearful of being last in line to convert their deposits into currency, staged runs on the banking system, leading to massive bank failures. In today's terms it would be a 'liquidity shock.' The collapse in money supply in turn led to a decline in spending and, in the face of nominal rigidities, especially of sticky money wages, a decline in employment and output. The process was aggravated by banks dumping their earning assets in a fire sale and by debt deflation. Both forces reduced the value of banks' collateral and weakened their balance sheets, in turn leading to weakening and insolvency of banks with initially sound assets.

According to Friedman and Schwartz, had the Fed acted as a proper lender of last resort, as it was established to be in the Federal Reserve Act of 1913, then it would have offset the effects of the banking panics on the money stock and prevented the Great Contraction. Since the publication of *A Monetary History*, a voluminous literature has arisen over the issues whether the banking panics were really panics in the sense of illiquidity shocks or whether they reflected endogenous insolvency responses to a recession caused by other forces, such as a collapse of autonomous expenditures or productivity shocks. If the panics really reflected insolvency rather than liquidity shocks, then the case Friedman and Schwartz made that expansionary monetary policy could have avoided the Great Contraction would be considerably weakened.

Ben Bernanke, the current Chairman of the Federal Reserve, also attributed the Great Contraction to monetary forces and especially the collapse of the banking system. However, he placed less emphasis on the effects via the quantity theory of money on spending as argued by Friedman and Schwartz, and more on the consequences of the collapse of the banking system in raising the cost of financial intermediation.

Thus the issue of whether illiquidity shocks triggering banking panics was at the heart of the Great Contraction is of crucial importance for the role of monetary policy in dealing with banking crises such as we recently witnessed. Indeed, in the crisis of 2007–8 the Bernanke Fed apparently learned the lesson from Friedman and Schwartz (Bernanke, 2002) by following expansionary monetary and credit policy and to a large extent prevented a repeat of the 1930s experience. Although there was not a classic Friedman and Schwartz banking panic in 2007–8, there was a panic in the shadow banking system and, unlike in the 1930s, many US banks deemed too big and too interconnected to fail were plagued with insolvency and were rescued by fiscal bail-outs.

In this chapter we revisit the debate over illiquidity versus insolvency in the Great Contraction. Section II discusses the recent debate and presents some econometric evidence that suggests that illiquidity shocks dominated in the banking panics in 1930 and 1931 while the last panic of 1933 was largely an insolvency event. In section III we examine why the US had so many bank failures and was so prone to banking failures in its history. Sections IV and V compare the financial crises of the 1930s in the US to the crisis of 2007–8. Section VI concludes with some lessons for policy.

II. The Recent Debate over US Banking Panics in the 1930s: Illiquidity versus Insolvency

In this section we survey recent literature on whether the clusters of bank failures that occurred between 1930 and 1933 were really panics in the sense of illiquidity shocks.[2] This has important implications for the causes of the Great Depression. If the clusters of bank failures were really panics, then it would support the original Friedman and Schwartz explanation. If the clusters of bank failures primarily reflected insolvency then other factors, such as a decline in autonomous expenditures or negative productivity shocks (Prescott, 1999), must explain the Great Contraction. We present some econometric evidence largely in support of the Friedman and Schwartz position.

Friedman and Schwartz viewed the banking panics as largely the consequence of illiquidity, especially in 1930–1. Their key evidence was a decline in the deposit–currency ratio, which lowered the money multiplier, money supply, and nominal spending. They describe the panic in the autumn of 1930 as leading to 'a contagion of fear' especially after the failure of the Bank of United States in New York City in December. They also discussed the effects of the initial banking panic leading to contagion by banks dumping their earning assets in a 'fire sale' in order to build up their reserves. This, in turn, led to the failure of otherwise solvent banks. Wicker (1996) disputes whether the 1930 panic and the spring 1931 Friedman and Schwartz panics were national in scope, but agrees with them that all four banking panics were liquidity shocks.

By contrast both Temin (1976) and White (1984), the latter using disaggregated data on a sample of national banks, argued that the original 1930 banking panic was not a liquidity event but a solvency event occurring in banks in agricultural regions in the South and the Midwest which had been weakened by the recession. These small unit banks came out of the 1920s in a fragile state, reflecting declining agricultural prices and oversupply after the First World War. As in Wicker (1980), they identify the locus of the crisis as the collapse, on 7 November 1930, of the Caldwell investment bank holding company of Nashville, Tennessee, a chain bank (in which one holding company had a controlling interest in a chain of banks), and its correspondent network across a half dozen states.

Calomiris and Mason (2003), following the approach taken in Calomiris and Mason (1997) to analyse a local banking panic in Chicago in June 1932, use disaggregated data on all of the individual member banks of the Federal Reserve System to directly address the question of whether the clusters of banking failures of 1930–3 reflected illiquidity or insolvency. Based on a survival-duration model on 8,700 individual banks, they relate the timing of bank failures to various characteristics of the banks as well as to local, regional and national shocks. They find that a list of fundamentals (including bank size, the presence of branch banking, net worth relative to assets as a measure of leverage, reliance on demand debt, market power, the value of the portfolio, loan quality, and the share of agriculture), as well as several macro variables, largely explains the timing of the bank failures. When they add into the regression as regressors the Friedman and Schwartz panic windows (or Wicker's amendments to them), they turn out to be of minimal significance. Thus they conclude that, with the exception of the 1933 banking panic, which, as Wicker (1996) argued, reflected a cumulative series of state bank suspensions in January and February leading to the national banking holiday on 6 March, that illiquidity was inconsequential.

Richardson (2007) provides a new comprehensive data source on the reasons for bank suspensions from the archives of the Federal Reserve Board of Governors including all Fed member banks and non-member banks (both state and local) from August 1929 to just before the bank holiday in March 1933. He also distinguished between temporary and permanent suspensions. Based on answers to a questionnaire used by bank examiners after each bank suspension, Richardson put together a complete list of the causes of each suspension. The categories include: depositor runs, declining asset prices, the failure of correspondents, mergers, mismanagement, and defalcations. Richardson then classified each bank suspension into categories reflecting illiquidity, insolvency, or both. With these data he then constructed indices of illiquidity and insolvency. His data show that 60 percent of the suspensions during the period reflected insolvency,

40 per cent illiquidity. Moreover, he shows that the ratio of illiquidity to insolvency spikes during the Friedman and Schwartz (and also Wicker) panic windows (see Figure 12.1). This evidence in some respects complements the Friedman and Schwartz and Wicker stories and those of Temin and White. During the panics, illiquidity rises relative to insolvency; between the panics insolvency increases relative to illiquidity. Consistent with the Friedman and Schwartz stories, the panics were driven by illiquidity shocks seen in increased hoarding, but after the panics, in the face of deteriorating economic conditions, bank insolvencies continued to rise. This is consistent with the evidence of Temin and White. The failures continued through the contraction until the banking holiday of the week of 6 March 1933 (with the exception of the spring of 1932 while the Fed was temporarily engaged in open-market purchases).

Richardson (2006) backs up the illiquidity story with detailed evidence on the 1930 banking panic. As described in Wicker (1980), the failure of Caldwell and Co. in November was the signature event of this crisis. Richardson uses his new database to identify the cascade of failures through the correspondent bank networks based on the Caldwell banks. During this period, most small rural banks maintained deposits on reserve with larger city banks that, in turn, would clear their cheques through big city clearinghouses and/or the Federal Reserve System. When Caldwell collapsed, so did the correspondent network. Moreover, Richardson and Troost (2009) clearly show that when the tidal wave from Caldwell hit the banks of the state of Mississippi in December, the banks in the southern half of the state, under the jurisdiction of the Federal Reserve Bank of Atlanta, fared much better (had a lower failure rate) than those in the northern half, under the jurisdiction of the Federal Reserve Bank of St Louis. The Atlanta Fed followed Bagehot's Rule, discounting freely the securities of illiquid but solvent member banks. The St Louis Fed followed the real bills doctrine and was reluctant to open the discount window to its member banks in trouble. This pattern holds up when the authors control for fundamentals using a framework like that in Calomiris and Mason (2003).[3]

Finally, Christiano et al. (2003) build a dynamic stochastic general equilibrium (DSGE) model of the Great Contraction, incorporating monetary and financial shocks. They find that the key propagation channels

FIGURE 12.1   Bank Failures and Suspensions

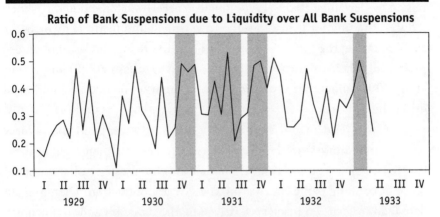

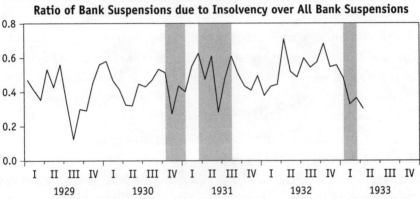

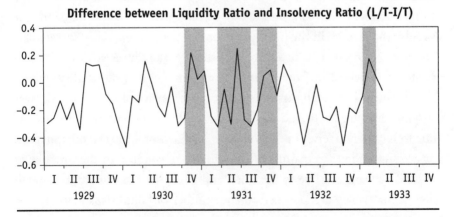

explaining the slump were the decline in the deposit–currency ratio, amplified by Bernanke et al.'s (1996) financial accelerator. The liquidity shock reduced funding for firms, lowering investment and firms' net worth. At the same time, the increased currency hoarding reduced consumption expenditure. Their simulations, like those of McCallum (1990) and Bordo et al. (1995) show that expansionary open-market purchases could have offset these shocks.

In sum, the debate over illiquidity versus insolvency in the failures of US banks hinges on the use of aggregate versus disaggregated data. Aggregate data tend to favour illiquidity and the presence of and importance of banking panics in creating the Great Contraction. Disaggregate data tend to focus on insolvency driven by the recession and to downplay the role of the panics in creating the Great Contraction. However, the recent more comprehensive data unearthed by Richardson, as well as the Christiano et al. model, suggest that the original Friedman and Schwartz story may well prevail.

(i) Empirical Evidence

In Bordo and Landon-Lane (2010) a vector autoregression (VAR) analysis of the determinants of bank failures is undertaken using the data of Richardson (2007). The VAR used includes the following six variables: bank failures/suspensions due to illiquidity; banks failures/suspensions due to insolvency; total bank failures/suspensions; the growth rate of money supply; the change in the unemployment rate; and the quality spread. The variables are ordered as listed above so that bank failures/suspensions will contemporaneously affect money, unemployment, and the quality spread.

The most important assumption is the ordering of the bank failures/suspensions due to illiquidity series before the bank failures/suspensions due to insolvency series in the VAR. In Richardson (2007) banks that fail or are suspended for reasons of illiquidity are counted in the number of failures/suspensions due to liquidity, and banks that fail or are suspended due to insolvency are assigned to the number of failures/suspensions due to insolvency. It is possible to imagine a situation where a bank run (an illiquidity shock) may cause banks that are otherwise solvent to fail due to illiquidity. Insolvent banks may also be caught up in the bank run and therefore it is natural to think that bank failures due to illiquidity will contemporaneously affect banks failures/suspensions due to insolvency.[4]

The failure of insolvent banks would not immediately affect illiquid but otherwise solvent banks, at least in the short run. However, the solvency shock may also cause, through contagion, a run on otherwise healthy banks, especially if there was a run-up of closures of insolvent banks preceding the bank run. Our identifying assumption is that if the insolvency shock causes a bank run then this will happen with a time lag. That is, the identifying assumption is that the illiquidity shock might cause some insolvent banks to fail contemporaneously, whereas the insolvency shock will lead to failures due to illiquidity only with a lag. The final variable is total bank failures and is not exactly equal to the sum of the previous two bank failure series. This is because not all bank failures are attributed to illiquidity or insolvency, as noted in the previous paragraph.

The ordering we choose for the last three variables is the following: the first variable is the growth rate of the money supply; the second is the change in the unemployment rate; and the third is the quality spread. The triangular ordering we use implies, then, that each variable contemporaneously affects each variable ordered below it, but not any variable ordered above it in the vector. Thus a change in the growth rate of money supply contemporaneously affects the change in unemployment and the quality spread, while the change in the unemployment rate contemporaneously affects the quality spread. These variables then affect bank failures/suspensions with a lag.

Thus we identify six shocks in total that we interpret as follows: the first shock is the illiquidity shock; the second is the insolvency shock; while the third is a bank failure/suspension residual shock. It is the shock to bank failures/suspensions that cannot be attributed to either illiquidity or insolvency. The next three shocks are a money growth rate shock, an aggregate real shock to unemployment that is orthogonal to the money growth shock, and a shock to the quality spread that is orthogonal to all the previous shocks. We might consider this shock to be a credit shock. Note that we cannot with this specification identify supply or demand shocks for both the money shocks and aggregate real shocks.

The reduced form VAR is estimated using ordinary least squares with two lags of each variable in each equation. It was determined that the money supply and unemployment series were non-stationary, so that all variables enter the VAR in log-levels except for money supply and the unemployment rate which enter as first differences of the log-level. The sample period used (based on Richardson's data) finished in February 1933 and so does not include the period of the bank holiday starting on 6 March 1933.

The lag structure was determined using various information criteria and the standard sequential likelihood ratio tests. All information criteria and the sequential likelihood ratio test suggest two lags should be included. The results suggest that there are a large number of significant contemporaneous relationships between the variables. All coefficients are significant except for the effect of the illiquidity and insolvency shocks on the growth rate of money supply.

Orthogonalized impulse response functions were computed, using the ordering described above, in order to determine the effect of the identified shocks on the variables of the system. It is clear from the results reported in Bordo and Landon-Lane (2010) that the illiquidity shock has a large and persistent effect on total bank failures/suspensions. The forecast error variance decompositions show that the illiquidity shock accounts for roughly 50 percent of the forecast error, with the insolvency shock only accounting for 16 percent. Thus it appears that the illiquidity shock is very important for explaining total bank failures/suspensions. Money supply shocks also have an effect on total bank failures/suspensions. A positive shock to money growth has the effect of lowering bank failures/ suspensions. This result is persistent and occurs for each of the bank failure/ suspension series. The effect of money is especially strong and persistent for the bank failures/suspensions due to insolvency series. This result suggests that monetary policy aimed at increasing the growth rate of money may have helped to mitigate some of the bank failures/suspensions that occurred during the early 1930s. This result reinforces the views of McCallum (1990), Bordo et al. (1995), and Christiano et al. (2003).

The other impulse response functions, reported in Bordo and Landon-Lane (2010), support the identification assumption that bank failures/ suspensions contemporaneously affect money, unemployment, and the quality spread, and that these three variables feed back into the bank failures/suspensions series with some lag. The illiquidity shock is seen to have a strong direct and indirect effect on total bank failures/suspensions due to insolvency, with the illiquidity shock affecting money supply which in turn affects bank failures/suspensions due to insolvency.

The impulse response functions together with the variance decompositions show that the illiquidity shock is very important in explaining the bank failures/suspensions during the early 1930s. In order to determine if the illiquidity shocks played a role during the particular financial crisis windows identified by Friedman and Schwartz (1963), we now turn to historical decompositions. Figure 12.2 contains historical decompositions for the total bank failures/suspensions series. Each panel of Figure 12.2 contains a simulated total bank failures/suspensions series under the hypothesis that only one orthogonalized shock was driving the stochastic component of the data. Thus the panel titled illiquidity shock shows the generated series if there was only an illiquidity shock.

The results of the historical decompositions clearly point to the illiquidity shock playing a significant role in the bank failures during the Friedman and Schwartz crisis windows. The most obvious case is during the first window from October 1930 to January 1931. Here the historical decomposition for the illiquidity series almost completely follows the actual data. The other shocks do not explain this first crisis window at all. For the next two crisis windows that take up most of 1931 the illiquidity shock does generate series that follow the actual series quite well. During these periods the money shock and the insolvency shock generate series that peak around the right time, but they do not generate series that closely follow the actual total bank failures/suspensions series. The only crisis window that the insolvency shock does predict well appears to be the final crisis of early 1933. In this case it does appear that the financial crisis in 1933 is more an insolvency story then an illiquidity story.

To summarize, we have estimated a VAR and used a triangular ordering to identify a set of shocks including illiquidity and insolvency shocks. The impulse response functions obtained from this orthogonalized VAR make sense and show that the illiquidity shock is an important shock for explaining the observed bank failures/suspensions series. Further, the historical decompositions show that the financial crises of late 1930 and all

FIGURE 12.2   Historical Decompositions of Total
Bank Failures/Suspensions

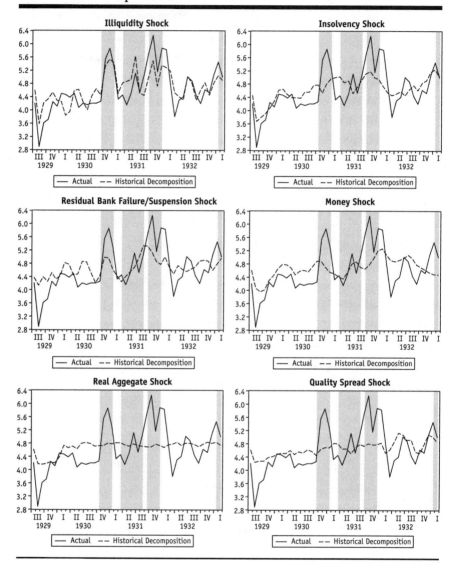

of 1931 are well modelled as illiquidity crises. The financial crisis of 1933 is better explained as an insolvency crisis.

Thus the evidence suggests that the banking panics of the 1930s were largely a liquidity event which massive monetary expansion could have avoided. The key policy lesson from the 1930s experience is that central banks need to attach prominent importance to their role as lenders of last resort. As we discuss in sections IV and V below, the Fed and other central banks learned this lesson well in the crisis of 2007–8.

III. Why Did the US Have So Many Banking Panics?

We have argued that the signature event in the US Great Contraction was the series of banking panics from 1930 to 1933. But this was nothing new in US financial history. From the early nineteenth century until 1914, the US had a banking panic every decade. There is a voluminous literature on US financial stability, and the lessons that come from that literature are that the high incidence of banking instability reflected two forces: unit banking and the absence of an effective lender of last resort.

(i) Unit Banking

Fear of the concentration of economic power largely explains why states generally prohibited branch banking and why since the demise of the Second Bank of the United States in 1836, there was until quite recently no interstate banking (White, 1983). Unit banks, because their portfolios were geographically constrained, were highly subject to local idiosyncratic shocks. Branching banks, especially those which extended across regions, can better diversify their portfolios and protect themselves against local/regional shocks.

A comparison between the experience of the US and Canadian banking systems makes the case (Bordo et al., 1996). The US until the 1920s has had predominantly unit banking and until very recently a prohibition on interstate banking. Canada since the late nineteenth century has had nationwide branch banking. Canada only adopted a central bank in 1934. The US established the Fed in 1914. Canada has had no banking panics since Confederation in 1867; the US has had nine. However, the Canadian chartered banks were always highly regulated and operated very much like a cartel under the guidance of the Canadian Bankers Association and the Department of Finance.

(ii) A Lender of Last Resort

From the demise of the Second Bank of the United States until the establishment of the Federal Reserve in 1914, the US had not had anything like a central bank to act as a lender of last resort, into which the Bank of England had evolved during the nineteenth century (Bordo, 2007). Clearinghouses, established first in New York City in 1857 and other major cities later, on occasion acted as a lender of last resort by pooling the resources of the members and issuing clearinghouse loan certificates as a substitute for scarce high-powered money reserves. However, on several prominent occasions before 1914 the clearinghouses did not allay panics (Timberlake, 2002). Panics were often ended in the National Banking era by the suspension of convertibility of deposits into currency. Also the US Treasury on a few occasions performed lender-of-last-resort functions.

The Federal Reserve was established to serve (among other functions) as a lender of last resort but, as documented above, failed in its task between 1930 and 1933. Discount window lending to member banks was at the prerogative of the individual Federal Reserve banks and, as discussed above, some Reserve banks did not follow through. Moreover, until the establishment of the National Credit Corporation in 1931 (which became the Reconstruction Finance Corporation in 1932), there was no monetary authority to provide assistance to non-member banks (Wicker, 1996). Wicker effectively argues that the panics pre-1914 were always centred in the New York money market and then spread via the vagaries of the National banking system to the regions. The New York Fed, according to him, learned the lesson of the panics of the national banking system and did prevent panics from breaking out in New York City during the Great Contraction. But, as he argues, it did not develop the tools to deal with the regional banking panics which erupted in 1930 and 1931.

(iii) Recent Evidence

There is considerable empirical evidence going back to the nineteenth century on the case linking unit banking to failures and panics (White, 1983). Cross-country regression evidence in Grossman (1994, 2010) finds that during the 1930s countries which had unit banking had a greater incidence of banking instability than those which did not. For the US, Wheelock (1995) finds, based on state- and county-level data, that states that allowed branching had lower bank failure rates than those which did not. However Carlson (2004) (also Calomiris and Mason, 2003) find, based on a panel of individual banks, that state branch banks in the US were less likely to survive the banking panics. The reason Carlson gives is that while state branch banks can diversify against idiosyncratic local shocks better than can unit banks, they were still exposed to the systemic shocks of the 1930s. He argues that branch banks used the diversification opportunities of branching to increase their returns but also followed more risky strategies such as holding lower reserves.

Carlson and Mitchener (2009) show, based on data on Californian banks in the 1930s (California was a state that allowed branch banking), that the entry of large branching networks, by improving the competitive environment actually improved the survival probabilities of unit banks. They explain the divergent results between studies based on individual banks and those based on state- and county-level data by the argument that the US banking system would have been less fragile in the 1930s had states allowed more branching, not because branch banks would have been more diversified but because the system would have had more efficient banks.

The recent financial crisis, although not a classic banking panic, did exhibit a large number of bank failures (mostly in small banks, as in the past, although there were a few large ones such as Countrywide). Most of the bank failures were resolved by the Federal Deposit Insurance Corporation (FDIC) set up in the aftermath of the Great Contraction. So, again, some lessons were learned from the 1930s experience. However, unlike in the 1930s, as we discuss below, a number of very large banks which became insolvent and were deemed too big and too interconnected to fail were bailed out by massive capital injections and partial nationalization.

IV. A Comparison of the Financial Crisis in the US to the 2007–8 Crisis

Many people have invoked the experience during the Great Contraction, and especially the banking crises of 1930–3, as a good comparison to the financial crisis and Great Recession of 2007–9. In several descriptive figures in this section we compare the behaviour of some key variables between the two events. We demarcate the crisis windows in the Great Contraction using Friedman and Schwartz's dates. For the recent period we use Gorton's (2010) characterization of the crisis as starting in the shadow bank repo market in August 2007 (dark grey shading) and then changing to a panic in the Universal banks after Lehman failed in September 2007 (light grey shading). In most respects, e.g., the magnitude of the decline in real GDP and the rise in unemployment (see Figures 12.3 and 12.4), the two events are very different, but there are some parallels between recent events and the 1930s. In Figure 12.3 we report real GNP for the 1930s and for 2007–9, normalized to be 100 at the start of each period. It is quite clear that the contraction in late 2007 was mild (only about 5 percent peak to trough) relative to the Great Contraction in the 1930s (roughly 35 percent peak to trough). The same is clear for unemployment which is depicted in Figure 12.4. Unemployment rose from near 0 percent at the start of the Great Contraction to slightly over 25 percent by the end of the contraction whereas the rise in unemployment from 4 to 10 percent for the most recent contraction is small in comparison.

As discussed above, the signature of the Great Contraction was a collapse in the money supply brought about by a collapse in the public's deposit–currency ratio, a decline in the banks deposit–reserve ratio, and a drop in the money multiplier (see Figures 12.5–12.7). In the recent crisis M2 did not collapse; indeed, it increased reflecting expansionary monetary policy. Moreover, the deposit–currency ratio did not collapse in the recent crisis, it rose. There were no runs on the commercial banks because depositors knew that their deposits were protected by federal deposit insurance, which was introduced in 1934 in reaction to the bank runs of the 1930s. The deposit–reserve ratio declined, reflecting an increase in banks' excess reserves induced by expansionary monetary policy, rather than a scramble for

FIGURE 12.3   Real GNP (Quarterly Data)

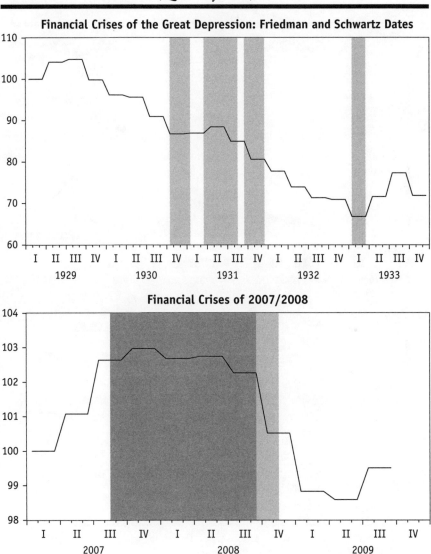

liquidity, as in the 1930s. The money multiplier declined in the recent crisis, largely explained by a massive expansion in the monetary base reflecting the Fed's doubling of its balance sheet in 2008. Moreover, although a few banks failed recently, they were minuscule relative to the 1930s, as were deposits in failed banks relative to total deposits (see Figure 12.8).[5]

FIGURE 12.4 Unemployment

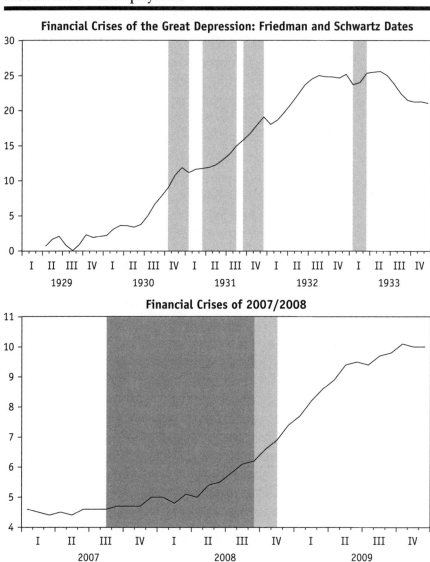

Thus the recent financial crisis and recession did not constitute a pure Friedman and Schwartz money story. It was not driven by an old-fashioned contagious banking panic. But, as in 1930–3, there was a financial crisis. It reflected a run in August 2007 on the shadow banking system, which was not regulated by the central bank nor covered by the

FIGURE 12.5   Money Stock (M2)

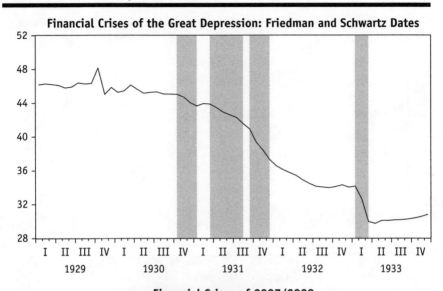

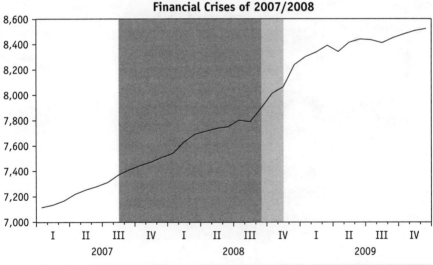

financial safety net. According to Eichengreen (2008), its rapid growth
was a consequence of the repeal in 1999 of the Depression-era Glass–
Steagall Act of 1935, which had separated commercial from investment
banking. These institutions held much lower capital ratios than the traditional commercial banks and hence were considerably more prone to risk.

FIGURE 12.6   Ratio of Deposits to Currency in Circulation

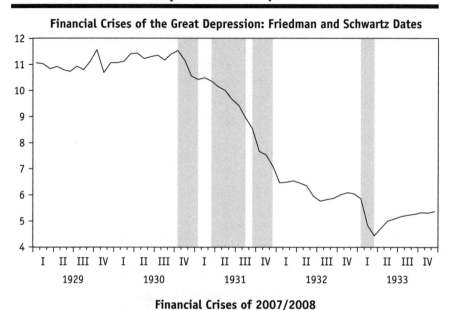

Financial Crises of the Great Depression: Friedman and Schwartz Dates

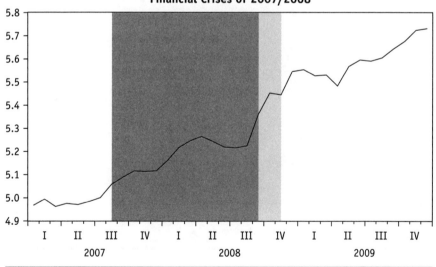

Financial Crises of 2007/2008

When the crisis hit, they were forced to engage in major deleveraging, involving a fire sale of assets into a falling market, which, in turn, lowered the value of their assets and those of other financial institutions. A similar negative feedback loop occurred during the Great Contraction, according to Friedman and Schwartz.

FIGURE 12.7   Monetary Base

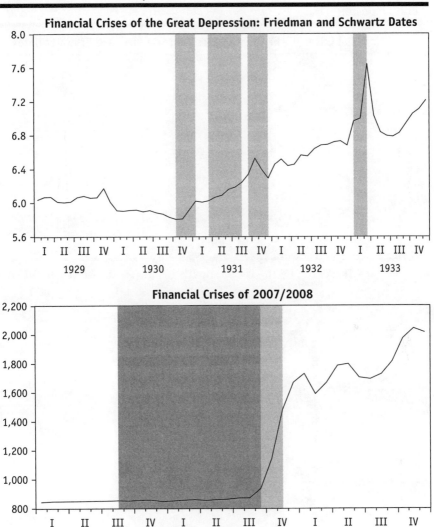

According to Gorton (2010), the crisis centred in the repo market (sale and repurchase agreements) which had been collateralized by opaque (sub-prime) mortgage-backed securities by which investment banks and some universal banks had been funded. The repo crisis continued through 2008 and then morphed into an investment/universal bank crisis after the failure

FIGURE 12.8   Deposits in Failed Banks as a Proportion of
Total Deposits

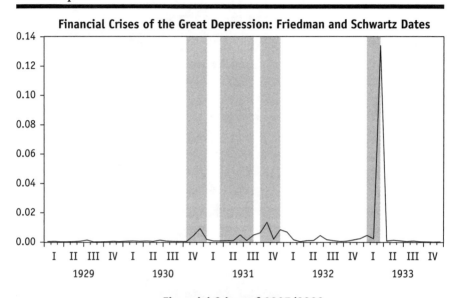

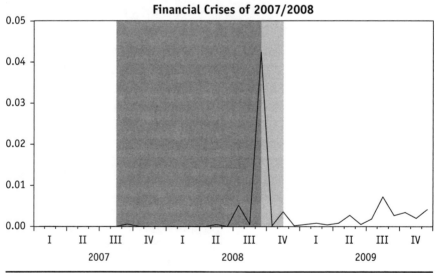

FIGURE 12.9 Quality Spread (Baa 10-Year T-Bill)

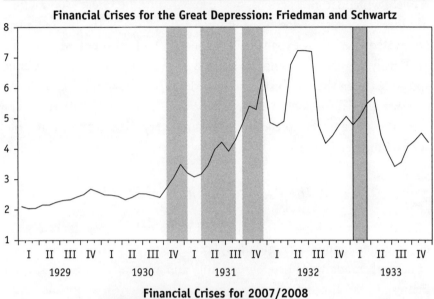

Financial Crises for the Great Depression: Friedman and Schwartz

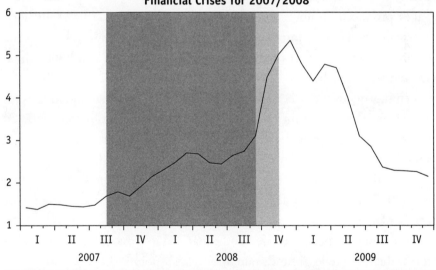

Financial Crises for 2007/2008

of Lehman Brothers in September 2008. The crisis led to a credit crunch, which led to a serious, but, compared to the Great Contraction, not that serious, recession (see Figures 12.3 and 12.4). The recession was attenuated in 2009 by expansionary monetary and fiscal policy.

Finally, Figure 12.9 compares the Baa 10-year composite Treasury bond spread between the two historical episodes. This spread is often used as a measure of credit-market turmoil (Bordo and Haubrich, 2010). As can be seen, the spike in the spread in 2008 is not very different from that observed in the early 1930s.

V. The Recent Crisis in More Detail

The crisis occurred following 2 years of rising policy rates. Its causes include: major changes in regulation, lax regulatory oversight, a relaxation of normal standards of prudent lending, and a period of abnormally low interest rates. The default on a significant fraction of subprime mortgages produced spillover effects around the world, via the securitized mortgage derivatives into which these mortgages were bundled, to the balance sheets of investment banks, hedge funds, and conduits (which are bank-owned but off their balance sheets) which intermediate between mortgage and other asset-backed commercial paper and long-term securities. The uncertainty about the value of the securities collateralized by these mortgages had the effect of spreading uncertainty about the soundness of loans for leveraged buy-outs through the financial system. All of this led to the freezing of the interbank lending market in August 2007 and substantial liquidity injections by the Fed and other central banks.

The Fed then both extended and expanded its discount-window facilities and cut the federal funds rate by 300 basis points. The crisis worsened in March 2008 with the rescue of Bear Stearns, an investment bank, by J.P. Morgan, backstopped by funds from the Federal Reserve. The rescue was justified on the grounds that the exposure of Bear Stearns to counterparties was so extensive that a worse crisis would follow if it were not bailed out. The March crisis also led to the creation of a number of new discount-window facilities whereby investment banks could access the window and which broadened the collateral acceptable for discounting. The next major event was a Federal Reserve–Treasury bail-out and partial nationalization of the insolvent government-sponsored enterprises (GSEs), Fannie Mae and Freddie Mac, in July 2008, on the grounds that they were crucial to the functioning of the mortgage market.

Events took a turn for the worse in September 2008 when the Treasury and Fed allowed the investment bank Lehman Brothers to fail, in order to discourage the belief that all insolvent institutions would be saved, in an attempt to prevent moral hazard. It was argued that Lehman was both in worse shape and less exposed to counterparty risk than Bear Stearns. The next day the authorities bailed out and nationalized the insurance giant AIG, fearing the systemic consequences for collateralized default swaps (insurance contracts on securities) if it were allowed to fail. The fall-out from the Lehman bankruptcy then turned the liquidity crisis into a fully fledged global credit crunch and stock-market crash, as interbank lending effectively seized up on the fear that no banks were safe.

In the ensuing atmosphere of panic, along with Fed liquidity assistance to the commercial paper market and the extension of the safety net to money market mutual funds, the US Treasury sponsored its Troubled Asset Relief Plan (TARP), whereby $700 billion could be devoted to the purchase of heavily discounted mortgage-backed and other securities to remove them from the banks' balance sheets and restore bank lending. As it later turned out, most of the funds were used to recapitalize the banks.

In early October 2008 the crisis spread to Europe and to the emerging-market countries as the global interbank market ceased functioning. The UK authorities responded by pumping equity into British banks, guaranteeing all interbank deposits and providing massive liquidity. The EU countries responded in kind. And on 13 October 2008 the US Treasury followed suit with a plan to inject $250 billion into the US banks, to provide insurance of senior interbank debt and unlimited deposit insurance for non-interest-bearing deposits. These actions ended the crisis. Expansionary Federal Reserve policy at the end of 2008, lowering the funds rate close to zero, followed by a policy of quantitative easing: the open-market purchases of long-term Treasury bonds and mortgage-backed securities finally attenuated the recession by the summer of 2009.

Unlike the liquidity panics of the Great Contraction, the deepest problem facing the financial system was insolvency. This was only recognized by the Fed after the September 2008 crisis. The problem stemmed from the difficulty of pricing securities backed by a pool of assets, whether mortgage loans, student loans, commercial paper issues, or credit card receivables. Pricing securities based on a pool of assets is difficult because the quality of individual components of the pool varies and, unless each component is individually examined and evaluated, no accurate price of the security can be determined.

As a result, the credit market, confronted by financial firms whose portfolios were filled with securities of uncertain value, derivatives that were so complex the art of pricing them had not been mastered, was plagued by the inability to determine which firms were solvent and which were not. Lenders were unwilling to extend loans when they could not be sure that a borrower was creditworthy. This was a serious shortcoming of the securitization process that was responsible for the paralysis of the credit market.

Finally, another hallmark of the recent crisis which was not present in the Great Contraction is that the Fed and other US monetary authorities engaged in a series of bail-outs of incipient and actual insolvent firms deemed too systemically connected to fail. These included Bear Stearns in March 2008, the GSEs in July, and AIG in September. Lehman Brothers had been allowed to fail in September on the grounds that it was both insolvent and not as systemically important as the others and, as was stated well after the event, that the Fed did not have the legal authority to bail it out. The extension of the 'too big to fail' doctrine, which had begun in 1984 with the bail-out of Continental Illinois bank, may be the source of future crises.

VI. Conclusion: Some Policy Lessons from History

In this chapter we have re-examined the issue of the role of the banking panics between 1930 and 1933 in creating the Great Contraction. We focused on the debate between those following the Friedman and Schwartz view that the banking crises were illiquidity shocks and those following the approach of Temin and others who view the clusters of banking failures as not being liquidity-driven panics but insolvencies caused by the recession.

Our survey of the evidence suggests that the banking crises did reflect contagious illiquidity, but also that endogenous insolvency was important between the panics. Bank failures regardless of their genesis contributed to the depression by reducing the money supply and by crippling the credit mechanism.

In Bordo and Landon-Lane (2010) we showed illiquidity played a major role in the financial crises of late 1930 and all 1931. We estimated a VAR and used a triangular ordering to identify a set of shocks including illiquidity and insolvency shocks. The impulse response functions obtained from this orthogonalized VAR make sense and show that the illiquidity shock is an important shock for explaining the observed bank failures/suspensions series. Further, the historical decompositions show that the financial crisis of late 1930 and all of 1931 are well modelled as illiquidity crises. The financial crisis of 1933 is better explained as an insolvency crisis.

The Federal Reserve learned the Friedman and Schwartz lesson from the banking panics of the 1930s of the importance of conducting expansionary open-market policy to meet all of the demands for liquidity (Bernanke, 2002). In the recent crisis the Fed conducted highly expansionary monetary policy in the autumn of 2007 and from late 2008 to the present. Also, based on Bernanke's (1983) view that the banking collapse led to a failure of the credit-allocation mechanism, the Fed, in conjunction with the Treasury, developed a plethora of extensions to its discount window referred to as credit policy (Goodfriend, 2009) to encompass virtually every kind of collateral in an attempt to unclog the blocked credit markets.

Some argue that for the first three quarters of 2008 Fed monetary policy was actually too tight, seen in a flattening of money growth and the monetary base and high real interest rates (Hetzel, 2009). Although the Fed's balance sheet surged, the effects on high-powered money were sterilized. This may have reflected concern that rising commodity prices at the time would spark inflationary expectations. By the end of the third quarter of 2008 the sterilization ceased, as evidenced by a doubling of the monetary base.

The Fed's credit policy involved providing credit directly to markets and firms the Fed deemed most in need of liquidity, and exposed the Fed to the temptation to politicize its selection of the recipients of its credit

(Schwartz, 2008). In addition, the Fed's balance sheet ballooned in 2008 and 2009 with the collateral of risky assets including those of non-banks. These assets were in part backed by the Treasury. The Fed also worked closely with the Treasury in the autumn of 2008 to stabilize the major banks with capital purchases and stress testing. Moreover, the purchase of mortgage-backed securities in 2009 (quantitative easing) combined monetary with fiscal policy. These actions, which many argue helped reduce the spreads and reopen the credit channels, impinged upon the Fed's independence and created problems for the Fed in the future (Bordo, 2010).

As discussed in Section V, the deepest problem of the recent crisis, however, was not illiquidity, as it was in the 1930s, but insolvency, and especially the fear of insolvency of counterparties. This has echoes in the correspondence-banking-induced panic of November 1930 (Richardson, 2006), but very different from the 1930s. The too-big-to-fail doctrine, which had developed in the 1980s, ensured that the monetary authorities would bail out insolvent large financial firms which were deemed too interconnected to fail. This is a dramatic departure from the original Bagehot's rule prescription to provide liquidity to illiquid but solvent banks. This new type of systemic risk (Tallman and Wicker, 2009) raises the spectre of moral hazard and future financial crises and future bail-outs.

(i) Policies to Prevent the Next Crisis

The crisis of 2007–8 had similarities to the 1930s experience in that there was a panic in the shadow banking system and the repo market in 2007, as argued by Gorton (2010), but also in investment banks and the universal banking system after Lehman failed in September 2008. But it was not a classic contagious banking panic. The decision to bail out large interconnected financial institutions in the autumn of 2008 does not have much resonance in the 1930s experience. The closest parallel from the 1930s was the Bank of United States, which failed in December 1930. It was one of the largest banks in the country but it was insolvent and it was allowed to fail (Lucia, 1985).

A key concern from the bail-outs of 2008 is that, in the future, the too-big-to-fail doctrine will lead to excessive risk-taking by such firms and future crises and bail-outs. This was a major concern in the debate leading to the recent Dodd Frank Wall Street Reform and Protection Act, passed in July 2010. The Act attempted to address the too-big-to-fail problem by establishing a Financial Stability Oversight Council made up of members from the Federal Reserve Board, the Treasury, the Securities and Exchange Commission, and a number of other financial agencies. The Council was charged with identifying and responding to emerging risks throughout the financial system. The Council would make recommendations to the Federal Reserve to impose increasingly strict rules for capital and leverage and other requirements to prevent banks from becoming too large and systemically exposed. It remains to be seen whether it will be effective in preventing future crises.

Notes

1. At the time the consensus view was that the slump was a consequence of the speculative boom of the 1920s. The boom was regarded as a manifestation of deep-seated structural imbalances seen in overinvestment. Indeed, according to the Austrian view which prevailed in the interwar period, depressions were part of the normal operation of the business cycle. Policy prescriptions from this view included tight money, tight fiscal policy, and wage cuts to restore balance. Keynes (1936) rejected these prescriptions and the classical view that eventually a return to full employment would be achieved by falling wages and prices. He attributed the slump to a collapse of aggregate demand, especially private investment. His policy prescription was to use fiscal policy—both pump priming and massive government expenditures. In the post-Second World War era, Keynesian views dominated the economics profession and the explanation given for the depression emphasized different components of aggregate expenditure.

2. Panics can arise because of exogenous illiquidity shocks in the context of the Diamond and Dybvig (1983) random withdrawals model, or in the context of asymmetric-information-induced runs and panics (Calomiris and Gorton, 1991).

3. Carlson (2008) shows that during the panic, banks that would otherwise have merged with stronger banks rather than fail were prevented from doing so.

4. These technically insolvent banks may still be operating owing to asymmetric information between depositors and bank operators.

5. The large spike in 1933 largely represents the bank holiday of 6–10 March in which the entire nation's banks were closed and an army of examiners determined

whether they were solvent or not. At the end of the week one-sixth of the nation's banks were closed. The relatively large spike in 2008 in the deposits in the failed banks series reflected the failure and reorganization by the FDIC of Countrywide Bank. Compared to the case in the 1930s failures, there were no insured depositor losses. With respect to the number of failed banks the current crisis was small with the maximum number of failed banks in the recent crisis being 25 compared with maximums 20 and 100 times greater during the banking crises of the 1930s.

References

Bernanke, B. (1983), 'Non Monetary Effects of the Financial Crisis in the Propagation of the Great Depression', *American Economic Review*, 73, 257–76.

———— (2002), 'On Milton's Ninetieth Birthday', speech given at the University of Chicago, 8 November.

———— Gilchrist, S., and Gertler, M. (1996), 'The Financial Accelerator and the Flight to Quality', *Review of Economics and Statistics*, **78**(1), 1–15.

Bordo, M. D. (2007), 'The History of Monetary Policy', *New Palgrave Dictionary of Economics*, 2nd edn, New York, Macmillan.

———— (2010), 'The Federal Reserve: Independence Gained, Independence Lost . . .', Shadow Open Market Committee 26 March.

———— Choudhri, E., and Schwartz, A. J. (1995), 'Could Stable Money Have Averted the Great Contraction?', *Economic Inquiry*, 33, 484–505.

———— Haubrich, J. (2010), 'Credit Crises, Money and Contractions: An Historical View', *Journal of Monetary Economics*, **57**(1), 1–18.

———— Landon-Lane, J. S. (2010), 'The Lessons from the Banking Panics in the United States in the 1930s for the Financial Crisis of 2007–2008', NBER Working Paper No. 16365, September.

———— Redish, A., and Rockoff, H. (1996), 'The US Banking System from a Northern Exposure: Stability versus Efficiency', *Journal of Economic History*, **54**(2), 325–41.

Calomiris, C., and Gorton, G. (1991), 'The Origins of Banking Panics: Models, Facts and Bank Regulation', in R. G. Hubbard (ed.), *Financial Markets and Financial Crises*, Chicago, IL, University of Chicago Press, 109–73.

———— Mason, J. (1997), 'Contagion and Bank Failures during the Great Depression: The June 1932 Chicago Banking Panic', *American Economic Review*, **87**(5), 863–83.

———— (2003), 'Fundamentals, Panics and Bank Distress during the Depression', *American Economic Review*, **93**(5), 1615–47.

Carlson, M. (2004), 'Are Branch Banks Better Survivors? Evidence from the Depression Era', *Economic Inquiry*, **42**(1), 111–26.

———— (2008), 'Alternatives for Distressed Banks and the Panics of the Great Depression', Finance and Economic Discussion Series, Washington, DC, Federal Reserve Board.

———— Mitchener, K. J. (2009), 'Branch Banking as a Device for Discipline: Competition and Bank Survivorship during the Great Depression', *Journal of Political Economy*, **117**(2), 165–210.

Christiano, L., Motto, R., and Rostagno, M. (2003), 'The Great Depression and the Friedman and Schwartz Hypothesis', *Journal of Money, Credit and Banking*, **35**, 1119–98.

Diamond, D., and Dybvig, P. (1983), 'Bank Runs, Deposit Insurance, and Liquidity', *Journal of Political Economy*, **91**(3), 401–19.

Eichengreen, B. (2008), 'Origins and Responses to the Crisis', UC Berkeley, mimeo, October.

Friedman, M., and Schwartz, A. (1963), *A Monetary History of the United States 1867 to 1960*, Princeton, NJ, Princeton University Press.

Galbraith, J. K. (1955), *The Great Crash 1929*, London, Hamish Hamilton.

Goodfriend, M. (2009), 'Central Banking in the Credit Turmoil: An Assessment of Federal Reserve Practice', Bank of Japan Conference, May.

Gorton, G. (2010), 'Questions and Answers about the Financial Crisis', NBER Working Paper 15787, February.

Grossman, R. S. (1994), 'The Shoe that Didn't Drop: Explaining Banking Stability in the Great Depression', *Journal of Economic History*, **54**, 654–82.

———— (2010), *Unsettled Account: The Evolution of Banking in the Industrial World since 1800*, Princeton, NJ, Princeton University Press.

Hetzel, R. (2009), 'Monetary Policy in the 2008–2009 Recession', *Federal Reserve Bank of Richmond Review*, September.

Keynes, J. M. (1936), *The General Theory of Employment, Interest and Money*, New York, Harcourt Brace.

Lucia, J. (1985), 'The Failure of the Bank of United States: A Reappraisal', *Explorations in Economic History*, **22**(4), 402–11.

McCallum, B. (1990), 'Could a Monetary Base Rule Have Prevented the Great Depression?', *Journal of Monetary Economics*, **26**, 3–21.

Prescott, E. C. (1999), 'Some Observations on the Great Depression', *Federal Reserve Bank of Minneapolis Quarterly Review*, **23**, 25–31.

Richardson, G. (2006), 'Correspondent Clearing and the Banking Panics of the Great Depression', NBER Working Paper 12716 December.

———— (2007), 'Categories and Causes of Bank Distress during the Great Depression, 1920–1935: The Illiquidity versus Solvency Debate Revisited', *Explorations in Economic History*, **44**(4), 588–607.

———— Troost, W. (2009), 'Monetary Intervention Mitigated Banking Panics during the Great Depression: Quasi Experimental Evidence from the Federal Reserve

District Border in Mississippi, 1929–1933', *Journal of Political Economy*, **117**(6), 1031–72.

Schwartz, A. (2008), 'Origins of the Financial Market Crisis of 2008', Cato Conference, October.

Tallman, E., and Wicker, E. (2009), 'Banking and Financial Crises in the United States History: What Guidance Can History Offer Policy Makers?', Indiana University, mimeo.

Temin, P. (1976), *Did Monetary Forces Cause the Great Depression?*, New York, W. W. Norton.

Timberlake, R., Jr (2002), 'Monetary Policy in the United States: An Intellectual and Institutional History', Chicago, IL, University of Chicago Press.

Wheelock, D. (1995), 'Regulation, Market Structure and the Bank Failures of the Great Depression', *Federal Reserve Bank of St Louis Review*, **77**, 27–38.

White, E. (1983), *The Regulation and Reform of the American Banking System, 1900–1929*, Princeton, NJ, Princeton University Press.

—————— (1984), 'A Reinterpretation of the Banking Crisis of 1930', *Journal of Economic History*, **44**, 119–38.

Wicker, E. (1980), 'A Reconsideration of the Causes of the Banking Panic of 1930', *Journal of Economic History*, **40**, 571–83.

—————— (1996), *The Banking Panics of the Great Depression*, New York, Cambridge University Press.

CHAPTER 13

Could Stable Money Have Averted the Great Contraction?

MICHAEL D. BORDO, EHSAN U. CHOUDHRI,
AND ANNA J. SCHWARTZ

I. Introduction

ALTHOUGH OVER FIFTY YEARS have elapsed since the onset of the Great Contraction, controversy still swirls about the factors responsible for its depth and long duration. A basic issue is the hypothesis due to Friedman and Schwartz [1963] that the Great Contraction would have been attenuated had the Federal Reserve not allowed the money stock to decline. Although the validity of the hypothesis has been a subject of much debate, there is little empirical evidence directly addressing it.

A direct test of the Friedman and Schwartz hypothesis requires simulating the behavior of output under a counterfactual policy of stable money. That approach was adopted by Warburton [1966], Friedman [1960], and Modigliani [1964], none of whom constructed a model of the economy on the basis of which to conduct his test. Recently, McCallum [1990] has used simulations from a macro model to show that his base rule (with feedback) would have avoided the severe decline in nominal income that occurred between 1929 and 1933.[1] The extent to which his rule would have improved

Originally published in "Could Stable Money Have Averted the Great Contraction?" *Economic Inquiry* 33, no. 3 (July 1995): 484–505.

the behavior of nominal income depends on the value of the feedback co-efficient. McCallum's simulations, however, do not address the issue considered here of how a stable-money rule would have performed.

In this chapter we present simulations that focus on the stable-money counterfactual. Our model is based on McCallum's, but we use a more general framework than his that (a) estimates separate relations for output and the price level, and (b) places no prior restrictions on the feedback from output and the price level to money. Our stable-money counterfactual does not change the long-term rate of money growth (from that actually experienced) and thus involves only short-run changes in the behavior of the money supply. We assume that dynamics embedded in the output and price relation are not especially sensitive to this type of policy change.

We simulate two variants of Milton Friedman's [1960] constant money growth rule. The first, a strong form of the rule, assumes that the Fed could quickly offset changes in the money multiplier by changes in high-powered money and thus keep the money stock on the constant growth rate path in each quarter. The second, a weaker form of the rule, assumes that the money multiplier is observed with a one-quarter lag and the Fed can only set the expected rate of growth of money (conditional on last-period information) equal to the constant rate.

Our basic simulation is derived from a model estimated for the 1921.1–1941.4 interwar period. The results of this simulation buttress the views of Friedman and Schwartz. Had a constant money growth rule (with an annual rate equal to the average 1921–41 rate of 2.95 percent) been followed throughout the interwar period the Great Contraction would have been avoided. Real output would have declined from 1929.3 to 1933.1, but the order of magnitude of the cumulative change (–11.1 to –21.6 percent) and the annual rate of change (–3.3 to –6.6 percent), when the actual cumulative change was –36.2 percent and the annual rate of change was –12.1 percent, would have been comparable to other recessions in the nineteenth and twentieth centuries.

In the basic simulation we assume that the output and price relations remained stable over the entire interwar period. The extraordinary economic conditions of the Great Contraction could have arguably shifted the output and price relations. Thus, we also present an alternative simulation that uses estimates of these relations based on the 1920s data. This simulation shows that a constant money growth rule (with an annual rate equal to the 1921–29 average of 3.29 percent) would have prevented even a mild recession during the Great Contraction period.

Section II contains a brief survey of the continuing debate over the cause and propagation mechanism of the Great Contraction and its implications for the stable-money hypothesis. Section III presents an overview of the behavior of the variables considered in our model. Section IV describes our methodology for performing counterfactual simulations for the interwar years 1921 to 1941. Section V provides basic simulations of the paths of output and the price level under different variants of the constant money growth rule. Section VI explores the sensitivity of our results to alternative specifications. Section VII contains a brief conclusion.

II. The Controversy over the Great Contraction

Since the publication of *A Monetary History* in 1963, a voluminous literature has appeared, some of it critical and some supportive of Friedman and Schwartz's contention that monetary forces—specifically the failure of the Federal Reserve to engage in expansionary open market operations to offset a series of banking panics beginning in October 1930—turned a not-unusual cyclical downturn in the United States into the greatest depression of all time. Various survey articles in recent years have dealt with many of the issues—notably Bordo [1989], Calomiris [1993], Eichengreen [1992a], Temin [1993], and Romer [1993]—so our discussion will be brief.

In the 1970s and 1980s debate focused on Peter Temin's [1976] contention that monetary forces could not have been the primary cause of the contraction because short-term interest rates fell rather than rose, as would be consistent with a leftward shift in the LM curve. For his alternative causal mechanism he posited a collapse of autonomous expenditures.

The consensus of the subsequent literature was that, although monetary forces were paramount, nonmonetary shocks should not be discounted. Thus, according to Hamilton [1987] and Field [1984], tight monetary policy initiated by the Fed in 1928 to counter the stock market boom and to stem a gold outflow to France, following her return to gold at an undervalued parity, initiated the contraction. The stock market crash of October 1929 then aggravated the downturn in the year following the crash by both increasing uncertainty and wealth-loss effects that led to a reduction in expenditures on consumer durables, as in Romer [1990] and Mishkin [1978]. Romer [1993] agreed that banking panics in 1930, 1931, and 1933 turned a severe recession into depression. Though consensus prevails on the primacy of monetary forces, debate still persists over the issues of the exogeneity of the money supply, as in Schwartz [1981], Bordo [1989], and Calomiris [1993], and of the propagation mechanism.

In the past decade, the focus of the literature has shifted to the mechanism by which monetary collapse was transmitted to the real economy. What is in contention is whether declining output responded to a bank-panic-induced (by a fall in the deposit-currency and deposit-reserve ratios) decline in money supply in the face of sticky wages and prices, or whether the bank failures themselves reduced output via the nonmonetary channel of the disruption of the process of financial intermediation, as suggested by Bernanke [1983].

This debate hinges on the issue of whether or not deflation was anticipated. If not, as Hamilton [1987; 1992] argued, based on evidence from commodity futures markets, and as Evans and Wachtel [1993] found for 1930–32, based on nominal interest rates, then debt deflation (by reducing the net worth of firms and banks) was the propagation mechanism, as in Fisher [1933], and Bernanke and Gertler [1989] and [1990]. If it was largely anticipated, as Nelson [1992] argued, based on an examination of the business press, and as Cecchetti [1992] found, based on time-series models of prices, then the mechanism worked through a rise in the ex ante real interest rate.

Another unsettled issue concerns the causal and propagation roles of international factors—whether the U.S. depression spread to the rest of the world or vice versa, as in Kindleberger [1973] and Temin [1993], with the consensus favoring the U.S. depression as the primary cause with reflex influences on the United States from declining output abroad, as Eichengreen [1992a] concluded. In addition, both Eichengreen [1992b] and Temin [1989] have argued that adherence to the gold standard rule of convertibility was crucial both in the international transmission of shocks and in preventing the monetary authorities of adherents from following reflationary policies.

Our approach in this chapter is compatible with much of the recent literature. We develop a methodology to ascertain the effect of the Friedman and Schwartz hypothesis of stable money on output and the price level. Such a framework is compatible with propagation mechanisms based on sticky wages and prices and on mechanisms stressing both unanticipated and anticipated deflation. It is also compatible with studies that identify the relative importance of different shocks, such as those of Cecchetti and Karras [1994] for the United States, and of Betts, Bordo and Redish [1996] for the United States and Canada. According to these studies, which identify the banking panics as supply shocks, output declines up to the middle of 1931 are generally accounted for by demand shocks and subsequent output declines mostly by supply shocks. Regardless of the source and importance of supply shocks, these results are not inconsistent with the Friedman and Schwartz hypothesis, since a stable money policy could have diminished the effect of all types of shocks to the economy.

One objection to our approach is that as long as the United States was committed to gold convertibility, it was beyond the Fed's power to undertake expansion of domestic credit to maintain stable money through the Great Contraction, as Eichengreen [1992b] argues.

For several reasons we do not believe this raises serious problems. First, given that the United States had the largest monetary gold stock in the world and that at its lowest point in 1932 the Federal Reserve gold reserve ratio was 56 percent, the threat of the United States being forced off the gold standard could not have been a binding constraint.

Second, we do not accept the view that Eichengreen [1992b] has revived, namely, that the Fed could not undertake an expansionary policy because of a shortage of "free gold"—gold not earmarked either as backing for Federal Reserve notes and deposits or as replacement for backing by ineligible assets. Had free gold been a genuine problem, why did not the Federal Reserve importune the Congress to alter the eligibility requirement before such legislation was enacted in February 1932? According to Friedman and Schwartz [1963, 406], free gold was "largely an ex post justification for policies followed, not an ex ante reason for them."[2]

Third, had the gold constraint been a real deterrent to pursuing expansionary monetary policy in the Great Contraction, the United States could have suspended convertibility, as Britain and other countries did. Once they did so, their economies rebounded, as described in Eichengreen and Sachs [1985] and Eichengreen [1992b].

A second objection to our approach, advanced by Calomiris [1993] among others, is that the Fed lacked the requisite understanding to maintain stable money. In favor of this view, Wicker [1965] and Brunner and Meltzer [1968] have argued that the Fed accepted the flawed Burgess-Riefler-Strong doctrine that focused on levels of member bank borrowing and short-term nominal interest rates as policy indicators. On this view the Fed conducted expansionary open market operations in the 1924 and 1927 recessions because neither member bank indebtedness nor nominal interest rates had declined. By contrast, in 1930 member bank borrowing and nominal interest rates fell. Hence the Fed believed no action was warranted, according to Wheelock [1992], and Bordo [1989].

Against this objection, we cite two facts: the connection between stable money and the real economy was well known at the time, as noted by Laidler [1991], even by isolated Federal Reserve officials; and other central banks had on earlier occasions acted successfully as lenders of last resort.

III. Output, Prices, and Money in the Interwar Years

Before discussing our model, we briefly review the behavior of real output, the price level, and the money supply during the interwar period. For data definitions and sources, see Appendix A.

Figure 13.1a shows quarterly time series of the log of real GNP (y) for the period 1921.1–1941.4. Output grew from 1921.1 to the cyclical peak in 1929.3 at an annual rate of 6.4 percent. The period was marked by two mild recessions: 1923.2 to 1924.3 and 1926.3 to 1927.4. Output then declined from 1929.3 to the cyclical trough in 1933.1 by 36.2 percent (at an annual rate of −12.1 percent), the sharpest and most prolonged decline in U.S. history. Rapid recovery then followed until the outbreak of World War II, with output growing at an annual rate of 8.6 percent. Recovery was marred by a brief, sharp recession from 1937.2 to 1938.2.[3]

Figure 13.1b presents the quarterly data for the log of the implicit GNP deflator (p) for the interwar period. Following a sharp post-World War I deflation, the price level was mildly deflationary until the summer of 1929 when it began a rapid plunge for the next three and a half years. It declined by 26.8 percent, or an annual rate of −8.5 percent. The deflation of 1929–1933 was the most severe in U.S. history. Fisher [1933] and Bernanke [1983] regard unanticipated deflation as an aggravating condition in the Great Contraction because of its deleterious effects on the balance sheets of households and firms. From the cyclical trough in 1933.1 until World War II prices advanced at an annual rate of 3.5 percent except for a deflationary episode from 1937.3 to 1939.2.

Figure 13.1c displays the behavior of the log of the M2 money supply (m).[4] Following a sharp policy-induced contraction after World War I, the money supply increased from 1922.2 until 1928.2 at an annual rate of 5.7 percent. The subsequent failure to grow in 1928–29 reflected contractionary Federal Reserve policy in reaction to the stock market boom and a gold flow to France after it returned to the gold standard at a parity that undervalued the franc as in Hamilton [1987] and Field [1984]. Money supply declined for the first year of the Great Contraction by 2.2 percent, a decline not much different from that experienced in earlier severe recessions (Friedman and Schwartz [1963]),[5] but, beginning in October 1930, with the onset of a series of banking panics, it began a plunge whereby m (in M2) fell by 12.4 percent at an annual rate. The fall in m did not end until the Banking Holiday of March 1933.

Beginning in March 1933, the money supply expanded rapidly at an annual rate of 7.8 percent until World War II, with the exception of a sharp contraction in 1937–38. According to Friedman and Schwartz, the Federal Reserve's decision to double reserve requirements in an attempt to soak up what it regarded as excess liquidity in the banking system was responsible for the monetary contraction.

Friedman and Schwartz link the severe decline of the money supply from 1930 to 1933 to a series of banking panics which ultimately caused one-third of the nation's banks to fail. The banking panics reduced the money supply by their effects on the money supply multiplier (see Figure 13.2a). The bank failures, attributed to the absence of Federal

FIGURE 13.1

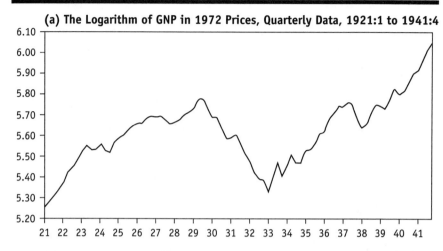

(a) The Logarithm of GNP in 1972 Prices, Quarterly Data, 1921:1 to 1941:4

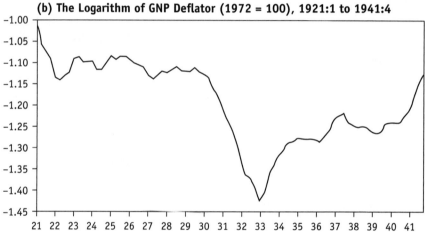

(b) The Logarithm of GNP Deflator (1972 = 100), 1921:1 to 1941:4

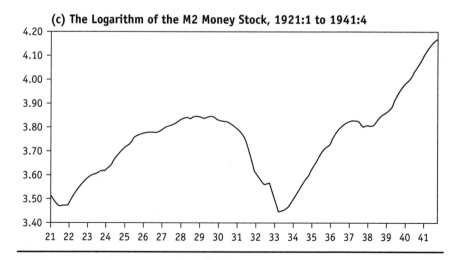

(c) The Logarithm of the M2 Money Stock, 1921:1 to 1941:4

FIGURE 13.2

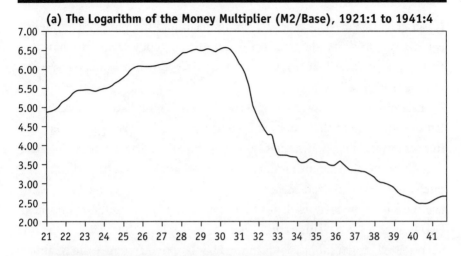

(a) The Logarithm of the Money Multiplier (M2/Base), 1921:1 to 1941:4

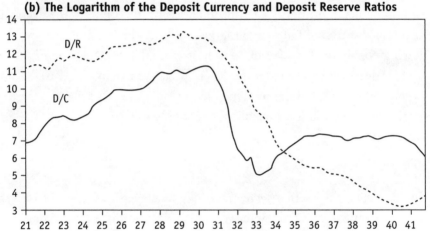

(b) The Logarithm of the Deposit Currency and Deposit Reserve Ratios

D/R

D/C

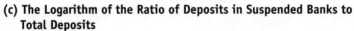

(c) The Logarithm of the Ratio of Deposits in Suspended Banks to Total Deposits

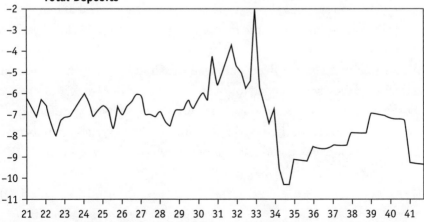

Reserve lender-of-last-resort action, undermined the public's confidence, leading to a massive decline in the deposit-currency ratio. The banks in turn reduced their loans, resulting in a sharp fall in the deposit-reserve ratio (see Figure 13.2b).

Friedman and Schwartz emphasize the bank failures as the force which led to a collapse of the money supply; for Bernanke [1983] they were also important for their nonmonetary role of impairing the financial interme- diation process and hence reducing the level and growth rate of real out- put.[6] As a standardized measure of the importance of bank failures, we use the log of the ratio of deposits in suspended banks to total deposits (s) (see Figure 13.2c).[7] This ratio, s, was quite high in the 1920s, reflecting deep-seated structural problems in the U.S. banking system—the weakness of unit banks in primarily agricultural areas of the country. The dramatic increase in s from 1930 to 1933 largely reflects the banking panics. Fol- lowing the Bank Holiday of March 1933 and the advent of FDIC in 1934, s declined to a much lower level.[8] That the rise in s in 1930–33 was accompanied by a fall in the money supply multiplier underscores the im- portance of bank failures in the money supply process.

IV. Methodology

In this section we describe the methodology we use to simulate counterfactual historical situations for the interwar period. We estimate a small quarterly model of the interwar U.S. economy. To keep our framework simple, our basic model includes only three variables: output, y, the price level, p and money, m. However, we also consider two variations of the basic model. In one variation, we introduce the rate of interest (r) as an additional variable while in the other we add the variable s to capture the role of bank failures. We assume that money affects output in the short run. The short-run non- neutrality of money is assumed to result from sticky prices or wages.[9]

We assume that y, p, m, r, and s are all stationary in first differences.[10] Also, we assume initially that the first four of these variables are cointe- grated via a money demand relation of the following form:

$$m_t - p_t = a_0 + a_1 y_t + a_2 r_t + v_t,$$

(1)

where v_t is a stationary component.[11] In view of (1), we include v_{t-1} as an error correction term in the equations that model the behavior of output and the price level as follows:

$$\Delta y_t = \beta_{10} + \beta_{11} v_{t-1} + a_{11}(L)\Delta y_{t-1} + a_{12}(L)\Delta p_t \\ + a_{13}(L)\Delta m_t + a_{14}(L)\Delta z_t + \delta_{11}\eta_t^d + \delta_{12}\eta_t^s, \tag{2}$$

$$\Delta p_t = \beta_{20} + \beta_{21} v_{t-1} + a_{22}(L)\Delta p_{t-1} + a_{21}(L)\Delta y_t \\ + a_{23}(L)\Delta m_t + a_{24}(L)\Delta z_t + \delta_{21}\eta_t^d + \delta_{22}\eta_t^s, \tag{3}$$

where $a_{ij}(L)$ are lag polynomials of order k, $z_t = r$, or s_p and η_t^d and η_t^s are mutually uncorrelated white-noise disturbances representing demand and supply shocks respectively.[12] The determination of the money supply is modeled as

$$\Delta m_t = \beta_{30} + a_{33}(L)\Delta m_{t-1} + a_{31}(L)\Delta y_t \\ + a_{32}(L)\Delta p_t + a_{34}(L)\Delta z_t + \eta_t^m, \tag{4}$$

where η_t^m is a white-noise money supply shock (uncorrelated with both η_t^d and η_t^s). Equation (4) allows for potential effects of y, p and z on m through high-powered money (via the Fed's reaction function) as well as the money multiplier.

In our basic model, we suppress the role of both the interest rate r and bank failures s by letting $\alpha_2 = 0$ in (1), and $\alpha_{i4}(L) = 0$, $i = 1,2,3$, in equations (2) through (4). Friedman and Schwartz [1963] treated bank panics as exogenous shocks to money supply and did not consider output and the price level as significant determinants of either high-powered money or the money multiplier. Their view suggests including bank panic shocks in η_t^m and setting $a_{31}(L) = a_{32}(L) = 0$ in (4).

Before discussing the estimation of our basic model, it is interesting to compare it with McCallum's [1990] model and to note the points of difference. First, McCallum estimates a relation for nominal income growth (i.e., $\Delta y_t + \Delta p_t$ in our notation), which depends on its own lagged values and lagged money growth. This relation can be thought of as a special case of our equations (1) and (2), which could be derived by placing restrictions on appropriate lag polynomials in (1) and (2). Second, McCallum models money growth differently from the way we do. He assumes that the growth of the money base is exogenous but allows growth in the money multiplier to depend on a bank failure variable (denoted by s in our model), which in turn is influenced by deviations of nominal income from its target path. Thus, there is a feedback from nominal income to money growth in his model, but this effect is restricted to the above channels and is not as general as our equation (3).

We estimate our basic model in the form of a vector error correction model. Letting $x_t \equiv [\Delta y_t, \Delta p_t, \Delta m_t]$ and $\eta_t \equiv [\eta_t^d, \eta_t^s, \eta_t^m]$, write equations (2) through (4) as $Ax_t = \beta_0 + \beta_1 v_{t-1} + \beta(L)x_{t-1} + \delta\eta_t$, and premultiply by A^{-1} to obtain

$$x_t = \gamma_0 + \gamma_1 v_{t-1} + C(L)x_{t-1} + e_t, \tag{5}$$

where $\gamma_i = A^{-1}\beta_i$, $i = 0, 1$, $C(L) = A^{-1}B(L)$ and $e_t \equiv [e_t^y, e_t^p, e_t^m]$ is a vector of reduced-form shocks. The reduced-form shocks are related to structural shocks by

$$e_t = D\eta_t, \tag{6}$$

where $D(=A^{-1}\delta) \equiv [D_{ij}]$, $i, j = 1, 2, 3$.

To perform counterfactual simulations of output, y, and prices, p, based on (5), we define the constant money growth policy as the Fed targeting a rate of growth of the money stock equal to θ, based on all available information. Under this policy

$$E(m_t \mid I_t) = m_{t-1} + \theta, \tag{7}$$

where I_t is the Fed's information set in period t. The degree of monetary control under a constant money growth policy clearly depends on the information available to the Fed. We consider several possibilities. At a minimum, we assume that the Fed observes all variables with a one-period lag (i.e., I_t contains values of all variables up to $t-1$). Using this weak informational assumption, the constant money growth rule (7) implies that the Δm equation of model (5) will change to

$$\Delta m_t = \theta + e_t^m. \tag{8}$$

We replace the Δm equation in (5) by (8) to simulate the behavior of output and the price level under this policy. This simulation does not require identification of structural shocks, and would be consistent with any view about the contemporaneous relationship between m, y, and p.

A stronger assumption about the Fed's monetary control is that it knows contemporaneous money supply shocks (i.e., I_t includes η_t^m in addition to information on all variables up to $t-1$). In this case the constant money growth policy would eliminate η_t^m shocks. Using (6), the constant money growth rule under the stronger informational assumption implies that

$$\Delta m_t = \theta + e_t^{m*}, \tag{9}$$

where $e_t^{m*} = D_{31}\eta_t^d + D_{32}\eta_t^s$. Moreover, with money supply shocks eliminated, Δy and Δp equations in (5) will be subject only to shocks $e_t^{y*} \equiv D_{11}\eta_t^d + D_{12}\eta_t^s$, and $e_t^{p*} \equiv D_{21}\eta_t^d + D_{22}\eta_t^s$, respectively. Note that the simulation based on (9) requires the identification of only η_t^m shocks as e_t^{w*} can be estimated as a residual in a projection of e_t^w on η_t^m, $w=y,p,m$.

A number of approaches can be used to identify η_t^m, the money supply shock term. One interesting possibility is suggested by the Friedman-Schwartz view that the behavior of the money supply was essentially independent of output and prices. If it is assumed that y and p do not affect m at least contemporaneously, then $a_{31}(0) = a_{32}(0) = 0$, and these exclusion restrictions imply that $D_{31} = D_{32} = 0$ while $D_{33} = 1$. Thus $e_t^m = \eta_t^m$, and (since $e_t^{m*} = 0$) the counterfactual money supply equation (9) reduces to

$$\Delta m_t = \theta. \tag{10}$$

As (8) and (10) represent polar assumptions about monetary control, the next section focuses on simulations based on these equations to present the least and the most favorable cases for stable money.

As extensions of our basic model, we include a fourth variable z representing either interest rates r or bank failures s. The behavior of the fourth variable is modeled as

$$
\begin{aligned}
\Delta z_t = \beta_{40} + a_{44}(L)\Delta z_{t-1} &+ a_{41}(L)\Delta y_t \\
&+ a_{42}(L)\Delta p_t + a_{43}(L)\Delta m_t + \eta_t^z,
\end{aligned}
\tag{11}
$$

where η_t^z is assumed to be white noise and uncorrelated with other shocks. In the case of $z_t = r_t$, η_t^z can be viewed as shocks to asset markets while for $z_t = s_t$, η_t^z can be thought of as financial shocks relevant to bank suspensions and failures. The model represented by (1), (2), (3), (4) and (11) [with $\alpha_2 = 0$ in (1) for $z_t = s_t$] can be estimated in the form of (5) with x_t and e_t redefined as $[\Delta y_t, \Delta p_t, \Delta m_t, \Delta z_t]$ and $[e_t^y, e_t^p, e_t^m, e_t^z]$. In this case, however, the restriction that y and p do not contemporaneously affect m is not sufficient to identify η_t^m since z could still exert a contemporaneous effect on m. While identification of η_t^m is not needed for counterfactual (8), additional assumptions would be required to justify counterfactual (10).

Our simulations assume that a change in the Δm equation does not alter other equations of the model. We suppose that the short-run adjustment process is not very sensitive to a change in monetary policy. The long-run rate of inflation would, however, depend on the long-run rate of money growth. Thus, in constructing our counterfactual, we avoid a change in the long-run money growth rate by setting θ equal to the average value of Δm for the period over which our model is estimated.

Our model does not explicitly constrain money to be neutral in the long run. One implication of long-run neutrality of money is that η^m would not permanently affect y. This restriction poses no problem for simulations based on (8) as any set of restrictions used to identify structural shocks would be consistent with this counterfactual. However, restrictions used to identify η_t^m for counterfactual (10) would not constrain the long-run effect of this shock to equal zero.

V. Basic Simulations

Before discussing our simulations, we present some evidence on the relationship between money and other variables in the model in the interwar period. Table 13.1 shows results of Granger causality tests between certain variables in the model for 1921.1 to 1941.4. Regressions in this table include the lagged value of the error correction term, v, and three lagged values of other regressors. Here, assuming that α_1 equals one and α_2 equals zero, we measure v by $(m-p-y)$.[13]

The first three regressions in the table are based on the three-variable framework of the basic model. In the first regression, we examine the influence of output and the price level on money. As the results show, three lagged values of both Δy and Δp as well as the lagged value of v, the error correction term, are insignificant in the regression explaining Δm. This evidence on the absence of Granger causality from output and the price level to money is consistent with the view that the money supply in this period was exogenous. The second and the third regressions in the table examine the links from money to output and the price level. The lagged values of Δm are significant (at the .011 level) in the Δy equation but insignificant in the Δp equation. However, even in the Δp equation, the lagged value of v is significant (at the .023 level), and thus money does exert an effect on the price level through the error correction term. Although we have suppressed the role of the interest rate in our basic model, we nevertheless explore the influence of this variable on money, output and the price level in regressions 4, 5 and 6. As the results show, interest rates do not improve the predictive content of any of these regressions.

The remaining regressions in the table explore the interaction of s with m, p and y. The results based on regressions 7 through 9 show that lagged Δs terms are significant in the Δm and Δp equations (at .017 and .060 levels, respectively) but not in the Δy equation. In regression 10, however, lagged values of both Δp and Δm are significant (at .015 and .052 levels) in the Δs equation. These results suggest a role for bank failures (s) in the model, but note that the effects operating between s and other variables are not very strong. For example, inclusion of this variable in the Δm and Δp equations increases the $\bar{R}^2$ of these equations only marginally: by

TABLE 13.1 Tests of Granger Causality

		Regressions			F-Tests		
No.	Dependent Variable	Regressors (no. of lags)	$\bar{R}^2$	Excluded Variable(s)	F-statistic	(p-value)	
1.	Δm	c, v(1), Δy(3), Δp(3), Δm(3)	.552	Δy(3)	1.55	(.208)	
				Δp(3)	.47	(.706)	
				v(1)	.10	(.920)	
2.	Δy	c, v(1), Δy(3), Δp(3), Δm(3)	.333	Δm(3)	4.02	(.011)	
				v(1)	3.37	(.070)	
3.	Δp	c, v(1), Δy(3), Δp(3), Δm(3)	.562	Δm(3)	.92	(.434)	
				v(1)	5.42	(0.23)	
4.	Δm	c, v(1), Δy(3), Δp(3), Δm(3) Δr(3)	.563	Δr(3)	1.16	(.332)	
5.	Δy	c, v(1), Δy(3), Δp(3), Δm(3), Δr(3)	.322	Δr(3)	.62	(.605)	
6.	Δp	c, v(1), Δy(3), Δp(3), Δm(3), Δr(3)	.554	Δr(3)	.55	(.650)	
7.	Δm	c, v(1), Δy(3), Δp(3), Δm(3), Δs(3)	.595	Δs(3)	3.63	(.017)	
8.	Δy	c, v(1), Δy(3), Δp(3), Δm(3), Δs(3)	.348	Δs(3)	1.56	(.206)	
9.	Δp	c, v(1), Δy(3), Δp(3), Δm(3), Δs(3)	.589	Δs(3)	2.59	(.060)	
10.	Δs	c, v(1), Δy(3), Δp(3), Δm(3), Δs(3)	.160	Δy(3)	1.39	(.253)	
				Δp(3)	3.76	(.015)	
				Δm(3)	2.70	(.052)	
				v(1)	1.42	(.237)	

NOTE: c is a constant, $v = m - p - y$, and r is the rate of interest. For regressors and excluded variable(s), the number in brackets represents the number of lagged values of the indicated variable. See Appendix A for sources of data.

.043 and .027, respectively (compare regression 7 with 1, and 9 with 3). The $\bar{R}^2$ of the Δs equation, moreover, is only .160.

We begin with simulations based on the basic vector error correction model (5) with three variables. We estimate this model using three lags for each variable.[14] Although our interest is primarily in the Great Contraction period, we simulate the behavior of Δy and Δp under the constant money growth policy for the whole interwar period. We focus on the two variants of the constant money growth policy discussed above. The weak case for this policy is represented by model I defined as model (5) with its Δm equation replaced by (8). Model II, on the other hand, represents the strong case. This model is defined as model (5) in which not only is the Δm equation replaced by (10) but also e_t^y and e_t^p in the Δy and Δp equations are replaced by e_t^{y*} and e_t^{p*} (estimated as residuals in regressions of e_t^y on e_t^m and e_t^p on e_t^m). In both models I and II, θ is set equal to .00738 (the mean value of Δm for 1921.1–1941.4).[15]

Figure 13.3 shows the simulated behavior of m, p, and y for models I and II, and compares it to the actual behavior of these variables. The actual and counterfactual monetary policies are contrasted in panel (a) of the figure. Note that even the weaker constant money growth rule (used in model I) would have resulted in only minor decreases in the money stock during 1931 to 1933.

The basic question raised in this chapter is addressed in panel (b) of Figure 13.3. As this figure shows, a fall in output would have occurred starting in 1929 in model I, but the simulated decline (−21.6 percent cumulative and −6.61 percent at an annual rate) would not have been as severe and prolonged as the decline in the Great Contraction (−36.2 percent cumulative and −12.1 percent at an annual rate). In fact, under this counterfactual a recovery would have begun in 1933 and output would have reached its 1929 level by early 1934. The 1929–33 output decrease in this case would have represented a major but not an exceptional recession. Model I assumes that the constant money growth policy would not have had any influence on money supply shocks. However, if this policy had eliminated these shocks according to the identifying assumptions of model II, then as the model II simulations in Figure 13.3B show, output would have declined only modestly (−11.1 percent cumulative and

−3.30 percent at an annual rate) during 1929 to 1931 and this episode would not have been considered a major recession. Interestingly, in both models a constant money growth policy does not appreciably change output until 1931, which is consistent with Romer's [1990] position that the 1929–30 contraction was due to nonmonetary forces—specifically, the stock market crash. It is also interesting to note that the simulated level of output in both models stays well above the actual level not only during the Great Contraction period but also throughout the subsequent recovery period. Figure 13.3C shows that the behavior of the price level would also be significantly altered under both counterfactuals, but deflation still persists in both cases.

As discussed above, money supply shocks in model II need not be neutral in the long run. Panel (a) of Figure 13.4 shows the impulse response of output to a (one standard deviation) money supply shock as identified in model II. The figure suggests that money supply shocks affect output permanently. One explanation of this result (indicating non-neutrality of money in the long run) is that monetary shocks led to a collapse of financial intermediation (highlighted by Bernanke [1983]) during the Great Contraction, and this collapse had long-term effects. We examine this issue further in the next section.

Table 13.2 presents some measures of the performance of the two models (as well as some other models discussed below). First, to examine the average difference between the counterfactual and actual output levels, the table shows the mean of $y_t^* - y_t$, where y_t^* represents the simulated value of y_t. This statistic is shown for the whole 1921.1–1941.4 period as well as subperiods 1929.3 to 1941.4 and 1929.3 to 1933.1. For both models I and II the mean difference for the subperiod including the recovery is even higher than the Great Contraction subperiod. Although the main issue is the effect of the constant money growth policy on the level of output, the table also shows the ratio of the variance of Δy_t^* to that of Δy_t for the whole period. As the table shows, this ratio of variances is below 1.0 for model I and much lower than 1.0 for model II. Finally, the table also provides estimates (for the whole period) of the ratio of the variance of Δp_t^* to that of Δp_t, where p_t^* is the simulated value of p_t. This ratio is also below 1.0 for both models I and II.

FIGURE 13.3

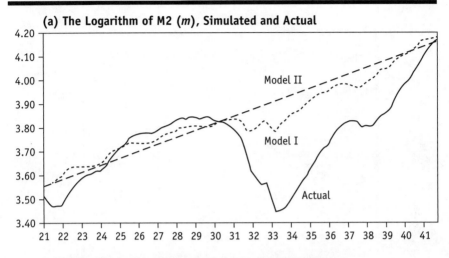

(a) The Logarithm of M2 (*m*), Simulated and Actual

Model II

Model I

Actual

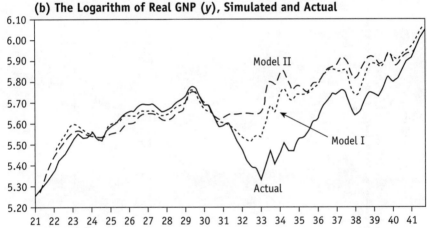

(b) The Logarithm of Real GNP (*y*), Simulated and Actual

Model II

Model I

Actual

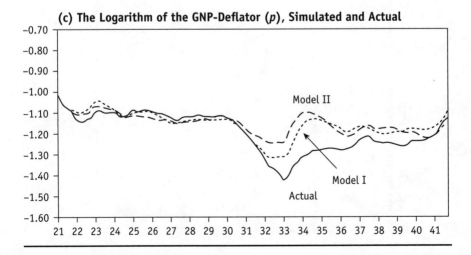

(c) The Logarithm of the GNP-Deflator (*p*), Simulated and Actual

Model II

Model I

Actual

TABLE 13.2 Performance Measures for Different Simulated Models

	Mean $(y^* - y)$			$\dfrac{var(\Delta y^*)}{var(\Delta y)}$	$\dfrac{var(\Delta p^*)}{var(\Delta p)}$
	1921.1–1941.4	1929.3–1941.4	1929.3–1933.1	1921.1–1941.4	1921.1–1941.4
Assuming Weak Monetary Control					
Model I	.067	.108	.043	.943	.961
Model IA	.061	.096	.033	.929	.970
Model IB	.067	.107	.048	.898	.967
Model IC	.075	.129	.061	1.082	1.130
Model ID	.093	.148	.114	1.085	1.048
Model IE	.198	.334	.220	.624	1.013
Assuming Strong Monetary Control					
Model II	.083	.149	.100	.765	.860
Model IIA	.080	.151	.080	.741	.868
Model IID	.101	.181	.219	.834	.941
Model IIE	.206	.347	.243	.526	.826

Note: A star (*) indicates a simulated value. Models I and II represent the basic three-variable version; IA and IIA exclude v; IB and IC include s and τ, respectively; ID and IID use data on industrial production and WPI (instead of the Balke-Gordon series on real GNP and the GNP deflator); and IE and IIE estimate parameters on the basis of 1921.1–1929.4 data. See text for further explanations of these models.

Our simulations also have implications for issues recently raised by Romer [1992]. Romer wishes to explain the determinants of the recovery from 1933 to 1941. Based on money-income multipliers calculated for the years 1921 and 1938 she simulates the behavior of real output from 1933 to 1941 if money growth had not deviated from the average (M1) growth rate of 1923 to 1927 of 2.88 percent. Such a money growth rate would have led to a 50 percent gap below potential in 1941. The fact that actual output grew substantially faster makes her case that gold-flow-induced expansionary money supply produced the recovery.

Our simulation also covers the recovery period from 1933 to 1941 but, unlike Romer, who assumed that the money supply collapsed from 1929 to 1933, as it did, our simulation assumes that a constant money growth rule for M2 was maintained over the entire interwar period. Our simulations suggest that the extra monetary stimulus Romer documents would have been unnecessary had stable money prevailed throughout the interwar period.

VI. Variations of the Basic Model

In this section we examine the sensitivity of our results to a number of variations of our model. First, as there is controversy about the view that the long-run money demand function is stable, we examine how our results would change if the assumption that $m - p$ and y are cointegrated is dropped. In this case the error correction term v will not appear in (2), (3) and (5). We thus resimulate models I and II using estimates of a three-variable VAR including y, p and m (without the error correction term). The performance measures for the resulting simulations (referred to as models IA and IIA) are also shown in Table 13.2. Compared to model I, the mean $(y^* - y)$ for model IA is lower by a small amount (.006) for the whole period but a somewhat larger amount (.010) during the Great Contraction. Comparison of model II with IIA shows similar results. The performance of a constant money growth policy thus deteriorates somewhat if the error correction term is removed from the model.

Next, we extend our model to include s or r as an additional variable as discussed in Section III. For this case we consider only the simulations

FIGURE 13.4

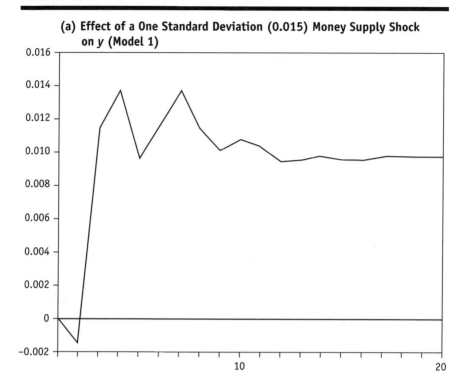

(a) Effect of a One Standard Deviation (0.015) Money Supply Shock on *y* (Model 1)

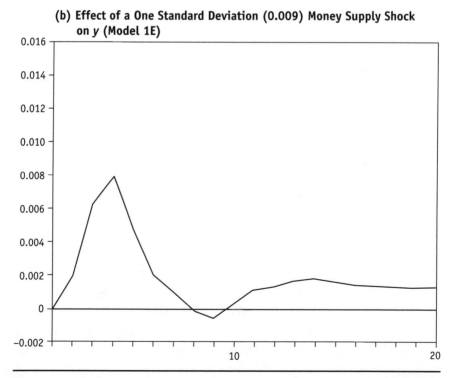

(b) Effect of a One Standard Deviation (0.009) Money Supply Shock on *y* (Model 1E)

based on the weak counterfactual since the strong counterfactual would require additional assumptions to identify money supply shocks. The four-variable vector error correction model under the weak monetary-control assumption is labelled model IB when the fourth variable represents s and model IC when it represents r.[16] Measures of performance for these two models are also shown in Table 13.2. Model IB leads to a slightly higher level of output than model I during the Great Contraction, but the overall performance of these two models is not much different. Thus the introduction of variable s does not make an appreciable difference to the results. The results change more significantly under model IC. While this model produces greater variability of both output growth and inflation, it also brings about a higher level of output. On balance, its performance compares favourably to that of model I.

Our data on y and p are the Balke-Gordon quarterly series on real GNP and the GNP deflator. As these series use interpolations of annual data, they allow future information to influence current values. To explore whether this data problem may have introduced a serious bias in our results, we also estimated our basic model using quarterly averages of monthly data on industrial production and the wholesale price index as alternative measures of y and p. The weak and strong versions of the basic model based on the alternative data set are labelled ID and IID. Measures of performance for these two models in Table 13.2 show that although the effect of the constant money growth policy on the variability of Δy and Δp differs between the two models, the policy substantially increases the level of output, especially during the Great Contraction, in both models. Indeed, in terms of the effect on the level of output, the case for the constant money growth policy is stronger if the data on industrial production and the wholesale price index are used instead of the Balke-Gordon estimates (compare model ID with I and IID with II).

Our simulations assume not only that a constant money growth policy would not have significantly altered the output and price equations but also that these equations were stable throughout the interwar period. This assumption is subject to the Lucas [1976] critique since the Great Contraction could have represented a regime shift that would have caused the parameters of the reduced-form relations to change. To explore this issue, we tested our model for possible breaks at three different dates, 1930.1, 1931.4 and 1933.2, which represent the beginning, the middle and the end of the Great Contraction. The Chow test of a break at a fixed date indicates a shift in both the output and price equations in 1930.1 as well as in 1933.2. It may be thought that an equation explaining nominal income would have been more stable than our separate output and price equations. However, testing a comparable nominal-income equation for stability, the Chow test indicates a break in this relation in 1933.2, though not in 1930.1.[17]

If, as the above evidence indicates, the Great Contraction was responsible for shifts in the output and price relations, then these shifts would not have occurred under a constant money growth policy that prevented the Contraction. This possibility suggests using relations estimated for the stable 1920s to construct the constant money growth counterfactual for the whole interwar period. For this simulation, the basic model was estimated separately for the subperiods 1921.1–1929.4 and 1930.1–1941.4 to calculate reduced-form shocks for the whole period. Then, using output and price equations estimated for the 1921.1–1929.4 subperiod and letting $\theta = .00822$ (the mean value of Δm for this subperiod), the behavior of m, y and p was simulated under both the weak and strong monetary control assumptions. These simulations are referred to as models IE and IIE, respectively, and are illustrated in Figure 13.5.

As Figure 13.5 shows, the behavior of output y and the price level p under both model IE and IIE is dramatically different from previous simulations. The most remarkable difference is in the behavior of y which, unlike in previous cases, does not exhibit any significant contraction during the 1929–33 period under both the weak and strong forms of the constant money growth rule. This result fully supports the underlying assumption of the simulation that by preventing the Great Contraction the constant money growth policy would have preserved the 1920s output and price relations. Performance measures for models IE and IIE in Table 13.2 show that although these models would have made a marginal difference to the variability of the price level, they would have produced a substantially higher level of output and a significantly lower output variability.

As noted above, the collapse of financial intermediation could have accounted for the result that money shocks had long-term effects on output in model II. If money is otherwise neutral in the long run, we would not expect money shocks to exert a permanent effect on output in a model based on the period before the financial collapse. This prediction is supported by panel (b) of Figure 13.4, which shows that in contrast to model II, η^m does not have a marked long-run effect on y in model IIE.

VII. Conclusion

This chapter reconsiders the long-debated question of whether stable money could have averted the Great Contraction in the United States. Our approach follows McCallum's methodology of using an empirical model of the economy based on interwar data to examine how a counterfactual policy would have performed. Our study, however, departs from McCallum's in considering a different monetary policy rule and estimating separate relations for output and the price level. We also allow the form of our rule to depend on information available to the Fed and on contemporaneous relations between money and other variables.

We consider two variants of Milton Friedman's constant money growth rule that represent limiting cases for a wide range of assumptions about monetary control. While one of these variants assumes that output and the price level do not affect money in the same period and lets the Fed observe money supply shocks contemporaneously, the other allows any pattern of instantaneous causality between money and economic activity and assumes that the Fed can react to shocks with only a one-period lag.

Basic simulations of both variants produce results consistent with claims that, had a stable money policy been followed, the Great Contraction would have been mitigated and shortened. A severe recession would have occurred but not of the extraordinary character of the Great Contraction. If it is further assumed that a stable money policy would have prevented shifts in the output and price relations, our alternative simulations produce the much stronger result that there would have been no recession at all during the Great Contraction under both variants of the constant money growth rule.

FIGURE 13.5

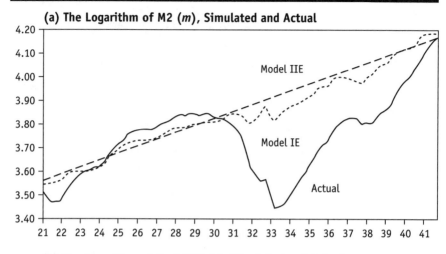

(a) The Logarithm of M2 (*m*), Simulated and Actual

Model IIE

Model IE

Actual

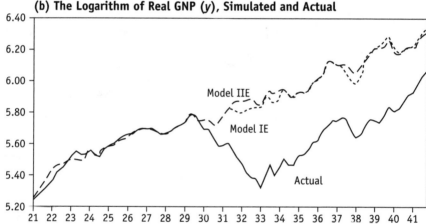

(b) The Logarithm of Real GNP (*y*), Simulated and Actual

Model IIE

Model IE

Actual

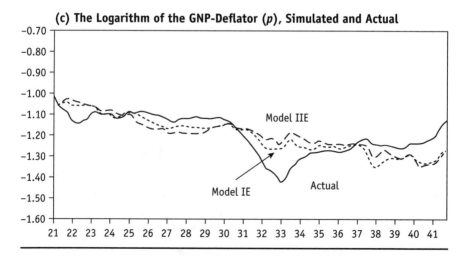

(c) The Logarithm of the GNP-Deflator (*p*), Simulated and Actual

Model IIE

Model IE

Actual

If our simulations are valid, then the extra monetary stimulus that Romer [1992] argues was essential to produce recovery after 1933 would not have been necessary. In fact, under all of our constant money growth counterfactuals, simulated output is well above the actual output throughout the 1933–41 period.

Eichenbaum [1992] has argued that, "After all, aside from the time consistency issue, there is little theoretical reason to recommend a k percent rule." The view that a k percent rule (our constant money growth rule) is suboptimal compares economic performance under constant money growth with alternative rules or discretion that yield a superior outcome. Our focus, however, is on the constant money growth policy relative to actual performance during the Great Depression. On that basis, constant money growth was clearly preferable.

Appendix A: Data Sources

Quarterly Data

Real Gross National Product and Gross National Product Implicit Price Deflator: Balke-Gordon [1986], Table 2.

Suspended Bank Deposits: *Federal Reserve Bulletin,* September 1937, 909; McCallum [1990].

Money Stock (M2): Friedman and Schwartz [1970], Table 2, 61–73.

Monetary Base: Friedman and Schwartz [1963], Appendix B, Table B-3, 799–808.

Interest Rate: Commercial paper rate in Balke-Gordon [1986], Table 2.

Monthly Data

Consumer Price Index: 1910–40, NBER Business Cycle Series no. 04072; 1941–61, NBER Business Cycle Series no. 04052.

Industrial Production: 1919–66, NBER Business Cycle Series no. 01303.

Money Stock (M2): Friedman and Schwartz [1970], Table 1, 8–52.

Notes

1. See also Feldstein and Stock [1994] who simulate the effect of an optimal monetary policy rule on nominal GDP over the 1959–92 period.

2. The argument in chapter 10 of Eichengreen [1992b], that the Federal Reserve would not have been able to expand the money supply in the 1931 episode because it would have violated the free gold constraint and forced the United States off the gold standard, is incorrect, as shown by Bordo [1994]. First, the author argues that since M1 fell by $2 billion between August 1931 and January 1932, a $2 billion open market operation would have been required to offset the decline, and this would have forced the United States, with only $400 million in free gold, off the gold standard. This argument ignores the arithmetic of money supply relationships. The ratio of M1 to high-powered money fell between August 1931 and January 1932 from 3.2 to 2.8— the average money multiplier over the period was approximately 3. Thus an open market operation to increase the monetary base by $600–650 million was all that would have been needed if no other forces were at work. According to Friedman and Schwartz [1963], other forces were present so that a $1 billion purchase would have been needed. But would the $1 billion purchase have exhausted free gold? It would have if the open market purchase, as Eichengreen assumes, were absorbed by a dollar-for-dollar increase in currency, which had to be backed 40 percent by gold and 60 percent by eligible paper. But if the purchase had increased bank reserves by $1 billion, which would have had the effect of calming depositors' fears about bank safety, then free gold would not have been exhausted.

3. We use the Balke-Gordon [1986] data based on the Kuznets-Commerce sources. Romer [1988] has criticized this data set and constructed her own series. Her data considerably reduce the severity of the 1923–24, 1926–27, and 1937–38 recessions but not that of the Great Contraction of 1929–33.

4. We also estimated the model using M1. The results were quite similar.

5. Romer [1990] attributes the decline in output from 1929 to 1930 to the effects of the stock market crash, not the decline in the money stock.

6. Temin [1978] disputes Friedman and Schwartz's contention that banking panics were the cause of the collapse in the money supply. His regressions show that the banking failures of the 1930s entirely reflected the decline in economic activity. A number of subsequent papers refute this finding, as in Anderson and Butkiewicz [1980], Wicker [1980], Mayer [1978], Boughton and Wicker [1979].

7. McCallum [1990] uses this measure. Bernanke [1983] uses the real value of suspended bank deposits as a proxy for the nonmonetary influence of the banking failures on economic activity.

8. According to White [1984], however, the majority of banks that failed after 1930 had characteristics similar to those that failed in the 1920s.

9. See, for example, Blanchard [1990].

10. For each of these variables, the augmented Dickey-Fuller test (both with and without a time trend) does not reject the hypothesis that the variable contains a unit root.

11. See Lucas [1988] who argues that U.S. long-run money demand is stable. Also see Hafer and Jansen [1991] for evidence supporting a cointegrated money demand relation for M2 over the period from 1915 to 1988. For a contrary view, see McCallum [1993] who argues that shocks to the money demand function are likely to include permanent stochastic changes in technology affecting transactions.

12. In the case where $z_t = s_t$, s is included in (2) and (3) for reasons discussed by Bernanke [1983].

13. Existing evidence, for example, Lucas [1988] and Hoffman and Rasche [1991], suggests that the income elasticity of money demand is close to one. The assumption that $\alpha_2 = 0$ is relaxed later in simulations based on the extended model that includes the interest rate. Note that α_0 (the intercept in the demand for money) is left out and is included in the constant terms of the regressions.

14. We also tried four lags for each variable but the additional lagged terms were not significant.

15. It might be argued that at the onset of the Great Contraction, the Fed would not have known the average interwar money growth rate and, thus, it would be more appropriate to set θ equal to some rate reflecting the 1920's experience. The average value of Δm for 1921-29 is, in fact, greater than the interwar average. As discussed above, however, we eschew using a higher rate of money growth in the present simulations on the grounds that estimated parameters of our model are likely to reflect the average experience of the whole interwar period. In the next section, we do set θ equal to the average Δm value for 1921.1-1929.4 in an alternative simulation based on a model estimated for the same period.

16. In model IC, v is measured as $m - p - y - \alpha_2 r$ with $\alpha_2 = -.04$. This estimate of α_2 was derived by applying the dynamic OLS procedure in Stock and Watson [1989] to the money demand relation (1), constraining α_1 equal to one and using four leads and lags.

17. Nominal income growth was regressed on a constant, lagged value of v, three lagged values of Δm and three of its own lagged values. McCallum's [1990] nominal-income equation is slightly different (it includes only one lagged value of Δm and no error-correction term) but this equation also breaks in 1933.2 according to the Chow test. However, as McCallum notes, a break at this date is not indicated if two dummy variables for the 1930.2 and 1930.3 quarters are also included in the equation.

References

Anderson, Barry, and James Butkiewicz. "Money, Spending, and the Great Depression." *Southern Economic Journal*, October 1980, 388–403.

Balke, Nathan S., and Robert J. Gordon. "Historical Data" in *The American Business Cycle: Continuity and Change*, edited by R. Gordon. Chicago: University of Chicago Press, 1986, 781–850.

Bernanke, Ben. "Nonmonetary Effects of the Financial Crisis in the Propagation of the Great Depression." *American Economic Review*, June 1983, 257–76.

Bernanke, Ben, and Mark Gertler. "Agency Costs, Net Worth and Business Fluctuations." *American Economic Review*, March 1989, 14–31.

———. "Financial Fragility and Economic Performance." *Quarterly Journal of Economics*, February 1990, 87–114.

Betts, Caroline, Michael Bordo and Angela Redish. "A Small Open Economy in Depression: Lessons from Canada in the 1930's." *Canadian Journal of Economics*, February 1996, 1–36.

Blanchard, Olivier. "Why Does Money Affect Output? A Summary," in *Handbook of Monetary Economics*, edited by B. M. Friedman and F. H. Hahn. Amsterdam: North Holland Publishers, 1990, vol. 2, chapter 15.

Bordo, Michael. "The Contribution of *A Monetary History of the United States, 1867–1960* to Monetary History," in *Money, History, and International Finance: Essays in Honor of Anna J. Schwartz*, edited by M. D. Bordo. Chicago: University of Chicago Press, 1989, 15–70.

———. "Review of Barry Eichengreen, *Golden Fetters: The Gold Standard and the Great Depression.*" *Journal of International Economics*, February 1994, 193–97.

Boughton, James M., and Elmus R. Wicker. "The Behavior of the Currency-Deposit Ratio during the Great Depression." *Journal of Money, Credit and Banking*, November 1979, 405–18.

Brunner, Karl, and Allan H. Meltzer. "What Did We Learn from the Monetary Experience of the United States in the Great Depression?" *Canadian Journal of Economics*, May 1968, 336–48.

Calomiris, Charles. "Financial Factors in the Great Depression." *Journal of Economic Perspectives*, 7(2), Spring 1993, 61–85.

Cecchetti, Stephen G. "Prices During the Great Depression: Was the Deflation of 1930–1932 Really Anticipated?" *American Economic Review*, March 1992, 141–56.

Cecchetti, Stephen G., and Georgios Karras. "Sources of Output Fluctuations during the Interwar Period: Further Evidence on the Causes of the Great Depression." *Review of Economics and Statistics*, February 1994, 80–102.

Eichenbaum, Martin. "Comment on 'Central Bank Behavior and the Strategy of Monetary Policy: Observations from Six Industrialized Countries' by Ben Bernanke and Frederic Mishkin," in *NBER Macroeconomics Annual 1992*, edited by O. Blanchard and S. Fisher, 1992, 233.

Eichengreen, Barry. "The Origins and Nature of the Great Slump Revisited." *Economic History Review*, May 1992(a), 213–39.

————. *Golden Fetters: The Gold Standard and the Great Depression, 1929–1939*. New York: Oxford University Press, 1992(b).

Eichengreen, Barry, and Jeffrey Sachs. "Exchange Rates and Economic Recovery in the 1930s." *Journal of Economic History*, December 1985, 925–46.

Evans, Martin, and Paul Wachtel. "Were Price Changes during the Great Depression Anticipated?" *Journal of Monetary Economics*, August 1993, 3–34.

Feldstein, Martin, and James Stock. "The Use of a Monetary Aggregate to Target Nominal GDP," in *Monetary Policy*, edited by N.G. Mankiw. Chicago: Chicago University Press, 1994, 7–62.

Field, Alexander J. "Asset Exchanges and the Transaction Demand for Money, 1919–1929." *American Economic Review*, March 1984, 43–59.

Fisher, Irving. "The Debt-Deflation Theory of Great Depressions." *Econometrica*, October 1933, 339–57.

Friedman, Milton. *A Program for Monetary Stability*. New York: Fordham University Press, 1960.

Friedman, Milton, and Anna J. Schwartz. *A Monetary History of the United States, 1867–1960*. Princeton: Princeton University Press, 1963.

————. *Monetary Statistics of the United States*. New York: Columbia University Press for NBER, 1970.

Hafer, Rik W., and Dennis W. Jansen. "The Demand for Money in the United States: Evidence from Cointegrating Tests." *Journal of Money, Credit and Banking*, May 1991, 155–68.

Hamilton, James D. "Monetary Factors in the Great Depression." *Journal of Monetary Economics*, March 1987, 145–70.

————. "Was the Deflation during the Great Depression Anticipated? Evidence from the Commodity Futures Market." *American Economic Review*, March 1992, 157–78.

Hoffman, Dennis, and Robert H. Rasche. "Long-Run Income and Interest Elasticities of Money Demand in the United States." *Review of Economics and Statistics*, November 1991, 665–74.

Kindleberger, Charles. *The World in Depression*. Berkeley: University of California Press, 1973.

Laidler, David. *The Golden Age of the Quantity Theory*. Princeton: Princeton University Press, 1991.

Lucas, Robert E., Jr. "Economic Policy Evaluation: A Critique," in *Carnegie-Rochester Conference Series on Public Policy*, edited by K. Brunner and A. H. Meltzer. Amsterdam: North-Holland, 1, 1976, 19–46.

————. "Money Demand in the United States: A Quantitative Review," in *Carnegie-Rochester Conference Series on Public Policy*, edited by K. Brunner and A. H. Meltzer, 29, 1988, 137–68.

Mayer, Thomas. "Money and the Great Depression: Some Reflections on Temin's Recent Book." *Explorations in Economic History,* April 1978, 127–45.

McCallum, Bennett T. "Could a Monetary Base Rule Have Prevented the Great Depression?" *Journal of Monetary Economics,* August 1990, 3–26.

———. "Unit Roots in Macro-economic Time Series: Some Critical Issues." *Federal Reserve Bank of Richmond Quarterly,* 79(2), Spring 1993, 13–44.

Mishkin, Frederic S. "The Household Balance Sheet and the Great Depression." *Journal of Economic History,* December 1978, 918–37.

Modigliani, Franco. "Some Empirical Tests of Monetary Management and Rules versus Discretion." *Journal of Political Economy,* April 1964, 211–45.

Nelson, Daniel B. "Was the Deflation of 1929–30 Anticipated? The Monetary Regime as Viewed by the Business Press." *Research in Economic History,* 13, 1992, 1–66.

Romer, Christina D. "World War I and the Postwar Depression: A Reinterpretation Based on Alternative Estimates of GNP." *Journal of Monetary Economics,* July 1988, 91–115.

———. "The Great Crash and the Onset of the Great Depression." *Quarterly Journal of Economics,* August 1990, 597–624.

———. "What Ended the Great Depression?" *Journal of Economic History,* December 1992, 757–84.

———. "The Nation in Depression." *Journal of Economic Perspectives,* 2, Spring 1993, 19–39.

Schwartz, Anna J. "Understanding 1929–1933," in *The Great Depression Revisited,* edited by K. Brunner. Boston: Martinus Nijoff, 1981, 5–48.

Stock, James H., and Mark W. Watson. "A Simple MLE of Cointegrating Vectors in General Integrated Systems." NBER Technical Working Paper No. 83, 1989.

Temin, Peter. *Did Monetary Factors Cause the Great Depression?* New York: Norton, 1978.

———. *Lessons from the Great Depression.* Cambridge: MIT Press, 1989.

———. "Transmission of the Great Depression." *Journal of Economic Perspectives,* 7(2), Spring 1993, 87–102.

U.S. Department of Commerce. *Long-Term Economic Growth,* 1860–1970. Washington, D.C.: U.S. Government Printing Office, 1973.

Warburton, Clark. "Monetary Theory, Full Production, and the Great Depression," in *Depression, Inflation, and Monetary Policy.* Baltimore: Johns Hopkins University Press, 1966, chapter 5.

Wheelock, David. "Monetary Policy in the Great Depression: What the Fed Did and Why." *Federal Reserve Bank of St. Louis Review,* March/April 1992, 3–28.

White, Eugene N. "A Reinterpretation of the Banking Crisis of 1930." *Journal of Economic History,* March 1984, 119–38.

Wicker, Elmus R. "Federal Reserve Monetary Policy, 1922–33: A Reinterpretation." *Journal of Political Economy,* August 1965, 325–43.

CHAPTER 14

Was Expansionary Monetary Policy Feasible during the Great Contraction?

An Examination of the Gold Standard Constraint

MICHAEL D. BORDO, EHSAN U. CHOUDHRI,

AND ANNA J. SCHWARTZ

1. Introduction

A MUCH-DEBATED HYPOTHESIS about the Great Depression is Friedman and Schwartz's (1963) contention that a severe but not unusual U.S. recession turned into the greatest contraction of all times because the Federal Reserve failed to undertake expansionary open-market operations. Controversy about the role of monetary factors in causing the Great Depression in the United States was a feature of the earlier literature, but the consensus of current literature is that monetary shocks (produced largely by a series of banking crises) played a major role in prolonging and deepening the Great Depression.[1]

Originally published in "Was Expansionary Monetary Policy Feasible during the Great Contraction? An Examination of the Gold Standard Constraint," *Explorations in Economic History* 39, no. 1 (January 2002): 1–28. © 2001 Elsevier Science.

International aspects of the Great Depression have also been the focus of attention in recent studies. Research on international experience shows conclusively that the countries that left the gold standard early suffered a less severe Depression than those that stayed on.[2] The international transmission of the Great Depression occurred for two key reasons. First, fixed exchange rates under the gold standard transmitted adverse shocks from one country to another. Second, commitment to the gold standard deterred countries from pursuing expansionary monetary policies to counteract these shocks.[3] This view of the transmission mechanism is supportive of the Friedman–Schwartz hypothesis insofar as it helps explain how banking panics in the United States could have produced a worldwide depression. However, this view also suggests that gold standard constraints might have prevented the Federal Reserve from increasing high-powered money sufficiently to offset decreases in the money stock induced by banking crises. A policy of expanding domestic credit to stabilize the stock of money might have aroused doubts about U.S. commitment to the gold standard and led to a loss of gold reserves. Eichengreen (1992) argues that the loss would have been sufficiently large to force the United States off the gold standard.

His argument points to the imperatives of the international gold standard rather than ineptness of the Federal Reserve as primarily responsible for not averting the Great Depression. For Friedman and Schwartz (1963), however, the Federal Reserve held so large a stock of gold that even had such a loss occurred, it would not have posed a serious threat to the U.S. commitment to the gold standard.

Although there is considerable interest in this issue, little empirical work exists on estimating the loss of gold reserves that might have resulted, had the Federal Reserve undertaken expansionary monetary policy to offset the banking panics during the Great Depression. The main purpose of this chapter is to undertake such an exercise.

Section 2 of the chapter briefly reviews the history of the interwar gold standard, discusses key developments before and during the Great Depression, and focuses on the international crises from 1931 to 1933. Section 3 then develops a model that identifies key determinants of gold flows from the United States. The model can be used to simulate the behavior of gold reserves had monetary policy been expansionary during banking panics. In view of the large size of the U.S. economy, the model explicitly takes into account the interaction between the United States and the rest of the world. Even in the special case of perfect capital mobility (which represents the most severe constraint for U.S. policy), the model shows that the expansion of U.S. domestic credit would have been only partially offset by gold flows and it would have been technically possible for the Federal Reserve to counter a decline in the stock of money.

Section 4 empirically implements the chapter's model using monthly data for four major countries, France, Germany, the United Kingdom, and the United States. We consider two hypothetical scenarios of expansionary monetary policy, one initiated after the first banking panic in October 1930, and the second, after the crises associated with sterling's devaluation in September 1931. We account for possible speculative attacks suggested by the recent literature. We simulate the time path of U.S. gold reserves (as well as that of the gold-reserve ratio) under the two hypothetical scenarios up to February 1933.

In the first simulation, we show that a $1 billion open market purchase over the period October 1930–February 1931 could have prevented the banking panics that followed by providing the banking system with additional reserves, and it would not have led to a gold drain in 1931–1933 sufficient to deplete U.S. gold reserves. In the second simulation, which omits the first hypothetical open market purchase, we assume that after the British devaluation the Federal Reserve would have increased domestic credit by $1 billion from September 1931 through January 1932. We show that U.S. gold reserves would have declined significantly but not sufficiently to reduce the gold ratio below the statutory minimum requirement. The reason for the hypothetical large gold outflows in this simulation is that the British devaluation could have shaken the market's confidence in the U.S. commitment to gold parity at a time when France was converting its dollar claims into gold.

2. Historical Background: Financial Crises of the Gold Exchange Standard

2.1. Overview

The gold standard dissolved during World War I as all major countries, with the exception of the United States, suspended gold convertibility de facto if not de jure. The gold exchange standard was restored worldwide in the period 1924–1927, when central bank statutes typically required a cover ratio for currencies between 30 and 40%, divided between gold and foreign exchange. Central reserve countries (the United States and United Kingdom) were to hold reserves only in the form of gold. By the end of 1928, 35 countries had their currencies officially convertible into gold.

The restoration of convertibility to sterling in 1925 at an overvalued parity and to the franc in 1928 at an undervalued parity led to maldistribution of gold, which was greatly aggravated by the inappropriate policies that France and the United States pursued. Each of them as well as other countries (Nurkse, 1944)[4] consistently sterilized gold inflows, which reduced gold reserves available to the rest of the world and enhanced deflationary pressure.

France was absorbing gold from the rest of the world at the same time as was the United States, the world's largest gold holder (see Figure 14.1). The Federal Reserve systematically sterilized gold inflows during the 1920s and 1930s (Friedman and Schwartz, 1963). In June 1928, the U.S. share of the world total monetary gold stock was 38.3%, and the French share, 11.7%. By June 1931, the shares were, respectively, 40.8 and 19.6% (see Figure 14.1).

The gold exchange standard collapsed in the face of the shocks of the Great Depression. Tight monetary policy by the Federal Reserve in 1928 to deflate the stock market boom and France's pro-gold policies precipitated a downturn in the United States and the rest of the world in 1929. A series of banking panics in the United States subsequently transmitted deflationary and contractionary pressures to the rest of the world on the gold standard.

FIGURE 14.1   Gold Reserves (U.S. Dollars), 1928–1933, Monthly

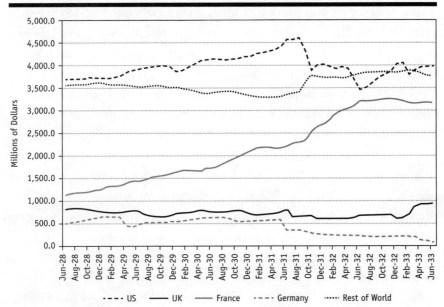

As soon as doubts began to surface about the stability of the reserve currencies, central banks scrambled to liquidate their foreign exchange reserves and replace them with gold. The share of foreign exchange in global central bank reserves plummeted from 37% at the end of 1930 to 13% at the end of 1931 and 11% at the end of 1932 (Nurkse, 1944, App. II). The implosion of the foreign-exchange component of the global reserve base exerted strong deflationary pressure on the world economy. Deflation stimulated gold output so total world gold reserves increased by $1 billion between 1930 and 1932, but it was not enough to satisfy the heightened central bank demand. To attract gold, they jacked up interest rates in the face of an unprecedented slump.

2.2. Chronology of the Breakdown of the Gold Exchange Standard

Against the background of the international gold exchange standard, we consider in more detail the events of 1931–1933, when U.S. adherence to gold may have been threatened. We focus on three episodes: Fall 1931,

Spring 1932, and Spring 1933, when the United States may have faced speculative attacks on the dollar. Early strains on the gold exchange standard appeared in 1927. An incipient run on sterling in July 1927, following massive capital flows to France, was averted by the cooperative action by the central banks of the four core countries. As its contribution to the cooperative arrangement, the Federal Reserve reduced the discount rate and the buying rate on bankers' acceptances.

Although the 1929 downturn produced strain on sterling, the defining crises of the gold exchange system occurred in 1931. The failure of the Austrian Creditanstalt in May 1931 led to a German crisis owing to internal drains from the banking system. Only later were foreign deposits withdrawn. The Bank of England extended short-term credits to the crisis-stricken central European countries, whose reserves had been declining in the face of persistent balance of payments deficits. A speculative attack in September 1931 on the Bank was successful (Capie, Mills, and Wood, 1986). Johnson (1997) notes that Britain gave up, not because of an immediate crisis—it floated after raising the discount rate to only 4½%—but because of the long-term problem in its balance of payments, with no foreseeable improvement.[5] French pressure then forced the Federal Reserve to raise the U.S. discount rate in two steps within a week by an unprecedented 2 percentage points from 1½ to 3½% as a quid pro quo for delaying conversion into gold of more than $500 million that the French held in dollar assets. This action halted the external drain but only served to exacerbate a domestic banking panic.

From March through June 1932, under Congressional pressure, the Federal Reserve pursued an expansionary open market policy, purchasing $1 billion in government securities. According to Friedman and Schwartz, the policy was successful in halting the downturn. It was ended, however, although much too soon, once Congress went into recess. Federal Reserve officials, who adhered to a deflationary real bills doctrine, did not believe that further purchases would help the banks or improve the economy. Eichengreen, however, contends that the Federal Reserve stopped the purchase program because of concern over its gold reserves, especially the level of free gold. Although gold reserves declined through June 1932, at

$3.5 billion they were still above the statutory limit, and July 1932 marked the end of central bank withdrawals from New York.

The final crisis of the dollar occurred in 1933. Massive banking panics across the United States led to a series of state bank holidays. Fears that the newly elected President Roosevelt would devalue the dollar upon taking office led mainly domestic residents to convert dollars into gold. Speculators in New York for the first time bought sterling. The decline in the gold reserves of the Federal Reserve Bank of New York below its statutory limit triggered the request by New York State for the governor to declare a Bank Holiday on Friday, March 3, and Roosevelt's decision to declare a 1-week national Bank Holiday on Monday, March 6. The Bank Holiday succeeded in allaying the banking panic and in halting the gold drain. Although the link with gold was cut in the following month, a modest gold drain did not resume until some months before the Gold Reserve Act was passed on January 31, 1934.

To examine in greater detail the view that expansionary monetary policy would have aroused speculative activity against the dollar, we look at the available sources of information on the subject.[6] The question about possible speculative activity centers on the Fall of 1931 and the Spring of 1932. That speculation arose in the weeks before the Roosevelt administration took office in March 1933 is unquestionable. The trigger, however, was not expansionary monetary policy, but rumors that the gold content of the dollar would be devalued, which turned out to be true.

At the earlier dates, suppose the data show a loss of gold by the United States. Is this evidence that the dollar was under attack? Suppose the data show an acceleration of a loss of gold. Is this evidence of a heightened attack on the dollar? The problem of interpretation arises because the official holders of dollar claims in the continental creditor countries had a motive other than doubts about the United States to want to increase their gold reserves. The motive to convert all dollar exchange into gold may well have been paramount—whatever the condition of the United States. Moreover, gold withdrawals from the United States were arranged with the consent of the United States. It was not necessarily the case that an increase in withdrawals spelled increased lack of confidence in the United States.

What do we learn from the sources at the two dates when the United States may have faced attacks on the dollar?

In the first of the three episodes, in the 6 weeks following British suspension of the gold standard in September 1931, short-term liabilities of U.S. banks to Europeans declined by $400 million, the U.S. monetary gold stock declined by $450 million, and the combined monetary gold stock of France, Belgium, Netherlands, and Switzerland rose by an equivalent amount. As Brown (1940, p. 1222) states, the gold drain has been described "incorrectly, as attacks upon the dollar." While the United States lost gold to the European gold standard countries, in September and October 1931, it still drew gold from Argentina, Canada, and Japan. The main drain was to France. France had an "uncompromising hostility to the gold exchange standard" (Brown, 1940, p. 1179), but it did not seek "wholesale conversion" of its dollar balances either before or after September 21, the date of British suspension. This was not a speculative attack, in the sense of the current use of those terms. According to Einzig (1937, p. 269) the forward dollar rate depreciated for 2 weeks from October 17 to 31, and then went to a premium for the rest of the year. This was a transitory dollar scare, at best, not a settled loss of confidence in the dollar.

Two emissaries of the Bank of France arrived in America in October to discuss with the Federal Reserve and the Treasury the terms under which its dollar balances would be withdrawn. At the end of the month a communiqué by Hoover and Laval on a visit to Washington emphasized the maintenance of the gold standard in France and the United States as essential for the restoration of economic stability and confidence. Randolph Burgess at the October meeting of the board of the BIS gave official assurance that the American gold standard was not in danger. In November and December 1931 the foreign drain temporarily ceased.

The second episode when the United States may have faced a speculative attack was during the Federal Reserve open market purchase from March to June 1932. During this period short-term liabilities of U.S. banks to Europeans declined by $550 million, the U.S. monetary gold stock declined by $535 million, and the combined increase in the European gold standard countries' gold was $280 million. The liquidation of dollar balances by France, Holland, Belgium, and Switzerland, which was completed by July 1932, was arranged to minimize disturbances to the American market. Was this a speculative attack, when the so-called attackers sought to achieve their objective with the least possible damage to the victim? During the period of gold loss to the continental creditor countries, and during the second half of 1932, Canada, South America, and the Far East continued to ship gold to the United States—a measure of confidence in the U.S. commitment to the gold standard. By the end of 1932, the U.S. gold stock was at a level higher than in October 1931. According to Henry Parker Willis (1934, p. 17), there was no threat to the gold standard even at the height of the continental withdrawals: "fears of a European drain, general among reserve bankers" in 1932, "had proven mythical."

Einzig (1937, p. 270) describes the forward dollar in the first half of 1932 as "abnormally undervalued, compared to its interest parities." This was the period when the Federal Reserve was actually conducting open market purchases that clearly did not drive the United States off gold even if the evidence in the forward rate is regarded as a possible speculative attack on the dollar. The putative attack failed, and post-June 1932, the forward rate was brought practically to parity with spot dollars.

Although there is little evidence that speculation against the dollar in the modern sense of the recent speculative attack literature was forthcoming from official sources, it is still possible that private agents in other countries or in the United States, acting alone or through investment banks and other intermediaries, could have taken a speculative position against the dollar in 1931 and 1932. The available data do not permit us to isolate these actions. Furthermore we were unable to find any mention of such activities in the narratives of knowledgeable contemporaries to which we had access.

The third episode of gold loss in February 1933, as indicated above, was unlike the earlier ones. Withdrawals by foreign countries had greatly reduced their U.S. balances. They were no longer a threat to the dollar, if they ever were. Foreigners had essentially completed their withdrawals by the beginning of August 1932, and had built up dollar holdings during the next half year.

The British Exchange Equalisation Account (which held dollars valued at 46 million pounds, at the current exchange rate of $3.36 per pound) in January 1933 began to replace dollars with gold. It did so partly at the request of the Federal Reserve Bank of New York, which was afraid of sudden gold withdrawals, and partly because of the possibility of an American devaluation (Howson, 1980, p. 35). The British withdrew only 8 million pounds equivalent in dollars during the next 2 months. During the 4 weeks from the beginning of February until the Bank Holiday, withdrawals amounted only to $150 million. Remaining balances were held to service ordinary transactions.

This time it was the U.S. banking crisis that began during the 1932 Presidential campaign that was one cause for concern. Another was that after Roosevelt's victory there was ground for the belief that the United States would leave the gold standard. Private investors and private bankers sold dollars short and used the proceeds to buy sterling. In addition, depositors who withdrew funds previously held as currency now demanded gold for dollars. Willis believed that it should have been possible "to offset and cancel the effects of such transactions and demands" (p. 19), given central bank tools, the size of the U.S. monetary gold stock, a favorable trade balance, and sizable foreign investments. Instead, he describes Federal Reserve managers as thrown "into a condition bordering on panic" (1934, p. 14). They were ready to surrender the gold standard, when there was no fundamental reason to do so.[7]

2.3. Could Expansionary Monetary Policy Have Averted the Crises of the Gold Exchange Standard?

Eichengreen (1992) argues that under the gold standard banking crises and currency crises were intertwined. In the Depression experiences of a number of European countries, incipient banking crises were aggravated by capital flight, as both domestic and foreign deposits were shifted abroad in anticipation of capital controls and devaluation. Central banks refrained from acting as lenders of last resort to provide liquidity to their banking systems because of fear that expansionary domestic credit would precipitate an attack on their gold reserves. The only solution to the dilemma was to cut the link with gold and devalue.[8]

This analysis, which seems sound for the experience of the small open economies of Europe, may not apply to the U.S. case, a large, relatively closed economy, with very substantial gold reserves. The issue is, how much gold would have been lost had the United States followed the requisite expansionary open market purchases to counter the banking panics, and would the gold losses have been sufficient to breach the required gold cover statute of 40% against Federal Reserve notes and 35% against Federal Reserve deposits.

An auxiliary issue relates to free gold, the excess of gold reserves over that required to meet the statutory 40% reserve requirement against notes and to cover the shortfall of eligible securities backing the remaining 60% of Federal Reserve notes. According to Eichengreen (1992), by the end of 1931 Federal Reserve free gold had fallen below what he regards as the critical level of $500 million. This level of free gold, he maintains, would not have allowed the Federal Reserve to conduct an open market purchase sufficient to make up the $2 billion decline in M1 that had occurred after the United Kingdom left gold. We find Eichengreen's conjecture to be mistaken, since he neglects the role of the money multiplier that, together with the change in high-powered money, determines the change in M1.

For two reasons we also are skeptical that the level of free gold was an actual constraint on Federal Reserve monetary policy. It never reported dollar amounts of free gold. Only in its 1932 annual report (p. 17), issued 4 months after the Glass–Steagall Act was passed, did it present a chart for 1929–1932, based on last-Wednesday-of-the-month total gold reserves, with different shading for required reserves, additional gold needed as collateral, and free gold. Reading from the chart, Eichengreen states that free gold in October 1931 was reduced to $400 million. If it were in fact at that low level that month, it is incomprehensible that the Federal Reserve did not move heaven and earth to force a change in eligibility requirements. The impression that free gold was not in fact the deterrent to expansionary monetary policy that the Federal Reserve and its supporters allege it to have been is further bolstered by Hoover's complaint (1952, pp. 115–118). He had proposed on October 6, 1931, that eligibility requirements be broadened, but no action had been taken until 4 months later. At a meeting at the White House with Governor Harrison of the New York Fed and Governor Meyer of the Board on February 8, 1932, the situation was said to be critical, and Hoover's proposal was finally agreed to. In addition, there is no evidence that the Federal Reserve during the months between the British abandonment of gold and the adoption of the Glass–Steagall Act was lobbying for this crucial legislative change. The failure of Congress to act on Hoover's proposal suggests the absence of any urgency. We therefore question whether free gold was truly a constraint on Federal Reserve performance.

The Federal Reserve acknowledged in the report that although free gold amounted to only $416 million on February 24, 1932, when the act was adopted, it could have been increased to $542 million simply by reducing the volume of Federal Reserve notes held by Federal Reserve banks in their own vaults. At no point did the Federal Reserve take such a step to increase free gold. Moreover, although the Federal Reserve held $740 million in U.S. government securities, they were not pledged as collateral backing for Federal Reserve notes until May 5, 1932 (p. 19), months after it had the authority to do so. The story that free gold was *the* reason it could not conduct open market purchases appears to be dubious. The statements by Secretary Ogden Mills and Randolph Burgess in the weeks before enactment of Glass–Steagall that Eichengreen cites about how close the United States was to being forced off the gold standard should be understood as political strong-arming to get the bill passed. Incidentally, as we noted at an earlier point, Randolph Burgess assured the BIS that the gold standard was not in danger in October 1931.[9]

A second issue of importance is whether Federal Reserve expansionary policies would have been sufficient to prevent banking panics in the United States from having effects on the rest of the world. Such policies would have prevented crises elsewhere. Had the U.S. money supply not collapsed, deflationary pressure on the rest of the world might have been avoided.

3. Basic Model

This section develops a simple model to determine U.S. gold flows and to provide a framework for simulating the behavior of U.S. gold reserves under alternative monetary policies. The model is used to derive the offset coefficient—that is, the proportion of an increase in U.S. domestic credit offset by gold outflows in the short run. For a large country like the United

States, the offset coefficient is always less than one. Under certain conditions, moreover, we show that the offset coefficient simply equals the rest-of-the-world share of the world gold stock.

We assume that the U.S. demand for money in period t is given by

$$m_t - p_t = a_0 + a_1 y_t + a_2 i_t + v_t, \quad a_1 > 0, \ a_2 < 0, \tag{1}$$

where m_t, p_t, and y_t represent logs of the money stock; the price level and real income; i_t denotes the interest rate; and v_t is the error term. The determinants of m_t can be expressed by the following two identities:

$$m_t \equiv \mu_t + \log(H_t), \tag{2}$$

$$H_t = G_t + D_t, \tag{3}$$

where μ_t is the log of the money multiplier while H_t, G_t, and D_t represent high-powered money, gold reserves, and domestic credit (defined as high-powered money excluding gold reserves).

Using (1)–(3) after expressing these relations in first differences, and utilizing the approximation that $\Delta \log(H_t) = \Delta H_t / \bar{H}_t$ with $\bar{H}_t \equiv (H_t + H_{t-1})/2$, we derive the following relation for determining U.S. gold flows:

$$\Delta G_t / \bar{H}_t = -\Delta D_t / \bar{H}_t - \Delta \mu_t + \Delta p_t + a_1 \Delta y_t + a_2 \Delta i_t + \Delta v_t. \tag{4}$$

Equation (4) can be utilized to examine the effect of an expansion in domestic credit on gold flows. Although the direct effect of ΔD_t on ΔG_t equals -1 in (4), ΔD_t could also exert an indirect effect through other variables on the right hand side of (4). Over a very short period (say, a month), it is plausible to assume that $\Delta \mu_t$, Δp_t, Δy_t, and Δv_t are exogenous to ΔD_t and Δi_t is the only potential channel for the indirect effect. We explicitly model the monetary relations in the rest of the world to explore this channel. To simplify the exposition, we treat the rest of the world as one country. Appendix 1 shows, however, that relations discussed below are valid for variables aggregated over the rest of the world under the assumption that all foreign countries have the same money demand functions (our simulations are based on the multicountry version discussed in Appendix 1).

Assuming that the money demand function in the rest of the world is of the same form as (1), representing the determinants of money stocks by identities similar to (2) and (3), and using an asterisk to denote rest-of-the-world variables and parameters, we obtain

$$\Delta G_t^* / \bar{H}_t^* = -\Delta D_t^* / \bar{H}_t^* - \Delta \mu_t^* + \Delta p_t^* + \alpha_1^* \Delta y_t^* + \alpha_2^* \Delta i_t^* + \Delta v_t^*, \tag{5}$$

where nominal variables, G_t^*, D_t^*, and $\bar{H}_t^* [\equiv (H_t^* + H_{t-1}^*) / 2]$ are expressed in foreign-currency units.[10] Assume that the world stock of gold is fixed and the U.S. price of gold is constant over time. These assumptions imply that gold flows in the United States and the rest of the world are linked as

$$\Delta G_t = -\Delta(e_t G_t^*), \tag{6}$$

where e_t denotes the exchange rate in representing the price of foreign currency in U.S. dollars.

We express the relationship between interest rates in the United States and abroad as

$$i_t = i_t^* + x_t + \varepsilon_t, \tag{7}$$

where x_t denotes the expected rate of U.S. dollar depreciation and ε_t represents departures from perfect capital mobility (or uncovered interest parity) caused by factors such as risk premia, transaction costs, information lags, and capital controls. If the gold standard had operated smoothly, no changes in gold parities would have been expected and x_t would have equaled zero. In this case, the Federal Reserve would still have been able to affect the interest rate differential, $i_t - i_t^*$, if departures from perfect capital mobility allowed it to systemically influence ε_t. However, even if capital were perfectly mobile and the interest rate differential could not have been changed by the Federal Reserve, the large size of the United States would have permitted it to affect the world interest rate and hence follow an independent monetary policy under the gold standard.

Using (4), (5), (6), and the first-difference form of (7), we derive the following relation that explicitly shows the key U.S. and rest-of-the-world variables which determine U.S. gold flows:

$$\Delta G_t / \bar{H}_t = \theta_t [-\Delta D_t / \bar{H}_t - \Delta\mu_t + \Delta p_t + \alpha_1 \Delta y_t + \alpha_2 (\Delta x_t + \Delta\varepsilon_t) + \Delta v_t]$$
$$+ (\theta_t \alpha_2 / \alpha_2^*)(\Delta D_t^* / \bar{H}_t^* + \Delta\mu_t^* - \Delta p_t^* - \alpha_1^* \Delta y_t^* - \Delta v_t^* + \gamma_t), \tag{8}$$

where $\theta_t \equiv \alpha_2^* e_t \bar{H}_t / (\alpha_2 \bar{H}_t + \alpha_2^* e_t \bar{H}_t^*)$ and $\gamma_t \equiv -\Delta e_t G_{t-1}^* / e_t \bar{H}_t^*$. Note that the term γ_t represents an adjustment for changes in the foreign price of gold and in periods when this price is constant, it equals zero.

We can use (8) to examine the offset coefficient, defined as the short-run change in G_t induced by a unit increase in D_t. In the short run, all variables in (8) except Δx_t and $\Delta\varepsilon_t$ are considered exogenous to ΔD_t. In the special case of no expected changes in gold parities and perfect capital mobility, both x_t and ε_t would equal zero, and the offset coefficient would simply equal $-\theta_t$.

As the U.S. stock of high-powered money represented a substantial portion of the world stock during the Great Depression, θ_t was significantly less than one. Thus, as long as there was no speculation against the dollar, even gold flows under perfect capital mobility would not have severely constrained the Federal Reserve's ability to determine the high-powered stock of money in the short run. The Federal Reserve would, of course, have been less constrained under imperfect mobility. In this case, we would expect that an increase in domestic credit would also lead to a decrease in ε_t (i.e., lower the interest-rate differential). This indirect effect of domestic credit expansion (via $\Delta\varepsilon_t$) would reduce the absolute value of the offset coefficient below θ_t.[11]

To simplify the model, suppose that the income and semi-interest elasticities of the money demand function are the same in both the United States and the rest of the world, and the income elasticity equals unity. For this case (assumed in our simulations discussed in the next section), setting $\alpha_1 = \alpha_1^* = 1$ and $\alpha_2 = \alpha_2^*$, and letting a prime denote the difference between the United States and foreign rates of inflation and output growth (i.e., $\Delta p_t' \equiv \Delta p_t - \Delta p_t^*$ and $\Delta y_t' \equiv \Delta y_t - \Delta y_t^*$), we can express equation (8) as

$$\Delta G_t = s_t \bar{H}_t [-\Delta D_t / \bar{H}_t + \Delta D_t^* / \bar{H}_t^* - \Delta \mu_t + \Delta \mu_t^* + \Delta p_t' + \Delta y_t' + \gamma_t + u_t], \tag{9}$$

where $s_t = e_1 \bar{H}_t^* / (e_t \bar{H}_t^* + \bar{H}_t)$ represents the foreign share of the world gold stock while $u_t \equiv \alpha_2 (\Delta x_t + \Delta \varepsilon_t) + \Delta v_t - \Delta v_t^*$ is a composite shock that includes not only shocks to money demand but also the influence of speculation and departures from uncovered interest parity. In the case of no speculation and perfect capital mobility, the offset coefficient now equals $-s_t$.

We use the above model to construct expansionary money counterfactuals, which would have allowed the Federal Reserve to pursue a monetary policy to prevent large decreases in the stock of money. Our counterfactuals distinguish policy needed during normal periods from policy needed during banking panics. During normal periods, small changes in domestic credit would suffice to produce money growth that is consistent with the gold standard. During banking panics, on the other hand, a key consideration would be to restore confidence in the banking system. An appropriate policy in these circumstances would be to expand domestic credit sufficiently to relieve shortages of bank reserves and avoid panic-induced bank failures. Expansionary monetary policy can thus be expressed as

$$\Delta D_t = \begin{cases} \delta_t^n \text{ during normal periods} \\ \delta_t^b \text{ during banking panics} \end{cases}, \tag{10}$$

where δ_t^b, determined by lender-of-the-last-resort considerations, would tend to be large relative to δ_t^n.[12] Note that expansionary actions are required only during banking panics. With appropriate policy during normal periods (i.e., suitable choice of δ_t^n), (10) would be compatible with fixed gold parities in the long run.

Given policy (10), U.S. gold flows would be determined by (9) and the following two relations implied by (3), its rest-of-the-world counterpart and (6) with $e_t = e$:

$$H_t = H_{t-1} + \Delta D_t + \Delta G_t, \tag{11}$$

$$H_t^* = H_{t-1}^* + \Delta D_t^* - \Delta G_t/e. \tag{12}$$

To construct our counterfactuals, we do not explicitly model the determinants of gold flows, ΔD_t^*, $\Delta \mu_t$, $\Delta \mu_t^*$, $\Delta p_t'$, $\Delta y_t'$, and u_t. However, we first make certain plausible assumptions (discussed below) about how expansionary monetary policy would affect their time paths. Given the assumed time paths, we solve the model represented by (9) and (10)–(12) for the time paths of ΔG_t, ΔD_t, Ht, and H_t^*. This solution is used to simulate the behavior of U.S. gold reserves, G_t, and the ratio of gold reserves to high-powered money, G_t/H_t.

4. Simulations of U.S. Gold Reserves and the Gold–Reserve Ratio

We now empirically implement our model using monthly data from 1926:7 to 1933:2, which period begins with all major countries adhering to the gold standard and ends with the United States leaving the gold standard. To estimate the rest-of-the-world variables in our model, we use data for three large countries, the United Kingdom, France, and Germany.[13] These countries accounted for a significant proportion of high-powered money and the monetary gold stock held outside the United States.[14] However, the omission of other countries with significant gold reserves could bias our estimates and we explore the magnitude of this bias later. The price levels and outputs were measured by indexes of consumer (retail) prices and industrial production. As monthly series for these indexes were very noisy, they were smoothed using the Hodrick–Prescott filter.

The Federal Reserve could have undertaken expansionary monetary policy, as represented by (10), at different stages of the Great Depression.[15] A critical time for the pursuit of such a policy was the onset of the first important constraint on U.S. monetary policy after the U.K. devaluation.[16] We thus also consider a second counterfactual in which expansionary policy is implemented in September 1931. For each counterfactual, we start with a number of plausible assumptions about the behavior of key variables, and later explore the sensitivity of our results to variations in these assumptions.

Before discussing our expansionary-money counterfactuals, we briefly examine how our model fits monthly data on U.S. gold flows. Dividing both sides of (9) by $s_t \bar{H}_t$, we can express it in the testable form

$$\Delta G_t / s_t \bar{H}_t = \beta_0 + \beta_1 z_t + u_t, \tag{13}$$

where $z_t = -\Delta D_t / \bar{H}_t + \Delta D_t^* / \bar{H}_t^* - \Delta \mu_t + \Delta \mu_t^* + \Delta p_t' + \Delta y_t' + \gamma_t$ represents an aggregate index of the determinants of U.S. gold flows. The model implies that $\beta_0 = 0$ and $\beta_1 = 1$. We estimated (13) by OLS, using our data from 1926:7 to 1933:2. The results of this estimation show that z_t exerts a significant positive effect on $\Delta G_t / s_t \bar{H}_t$.[17] The coefficient β_1, however, is significantly less than 1. Our monthly data—especially, the indexes for the rest-of-the-world variables—are likely to involve substantial measurement errors and these errors could have biased the estimate of β_1 downward. Imperfect capital mobility could also account for the bias in β_1 since μ_t would be correlated with z_t in this case (because ΔD_t and ΔD_t^* would influence $\Delta \varepsilon_t$). However, as perfect capital mobility represents the most unfavorable case for the feasibility of expansionary monetary policy in the United States, we use this assumption in our simulations below.

It is also interesting to examine the behavior of u_t over time. According to (9), u_t includes not only the effect of shocks to money demand (Δv_t and Δv_t^*) but also the influence of speculation and departures from uncovered interest parity (via Δx_t and $\Delta \varepsilon_t$). Figure 14.2 shows the values of u_t from 1926:7 to 1933:2, estimated from (13) with the constraint (implied by the model) that $\beta_0 = 0$ and $\beta_1 = 1$. During the early 1930s (the period relevant to our counterfactuals discussed below), Figure 14.2 shows large negative values of u_t for the months of October 1931, June 1932, and February 1933. One possible explanation of the three large negative residuals is that they were caused by speculative attacks (resulting from shifts in x_t). If speculative attacks did occur, it is interesting to examine what the source of these attacks was and how dollar speculation would have been influenced by our counterfactuals. We explore these questions below. However, since the historical evidence (discussed in Section 2) that speculative attacks

FIGURE 14.2   The Behavior of the Residual (u_t) 1926:07–1933:02

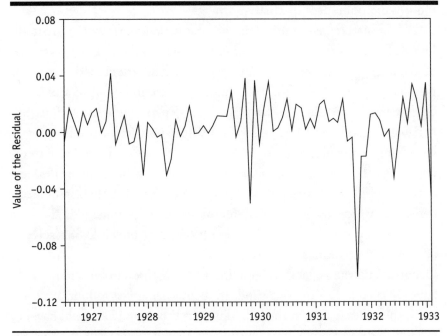

occurred is not compelling, we also consider the possibility that the three residuals were produced by large exogenous shocks that would not have been affected by our counterfactuals.

To explore the role of dollar speculation, we first consider a first-generation speculative attack model, which assumes that the United States would have left the gold standard if the G_t/H_t ratio fell to some critical proportion (e.g., determined by legal reserve requirements). Following the approach of Flood and Garber (1984) and Blanco and Garber (1986), we develop such a model for our large-country case.[18] A critical variable in this model is the shadow exchange rate—that is, the hypothetical exchange rate that would prevail (under permanently flexible exchange rates) if U.S. gold reserves fell to the critical level. The probability of U.S. devaluation equals the probability that the shadow exchange rate exceeds the actual exchange rate. According to our estimates, the probability of U.S. devaluation was almost zero throughout our simulation period (1930:1–1933:2) including the critical months of October 1931, June 1932, and February 1933.

Thus, this model suggests that the large residuals observed in these months did not reflect speculative attacks.

A problematic assumption of the first-generation model is that the United States was fully committed to the gold standard as long as the reserve ratio stayed above a constant fraction. Indeed, the second-generation models of speculative attack assume that the commitment to a fixed exchange rate is not state invariant but can depend on a number of state variables (Flood and Marion, 1996). In this approach, a combination of worsening economic conditions and certain events could give rise to expectations of dollar devaluation. A speculative attack in October 1931, for example, might have been triggered by the U.K. devaluation in September 1931, which weakened the international commitment to the gold standard, and could have suggested a weakening of the U.S. resolve to adhere to the gold standard during a depression. Actions by the U.S. Congress and the Federal Reserve from March through June 1932 might have signaled a shift in policy and led to another attack in June 1932. Finally, speculation against the U.S. dollar in February 1933 could have resulted from the internal drain in that month and the expectation that the Roosevelt administration would abandon the gold standard in an effort to check the deepening depression.

It is not obvious, however, how expectations of devaluation would have been affected under our counterfactual of a monetary expansion in October 1931. One possibility is Eichengreen's contention that such an expansion would have further eroded confidence in U.S. commitment to gold and led to large gold outflows. Another possibility is that by preventing banking panics and restoring financial stability, this policy would have been viewed as improving economic conditions and increasing the likelihood of the United States staying on gold. Speculative pressures would have eased in this case. As it is difficult to resolve this issue on the basis of a priori arguments, we consider evidence on actual monetary expansions. Interestingly, expansionary open market operations (of a magnitude similar to our counterfactual) were undertaken in the spring of 1932. Hsieh and Romer (2001) have carefully examined this episode and find little evidence that the monetary expansion led to expectations of devaluation. This case study suggests that a similar monetary expansion in October 1931 would not have significantly affected dollar speculation and we make this assumption in our counterfactual.

4.1. Counterfactual 1: Expansionary Policy, October 1930–February 1931

Our basic assumption is that if the Federal Reserve had increased domestic credit sufficiently in response to the first wave of banking panics, subsequent banking panics would have been averted. Although it is difficult to determine the precise amount of change in domestic credit that would have been adequate to restore confidence in the banking system, we suppose that a $1 billion increase in domestic credit from October 1930 to February 1931 (instead of an actual decrease of $37 million over this period) would have been more than enough for this purpose.[19] Domestic credit expansion of this magnitude would have easily met the need for additional bank reserves and more than offset the money–supply effect of the decrease in the money multiplier during the crisis. Furthermore, if the open market purchase had been directed to the provision of bank reserves, there would have been no direct offset on free gold.[20]

We expect that this policy would have produced a number of important effects. The money multiplier would have reverted to its normal level after the restoration of financial stability. The decline in the stock of money would thus have been arrested and the severity of the Depression in the United States as well as the rest of the world would have been significantly reduced. Improved economic conditions would have allowed the United Kingdom to stay on gold and there would have been no reason for speculation against the dollar. Without the U.K. devaluation and the putative fear of U.S. devaluation, there would also have been no reason for France to significantly decrease its domestic credit after September 1931.[21] Our basic simulation makes four assumptions to incorporate these effects.

First, we assume that the money multiplier would have started recovering by March 1931 and then move gradually toward its normal level. To simulate the time path of the multiplier (in logs) from 1931:3 to 1933:2 we use the model

$$\mu_t = a(\bar{\mu} - \mu_{t-1}) + \mu_{t-1},$$
(14)

FIGURE 14.3 The Actual and Simulated Values of the Money Multiplier 1926:07–1933:02

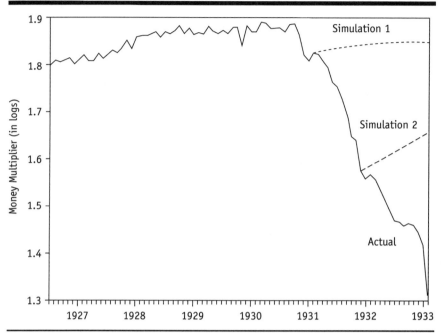

where $\bar{\mu}$ is the average value of μ_t for the precrises period 1926:7–1930:9. The speed of adjustment toward this normal level $\bar{\mu}$ depends on the parameter a, and we initially set it equal to a conservative value of 0.1 (see Figure 14.3 for the path of μ_t generated by this model). Second, because the United States experienced a worse contraction than other countries, especially the countries (such as the United Kingdom) that left the gold standard in 1931, we assume that the expansionary policy would have brought about a stronger improvement in U.S. economic activity relative to the rest of the world. We thus set the values of $\Delta p'_t$ and $\Delta y'_t$ from 1931:3 to 1933:2 equal to their mean rate of change for the precrises 1926:7–1930:9 period.

Our third assumption is based on the view that the three large negative u_t shocks for October 1931, June 1932, and February 1933 might have resulted from speculation. As there would have been no speculation under our counterfactual, we set u_t (as estimated in Figure 14.3) equal to zero

FIGURE 14.4   The Actual and Simulated Values of U.S. Gold Reserves
1930:01–1933:02

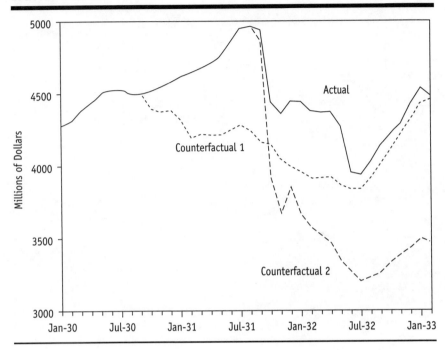

for these 3 months but otherwise assume no change in the behavior of u_t. Finally, our fourth assumption is that the average change in French domestic credit for the 1931:10–1933:2 period would have been the same as it was in the 1926:7–1931:9 period, and we adjust the mean of the series on French domestic credit (for the postdevaluation period) accordingly in calculating ΔD_t^*.

Given these assumptions, we use (9)–(12) to construct smooth money counterfactual 1. The main results of this counterfactual are presented in Figures 14.4 and 14.5. Figure 14.4 shows that gold reserves under counterfactual 1 fall after the first banking crisis and again after U.K. devaluation, reaching their lowest level in July 1932. However, even at their lowest level, simulated gold reserves are only about $100 million less than the actual shock. The behavior of the gold–reserve ratio under counterfactual 1 is shown in Figure 14.5. After falling sharply during the domestic credit expansion up to February 1931, this ratio stabilizes until August 1932 and

FIGURE 14.5 The Actual and Simulated Values of the U.S. Gold–
Reserve Ratio 1930:01–1933:02

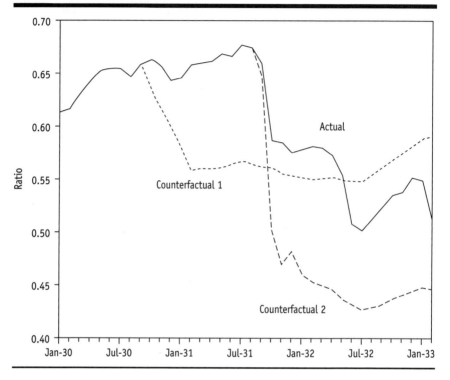

increases moderately afterward. The ratio stays above 54% throughout the
simulation period, and thus there would clearly have been an adequate supply of free gold—that is, gold not required for the backing of eligible
liabilities—under counterfactual 1.

We performed a large number of simulations to explore the sensitivity
of our results to different assumptions. We relaxed assumption one to
allow for a slower recovery in the money multiplier and assumption two to
permit a more modest improvement in the relative U.S. macroeconomic
performance (i.e., the behavior of $\Delta y_t'$ and $\Delta p_t'$). It could be argued that
the three large negative residuals represent exogenous shocks that would
not have been eliminated under expansionary policy. We thus constructed
a counterfactual without assumption three (i.e., set u_t equal to its actual
value for all periods). We also constructed counterfactuals without as-

sumption four to allow for the possibility that post-September 1931 changes in French policy were exogenous and would not have changed in response to expansionary policy (actual values of ΔD_t^* for the whole period are used in these simulations). The results of this analysis are summarized in Appendix 2. The analysis shows that even under the most unfavorable assumptions, the gold–reserve ratio stays well above 50% in counterfactual 1.

4.2. Counterfactual 2: Expansionary Policy, September 1931–January 1932

We assume that the Federal Reserve increased domestic credit by about an additional billion dollars from September 1931 to January 1932.[22] Expansion of domestic credit by an extra billion dollars would have allowed high-powered money to increase by more than the actual increase in the public's holding of currency and would have considerably eased the pressure on bank reserves. It is thus plausible to suppose that the money multiplier would have recovered after some lag, perhaps at a lower pace as compared to the first counterfactual. We modify our assumption one as follows. We assume that that multiplier would have fallen, as it actually did, up to December 1931, and from January 1932 on, it would have started adjusting toward its normal level at a rate slower than counterfactual 1. We again use model (14) to simulate the behavior of the multiplier but assume a smaller value of 0.025 for the adjustment parameter, a. We would also expect some improvement in relative U.S. economic performance under this counterfactual. Our assumption two is modified to let this improvement take place by the beginning of 1932, and starting January 1932, we set both $\Delta p_t'$ and $\Delta y_t'$ equal to their average rates for the 1926:07–1931:09 period (which are lower than the corresponding rates assumed in the first counterfactual).

It is less clear how to modify our assumption three regarding the residuals in the 3 critical months. As discussed above, it is difficult to determine on a priori grounds whether counterfactual 2 would have been seen as weakening or strengthening the U.S. commitment to gold. We appeal to the Hsieh–Romer evidence that the $1 billion expansionary open market operation in the spring of 1932 had little effect on expectations of devaluation. We assume that a similar expansion in the fall of 1931 would also not have significantly altered devaluation expectations. In our basic simulation of counterfactual 2, we let the u_t shock for October 1931 equal its actual value but set (as in counterfactual 1) the u_t shocks for June 1932 and February 1933 equal to zero. We do not use assumption four (i.e., do not adjust the path of ΔD_t^*) as it is not obvious that counterfactual 2 would have changed French policy.

The behavior of gold reserves and the gold–reserve ratio under counterfactual 2 is also shown in Figures 14.4 and 14.5. In this counterfactual, both gold reserves and the gold–reserve ratio would have declined sharply during the 9 months after the U.K. devaluation, falling to their lowest values in July 1932. Even at this critical stage, however, gold reserves would have been only about $750 million below their actual level and the gold–reserve ratio would still have been above 42.5%. Counterfactual 2 would, therefore, not have posed a serious problem for the United States to stay on the gold standard.

The results for our second counterfactual differ significantly from Eichengreen's (1992, pp. 295, 296) estimate that a policy designed to offset the decline in the stock of (M1) money from August 1931 to January 1932 would have decreased U.S. gold reserves by $2 billion and forced the United States off the gold standard. His calculations ignore the role of the money multiplier (see Bordo, 1994), and do not use a model to determine gold flows. Nevertheless, his estimate differs from ours largely because the policy that he considers differs from the one we simulate. Our counterfactual is based on a policy, similar to the one suggested by Friedman and Schwartz (1963), which focuses on the need for an adequate domestic-credit expansion to respond to the banking crises but does not require the money stock to stay at the initial level. Indeed, the (M2) money stock in our simulation falls from September 1931 to July 1932 but then increases gradually up to February 1933 to reach a level only about $300 million below its initial value. The Eichengreen experiment, on the other hand, involves offsetting the August 1931 to January 1932 decline in the money stock over a short period and hence requires a much bigger expansion in domestic credit.[23] In our view, if the Federal Reserve had acted only after the U.K. devaluation, an expansionary program of the order of magnitude assumed in our counterfactual [and suggested by Friedman and Schwartz (1963)] would have been appropriate at this late stage. Such a program would have improved economic conditions without driving the United States off the gold standard.

We also explored the sensitivity of the results of counterfactual 2 to a number of variations. Our discussion below focuses on key variations (see Appendix 2 for other variations and details). A key argument against counterfactual 2 is that it would have induced further speculation and increased the value of u_t in October 1931. A possible estimate of this increase is the June 1932 residual on the assumption that it represented the effect of similar open market operations from March through June 1932.[24] To explore this possibility, we set the u_t shock for October 1931 equal to the sum of the actual residuals for both October 1931 and June 1932. This variation of counterfactual 2 lowers the path of the gold–reserve ratio, but the ratio still stays above 41.5%. However, the large gold outflow in October 1931 (induced by the bigger u_t shock) would now lower the path of H_t (as well as M_t). We thus consider another variation in which domestic credit is increased by another $300 million in October 1931 to keep the path of H_t roughly the same as in our basic counterfactual. The gold–reserve ratio in this variant (which combines a bigger shock with a greater injection of domestic credit) falls at its lowest level to 38.6%. If a slower recovery is also assumed, the lowest value of the ratio would be further reduced to 38.8%. The statutory requirement, which was a weighted average of the 40% requirement for currency and the 35% requirement for deposits at the Federal Reserve, depending on the relative shares of currency and deposits was about 37% in October 1931. The statutory requirement would not have been breached.

In the worst case scenario, even if the statutory reserve requirement had been breached temporarily, the Federal Reserve had ample powers to deal with this without having to abandon gold convertibility. Indeed in March 1933, when the New York Federal Reserve Bank's gold reserves fell below its statutory limit, it applied to the Board in Washington for a suspension of the requirement, which the Board granted for 30 days at a negligible cost to the New York Reserve Bank. This action did not in any way suggest an abandonment of the gold standard.

It should be emphasized that our simulation assumes the case of perfect capital mobility (i.e., considers u_t exogenous to domestic-credit policy), which implies a high offset coefficient (equal to the rest-of-the-world share in world high-powered money). There were likely significant departures from this assumption, especially after the U.K. devaluation which led to a wide range of restrictions on international capital flows. Austria, Germany, and Hungary instituted capital controls in the summer of 1931. The United Kingdom and the sterling area introduced controls at the end of 1931, as did Japan in 1932. Thus, the estimate of gold loss resulting from domestic credit expansion in our second counterfactual is likely to be overstated.

Our estimates omit a significant portion of the rest of the world. To explore the bias resulting from this omission, we modified our basic simulations to increase the size of $\bar{H}_t^*$ such that the aggregate high-powered money for the United Kingdom, France, and Germany is always 60% of $\bar{H}_t^*$ [this percentage reflects the approximate share of the three countries in non-U.S. world high-powered money based on the 21-country sample in Bordo and Eichengreen (1998)]. Holding other factors constant, we find that this adjustment decreases the gold–reserve ratio only slightly and does not alter the implications of our results for the feasibility of expansionary money (see Appendix 2).[25]

5. Conclusions

The recent consensus view is that the gold standard is the key cause of the Great Depression. This view has merit, first in the sense that deflationary shocks were transmitted by the gold standard and, second, in the sense that for most countries continued adherence to gold blocked their recoveries. These were small, open economies, with limited gold reserves. This was not, however, the case for the United States. The United States had the largest economy in the world, held massive gold reserves, and hence was not constrained from using expansionary policy to offset banking panics. Indeed, under Benjamin Strong, the Federal Reserve had demonstrated its understanding of the need to pursue such policies.

This conclusion holds even in the face of perfect international capital flows. Dollar claims against the United States were minor relative to the size of its gold reserves in contrast to the situation today. Emerging countries that recently experienced crises hold outstanding international liabilities far in excess of their international reserves. This made it hard for them to alleviate domestic banking difficulties using domestic monetary policy.

The simulations we constructed, based on a model of a large open economy, indicate that expansionary open market operations at two critical junctures of the Great Depression would have been successful in every scenario in averting the banking panics without endangering convertibility. Indeed, had expansionary open market purchases been conducted in 1930, the Depression would not have led to the international crises that followed.

APPENDIX 1: MULTICOUNTRY VERSION

Letting superscript j index countries in the rest of the world, the relations for individual foreign countries corresponding to (5) and (7) are

$$\Delta G_t^j / \bar{H}_t^j = - \Delta D_t^j / \bar{H}_t^j - \Delta \mu_t^j + \Delta p_t^j + \alpha_1^* \Delta y_t^j + \alpha_2^* \Delta i_t^j + \Delta v_t^j, \tag{5'}$$

$$\Delta i_t = \Delta i_t^j + \Delta x_t^j + \Delta \varepsilon_t^j, \tag{7'}$$

where (5′) assumes that the money demand for each country is the same form as (1). Letting e_t^j denote the exchange rate of country j in terms of a reference foreign currency, define the weight for each country as $w_t^j \equiv e_t^j \bar{H}_t^j / \bar{H}_t^*$, with $\bar{H}_t^* \equiv \sum_j e_t^j \bar{H}_t^j$. Multiplying both sides of (5′) and (7′) by w_t^j and aggregating over all countries in the rest of the world, we obtain (5) and the first difference form of (7) with $\xi_t^* = \sum_j w_t^j \xi_t^j$ for $\xi = \Delta\mu, \Delta p, \Delta y, \Delta i, \Delta v; \Delta G_t^* / \bar{H}_t^* = \sum_j w_t^j \Delta G_t^j / \bar{H}_t^j; \Delta D_t^* / \bar{H}_t^* = \sum_j w_t^j \Delta D_t^j / \bar{H}_t^j; \Delta x_t = \sum_j w_t^j \Delta x_t^j;$ and $\Delta \epsilon_t = \sum_j w_t^j \Delta \epsilon_t^j$. Relation (6) changes to $\Delta G_t = -e \sum_j \Delta(e_t^j G_t^j)$, where e is the price of the reference currency in U.S. dollars (assumed, for simplicity, to be constant over time). Then using revised (6) along with (4), (5), and the first difference form of (7), we

TABLE 14.A1   Sensitivity Analysis for Counterfactual 1

	Lowest Simulated Values of	
	Gold Reserves (mill. U.S. $)	Gold–Reserve Ratio (%)
Basic simulation (as discussed in the text)	3834	54.8
Variation A (slower recovery of the money multiplier)	3859	55.0
Variation B (no change in French policy)	3637	53.5
Variation C (slower recovery of U.S. economy)	3678	53.8
Variation D (Variations B and C combined)	3485	52.5
Variation E (three large residuals not eliminated)	3306	51.1
Variation F (non-U.S. high-powered money adjusted)	3533	52.8

NOTE: Each variation differs from the basic simulation as indicated below. Variation A: a is set equal to 0.05 in (14) to determine $\Delta\mu$ from 1931:3. Variation B: French domestic credit series not adjusted in calculating ΔD_t^*. Variation C: $\Delta p_{t'}$ and $\Delta y_{t'}$ equal the average of their actual and simulated values. Variation D: changes in Variations B and C combined. Variation E: u_t is not set equal to zero for 1931:10, 1932:6, and 1933:2. Variation F: set $\bar{H}_t^*$ equal to 1.66 times the aggregate high-powered money of the United Kingdom, France, and Germany.

obtain (8) with $\gamma_t = -\sum_j w_t^j \Delta e_t^j G_{t-1}^j / e_t^j \bar{H}_t^j$. In the multicountry case, rest-of-the-world variables represent weighted averages of country variables with each country's weight equal to its share of the rest-of-the-world stock of high-powered money. This weighting scheme is used in our simulations.

APPENDIX 2: SENSITIVITY ANALYSIS

The key results of our sensitivity analysis for the two counterfactuals are summarized in Tables 14.A1 and 14.A2. For a number of variations of the basic simulations, the tables show the lowest levels to which gold reserves and the gold–reserve ratio would have fallen during the simulation period.

Variations A–C in Table 14.A1 modify the assumptions of the first counterfactual one at a time: Variation A considers a slower recovery of the money multiplier (from March 1931); Variation B assumes that French domestic credit policy after September 1931 would not have changed; and Variation C makes a more conservative assumption about the improvement in the relative performance of U.S. output and prices. Variation D combines the unfavorable assumptions of Variations B and C. Variation E explores the possibility that the three large negative residuals would not have been eliminated. Finally, Variation F adjusts $\bar{H}_t^*$ according to the share of the United Kingdom, France, and Germany in the non-U.S. world high-powered money but this adjustment does not much affect the results of the basic simulation. The table shows that the gold–reserve ratio stays well above 50% in all cases.

Variations of counterfactual 2 are shown in Table 14.A2. These variations include the case of a larger shock in October 1931 (equal to the sum of October 1931 and June 1932 residuals) as well as the case that combines the larger shock with a more expansionary policy (involving an additional in-

TABLE 14.A2   Sensitivity Analysis for Counterfactual 2

	Lowest Simulated Values of	
	Gold Reserves (mill. U.S. $)	Gold–Reserve Ratio (%)
Basic simulation (as discussed in the text)	3196	42.6
Variation A (constant money multiplier)	3383	44.0
Variation B (larger shock for October 1931)	3060	41.6
Variation C (larger shock, more expansionary policy)	2892	38.6
Variation D (slower recovery of U.S. economy)	3165	42.4
Variation E (Variations C and D combined)	2859	38.3
Variation F (non-U.S. high-powered money adjusted)	3085	41.8

NOTE: Each variation differs from the basic simulation as indicated below. Variation A: $\Delta\mu$ is set equal to zero from 1932:1. Variation B: u_t for 1931:10 set equal to the sum of 1931:10 and 1932:6 residuals. Variation C: Variation B plus domestic credit increased by $300 Million. Variation D: Δp_t and Δy_t equal the average of their actual and simulated values. Variation E: changes in Variations C and D combined. Variation F: $\bar{H}_{t^*}$ equals 1.66 times the aggregate high-powered money of the United Kingdom, France, and Germany.

jection of $300 million). The possibility that counterfactual 2 would not have affected any of the three residuals was also examined but this variation (not shown in the table) produces results similar to those of Variation B.

DATA APPENDIX

The source of monthly U.S., U.K., French, German, and rest of world gold reserves in Figure 14.1 is Federal Reserve (1943).

The source of monthly data for the United Kingdom, France, Germany, and the United States used in Section 4 is the database developed by Kwiecinska–Kalita (see her 1995 thesis for detailed description and sources of these data). Money supply series are based on an M3 definition of money for the United Kingdom, M2 for the United States and Germany, and M1 for France (time and saving deposits for France are not available for the whole period). The money supply and high-powered money data for the United States are the same as in Friedman and Schwartz (1963) and are already seasonally adjusted. These data for other countries were seasonally adjusted using a procedure based on moving averages. Domestic credit was defined as the difference between high-powered money and gold reserves. Gold reserve monthly data for France are available only since June 1928. French gold reserves before this date were estimated using the assumption that they were a fixed proportion of French high-powered money. Price level and output for each country were measured by indexes of consumer (retail) prices and industrial production. These indexes were smoothed using the Hodrick–Prescott filter with the smoothing parameter equal to 14,400.

Notes

1. For a recent review of the causes of the U.S. Depression, see Romer (1993).

2. See, for example, Choudhri and Kochin (1980), Eichengreen and Sachs (1985), Bernanke and James (1991), and Bernanke (1995).

3. Eichengreen (1992) documents the case of the central European countries (Austria, Germany, and Hungary), each of which in the summer of 1931 suffered banking crises. When the monetary authorities attempted to use expansionary policy to allay the banking crises, their currencies were subjected to speculative attacks,

forcing them to abandon unrestricted convertibility to gold. Belgium in 1935 was forced off the gold standard under similar conditions.

4. For example, the German Reichsbank, which adopted policies to accumulate gold and rebuild its reserve position following the German hyperinflation.

5. According to Eichengreen and Jeanne (1998), the British devalued sterling because of rising unemployment, which made it impossible to pursue the contractionary policies required to defend the parity.

6. There are two main sources of statistical information about the willingness of foreigners to hold dollar exchange. One source is a table showing outstanding amounts of short-term foreign liabilities reported by banks in New York City, including the Federal Reserve Bank of New York, at end-of-month dates beginning May 1929 through June 1931, thereafter weekly (*Banking and Monetary Statistics 1943*, Table 161). Detail is available through mid-February 1932 for 6, subsequently 9 European countries, the rest, and total Europe, and 4 other areas. The second source is a monthly table from 1914 on, showing the U.S. monetary gold stock, net gold imports, and gold under earmark (ibid., Table 156). In addition, weekly Saturday quotations of spot and forward rates for 1 month and 3 months of the dollar and six other European currencies are available (Einzig, 1937). The forward rates show the premium or discount in relation to sterling.

The sources do not distinguish private from official holders of dollar exchange nor when the United States lost gold how much was transferred to private or official claimants. Under the gold exchange standard, official holders of dollar exchange were clearly significant participants in the foreign exchange market and data on their gold holdings can be correlated with opposite movements in U.S. gold.

7. Willis (p. 18) believed that "the Reserve system should have been strong enough to resist any demands originating in the ordinary course of business. Foreign countries were not in a position to weaken it. They had already earmarked about all the gold to which they could successfully lay claim without crippling their American balances. . . . The danger lay entirely in the possibility of domestic withdrawals of gold or in a flight of capital [by domestic holders] which might result in eventual shipments. Immediate withdrawals for domestic hoarding were of course minor in importance."

8. In his conclusion Eichengreen (1992, pp. 392, 393) states: ". . . the failure of monetary . . . authorities to take offsetting action once the Depression was underway is no longer perplexing once one acknowledges the role of gold standard constraints. Unilateral action to . . . make available additional money and credit was certain to create balance of payments deficits where they did not already exist and to magnify these deficits with which central banks were already attempting to cope . . . gold convertibility would be threatened. Even the provision of liquidity to a banking system in distress might cast doubt over the official commitment to gold, prompting the transfer of bank deposits out of the country and aggravating the problem of

domestic financial instability. The Federal Reserve and the Bank of France, possessing extensive gold reserves, were less immediately threatened than other central banks. But *even* they had very limited room for maneuver (our emphasis)." And earlier he comments (p. 295): "In principle, the Fed could have used expansionary open market operations to prevent the decline in the money supply. It *refused* to do so for fear of endangering the gold parity," although he does not cite any supporting statement by a Fed official. The United States of course had a balance of payments surplus, not a deficit, throughout the Great Contraction.

9. Meltzer (2001) also argues that, if free gold was in fact a binding constraint, the Federal Reserve could have followed earlier precedent and temporarily suspended gold reserve requirements.

10. In this relation nongold international reserves are included in D_t^*.

11. Suppose that under imperfect capital mobility, the influence of domestic credit expansion on ε_t can be simply represented as $\varepsilon_t = \pi D_t / \bar{H}_t + \varepsilon_{t-1}$, with $\pi < 0$. Using this relation to substitute for $\Delta\varepsilon_t$ in (8), we can derive the offset coefficient as $-\theta_t(1 - \pi\alpha_2)$, where the expression in the parentheses is less than one.

12. To increase bank reserves, δ_t^b would have to be large enough to exceed $\Delta C_t - \Delta G_t$, where C is the currency held by the public. The amount needed to satisfy this condition would be especially large if a currency drain during a banking panic is accompanied by gold outflows caused by speculation.

13. For the data used, see the Data Appendix.

14. The share of the United Kingdom, France, and Germany in central bank gold reserves minus the U.S. share in 1929–1931 is 57%. The world consists of the 21 countries included in Bordo and Eichengreen (1998), which accounts for about 75% of the 1928 total in Federal Reserve (1943). The same share for high-powered money for the three countries as a share of the world less the United States is 55% (League of Nations, various issues).

15. Such knowledge was available and was used in the 1920s by Benjamin Strong to conduct open market operations to smooth economic activity, to maintain price stability, and to prevent banking panics. This knowledge could have been utilized by his successors to mitigate the deflationary experience of the Great Depression and to prevent its transmission to the rest of the world.

16. See, for example, Romer (1993). Eichengreen (1992) also focuses on this period in discussing the gold-standard constraint for U.S. monetary policy.

17. Estimates of the regression are

$$\Delta G_t / s_t \bar{H}_t = \underset{(0.966)}{0.002} + \underset{(4.125)}{0.546} z_t + u_t,$$

$R^2 = 0.179$, standard error of regression $= 0.020$, DW Statistics $= 1.516$, (t values in parentheses).

18. For derivation and estimation of this model, see Appendix 1 in Bordo, Choudhri, and Schwartz (1999).

19. Open market operations of similar amounts are suggested by Friedman and Schwartz (1963) for the first 8 months of 1930 or the first 6 months of 1931. In our counterfactual, we set δ_t^b equal to \$200 million from October 1930 to February 1931 and δ_t^n equal to −\$10 million from March 1931 to February 1933. These values yield a rate of money growth (M2) of about 2.4% over the simulation period, which is approximately equal to the growth rate in the presimulation period.

20. However, there would have been a small indirect effect, to the extent that member banks reduced their borrowing, and hence that eligible paper would have declined.

21. Of the three countries, the average value of domestic credit change decreased significantly after the U.K. devaluation only in the case of France.

22. A similar counterfactual is discussed by Friedman and Schwartz (1963). In our simulation, we assume the following values of δ_t^b from September 1931 to January 1932 to ensure that high-powered money exceeds the actual increase in currency held by public in each month: 250 in 1931:9, 1250 in 1931:10, 250 in 1931:11, 0 in 1931:12, and 150 in 1932:1. The assumed increase in domestic credit over this period exceeds the actual increase by about \$1050 million. For the remaining simulation period, δ_t^n is set equal to 0 to produce almost a zero rate of money growth of the presimulation period.

23. Using our model, for example, we calculate that an increase in domestic credit of about 2300 million dollars (in addition to the actual increase from September 1931 to January 1932) would have been needed to raise the stock of (M2) money in January 1932 to the August 1931 level.

24. If residuals in October 1931 and June 1932 did not arise from speculation, then an appropriate simulation would set u_t equal to its actual values for these months. This variation of the simulation was also performed but is not reported in Appendix 2 as it is more favorable for counterfactual 2 than the one discussed below (which sets u_t in October 1931 equal to the sum of the two residuals and u_t in June 1932 equal to zero).

25. The adjustment in $\bar{H}_t^*$ affects s_t and [via (13)] u_t. We assume that the behavior of ΔD_t^*, $\Delta \mu_t^*$, $\Delta p_t'$, and $\Delta y_t'$ is unchanged.

References

Bernanke, B. (1995), "The Macroeconomics of the Great Depression: A Comparative Approach." *Journal of Money, Credit and Banking*, **27**, 1–28.

Bernanke, B., and James, H. (1991), "The Gold Standard, Deflation, and Financial Crisis in the Great Depression: An International Comparison." In: R. G. Hubbard (Ed.), *Financial Markets and Financial Crises*. Chicago: Univ. of Chicago Press.

Blanco, H., and Garber, P. M. (1986), "Recurrent Devaluation and Speculative Attacks on the Mexico Peso." *Journal of Political Economy* 94(1), 148–166.

Board of Governors of the Federal Reserve System (1943), *Banking and Monetary Statistics, 1914–1941.* P. 544.

Bordo, M. D. (1994), "Review of Barry Eichengreen, *Golden Fetters: The Gold Standard and the Great Depression.*" *Journal of International Economics* **36**, 193–197.

Bordo, M. D., Choudhri, E. U., and Schwartz, A. J. (1999), "Was Expansionary Monetary Policy Feasible during the Great Contraction? An Examination of the Gold Standard Constraint." NBER Working Paper No. 7125.

Bordo, M. D., and Eichengreen, B. (1998), "Implications of the Great Depression for the Development of the International Monetary System." In: Bordo, Goldin, and White (Eds.), *The Defining Moment: The Great Depression and the American Economy in the Twentieth Century.* Chicago: Chicago Univ. Press.

Brown, W. A., Jr. (1940), *The International Gold Standard Reinterpreted 1919–1934.* New York: NBER.

Capie, F., Mills, T. C., and Wood, G. E. (1986), "What Happened in 1931?" In: F. Capie and G. E. Wood (Eds.), *Financial Crises and the World Banking System.* London: Macmillan. Pp. 120–148.

Choudhri, E. U., and Kochin, L. A. (1980), "The Exchange Rate and the International Transmission of Business Cycle Disturbances: Some Evidence from the Great Depression." *Journal of Money, Credit and Banking* **12**, 565–574.

Eichengreen, B. (1990), *Elusive Stability.* New York: Cambridge Univ. Press.

Eichengreen, B. (1992), *Golden Fetters: The Gold Standard and the Great Depression, 1919–1939.* New York: Oxford Univ. Press.

Eichengreen, B., and Jeanne, A. (1998), "Currency Crisis and Unemployment: Sterling in 1931." In: P. Krugman (Ed.), *Currency Crises.* Chicago: University of Chicago Press. Pp. 7–43.

Eichengreen, B., and Sachs, J. (1985), "Exchange Rates and Economic Recovery in the 1930's." *Journal of Economic History* **45**, 925–946.

Einzig, P. (1937), *The Theory of Forward Exchange.* London: Macmillan.

Flood, R. P., and Garber, P. M. (1984), "Collapsing Exchange Rate Regimes: Some Linear Examples." *Journal of International Economics* **17**, 1–13.

Flood, R. P., and Marion, N. P. (1996), "Speculative Attacks: Fundamentals and Self-Fulfilling Prophecies." NBER Working Paper No. 5789.

Friedman, M., and Schwartz, A. J. (1963), *A Monetary History of the United States, 1867–1960.* Princeton: Princeton Univ. Press.

Hoover, H. (1952), *The Memoirs of Herbert Hoover: The Great Depression 1929–1941.* New York: Macmillan.

Howson, S. (1980), "Sterling's Managed Float: The Operations of the Exchange Equalisation Account, 1932–39." *Princeton Studies in International Finance* No. 46 (November).

Hsieh, C.-T., and Romer, C. D. (2001), "Was the Federal Reserve Fettered? Devaluation Expectations in the 1932 Monetary Expansion." NBER Working Paper No. 8113.

Johnson, H. C. (1997), *Gold, France, and Great Depression, 1919–1932*. Oxford: Oxford Univ. Press.

Kwiecinska-Kalita, H. (1995), "Monetary Independence under a Fixed Exchange Rate: The Interwar Experience, 1925:5–1931:4." Ph.D. thesis, University of Toronto.

Meltzer, A. H. (2001), "Why Did Monetary Policy Fail in the Thirties?" In: *A History of the Federal Reserve 1913–51*, Vol. 1, Chap. 5. Carnegie Mellon (Mimeo). Chicago: Univ. of Chicago Press.

Nurkse, R. (1944), *International Currency Experience*. Geneva: League of Nations.

Romer, C. (1993), "The Nation in Depression." *Journal of Economic Perspectives* **7**, 19–40.

Willis, H. P., and Chapman, J. M. (1934), *The Banking Situation*. New York: Columbia Univ. Press.

CHAPTER 15

Could the United States Have Had a Better Central Bank?

An Historical Counterfactual Speculation

MICHAEL D. BORDO

1. Introduction

THE FEDERAL RESERVE'S CENTENARY will be in 2014. It is time to reflect on how the institution has done in its first 100 years—on its successes and failures. Much has been written on the history of the Federal Reserve. The key books are by Milton Friedman and Anna Schwartz in A Monetary History of the United States (1867–1960) and Allan Meltzer, A History of the Federal Reserve (2003) and (2009) and two recent books are also important: John Wood, A History of Central Banking in Great Britain and the United States (2005) and Robert Hetzel, The Monetary Policy of the Federal Reserve: A History (2008).

The general thrust of the evaluation of the Fed's performance is that it did well in the 1920s, the 1950s, and from the mid 1980s to 2006 (the Great Moderation) but that it performed badly in the Great Depression of the 1930s and the Great Inflation from 1965 to 1980. Many also have

Originally published in "Could the United States Have Had a Better Central Bank? An Historical Counterfactual Speculation," *Journal of Macroeconomics* 34, no. 3 (September 2012): 597–607. © 2012 Elsevier Inc. All rights reserved.

criticized the Fed for its performance during the recent financial crisis and Great Recession (e.g., Meltzer, 2009; Taylor, 2009; Hetzel, 2012) but it will take more time to conclude that this experience should be ranked as badly as the Great Depression and Great Inflation.

This literature is critical of the Fed for following flawed doctrine, for its lack of independence from political pressure and for flaws in its structure. However despite its serious failures the consensus would argue that the Fed during its 100 years has exhibited the ability to learn from its past errors.

Selgin et al. (2010) go farther than the main stream view. They argue that the Fed has never done better with respect to price stability, real economic stability and financial stability compared to the regime which preceded it—the classical gold standard, national banking, US Treasury and Clearing House regime.

This chapter does not directly engage into the debate over how well or badly the Fed did in its first 100 years. Rather I focus on whether the track record of economic performance could have been improved if the development of a US central bank had followed two quite different historical paths which were presented at key conjunctures in the past. The first scenario is to assume that the charter of the Second Bank of the United States had not been revoked by Andrew Jackson in 1836 and the Second Bank had survived. This is not a totally unrealistic scenario since absent Jackson's veto the Bank would have survived and the Congress came reasonably close to overriding the veto. The second scenario takes as given that the Second Bank did not survive and history had evolved as it did, but considers the situation in which the Federal Reserve Act of 1913 was closer to the original plan for a central bank for the United States proposed by Warburg (1910a). Both of these scenarios would have led to greater financial stability than we had in the twentieth century and possibly better overall macro-performance and price stability.

Section 2 develops the Second Bank counterfactual. Section 3 considers the Warburg scenario. Section 4 speculates on whether these alternative arrangements would have given us better overall financial, macroeconomic and price stability performance throughout the twentieth century than we had. Section 5 concludes with some policy relevant lessons from history.

2. Had the Second Bank of the United States Survived

In 1790 Alexander Hamilton proposed a financial reform package for the US to overcome the economic paralysis of the Confederacy. It would serve as the basis for US financial development and lead to a financial revolution which underpinned long run economic growth (Rousseau and Sylla, 2003). A key plank of Hamilton's plan was the creation of a national bank, the First Bank of the United States. This bank, modeled after the Bank of England, would have both public and private ownership and would provide loans to both sectors. It would be sufficiently well capitalized to be able to provide the government with medium term bridge loans to finance shortfalls in government tax receipts. It was also hoped that its loans to the private sector would spur economic development but it was deemed imperative that it also hold sufficient specie reserves to always maintain convertibility of the notes. The First Bank of the United States was chartered in 1791 with a capital of $10 million (it was the largest business enterprise in the country) (Bordo and Vegh, 2002).

There was strong opposition to the First Bank from Hamilton's initial proposal. The opposition was on both constitutional issues and populist distrust of the concentration of economic power. The Constitution had merely said that the Federal government could coin money and regulate its value; it said nothing about setting up banks. The constitutional debate that has followed since then reflected the fundamental political question of how power was to be divided between the Federal government and the States. The second source of opposition was a deep seated populist distrust of the concentration of economic power in a national bank located in Philadelphia with branches in every state. As a consequence of this opposition the First Bank had its charter revoked after 20 years in 1811.

A Second Bank of the United States with terms similar to the First Bank was chartered in 1816, in the face of financial disarray following the War of 1812, with a capital of $50 million. Once again opposition to the Second Bank arose from politicians, especially in the South, who wished to preserve as much power in the States as possible, and from citizens concerned about the concentration of power. This pressure was taken up by

Andrew Jackson who made it a centerpiece of his agenda to close the Second Bank under Nicholas Biddle.

As a result of this opposition the charter of the Second Bank was not
renewed and the chartering of banks became the sole prerogative of the
States. The succeeding 80 years were characterized by considerable financial instability—the Free Banking era from 1836 to 1863—with a flawed
payments system, numerous bank failures and several notable banking
panics, followed by the National Banking era which did create a uniform
currency but was punctuated by four serious banking panics and several
minor ones. The system did not solve the problem of "the inelasticity of
high powered money" (Friedman and Schwartz, 1963). The outcry following the Panic of 1907 led to the reforms leading to the Federal Reserve.

My counterfactual, which is close to that of Hammond (1957), is that had
the Second Bank not been destroyed by Andrew Jackson in 1836, that US
monetary history would have been very different. Monetary and financial
instability would have been considerably less.

The Second Bank of the United States under Nicholas Biddle in the
decade before the Bank War had developed into a first rate central bank.
According to Redlich (1951) Biddle had read Thornton's (1802) and understood the principle tenets of monetary theory. Biddle had a remarkably
clear understanding of the role of the Bank in stabilizing exchange rates
and maintaining adherence to the gold standard, smoothing seasonal and
cyclical shocks and acting as a lender of last resort to the banking system.
In many respects he was ahead of his contemporaries at the Bank of
England.

Had the Second Bank survived, the US may have adopted nationwide
branch banking as Canada did. The state banks were already competing
with the Second Bank in the 1830s and it is likely that the Second Bank
would have expanded and extended its branching network. It is unlikely
that the federal government would have blocked chartering competitors
for the Second Bank as happened in France in this period. Moreover the
states would likely have moved to promote interregional branching because
their banks would have found it difficult to compete with the Second Bank
without cross state branching. Had nationwide branch banking come on
the scene the US would have developed a more resilient banking system

as in Canada where banks could pool risk across regions and the incidence of banking panics would have been less (Bordo et al., 2011).

In addition the Second Bank would have learned to act as a lender of last resort just as the Bank of England did. Thus even if the States had developed free banking and not gone the Canadian route, the Second Bank would have learned to stem incipient panics, the interstate branching network of the Second Bank would have continued to create a unified national currency and also an efficient payments mechanism. Moreover the Second Bank under Biddle had been developing and strengthening the two name bill of exchange market which in Europe developed into the deep and liquid bankers acceptance market. A unified money market would have developed more rapidly than it did (Knodell, 2003). Given the development of a deep and liquid money market the Second Bank would have been able to use its discount rate to backstop the market and provide liquidity when needed. It would also have developed open market operations as the Bank of England did to make 'Bank Rate effective' (Sayers, 1976).

Had the Second Bank learned to deal with the financial crisis problem as was the case of the Bank of England after the Overend Gurney crisis of 1866 (when the Bank heeding Bagehot's (1873) criticism of its actions in not allaying the panic), and adopted his Responsibility doctrine to subsume its private interest to that of the public. It also learned to follow Bagehot's rule to lend freely to the money market on the basis of sound collateral. Had the Second Bank adopted similar strictures, the US would not have needed to found the Federal Reserve and the US central bank would likely not have made the mistakes it did between 1929 and 1933. In addition the Second Bank had already begun by 1830 to iron out the seasonal in the money market removing another reason to establish a new central bank.

Had the Second Bank developed into a best practice mid-nineteenth-century central bank then the Civil War would have been financed in a more efficient way than it was, just as the Bank of England learned to do in the Napoleonic Wars by freely discounting exchequer bills at a low pegged discount rate (Bordo and White, 1991). This may have obviated the need to issue greenbacks. Moreover there would not have been the need to develop the National Banking system to provide a new source of currency. The gold standard would have been temporarily suspended according to the gold standard contingent rule (Bordo and Kydland, 1995) and given the credibility of the Second Bank the Federal government would have been able to issue debt at higher prices than would otherwise have been the case.

Finally the Second Bank would have continued to adhere to the gold standard convertibility rule and to follow the rules of the game as the other central banks learned to do in the nineteenth century, as Biddle had learned to do in the 1830s. He intervened in the foreign exchange market to smooth balance of payments adjustment (Bordo et al., 2007). By adhering to the convertibility rule, the Second Bank would have gained the credibility to use its tools to temporarily smooth interest rates and offset shocks to the real economy acting within the target zone provided by the gold points (Bordo and MacDonald 2007). This suggests that the Second Bank could have smoothed the price level and dampened the international price and output shocks that characterized the experience under the pre-1914 classical gold standard. Business cycles in the US would have been milder than they were both because banking panics would have been prevented by the Second Bank and because of its smoothing operations.

The Second Bank, by following the gold standard rules, would have aided in the implicit international cooperation that strengthened the system (Eichengreen, 1992). Indeed the creation and backstopping of the bankers acceptance market would have facilitated the ability of US merchant banks to issue dollar denominated trade and bankers acceptances and would have reduced the reliance on and transfers to the British merchant banks who supplied the sterling bills needed to finance US trade with the rest of the world (Lawrence, 1997). This would have allowed the dollar to become an international currency sooner than it did. This would also have obviated the need for establishing the Fed in 1913.

Counter to my Second Bank counterfactual, one could argue that deep seated American populism and distrust of centralized power as well as states' rights sentiment would have eventually terminated the Second Bank even if the Bank War between Andrew Jackson and Nicholas Biddle had not happened. A possible response to this objection is that, as was the case with the Bank of England in the eighteenth and nineteenth centuries, the Second Bank would have learned some self-protective skills to create a constituency in the nation and especially in the Congress, to ward off incipient threats to its charter. This would suggest that the Jackson Biddle War was sui generis, reflecting a head on collision of two very strong willed individuals that would not necessarily have repeated itself.[1]

2.1. The Second Bank in the Twentieth Century

With the Second Bank as the US central bank, assuming that it evolved in the way other advanced country central banks had evolved, the events of the twentieth century may have been different than they were. World War I would likely have been financed in the way it was and the gold standard would have been suspended as it was during the Civil War or partially suspended as it was under the embargo on gold exports from 1917 to 1919. The postwar instability in Europe would not have been much different than it was and the real exchange rate misalignments would not have been much different than they were. The gold exchange standard would likely have been established as it was and would have had the same problems as it had, although a longstanding US central bank might not have sterilized gold inflows in the 1920s and would have allowed the adjustment mechanism to work (although if France had followed its pro gold sterilization policies, deflationary pressure would have still been prevalent [Irwin, 2010]). Bordo and Eichengreen (1998) argue that if the Great Depression had not happened, the gold exchange standard could have lasted much longer, at least until the 1960s when it would have collapsed because of the Triffin Dilemma and the world would then have moved towards a fiat money system.

Most important for the monetary history of the twentieth century is the likelihood that the US central bank would not have allowed the Great Depression to happen because it would not have been hobbled by the orthodoxy of the real bills doctrine embedded in the Federal Reserve Act (Meltzer, 2003). This suggests that it would not have followed the tight monetary policies it did in 1928–1929 to stem the stock market boom and it would have learned to follow orthodox lender of last resort policy—to use open market operations to provide liquidity to the money market or else discount freely to all commercial banks on the basis of sound collateral—to prevent the type of banking panics that occurred in the early 1930s. Moreover the flaws in the structure of the Fed emphasized by Friedman and Schwartz (1963) would have been absent. Had the Great Depression not happened then monetary history would have been very different indeed and we might not have had World War II, Keynesian economics and the Great Inflation.

3. Had Paul Warburg's Plan for a US Central Bank Been Adopted

Our second counterfactual scenario for a US central bank is somewhat less radical than the previous one. We assume that the Second Bank was destroyed and the financial history of the nineteenth century played out as it did. During the Civil War the framers of the National Banking system wanted to rectify the perceived major shortcoming of the Free Banking system which prevailed from 1836 to 1863—the absence of a uniform currency. This was achieved by the creation of National banks which issued national bank notes fully backed by US government securities. National banks were also required to have higher capital requirements than did the state banks as well as higher reserve requirements. They were also tightly supervised by the Comptroller of the Currency (White 2011).

However the National Banking system had a number of fatal flaws which contributed greatly to the frequent serious banking panics which occurred in the succeeding 50 years. The two fatal flaws of an inelastic monetary base and the inverted pyramid of credit engendered several reform movements in the 40-year period.

The inelasticity of the monetary base (high powered money) problem stemmed from the fact that there was no institutional mechanism in place to serve as a lender of last resort in the face of a banking panic when the public en masse attempted to convert their deposits into currency. The only way to increase national bank notes was by increasing the value or quantity of government bonds backing the notes. This would be hard to do in the conditions of a banking panic (Cagan, 1963). Two mechanisms were developed in the national banking era to provide emergency currency: the Clearing Houses in New York City and other major financial centers would issue Clearing House loan certificates based on the pooled assets of the member banks. These would serve as a substitute for bank reserves thus allowing the banks to pay out cash to the public. The other mechanism was the independent US Treasury which had some rudimentary tools of monetary policy at its disposal (especially lending tax and customs receipts to commercial banks for short periods, which were held in gold at its branches [Timberlake, 1993]). These substitutes for a central bank engaging in Discount Window Lending or conducting open market operations (as was done at the time by the Bank of England and other European central banks) were successful in allaying panics on several occasions (1884 and 1890) but were used too little and too late to prevent major panics from erupting in 1873, 1893 and 1907 (Schwartz 1986). Under the national banking system the Country national banks in small cities could hold half of their 25% reserve requirements as correspondent balances earning interest in Reserve City banks (larger cities), Reserve City banks in turn could hold half of their reserves as correspondent balances earning interest in the Central Reserve City banks in New York, Chicago and St. Louis (Bordo et al., 1992). As it turned out much of the nation's reserves ended up in the New York money center banks who would invest them in the call loan market. Call loans (viewed as highly liquid) were used to finance purchases of stocks on the New York stock exchange. The tight connection between the nation's bank reserves and the stock market linked stock market crashes to banking panics (Sprague, 1910).

A third problem of the National Banking system was seasonal stringency in the money markets which could exacerbate financial crises. In the autumn crop moving season, the demand for credit would tend to push up short-term interest rates. If other factors leading to financial stringency occurred at the same time (such as the Bank of England raising its discount rate to protect its gold reserves, hence reducing the supply of sterling bills of exchange used to finance the export of grain from the US), then a panic could arise. Most of the panics under the National Banking system occurred in the fall (Miron, 1986).

These three flaws of the National Banking system led to a series of proposals following each major panic for reform of the financial system (West, 1977). However nothing substantive was changed until the Panic of 1907 which was 'the straw that broke the camel's back'. The Panic of 1907 led to the Aldrich Vreeland Act of 1908 which institutionalized the emergency currency creation procedures developed by the Clearing Houses. Groups of banks were allowed to form National Currency Associations to temporarily issue emergency currency in the face of a panic on permission from the Secretary of the Treasury. In addition to the creation of National Currency Associations, the Aldrich Vreeland Act created the National Monetary Commission with a mandate to draft by 1912 a plan for a US style central bank.

Paul Warburg, a successful German investment banker who had immigrated to the US, proposed a plan for reform of the US system along the lines of the European financial systems that he was familiar with. Warburg succeeded in convincing Nelson Aldrich, the Chairman of the Senate banking committee, of the efficacy of his plan at a secret meeting of prominent bankers held at Jekyll Island, Georgia (Wicker, 2005).

Warburg made the case for a European style central bank for the US. He argued that in the advanced countries of Europe the presence of a discount market and a central bank providing the liquidity to back it up, and serve as lender of last resort in times of stringency, would prevent the type of financial instability experienced in the US. Warburg believed that a market for bills of exchange (two name bills) like the market for bankers acceptances in use in Europe would be more liquid than the existing US commercial bill market (based on single name promissory notes). Warburg argued that the US money market would be more liquid if national banks were permitted to issue bankers acceptances. Moreover he believed that the creation of a US acceptance market would break the monopoly that sterling bills had over US international commerce and would help the dollar become an international currency (Broz, 1997; Eichengreen, 2010).

The European financial systems that Warburg wanted the US to emulate were highly sophisticated ones that had taken centuries to evolve. In the English system the Bank of England would discount paper for the discount houses on the basis of the quality of the collateral offered. The discount houses in turn would then provide liquidity to the banking system. In times of panic the Bank of England would lend anonymously to the money market, as if through a frosted glass window.

The mechanism can be envisaged as the central bank having a discount window made of frosted glass and raised just a few inches. Representatives of institutions could appear at the window and push through the paper they wanted discounted. The central banker would return the appropriate amount of cash, reflecting the going rate of interest. The central banker does not know, nor does he care, who is on the other side of the window. He simply discounts good quality paper or lends on the basis of good collateral. In this way, institutions holding good quality assets will have no difficulty in obtaining the funds they need. Institutions with poor quality are likely to suffer. In times of panic the interest rate would rise. (Capie, 2002, p. 311)

In addition to not having a unified money market based on bankers acceptances and a central bank using its discount rate to back it up and serve as lender of last resort, the institutional framework of the European banking systems was very different from the US in the National banking era. The European banking system was relatively concentrated in a few large nationwide branching banks versus the US with thousands of unit banks.

With these institutional differences in mind Warburg (1910b) proposed the creation of a central bank with 20 regional branches controlled by bankers but regulated to some extent by government officials. His proposed United Reserve Bank would rediscount bills of exchange for its member banks, thereby providing liquidity to the market and establishing a lender of last resort following Bagehot's rule to lend freely in a banking panic.

The relationship between the central bank and the discount market is a most important one. While in normal times only a small proportion of the business is done by the central bank, the existence of this bank is all important to the whole financial structure, because even if a bank makes it a rule not to rediscount with the central bank and in its general business keeps independent of this institution, the fact remains that in case of need it can nevertheless rediscount with the central bank every legitimate bill, both bankers or mercantile acceptance, so that every legitimate bill represents a quick asset, on the realization of which every bank or banker can rely. Consequently no investor, bank, banker, private capitalist or financial institution will ever hesitate to buy good bills.

Furthermore, there will not be in critical times any rush to sell good bills, as everybody in these countries knows that there is no better and safer investment, because for no other investment is there an equally reliable market. (Warburg, 1910a, p. 37)

Under Warburg's plan the discount rate would be the key instrument of monetary policy and it would be supplemented by open market operations to help make the discount rate effective, i.e., to ensure that changes in the discount rate could always determine the behavior of market interest rates. He wanted the discount market to replace the call loan market as the key source of liquidity for US banks and hence eliminate the link between the stock market and the banking system under the inverted pyramid of credit. As in Europe adherence to the official gold parity would anchor the price level and the new central bank would issue currency backed by bills of exchange and gold, and would manage the gold standard by intervening in the foreign exchange market and manipulating the gold points according to the 'rules of the game'.

Nelson Aldrich incorporated much of the Warburg Plan into the Aldrich bill which was presented to the Senate in 1912 and rejected. The succeeding Democratic Congress put forward a bill drafted by Carter Glass and H. Parker Willis which, with some minor alterations, became the Federal Reserve Act. The Federal Reserve Act took on board many of the key monetary and international policy provisions of the Aldrich bill but differed from it radically in terms of structure and governance. Rather than a central bank with many branches, the Federal Reserve System had 12 regional Reserve Banks and the Federal Reserve Board in Washington. The key monetary policy difference between the Federal Reserve Act and the Aldrich Plan was that individual Reserve Banks would set their own discount rates and keep a minimum reserve in terms of gold and 'eligible' paper against its notes and deposits.

The Federal Reserve Act incorporated many of Warburg's ideas but left out or downgraded others. First, consistent with his views, member banks were required to maintain reserve balances with the Reserve Banks which would reduce the concentration of correspondent balances in the New York call loan market and the transmission of instability from the stock market to the banking system.

Second, consistent with Warburg's plan to address the problem of inelastic currency, the Act permitted member banks to rediscount eligible paper with the Reserve Banks in exchange for currency or reserve deposits. Third, Warburg's views were also reflected in the sections of the Act that permitted member banks to offer bankers acceptances based on international trade and which authorized the Reserve Banks to rediscount or purchase acceptances in the open market. The Reserve Banks would set the 'bill buying rates' on acceptances they offered to purchase in the open market. The Fed's acceptance buying facility was closer in form to the Bank of England's discount facility than the Fed's discount window. Typically Reserve Banks would purchase all of the eligible acceptances offered to them at their set bill buying rates.

In other respects the Act departed from Warburg's vision. First, it did not contain explicit instructions for how the Fed should respond in the event of a banking panic, i.e., how it should serve as a lender of last resort. Unlike Warburg (1910a) it does not state Bagehot's rule.

> Thus certain periodic and normal demands for cash, as well as a domestic drain caused by distrust, must be met by paying out freely. A foreign drain, on the other hand, must generally be met by an energetic increase of the rate, while a drain both domestic and foreign must be treated by various combinations of both methods. (Warburg, 1910a, p. 37)

The framers believed that they had created a foolproof mechanism that would prevent panics from occurring in the first place.

Second, the Act did not address sources or forms of financial instability outside the banking system, e.g., from the trust companies. Moreover only member banks were given access to the Fed's services and this left out nonmember state banks (as well as trust companies and other financial institutions).

Third, the Federal Reserve Act limited the types and maturities of loans and securities that member banks could rediscount with the Reserve Banks.

Glass and Willis were strong proponents of the real bills doctrine. They believed that Federal Reserve Credit should be extended only by rediscounting self-liquidating commercial and agricultural loans. The Federal Reserve Act allowed the rediscounting of notes based on commercial transactions but forbade the rediscounting of loans and securities from the financing of financial assets except US government bonds. The provisions of the Federal Reserve Act defining eligible paper were similar to those in the Aldrich bill but the Aldrich bill would have permitted the rediscounting of any direct obligations of the borrowing bank if approved by the Secretary of the Treasury. Thus the lender of last resort function envisaged by the Federal Reserve Act fell short of what Warburg had planned. This became an issue in the Great Depression (Bordo and Wheelock, 2011).

3.1. The Federal Reserve's Performance in the 1920s and 1930s

The Federal Reserve began operating in 1914. It successfully helped finance World War I by discounting loans secured by government securities and by using open market operations. After the war the Fed, according to Friedman and Schwartz, made its first policy mistake by delaying tightening in 1919 in the face of rising inflation, and then once it did tighten in late 1919, it waited too long to ease precipitating a serious recession in 1920–1921. The Fed tightened in 1919 when it observed its gold reserves declining. It raised its discount rates in classic European central bank style. Friedman and Schwartz gave the Fed high marks for maintaining price and real economic stability in the 1920s, for conducting countercyclical monetary policy to offset two minor business cycles. They also praise the Fed for smoothing out the seasonal cycle in interest rates and thereby achieving one of the goals of its framers.

Meltzer (2003) criticizes the Fed for basing its policy actions in the 1920s and 1930s on a variant of the Real Bills doctrine—the Burgess Rieffler Strong doctrine—which encouraged the Fed to base its decisions to tighten or ease policy on the level of short-term nominal interest rates and the level of member bank borrowing in the key money market cities. Following this rule, according to Meltzer (2003), Wheelock (1991) and Wicker (1966), worked well in the tranquil 1920s but created problems in the 1930s in the face of deflation and a collapsed demand for loans. Friedman and Schwartz also criticized the Fed for following the Real Bills proscription against discounting financial paper.

The Fed largely adhered to gold standard orthodoxy in the 1920s and attached higher weight to external than internal balance (Wicker, 1966). Its major departure from orthodoxy was sterilization of gold inflows which impeded the classical price specie flow adjustment mechanism from working and also imposed deflationary pressure on the rest of the world (Meltzer, 2003).

Federal Reserve policy during the Great Contraction departed radically from what Warburg had in mind for a lender of last resort. Following the stock market crash of October 1929 the New York Fed used its discount window lending and open market operations to inject reserves into the banking system and prevented the crash from turning into a liquidity panic. Thereafter, the Fed did not use its policy tools to effectively prevent a series of banking panics from playing out—leading to a collapse of money supply, prices and real output.

There is a vast literature considering why the Federal Reserve failed to act effectively as a lender of last resort during the Great Contraction. Friedman and Schwartz (1963) emphasize the Fed's flawed structure and lack of strong leadership. After the death of Benjamin Strong, Governor of the New York Fed, who had exerted powerful control over the key Open Market Investment committee, the System became paralyzed by in-fighting, petty jealousies and sharp differences of opinion. Other studies contended that the policies followed by the Fed during the Depression were fundamentally consistent with those of the 1920s (Wicker, 1966; Wheelock, 1991; Meltzer, 2003). Those studies posit that Fed officials misinterpreted the behavior of nominal interest rates and the level of borrowing from the Fed's discount window. Low nominal interest rates after 1930 and little borrowing at the discount window were treated as evidence that monetary conditions were exceptionally easy and that there was little more the Fed could or should do to promote recovery.

Temin (1989) and Eichengreen (1992) focus on the role of the gold standard. The Federal Reserve Act affirmed the fundamental role that the gold standard played in the US monetary system. The Reserve Banks were required to maintain gold reserves to back their note and deposit liabilities. Although the Act permitted the Federal Reserve Board to suspend the System's gold reserve requirement, Fed officials were very reluctant to take any action that would threaten the gold standard.

In addition to these factors a key reason why the Fed failed was because it did not recreate the features of the European banking system that made the Bank of England, the Reichsbank and other central banks effective lenders of last resort (Bordo and Wheelock, 2011). The framers of the Federal Reserve Act intended the discount window to be the primary means by which the Fed would furnish an elastic currency. They sought to provide a mechanism that would ensure ample supplies of currency and bank reserves to support commercial and agricultural activity, but not be a source of funds for speculation or long-term investment. Thus the types of paper that were eligible for rediscounting with Federal Reserve Banks were restricted to short-term commercial and agricultural paper (and US government securities). During the Depression, many banks apparently lacked paper that was acceptable for rediscounting with the Federal Reserve Banks.

The second problem with the discount mechanism under the Federal Reserve Act was that member banks were quite reluctant to borrow from the Fed in a crisis. In part this reluctance stemmed from the Fed's administration of the discount window. Throughout the 1920s, according to Meltzer (2003, pp. 161–165), Fed officials had tried to discourage banks from continuous borrowing and wished to instill the idea that banks are hesitant to borrow from the Fed and do so reluctantly when confronted with a short-term liquidity need. Fed officials also were concerned that banks were borrowing from the Fed to finance loans for the purchase of stocks.

A third problem was that of stigma; during the Depression banks became reluctant to turn to the discount window because they feared that depositors would interpret this as a sign of weakness hence increasing the likelihood of a run on the bank (Friedman and Schwartz, 1963, pp. 318–319).

The Fed had a second mechanism to supply currency or reserves during a crisis—the purchase of bankers acceptances, the mechanism that Warburg favored. Although the Fed did make large purchases of bankers acceptances during the banking panics in the fall of 1931 and the spring of 1933, these purchases were not large enough to offset the effects of currency and gold withdrawals from the banking system.

Although the Fed's purchases of bankers acceptances provided some support to the banking system during the panics, the acceptance market was small and highly concentrated in New York City, which limited the usefulness of Fed purchases during a crisis. Conceivably the Fed could have made it more attractive for banks to sell acceptances to the Reserve Banks by lowering their bill buying rates, but it seems doubtful that they could have purchased enough acceptances to prevent declines in bank reserves (Bordo and Wheelock, 2011, p. 30).

The Federal Reserve's decentralized system also created problems in responding to a financial crisis. The framers wanted a federal system of Reserve Banks to respond to and support the banking and currency needs of their individual districts. Thus, each Federal Reserve Bank had the discretion to set its own discount rate and administer its discount window. The Fed's decentralized structure proved unwieldy in responding to financial crises. The individual Reserve Banks acted competitively rather than cooperatively at critical points during the Depression. For example, in March 1933, the Federal Reserve Bank of Chicago refused a request from the New York Fed to exchange gold for US government securities when gold outflows threatened to push the New York Fed's reserve ratio below its legal minimum (Meltzer, 2003, p. 287).

The Act left considerable discretion to the individual Reserve Banks and the Federal Reserve Board for implementing policy. Some of the Reserve Banks moved more aggressively than others to supply currency to banks threatened by a panic. Richardson and Troost (2009) compare the liberal lending policies of the Atlanta Fed to those of the St. Louis Fed. They find the incidence of bank failures to be much greater in the half of Mississippi under St. Louis's jurisdiction than the half under Atlanta's jurisdiction. Another example of discretion by a Reserve Bank was the New York Fed's aggressive response to the 1929 stock market crash.

The actions by the New York and Atlanta Reserve Banks suggest that the Federal Reserve had the tools and the power to respond effectively to financial crises. However an effective response required leaders who were willing to improvise and test the limits of the Federal Reserve Act. The Act did not provide an automatic, foolproof mechanism for dealing with crisis, as the founders had hoped. Instead, effective lender of last resort action depended a great deal on the discretion of individual policy makers (Bordo and Wheelock, 2011).

The Fed's early history shows that a lender of last resort system that works well in one environment may not work in another environment. Paul Warburg sought to emulate the European Central bank mechanism and discount market. For political economy reasons (especially the ingrained fear of concentration of power) US banking institutions were not fully adapted to the European system. The Federal Reserve Act overcame some of the flaws of the National Banking system (e.g., the inelastic currency and the seasonal in short-term interest rates) that promoted instability, but not all of them. Perhaps the Fed's lender of last resort mechanism would have performed better with a Canadian/European style branch banking system coupled with a deep acceptance market.

Had Warburg's original plan been adopted many of the barriers to effective LLR action would have been overcome. These include: decision-making authority concentrated in a unique central bank with many branches, a uniform discount window policy, access to the discount window for all commercial banks, a much wider range of eligible securities, a more extensive market for acceptances, a US central bank acting to provide liquidity to the money market as a whole, and the explicit adherence to a Bagehot type rule. These institutional changes would very likely have prevented the banking panics of the Great Depression. Similar to the Second Bank scenario discussed above, had the Great Depression been avoided the rest of the monetary history of the twentieth century would have been very different than it was.

3.2. The Legacy of the Great Depression

Amendments to the Federal Reserve Act in the 1930s addressed many of the technical flaws that caused the Fed to be an effective lender of last resort in the Great Depression. These included a new authority to lend to member banks (relaxed collateral requirements); a new authority to lend to nonmember banks; a new authority to lend to nonbank firms and individuals (Section 13(3)), which in the 2008 crisis was used to justify many of the Fed's credit operations; and increased authority of the Board of Governors to determine Reserve Bank discount rates and lending policy. The problem of decentralization was dealt with by greatly increasing the power of the Board of Governors in Washington.

In addition other reforms promoted stability of the banking system such as Federal deposit insurance, the Glass-Steagall separation of commercial and investment banking, deposit interest ceilings and enhanced supervision. There were no changes to the dual banking system or to the prohibition to interstate banking and hence the US banking system did not move in the direction of a Canadian or European style nationwide branch banking system. These changes created a banking system that was slow to innovate and lost business to less regulated financial institutions and markets (the shadow banking system) (Bordo and Wheelock, 2011).

These reforms and a regime of low inflation under the Bretton Woods system led to three decades of both financial and macroeconomic stability. Beginning in the 1970s with the breakdown of the Bretton Woods system and the run up in inflation, financial stress reappeared in the mid 1970s with several important bank failures. In dealing with banking instability for the next three decades the Fed moved away from the classic Bagehot's rule LLR doctrine posited by Warburg towards concern over systemic risk and 'too big to fail'.

The reforms of the 1930s focused on protecting bank depositors and preventing runs by depositors and hence they proved only partly helpful during the crisis of 2007–2008. As with the original Federal Reserve Act, the 1930s reforms did not contemplate how to protect the banking system from instability coming from outside the banking system (e.g., runs on investment banks). The Section 13(3) lending programs created by the Fed in 2007–2008 were, for the most part, helpful in alleviating the crisis, but required considerable discretion and judgement on the part of Fed officials. Moreover the Fed seemed to have had no way to save the financial system without resorting to bailouts and these actions both led to moral hazard and a compromise of the Fed's independence (Bordo and Wheelock, 2011). Thus the reforms that followed the Great Depression only went part way in moving the Fed closer to Warburg's original vision.

4. Could the Alternative Scenarios for a US Central Bank Have Delivered Better Inflation and Overall Macro-performance than Did the Fed?

A key part of the Federal Reserve Act was that the Fed would adhere to the gold standard as did all other major central banks in 1914. Adhering to the gold standard provided a credible nominal anchor to the price level. There is considerable evidence that world price levels under the gold standard tended to be mean reverting reflecting the stabilizing properties of the commodity theory of money (Bordo, 1981; Bordo and Gavin, 2007). Although prices reverted towards the mean, in the short run there was considerable price variability reflecting the operation of the price specie flow mechanism and shocks to the gold market. There were also long swing movements in prices consequent upon major gold discoveries and countries joining the gold standard.

The Fed was set up like the European central banks to credibly adhere to gold and to manage the gold standard, i.e., to smooth interest rates and offset temporary real shocks (Goodfriend, 1988). Adherence to the gold standard was ended during World War I by most countries, although the US never formally left gold but an embargo on gold exports was imposed from 1917 to 1919. The price level in the US more than doubled during the war years but increased less than in the major other belligerents. After the war in 1919 the Fed, like other central banks, followed contractionary policy to reduce prices and return to the prewar status. Tight Fed policy led to a massive deflation and sharp recession from 1920 to 1921. The ensuing decade of the 1920s exhibited stable prices and relatively stable and rapid real economic growth.

The Great Contraction from 1929 to 1933 experienced both a massive deflation of close to 35% and an unprecedented drop in real activity of similar magnitude. As mentioned above fatal policy errors by the Fed and "golden fetters" were largely responsible for the debacle. After the Depression the US had both rapid growth and reflation. The US left the gold standard in April 1933 and then returned in January 1934 after a massive devaluation. World War II, like World War I, exhibited rapid inflation. After the war the US became part of the Bretton Woods System with the dollar anchored to gold and the rest of the world pegged to the dollar. The US returned to price stability in the 1950s and early 1960s. Chairman McChesney Martin and Presidents Eisenhower and Kennedy believed in adhering to gold standard rules and the primacy of price stability. The 1950s also were characterized by good overall macro-performance very similar to the 1920s. Business cycles were mitigated by well-timed countercyclical monetary policy (Meltzer, 2003; Bordo and Landon-Lane, 2010).[2]

Price stability ended with the Great Inflation which began in 1965. The initial run up in inflation reflected the Martin's Fed decision to give up its independence and coordinate monetary policy with the expansionary fiscal policy of the Johnson administration (Meltzer, 2009). It also reflected the growing acceptance in the Fed and the Administration in the Phillips curve tradeoff between unemployment and inflation. The Great Inflation worsened in the 1970s, peaking at 15% in 1980.

There are a number of competing explanations for it (Bordo and Orphanides, 2013). These include accommodation of the oil price shocks of 1973 and 1979, and the Fed's unwillingness, in the face of political pressure, to follow through on the contractionary monetary policy needed to break the back of inflationary expectations. This was because of the concern over the rise in unemployment that would ensue. By the end of the 1970s inflationary expectations became unanchored and the US dollar plunged dramatically. In response President Carter appointed Paul Volcker as chairman of the Federal Reserve with the prescription to break the back of inflation and inflationary expectations.

The Volcker shock of 1979 involved a shift in monetary control procedure away from the traditional use of short-term interest rates towards monetary aggregates. Tight money produced a spike in interest rates, a severe recession and by 1982 inflation had been halved. From the mid 1980s until 2007 the Fed kept inflation low (close to 2%) and stable. Inflationary expectations declined drastically by the end of the 1980s and the real economy grew rapidly, punctuated by two mild recessions. In this Great Moderation period the Fed was acclaimed for adopting a credible low inflation rule-like policy which echoed the experience of the 1920s and 1950s, and in some respects the pre-1914 gold standard (Bordo and Schwartz, 1999).

The benign environment of the Great Moderation was shattered by the Subprime Mortgage Financial Crisis of 2007–2008 and the Great Recession of 2007–2009 followed by a still anemic recovery. The Fed dealt with the liquidity crisis using both its traditional DWL tools and, by the use of unconventional credit policy. Its role in the crisis has been criticized for compromising its independence by conducting fiscal policy and for moving away from the rule-like behavior that it had followed in the Great Moderation towards the use of discretion (Meltzer, 2009). It has also been criticized for keeping interest rates artificially low from 2002 to 2006 to offset an imaginary threat of deflation (Taylor, 2009), and then pausing in its expansionary actions in early 2008 and keeping interest rates too high until late 2008 thereby guaranteeing a serious recession (Hetzel, 2008). The Fed's shift to Quantitative Easing (QE1) and purchasing massive amounts of long-term Treasuries and mortgage backed securities in December 2009, once it had reached the zero lower bound, may be largely responsible for ending the recession. A second round of QE in response to a sluggish recovery in the fall of 2010 has not been viewed as successful in stimulating the economy (Goodfriend, 2011). This also seems to be the case with its 2011 policy of twisting the yield curve by substituting long term for short-term securities in its portfolio (Goodfriend, 2011).

The present recovery differs markedly from past recoveries following deep recessions. What seems to be different is the moribund housing sector after the massive nationwide housing bust since 2006 (reflected in a collapse in residential investment) (Bordo and Haubrich, 2011)—a problem which monetary policy may not be able to address.

An open question is whether the expansionary policies that the Fed has been following will eventually lead to a run up in inflationary expectations in the future. What also is an open question is whether the Fed's lapses from rule-like behavior between 2007 and 2011 and its extensive use of fiscal policies, which has undermined its independence and exposed its balance sheet to credit risk, will end its good track record of maintaining price stability during the Great Moderation.

Would the revived Second Bank or the Warburg inspired central bank have performed better than the Fed did with respect to price stability and overall macro-performance? Both hypothetical central banks were based on the gold standard as was the original Fed, so the answer depends on whether the gold standard would have survived if the Great Depression (which many believe was caused by the failures of Fed policy) had not happened. Bordo and Eichengreen (1998) have argued that the gold exchange standard would have survived and, assuming that World War II had happened (which is also questionable given that Hitler's electoral success had a lot to do with the fact that Germany suffered badly in the Great Depression (Temin, 1998)), it would have been suspended during the war and then, following the gold standard contingent rule (Bordo and Kydland, 1995) it would have been restored. The counterfactual exercise that Bordo and Eichengreen conducted, based on a model of the global gold exchange standard, showed that the gold exchange standard could have lasted until the mid 1960s but would then have collapsed because of the Triffin Dilemma. The US would have been the key reserve country as it was since the mid 1920s (Eichengreen and Flandreau, 2008) and the US gold reserves would have been threatened as the rest of the world used dollars as their reserve currencies.

Moreover the world would have shifted to a fiat regime to overcome the resource costs and vagaries of the gold standard that the great economists, Irving Fisher, Alfred Marshall, Knut Wicksell, John Maynard Keynes and Milton Friedman had posited. Also the financial innovation that began pre-1914, with the gold points serving as a credible target zone to allow central banks to use monetary policy to offset shocks and smooth interest rates, would have continued (Bordo and Flandreau, 2003). In addition if we had not had the Great Depression then Keynes would not have published the General Theory and Keynesian economics and the Phillips curve would never have developed. This would mean that the Fed would have learned to follow a stable nominal anchor with fiat money several decades before they did.

The examples of Germany and Switzerland, both of whom had a much better record of maintaining price stability in the post-war than the Fed and many other central banks, suggests that it could have been done (Beyer et al., 2008; Bordo and James, 2007). Germany's stability culture came out of its drastic experience with hyperinflation in the 1920s. Switzerland's stability culture goes back to the founding of the Swiss National Bank in

1907 and the importance that price stability meant to a country whose major industry was providing financial services (Bordo and James, 2007).

Thus a reasonable case could be made that either variants of alternative models for a US central bank could have done a better job in maintaining price stability and overall macro-stability to the extent that price instability is an important cause of real instability (Lucas, 1973; Schwartz, 1995).[3] This analysis is based on the path dependency that follows from key innovations in the past which set the economy on trajectories that would otherwise have been different.

My story about what would have happened assumes that both counterfactual historic central banks would have learned to be effective central banks as was the case with the Bank of England and other long-lived institutions during the nineteenth century and then painfully, in the twentieth century, by the Federal Reserve. This is not to say that the Bank of England was perfect. It had a worse record than the Fed in the post-World War II period but its poor inflation performance had a lot to do with the Keynesian legacy of the Great Depression and the aftermath of World War II and the creation of the welfare state (Capie, 2010). Had the Great Depression not happened it seems reasonable to hypothesize that the Bank of England, the Banque de France and other central banks would have had better records too.

5. Conclusion: Some Lessons from History

In this chapter I have argued that had the Second Bank of the United States not been destroyed in 1836 that the US could have had a better history with respect to financial stability, price stability and overall macro-performance. Had history played out as it did and the Second Bank been terminated then a second more modest counterfactual, which assumes that a US central bank closer to the Warburg plan of 1910, would also have done better than the Fed throughout much of the twentieth century.

These hypothetical central banks had several key features which were crucial to their hypothetical success. The first was adherence to a commitment to a credible nominal anchor, the gold standard, and then a fiat money standard operated on lines like the gold standard. The second was following a rule to preserve financial stability—following Bagehot's rule as interpreted by the Bank of England in the second half of the nineteenth century—to provide liquidity freely to the money market in the face of a panic. Third was independence from the fiscal authorities which was a key tenet of the classical gold standard.

The Fed departed from these rules over much of its history. It learned to be a lender of last resort after the Great Depression but has pushed that notion way beyond what the framers expected of it, to protect the integrity of the payments system. Today it has expanded its mandate to the guarantee of the stability of the entire financial system.

The Fed achieved price stability in the 1920s, 1950s and between 1985 and 2007. It also learned from its bad behavior in the Great Inflation to follow a credible rule like commitment to maintain low inflation during the Great Moderation. It then followed a period of keeping interest rates too low for fear of deflation between 2002 and 2006 which added fuel to the fire of the subprime crisis and since the recession has ended may have kept policy too loose to not avoid future inflation.

The Fed was granted considerable independence at its inception. It abused this independence during the 1930s and from the mid 1930s to 1951 it effectively became a branch of the Treasury. It regained its independence in the 1951 Treasury Federal Reserve Accord but under Chairmen McChesney Martin, Arthur Burns and G. William Miller it again allowed monetary policy to become subservient to the needs of the Treasury. Since Paul Volcker became chairman in 1979 the Fed's independence has been restored and the Fed between 1985 and the early 2000s has conducted monetary policy as good as any contemporary or historic central bank. Its record since 2007 once again suggests that its independence has been sacrificed. It is too soon to tell how permanent this will be.

The hypothetical examples that I have constructed suggest that the US could have had a better central bank. The actual history of the Federal Reserve suggests that with considerable effort the Fed by the early 2000s had learned from its past mistakes and had moved closer to these history based hypothetical examples. It may have regressed in the run up, the management, and the aftermath of the recent Financial Crisis and the Great Recession. Whether it will return to this path is an open question.

Notes

1. Had the Bank War not happened, the financial turmoil that led to the Panic of 1837 (especially the Distribution of the Treasury's Specie Surplus in 1836 [Rousseau, 2002]) and the debt defaults by eight states in 1841 (due to their faulty public finances) likely would still have been present. Moreover Biddle might still have engaged in the same cotton speculations and bad investments that brought down the Pennsylvania chartered Second Bank in 1841.

2. This was not generally the case in other periods where the Fed often tightened monetary policy too late in the business cycle upswing to prevent inflation and loosened too late in the downswing to mitigate recession (Bordo and Landon-Lane, 2010).

3. It is also not clear that these alternative central bank scenarios would have done better than did the Fed in following countercyclical monetary policy since such policies as a general rule were not followed by central banks before World War I. Given that the flaws of the Fed with respect to financial stability would have been avoided, the need for countercyclical monetary policy may have been less.

References

Bagehot, W., 1873. Lombard Street. London.

Beyer, A., Gaspar, V., Gerberding, C., Issing, O., 2008. Opting out of the Great Inflation: German Monetary Policy after the Breakdown of Bretton Woods. NBER Working Paper 14596.

Bordo, M.D., 1981. The classical gold standard: some lessons for today. Federal Reserve Bank of St. Louis Review 63 (6).

Bordo, M.D., Eichengreen, B., 1998. Implications of the Great Depression for the development of the international monetary system. In: Bordo, M.D., Goldin, C., White, E.N. (Eds.), The Defining Moment: The Great Depression and the American Economy in the Twentieth Century. University of Chicago Press for the NBER, Chicago.

Bordo, M.D., Flandreau, M., 2003. Core, periphery, exchange rate regimes and globalization. In: Bordo, M.D., Taylor, A., Williamson, J. (Eds.), Globalization in Historical Perspective. University of Chicago, Chicago.

Bordo, M.D., Gavin, W., 2007. Gold, fiat money and price stability. Berkeley Electronic Journal of Macroeconomics: Topics in Macroeconomics (June).

Bordo, M.D., Haubrich, J., 2011. Deep Recessions, Fast Recoveries and Financial Crises: Evidence from the American Record. Federal Reserve Bank of Cleveland (mimeo).

Bordo, M.D., Humpage, O., Schwartz, A., 2007. The historical origins of US exchange market intervention. International Journal of Finance and Economics 12 (2), 109–132.

Bordo, M.D., James, H., 2007. From 1907 to 1946: a happy childhood or a troubled adolescence? In: The Swiss National Bank 1907–2007, Swiss National Bank. Zurich, Neue Zurcher Zeitung (Chapter 2).

Bordo, M.D., Kydland, F., 1995. The gold standard as a rule: an essay in exploration. Explorations in Economic History (October).

Bordo, M.D., Landon-Lane, J., 2010. Exits from Recessions: the US Experience 1920–2007. NBER Working Paper 15731, February.

Bordo, M.D., Orphanides, A., 2013. The Great Inflation. University of Chicago Press, Chicago.

Bordo, M.D., Rappoport, P., Schwartz, A.J., 1992. Money and credit during the national banking era-1880–1914. In: Goldin, C., Rockoff, H. (Eds.), Strategic factors in nineteenth century American economic history. University of Chicago Press, Chicago.

Bordo, M.D., Schwartz, A.J., 1999. Monetary policy regimes and economic performance: the historical record. In: Taylor, J., Woodford, M. (Eds.), North Holland Handbook of Macroeconomics. North Holland, New York (Chapter 2).

Bordo, M.D., Vegh, C., 2002. What if Alexander Hamilton had been Argentinian? A comparison of the early monetary experience of Argentina and the United States. Journal of Monetary Economics (April).

Bordo, M.D., Wheelock, D.C., 2011. The Promise and Performance of the Federal Reserve as Lender of Last Resort. NBER Working Paper 16743, February.

Bordo, M.D., White, E., 1991. A tale of two currencies: British and French finances during the Napoleonic wars. Journal of Economic History (June).

Cagan, P., 1963. The first fifty years of the Federal Reserve. In: Carson, D. (Ed.), Banking and Monetary Studies. Richard D. Irwin, Homewood, Illinois.

Capie, F., 2002. The emergence of the Bank of England as a mature central bank. In: The Political Economy of British Historical Experience, 1688–1914. Oxford University Press, London, pp. 295–315.

Capie, F., 2010. A History of the Bank of England: 1950s to 1979. Cambridge University Press, Cambridge.

Eichengreen, B., 1992. Golden Fetters: The Gold Standard and the Great Depression. Oxford University Press, New York.

Eichengreen, B., 2010. Exorbitant Privilege. Oxford University Press, New York.

Eichengreen, B., Flandreau, M., 2008. The Rise and Fall of the Dollar, or When Did the Dollar Replace Sterling as the Leading International Currency? NBER Working Paper 14154, July.

Friedman, M., Schwartz, A.J., 1963. A Monetary History of the United States 1867–1960. Princeton University Press, Princeton.

Goodfriend, M., 1988. Central banking under the gold standard. In: Brunner, K., Meltzer, A. (Eds.), Money, Cycles and Exchange Rates: Essays in Honor of

Allan H. Meltzer. Carnegie Rochester Conference Series in Public Policy, vol. 29, pp. 85–124.

Goodfriend, M., 2011. Central banking in credit turmoil: an assessment of Federal Reserve practice. Journal of Monetary Economics.

Hammond, B., 1957. Banks and Politics in America. Princeton University Press, Princeton.

Hetzel, R.L., 2008. The Monetary Policy of the Federal Reserve: A History. Cambridge University Press, New York.

Hetzel, R.L., 2012. The Great Recession: Failure of Markets or Policy? Cambridge University Press, New York.

Irwin, D., 2010. Did France Cause the Great Depression? NBER Working Paper 16350, September.

Knodell, J., 2003. Profit and Duty in the Second Bank of the United States' exchange operations. Financial History Review 10, 5–30.

Lawrence B, J., 1997. The International Origins of the Federal Reserve System. Cornell University Press, Ithaca.

Lucas Jr., R.E., 1973. Some international evidence on output inflation tradeoffs. American Economic Review (June).

Meltzer, A.H., 2003. A History of the Federal Reserve, 1913–1951, vol. 1. University of Chicago Press, Chicago.

Meltzer, A.H., 2009. A History of the Federal Reserve, 1951–1986, vol. 2. University of Chicago Press, Chicago.

Miron, J.A., 1986. Financial panics, the seasonality of the nominal interest rate, and the founding of the Fed. American Economic Review 76 (1), 125–140.

Redlich, F., 1951. The Molding of American Banking: Man and Ideas. Hafner Publishers, New York.

Richardson, G., Troost, W., 2009. Monetary intervention mitigated banking panics during the great depression; quasi-experimental evidence from a Federal Reserve District Border, 1929–33. Journal of Political Economy 117 (6), 1031–1073.

Rousseau, P.L., 2002. Jacksonian monetary policy, specie flows, and the Panic of 1837. Journal of Economic History 2 (June), 457–488.

Rousseau, P.L., Sylla, R., 2003. Financial systems, economic growth and globalization. In: Bordo, M.D., Taylor, A.M., Williamson, J. (Eds.), Globalization in Historical Perspective. University of Chicago Press, Chicago.

Sayers, R.S., 1976. Bank of England Operations 1891–1944, vol. I. Cambridge University Press, Cambridge.

Schwartz, A.J., 1986. Real versus pseudo financial crises. In: Wood, G., Capie, F. (Eds.), Crises in the World Banking System. Macmillan, London.

Schwartz, A.J., 1995. Why financial stability depends on price stability. Economic Affairs Autumn, 21–25.

Selgin, G., Lastrapes, W., White, L.H., 2010. Has the Fed Been a Failure? University of Georgia (mimeo).

Sprague, O.M.W., 1910. History of Crises under the National Banking System. US National Monetary Commission, Senate Document No. 538, 61 Congress 2 Session Washington: Government Printing Office.

Taylor, J.B., 2009. Getting Off Track: How Government Actions and Interventions Caused, Prolonged, and Worsened the Financial Crisis. Hoover Institution Press, Stanford.

Temin, P., 1989. Lessons from the Great Depression. MIT Press, Cambridge, Mass.

Temin, P., 1998. Comment. In: Bordo, M.D., Goldin, C., White, E.N. (Eds.), The Defining Moment: The Great Depression and the American Economy in the Twentieth Century. University of Chicago Press, Chicago.

Thornton, H., 1962, 1802. An Inquiry into the Nature and Effects of the Paper Credit of Great Britain. Kelley, New York (Reprint).

Timberlake Jr., R.H., 1993. Monetary Policy in the United States: An Intellectual and Institutional History. University of Chicago Press, Chicago.

Warburg, P.M., 1910a. The Discount System in Europe. National Monetary Commission. US Senate Document No. 402. Washington DC: US Government Printing Office.

Warburg, P.M., 1910b. The United Reserve Bank plan. In: Warburg, Paul (Ed.), The Federal Reserve, vol. 1. Macmillan, New York (Chapter III).

West, R.C., 1977. Banking Reform and the Federal Reserve, 1863–1927. Cornell University Press, Ithaca.

Wheelock, D.C., 1991. The Strategy and Consistency of Federal Reserve Monetary Policy, 1924–1933. Cambridge University Press, New York.

White, E.N., 2011. To Establish a More Effective Supervision of Banking: How the Birth of the Fed Altered Bank Supervision. NBER Working Paper 16825.

Wicker, E., 1966. Federal Reserve Monetary Policy, 1917–1933. Random House, New York.

Wicker, E., 2005. The Great Debate on Banking Reform: Nelson Aldrich and the Origins of the Fed. Ohio State University Press, Columbus.

ABOUT THE AUTHOR

Michael D. Bordo is a Board of Governors' Professor of Economics and director of the Center for Monetary and Financial History at Rutgers University, New Brunswick, New Jersey. He is currently a distinguished visiting fellow at the Hoover Institution, Stanford University. He recently served as *president of the Economic History Association*. He has held academic positions at the University of South Carolina and Carleton University in Ottawa, Canada. Bordo has been a visiting professor at the University of California at Los Angeles, Carnegie Mellon University, Princeton University, Harvard University, and Cambridge University, where he was the Pitt Professor of American History and Institutions. He has been a visiting scholar at the International Monetary Fund; the Federal Reserve Banks of St. Louis, Cleveland, and Dallas; the Federal Reserve Board of Governors; the Bank of Canada; the Bank of England; and the Bank for International Settlement. He is a research associate of the National Bureau of Economic Research, Cambridge, Massachusetts, and a member of the Shadow Open Market Committee. He is also a member of the Federal Reserve Centennial Advisory Committee. He has a BA degree from McGill University, an MSc in economics from the London School of Economics, and a PhD from the University of Chicago in 1972.

He has published many articles in leading journals including the *Journal of Political Economy*, the *American Economic Review*, the *Journal of Monetary Economics*, and the *Journal of Economic History*. He has authored and coedited sixteen books on monetary economics and monetary history. These include (with Owen Humpage and Anna J. Schwartz) *Strained Relations: US Foreign Exchange Operations and Monetary Policy in the Twentieth Century* (2014); (with Athanasios Orphanides) *The Great Inflation* (2013); (with Will Roberds) *A Return to Jekyll Island* (2013); (with Ronald MacDonald) *Credibility and the International Monetary Regime* (2012); and (with Alan Taylor and Jeffrey Williamson) *Globalization in Historical Perspective* (2003). He is also editor of a series of books for Cambridge University Press: Studies in Macroeconomic History.

He is currently doing research on *the evolution of central banks; the profiles of Federal Open Market Committee members; and the timing of exits from episodes of loose monetary policy: a comparison of the 1932 open market operations with QE1.*

SOURCE NOTES

The following articles were reprinted in the chapters in this volume. We thank the various presses for permission to reprint them.

(Chapter 2) Originally published in "The Importance of Stable Money: Theory and Evidence," *Cato Journal* 3, no. 1 (Spring 1983). Copyright © Cato Institute. All rights reserved.

(Chapter 3) Originally published in "Monetary Policy Regimes and Economic Performance: The Historical Record," chap. 2 in *Handbook of Macroeconomics, Volume I*, ed. John Taylor and Michael Woodford (New York: North Holland, 1999). © 1999 Elsevier Science B.V. All rights reserved.

(Chapter 4) Originally published in "Introduction to *The Great Inflation*" in *The Great Inflation: The Rebirth of Modern Central Banking*, ed. Michael D. Bordo and Athanasios Orphanides (Chicago: University of Chicago Press, 2013), 1–22. This chapter is a selection from a published volume from the National Bureau of Economic Research.

(Chapter 5) Originally published in "Exits from Recessions: The US Experience, 1920–2007," chap. 8 in *No Way Out: Persistent Government Interventions in the Great Contraction*, ed. Vincent R. Reinhart (Washington, DC: AEI Press), 117–62. Copyright 2013 by the American Enterprise Institute for Public Policy Research, Washington DC.

(Chapter 6) Originally published in "Deep Recessions, Fast Recoveries, and Financial Crises: Evidence from the American Record," *Economic Inquiry* 55, no. 1 (January 2016): 527–41.

(Chapter 7) Originally published in "Credit Crises, Money and Contractions: An Historical View," *Journal of Monetary Economics* 57, no. 1 (March 2010): 1–18. © 2009 Elsevier B.V. All rights reserved.

(Chapter 8) Originally published in "Three Great American Disinflations," NBER Working Paper (2008).

(Chapter 9) Originally published in "Aggregate Price Shocks and Financial Instability: An Historical Analysis," *Economic Inquiry* 40, no. 4 (2002): 521–38.

(Chapter 10) Originally published in "Does Expansionary Monetary Policy Cause Asset Price Booms: Some Historical and Empirical Evidence," in *Macroeconomic and Financial Stability: Challenges for Monetary Policy*, ed. Sofía Bauducco, Lawrence Christiano, and Claudio Raddatz (Central Bank of Chile: Santiago, Chile). © 2014. Central Bank of Chile.

(Chapter 11) Originally published in "The History of Monetary Policy," in *New Palgrave Dictionary of Economics*, 2nd ed., ed. Steven N. Durlauf and Lawrence E. Blume (New York: Palgrave Macmillan, 2008), 205–15.

(Chapter 12) Originally published in "The Banking Panics in the United States in the 1930s: Some Lessons for Today," *Oxford Review of Economic Policy* 26, no. 3 (2010): 486–509. © The Authors 2010. Published by Oxford University Press. For permissions please e-mail: journals.permissions@oxfordjournals.org.

(Chapter 13) Originally published in "Could Stable Money Have Averted the Great Contraction?" *Economic Inquiry* 33, no. 3 (July 1995): 484–505.

(Chapter 14) Originally published in "Was Expansionary Monetary Policy Feasible during the Great Contraction? An Examination of the Gold Standard Constraint," *Explorations in Economic History* 39, no. 1 (January 2002): 1–28. © 2001 Elsevier Science.

(Chapter 15) Originally published in "Could the United States Have Had a Better Central Bank? An Historical Counterfactual Speculation," *Journal of Macroeconomics* 34, no. 3 (September 2012): 597–607. © 2012 Elsevier Inc. All rights reserved.

INDEX